Using and Administering Linux: Volume 2

Zero to SysAdmin: Advanced Topics

Second Edition

David Both

Apress®

Using and Administering Linux: Volume 2: Zero to SysAdmin: Advanced Topics

David Both
Raleigh, NC, USA

ISBN-13 (pbk): 978-1-4842-9614-1   ISBN-13 (electronic): 978-1-4842-9615-8
https://doi.org/10.1007/978-1-4842-9615-8

Managing Director, Apress Media LLC: Welmoed Spahr
Acquisitions Editor: James Robinson-Prior
Development Editor: Jim Markham
Editorial Assistant: Gryffin Winkler

Cover image designed by the author

Distributed to the book trade worldwide by Springer Science+Business Media New York, 1 New York Plaza, 1 FDR Dr, New York, NY 10004. Phone 1-800-SPRINGER, fax (201) 348-4505, e-mail orders-ny@springer-sbm. com, or visit www.springeronline.com. Apress Media, LLC is a California LLC and the sole member (owner) is Springer Science + Business Media Finance Inc (SSBM Finance Inc). SSBM Finance Inc is a **Delaware** corporation.

For information on translations, please e-mail booktranslations@springernature.com; for reprint, paperback, or audio rights, please e-mail bookpermissions@springernature.com.

Apress titles may be purchased in bulk for academic, corporate, or promotional use. eBook versions and licenses are also available for most titles. For more information, reference our Print and eBook Bulk Sales web page at http://www.apress.com/bulk-sales.

Any source code or other supplementary material referenced by the author in this book is available to readers on GitHub (https://github.com/Apress). For more detailed information, please visit https://www.apress.com/gp/services/source-code.

Paper in this product is recyclable.

This book is dedicated to all

Linux and open source developers, system administrators, course developers, and trainers.

:(){ :|:& };:

Table of Contents

About the Author

David Both is an open source software and GNU/Linux advocate, trainer, writer, and speaker. He has been working with Linux and open source software for more than 25 years and has been working with computers for over 50 years. He is a strong proponent of and evangelist for the "Linux Philosophy for System Administrators."

He worked for IBM for 21 years and, while working as a course development representative in Boca Raton, FL, in 1981, wrote the training course for the first IBM PC. He has taught RHCE classes for Red Hat and has taught classes on Linux ranging from Lunch'n'Learns to full five-day courses.

David's books and articles are a continuation of his desire to pass on his knowledge and to provide mentoring to anyone interested in learning about Linux.

David prefers to purchase the components and build his own computers from scratch to ensure that each new computer meets his exacting specifications. Building his own computers also means not having to pay the Microsoft tax. His latest build is an ASUS TUF X299 motherboard and an Intel i9 CPU with 16 cores (32 CPUs) and 64GB of RAM in a Cooler Master MasterFrame 700.

David is the author of *The Linux Philosophy for SysAdmins* (Apress, 2018) and co-author of *Linux for Small Business Owners* (Apress, 2022) and can be found on Mastodon @linuxgeek46@LinoxRocks.online.

About the Technical Reviewers

Branton Brodie started his Linux journey last year while attending All Things Open 2022. Getting into the IT world was something he wanted to do for a while but didn't know where to start until he went there and saw all the opportunities shown. Linux stood out to him the most, and he is now studying to become a SysAdmin. He enjoys reading about tech and how the future of tech will shape the world around us. He lives in the calming town of Wake Forest, NC.

Seth Kenlon is a Unix and Linux geek, SysAdmin, open source and free culture advocate, music producer, Java and Lua programmer, game designer, and tabletop gamer. He arrived in the computer industry by way of film production.

Acknowledgments

Writing a book – and especially a three-volume second edition – is not a solitary activity, and this massive Linux training course required a team effort much more so than most.

The most important person in this effort has been my awesome wife, Alice, who has been my head cheerleader and best friend throughout. I could not have done this without your support and love. Again!

I owe many thanks to my editors at Apress, James Robinson-Prior and Gryffin Winkler, for seeing the need for a second edition and especially for being supportive as I worked my way through some major restructuring and a significant amount of new material. I especially thank you for your immediate support when I suggested having a student as second technical editor.

Seth Kenlon, my amazing technical reviewer, and I have worked together before on previous books as well as many of the articles I wrote for the now defunct Opensource.com website. I am grateful for his contributions to the technical accuracy of all three volumes of this course. Seth also made some important suggestions that improved the flow and accuracy of this course. I once said that Seth was on the "ragged edge of being brutally honest" in his editorial tasks; he responded that he had been aiming for "completely brutal," but had apparently failed. You still have my ongoing gratitude for the work you do.

I also owe many thanks to Branton Brodie, my second technical editor for all three volumes. Branton and I met as part of his desire to learn about Linux at a time when I was just starting on this second edition. I thought that having a student who wanted to take the course anyway act as a technical editor could provide me with some insight into how students view the course. His contributions have been valuable to my work as I was able to revise descriptions and explanations that made sense to me but not necessarily to anyone who has never been exposed to Linux or system administration.

Of course any remaining errors, omissions, and poor explanations are my responsibility alone.

Introduction

This Linux training course, "Using and Administering Linux – Zero to SysAdmin," is significantly different from other courses. It consists of three volumes. Each of these three volumes is closely connected, and they build upon each other.

This Linux training course differs from others because it is a complete self-study course. You should start at the beginning of Volume 1 and read the text, perform all of the experiments, and do all of the chapter exercises through to the end of Volume 3. If you do this, even if you are starting from zero knowledge about Linux, you can learn the tasks necessary to becoming a Linux system administrator, a SysAdmin.

Another difference this course has over others is that all of the experiments are performed on one or more virtual machines (VMs) in a virtual network. Using the free software VirtualBox, you will create this virtual environment on any reasonably sized host, whether Linux or Windows. In this virtual environment, you are free to experiment on your own, make mistakes that could damage the Linux installation of a hardware host, and still be able to recover completely by restoring the Linux VM host from any one of multiple snapshots. This flexibility to take risks and yet recover easily makes it possible to learn more than would otherwise be possible.

These course materials can also be used as reference materials. I have used my previous course materials for reference for many years, and they have been very useful in that role. I have kept this as one of my goals in this set of materials.

Not all of the review exercises in this course can be answered by simply reviewing the chapter content. For some questions you will need to design your own experiment in order to find a solution. In many cases there will very probably be multiple solutions, and all that produce the correct results will be the "correct" ones.

The Process

The process that goes with this format is just as important as the format of the course – really even more so. The first thing that a course developer must do is generate a list of requirements that define both the structure and the content of the course. Only then can the process of writing the course proceed. In fact, many times I find it helpful to write the review questions and exercises before I create the rest of the content. In many chapters of this course, I have worked in this manner.

These courses present a complete, end-to-end Linux training course for students like you who know before you start that you want to learn to be a Linux system administrator – a SysAdmin. This Linux course will allow you to learn Linux right from the beginning with the objective of becoming a SysAdmin.

Many Linux training courses begin with the assumption that the first course a student should take is one designed to start them as a user. Those courses may discuss the role of root in system administration, but ignore topics that are important to future SysAdmins. Other courses ignore system administration altogether. A typical second course will introduce the student to system administration, while a third may tackle advanced administration topics.

Frankly, this baby step approach did not work well for many of us who are now Linux SysAdmins. We became SysAdmins, in part at least, due to our intense desire to learn as much as possible as quickly as possible. It is also, I think in large part, due to our highly inquisitive natures. We learn a basic command and then start asking questions, experimenting with it to see what its limits are, what breaks it, what using it can break. We explore the man(ual) pages and other documentation to learn the extreme usages to which it might be put. If things don't break by themselves, we break them intentionally to see how they work and to learn how to fix them. We relish our own failures because we learn more from fixing them than we do when things always work as they are supposed to.

In this course we will dive deep into Linux system administration almost from the very beginning. You will learn many of the Linux tools required to use and administer Linux workstations and servers – usually multiple tools that can be applied to each of these tasks. This course contains many experiments to provide you with the kind of hands-on experiences that SysAdmins appreciate. All of these experiments guide you one step at a time into the elegant and beautiful depths of the Linux experience. You will learn that Linux is simple and that simplicity is what makes it both elegant and knowable.

Based on my own years working with Unix and Linux, the course materials contained in these three volumes are designed to introduce you to the practical, daily tasks you will perform as a Linux user and, at the same time, as a Linux system administrator – SysAdmin.

But I don't know everything – that's just not possible. No SysAdmin does. Further, no two SysAdmins know exactly the same things because that, too, is impossible. We have each started with different knowledge and skills; we have different goals; we have different experiences because the systems on which we work have failed in different ways, had different hardware, were embedded in different networks, had different distributions installed, and many other differences. We use different tools and approaches to problem solving because the many different mentors and teachers we had used different sets of tools from each other; we use different Linux distributions; we think differently; and we know different things about the hardware on which Linux runs. Our past is much of what makes us what we are and what defines us as SysAdmins.

So I will show you things in this course – things that I think are important for you to know, things that, in my opinion, will provide you with the skills to use your own curiosity and creativity to find solutions that I would never think of to problems I have never encountered.

I have always found that I learn more from my mistakes than I ever have when things work as they are supposed to. For this reason I suggest that, rather than immediately reverting to an earlier snapshot when you run into trouble, you try to figure out how the problem was created and how best to recover from it. If, after a reasonable period of time, you have not resolved the problem, that would be the point at which reverting to a snapshot would make sense.

What This Course Is Not

This course is not a certification study guide. It is not designed to help you pass a certification test of any type. This course is intended purely to help you become a good or perhaps even great SysAdmin, not to pass a test.

There are a few good certification tests. Red Hat and Cisco certifications are among the best because they are based on the test-taker's ability to perform specific tasks. I am not familiar with any of the other certification tests because I have not taken them. But the courses you can take and books you can purchase to help you pass those tests are designed to help you pass the tests and not to administer a Linux host or network. That does not make them bad – just different from this course.

Content Overview

This quick overview of the contents of each volume should serve as a quick orientation guide if you need to locate specific information. If you are trying to decide whether to purchase this book and its companion volumes, it will give you a good overview of the entire course.

Using and Administering Linux: Volume 1 – Zero to SysAdmin: Getting Started

Chapters 1 through 3 of Volume 1 introduce operating systems in general and Linux in particular and briefly explore the Linux Philosophy for SysAdmins in preparation for the rest of the course.

Chapter 4 then guides you through the use of VirtualBox to create a virtual machine (VM) and a virtual network to use as a test laboratory for performing the many experiments that are used throughout the course. In Chapter 5, you will install the Xfce version of Fedora – a popular and powerful Linux distribution – on the VM. Chapter 6 shows you how to use the Xfce desktop, which will enable you to leverage your growing command-line interface (CLI) expertise as you proceed through the course.

Chapters 7 and 8 will get you started using the Linux command line and introduce you to some of the basic Linux commands and their capabilities. In Chapter 9 you will learn about data streams and the Linux tools used to manipulate them. And in Chapter 10 you will learn a bit about several text editors, which are indispensable to advanced Linux users and system administrators. You will also learn to use the Vim text editor to create and modify the many ASCII plain text files that Linux uses for configuration and administrative programming.

Chapters 11 through 13 start your work as a SysAdmin and take you through some specific tasks such as working as root and installing software updates and new software. Chapters 14 and 15 discuss more terminal emulators and some advanced shell skills. In Chapter 16 you will learn about the sequence of events that take place as the computer boots and Linux starts up. Chapter 17 shows you how to configure your shell to personalize it in ways that can seriously enhance your command-line efficiency.

Finally, Chapters 18 and 19 dive into all things files and filesystems.

1. Introduction

2. Introduction to Operating Systems

Using and Administering Linux: Volume 2 – Zero to SysAdmin: Advanced Topics

Volume 2 of *Using and Administering Linux* introduces you to some incredibly powerful and useful advanced topics that every SysAdmin must know.

In Chapters 20 and 21, you will experience an in-depth exploration of logical volume management (LVM) – and what that even means – as well as the use of file managers to manipulate files and directories. Chapter 22 introduces the concept that, in Linux, everything is a file. You will also learn some fun and interesting uses of the fact that everything is a file.

In Chapter 23 you will learn to use several tools that enable the SysAdmin to manage and monitor running processes. Chapter 24 enables you to experience the power of the special filesystems, such as /proc, which enable us as SysAdmins to monitor and tune the kernel while it is running – without a reboot.

Chapter 25 will introduce you to regular expressions and the power that using them for pattern matching can bring to the command line, while Chapter 26 discusses managing printers and printing from the command line. In Chapter 27 you will use several tools to unlock the secrets of the hardware on which your Linux operating system is running.

Chapters 28 and 29 show you how to do some simple – and not so simple – command-line programming and how to automate various administrative tasks. In Chapter 30 you will learn to use Ansible, a powerful tool that makes automating tasks for thousands of computers just as easy as for one. Chapter 31 discusses the tools you will use to perform repetitive and automated tasks at specific times.

You will begin to learn the details of networking in Chapter 32, and Chapter 33 covers use of the powerful NetworkManager tool.

Chapter 34 introduces the B-Tree Filesystem (BTRFS) and covers its very interesting features. This chapter also informs you why BTRFS is not an appropriate choice for a filesystem in most use cases.

Chapters 35 through 37 allow you to explore systemd, the modern tool for starting Linux at boot time and which is also used to manage system services and tools. Chapter 38 discusses dbus and udev and how Linux uses them to treat all devices as plug and play (PnP).

In Chapter 39 you will learn to use and manage traditional log files. You will also learn to configure and use the logwatch facility to assist you with sorting through the many log messages to get to the important ones.

Chapter 40 covers the tasks required to manage users, while Chapter 41 introduces you to some basic tasks needed to manage the firewall. You will use the firewalld command-line tool to create and manage zones to which the network interfaces will be assigned based on various security needs such as internal and external networks.

20. Logical Volume Management (LVM)

21. File Managers

22. Everything Is a File

23. Managing Processes

Using and Administering Linux: Volume 3 – Zero to SysAdmin: Network Services

In Volume 3 of *Using and Administering Linux*, you will start by creating a new VM in the existing virtual network. This new VM will be used as a server for the rest of this course, and it will replace some of the functions performed by the virtual router that is part of our virtual network.

Chapter 42 begins this transformation from simple workstation to server by adding a second network interface card (NIC) to the new VM so that it can act as a firewall and router and then changing its network configuration from Dynamic Host Configuration Protocol

(DHCP) to static IP addressing. This includes configuring both NICs so that one is connected to the existing virtual router so as to allow connections to the outside world and so that the other NIC connects to the new "inside" network that will contain the existing VM.

Chapter 43 discusses Domain Name Services (DNS) in detail both from client and server standpoints. You'll learn to use the /etc/hosts file for simple name resolution and then create a simple caching name server. You will then convert the caching name server into a primary name server for your internal network.

In Chapter 44 you will convert the new server into a router using kernel parameters and a simple firewall configuration change.

Chapter 45 shows how to use SSHD to provide secure remote access between Linux hosts. It also provides some interesting insights into using commands remotely and creating a simple command-line program to back up specific directories of a remote host to the local host.

Although we have incorporated security in all aspects of what has already been covered, Chapter 46 covers some additional security topics. This includes physical hardening as well as further hardening of the host to provide enhanced protection from network intrusions.

In Chapter 47 you will learn techniques and strategies for creating backups that use easily available open source tools, which are easy to use for both creating backups and restoring complete filesystems or individual files.

You will learn to install and configure an enterprise-class email server that can detect and block most spam and malware in Chapters 48 through 50. Chapter 51 takes you through setting up a web server, and in Chapter 52 you will set up WordPress, a flexible and powerful content management system.

In Chapter 53 you return to email by setting up a mailing list using Mailman.

Sometimes accessing a desktop remotely is the only way to do some things, so in Chapter 54 you will do just that.

Chapter 55 discusses package management from the other direction by guiding you through the process of creating an RPM package for the distribution of your own scripts and configuration files. Then Chapter 56 guides you through sharing files to both Linux and Windows hosts.

Finally, Chapter 57 will get you started in the right direction because I know you are going to ask, "Where do I go from here?"

42.   Server Preparation

43.   Name Services

Taking This Course

Although designed primarily as a self-study guide, this course can be used effectively in a classroom environment. This course can also be used very effectively as a reference. Many of the original course materials I wrote for Linux training classes I used to teach as an independent trainer and consultant were valuable to me as references. The experiments became models for performing many tasks and later became the basis for automating many of those same tasks. I have used many of those original experiments in parts of this course, because they are still relevant and provide an excellent reference for many of the tasks I still need to do.

You will see as you proceed through the course that it uses many software programs considered to be older and perhaps obsolete like Sendmail, Procmail, BIND, the Apache web server, and much more. Despite their age, or perhaps because of it, the software I have chosen to run my own systems and servers and to use in this course has been well-proven and is all still in widespread use. I believe that the software we will use in these experiments has properties that make it especially valuable in learning the in-depth details of how Linux and those services work. Once you have learned those details, moving to any other software that performs the same tasks will be relatively easy. In any event, none of that "older" software is anywhere near as difficult or obscure as some people seem to think that it is.

Who Should Take This Course

If you want to learn to be an advanced Linux user and even a SysAdmin, this course is for you. Most SysAdmins have an extremely high level of curiosity and a deep-seated need to learn Linux system administration. We like to take things apart and put them back together again to learn how they work. We enjoy fixing things and are not hesitant about diving in to fix the computer problems that our friends and co-workers bring us.

We want to know what happens when some computer hardware fails, so we might save defective components such as motherboards, RAM, and storage devices. This gives us defective components with which we can run tests. As I write this, I have a known defective hard drive inserted in a hard drive docking station connected to my primary workstation and have been using it to test failure scenarios that will appear in this course.

Most importantly, we do all of this for fun and would continue to do so even if we had no compelling vocational reason for doing so. Our intense curiosity about computer hardware and Linux leads us to collect computers and software like others collect stamps or antiques. Computers are our avocation – our hobby. Some people like boats, sports, travel, coins, stamps, trains, or any of thousands of other things, and they pursue them relentlessly as a hobby. For us – the true SysAdmins – that is what our computers are. That does not mean we are not well-rounded and don't do other things. I like to travel, read, go to museums and concerts, and ride historical trains, and my stamp collection is still there, waiting for me when I decide to take it up again.

In fact, the best SysAdmins, at least the ones I know, are all multifaceted. We are involved in many different things, and I think that is due to our inexhaustible curiosity about pretty much everything. So if you have an insatiable curiosity about Linux and want to learn about it – regardless of your past experience or lack thereof – then this course is most definitely for you.

Who Should Not Take This Course

If you do not have a strong desire to learn about how to use or administer Linux systems, this course is not for you. If all you want – or need – to do is use a couple apps on a Linux computer that someone has put on your desk, this course is not for you. If you have no curiosity about what superpowers lie behind the GUI desktop, this course is not for you.

Why This Course

Someone asked me why I wanted to write this course. My answer is simple – I want to give back to the Linux community. I have had several amazing mentors over the span of my career, and they taught me many things – things I find worth sharing with you along with much that I have learned for myself.

This course – all three volumes of it – started its existence as the slide presentations and lab projects for three Linux courses I created and taught. For a number of reasons, I do not teach those classes anymore. However, I would still like to pass on my knowledge and as many of the tips and tricks I have learned for the administration of Linux as possible. I hope that with this course I can pass on at least some of the guidance and mentoring that I was fortunate enough to have in my own career.

About Fedora Releases

The first edition of this self-study course was originally written for Fedora 29, and we are now up to Fedora 38. As I have worked through the second edition of this course, I have added new materials I thought appropriate and incorporated as many errata corrections as possible.

Where it was necessary, I have also included revised graphics such as screenshots used for illustrative purposes. In many cases the graphics for earlier releases of Fedora are still applicable although the background images and some nonessential visual elements have changed. In those cases I have retained the original graphics.

I have only replaced older graphics with newer ones where necessary to ensure the accuracy and clarity of the illustrated points. Some of the illustrations in this course are from Fedora 29. If you are using later releases of Fedora, such as Fedora 37, 38, or later, the background and other cosmetic elements may be different from Fedora 29.

David Both

CHAPTER 20

Logical Volume Management (LVM)

Objectives

In this chapter you will learn

- The advantages of logical volume management (LVM)

- The structure of LVM

- To manage LVM systems

- To create new volume groups (VGs) and logical volumes (LVs) with EXT4

- To add space to existing volume groups and logical volumes

The Need for Logical Volume Management

Managing disk space has always been a significant task for SysAdmins. Running out of disk space used to be the start of a long and complex series of tasks to increase the space available to a disk partition. It also required taking the system offline. This usually involved installing a new hard drive, booting to recovery or single-user mode, creating a partition and a filesystem on the new hard drive, using temporary mountpoints to move the data from the too-small filesystem to the new, larger one, changing the content of the /etc/fstab file to reflect the correct device name for the new partition, and rebooting to remount the new filesystem on the correct mountpoint.

© David Both 2023
D. Both, *Using and Administering Linux: Volume 2*, https://doi.org/10.1007/978-1-4842-9615-8_20

I have to tell you that, when LVM first made its appearance in Fedora, I resisted it rather strongly. My initial reaction was that I did not need this additional layer of abstraction between me and the storage devices. It turns out that I was wrong and that logical volume management is very useful.

Logical volume management (LVM) allows for very flexible disk space management. It provides features like the ability to add (or remove) disk space to a filesystem, and it allows for the collection of multiple physical storage devices and partitions into a single volume group (VG), which can then be divided into logical volumes (LV). LVM also allows us to create entirely new volume groups and logical volumes. It can do all of this without rebooting or unmounting the existing filesystems, so long as drive space is available or a physical device can be hot-plugged.

Running Out of Disk Space in VirtualBox

I like to run a new distribution in a VirtualBox virtual machine for a few days or weeks to ensure that I will not run into any significant problems when I start installing it on my production machines.

The morning after a new release, I started installing Fedora on a new virtual machine on my primary workstation, thinking I had enough disk space allocated to the filesystem of the host computer on which it was being installed. I did not. About a third of the way through the installation, I ran out of space on that host's filesystem. Fortunately, VirtualBox is great software itself. It detected the out-of-space condition, paused the virtual machine, and even displayed an error message indicating the exact cause of the problem.

Recovery

Since Fedora and most modern distributions use logical volume management, and I had some free space available on the hard drive, I was able to assign additional disk space to the appropriate filesystem on the fly. This means that I did not have to reformat the entire hard drive and reinstall the operating system or even reboot. I simply assigned some of the available space to the appropriate logical volume and resized the filesystem – all while the filesystem was mounted and active and the running program, VirtualBox, was using the filesystem and waiting. I resumed running the virtual machine, and the installation continued as if nothing had occurred.

Running out of disk space while a critical program is running has happened to almost all SysAdmins. And while many programs are not as well written and resilient as VirtualBox, Linux logical volume management made it possible to recover without losing any data and without having to restart the time-consuming VM installation.

LVM Structure

The structure of a logical volume manager (LVM) disk environment is illustrated in Figure 20-1. Logical volume management enables the combination of multiple individual storage devices and/or disk partitions into a single volume group. That volume group can then be subdivided into logical volumes or used as a single large volume. Regular filesystems, such as EXT3 or EXT4, can then be created on a logical volume.

Logical volume management allows combining partitions and entire storage devices into volume groups. In Figure 20-1, two complete physical storage devices and one partition from a third hard drive have been combined into a single volume group. Two logical volumes have been created from the space in the volume group, and a filesystem, such as an EXT4 filesystem, has been created on each of the two logical volumes.

To add space to a logical volume, we can extend the LV into an existing space in the volume group (VG) if there is any available. If there's none available, we might need to install a new hard drive and extend an existing VG to include at least part of the new drive. Then we can extend the LV within the VG.

A logical volume cannot be larger than the volume group in which it resides. A volume group may contain multiple partitions and physical volumes (PVs) that encompass parts or all of multiple storage devices. This enables overall more efficient use of the physical disk space available. Volume groups may also be extended to provide additional disk space for the contained logical volumes.

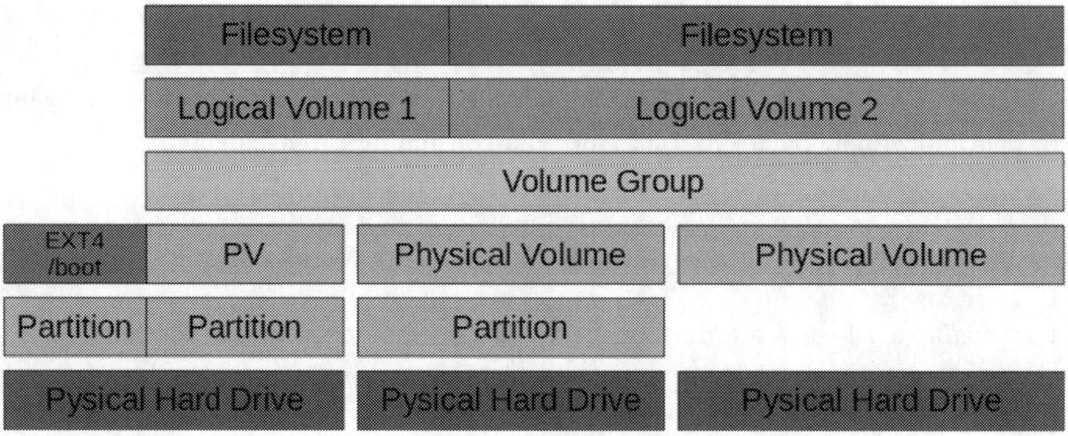

Figure 20-1. *Logical volume management allows combining partitions and entire storage devices into volume groups*

Extending a Logical Volume

The need to resize – especially to expand – an existing filesystem has been around since the beginnings of Unix, and probably back to the very first filesystems, and has not gone away with Linux. It has gotten easier, however, with logical volume management and the ability to expand an active, mounted filesystem. The steps required to do this are fairly simple but will differ depending upon specific circumstances.

Let's start with a simple logical volume extension where space is already available in the volume group. This section covers extending an existing logical volume in an LVM environment using the command-line interface (CLI). This is the simplest situation in which we might find ourselves and the easiest to accomplish.

This procedure can be used on a mounted, live filesystem only with the Linux 2.6 kernel (and higher) and EXT3, EXT4, and BTRFS filesystems. These requirements should not be hard to meet because the most recent kernel series is 5.x.x and most distributions use the EXT3, EXT4, or BTRFS filesystem by default.

I do not recommend that you resize a mounted and active volume on any critical system, but it can be done and I have done so many times, even on the root (/) filesystem. Use your judgment, but consider how much pain might be experienced if there were a failure during the resizing vs. the pain related to taking an active system offline to perform the resizing.

Warning   Not all filesystem types can be resized. The EXT3, EXT4, BTRFS, and XFS filesystems can be expanded on an active, mounted filesystem. These filesystems can be reduced on unmounted filesystems. Other filesystems may not be able to be resized. Be sure to check the documentation for the filesystem you want to resize to ensure that it can be done.

Note that volume groups and logical volumes can be extended while the system is up and running, and the filesystem being expanded can be mounted and active during this process. Let's add 2GB of space to the /home filesystem.

All of the experiments in this chapter must be performed as root.

EXPERIMENT 20-1: EXTENDING A LOGICAL VOLUME

In a real-world environment, we would need to explore a little to determine whether the volume group in which our /home logical volume exists has enough space to do so. Let's start with that. The vgs command lists all volume groups, and the lvs command lists all logical volumes:

```
[root@studentvm1 ~]# lsblk -i
NAME                          MAJ:MIN RM   SIZE RO TYPE MOUNTPOINTS
sda                               8:0   0   60G  0 disk
|-sda1                            8:1   0    1M  0 part
|-sda2                            8:2   0    1G  0 part /boot
|-sda3                            8:3   0    1G  0 part /boot/efi
`-sda4                            8:4   0   58G  0 part
  |-fedora_studentvm1-root 253:0   0    2G  0 lvm  /
  |-fedora_studentvm1-usr  253:1   0   15G  0 lvm  /usr
  |-fedora_studentvm1-tmp  253:2   0    5G  0 lvm  /tmp
  |-fedora_studentvm1-var  253:3   0   10G  0 lvm  /var
  |-fedora_studentvm1-home 253:4   0    2G  0 lvm  /home
  `-fedora_studentvm1-test 253:5   0  500M  0 lvm  /test
sdb                              8:16   0   20G  0 disk
|-sdb1                           8:17   0    2G  0 part
`-sdb2                           8:18   0    2G  0 part
sr0                              11:0   1 1024M  0 rom
zram0                           252:0   0    8G  0 disk [SWAP]
```

5

```
[root@studentvm1 ~]# vgs
 VG                      #PV #LV #SN Attr   VSize    VFree
 fedora_studentvm1   1   6    0 wz--n- <58.00g <23.51g
[root@studentvm1 ~]# lvs
  LV   VG                  Attr       LSize  Pool Origin Data%  ...
  home fedora_studentvm1 -wi-ao----   2.00g
  root fedora_studentvm1 -wi-ao----   2.00g
  test fedora_studentvm1 -wi-ao---- 500.00m
  tmp  fedora_studentvm1 -wi-ao----   5.00g
  usr  fedora_studentvm1 -wi-ao----  15.00g
  var  fedora_studentvm1 -wi-ao----  10.00g
[root@studentvm1 ~]#
```

These commands show that the /home filesystem is located in the fedora_studentvm1 volume group and that there is 23.51GB of space available in that VG. That makes this task simple.

First, expand the logical volume using the existing free space within the volume group. The following command expands the LV by 2GB. The volume group name is fedora_studentvm1, and the logical volume name is home:

```
[root@studentvm1 ~]# lvextend -L +2G /dev/fedora_studentvm1/home
  Size of logical volume fedora_studentvm1/home changed from 2.00 GiB (512
  extents) to 4.00 GiB (1024 extents).
  Logical volume fedora_studentvm1/home successfully resized.
[root@studentvm1 ~]# lvs
  LV   VG                  Attr       LSize  Pool Origin Data% ...
  home fedora_studentvm1 -wi-ao----   4.00g
  root fedora_studentvm1 -wi-ao----   2.00g
  test fedora_studentvm1 -wi-ao---- 500.00m
  tmp  fedora_studentvm1 -wi-ao----   5.00g
  usr  fedora_studentvm1 -wi-ao----  15.00g
  var  fedora_studentvm1 -wi-ao----  10.00g
[root@studentvm1 ~]# df -h
Filesystem                          Size  Used Avail Use% Mounted on
devtmpfs                            4.0M     0  4.0M   0% /dev
tmpfs                               7.9G   12K  7.9G   1% /dev/shm
tmpfs                               3.2G  1.2M  3.2G   1% /run
/dev/mapper/fedora_studentvm1-root  2.0G  631M  1.2G  35% /
/dev/mapper/fedora_studentvm1-usr    15G  5.8G  8.2G  42% /usr
```

```
/dev/sda2                              974M  280M   628M  31% /boot
/dev/mapper/fedora_studentvm1-var      9.8G  659M   8.6G   7% /var
/dev/sda3                             1022M   18M  1005M   2% /boot/efi
/dev/mapper/fedora_studentvm1-test     459M  1.1M   429M   1% /test
/dev/mapper/fedora_studentvm1-home     2.0G  1.4G   457M  75% /home
/dev/mapper/fedora_studentvm1-tmp      4.9G  160K   4.6G   1% /tmp
tmpfs                                  1.6G   72K   1.6G   1% /run/user/984
tmpfs                                  1.6G   64K   1.6G   1% /run/user/0
[root@studentvm1 ~]#
```

That extends the size of the logical volume but does not change the size of the EXT4 filesystem. Notice the logical volume has increased to 4GB, but the filesystem is still 2GB in size. The following command expands the size of the filesystem to fill the space on the volume:

```
[root@studentvm1 ~]# resize2fs /dev/fedora_studentvm1/home ; df -h
resize2fs 1.46.5 (30-Dec-2021)
Filesystem at /dev/fedora_studentvm1/home is mounted on /home; on-line
resizing required
old_desc_blocks = 1, new_desc_blocks = 1
The filesystem on /dev/fedora_studentvm1/home is now 1048576 (4k)
blocks long.

Filesystem                            Size  Used  Avail Use% Mounted on
devtmpfs                              4.0M     0   4.0M   0% /dev
tmpfs                                 7.9G   12K   7.9G   1% /dev/shm
tmpfs                                 3.2G  1.2M   3.2G   1% /run
/dev/mapper/fedora_studentvm1-root    2.0G  631M   1.2G  35% /
/dev/mapper/fedora_studentvm1-usr      15G  5.8G   8.2G  42% /usr
/dev/sda2                             974M  280M   628M  31% /boot
/dev/mapper/fedora_studentvm1-var     9.8G  659M   8.6G   7% /var
/dev/sda3                            1022M   18M  1005M   2% /boot/efi
/dev/mapper/fedora_studentvm1-test     459M  1.1M   429M   1% /test
/dev/mapper/fedora_studentvm1-home     3.9G  1.4G   2.4G  37% /home
/dev/mapper/fedora_studentvm1-tmp      4.9G  160K   4.6G   1% /tmp
tmpfs                                 1.6G   72K   1.6G   1% /run/user/984
tmpfs                                 1.6G   64K   1.6G   1% /run/user/0
[root@studentvm1 ~]#
```

We have added 2GB of space to the active /home filesystem without rebooting or unmounting it.

This ability to expand the logical volume and the filesystem on that LV without rebooting or even taking the filesystem offline means that users' work can continue without interruption. I have expanded the size of many filesystems over the years including some on running servers of various types such as web and email servers.

Creating and Extending Volume Groups

The use of volume groups provides us a great deal of flexibility in managing disk space, especially when we need to add more space to one or more logical volumes.

In this section we explore multiple options for expanding disk space using volume groups. We will extend existing volume groups and create new ones to provide additional space for logical volumes. We will then create a new volume or extend an existing one.

Create a New Volume Group

There are times when it will be necessary to create a new volume group to contain one or more new logical volumes. Sometimes there is already space available on an existing hard drive, which there is on /dev/sdb. We have one unused partition of 2GB and approximately 16GB of as yet partitioned space.

In Experiment 20-2 we use an existing but unused partition to create a volume group.

EXPERIMENT 20-2: CREATING A NEW VOLUME GROUP

Before beginning, verify the amount of space left on /dev/sdb. I know that we just did this in Experiment 20-1, but we should never make any assumptions about the current state of the system, so I make it a practice to check before doing anything:

```
[root@studentvm1 ~]# lsblk
NAME                      MAJ:MIN RM  SIZE RO TYPE MOUNTPOINT
sda                           8:0  0   60G  0 disk
|-sda1                        8:1  0    1G  0 part /boot
`-sda2                        8:2  0   59G  0 part
  |-fedora_studentvm1-root  253:0  0    2G  0 lvm  /
  |-fedora_studentvm1-swap  253:1  0    4G  0 lvm  [SWAP]
  |-fedora_studentvm1-usr   253:2  0   15G  0 lvm  /usr
  |-fedora_studentvm1-home  253:3  0    4G  0 lvm  /home
```

```
  |-fedora_studentvm1-var   253:4   0   10G  0 lvm  /var
  `-fedora_studentvm1-tmp   253:5   0    5G  0 lvm  /tmp
sdb                          8:16   0   20G  0 disk
|-sdb1                       8:17   0    2G  0 part /TestFS
`-sdb2                       8:18   0    2G  0 part
```

The lsblk command tells us that the /dev/sdb drive has a total of 20GB of space and that the /TestFS partition, /dev/sdb1, that we created in Chapter 19 of Volume 1 uses 2GB as does the /dev/sdb2 partiton. The remaining unallocated space is about 16GB in size. Note that if you unmounted the /TestFS filesystem, the mountpoint would not show up, but it would be /dev/sdb1.

We want to allocate the rest of the space on the /dev/sdb drive to this new volume group. Normally we would just delete the /dev/sdb2 partition to allow creation of a new partition consisting of the rest of the space on the hard drive. That would be too easy and definitely much less fun and informative. Instead, we will create a third partition on the drive, and these two partitions will be combined into a single volume group in which we will create a logical volume.

Create a new primary partition on /dev/sdb that uses the rest of the space on the drive. This new /dev/sdb3 partition will be 16GB in size. You should be able to do this now without explicit instructions. Then verify that the partition was created.

Create one physical volume (PV) on each partition, /dev/sdb2 and /dev/sdb3. We can do this with a single command. The pvcreate command will warn that the btrfs partition created in Volume 1, Chapter 19, is detected, and be sure you want to delete it:

```
[root@studentvm1 ~]# pvcreate /dev/sdb2 /dev/sdb3
WARNING: btrfs signature detected on /dev/sdb2 at offset 65600. Wipe it?
[y/n]: y
  Wiping btrfs signature on /dev/sdb2.
  Physical volume "/dev/sdb2" successfully created.
  Physical volume "/dev/sdb3" successfully created.
```

Now create a volume group encompassing both of the partitions /dev/sdb2 and /dev/sdb3. A volume group can contain physical volumes spanning multiple storage devices such as two or more hard drives or SSDs:

```
[root@studentvm1 ~]# vgcreate NewVG-01 /dev/sdb2 /dev/sdb3
  Volume group "NewVG-01" successfully created
```

Verify the new volume group:

```
[root@studentvm1 ~]# vgs
  VG                #PV #LV #SN Attr   VSize    VFree
  NewVG-01            2   0   0 wz--n-  17.99g  17.99g
  fedora_studentvm1   1   6   0 wz--n- <58.00g <21.51g
```

Notice that the combined size of the volume group NewVG-01 is almost 18GB, all of which is available. Now create a new logical volume in this volume group. The -L 2G option defines the size of the new volume. Obviously, NewVG-01 is the name of the volume group in which the volume is to be created, and --name TestVol1 specifies the name of the new logical volume:

```
[root@studentvm1 ~]# lvcreate -L 2G NewVG-01 --name TestVol1
  Logical volume "TestVol1" created.
[root@studentvm1 ~]# lvs
  LV       VG                Attr       LSize   Pool Origin Data%   ...
  TestVol1 NewVG-01          -wi-a-----   2.00g
  home     fedora_studentvm1 -wi-ao----   4.00g
  root     fedora_studentvm1 -wi-ao----   2.00g
  test     fedora_studentvm1 -wi-ao---- 500.00m
  tmp      fedora_studentvm1 -wi-ao----   5.00g
  usr      fedora_studentvm1 -wi-ao----  15.00g
  var      fedora_studentvm1 -wi-ao----  10.00g
```

That was easy. However, the man page for lvcreate is long and complex and it is not clear, even from the examples, that this simple command can create a new volume.

Now create an EXT4 filesystem on the new volume, mount it temporarily on /mnt, and test it by creating a few files with some test data there. There is no need to create a permanent mountpoint for this filesystem or to add an entry in /etc/fstab because this filesystem will not be used for anything more than a bit of testing. Note that this is the exact type of use case for which the /mnt mountpoint is intended by the Linux Filesystem Hierarchy Standard (FHS) as we saw in Chapter 19 of Volume 1:

```
[root@studentvm1 ~]# mkfs -t ext4 /dev/mapper/NewVG--01-TestVol1
mke2fs 1.46.5 (30-Dec-2021)
Creating filesystem with 524288 4k blocks and 131072 inodes
Filesystem UUID: 67e5badd-933b-4bb8-9851-3eed9cb16553
Superblock backups stored on blocks:
        32768, 98304, 163840, 229376, 294912
```

```
Allocating group tables: done
Writing inode tables: done
Creating journal (16384 blocks): done
Writing superblocks and filesystem accounting information: done

[root@studentvm1 ~]# mount /dev/mapper/NewVG--01-TestVol1 /mnt
[root@studentvm1 ~]# ll /mnt
total 16
drwx------ 2 root root 16384 Feb 16 16:04 lost+found
[root@studentvm1 ~]# lsblk -f
NAME                        MAJ:MIN RM   SIZE RO TYPE MOUNTPOINT
sda                             8:0  0    60G  0 disk
|-sda1                          8:1  0     1M  0 part
|-sda2                          8:2  0     1G  0 part /boot
|-sda3                          8:3  0     1G  0 part /boot/efi
`-sda4                          8:4  0    58G  0 part
  |-fedora_studentvm1-root 253:0  0     2G  0 lvm  /
  |-fedora_studentvm1-usr  253:1  0    15G  0 lvm  /usr
  |-fedora_studentvm1-tmp  253:2  0     5G  0 lvm  /tmp
  |-fedora_studentvm1-var  253:3  0    10G  0 lvm  /var
  |-fedora_studentvm1-home 253:4  0     4G  0 lvm  /home
  `-fedora_studentvm1-test 253:5  0   500M  0 lvm  /test
sdb                            8:16  0    20G  0 disk
|-sdb1                         8:17  0     2G  0 part
|-sdb2                         8:18  0     2G  0 part
`-sdb3                         8:19  0    16G  0 part
  `-NewVG--01-TestVol1     253:6  0     2G  0 lvm  /mnt
sr0                           11:0   1 1024M  0 rom
zram0                        252:0   0     8G  0 disk [SWAP]
[root@studentvm1 ~]#
```

It is not necessary to spend a lot of time, but do a bit of testing on this new volume. Just create a few files with some data in them and verify that all is working. When you are finished testing, unmount the volume.

Although the two partitions we used to create the new volume group in Experiment 20-2 are both on the same hard drive, it does illustrate that multiple partitions and even entire storage devices can be combined into a single volume group.

Extend an Existing Volume Group

In situations in which there is no existing space to be found, it will be necessary to add a new drive in order to create that space. Experiment 20-3 takes us through the process of adding a new hard drive and then creating a volume group and a logical volume in the new space.

EXPERIMENT 20-3: EXTENDING AN EXISTING VOLUME GROUP

In Experiment 19-8 we created a new virtual hard drive for the VM. We added one hard drive in that experiment, and now we add another virtual hard drive to that SATA controller. If necessary you can refer to the instructions in Experiment 19-8. Allocate 2GB of space to this device.

Use the `lsblk` command to determine the drive identifier. On my StudentVM1 host, it is /dev/sdc, and it should be on your virtual machine as well. You should be sure to use the correct device for your computer.

Now create a new physical volume (PV) on the new hard drive:

```
[root@studentvm1 ~]# pvcreate /dev/sdc
  Physical volume "/dev/sdc" successfully created.
```

Extend the NewVG-01 volume group to include the new physical volume:

```
[root@studentvm1 ~]# vgextend NewVG-01 /dev/sdc
  Volume group "NewVG-01" successfully extended
[root@studentvm1 ~]#
```

Extend the logical volume. This command extends the logical volume by adding all of the space on the new /dev/sdc physical volume:

```
[root@studentvm1 ~]# lvextend /dev/NewVG-01/TestVol1 /dev/sdc
  Size of logical volume NewVG-01/TestVol1 changed from 2.00 GiB (512
  extents) to <4.00 GiB (1023 extents).
  Logical volume NewVG-01/TestVol1 successfully resized.
[root@studentvm1 ~]#
```

Finally, resize the filesystem:

```
[root@studentvm1 ~]# resize2fs /dev/NewVG-01/TestVol1
resize2fs 1.44.3 (10-July-2018)
Filesystem at /dev/NewVG-01/TestVol1 is mounted on /mnt; on-line resizing
required
old_desc_blocks = 1, new_desc_blocks = 1
The filesystem on /dev/NewVG-01/TestVol1 is now 1047552 (4k) blocks long.
```

If the resize2fs command fails, run **e2fsck -f /dev/NewVG-01/TestVol1** and then retry the resizing:

```
[root@studentvm1 ~]# lsblk -i
NAME                          MAJ:MIN RM   SIZE RO TYPE MOUNTPOINT
sda                               8:0   0    60G  0 disk
|-sda1                            8:1   0     1M  0 part
|-sda2                            8:2   0     1G  0 part /boot
|-sda3                            8:3   0     1G  0 part /boot/efi
`-sda4                            8:4   0    58G  0 part
  |-fedora_studentvm1-root    253:0   0     2G  0 lvm  /
  |-fedora_studentvm1-usr     253:1   0    15G  0 lvm  /usr
  |-fedora_studentvm1-tmp     253:2   0     5G  0 lvm  /tmp
  |-fedora_studentvm1-var     253:3   0    10G  0 lvm  /var
  |-fedora_studentvm1-home    253:4   0     4G  0 lvm  /home
  `-fedora_studentvm1-test    253:5   0   500M  0 lvm  /test
sdb                              8:16   0    20G  0 disk
|-sdb1                           8:17   0     2G  0 part
|-sdb2                           8:18   0     2G  0 part
`-sdb3                           8:19   0    16G  0 part
  `-NewVG--01-TestVol1        253:6   0     4G  0 lvm  /mnt
sdc                              8:32   0     2G  0 disk
`-NewVG--01-TestVol1          253:6   0     4G  0 lvm  /mnt
sr0                              11:0   1  1024M  0 rom
zram0                           252:0   0     8G  0 disk [SWAP]
[root@studentvm1 ~]#
```

We have expanded the capacity of a logical volume by adding space to the volume group from a new drive.

Notice that none of the experiments in this chapter required rebooting the computer. All of the experiments were performed with the system fully functional.

Tips

Using LVM is already quite easy, but I have found a few things that can make it even more so.

I use the Extended filesystems unless there is clear reason to use another filesystem. Not all filesystems support resizing, but XFS, BTRFS, EXT3, and EXT4 do. The EXT filesystems are also very fast and efficient. The EXT filesystems can be tuned by a knowledgeable SysAdmin to meet the needs of most environments if the default tuning parameters do not.

I use meaningful volume and volume group names to help make identification of groups and volumes easy while working on them. I also use EXT filesystem labels for the same reason. Filesystem labels can make mounting filesystems easy by reducing the amount of typing required to mount them manually or to add the specification to the /etc/fstab file.

Be aware that volume groups that span multiple physical volumes will fail completely if one of the physical devices composing them fails. LVM is not inherently fault tolerant although a properly designed software Redundant Array of Independent/Inexpensive Disks (RAID) system using LVM can be. As always, make frequent backups of everything; see Chapter 40 in this volume of the course.

Advanced Capabilities

LVM has some additional very powerful and interesting advanced features that are beyond the scope of this course. However, here's an overview of some of those features.

It is possible to create hybrid volumes that consist of rotating storage devices along with SSDs in which the SSD acts as a data cache for the slower hard disk drive (HDD). This can speed up access to frequently used data.

LVM can be used to create RAID (Redundant Array of Independent/Inexpensive Disks) volumes in various configurations. RAID is a tool that allows combining two or more identical physical devices into logical groups. These groups can be used to speed access to data on the storage devices and to add a level of redundancy that helps prevent data loss in the event of the failure of one device. RAID is most useful for providing redundancy with SSDs and both speed and redundancy for HDDs.

Mirror volumes are simply two storage devices that LVM keeps identical in as close to real time as possible. This redundancy provides protection against the failure of one of those devices.

Snapshot volumes are a snapshot of a storage device taken at a point in time. This enables you to do a rollback to the snapshot if the original device is corrupted.

There is a lot of overlap in the capabilities of RAID and LVM. RAID itself can be implemented at the hardware level or via LVM. Most storage controller hardware contains built-in RAID capabilities. RAID also provides two-device mirroring.

Chapter Summary

Logical volume management (LVM) provides a high-level tool for the advanced management of disk space on modern Linux hosts. By abstracting the hardware into volume groups and logical volumes, it enables the SysAdmin to create volumes that are not limited by the physical space on individual storage devices. It provides the capability to manage logical volumes by adding space when and where it is needed without disturbing ongoing operations.

The LVM facility has many more functions than we have used in this chapter. They enable capabilities such as creating and restoring backups of volume groups and deleting, renaming, resizing, and more of the groups and volumes that make up the whole of an LVM system.

I suggest reading the man pages for these commands to at least get a fair idea of the vast amount of control that can be exerted over an LVM system. You can use tab completion to locate other LVM-related commands: lv<tab><tab>.

Exercises

Perform these exercises to complete this chapter:

1. What are some of the reasons for using logical volume management?

2. How does the information available with the `vgdisplay` command differ from that of the `vgs` command?

3. I sometimes use a drive docking station to test storage devices I
    suspect may have errors or that I want to attempt data recovery
    from. How would I access the data on a hard drive if the drive had
    been configured as the only member of a volume group?

4. Expand the /tmp filesystem by 5GB into some of the remaining
    and yet unused space on /dev/sdc.

CHAPTER 21

File Managers

Objectives

In this chapter you will learn

- The functions of a file manager

- Basic usage of Midnight Commander (MC), a text-mode file manager

- Basic usage of Krusader, a graphical file manager based on Midnight Commander

- Basic usage of Thunar, the graphical default file manager for the Xfce desktop

- Short introductions to a few other file managers.

Introduction

One of the most common administrative tasks that end users and administrators alike need to perform is file management. Managing files can consume a major portion of your time. Locating files, determining which files and folders (directories) are taking the most disk space, deleting files, moving files, and simply opening files for use in an application are some of the most basic yet frequent tasks we do as computer users. File management programs are tools that are intended to streamline and simplify those necessary chores.

This chapter will be mostly about learning the Midnight Commander text-mode file manager. The reason for this is that, as SysAdmins, we work mostly on the command line, and Midnight Commander will be available even if it might need to be installed. We will also look at the Thunar graphical file manager, which is the default for the Xfce desktop, and we will take a very brief look at some other available file managers.

17

© David Both 2023
D. Both, *Using and Administering Linux: Volume 2*, https://doi.org/10.1007/978-1-4842-9615-8_21

As with every aspect of Linux, there are many options available for file managers. A few of those provided by my usual distribution, Fedora, are listed in the following. Some are text and others are graphical interfaces.

Text-Mode Interface

- Midnight Commander

- Vifm

- nnn

Graphical Interface

- Thunar

- Krusader

- Dolphin

- XFE

I have used each of these at different times for various reasons, and they all have qualities to recommend them. Ranging from very simple to feature-packed, there is a file manager available that will meet your needs. This chapter looks briefly at each of the file managers listed.

Default File Manager

Like most Linux distributions, Fedora has a default graphical desktop file manager, currently Thunar[1] for the Xfce desktop. The Linux desktop usually has an icon that looks like a little house; that is your "home" directory, that is, folder. Click the Home icon, and the default file manager opens with your home directory as the PWD, or present working directory. The Home icon is located on the desktop along with the Trash icon and some drive icons, as shown in Figure 21-1.

---

[1] Xfce.org, Thunar File Manager, `https://docs.xfce.org/xfce/thunar/start`

Figure 21-1. *The Xfce desktop with the Home icon and the Thunar file manager open*

Each desktop, such as Xfce, KDE Plasma, Cinnamon, LXDE, and so on, has a default graphical file manager. In Xfce and most other desktop environments, the default file manager can be changed using **Applications ➤ Settings ➤ Preferred Applications ➤ Utilities ➤ File Manager**. We will cover Thunar in more detail later in this chapter along with installing and using some of the other graphical file managers.

Text-Mode File Managers

Because we SysAdmins spend so much time using the command-line interface, we will spend most of our time in this chapter on text-mode file managers. Text-mode file managers are particularly useful when a GUI is not available, but they can also be used as a primary file manager in a desktop terminal emulator session even when you are using a GUI.

There are several fine text-mode file managers to choose from. My personal favorite is Midnight Commander, but there are others that are also powerful, usable, and well respected.

Midnight Commander

Midnight Commander[2] is a text-based program that I use frequently because I often need to interact with local and remote Linux computers using the CLI. It can be used locally with almost any of the common shells and remotely through SSH.

Midnight Commander provides an interactive, visually based, text-mode user interface for navigating the filesystem and managing files. It can be used to copy, edit, move, or delete files and complete directory trees. It can also be used to expand archive files of various types and explore their contents.

You can start Midnight Commander from the CLI with the mc command. Figure 21-2 shows Midnight Commander in the Konsole terminal emulator program. The user interface for Midnight Commander is two text-mode panels, left and right, which each display the contents of a directory. Along the very top of the Midnight Commander (a.k.a. MC) interface is a menu bar containing menu items for configuring Midnight Commander and the current panel, and a selection bar that highlights one line of the current directory is displayed in the current panel.

The top of each panel displays the name of the current directory for that panel. The directory entry for the current panel is highlighted.

Navigation is accomplished with the arrow and Tab keys. The Enter key can be used to enter a highlighted directory. The bottom portion of the interface displays information about the file or directory highlighted in each panel, a hint feature, and a line of function

---

[2] Midnight Commander, `https://midnight-commander.org/`

key labels; you can simply press the function key on your keyboard that corresponds to the function you want to perform. Between the hint line and the function keys is a command line. You can type any CLI command here as you would at the standard Bash or some other shell prompt; it is, after all, a Bash prompt.

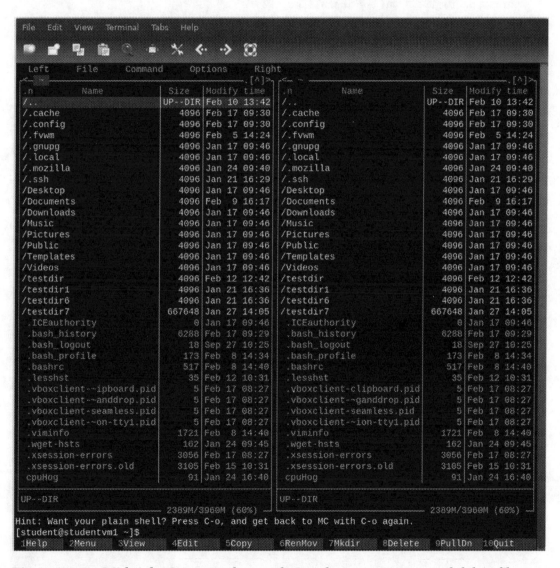

Figure 21-2. *Midnight Commander can be used to move, copy, and delete files*

EXPERIMENT 21-1: INTRODUCING MIDNIGHT COMMANDER

As the root user, install Midnight Commander:

```
[root@studentvm1 ~]# dnf -y install mc
```

Then as the user student, ensure that the PWD is your home directory. Start Midnight Commander with the mc command.

Midnight Commander starts with two open panels. Switch between the panels using the **Tab** key. Use the arrow keys to move the highlight bar (cursor) up and down the list of files and directories in the current panel. Highlight the Documents directory in the right panel and press the Enter key to change into that directory.

Moving up to the parent directory can be accomplished by highlighting the double-dot (..) entry at the top of the list in the panel and pressing the Enter key. In the left panel in Figure 21-3, this entry is shown at the top, and the Size column shows "UP--DIR". But don't do that now.

```
   Left      File    Command    Options    Right
+<- ~ ------------------------------.[^]>++<- ~/Documents ----------------------.[^]>+
|.n        Name       | Size |Modify time ||.n        Name       | Size |Modify time |
|/..                  |UP--DIR|Dec 22 11:06|| test10             |     0|Dec 30 16:32|
|/.cache              |  4096|Jan 24 21:21|| test11             |     0|Dec 30 16:32|
|/.config             |  4096|Jan 25 09:55|| test12             |     0|Dec 30 16:32|
|/.gnupg              |  4096|Dec 22 13:15|| test13             |     0|Dec 30 16:32|
|/.local              |  4096|Dec 22 13:15|| test14             |     0|Dec 30 16:32|
|/.mozilla            |  4096|Oct 29 14:28|| test15             |     0|Dec 30 16:32|
|/.ssh                |  4096|Dec 22 21:30|| test16             |     0|Dec 30 16:32|
|/Desktop             |  4096|Dec 24 08:19|| test17             |     0|Dec 30 16:32|
|/Documents           |  4096|Jan 25 22:05|| test18             |     0|Dec 30 16:32|
|/Downloads           |  4096|Dec 22 13:15|| test19             |     0|Dec 30 16:32|
|/Music               |  4096|Dec 22 13:15|| test20             |     0|Dec 30 16:32|
|/Pictures            |  4096|Dec 22 13:15|| testfile01         | 41876|Dec 30 16:32|
|/Public              |  4096|Dec 22 13:15|| testfile02         | 41876|Dec 30 16:32|
|/Templates           |  4096|Dec 22 13:15|| testfile03         | 41876|Dec 30 16:32|
|/Videos              |  4096|Dec 22 13:15|| testfile04         | 41876|Dec 30 16:32|
|/testdir             |  4096|Dec 30 16:48|| testfile05         | 41876|Dec 30 16:32|
|/testdir1            |  4096|Dec 30 16:36|| testfile06         | 41876|Dec 30 16:32|
|/testdir6            |  4096|Dec 30 16:36|| testfile07         | 41876|Dec 30 16:32|
|/testdir7            |  4096|Dec 30 16:36|| testfile08         | 41876|Dec 30 16:32|
| .ICEauthority       |  1864|Jan 24 21:21|| testfile09         | 41876|Dec 30 16:32|
|---------------------------------------||----------------------------------------|
|UP--DIR                               || testfile03                             |
+--------------------- 3758M/3968M (94%) -++-------------------- 3758M/3968M (94%) -+
       Hint: Want your plain shell? Press C-o, and get back to MC with C-o again.
[student@studentvm1 Documents]$                                             [^]
 1Help   2Menu   3View   4Edit   5Copy   6RenMov  7Mkdir   8Delete  9PullDn 10Quit
```

Figure 21-3. *Midnight Commander with two panels. The **Tab** key switches between panels*

Note   I started Midnight Commander using the -a option, which uses ASCII plain text characters to draw lines instead of advanced line drawing characters as shown in Figure 21-2. Those line drawing characters do not line up quite as well when copied from the terminal session into a document.

To enter a command at the Midnight Commander command prompt, just start typing. Let's look at the value of the $SHELL variable:

```
|---------------------------------------||---------------------------------------|
|UP--DIR                                ||UP--DIR                                |
+----------.--------- 3690M/3968M (92%) -++---------------- 3690M/3968M (92%) -+
Hint: Want your plain shell? Press C-o, and get back to MC with C-o again.
[student@studenlvm1 ~]$ echo $SHELL                                     [^]
 1Help    2Menu   3View   4Edit    5Copy    6RenMov
 7Mkdir  8Delete  9PullDn 10Quit
```

The result is shown in a sub-shell. Press Enter to exit the sub-shell and return to MC.

In the right panel, scroll down to highlight one of the files that has some content. The size of a file is shown in the Size column. View the file content by pressing the **F3** key as seen in Figure 21-4. This is a viewer only, and you cannot edit the file from within this window. The F4 key opens the file in an editor.

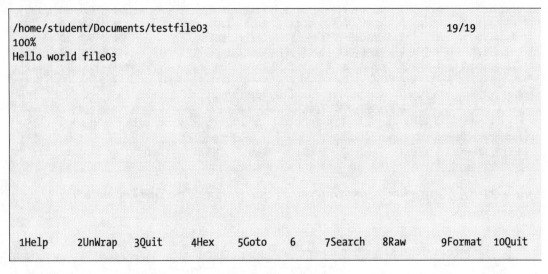

```
/home/student/Documents/testfile03                              19/19
100%
Hello world file03




















 1Help     2UnWrap   3Quit    4Hex    5Goto    6    7Search   8Raw    9Format  10Quit
```

Figure 21-4. *Press the F3 key to view the content of a file*

The top line of the viewer shows the path and file name, the distance into the file being viewed compared to the total amount of data in the file, and the percentage of the distance into the file being viewed.

There are navigation, search, and viewing options that can be accessed using the function keys as shown on the bottom line. Press **F3** again or **F10** to quit the viewer and return to the main MC window.

Notice the function key assignments at the bottom of the MC window. **F1** will display some help. There are also function keys for Move, Copy, Delete, and Quit, among others. Press the corresponding function key on the keyboard to perform that function.

Be sure that the F1 and F10 keys are not being captured by the terminal emulator. Use the menu bar of the Xfce4-terminal emulator session and select **Edit ➤ Preferences** and then select the **Advanced** tab. Add check marks to the "**Disable menu shortcut key (F10 by default)**" and "**Disable help window shortcut key (F1 by default)**" options to allow Midnight Commander to capture these keystrokes.

This should not be an issue for virtual consoles and, if you're using a GUI terminal emulator, you can also click the F1 or F10 using the mouse.

Highlight one of the files in the right panel and press **F5** to start the copy of the file. This opens the Copy dialog shown in Figure 21-5.

```
   Left      File    Command    Options    Right
+<- ~ -------------------------------.[^]>++<- ~/Documents --------------------.[^]>+
|.n       Name      | Size |Modify time ||.n      Name      | Size |Modify time |
|/..                |UP--DIR|Dec 22 11:06|| test11          |      0|Dec 30 16:32|
|/.cache            |   4096|Jan 24 21:21|| test12          |      0|Dec 30 16:32|
|/.config           |   4096|Jan 25 09:55|| test13          |      0|Dec 30 16:32|
|/.gnupg                                                              c 30 16:32|
|/.local   +----------------------------- Copy ------------------------------+ c 30 16:32|
|/.mozilla | Copy file "testfile03" with source mask:                  | c 30 16:32|
|/.ssh     | *                                                         | c 30 16:32|
|/Desktop  |                              [x] Using shell patterns     | c 30 16:32|
|/Document | to:                                                       | c 30 16:32|
|/Download | /home/student/                                            | c 30 16:32|
|/Music    |---------------------------------------------------------- | c 30 16:32|
|/Pictures | [ ] Follow links            [ ] Dive into subdir if exists| c 30 16:32|
|/Public   | [x] Preserve attributes     [ ] Stable symlinks           | c 30 16:32|
|/Template |---------------------------------------------------------- | c 30 16:32|
|/Videos   |        [< OK >] [ Background ] [ Cancel ]                  | c 30 16:32|
|/testdir  +-----------------------------------------------------------+ c 30 16:32|
|/testdir1                                                             c 30 16:32|
|/testdir6          |   4096|Dec 30 16:36|| testfile08      | 41876|Dec 30 16:32|
|/testdir7          |   4096|Dec 30 16:36|| testfile09      | 41876|Dec 30 16:32|
| .ICEauthority     |   1864|Jan 24 21:21|| testfile10      | 41876|Dec 30 16:32|
| .bash_history     |   2340|Jan 25 22:04|| testfile11      | 41876|Dec 30 16:32|
|-------------------------------------------||----------------------------------|
|UP--DIR                                    || testfile03                        |
+-------------------- 3758M/3968M (94%) -++---------------------- 3758M/3968M (94%) -+
Hint: Want your plain shell? Press C-o, and get back to MC with C-o again.
[student@studentvm1 Documents]$                                            [^]
 1Help   2Menu   3View   4Edit   5Copy   6RenMov  7Mkdir  8Delete  9PullDn 10Quit
```

Figure 21-5. *The Copy dialog provides some options for the copy command*

Multiple files can be selected on which to perform the move, copy, or delete operation. Highlight each file and press the **Insert** key to select each desired file. In this case we only want to copy the one file. Use the down arrow key to sequence through the options and highlight **OK**; then press **Enter** to complete the operation.

Switch to the left panel and scroll down until you can see the file you copied to verify that it is in the directory there. Highlight the copied file in the left panel and press **F8** to delete that file. A dialog opens to allow verification that you want to delete the selected file or files. Select **Yes** and press **Enter**.

Switch back to the right panel and select several non-adjacent files using the Insert key. Highlight each desired file and press the Insert key to "tag" it, as the MC documentation terms selecting a file or directory. Your results should be similar to those in Figure 21-6.

```
   Left     File     Command     Options     Right
 +<- ~ ------------------------------.[^]>++<- ~/Documents ----------------------.[^]>+
 |.n      Name          | Size  |Modify time ||.n        Name        | Size  |Modify time |
 | .bashrc              |   350|Dec 25 14:26|| test16               |     0|Dec 30 16:32|
 | .esd_auth            |    16|Dec 22 13:15|| test17               |     0|Dec 30 16:32|
 | .vboxclien~board.pid |     6|Jan 24 21:21|| test18               |     0|Dec 30 16:32|
 | .vboxclien~splay.pid |     6|Jan 24 21:21|| test19               |     0|Dec 30 16:32|
 | .vboxclien~ddrop.pid |     6|Jan 24 21:21|| test20               |     0|Dec 30 16:32|
 | .vboxclien~mless.pid |     6|Jan 24 21:21|| testfile01           | 41876|Dec 30 16:32|
 | .viminfo             |  3383|Jan 16 13:43|| testfile02           | 41876|Dec 30 16:32|
 | .xscreensaver        |  8816|Dec 23 17:13|| testfile03           | 41876|Dec 30 16:32|
 | .xsession-errors     |  2939|Jan 24 21:24|| testfile04           | 41876|Dec 30 16:32|
 | .xsession-errors.old |  2405|Jan 17 21:27|| testfile05           | 41876|Dec 30 16:32|
 | dmesg.txt            | 41876|Dec 30 16:37|| testfile06           | 41876|Dec 30 16:32|
 | dmesg1.txt           | 41936|Jan 16 14:08|| testfile07           | 41876|Dec 30 16:32|
 | dmesg2.txt           | 41876|Dec 30 16:37|| testfile08           | 41876|Dec 30 16:32|
 | dmesg3.txt           | 41876|Dec 30 16:37|| testfile09           | 41876|Dec 30 16:32|
 | link3                |     0|Dec 30 16:40|| testfile10           | 41876|Dec 30 16:32|
 | newfile.txt          |     0|Dec 30 16:37|| testfile11           | 41876|Dec 30 16:32|
 |!softlink1            |     5|Dec 30 16:48|| testfile12           | 41876|Jan 27 08:52|
 |------------------------------------------||---------- 209,380 B in 7 files -----------|
 |-> link1                                  || testfile09                                |
 +-------------------- 3758M/3968M (94%) -++-------------------- 3758M/3968M (94%) -+
          Hint: Want to do complex searches? Use the External Panelize command.
 [student@studentvm1 Documents]$                                                    [^]
  1Help   2Menu    3View    4Edit    5Copy    6RenMov  7Mkdir   8Delete  9PullDn 10Quit
```

Figure 21-6. *Select – or "tag" – several files in the right panel*

After tagging some files in the right directory panel, press the **F8** key and then verify that you want to delete the files. All of the tagged files will be deleted. If the selection bar is highlighting an untagged file, that file will not be deleted. We could have copied or moved the files instead of deleting them. You could also simply run the commands from the MC command line.

New directories can be created in a couple ways. First, just type the following command at the Midnight Commander command line as shown in Figure 21-7. Just start typing as the selection bar is only used within the directory panels. Press **Enter**.

```
+--------------------- 3758M/3968M (94%) -++--------------------- 3758M/3968M (94%) -+
       Hint: Do you want Lynx-style navigation? Set it in the Configuration dialog.
[student@studentvm1 Documents]$ mkdir Directory01                                [^]
  1Help   2Menu   3View   4Edit   5Copy   6RenMov 7Mkdir   8Delete 9PullDn 10Quit
```

Figure 21-7. *Commands can be entered on the MC command line*

Another way to create a directory is to use the **F7** key and use the dialog box in Figure 21-8. The name of the directory or file that is under the selection bar will be displayed in the dialog. Delete that, type in the directory name, and select **OK** and press **Enter** to complete creating the directory.

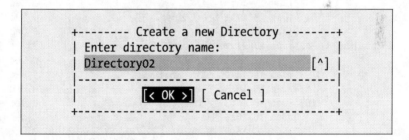

```
+--------- Create a new Directory ---------+
| Enter directory name:                    |
| Directory02                         [^]  |
|------------------------------------------|
|        [< OK >] [ Cancel ]               |
+------------------------------------------+
```

Figure 21-8. *Type a new directory name in this dialog*

Take a few moments to look at the menu items across the top of the MC interface. The Left and Right menus allow you to personalize the display of data in the left and right panels, respectively. The File menu allows file operations such as creating links, changing the file mode and ownership, displaying only files that match a filter, making new directories, deleting and copying files, and more. Some of these functions are duplicated by the function keys.

There are a couple changes I like to make to the MC interface. I do like to view the file mode (permissions) and size when the selection bar is on a file. This data is shown on the mini status line. It is necessary to make this configuration change to each panel separately. In Figure 21-9 I have already made this change to the left panel, and you can see mode and size of the file dmesg1.txt at the bottom of the left panel. Although the selection bar is in the right panel at the moment, the last selection in the left panel is the one shown on the mini status line.

To access the top menu bar, press the **F9** key. Use the right and left arrow keys to move the highlight between the main menu items; select the **Right** menu and then use the down arrow key to open the drop-down menu under the Right menu as shown in Figure 21-9. Continue to use the down arrow key to select the **Listing format** menu item and press **Enter**.

```
   Left      File    Command    Options     Right
+<- ~ --------------------------------.[^]+----------------------+--------------.[^]>+
|.n       Name       | Size  |Modify time| File listing          |Size  |Modify time |
| .bashrc            |    350|Dec 25 14:2| Quick view      C-x q|P--DIR|Jan 27 08:34|
| .esd_auth          |     16|Dec 22 13:1| Info            C-x i|  4096|Jan 27 13:52|
| .vboxclien~board.pid|     6|Jan 24 21:2| Tree                  |  4096|Jan 27 13:53|
| .vboxclien~splay.pid|     6|Jan 24 21:2|----------------------|     0|Dec 30 16:32|
| .vboxclien~ddrop.pid|     6|Jan 24 21:2| Listing format...     |     0|Dec 30 16:32|
| .vboxclien~mless.pid|     6|Jan 24 21:2| Sort order...         |     0|Dec 30 16:32|
| .viminfo           |   3383|Jan 16 13:4| Filter...             |     0|Dec 30 16:32|
| .xscreensaver      |   8816|Dec 23 17:1| Encoding...      M-e  |     0|Dec 30 16:32|
| .xsession-errors   |   2939|Jan 24 21:2|----------------------|     0|Dec 30 16:32|
| .xsession-errors.old|  2405|Jan 17 21:2| FTP link...           |     0|Dec 30 16:32|
| dmesg.txt          |  41876|Dec 30 16:3| Shell link...         |     0|Dec 30 16:32|
| dmesg1.txt         |  41936|Jan 16 14:0| SFTP link...          |    13|Dec 30 16:33|
| dmesg2.txt         |  41876|Dec 30 16:3| SMB link...           |     0|Dec 30 16:32|
| dmesg3.txt         |  41876|Dec 30 16:3| Panelize              |     0|Dec 30 16:32|
| link3              |      0|Dec 30 16:4|----------------------|     0|Dec 30 16:32|
| newfile.txt        |      0|Dec 30 16:3| Rescan          C-r  |     0|Dec 30 16:32|
|!softlink1          |      5|Dec 30 16:4+----------------------+     0|Dec 30 16:32|
|-------------------------------------||--------------------------------------------|
| dmesg1.txt          | 41936|-rw-rw-r--|| file02                                     |
+-------------------- 3758M/3968M (94%) -++---------------------- 3758M/3968M (94%) -+
       Hint: Want your plain shell? Press C-o, and get back to MC with C-o again.
[student@studentvm1 Documents]$
 1Help  2Menu   3View   4Edit   5Copy    6RenMov  7Mkdir   8Delete  9PullDn 10Quit
```

Figure 21-9. *To view the file mode and size, press F9 to access the top menu bar and select **Listing format** for the left and right panel settings*

The Listing format dialog is shown in Figure 21-10. Use the arrow keys to highlight **User mini status**. Press the **space bar** to place an X in the check box. Select **OK** and press Enter. Now do this for the left panel as well.

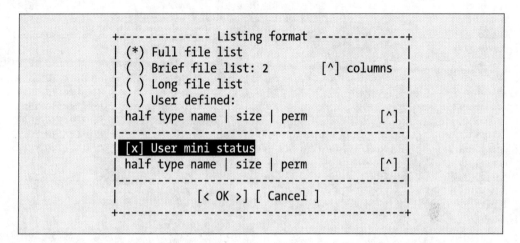

```
         +-------------- Listing format --------------+
         | (*) Full file list                        |
         | ( ) Brief file list: 2        [^] columns  |
         | ( ) Long file list                        |
         | ( ) User defined:                         |
         | half type name | size | perm         [^]  |
         |-------------------------------------------|
         | [x] User mini status                      |
         | half type name | size | perm         [^]  |
         |-------------------------------------------|
         |            [< OK >] [ Cancel ]            |
         +-------------------------------------------+
```

Figure 21-10. *Place an X in the User mini status check box to view file size and mode*

I also like to use the Vim editor rather than the default MC internal editor. That internal editor is perfectly fine, but my fingers prefer the Vim key combinations because they remember them after 25 years working with Vi and Vim. This can be changed too.

From the top menu bar, select **Options ➤ Configuration**, and you will see the **Configure options** dialog in Figure 21-11. Use the arrow keys to select **Use internal edit** and press the space bar to remove the X from the check box. Select **OK** and press **Enter** to complete this change.

```
   Left      File     Command     Options     Right
+<- ~ -------------------------------.[^]>++<- ~/Documents ----------------------.[^]>+
|.n      Name                                                         |Modify time |
| .bashrc        +----------------- Configure options ----------------+|Dec 30 16:32|
| .esd_auth      | + File operations ---------+ + Other options ----------+ ||Dec 30 16:32|
| .vboxclien~b   | | [x] Verbose operation  | |[ ] Use internal edit    | ||Dec 30 16:32|
| .vboxclien~s   | | [x] Compute totals     | |[x] Use internal view    | ||Dec 30 16:32|
| .vboxclien~d   | | [x] Classic progressbar| |[ ] Ask new file name    | ||Dec 30 16:32|
| .vboxclien~m   | | [x] Mkdir autoname     | |[ ] Auto menus           | ||Dec 30 16:32|
| .viminfo       | | [ ] Preallocate space  | |[ ] Drop down menus      | ||Dec 30 16:32|
| .xscreensave   | +------------------------+ |[x] Shell patterns       | ||Dec 30 16:32|
| .xsession-er   | + Esc key mode -----------+ |[ ] Complete: show all   | ||Dec 30 16:32|
| .xsession-er   | | [x] Single press       | |[x] Rotating dash        | ||Dec 30 16:32|
| dmesg.txt      | | Timeout: 1000000       | |[x] Cd follows links     | ||Dec 30 16:32|
| dmesg1.txt     | +------------------------+ |[ ] Safe delete          | ||Dec 30 16:32|
| dmesg2.txt     | + Pause after run --------+ |[ ] Safe overwrite       | ||Dec 30 16:32|
| dmesg3.txt     | | ( ) Never              | |[x] Auto save setup      | ||Dec 30 16:32|
| link3          | | (*) On dumb terminals  | |                         | ||Dec 30 16:32|
| newfile.txt    | | ( ) Always             | |                         | ||Dec 30 16:32|
|!softlink1      | +------------------------+ +-------------------------+ ||Dec 30 16:32|
|-------------   |-----------------------------------------------------| -----------|
|-> link1        |             [< OK >] [ Cancel ]                      |            |
+-------------   +-----------------------------------------------------+ 3968M (94%) -+
      Hint: Want to
[student@studentvm1 Documents]$                                               [^]
 1Help   2Menu    3View    4Edit    5Copy    6RenMov  7Mkdir   8Delete  9PullDn 10Quit
```

Figure 21-11. *Remove the X from "Use internal edit" to use an external editor instead*

The F4 key is used to edit an existing, selected file. If you have an F14 key on your keyboard, it can be used to start the editor with a new, empty file, or you can use Shift+F4 to simulate the F14 key. These keys invoke the Vim editor now that we have changed the editor option to external. A different external editor may be specified in the $EDITOR environment variable.

There are other options I sometimes change, such as the colors. Select **Options ➤ Appearance** as shown in Figure 21-12. The resulting dialog has the current skin (color combination) highlighted. To choose a new skin, press **Enter** to view the list. Scroll to the one you want and press **Enter**. The change is immediate, and if it looks like it will be what you want, select **OK** and press **Enter**.

```
   Left      File     Command    Options      Right
+<- ~ ------------------------------------------+ocuments ----------------------.[^]>+
|.n        Name      | Size |  Configuration...      Name     | Size  |Modify time |
|/..                 |UP--DIR| Layout...           |0         |      0|Dec 30 16:32|
|/.cache             |  4096| panel options...      |1         |      0|Dec 30 16:32|
|/.config            |  4096| Confirmation...      |2         |      0|Dec 30 16:32|
|/.gnupg             |  4096| Appearance...        |3         |      0|Dec 30 16:32|
|/.local             |  4096| Display bits...      |4         |      0|Dec 30 16:32|
|/.mozilla           |  4096| Learn keys...        |5         |      0|Dec 30 16:32|
|/.ssh               |  4096| Virtual FS...        |6         |      0|Dec 30 16:32|
|/Desktop            |  4096|-------------------   |7         |      0|Dec 30 16:32|
|/Documents          |  4096| Save setup           |8         |      0|Dec 30 16:32|
|/Downloads          |  4096+-------------------+   |9         |      0|Dec 30 16:32|
|/Music              |  4096|Dec 22 13:15|| test20            |      0|Dec 30 16:32|
|/Pictures           |  4096|Dec 22 13:15|| testfile01        | 41876|Dec 30 16:32|
|/Public             |  4096|Dec 22 13:15|| testfile02        | 41876|Dec 30 16:32|
|/Templates          |  4096|Dec 22 13:15|| testfile03        | 41876|Dec 30 16:32|
|/Videos             |  4096|Dec 22 13:15|| testfile04        | 41876|Dec 30 16:32|
|/testdir            |  4096|Dec 30 16:48|| testfile05        | 41876|Dec 30 16:32|
|/testdir1           |  4096|Dec 30 16:36|| testfile06        | 41876|Dec 30 16:32|
|/testdir6           |  4096|Dec 30 16:36|| testfile07        | 41876|Dec 30 16:32|
|/testdir7           |  4096|Dec 30 16:36|| testfile08        | 41876|Dec 30 16:32|
| .ICEauthority      |  1864|Jan 24 21:21|| testfile09        | 41876|Dec 30 16:32|
| .bash_history      |  2340|Jan 25 22:04|| testfile10        | 41876|Dec 30 16:32|
|----------------------------------------||-------------------------------------------|
|UP--DIR                                 || test13                                    |
+--------------------- 3758M/3968M (94%) -++--------------------- 3758M/3968M (94%) -+
Hint: Want your plain shell? Press C-o, and get back to MC with C-o again.
[student@studentvm1 Documents]$                                              [^]
 1Help   2Menu   3View   4Edit   5Copy   6RenMov  7Mkdir  8Delete 9PullDn 10Quit
```

Figure 21-12.   *The **Options ➤ Appearance** dialog allows selection of "skins" for various colors*

Any changes you make to viewing modes or options must be saved because they are only temporary otherwise and will no longer be in effect the next time Midnight Commander is started. Save the changes you have made by accessing the top menu bar and then selecting **Options ➤ Save setup**.

MC is very powerful with many features that make it one of the most useful tools I have in my toolbox. Midnight Commander has a man page (**man mc**) that is over 2600 lines long. Be sure to read it to discover all of the capabilities and options available.

Like the rest of Linux, there is much more to MC than we have time for in this experiment. You should spend more time experimenting on your own with MC to learn more about it.

Exit from Midnight Commander by pressing the **F10** key. You may need to then press **Enter** to answer "Yes" to the question.

Midnight Commander has a virtual filesystem that enables connecting a local instance with remote hosts using FTP, SMB (Samba), and SSH protocols. This allows files to be copied from one host to another. Files on a remote host can be managed with MC on your local host using those protocols. I always use SSH.

Other Text-Mode File Managers

There are a number of other text-mode file managers available. Other than while researching this chapter, I have never used any of them because I find MC meets all of my text-mode file manager needs. We will only look at a couple that have Fedora packages available, which makes them easy to install and, in my opinion at least, reasonably easy to use.

Vifm

Vifm is a dual-pane file manager that provides a Vim-like environment. If you like Vim and its commands are embedded in your muscle memory, this is the file manager for you. Figure 21-13 illustrates the very minimalistic interface. The panes can be split horizontally or vertically.

Figure 21-13. *Vifm is a dual-pane file manager that uses Vim-like key combinations*

You can highlight a file and use a command like **dd** to delete a file. Vifm pops up a verification dialog, and you can respond Yes or No to complete the action. The **yy** command yanks (copies) a file in one pane, and the **p** command pastes it in the other pane. The **Tab** key is used to switch between active panes. Select a file and press the **Enter** key to open the file for editing with Vim. Exit from Vim in the normal manner. You can also exit from Vifm using the same keystrokes as used to exit from Vim itself. Vifm supports multi-file operations like delete, move, and copy.

The Fedora package name is vifm if you want to install it.

nnn

The nnn file manager is a very simple, single-pane tool that offers no frills. Only one directory and its content are displayed at a time. Use the arrow keys to select a directory, as shown in Figure 21-14, and press the **Enter** key to make that directory the PWD. Select a file and press **e** to edit the file in Vim.

```
[1 2 3 4] /home/student/Documents

    2019-01-27 13:52         /   Directory01/
    2019-01-27 13:53         /   Directory02/
    2018-12-30 16:32        0B   file01
    2018-12-30 16:32        0B   file02
    2018-12-30 16:32        0B   file03
>   2018-12-30 16:32        0B   file04
    2018-12-30 16:32        0B   file05
    2018-12-30 16:32        0B   file06
    2018-12-30 16:32        0B   file07
    2018-12-30 16:32        0B   file08
    2018-12-30 16:33       13B   file09
    2018-12-30 16:32        0B   file10
    2018-12-30 16:32        0B   file11
    2018-12-30 16:32        0B   file12
    2018-12-30 16:32        0B   file13
    2018-12-30 16:32        0B   file14
    2018-12-30 16:32        0B   file15
    2018-12-30 16:32        0B   file16
    2018-12-30 16:32        0B   file17
    2018-12-30 16:32        0B   file18
    2018-12-30 16:32        0B   file19
    2018-12-30 16:32        0B   file20

6/55 [file04]
```

Figure 21-14. nnn is a single-pane file manager with a very simple interface

A press of the **n** key opens a dialog to create a new file or directory. The package name is nnn to install this file manager.

Graphical File Managers

Like all Linux tools, there are plenty of choices when it comes to graphical file managers. We will discuss a few of these here, but these are not all of the ones from which you might choose.

Krusader

Krusader is an exceptional file manager that is modeled after Midnight Commander. It uses a similar two-panel layout but in a graphical interface as shown in Figure 21-15 instead of a text-mode interface. Krusader allows you to use the same keyboard navigation and command structure as Midnight Commander and also allows you to use the mouse or trackball to navigate and perform all of the standard drag-and-drop operations you would expect on files.

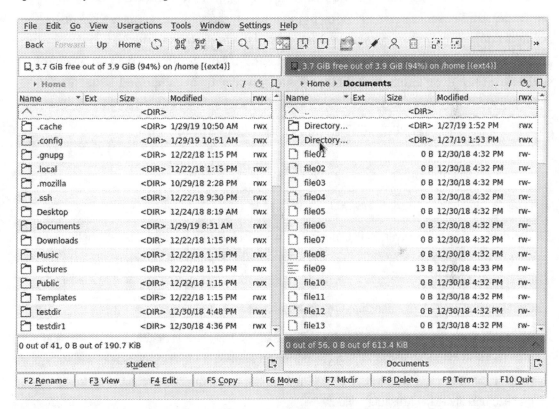

Figure 21-15. *Krusader is much like Midnight Commander, but uses a GUI interface and provides significantly more flexibility*

The user interface for Krusader, much like that of Midnight Commander, is two GUI-mode panels, left and right, which each display the contents of a directory. The top of each panel contains the name of the current directory for that panel. In addition, tabs can be opened for each panel, and a different directory can be opened in each tab. Navigation is accomplished with the arrow and Tab keys or with the mouse. The Enter key can be used to enter a highlighted directory, or you can double-click the desired directory. Each tab and panel can be configured to show files in one of two different modes. In Figure 21-15, files are displayed in the detailed view, which, in addition to the file name and an icon or preview, shows the file size, the date it was last modified, the owner, and the file permissions.

Along the very top of the Krusader graphical user interface are a menu bar and a tool bar containing menu items for configuring Krusader and managing files. The bottom portion of the interface displays a line of function key labels; you can simply press the function key on your keyboard that corresponds to the function you want to perform.

By default Krusader saves the current tab and directory locations as well as other configuration items when you exit so that you will always return to the last configuration and set of directories when restarting the application. This configuration can be changed so that your home or some other directories are always the ones opened at startup.

EXPERIMENT 21-2: INTRODUCING KRUSADER

As root, install Krusader:

```
[root@studentvm1 ~]# dnf install -y krusader
```

This command installed over 75 packages on my StudentVM1 virtual machine although that number may be significantly different for you. Krusader was written to integrate with the KDE desktop. Many of the packages are needed to support the KDE base functions of Krusader.

Start Krusader on the Xfce desktop through **Applications ➤ Accessories ➤ Krusader**.

Since this is the first time you will have used Krusader, it will show you a Welcome dialog and then take you through a dialog to help you perform a starting configuration. It is not necessary to make any changes at this time, so click the **Ok** buttons and then the **Close** button to proceed directly to the Krusader window.

Krusader, like Midnight Commander, starts with two open panels. Switch between the panels using the **Tab** key or by clicking with the mouse.

Highlight the Documents directory in the right panel and press the **Enter** key or just double-click it.

Change directories by double-clicking the desired directory. Moving up to the parent directory can be accomplished by double-clicking the double-dot (..) entry. You can also move to the parent of the directory in the highlighted panel by clicking the arrow icon in the tool bar.

Notice the function key assignments at the bottom of the Krusader window. These function keys provide functions similar to those of Midnight Commander. F1 will display some help. There are also function keys for Move, Copy, Delete, and Quit, among others. Simply press the corresponding function key on the keyboard or click the button to perform that function. You can also right-click a desired file to pop up a context menu and then take one of the actions from the menu.

Figure 21-16 shows how to configure Krusader to display the embedded Konsole terminal session and the command line. Go ahead and configure those both, now.

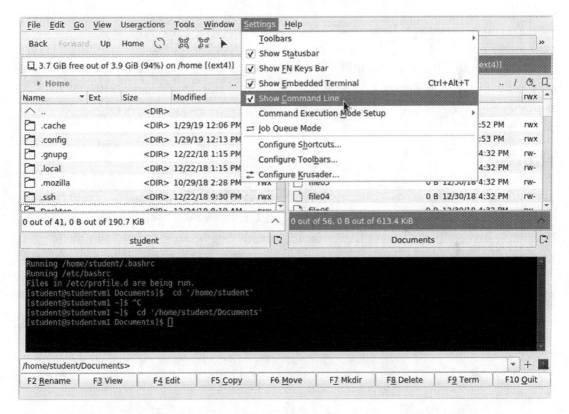

Figure 21-16. *Configuring Krusader to show both the built-in command-line interface and the Konsole terminal window panel*

After having configured the terminal session and the simple command line, you can issue CLI commands simply by typing them; the CLI entry text box is at the bottom, just above the function key assignment line. The cursor there is always active while you are in navigation mode. To change the PWD of the current panel to the /tmp directory, type cd /tmp and press the **Enter** key, just as you would from the shell prompt.

Using the GUI, navigate to your ~/Documents directory. Highlight the file dmesg1.txt and press F3. This shows the contents of that file. Scroll up and down the file using the Page Up and Page Down keys or using the scroll bar. Click the **X** in the View tab to close the view of the file and return to the main Krusader window. In order to edit a file, the Kate GUI text editor would need to be installed.

Locate the dmesg2.txt or similar file and press **F8** to delete it. Click the Delete button to complete the deletion.

Take some time to explore Krusader on your own.

Press the **F10** key to exit from Krusader.

I use Krusader as one of my main GUI file managers. It is powerful and easy to use, especially to someone familiar with Midnight Commander. The biggest drawback to Krusader is the large number of other KDE programs required to support it.

Thunar

Thunar is a lightweight file manager that is the default for the Xfce desktop. Thunar has a single-directory pane with which to work. It also has a sidebar for navigation. Thunar is a simple, decent file manager that is good for many beginners due to its simplicity while providing enough features to enable you to perform many of the functions of more complex file managers. Thunar is shown in Figure 21-17.

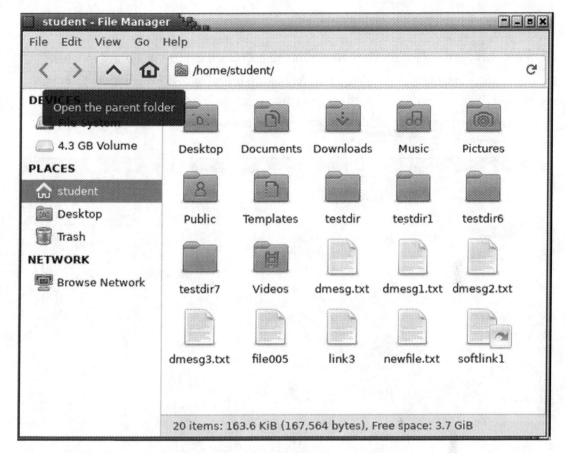

Figure 21-17. *Thunar is the default file manager for the Xfce desktop*

The primary user interface for Thunar is fairly simple with a navigation sidebar and a single-directory window in which to work. It does support multiple tabs but not splitting the panel into two. Navigation is accomplished with the arrow and Tab keys or the mouse. The Enter key can be used to enter a highlighted directory.

Having used the Xfce desktop and Thunar for a couple years after this book was first written, I now find that Thunar is one of my favorite graphical file managers. This is, in part at least, due to its relative simplicity and clean interface.

Dolphin

Dolphin, shown in Figure 21-18, is somewhat like Krusader. It can be configured for two directory navigation panels, and it adds a sidebar that allows for easy filesystem navigation. It also supports tabs; however, when restarted it always reverts to the default of one pair of directory panels that display your home directory.

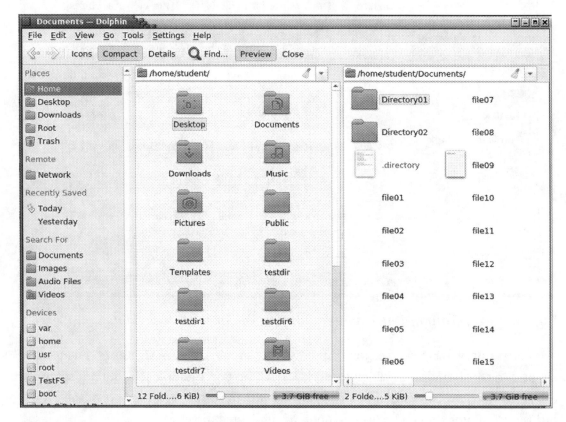

Figure 21-18. *After some configuration, the Dolphin file manager uses two directory navigation panels and a navigation sidebar*

The primary user interface for Dolphin can be configured to be very similar to Krusader. Navigation is accomplished with the arrow and Tab keys or the mouse. The Enter key can be used to enter a highlighted directory. Dolphin also supports expanding the directory trees in both the sidebar navigation panel and the directory panels.

Dolphin is not installed by default from the Xfce live image, so it needs to be installed manually. Dolphin requires about 35 additional dependencies, which are also installed. The package name is "dolphin" in case you want to install and test it. I did find that Dolphin has problems with display of some icons; you can see this in Figure 21-18. I did not try to fix this problem.

XFE

XFE is one of the more interesting of the file managers as it has an interface all its own and is a bit more flexible than some of the other file managers. Figure 21-19 shows the unique interface of the XFE file manager.

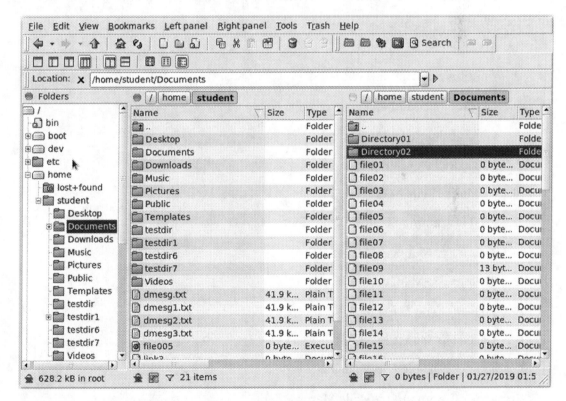

Figure 21-19. *The XFE file manager has its own unique interface*

XFE may be configured to display one or two directory panels and the navigation bar, which is optional. It performs all the expected drag-and-drop functions, but it requires some manual configuration to link some desired applications like LibreOffice with specific file types. It has a reasonable set of configuration options, but nowhere near those of Krusader.

XFE is also quite restrictive about retaining its own set of "themes" and has no option to use the desktop color scheme, icons, decorations, or widgets. This also makes it incapable of adjusting the font size it uses so that in Hi-DPI environments, such as my 3840 × 2160 32-inch display, the text is tiny and difficult to read.

Install the "xfe" package to experiment with this file manager.

Other File Managers

Here is a list of file managers I found on Tecmint. Their article, "30 Best File Managers and Explorers [GUI + CLI] for Linux,"[3] not only lists them but also offers a short description of each. You may find one – or more – that suits you better than the ones I have covered here:

1. Konqueror File Manager

2. Nautilus File Manager

3. Dolphin File Manager

4. GNU Midnight Commander

5. Krusader File Manager

6. PCManFM File Manager

7. X File Explorer (XFE)

8. Nemo File Manager

9. Thunar File Manager

10. SpaceFM File Manager

11. Caja – File Manager

12. Ranger Console File Manager

13. Linux Command Line File Manager

14. Deepin File Manager

15. Polo File Manager

---

[3] Kili, Aaron, "30 Best File Managers and Explorers [GUI + CLI] for Linux," www.tecmint.com/linux-file-managers/, Tecmint, 2023

16.   cfiles – Terminal File Manager

17.   Double Commander

18.   Emacs File Manager

19.   Pantheon Files

20.   Vifm File Manager

21.   Worker File Manager

22.   nnn – Terminal File Manager

23.   WCM Commander

24.   4Pane File Manager

25.   lf – Terminal File Manager

26.   jFileProcessor

27.   qtfm File Manager

28.   PCManFM-qt

29.   fman

30.   Liri Files

31.   Ytree

Chapter Summary

There are many file managers, and one that I have not covered may already be your favorite. Your choice of file manager should be the one that works best for you. GNU/Linux provides many viable choices, and one will most likely meet most of your needs. If your favorite does not meet your needs for a particular task, you can always use the one that does.

All of the file managers I covered in this chapter are free of charge and distributed under some form of open source license. All are available from common, trusted repositories for Fedora and CentOS.

Exercises

Perform these exercises to complete this chapter:

1. For single-panel GUI file managers like Thunar, is it possible to use a second instance to drag and drop actions such as copy or move?

2. Configure the right pane of Midnight Commander to view the Info of the file highlighted by the selection bar in the left panel. What information does this Info panel display about the filesystem?

3. Is the configuration you have just done in Experiment 21-2 persistent between restarts of MC?

4. Continuing with Midnight Commander, switch the two panels so that the Info panel is on the right.

5. Convert the MC Info panel to show a directory tree. Are the subdirectories displayed when the directory tree is first entered?

CHAPTER 22

Everything Is a File

Objectives

In this chapter you will learn

- The definition of a file

- What "everything is a file" really means and why it is important

- The implications of "everything is a file"

- How to use common Linux file management tools to access hardware as files

This is one of the most important concepts that makes Linux especially flexible and powerful: everything is a file. That is, everything can be the source of a data stream, the target of a data stream, or in many cases both. In this chapter you will explore what "everything is a file" really means and learn to use that to your advantage as a SysAdmin.

> *The whole point with "everything is a file" is …the fact that you can use common tools to operate on different things.*
>
> —Linus Torvalds in an email

© David Both 2023
D. Both, *Using and Administering Linux: Volume 2*, https://doi.org/10.1007/978-1-4842-9615-8_22

What Is a File?

Here is a trick question for you. Which of the following are files?

- Directories

- Shell scripts

- Running terminal emulators

- LibreOffice documents

- Serial ports

- Kernel data structures

- Kernel tuning parameters

- Storage devices like /dev/sda

- /dev/null

- Partitions – /dev/sda1

- Logical volumes (LVM) such as /dev/mapper/volume1-tmp

- Printers

- Sockets

To Unix and Linux, they are all files, and that is one of the most amazing concepts in the history of computing. It makes possible some very simple yet powerful methods for performing many administrative tasks that might otherwise be extremely difficult or impossible.

Linux handles almost everything as a file. This has some interesting, powerful, and amazing implications. This concept makes it possible to copy an entire hard drive, boot record included, because the entire hard drive is a file, just as are the individual partitions.

"Everything is a file" is possible because all devices are implemented by Linux as these things called device files. Device files are not device drivers; rather, they are gateways to devices that are exposed to the user.[1]

---

[1] Hoffman, Chris, "What Does 'Everything Is a File' Mean in Linux?," www.howtogeek.com/117939/htg-explains-what-everything-is-a-file-means-on-linux/, 2016

Device Files

Device files are technically known as device special files.[2] Device files are employed to provide the operating system and the users an interface to the devices that they represent. All Linux device files are located in the /dev directory, which is an integral part of the root (/) filesystem because they must be available to the operating system during early stages of the boot process – before other filesystems are mounted.

Device File Creation

Over the years, chaos overtook the /dev directory with huge numbers of mostly unneeded devices. The udev daemon was created to simplify this problem. Understanding how udev works is key to dealing with devices, especially hot-plug devices and how they can be managed.

The /dev directory has always been the location for the device files in all Unix and Linux operating systems. In the past, device files were created at the time the operating system was installed on the system. This meant that all possible devices that might ever be used on a system needed to be created in advance. In fact, tens of thousands of device files needed to be created to handle all of the possibilities. It became very difficult to determine which device file actually related to a specific physical device or if one were missing.

udev Simplification

udev is designed to simplify this problem by creating entries in /dev only for those devices that actually currently exist at boot time or that have a high probability of actually existing on the host. This significantly reduces the total number of device files required.

In addition, udev assigns names to devices when they are plugged into the system, such as Universal Serial Bus (USB) storage and printers and other non-USB types of devices as well. In fact, udev treats all devices as plug and play (PnP), even at boot time. This makes dealing with devices consistent at all times, whether at boot time or when

---

[2]Wikipedia, Device File, https://en.wikipedia.org/wiki/Device_file

they are hot-plugged later. It is not necessary for us as SysAdmins to do anything else for the device files to be created. The Linux kernel takes care of everything. It is only possible to mount the partition in order to access its contents after the device file such as /dev/sdb1 has been created.

Kernel developer and maintainer Greg Kroah-Hartman, one of the creators of udev, wrote a paper[3] that provides some insight into the details of udev and how it is supposed to work. Note that udev has matured since the article was written and some things have changed, such as the udev rule locations and structure. Regardless, this paper provides some deep and important insight into udev and current device naming strategies, which I'll attempt to summarize in this chapter.

Naming Rules

In modern versions of Fedora and CentOS, udev stores its default naming rules in files in the /usr/lib/udev/rules.d directory and its local rules and configuration files in the /etc/udev/rules.d directory. Each file contains a set of rules for a specific device type. CentOS 6 and earlier stored the global rules in /lib/udev/rules.d/. The location of the udev rule files may be different on your distribution.

In earlier versions of udev, there were many local rule sets created, including a set for network interface card (NIC) naming. As each NIC was discovered by the kernel and renamed by udev for the very first time, a rule was added to the rule set for the network device type. This was initially done to ensure consistency before names had changed from "ethX" to more consistent ones.

Rule Change Blues

One of the main consequences of using udev for persistent plug-and-play naming is that it makes things much easier for the average non-technical user. This is a good thing in the long run; however, there have been migration problems, and many SysAdmins were – and still are – not happy with these changes.

---

[3] Kroah-Hartman, Greg, "Kernel Korner: udev – Persistent Naming in User Space," `www.linuxjournal.com/article/7316`, Linux Journal

The rules changed over time, and there were at least three significantly different naming conventions for network interface cards. That naming disparity caused a great deal of confusion, and many configuration files and scripts had to be rewritten multiple times during the period of these changes.

For example, the name of a NIC that was originally eth0 would have changed from that to em1 or p1p2 and finally to eno1. I wrote an article[4] on my website that goes into some detail about these naming schemes and the reasons behind them.

Now that udev has multiple consistent default rules for determining device names, especially for NICs, storing the specific rules for each device in local configuration files is no longer required to maintain that consistency.

Device Data Flow

Let's look at the data flow of a typical command to visualize how device special files work. Figure 22-1 illustrates a simplified data flow for a simple command. Issuing the # cat /etc/resolv.conf command from a GUI terminal emulator such as Konsole or xterm causes the resolv.conf file to be read from the disk with the disk device driver handling the device-specific functions such as locating the file on the hard drive and reading it. The data is passed through the device file and then from the command to the device file and device driver for pseudo-terminal 6 where it is displayed in the terminal session.

Of course the output of the cat command could have been redirected to a file in the following manner, cat /etc/resolv.conf > /etc/resolv.bak, in order to create a backup of the file. In that case the data flow on the left side of Figure 22-1 would remain the same, while the data flow on the right would be through the /dev/sda2 device file, the hard drive device driver, and then back onto the hard drive in the /etc directory as the new file, resolv.bak.

---

[4] Both, David, "Network Interface Card (NIC) name assignments," www.linux-databook.info/?page_id=4243

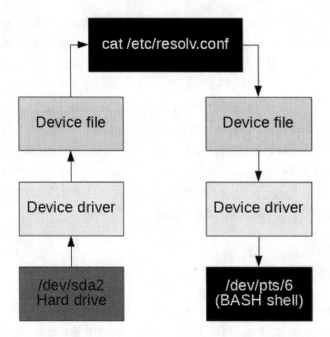

Figure 22-1. *Device data flow*

These device special files make it very easy to use standard streams (STDIO) and redirection to access any and every device on a Linux or Unix computer. They provide a consistent and easy-to-access interface to every device. Simply directing a data stream to a device file sends the data to that device.

One of the most important things to remember about these device special files is that they are not device drivers. They are most accurately described as portals or gateways to the device drivers. Data is passed from an application or the operating system to the device file, which then passes it to the device driver, which then sends it to the physical device.

By using these device files that are separate from the device drivers, it is possible for users and programs to have a consistent interface to every device on the host computer. This is how common tools can be used to operate on different things as Linus says.

The device drivers are still responsible for dealing with the unique requirements of each physical device. That is, however, outside the scope of this book.

Device File Classification

Device files can be classified in at least two ways. The first and most commonly used classification is that of the type of data stream commonly associated with the device. For example, teletype (tty) and serial devices are considered to be character based because the data stream is transferred and handled one character or byte at a time. Block-type devices such as storage devices transfer data in blocks, typically a multiple of 256 bytes.

Let's take a look at the /dev directory and some of the devices in it.

EXPERIMENT 22-1: VIEWING DEVICE SPECIAL FILES

This experiment should be performed as the user student. Open a terminal session and display a long listing of the /dev directory:

```
[student@studentvm1 ~]$ ls -l /dev | less
<SNIP>
brw-rw----. 1 root     disk      8,    0 Jan 30 06:53 sda
brw-rw----. 1 root     disk      8,    1 Jan 30 06:53 sda1
brw-rw----. 1 root     disk      8,    2 Jan 30 06:53 sda2
brw-rw----. 1 root     disk      8,   16 Jan 30 06:53 sdb
brw-rw----. 1 root     disk      8,   17 Jan 30 06:53 sdb1
brw-rw----. 1 root     disk      8,   18 Jan 30 06:53 sdb2
brw-rw----. 1 root     disk      8,   19 Jan 30 06:53 sdb3
brw-rw----. 1 root     disk      8,   32 Jan 30 06:53 sdc
<SNIP>
crw-rw-rw-. 1 root     tty       5,    0 Jan 30 06:53 tty
crw--w----. 1 root     tty       4,    0 Jan 30 06:53 tty0
crw--w----. 1 root     tty       4,    1 Jan 30 11:53 tty1
crw--w----. 1 root     tty       4,   10 Jan 30 06:53 tty10
crw--w----. 1 root     tty       4,   11 Jan 30 06:53 tty11
crw--w----. 1 root     tty       4,   12 Jan 30 06:53 tty12
<SNIP>
```

The results from this command are too long to show here in full, but you will see a list of device files with their file permissions and their major and minor identification numbers.

The voluminous output of the `ls -l` command is piped through the `less` utility to allow you to page through the results; use the Page Up, Page Down, and up and down arrow keys to move around. Type **q** to quit and get out of the `less` display.

The pruned listing of device files shown in Experiment 22-1 are just a few of the ones in the /dev directory on my StudentVM1 virtual machine. The ones on your VM should be very similar if not identical. They represent disk- and tty-type devices among many others. Notice the leftmost character of each line in the output. The ones that have a "b" are block-type devices, and the ones that begin with "c" are character devices.

The more detailed and explicit way to identify device files is using the device major and minor numbers. The disk devices have a major number of 8, which designates them as SCSI block devices. Note that all parallel ATA (PATA)[5] and serial ATA (SATA)[6] storage devices and SSDs have been managed by the SCSI subsystem because the old ATA subsystem was deemed many years ago as not maintainable due to the poor quality of its code. As a result storage devices that would have previously been designated as "hd[a-z]" are now referred to as "sd[a-z]".

You can probably infer the pattern of disk drive minor numbers in the small sample shown. Minor numbers 0, 16, 32, and so on up through 240 are the whole disk numbers. So major/minor 8/16 represents the whole disk /dev/sdb, and 8/17 is the device file for the first partition, /dev/sdb1. Major/minor 8/34 would be /dev/sdc2.

The tty device files in the preceding list are numbered a bit more simply from tty0 through tty63. I find the number of tty devices a little incongruous because the whole point of the new udev system is to create device files for only those devices that actually exist; I am not sure why it is being done this way. However, you can also see from the listing that all of these device files were created on the same date, which was when the host was last booted. The device files on your host should also have a timestamp that is the same as the last boot time.

The Linux Allocated Devices[7] file at Kernel.org is the official registry of device types and major and minor number allocations. It can help you understand the major/minor numbers for all currently defined devices.

---

[5] Wikipedia, Parallel ATA, https://en.wikipedia.org/wiki/Parallel_ATA

[6] Wikipedia, Serial ATA, https://en.wikipedia.org/wiki/Serial_ATA

[7] www.kernel.org/doc/html/v4.11/admin-guide/devices.html

Fun with Device Files

Let's take a few minutes now and have some fun with some of these device files. We will perform a couple fun experiments that illustrate the power and flexibility of the Linux device files.

Most Linux distributions have multiple virtual consoles, 1 through 7, that can be used to log into a local console session with a shell interface. These can be accessed using the key combinations HostKey+F1 for console 1, HostKey+F2 for console 2, and so on. Virtual consoles were introduced in Volume 1, Chapter 7, of this course, so you should have already had some exposure to them. The default HostKey is the right Ctrl key, but I have reconfigured mine to be the left Win key, a.k.a., the super key, because I find it easier. You can change the default HostKey with the VirtualBox Manager.

EXPERIMENT 22-2: FUN WITH DEVICE FILES

In this experiment we will show that simple commands can be used to send data between devices, in this case, different console and terminal devices. Perform this experiment as the student user.

In the StudentVM1 desktop window, press **HostKey+F2** to switch to console 2. On some distributions like Fedora, the login information includes the tty (teletype) device associated with this console, but some do not. It should be tty2 because you are in console 2.

Log into console 2 as the student user. Then use the who am i command – yes, just like that, with spaces – to determine which tty device is connected to this console:

```
[student@studentvm1 ~]$ who am i
student  tty2        2019-01-30 15:32
```

This command also shows the date and time that the user on the console logged in.

Before we proceed any further with this experiment, let's look at a listing of the tty2 and tty3 devices in /dev. We do that by using a set [23] so that only those two devices are listed:

```
[student@studentvm1 ~]$ ls -l /dev/tty[23]
crw--w---- 1 student tty 4, 2 Feb 18 12:03 /dev/tty2
crw--w---- 1 root    tty 4, 3 Feb 18 12:05 /dev/tty3
```

There are a large number of tty devices defined at boot time, but we do not care about most of them for this experiment, just the tty2 and tty3 devices. As device files there is nothing special about them; they are simply character-type devices. Note the "c" in the first column of the results. We will use these two TTY devices for this experiment. The tty2 device is attached to virtual console 2, and the tty3 device is attached to virtual console 3.

Press **HostKey+F3** to switch to console 3 and log in again as the student user. Use the who am i command again to verify that you really are in console 3 and then enter the echo command:

```
[student@studentvm1 ~]$ who am i
student   tty3          2019-01-30 15:38
[student@studentvm1 ~]$ echo "Hello world" > /dev/tty2
```

Press **HostKey+F2** to return to console 2. The string "Hello world" (without quotes) should display in console 2.

This experiment can also be performed with terminal emulators on the GUI desktop. Terminal sessions on the desktop use pseudo-terminal devices in the /dev tree, such as /dev/pts/1, where pts stands for "pseudo-terminal session."

Return to your graphical desktop using HostKey+F1. Open at least two terminal sessions on the GUI desktop using Konsole, Tilix, xterm, or your other favorite graphical terminal emulator. You may open several if you wish. Determine which pseudo-terminal device files they are connected to with the who am i command and then choose one pair of terminal emulators to work with for this experiment. Use one to send a message to the another with the echo command:

```
[student@studentvm1 ~]$ who am i
student   pts/2          2023-02-18 12:01 (192.168.0.1)
```

However, it is possible that you will get no result from the who am i command. This occurs because who am i only seems to work on login terminal sessions and not on a non-login session such as one started from the desktop. So a virtual console session or a remote SSH login session would work with this. But there are at least two ways to circumvent this – as is usual in Linux.

We will use the w command. The w command lists the tasks being run on each terminal session, so the terminal session that shows w in the WHAT column is the one you are looking for. In my case it is pts/2, as shown in the following:

```
[student@studentvm1 ~]$ w
 12:11:53 up 1 day, 14:41,  6 users,  load average: 0.01, 0.11, 0.09
USER     TTY       LOGIN@   IDLE   JCPU   PCPU WHAT
student  tty1      Fri08    43:40m 55.40s 10.93s xfce4-session
root     pts/1     Fri16    3:31m  0.03s  0.03s -bash
student  pts/2     12:01    1.00s  0.03s  0.01s w
student  tty2      12:03    4:16   0.03s  0.03s -bash
student  tty3      12:06    4:24   0.02s  0.02s -bash
student  pts/3     12:09    1:20   0.02s  0.02s -bash
[student@studentvm1 ~]$
[student@studentvm1 ~]$ echo "Hello world" > /dev/pts/3
```

On my test host, I sent the text "Hello world" from /dev/pts/2 to /dev/pts/3. Your terminal devices may be different from the ones I have used on my test VM. Be sure to use the correct devices for your environment for this experiment.

Another interesting experiment is to print a file directly to the printer from the command line. We will do this in Chapter 26.

The /dev directory contains some very interesting device files that are portals to hardware that one does not normally think of as a device like a hard drive or display. For one example, system memory – RAM – is not something that is normally considered as a "device," yet /dev/mem is the device special file through which direct access to memory can be achieved.

EXPERIMENT 22-3: A DIRECT LOOK AT RAM CONTENTS

This experiment must be run as the root user. Because you are only reading the contents of memory, this experiment poses little danger.

If a root terminal session is not already available, open a terminal emulator session and escalate your privilege to root. The next command will dump the first 200K of RAM to Standard Output (STDOUT):

```
[root@studentvm1 ~]# dd if=/dev/mem bs=2048 count=100
```

It may not look like that much, and what you do see will be unintelligible. To make it a bit more intelligible – to at least display the data in a decent format that might be interpreted by an expert – pipe the output of the previous command through the od (Octal Display) utility:

```
[root@studentvm1 ~]# dd if=/dev/mem bs=2048 count=100 | od -c
```

Root has more access to read memory than a non-root user, but most memory is protected from being written by any user, including root.

The dd command provides significantly more control than simply using the cat command to dump all of memory, which I have also tried. The dd command provides the ability to specify how much data is read from /dev/mem and would also allow me to specify the point at which to start reading data from memory. Although some memory was read using the cat command, the kernel eventually responded with the error in Figure 22-2.

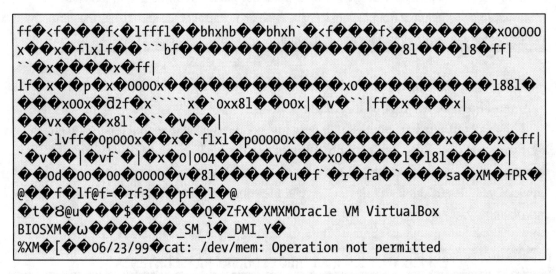

Figure 22-2. *The error on the last line was displayed when the **cat** command attempted to dump protected memory to STDOUT*

You can also log in as the non-root user, student, and try this command. You will get an error message because the memory you are trying to access does not belong to the user. This is a memory protection feature of Linux that keeps other users from reading or writing memory that does not belong to them.

These memory errors mean that the kernel is doing its job by protecting memory that belongs to other processes, which is exactly how it should work. So, although you can use /dev/mem to display data stored in RAM, access to most memory space is protected and will result in errors. Only that virtual memory that is assigned by the kernel memory manager to the bash shell running the dd command should be accessible without causing an error. Sorry, but you cannot snoop in memory that does not belong to you unless you find a vulnerability to exploit.

Many types of malware depend upon privilege escalation to allow them to read the contents of memory that they would not normally be able to access. This allows the malware to find and steal personal data such as account numbers, user ID (UID), and stored passwords. Fortunately, Linux protects against memory access by non-root users. It also protects against privilege escalation. But even Linux security is not perfect. It is important to install security patches to protect against vulnerabilities that allow privilege escalation. You should also be aware of human factors such as the tendency people have to write down their passwords, but that is all another book.[8]

You can now see that memory is also considered to be a file and can be treated as such using the memory device file.

Randomness, Zero, and More

There are some other very interesting device files in /dev. The device special files null, zero, random, and urandom are not associated with any physical devices. These device files provide sources of zeros, nulls, and random numbers.

The null device /dev/null can be used as a target for the redirection of output from shell commands or programs so that it is not displayed on the terminal.

EXPERIMENT 22-4: USING /DEV/NULL

I frequently use /dev/null in my bash scripts to prevent users from being presented with output that is irrelevant or that might be confusing to them. Enter the following command to redirect the output to the null device. Nothing will be displayed on the terminal. The data is just dumped into the big bit bucket in the sky:

```
[student@studentvm1 ~]$ echo "Hello world" > /dev/null
```

There is no visible output from the /dev/null because the null device simply returns an end of file (EOF) character. Note that the byte count is zero. The null device is much more useful as a place to redirect unwanted output so that it is removed from the data stream.

---

[8] Apress has a number of good books on security at www.apress.com/us/security

The /dev/random and /dev/urandom devices are both useful as data stream sources. As their names imply, they both produce essentially random output – not just numbers but any and all byte combinations. The /dev/urandom device produces a deterministic[9] stream of random output and is very fast, while /dev/random produces a non-deterministic[10] stream but is slower.

EXPERIMENT 22-5: USING /DEV/URANDOM

Use this command to view typical output from /dev/urandom. You can use Ctrl+C to break out:

```
[student@studentvm1 ~]$ cat /dev/urandom
,3��  VwM
N�g�/�1�ş�!��'⚦'�:�|R��[塚t��Z��F.:H�7�,��
��z/��|�7q�Sp�"�(1_c��π��-
�������ś�Y���D^5�i8��"%���&ŋ|C9!y���f�5bPp;��C
��x��1���U��3~��ꙅ
<SNIP>
```

I have shown only a part of the data stream from the command, but it should give you a sense for what you should see on your system.

You could also pipe the output of Experiment 22-6 through the od (Octal Display) command to make it a little more human readable for this experiment. That makes little sense for most real-world applications because it is, after all, random data.

The man page for od shows that it can be used to obtain data directly from a file as well as specify the amount of data to be read.

---

[9] Deterministic means the output is determined by a known algorithm and uses a seed string as a starting point. Each unit of output is dependent upon the previous output and the algorithm, so if you know both the seed and the algorithm, the entire data stream can be reproduced. As a result it is possible, although difficult, for a cracker to reproduce the output if the original seed is known.

[10] Non-deterministic results are not dependent upon the previous data in the random data stream. Thus, they are more truly random than if they were deterministic.

EXPERIMENT 22-6: USING THE OD COMMAND ON RANDOM DATA

In this case I have used -N 128 to limit the output to 128 bytes:

```
[student@studentvm1 ~]$ od /dev/urandom -N 128
0000000 043514 022412 112660 052071 161447 057027 114243 061412
0000020 154627 105675 154470 110352 135013 127206 103057 136555
0000040 033417 011054 014334 040457 157056 165542 027255 121710
0000060 125334 065600 165447 165245 020756 101514 042377 132156
0000100 116024 027770 000537 014743 170561 011122 173454 102163
0000120 074301 104771 123476 054643 105211 151753 166617 154313
0000140 103720 147660 012644 037363 077661 076453 104161 033220
0000160 056501 001771 113557 075046 102700 043405 132046 045263
0000200
```

The dd command could also be used to specify a limit to the amount of data taken from the [u]random devices, but it cannot directly format the data.

The /dev/random device file produces non-deterministic random output, but it produces output more slowly. This output is not determined by an algorithm that is dependent only upon the previous number that was generated, but it is generated in response to keystrokes and mouse movements. This method makes it far more difficult to duplicate a specific series of random numbers. Use the cat command to view some of the output from the /dev/random device file. Try moving the mouse to see how it affects the output.

The random data generated from /dev/random and /dev/urandom, regardless of how it is read from those devices, is usually redirected to a file on some storage media or to STDIN of another program. Random data seldom needs to be viewed by the SysAdmin, developer, or end user. But it does make a good demonstration for this experiment.

As its name implies, the /dev/zero device file produces an unending string of zeros as output. Note that these are octal zeros and not the ASCII character zero (0).

EXPERIMENT 22-7: USING /DEV/ZERO

Use the dd command to view some output from the /dev/zero device file. Note that the byte count for this command is non-zero:

```
[student@studentvm1 ~]$ dd if=/dev/zero  bs=512 count=500 | od -c
0000000  \0  \0  \0  \0  \0  \0  \0  \0  \0  \0  \0  \0  \0  \0  \0  \0
*
500+0 records in
500+0 records out
256000 bytes (256 kB, 250 KiB) copied, 0.00126996 s, 202 MB/s
0764000
```

Back Up the Master Boot Record

Consider, for example, the simple task of making a backup of the master boot record (MBR) of a hard drive. I have had, on occasion, needed to restore or recreate my MBR, particularly the partition table. Recreating it from scratch is very difficult. Restoring it from a saved file is easy. So let's back up the boot record of the hard drive. Although the modern GUID partition table (GPT) does not have the same problem as the old MBR because there are multiple copies stored across the disk, Experiments 22-8 and 22-9 are still a good illustration of the uses of the dd command and the implications of "everything is a file." Many systems still use the old MBR, and the sda storage device for StudentVM1 was created using partition type 83, Linux, which automatically uses the MBR. The GPT does still use the first sector on the disk as a "protective" MBR for a bit of backward compatibility.

Note that all of the experiments in this section must be performed as root.

EXPERIMENT 22-8: BACKING UP THE MASTER BOOT RECORD (MBR)

Perform this experiment as the root user. We are going to create a backup of the master boot record (MBR) for /dev/sda, but we will not attempt to restore it.

The dd command must be run as root because for security reasons non-root users do not have access to the hard drive device files in the /dev directory. The bs value is not what you might think; it stands for block size. Count is the number of blocks to read from the source file:

```
[root@studentvm1 ~]# dd if=/dev/sda of=/tmp/myMBR.bak bs=512 count=1
```

This command creates a file, myMBR.bak, in the /tmp directory. The file is 512 bytes in size and contains the contents of the MBR including the bootstrap code and partition table. Look at the contents of the file you just created:

```
[root@studentvm1 ~]# cat /tmp/myMBR.bak
�c��M����  |����!��8u
Z�����}�f�cd�@f�D��������@�����f�f`|fL��uNf�\|
f1�f�4��1�f�t;}7���0����Z�2p��1 Λ�r��`���1�����
�a�&Z|��}���}�4��}�.���GRUB GeomHard DiskRead Error
����<u��}����  !��( �)����  ��U�[root@studentvm1 ~]#
```

Because there is no end of line (EOL) character at the end of the boot sector, the command prompt is on the same line as the end of the boot record.

If the MBR were damaged, it would be necessary to boot to a rescue disk and use the command in Figure 22-3, which would perform the reverse operation of the one earlier. Notice that it is not necessary to specify the block size and block count as in the first command because the dd command will simply copy the backup file to the first sector of the hard drive and stop when it reaches the end of the source file.

```
#  dd if=/tmp/myMBR.bak of=/dev/sda
```

Figure 22-3. *This command would restore the backup of the boot record*

So now that you have performed a backup of the boot record of your hard drive and verified the contents of that backup, let's move to a safer environment to destroy the boot record and then restore it.

EXPERIMENT 22-9: SAVING AND RESTORING THE MBR

This is a rather long experiment, and it must be performed as root. You are going to make a backup of the MBR for a new virtual hard drive, partition, and filesystem you will create for your VM, damage the MBR on the device, try to read the device, and then restore the MBR.

Start by creating a new virtual hard drive of 2GB in size using the VirtualBox Manager. This virtual hard drive should be dynamically allocated and be automatically named StudentVM1_3.vdi.

After creating the new virtual hard drive, verify that its device special file is /dev/sdd. If your new virtual disk is not /dev/sdd, be sure to use the device special file for the one you just created.

The output from dmesg looks like this:

```
[206061.164672] ata4: SATA link up 3.0 Gbps (SStatus 123 SControl 300)
[206061.164815] ata4.00: ATA-6: VBOX HARDDISK, 1.0, max UDMA/133
[206061.164821] ata4.00: 4194304 sectors, multi 128: LBA48 NCQ (depth 32)
[206061.164998] ata4.00: configured for UDMA/133
[206061.165136] scsi 3:0:0:0: Direct-Access     ATA      VBOX
HARDDISK    1.0  PQ: 0 ANSI: 5
[206061.165574] scsi 3:0:0:0: Attached scsi generic sg4 type 0
[206061.166865] sd 3:0:0:0: [sdd] 4194304 512-byte logical blocks: (2.15
GB/2.00 GiB)
[206061.166879] sd 3:0:0:0: [sdd] Write Protect is off
[206061.166883] sd 3:0:0:0: [sdd] Mode Sense: 00 3a 00 00
[206061.166903] sd 3:0:0:0: [sdd] Write cache: enabled, read cache: enabled,
doesn't support DPO or FUA
[206061.166928] sd 3:0:0:0: [sdd] Preferred minimum I/O size 512 bytes
[206061.175778] sd 3:0:0:0: [sdd] Attached SCSI disk
```

The new drive will also show up with the lsblk command as /dev/sdd.

Look at the boot record to provide a basis for later comparison. Note that there is no data in the boot record of this new drive:

```
[root@studentvm1 ~]# dd if=/dev/sdd bs=512 count=1
1+0 records in
1+0 records out
512 bytes copied, 0.000348973 s, 1.5 MB/s
```

Create a partition of type 83, Linux filesystem, that fills the entire 2GB of the /dev/sdd virtual drive and save the new partition table:

```
[root@studentvm1 ~]# fdisk /dev/sdd

Welcome to fdisk (util-linux 2.38.1).
Changes will remain in memory only, until you decide to write them.
Be careful before using the write command.

Device does not contain a recognized partition table.
Created a new DOS disklabel with disk identifier 0x9515fe71.
```

```
Command (m for help): p
Disk /dev/sdd: 2 GiB, 2147483648 bytes, 4194304 sectors
Disk model: VBOX HARDDISK
Units: sectors of 1 * 512 = 512 bytes
Sector size (logical/physical): 512 bytes / 512 bytes
I/O size (minimum/optimal): 512 bytes / 512 bytes
Disklabel type: dos
Disk identifier: 0x9515fe71

Command (m for help):
Command (m for help): n
Partition type
   p   primary (0 primary, 0 extended, 4 free)
   e   extended (container for logical partitions)
Select (default p): <press Enter>

Using default response p.
Partition number (1-4, default 1): <press Enter>
First sector (2048-4194303, default 2048): <press Enter>
Last sector, +sectors or +size{K,M,G,T,P} (2048-4194303, default 4194303):
<press Enter>

Created a new partition 1 of type 'Linux' and of size 2 GiB.

Command (m for help): w
The partition table has been altered.
Calling ioctl() to re-read partition table.
Syncing disks.
```

Check the boot record again, which is no longer completely empty:

```
[root@studentvm1 ~]# dd if=/dev/sdd bs=512 count=1 | od -c
1+0 records in
1+0 records out
512 bytes copied, 0.0131589 s, 38.9 kB/s
0000000  \0  \0  \0  \0  \0  \0  \0  \0  \0  \0  \0  \0  \0  \0  \0  \0
*
0000660  \0  \0  \0  \0  \0  \0  \0  \0   q 376 025 225  \0  \0  \0
0000700   !  \0 203 025   P 005  \0  \b  \0  \0  \0 370   ?  \0  \0  \0
0000720  \0  \0  \0  \0  \0  \0  \0  \0  \0  \0  \0  \0  \0  \0  \0  \0
*
```

```
0000760  \0  \0  \0  \0  \0  \0  \0  \0  \0  \0  \0  \0  \0  \0  U 252
0001000
```

Verify that the partition is /dev/sdd1 and then create an EXT4 filesystem on the partition:

```
[root@studentvm1 ~]# mkfs -t ext4 /dev/sdd1
mke2fs 1.44.3 (10-July-2018)
Creating filesystem with 524032 4k blocks and 131072 inodes
Filesystem UUID: 3e031fbf-99b9-42e9-a920-0407a8b34513
Superblock backups stored on blocks:
    32768, 98304, 163840, 229376, 294912

Allocating group tables: done
Writing inode tables: done
Creating journal (8192 blocks): done
Writing superblocks and filesystem accounting information: done
```

Mount the new filesystem on the /mnt mountpoint and store some data on the device. This will verify that the new filesystem is working as it should:

```
[root@studentvm1 ~]# mount /dev/sdd1 /mnt ; ll /mnt
total 16
drwx------. 2 root root 16384 Jan 31 08:08 lost+found
[root@studentvm1 ~]# dmesg > /mnt/testfile001 ; ll /mnt
total 60
drwx------. 2 root root 16384 Jan 31 08:08 lost+found
-rw-r--r--. 1 root root 44662 Jan 31 08:12 testfile001
[root@studentvm1 ~]#
```

Copy the MBR:

```
[root@studentvm1 ~]# dd if=/dev/sdd of=/tmp/sddMBR.bak bs=512 count=1
1+0 records in
1+0 records out
512 bytes copied, 0.0171773 s, 29.8 kB/s
```

Check the file containing the MBR. Note that there is not a lot there:

```
[root@studentvm1 ~]# cat /tmp/sddMBR.bak

f��� !��?U�[root@studentvm1 ~]#
```

Now is the fun part. We unmount the partition, overwrite the MBR of the device with one 512-byte block of random data, and then view the new content of the MBR to verify the change. This time there is a significant amount of random data:

```
[root@studentvm1 ~]# umount /mnt
[root@studentvm1 ~]# dd if=/dev/urandom of=/dev/sdd bs=512 count=1
512+0 records in
512+0 records out
262144 bytes (262 kB, 256 KiB) copied, 0.10446 s, 2.5 MB/s
[root@studentvm1 ~]# dd if=/dev/sdd bs=512 count=1

 _Cv3�X��qQ��������������4p|�?
kn��x�-�
            �
         �N���Y��9��]�i���\�TXSqy4�AK�_�o{j�l����p·\
A�u�-w��3�#99�]ʞ���K'�(�Qτ,10�H�jp
����a!�)�0�^o�]�y��S�B�IAu3S��QU���}�����
                           �9I�Ā��IBQ��ZZ�3
�H
  ��xʃ�0�_PX�>�.�m���\�

���z�QfYU��c�f�s�hW�yvR���/���m�m�����T)�_���>
�J�Z�Xv2�бqu[,����t�����m)�a�5p����j��*��K��Z{��
8�����#(UOh8*V��
�<N����7��'#4���G:����+�I��T���z�9t��~��i!
����."=�� �c�,7:�v��l<�(��U�P*
w�4�+\���Q��������V���1+0 records in
1+0 records out
512 bytes copied, 0.000603043 s, 849 kB/s
[root@studentvm1 ~]#
```

Let's try a couple more things to test out this state of affairs before we restore this MBR. First, we use fdisk to verify that the drive no longer has a partition table, which means that the MBR has been overwritten:

```
[root@studentvm1 ~]# fdisk -l /dev/sdd
Disk /dev/sdd: 2 GiB, 2147483648 bytes, 4194304 sectors
Units: sectors of 1 * 512 = 512 bytes
```

```
Sector size (logical/physical): 512 bytes / 512 bytes
I/O size (minimum/optimal): 512 bytes / 512 bytes
[root@studentvm1 ~]#
```

An attempt to mount the original partition will fail. The error message indicates that the special device does not exist. This shows that most of the special device files are created and removed as necessary, on demand:

```
[root@studentvm1 ~]# mount /dev/sdd1 /mnt
mount: /mnt: special device /dev/sdd1 does not exist.
```

It is time to restore the boot record you backed up earlier. Because you used the **dd** command to carefully overwrite with random data only the MBR that contained the partition table for the drive, all of the other data remains intact. Restoring the MBR will make it available again. Restore the MBR, view the MBR on the device, then mount the partition, and list the contents:

```
[root@studentvm1 ~]# dd if=/tmp/sddMBR.bak of=/dev/sdd
1+0 records in
1+0 records out
512 bytes copied, 0.0261115 s, 19.6 kB/s
```

```
[root@studentvm1 ~]# fdisk -l /dev/sdd
Disk /dev/sdd: 2 GiB, 2147483648 bytes, 4194304 sectors
Units: sectors of 1 * 512 = 512 bytes
Sector size (logical/physical): 512 bytes / 512 bytes
I/O size (minimum/optimal): 512 bytes / 512 bytes
Disklabel type: dos
Disk identifier: 0xb1f99266

Device     Boot Start     End Sectors Size Id Type
/dev/sdd1          2048 4194303 4192256   2G 83 Linux
[root@studentvm1 ~]#
```

The fdisk command shows that the partition table has been restored. Now mount the partition and verify that the data we stored there still exists:

```
[root@studentvm1 ~]# mount /dev/sdd1 /mnt ; ll /mnt
total 60
drwx------. 2 root root 16384 Jan 31 08:08 lost+found
-rw-r--r--. 1 root root 44662 Jan 31 08:12 testfile001
[root@studentvm1 ~]#
```

Wow – how cool is that! This series of experiments is designed to illustrate that you can use the fact that all devices can be treated like files and therefore use some very common but powerful CLI tools in some very interesting ways.

It is not necessary to specify the amount of data to be copied with the sb= and count= parameters because the dd command only copies the amount of data available, in this case a single 512-byte sector.

Unmount the /dev/sdd1 device because we are finished with it.

Implications of Everything Is a File

The implications of "everything is a file" are far-reaching and much greater than can be listed here. You have already seen some examples in the preceding experiments. But here is a short list that encompasses those and more:

- Clone storage devices.

- Back up partitions.

- Back up the master boot record (MBR).

- Install ISO images onto USB thumb drives.

- Communicate with users on other terminals.

- Print files to a printer.

- Change the contents of certain files in the /proc pseudo-filesystem to modify configuration parameters of the running kernel.

- Overwrite files, partitions, or entire storage devices with random data or zeros.

- Redirect unwanted output from commands to a null device where it disappears forever.

- Etc., etc., etc.

There are so many possibilities here that any list can really only scratch the surface. I am sure that you have figured – or will figure – out many ways to use this tenet of the Linux Philosophy far more creatively than I have discussed here.

Chapter Summary

It is all part of a filesystem. Everything on a Linux computer is accessible as a file in the filesystem space. The whole point of this is to be able to use common tools to operate on different things – common tools such as the standard GNU/Linux utilities and commands that work on files will also work on devices – because, in Linux, they are files.

Exercises

Perform the following exercises to complete this chapter:

1. Why does even root have restricted access to RAM?

2. What is the difference between the device special files /dev/sdc and /dev/sdc1?

3. Can the cat command be used to dump the data from a partition?

4. Can the cat command be used to dump the data from a hard drive?

5. Is it possible to use standard Linux commands to clone complete storage devices in the manner of tools like Ghost, Clonezilla, or Paragon Drive Copy 15 Professional? Don't worry – skip this question if you are not familiar with any of these tools.

6. Create a backup file of the entire partition /dev/sdd1 (or the equivalent device on your VM) and store the data file on /tmp, which should have more than enough space to contain this backup file.

7. What would happen if the backup file from #6 were restored to a new partition that was created to be larger than the original partition?

CHAPTER 23

Managing Processes

Objectives

In this chapter you will learn

- What is a process
- How processes are represented to the kernel
- Kernel process scheduling
- How processes use system resources
- To use common Linux tools for exploring and managing processes

Processes

The function of an operating system like Linux is to run programs that perform tasks for the users. Behind the scenes, the operating system runs its own programs that are used to manage the computer hardware, the devices attached to it, and the running programs themselves.

Each program consists of one or more processes. A process is a running program and consumes resources such as memory and CPU time. In this chapter we look at how the kernel schedules processes to receive CPU time.

© David Both 2023
D. Both, *Using and Administering Linux: Volume 2*, https://doi.org/10.1007/978-1-4842-9615-8_23

Process Scheduling in the Kernel

The Linux kernel provides scheduling services that determine which processes get CPU time, how much, and when. Most Linux distributions of the last 15 years use the Completely Fair Scheduler (CFS), which was introduced into the kernel in October of 2007.[1]

The overall objective of CPU scheduling in a modern operating system is to ensure that critical processes such as memory allocation or emptying a full communications buffer get CPU time immediately when they need it while ensuring that system administration and user-level processes get CPU time and are responsive to the users including the root user. The scheduling of processes for access to CPU time is managed by a complex algorithm that considers many factors.

Each process has its existence in a kernel data structure as an abstraction consisting of data about the process including its process ID (PID) number, memory locations assigned to it, its priority and nice number, how much CPU time it has recently used, how long ago it was actually on CPU, files opened by the process, as well as other necessary data. Like the processes they represent, the kernel data structures that form the abstraction are ephemeral, and the RAM assigned to them is reassigned to the pool of free memory when the processes are terminated.

Opensource.com has published an excellent article[2] that provides a good overview of the CFS and compares it to the older and more simple preemptive scheduler. For a more detailed description of the Linux CFS, Nikita Ishkov, a graduate student at University of Tampere School of Information Sciences in Finland, has written his master's thesis, "A complete guide to Linux process scheduling,"[3] about this.

---

[1] Wikipedia, Completely Fair Scheduler, `https://en.wikipedia.org/wiki/Completely_Fair_Scheduler`

[2] Kalin, Marty, "CFS: Completely fair process scheduling in Linux," `https://opensource.com/article/19/2/fair-scheduling-linux`

[3] Ishkov, Nikita, "A complete guide to Linux process scheduling," `https://tampub.uta.fi/bitstream/handle/10024/96864/GRADU-1428493916.pdf`, University of Tampere School of Information Sciences, 2015

Tools

We SysAdmins have access to tools that allow us to view and manage the running processes. For me, these are `top`, `atop`, `htop`, and `glances`. All of these tools monitor CPU and memory usage, and most of them list information about running processes at the very least. Some monitor other aspects of a Linux system as well. All provide near-real-time views of system activity. Although these tools can generally be run by any non-root user, the root user has more control over all processes, while non-root users can only manage their own processes and have some limitations on that.

Processes sometimes misbehave and need to be brought under control. Sometimes we just want to satisfy our curiosity in our efforts to more fully understand the workings of a properly functioning Linux computer so that we will be able to identify when it is malfunctioning. These tools can help us do both.

Let's start by looking at `top`, arguably the oldest of these tools and the one that is most likely to be always available on a modern Linux host. I will use `top` in the chapter to introduce a number of concepts pertaining to process management and to familiarize you with its use and then move on to other tools that you will find useful in monitoring and managing processes.

top

One of the first tools I use when performing problem determination is `top`. I like it because it has been around since forever – well, 1984, anyway – and is always available while the other tools may not be installed. The `top` program is a very powerful utility that provides a great deal of information about your running system. This includes data about memory usage, CPU loads, and a list of running processes including the amount of CPU time and memory being utilized by each process. Top displays system information in near real time, updating (by default) every three seconds. Fractional seconds are allowed by `top`, although very small values can place a significant load on the system. It is also interactive, and the data columns to be displayed and the sort column can be modified.

The output from `top`, shown in Figure 23-1, is divided into two sections – the "Summary" section, which is the upper section of the output, and the "Process" section, which is the lower portion of the output. I will use this terminology for `top`, `atop`, `htop`, and `glances` in the interest of consistency.

```
top - 21:49:11 up 1 day,  9:55,  6 users,  load average: 0.00, 0.00, 0.00
Tasks: 201 total,   1 running, 200 sleeping,   0 stopped,   0 zombie
%Cpu(s):  0.0 us,  0.3 sy,  0.0 ni, 98.7 id,  0.0 wa,  0.3 hi,  0.7 si,  0.0 st
MiB Mem :   3942.5 total,    234.4 free,    468.9 used,   3239.2 buff/cache
MiB Swap:   4096.0 total,   4094.7 free,      1.3 used.   3230.5 avail Mem
```

PID	USER	PR	NI	VIRT	RES	SHR	S	%CPU	%MEM	TIME+	COMMAND
1738	student	20	0	293564	3156	2708	S	0.3	0.1	2:03.22	VBoxClient
2845	root	20	0	40128	6512	4236	S	0.3	0.2	0:01.47	sshd
11630	root	20	0	0	0	0	I	0.3	0.0	0:00.17	kworker/0:2-
11901	root	20	0	228752	4532	3912	R	0.3	0.1	0:00.05	top
1	root	20	0	171396	14216	9120	S	0.0	0.4	0:13.70	systemd
2	root	20	0	0	0	0	S	0.0	0.0	0:00.21	kthreadd
3	root	0	-20	0	0	0	I	0.0	0.0	0:00.00	rcu_gp
4	root	0	-20	0	0	0	I	0.0	0.0	0:00.00	rcu_par_gp
6	root	0	-20	0	0	0	I	0.0	0.0	0:00.00	kworker/0:0H
8	root	0	-20	0	0	0	I	0.0	0.0	0:00.00	mm_percpu_wq
9	root	20	0	0	0	0	S	0.0	0.0	0:05.03	ksoftirqd/0
10	root	20	0	0	0	0	I	0.0	0.0	0:04.95	rcu_sched
11	root	20	0	0	0	0	I	0.0	0.0	0:00.00	rcu_bh
12	root	rt	0	0	0	0	S	0.0	0.0	0:00.04	migration/0
14	root	20	0	0	0	0	S	0.0	0.0	0:00.00	cpuhp/0
15	root	20	0	0	0	0	S	0.0	0.0	0:00.00	cpuhp/1

Figure 23-1. *Typical output from the top utility*

EXPERIMENT 23-1: INTRODUCING TOP

In order to more fully understand the descriptions of top and the other process management tools that will be covered in this chapter, start top as root in a terminal session on the desktop:

[root@studentvm1 ~]# **top**

Refer to this instance of top as we proceed through the following sections that describe its output.

Much of the description of the display generated by top is similar to that of the other tools covered in this chapter. We will spend the most time with top for this reason and because it is always available while the other tools may need to be installed. We will then cover some of the differences between top and the other tools.

Summary Section

The Summary section of the output from top is an overview of the system status. The first line shows the system uptime and the 1-, 5-, and 15-minute load averages. We will discuss load averages in more detail later in this chapter.

The second line shows the number of processes currently active and the status of each. The lines containing CPU statistics are shown next. There can be a single line that combines the statistics for all CPUs present in the system or one line for each CPU; in the case of the VM used for the example, this is a single dual-core CPU. Press the **1** key to toggle between the consolidated display of CPU usage and the display of the individual CPUs. The data in these lines is displayed as percentages of the total CPU time available.

The other fields for these CPU data have changed over time, and I had a difficult time locating information about the last three as they are relatively new. So here are descriptions of all those fields:

- **us – userspace:** Applications and other programs running in user space, that is, not in the kernel.

- **sy – system calls:** Kernel-level functions. This does not include CPU time taken by the kernel itself, just the kernel system calls.

- **ni – nice:** Processes that are running at a positive nice level.

- **id – idle:** Idle time, that is, time not used by any running process.

- **wa – wait:** CPU cycles that are spent waiting for I/O to occur. This is wasted CPU time.

- **hi – hardware interrupts:** CPU cycles that are spent dealing with hardware interrupts.

- **si – software interrupts:** CPU cycles spent dealing with software-created interrupts such as system calls.

- **st – steal time:** The percentage of CPU cycles that a virtual CPU waits for a real CPU while the hypervisor is servicing another virtual processor.

The last two lines in the Summary section are memory usage. They show the physical memory usage including both RAM and swap space.

Process Section

The Process section of the output from top is a listing of the running processes in the system – at least the number of processes, or processes, for which there is room on the terminal display. The default columns displayed by top are described in the following. Several other columns are available, and each can usually be added with a single keystroke; refer to the top man page for details:

- **PID:** The process ID.

- **USER:** The username of the process owner.

- **PR:** The priority of the process.

- **NI:** The nice number of the process.

- **VIRT:** The total amount of virtual memory allocated to the process.

- **RES:** Resident size (in kb unless otherwise noted) of non-swapped physical memory consumed by a process.

- **SHR:** The amount of shared memory in kb used by the process.

- **S:** The status of the process. This can be R for running, S for sleeping, and Z for zombie. Less frequently seen statuses can be T for traced or stopped and D for uninterruptable sleep.

- **%CPU:** The percentage of CPU cycles, or time used by this process during the last measured time period.

- **%MEM:** The percentage of physical system memory used by the process.

- **TIME+:** Total CPU time to 100ths of a second consumed by the process since the process was started.

- **COMMAND:** This is the command that was used to launch the process.

Now that we know a little about the data displayed by top, let's do an experiment to illustrate some of its basic capabilities.

EXPERIMENT 23-2: EXPLORING TOP

The top program should already be running in a root terminal session. If not, make it so. Start by observing the Summary section.

The top program has a number of useful interactive commands you can use to manage the display of data and to manipulate individual processes. Use the **h** key to view a brief help page for the various interactive commands. Be sure to press **h** twice to see both pages of the help. Use the **q** command to quit top.

Use the **1** (one) key to display CPU statistics as a single, global number as shown in Figure 23-1 or by individual CPU as seen in Figure 23-2. The **l** (el) key turns load averages on and off. Use the **t** and **m** keys to rotate the process/CPU and memory lines of the Summary section, respectively, through off, text only, and a couple types of bar graph formats.

The **d** and **s** keys are interchangeable and can be used to set the delay interval between updates. The default is three seconds, but I prefer a one-second interval. Interval granularity can be as low as one-tenth (0.1) of a second, but this will consume more of the CPU cycles you are trying to measure. Try setting the delay interval to 5, 1, .5, and other intervals you think might be interesting. When you have finished, set the delay interval to one second.

Use the **Page Up** and **Page Down** keys to scroll through the list of running processes.

By default the running processes are sorted by CPU usage. You can use the **<** and **>** keys to sequence the sort column to the left or right. By default there is no highlight or some other mark to indicate by which column the results are being sorted. You can add highlighting – press the **x** key, which will show the current sort column in bold – the entire column.

```
top - 10:23:10 up 1 day, 22:29,  6 users,  load average: 0.00, 0.00, 0.00
Tasks: 202 total,   1 running, 201 sleeping,   0 stopped,   0 zombie
%Cpu0  :   0.7/2.6     3[|||                                                ]
%Cpu1  :   0.3/1.3     2[|                                                  ]
MiB Mem : 18.4/3942.5  [|||||||||||||||                                     ]
MiB Swap:  0.0/4096.0  [                                                    ]
```

PID	USER	PR	NI	VIRT	RES	SHR	S	%CPU	%MEM	TIME+	COMMAND
1	root	20	0	171396	14224	9120	S	0.7	0.4	0:17.96	systemd
799	root	20	0	231324	2860	2044	S	0.3	0.1	0:09.38	screen
900	dbus	20	0	42300	6052	4428	S	0.3	0.1	0:21.26	dbus-daemon
962	root	20	0	588844	14960	13264	S	0.3	0.4	0:00.27	abrt-dump-journ
1006	root	20	0	273668	35524	34192	S	0.3	0.9	0:11.58	sssd_nss
1054	root	20	0	547304	19192	16336	S	0.3	0.5	0:10.18	NetworkManager
2054	root	20	0	253960	11900	10172	S	0.3	0.3	0:01.11	abrt-dbus
11940	root	20	0	228752	4960	4092	R	0.3	0.1	1:30.09	top
27130	root	20	0	0	0	0	I	0.3	0.0	0:00.01	kworker/u4:0-ev
2	root	20	0	0	0	0	S	0.0	0.0	0:00.31	kthreadd
3	root	0	-20	0	0	0	I	0.0	0.0	0:00.00	rcu_gp
4	root	0	-20	0	0	0	I	0.0	0.0	0:00.00	rcu_par_gp
6	root	0	-20	0	0	0	I	0.0	0.0	0:00.00	kworker/0:0H
8	root	0	-20	0	0	0	I	0.0	0.0	0:00.00	mm_percpu_wq
9	root	20	0	0	0	0	S	0.0	0.0	0:07.30	ksoftirqd/0
10	root	20	0	0	0	0	I	0.0	0.0	0:06.84	rcu_sched
11	root	20	0	0	0	0	I	0.0	0.0	0:00.00	rcu_bh
12	root	rt	0	0	0	0	S	0.0	0.0	0:00.05	migration/0
14	root	20	0	0	0	0	S	0.0	0.0	0:00.00	cpuhp/0
15	root	20	0	0	0	0	S	0.0	0.0	0:00.00	cpuhp/1
16	root	rt	0	0	0	0	S	0.0	0.0	0:00.22	migration/1

Figure 23-2. *Use the t and m keys to change the CPU and memory summaries to bar graphs*

Use the **>** key to move the column all the way to the right and then the **<** key to move it back to the desired column. Move the sort index to various columns. When finished set the CPU usage as the sort column again.

If you alter the **top** display configuration, you can use the **W** (in uppercase) key to write the changes to the configuration file ~/.toprc in your home directory. Leave **top** running.

More About Load Averages …

Before we continue it is important to discuss load averages in more detail. Load averages are important criteria for measuring CPU usage. But what does this really mean when I say that the one (or five or ten)-minute load average is 4.04, for example? Load average can be considered a measure of demand for the CPU; it is a number that represents the average number of instructions waiting for CPU time. So this is a true measure of CPU performance, unlike the standard "CPU percentage," which includes I/O wait times during which the CPU is not really working.

For example, a fully utilized single-processor system CPU would have a load average of 1. This means that the CPU is keeping up exactly with the demand; in other words it has perfect utilization. A load average of less than one means that the CPU is underutilized, and a load average of greater than 1 means that the CPU is overutilized and that there is pent-up, unsatisfied demand. For example, a load average of 1.5 in a single-CPU system indicates that one-third of the CPU instructions are forced to wait to be executed until the one preceding it has completed.

This is also true for multiple processors. If a four-CPU system has a load average of 4, then it has perfect utilization. If it has a load average of 3.24, for example, then three of its processors are fully utilized and one is utilized at about 24%. In the preceding example, a four-CPU system has a one-minute load average of 4.04, meaning that there is no remaining capacity among the four CPUs and a few instructions are forced to wait. A perfectly utilized four-CPU system would show a load average of 4.00 so that the system in the example is fully loaded but not overloaded.

The optimum condition for load average is for it to equal the total number of CPUs in a system. That would mean that every CPU is fully utilized and yet no instruction must be forced to wait. But reality is messy, and optimum conditions are seldom met. If a host were running at 100% utilization, this would not allow for spikes in CPU load requirements.

The longer-term load averages provide indication of the overall utilization trend.

Linux Journal has an excellent article[4] describing load averages, the theory, the math behind them, and how to interpret them in the December 1, 2006, issue.

---

[4] Linux Journal, Examining Load Average, www.linuxjournal.com/article/9001?page=0,0

...and Signals

The top utility and all of the other monitors discussed here allow you to send signals[5] to running processes. Each of these signals has a specific function though some of them can be defined by the receiving program using signal handlers.

The separate **kill** command can also be used to send signals to processes outside of the tools like top. The **kill -l** command can be used to list all possible signals that can be sent. Three of these signals can be used to kill a process:

- **SIGTERM (15)**: Signal 15, SIGTERM, is the default signal sent by top and the other monitors when the **k** key is pressed. The program's signal handler may intercept incoming signals and act accordingly by terminating itself, or the signal handler may simply ignore the signal and continue to run. If the program does not have a signal handler, SIGTERM will terminate the program. The idea behind SIGTERM is that by signaling the program that you want it to terminate itself, it will take advantage of that and clean up things like open files and then terminate itself in a controlled and nice manner.[6]

- **SIGKILL (9)**: Signal 9, SIGKILL, provides a means of killing even the most recalcitrant programs, including scripts and other programs that have no signal handlers. For scripts and other programs with no signal handler, however, it not only kills the running script but it also kills the shell session in which the script is running; this may not be the behavior that you want. If you want to kill a process and you don't care about being nice, this is the signal you want. This signal cannot be intercepted by a signal handler in the program code.

- **SIGINT (2)**: Signal 2, SIGINT, can be used when SIGTERM does not work and you want the program to die a little more nicely, for example, and without killing the shell session in which a script is running. SIGINT sends an interrupt to the session in which the program is running. This is equivalent to terminating a running program, particularly a script, with the **Ctrl+C** key combination.

---

[5] Wikipedia, Unix Signals, `https://en.wikipedia.org/wiki/Unix_signal`

[6] Thanks to reader and student Xie Pan for improving my understanding of how this signal works with scripts.

CPU Hogs

Now that we know a bit more, let's experiment. We will create a program that hogs CPU cycles and then run multiple instances of it so that we can use our tools on it, starting with top.

EXPERIMENT 23-3: THE CPU HOG

Start two terminal sessions on the desktop as the student user. In one terminal session, run top and position this window so you can see it as you perform the following tasks in the second terminal session. Observe the load averages displayed in top as you progress through this experiment.

Create a Bash shell program file in your home directory named cpuHog and make it executable with the permissions rwxr_xr_x:

```
[student@studentvm1 ~]$ touch ./cpuHog
[student@studentvm1 ~]$ chmod 755 cpuHog
```

Edit the file with Vim and add to it the content shown in Figure 23-3. Using while [1] forces this program to loop forever. Also the Bash syntax is very picky; be sure to leave spaces around the "1" in this expression; [1] will work but [1] will not work. Save the file and exit from Vim.

```
#!/bin/bash
# This little program is a cpu hog
X=0;while [ 1 ];do echo $X;X=$(((X+1));done
```

Figure 23-3. *The cpuHog program will enable us to explore the tools used to manage processes*

This program simply counts up by one and prints the current value of X to STDOUT. As a side effect, it sucks up CPU cycles. The terminal session in which cpuHog is running should show a very high CPU usage in top. Observe the effect this has on system performance in top. CPU usage should immediately go way up, and the load averages should also start to increase over time. If you want, you can open additional terminal sessions and start the cpuHog program in them so that you have multiple instances running.

Now start the cpuHog program:

[student@studentvm1 ~]$ **./cpuHog**

This program will run until we stop it. Use the top program to show CPU usage. As you can see in Figure 23-4, this should show that one cpuHog instance is taking up a very large amount of CPU time. Record the PID – 5036 in Figure 23-4, but it will be different on your VM – for this instance of the cpuHog. You should also notice that the nice number of this instance is 0.

```
top - 21:05:39 up 2 days,  9:12,  8 users,  load average: 0.71, 0.44, 0.19
Tasks: 206 total,   5 running, 201 sleeping,   0 stopped,   0 zombie
%Cpu0  :  36.0/64.0   100[                                                     ]
%Cpu1  :   2.2/89.1    91[                                                     ]
MiB Mem : 18.6/3942.5   [                                                      ]
MiB Swap:  0.0/4096.0   [                                                      ]

  PID USER      PR  NI    VIRT    RES    SHR S  %CPU  %MEM     TIME+ COMMAND
 5036 student   20   0  216332   3188   2940 R  97.1   0.1   0:09.51 cpuHog
30678 student   20   0  231284   2876   2044 R  72.5   0.1   0:34.54 screen
 7964 root      20   0       0      0      0 I   7.8   0.0   0:07.59 kworker/u4:0-events_unbound
 7833 root      20   0       0      0      0 R   6.9   0.0   0:04.94 kworker/u4:2-events_unbound
 8144 student   20   0  228752   5000   4136 R   1.0   0.1   0:00.75 top
    1 root      20   0  171396  14228   9120 S   0.0   0.4   0:21.80 systemd
<snip>
```

Figure 23-4. *One instance of cpuHog is running and takes over 97% of CPU cycles on one CPU*

Open four new screen or terminal sessions and start an instance of cpuHog in each. Both CPUs should be running at 100%. You will also notice that other programs such as screen, if you are using it, also take CPU time.

Watch the load averages as they climb over time.

Tip   If you need to go do other things while working in this chapter, it would be fine to terminate any running cpuHog instances and restart them later when you come back.

Process Scheduling

Linux schedules each task for time on the CPU using an algorithm that considers some basic factors, including its nice number. These factors are combined into a priority by the algorithm. The factors considered by the Linux kernel scheduler include the following for each process:

- Length of time waiting for CPU time

- Amount of CPU time recently consumed

- Nice number

- The priority of the process in question

- The priorities of the other processes waiting for CPU time

The algorithm, which is a part of the kernel scheduler, determines the priority of each process running in the system. Programs or processes with higher priorities are more likely to be allocated CPU time. Priorities are very dynamic and can change rapidly based on the factors listed.

Linux process priorities run from 0 through 39 with 39 being the lowest priority and 0 the highest. This seems to be reversed from common logic, but you should consider that higher numbers mean a "nicer" priority.

There is also an RT, or RealTime, priority that is used by some processes that need to get CPU time immediately when some event occurs. This might be a process that handles hardware interrupts for the kernel. In order to ensure that data is not lost as it arrives from a disk drive or network interface, for example, a high-priority process is used to empty the data buffer when it becomes full and store the data in some specific memory location where it can be accessed as needed. Meanwhile, the empty input buffer can be used to store more incoming data from the device.

Nice Numbers

Nice numbers are the mechanism used by administrators to affect the priority of a process. It is not possible to change the priority of a process directly, but changing the nice number can modify the results of the kernel scheduler's priority setting algorithm. Nice numbers run from –20 to +19 where higher numbers are nicer.

The default nice number is 0 and the default priority is 20. Setting the nice number higher than zero increases the priority number somewhat, thus making the process nicer and therefore less greedy of CPU cycles. Setting the nice number to a more negative number results in a lower priority number, making the process less nice. Nice numbers can be changed using the renice command or from within top, atop, and htop.

Now that we know a bit more about priorities and nice numbers, we can explore them in this next experiment.

EXPERIMENT 23-4: EXPLORING PRIORITIES AND NICE NUMBERS

Start this experiment in the terminal session that is already running top as the student user. Be sure to use the PID numbers that pertain to your VM rather than the ones I used on my VM.

Set the sort column to TIME+ so that you can more easily observe the steadily increasing total amount of CPU time accumulated by the cpuHogs.

Renice the oldest process, in my case the one with PID 5036, from within top. Simply type **r**, and top asks you which process to renice. Enter the PID of the process and hit the **Enter** key. In my case the PID is 5036; the PID will definitely be different for you. Then it asks "Renice PID 5036 to value:" Now type the number **10** and hit the **Enter** key.

Verify that the nice number is now 10 and look at the priority number. On my VM the priority is now 30, which is lower than the default priority of 20. Switch to a different terminal session, one that is not running top or the cpuHog, and change the nice number from the command line:

```
[student@studentvm1 ~]$ renice 15 5036
5036 (process ID) old priority 10, new priority 15
[student@studentvm1 ~]$
```

Verify that the new nice number is 15. What is the priority number for this process now? On my VM the priority is now 35.

Now use the renice command to set the nice number of PID 5036 to –20:

```
[student@studentvm1 ~]$ renice -20 5036
renice: failed to set priority for 5036 (process ID): Permission denied
[student@studentvm1 ~]$
```

You should receive an error indicating that you don't have permission to do this. A non-root user cannot renice their own processes to a lower (less nice) number. Why do you think that this might be the case?

Start top in a root terminal session. Now, as root, reset the nice number of the cpuHog on your VM to −20. This will work this time because root can do anything. Observe the nice number of this process. Again the system is no more or less responsive, but in a real environment, a program that has a −20 nice number might cause the rest of the system to become sluggish.

Open another terminal session − as a new tab, as a new window, or in a screen session − it does not matter which. Start another instance of the cpuHog program, but let's do it a bit differently:

```
[student@studentvm1 ~]$ nice -n +20 ./cpuHog
```

When we know we want to start a program with a different nice number than the default of 0 (zero), we can use the nice command to start it and specify the nice number. Verify the nice number and the priority number in the top display.

Note that any nice number higher than 19 is interpreted to be 19 regardless of which tool is used to set it. Although the system is no more or less responsive because this is a shell script and there is plenty of CPU available, this is one way to make a process behave more nicely.

Open more terminal sessions as the student user and start at least five more instances of the cpuHog without changing the nice number. Allow all of these processes to run. As you watch these cpuHog processes, you should observe that in our artificial environment, each of the cpuHog processes receives from about 15% to 24% of the overall CPU time.

I found in my own experiments that little changed in terms of the amount of CPU time accrued to the cpuHog with the highest nice number vs. the cpuHog with the lowest. This experiment does show how to set nice numbers and the resultant changes in the priority of the processes, but there are other factors that the kernel uses in its allocation of CPU resources. Those factors make it impossible to state with certainty that changing the nice number of a particular process will have a specific effect. This is especially true in an artificially created situation such as an experiment like this one.

With that said, however, in a production environment, I have found that increasing the nice number of a particularly greedy hog process can improve the responsiveness of other processes.

Killing Processes

Sometimes a process must be killed because it cannot otherwise be controlled. There are a number of ways to do this.

EXPERIMENT 23-5: KILLING PROCESSES

Be sure that you can see the top utility running in a separate terminal session. Switch to one terminal session that is running an instance of cpuHog as the student user.

As the student user, choose one current instance of the cpuHog and determine its PID. Now let's kill this newest cpuHog process from within top.

In the screen session in which top is running as the student user, type **k**. Now top asks "PID to kill:" Type in the PID of the process and press the **Enter** key. On my VM I chose a cpuHog with PID 5257, but you must use the PID of one of your cpuHog instances. The top program now displays "Kill PID 5257 with signal [15]:" At this point you could choose another signal or just press Enter. For now, just press **Enter** and the program disappears from the top process list.

Signal 15 is used to terminate a program nicely and give it a chance to clean up after itself and close open files if there are any. This is the nicest way of killing a process if it has no option to terminate itself within its own interface.

For processes that are a bit more recalcitrant and that don't respond to Signal 15, we can use Signal 9, which tells the kernel to just kill the program without being nice. Go to an unused screen session and enter the command and locate the PID of one of the cpuHogs. On my VM this was 7533, but be sure to use the correct PID for one of the cpuHogs on your system. This time we will use the kill command to send Signal 9:

[student@testvm1 ~]$ **kill -9 7533**

Choose another running cpuHog instance and let's use Signal 2 with the kill command:

[student@testvm1 ~]$ **kill -2 12503**

This sends the SIGINT (2) signal to process 12503. Switch to the screen session in which the program was running and verify that it has been killed. Note the message that says "Killed."

While still in that same terminal session, restart the program. After it has run for a couple seconds, press **Ctrl+C**, and the running program is killed:

```
6602
6603
6604
6605
6606
6607
6608
6609
6610
6611
^C
[student@studentvm1 ~]$
```

Using kill -2 is the same as pressing Ctrl+C from within the session running the program.

You should still have some cpuHogs running on your VM. Let them run for now as we can use them while exploring other tools for process management.

Other Interactive Tools

As we have seen with other tools, Linux provides plenty of options for managing processes. The following tools are also interactive ones that provide different approaches and data displays. All are good, and these only represent some of the many tools available.

atop

The atop tool is an excellent monitor to use when you need more details about I/O activity. The default refresh interval is ten seconds, but this can be changed using the interval (**i**) command to whatever is appropriate for what you are trying to do. atop cannot refresh at sub-second intervals like top can.

Use the **h** key to display help. Be sure to notice that there are multiple pages of help, and you can use the space bar to scroll down to see the rest.

One nice feature of atop is that it can save raw performance data to a file and then play it back later for close inspection. This is handy for tracking down intermittent problems, especially ones that occur during times when you cannot directly monitor the system. The **atopsar** program is used to play back the data in the saved file.

```
ATOP - studentvm1              2019/02/06  08:57:36         --------------            10s elapsed
PRC | sys     16.15s | user    2.78s | #proc     211 | #tslpu      0 | #zombie     0 | #exit       2 |
CPU | sys      166%  | user     24%  | irq       10% | idle       0% | wait       0% | curscal     ?% |
cpu | sys       78%  | user     16%  | irq        6% | idle       0% | cpu000 w   0% | curscal     ?% |
cpu | sys       88%  | user      8%  | irq        4% | idle       0% | cpu001 w   0% | curscal     ?% |
CPL | avg1     6.95  | avg5     7.01 | avg15    7.00 | csw   1744707 | intr   460106 | numcpu      2 |
MEM | tot      3.9G  | free     2.3G | cache  713.3M | buff   188.2M | slab   222.4M | hptot    0.0M |
SWP | tot      4.0G  | free     4.0G |               |               | vmcom    1.8G | vmlim    5.9G |
LVM | udentvm1-var   | busy      3%  | read        0 | write      20 | MBw/s     0.0 | avio 12.9 ms |
DSK |          sda   | busy      3%  | read        0 | write       7 | MBw/s     0.0 | avio 37.1 ms |
NET | transport      | tcpi      3   | tcpo        5 | udpi        6 | udpo        2 | tcpao       0 |
NET | network        | ipi       9   | ipo         5 | ipfrw       0 | deliv       9 | icmpo       0 |
NET | enpos8    0%   | pcki      5   | pcko        7 | sp 1000 Mbps | si   0 Kbps | so   3 Kbps |
NET | enpos3    0%   | pcki      2   | pcko        0 | sp 1000 Mbps | si   0 Kbps | so   0 Kbps |

  PID SYSCPU USRCPU  VGROW  RGROW  RDDSK  WRDSK RUID       ST EXC  THR S CPUNR  CPU CMD          1/2
 5096  2.70s  0.40s     OK     OK     OK     OK student    --  -    1 R     0  38% cpuHog
 4939  2.49s  0.60s     OK     OK     OK     OK student    --  -    1 R     0  37% screen
 5162  2.57s  0.52s     OK     OK     OK     OK student    --  -    1 R     0  37% cpuHog
 5036  1.87s  0.37s     OK     OK     OK     OK student    --  -    1 R     1  27% cpuHog
 5314  1.85s  0.38s     OK     OK     OK     OK student    --  -    1 R     1  27% cpuHog
 5285  1.75s  0.48s     OK     OK     OK     OK student    --  -    1 R     1  27% cpuHog
30591  1.43s  0.00s     OK     OK     OK     OK root       --  -    1 I     1  17% kworker/u4:3-e
32018  1.42s  0.00s     OK     OK     OK     OK root       --  -    1 I     1  17% kworker/u4:2-e
 5087  0.04s  0.01s     OK     OK     OK     OK root       --  -    1 S     0   1% top
  558  0.02s  0.01s  8824K  4812K     OK     OK root       --  -    1 R     0   0% atop
26067  0.00s  0.01s     OK     OK     OK     OK student    --  -    3 S     0   0% VBoxClient
  552  0.01s  0.00s     OK     OK     OK     OK root       --  -    1 I     0   0% kworker/0:2-ev
```

Figure 23-5. *The atop system monitor provides information about disk and network activity in addition to CPU and process data*

Summary Section

atop contains much of the same information as top but also displays information about network, raw disk, and logical volume activity. Figure 23-5 shows these additional data in the columns at the top of the display. Note that if you have the horizontal screen real estate to support a wider display, additional columns will be displayed. Conversely, if you have less horizontal width, fewer columns are displayed. I also like that atop displays the current CPU frequency and scaling factor – something I have not seen on any other of these monitors – on the second line in the rightmost two columns in Figure 23-5.

Process Section

The atop process display includes some of the same columns as those for top, but it also includes disk I/O information and thread count for each process as well as virtual and real memory growth statistics for each process. As with the Summary section, additional columns will display if there is sufficient horizontal screen real estate. For example, in Figure 23-5, the RUID (real user ID) of the process owner is displayed. Expanding the display will also show the EUID (effective user ID), which might be important when programs run SUID (set user ID).

atop can also provide detailed information about disk, memory, network, and scheduling information for each process. Just press the **d**, **m**, **n**, or **s** key, respectively, to view that data. The **g** key returns the display to the generic process display.

Sorting can be accomplished easily by using **C** to sort by CPU usage, **M** for memory usage, **D** for disk usage, **N** for network usage, and **A** for automatic sorting. Automatic sorting usually sorts processes by the most busy resource. The network usage can only be sorted if the netatop kernel module is installed and loaded.

You can use the **k** key to kill a process but there is no option to renice a process.

By default, network and disk devices for which no activity occurs during a given time interval are not displayed. This can lead to erroneous assumptions about the hardware configuration of the host. The **f** command can be used to force atop to display the idle resources.

EXPERIMENT 23-6: USING ATOP

Install atop if it is not already, and then start it:

```
[root@studentvm1 ~]# dnf -y install atop ; atop
```

Observe the atop display for a few minutes. Start a couple additional cpuHogs and kill them after observing their effects on the system. Do not delete the cpuHogs that have been running for a long time.

Be sure to look at the csw (Context Switches) and intr (Interrupts) data. Context switches are the number of times per interval that the CPU switches from one program to another. Interrupts display the number of times per interval that software or hardware interrupts occur and cause the CPU to handle those interrupts.

Read the man page for `atop` to learn more about any data items and interactive commands that you find interesting.

Do not kill the remaining cpuHog instances. Exit from `atop`.

Configuration

The atop man page refers to global and user-level configuration files, but none can be found in my own Fedora or CentOS installations. There is also no command to save a modified configuration, and a save does not take place automatically when the program is terminated. So there appears to be no way to make configuration changes permanent.

htop

The htop program seen in Figure 23-6 is much like top on steroids. It does look a lot like top, but it also provides some capabilities that top does not. It can also be configured to provide disk, network, and I/O information.

```
 1 [||||||||||||||||||||||||||||||||||100.0%]    Tasks: 122, 126 thr; 2 running
 2 [||||||||||||||||||||||||||||||||||100.0%]    Load average: 6.93 6.97 6.99
Mem[|||||||||||||||||||             523M/3.85G]   Uptime: 3 days, 18:18:35
Swp[                                0K/4.00G]

  PID USER      PRI  NI   VIRT    RES   SHR S CPU% MEM%   TIME+  Command
 5036 student     0 -20   211M   1132   988 R 35.9  0.0 19h37:26 /bin/bash ./cpuHog
 4939 student    20   0   227M   4236  2048 S 35.2  0.1 21h36:44 SCREEN
 5285 student    20   0   211M   1072   924 R 32.8  0.0 19h35:32 /bin/bash ./cpuHog
 5314 student    20   0   211M   1136   988 R 31.2  0.0 19h29:25 /bin/bash ./cpuHog
 5162 student    20   0   211M   1132   988 R 27.3  0.0 19h33:59 /bin/bash ./cpuHog
 5096 student    32  12   211M   3152  2912 R 27.3  0.1 19h41:37 /bin/bash ./cpuHog
  866 root        0 -20 17044  16984 12580 S  2.3  0.4  3:02.08 atop
 4962 root       20   0   220M   4392  3712 R  1.6  0.1  0:00.07 htop
    1 root       20   0   103M  14660  9196 S  0.8  0.4  0:32.39 /usr/lib/systemd/systemd --
  653 root       20   0   197M   125M  112M S  0.8  3.2  0:20.94 /usr/lib/systemd/systemd-
  901 root       20   0   665M  78208 76220 S  0.8  1.9  0:20.35 /usr/sbin/rsyslogd -n
  930 dbus       20   0 42272   6632  4856 S  0.8  0.2  0:40.63 /usr/bin/dbus-daemon --system
 4967 root       20   0   159M   8656  7692 S  0.8  0.2  0:00.01 /usr/libexec/nm-dispatcher
 4797 root       20   0 39180   5040  3804 S  0.0  0.1  2:47.35 sshd: root@pts/0
 5068 root       20   0   225M   2908  1900 S  0.0  0.1  1:52.78 SCREEN
  678 root       20   0 33300  12232  8008 S  0.0  0.3  0:02.01 /usr/lib/systemd/systemd-udevd
  879 root       16  -4   104M   1824  1220 S  0.0  0.0  0:00.01 /sbin/auditd
  881 root       16  -4   104M   1824  1220 S  0.0  0.0  0:00.21 /sbin/auditd
  878 root       16  -4   104M   1824  1220 S  0.0  0.0  0:01.22 /sbin/auditd
  880 root       16  -4  7068   3412  3016 S  0.0  0.1  0:00.47 /usr/sbin/sedispatch
  926 root       20   0   308M   9796  8368 S  0.0  0.2  0:00.00 /usr/sbin/ModemManager
```

Figure 23-6. *htop has nice bar charts to indicate resource usage, and it can show the process tree*

If you get into a menu or dialog that you want to get out of without making any changes, you can always press the Escape (**Esc**) key once to back up.

Summary Section

The Summary section of htop is displayed in two columns by default although that can be changed to three columns. It is very flexible and can be configured with several different types of information in pretty much any order you like. htop has a number of different options for the CPU display, including a single combined bar, a bar for each CPU, and various combinations in which specific CPUs can be grouped together into a single bar.

I think this is a cleaner summary display than some of the other system monitors and it is easier to read. The drawback to this Summary section is that some information is not available in htop that is available in the other monitors, such as CPU percentages by user, idle, and system time. I don't think that is a serious issue, just something to be aware of.

Recent versions of htop can also display the processor clock speed and temperature of each core. You can also choose to display network and disk I/O data. The configuration I use on my systems is shown in Figure 23-7. This image is from my primary workstation.

```
 0[||||||||||100.0%|3600MHz*60°C]   16[||||||||||100.0%|3599MHz*60°C]  Hostname: david.both.org
 1[||||||||||100.0%|3600MHz*62°C]   17[||||||||||100.0%|3599MHz*62°C]  Date & Time: 2023-02-20 16:38:13
 2[||||||||||100.0%|3600MHz*59°C]   18[||||||||||100.0%|3599MHz*59°C]  Uptime: 5 days, 01:07:42
 3[||||||||||100.0%|3599MHz*61°C]   19[||||||||||100.0%#3600MHz*61°C]
 4[||||||||||100.0%|3599MHz*58°C]   20[||||||||||100.0%|3599MHz*58°C]  Tasks: 220, 1085 thr, 378 kthr; 32
 5[||||||||||100.0%*3599MHz*59°C]   21[||||||||||100.0%*3600MHz*59°C]  Load average: 37.14 36.33 36.25
 6[||||||||||100.0%#1399MHz*48°C]   22[||||||||||100.0%#1400MHz*48°C]  Disk IO: 3.5% read: 0KiB/s write:
 7[|||||*****100.0%*1200MHz*48°C]   23[||||||||||100.0%*1200MHz*48°C]  Network: rx: 1KiB/s tx: 0KiB/s (7/
 8[||||||||||100.0%#3599MHz*60°C]   24[||||||||||100.0%*3600MHz*60°C]
 9[||||||||||100.0%|3599MHz*64°C]   25[||||||||||100.0%|3599MHz*64°C]  Systemd: running (0/655 failed) (0
10[||||||||||100.0%*3600MHz*60°C]   26[||||||||||100.0%*3600MHz*60°C]
11[||||||||||100.0%|3599MHz*60°C]   27[||||||||||100.0%|3599MHz*60°C]  Mem[||||||#*@@@@      11.4G/62.5G]
12[||||||||||100.0%#3599MHz*59°C]   28[||||||||||100.0%|3600MHz*59°C]  zrm[||          1.56M(7.68M)/8.00G]
13[||||||||||100.0%#3600MHz*59°C]   29[||||||||||100.0%|3600MHz*59°C]  Swp[|#              8.73M/8.00G]
14[||||||||||100.0%#3600MHz*56°C]   30[||||||||||100.0%#3599MHz*56°C]  Avg[||||||||||100.0%#3312MHz*64°C]
15[||||||||||100.0%|3599MHz*57°C]   31[||||||||||100.0%|3599MHz*57°C]

[Main] [I/O]
  PID USER      PRI  NI  VIRT   RES   SHR S  CPU%▽MEM%   TIME+   Command
51601 dboth      20   0 5063M 1531M 1419M S 200.0  2.4  3h28:28 VirtualBoxVM --comment StudentVM1 --start
51646 dboth      21   1 5063M 1531M 1419M R  99.0  2.4  1h39:42 VirtualBoxVM --comment StudentVM1 --start
51647 dboth      21   1 5063M 1531M 1419M R  98.3  2.4  1h38:34 VirtualBoxVM --comment StudentVM1 --start
65212 boinc      39  19 71336 70512  2388 R  95.1  0.1  1h22:36 wcgrid_mcm1_map_7.61_x86_64-pc-linux-gnu
58864 boinc      39  19 75776 74964  2388 R  93.5  0.1  2h50:30 wcgrid_mcm1_map_7.61_x86_64-pc-linux-gnu
61969 boinc      39  19 73656 72952  2388 R  93.4  0.1  2h09:32 wcgrid_mcm1_map_7.61_x86_64-pc-linux-gnu
53999 boinc      39  19 80068 79300  2388 R  93.2  0.1  4h15:33 wcgrid_mcm1_map_7.61_x86_64-pc-linux-gnu
37214 boinc      39  19 90316 89556  2388 R  93.1  0.1  7h42:14 wcgrid_mcm1_map_7.61_x86_64-pc-linux-gnu
48228 boinc      39  19 83232 82428  2388 R  93.0  0.1  5h19:30 wcgrid_mcm1_map_7.61_x86_64-pc-linux-gnu
71571 boinc      39  19 73708 72916  2388 R  93.0  0.1 12:16.99 wcgrid_mcm1_map_7.61_x86_64-pc-linux-gnu
61780 boinc      39  19 73888 73000  2388 R  92.7  0.1  2h12:02 wcgrid_mcm1_map_7.61_x86_64-pc-linux-gnu
57402 boinc      39  19 76612 75728  2388 R  92.5  0.1  3h08:40 wcgrid_mcm1_map_7.61_x86_64-pc-linux-gnu
57205 boinc      39  19 76864 76004  2388 R  92.5  0.1  3h11:27 wcgrid_mcm1_map_7.61_x86_64-pc-linux-gnu
56661 boinc      39  19 77388 76512  2388 R  92.3  0.1  3h23:17 wcgrid_mcm1_map_7.61_x86_64-pc-linux-gnu
60947 boinc      39  19 74504 73688  2388 R  92.2  0.1  2h25:40 wcgrid_mcm1_map_7.61_x86_64-pc-linux-gnu
48362 boinc      39  19 83020 82172  2388 R  92.1  0.1  5h17:29 wcgrid_mcm1_map_7.61_x86_64-pc-linux-gnu
48565 boinc      39  19 83088 82248  2388 R  92.0  0.1  5h16:37 wcgrid_mcm1_map_7.61_x86_64-pc-linux-gnu
64022 boinc      39  19 72340 71424  2388 R  91.9  0.1  1h41:40 wcgrid_mcm1_map_7.61_x86_64-pc-linux-gnu
62339 boinc      39  19 73420 72464  2388 R  91.5  0.1  2h03:59 wcgrid_mcm1_map_7.61_x86_64-pc-linux-gnu
57614 boinc      39  19 76584 75752  2388 R  91.5  0.1  3h06:10 wcgrid_mcm1_map_7.61_x86_64-pc-linux-gnu
51365 boinc      39  19 81616 80740  2388 R  91.4  0.1  4h49:02 wcgrid_mcm1_map_7.61_x86_64-pc-linux-gnu
60212 boinc      39  19 75108 74248  2388 R  91.3  0.1  2h36:29 wcgrid_mcm1_map_7.61_x86_64-pc-linux-gnu
71865 boinc      39  19 73708 72856  2328 R  91.1  0.1  7:05.62 wcgrid_mcm1_map_7.61_x86_64-pc-linux-gnu
F1Help  F2Setup F3Search F4Filter F5Tree  F6SortBy F7Nice - F8Nice + F9Kill  F10Quit
```

Figure 23-7. *My personal htop configuration displays a lot more information than the default setup. This system does have a lot of CPUs*

The **F2** (Setup) key is used to configure the Summary section of htop. A list of available data displays is shown, and you can use various keys to add them to the left or right column and to move them up and down within the selected column.

Be sure to look at the csw (Context Switches) and intr (Interrupts) data. Context switches are the number of times per interval that the CPU switches from one program to another. Interrupts display the number of times per interval that software or hardware interrupts occur and cause the CPU to handle those interrupts.

Process Section

The Process section of htop is very similar to that of top. As with the other monitors, processes can be sorted by any of several factors, including CPU or memory usage, user, or PID. Note that sorting is not possible when the tree view is selected.

The **F6** key allows you to select the sort column; it displays a list of the columns available for sorting, and you select the column you want and press the **Enter** key.

You can use the **up** and **down** arrow keys to select a process. The cursor bar moves up and down to highlight individual processes. The **space bar** can be used to tag multiple processes on which commands may be performed.

To kill a process, use the arrow keys to select the target process and press the **F9** or the **k** key. A list of signals to send the process is displayed down the left side of the terminal session with 15, SIGTERM, selected. You can specify the signal to use, if different from SIGTERM, using the **up** and **down** arrow keys. You could also use the **F7** and **F8** keys to renice the selected process.

One option I especially like is **F5**, which displays the list of running processes in a tree format making it easy to determine the parent/child relationships of running processes.

```
┌─────────────────────────────────────────────────────────────────────┐
│         EXPERIMENT 23-7: GETTING STARTED WITH HTOP                    │
└─────────────────────────────────────────────────────────────────────┘
```

Perform this experiment as root. Install htop and then start it:

[root@studentvm1 ~]# **dnf -y install htop ; htop**

Observe the htop display for a few minutes. Press the **T** (uppercase) key to sort the processes on their total accumulated CPU time. Start at least four new cpuHogs. If the new cpuHog instances are not immediately visible, it may take a few minutes, but the new cpuHogs will climb up the list of running processes so that they are visible. Their positions in the list will be more stable this way and make it easier to select one or more of them.

But we do not need to wait in order to locate these cpuHog instances. We could just use the **Page Down** and **Page Up** keys to do an eyeball search, but there is a better way.

Press the **F3** key and type in the search term "cpuH" (without the quotes). The cursor will move to the first cpuHog instance, which will be highlighted. Press **F3** to search through the list of running processes to locate the other cpuHog instances. Pressing any other key will exit from search mode and leave the cursor on the selected process.

Now use the **up** and **down** arrow keys to move the cursor to another of the new cpuHog instances. On my VM this is the cpuHog with a PID of 2325. Notice that the cursor remains on this process even it changes position in the display. The PID of your cpuHog instance will be different.

We are going to kill this process, so press **F9** to list the signals that can be sent to the highlighted cpuHog process. Move the cursor up to **SIGKILL** (Signal 9) as shown in Figure 23-8, and press **Enter** to kill this process.

Move the cursor to one of the remaining new cpuHogs. Press the **space bar** to tag this process. Tag two more of the new cpuHogs. Do not tag any of the cpuHog instances that have been running for a longer time.

Kill the tagged cpuHogs. Press the **k** key. This time leave the cursor on SIGTERM (Signal 15), and press **Enter** to kill all of the tagged processes. Look through the terminal sessions in which you started these cpuHogs to verify that they have been killed.

It is possible to set the delay interval but only from the command line. There is not an interactive command in any of the tools like top or htop that provides this capability. The -d option sets the delay time in tenths of a second – that is tenths, not full seconds.

Press **q** to quit from htop. Then enter the following command to start htop with a one-second interval:

```
[root@studentvm1 ~]# htop -d 10
```

```
1 [|||||||||||||||||||||||||||||||||100.0%]   Hostname: studentvm1
2 [|||||||||||||||||||||||||||||||||100.0%]   Tasks: 130, 124 thr; 2 running
Swp[                              0K/4.00G]   Load average: 13.26 13.08 12.59
Mem:3.85G used:538M buffers:193M cache:873M   Uptime: 4 days, 19:30:12

Send signal:     PID USER     PRI  NI   VIRT   RES   SHR S CPU% MEM%    TIME+  Command
 0 Cancel       4939 student   20   0  227M  4820  2048 R 17.9  0.1 28h55:00 SCREEN
 1 SIGHUP       5096 student   32  12  211M  3152  2912 R 17.9  0.1 26h25:20 /bin/bash ./cpuH
 2 SIGINT       5036 student    0 -20  211M  1132   988 R 14.0  0.0 26h19:00 /bin/bash ./cpuH
 3 SIGQUIT      5285 student   20   0  211M  1072   924 R 13.7  0.0 26h18:04 /bin/bash ./cpuH
 4 SIGILL       5162 student   20   0  211M  1132   988 R 14.0  0.0 26h12:58 /bin/bash ./cpuH
 5 SIGTRAP      5314 student   20   0  211M  1136   988 R 17.9  0.0 26h08:28 /bin/bash ./cpuH
 6 SIGABRT      2277 student   20   0  211M  3200  2960 R 17.9  0.1  7:24.16 /bin/bash ./cpuH
 6 SIGIOT       2325 student   20   0  211M  1136   988 R 17.8  0.0  7:22.45 /bin/bash ./cpuH
 7 SIGBUS       2272 student   20   0  211M  1072   924 R 13.8  0.0  7:21.19 /bin/bash ./cpuH
 8 SIGFPE       2273 student   20   0  211M  3292  3048 R 13.8  0.1  7:17.76 /bin/bash ./cpuH
 9 SIGKILL     26067 student   20   0  286M  3176  2724 S  0.1  0.1  6:49.95 /usr/bin/VBoxCli
10 SIGUSR1     26069 student   20   0  286M  3176  2724 S  0.0  0.1  6:49.47 /usr/bin/VBoxCli
11 SIGSEGV      1105 root      20   0  386M 82840 38908 S  0.0  2.1  5:07.76 /usr/libexec/Xor
12 SIGUSR2      4881 student   20   0 39180  5072  3840 S  0.1  0.1  5:01.21 sshd: student@pt
13 SIGPIPE      2848 student   20   0  211M  1072   924 R 17.8  0.0  3:35.51 /bin/bash ./cpuH
14 SIGALRM      2845 student   20   0  211M  1196  1052 R 13.8  0.0  3:32.45 /bin/bash ./cpuH
15 SIGTERM      4797 root      20   0 39180  5040  3804 S  0.0  0.1  3:04.67 sshd: root@pts/0
16 SIGSTKFLT    5068 root      20   0  226M  2908  1900 S  0.0  0.1  2:00.10 SCREEN
17 SIGCHLD       905 root      20   0  491M  4356  3904 S  0.0  0.1  1:15.09 /usr/sbin/VBoxSe
18 SIGCONT       930 dbus      20   0 42272  6632  4856 S  0.0  0.2  0:51.88 /usr/bin/dbus-da
19 SIGSTOP       919 root      20   0  491M  4356  3904 S  0.0  0.1  0:46.71 /usr/sbin/VBoxSe
20 SIGTSTP     26122 student   20   0  406M 32612 25496 S  0.0  0.8  0:43.36 xfwm4 --display
21 SIGTTIN         1 root      20   0  103M 14660  9196 S  0.0  0.4  0:40.62 /usr/lib/systemd
22 SIGTTOU     26205 student   20   0  678M 73684 42960 S  0.0  1.8  0:32.88 /usr/bin/python3
EnterSend    EscCancel
```

Figure 23-8. *Select a cpuHog instance and press F9 to list the signals that can be sent*

Read the man page for htop to learn more about any data items and interactive commands that you find interesting.

Do not kill the remaining cpuHog instances and leave htop running.

Configuration

Each user has their own htop configuration file, ~/.config/htop/htoprc, and changes to the htop configuration are stored there automatically. There is no global configuration file for htop.

The htop utility has a very flexible configuration. The CPUs and Memory meters in the header section can be configured in the **F2** Setup dialog page as seen in Figure 23-9.

Let's take some time to explore this setup capability in Experiment 23-8.

EXPERIMENT 23-8: CONFIGURING HTOP

Perform this experiment as the root user, but everything will work the same way with a non-root user except that non-root users will be unable to change nice numbers in a negative direction.

Press the F2 key to open the Setup dialog, which is shown in Figure 23-9. The Meters option in the Setup column allows us to add, delete, and configure the various available meters.

Use the up and down arrow keys to select one of the four options in the Setup column. After you check that out, return the cursor to the Meters dialog and look at the meters in each of the Left and Right columns.

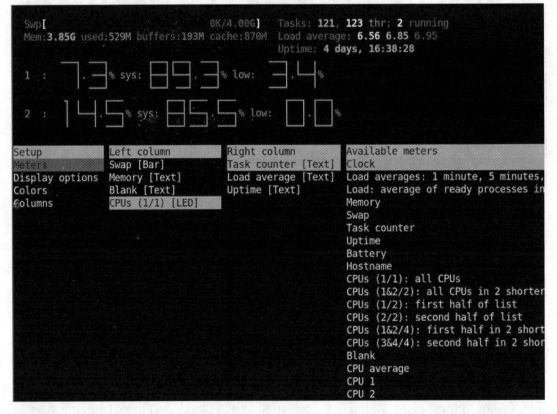

Figure 23-9. *The htop Setup dialog showing some different meter styles in the Summary section*

On your display the CPUs meter will be at the top. Ensure that it is highlighted and press **Enter**. The CPUs meter is highlighted with a different color and a double up/down arrow symbol (↕). First, press the **space bar** to rotate through the available meter types. Choose one you like. Use the **up** and **down** keys on the keyboard to move this meter to a location you prefer in the current column. Use the **right arrow** and **left arrow** keys to change the column in which the meter is displayed. Press **Enter** again to lock the meter into position.

The rightmost column in the Meters dialog displays all of the available meters. Move the highlight bar to the Hostname meter and press **Enter**. Use the arrow keys to move the Hostname meter to the top of the Right column and press Enter to lock it into position.

Move the cursor back to the Setup column and place it on **Display options**. Move the cursor to the Display options column and remove the x from **Hide kernel threads**. This enables htop to display kernel-related process threads. You could also press **K** (uppercase) when in the main htop screen to toggle the showing of kernel threads. The kthr item now appears on the Tasks line of the Summary section.

I also like to enable **Leave a margin around header**, **Detailed CPU time**, and **Count CPUs from 0 instead of 1**. Try these and some of the other options in this dialog.

Try out some of the different color schemes in the **Colors** dialog. The Columns dialog allows you to configure the specific columns to be displayed in the process list and in what sequence they appear.

Be sure to spend plenty of time experimenting with htop because it is very useful. Exit from htop when you are finished.

Glances

The Glances utility can display more information about your computer than any of the other text-mode monitors with which I am currently familiar. This includes filesystem I/O, network I/O, and sensor readouts that can display CPU and other hardware temperatures as well as fan speeds and disk usage by hardware device and logical volume.

The drawback to having all of this information is that Glances uses a significant amount of CPU resources itself. On my systems I find that it can use from about 10% to 20% of CPU cycles. That is a lot, so you should consider that impact when you choose your monitoring tool. Glances can also explore your network using SNMP protocols to discover and query other network nodes.

Summary Section

The Summary section of Glances contains most of the same information as the Summary sections of the other monitors. If you have enough horizontal screen real estate, it can show CPU usage with both a bar graph and a numeric indicator; otherwise, it will show only the number.

I like this Summary section better than those of the other monitors; I think it provides the right information in an easily understandable format. As with atop and htop, you can press the 1 key to toggle between a display of the individual CPU cores or a global one with all of the CPU cores as a single average as shown in Figure 23-10.

Process Section

The Process section displays the standard information about each of the running processes. Processes can be sorted automatically (a) or by CPU (c), memory (m), name (p), user (u), I/O rate (i), or time (t). When sorted automatically processes are first sorted by the most used resource. In Figure 23-10 the default sort column, TIME+, is highlighted. As with htop TIME+ is the accumulated CPU time for the process.

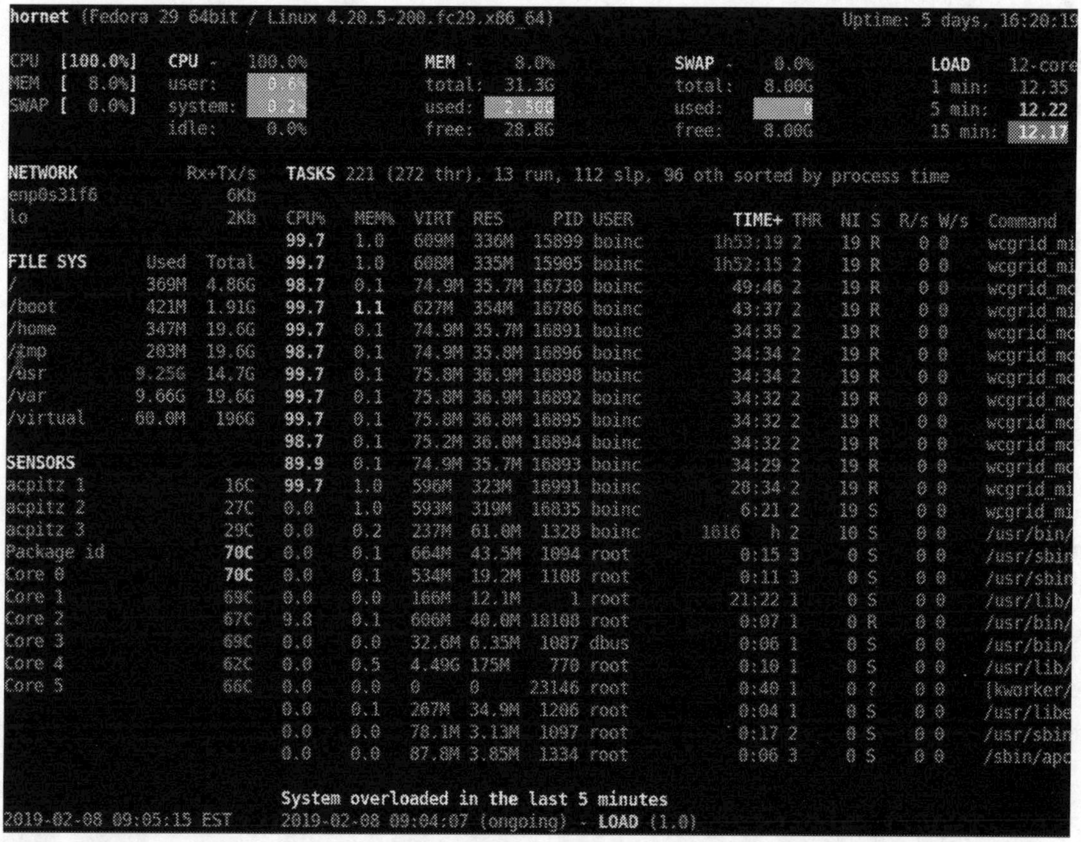

Figure 23-10.   *The Glances interface with network, filesystem, and sensor information*

Glances also shows warnings and critical alerts at the very bottom of the screen, including the time and duration of the event. This can be helpful when attempting to diagnose problems when you cannot stare at the screen for hours at a time. These alert logs can be toggled on or off with the **l** (El) key, warnings can be cleared with the **w** key, while alerts and warnings can all be cleared with **x**.

To kill a process, use the up/down arrow keys to highlight the desired process and press **k** and respond appropriately on the little confirmation dialog.

Sidebar

Glances has a very nice sidebar that displays information that is not available in top or htop. atop and htop both display some of this data, but Glances is the only monitor that displays all of the sensor data. Sometimes it is nice to see temperatures and fan speeds.

The individual modules, disk, filesystem, network, and sensors, can be toggled on and off using the **d**, **f**, **n**, and **s** commands, respectively. The entire sidebar can be toggled using **2**. Docker stats can be displayed in the sidebar with uppercase **D**.

Note that the hardware sensors are not displayed when Glances is running on a virtual machine. For this reason I have used a screenshot of Glances from one of my physical hosts.

Configuration

The system-wide instance of the configuration file is located in the /etc/glances/ glances.conf directory. Individual users can have a local instance at ~/.config/glances/ glances.conf, which will override the global configuration. The primary purpose of these configuration files is to set thresholds for warnings and critical alerts. There is no way I can find to make other configuration changes – such as sidebar modules or the CPU displays – permanent. It appears that you must reconfigure those items every time you start Glances.

There is a document, /usr/share/doc/Glances/Glances-doc.html, that provides a great deal of information about using Glances, and it explicitly states that you can use the configuration file to configure which modules are displayed. However, neither the information given nor the examples describe just how to do that.

EXPERIMENT 23-9: EXPLORING GLANCES

Perform this experiment as the root user. To begin, install Glances and then start it.

Note that, due to the CPU load overhead incurred by Glances, there may be some delay before the Glances display appears. View the Glances output for a few minutes and locate the various types of data that you have already seen in the previous monitors. Press the **h** key to display a Help menu. Most of the options here are simply show/hide various data displays or to select a sort column. Press **h** again to exit from the Help menu.

Press the **f** key to hide the filesystem usage statistics. Press **f** again to display them again. Note that the disk I/O statistics are not shown – I am not sure why this is the case. Because this is a VM, the sensor data will not be displayed because there is no physical hardware.

Take some time to experiment with Glances until you feel comfortable with it.

Press **q** or Esc to **exit** from Glances.

Despite its lack of interactive capabilities such as the ability to renice or kill processes and its own high CPU load, I find Glances to be a very useful tool. The complete Glances documentation[7] is available on the Internet, and the Glances man page has startup options and interactive command information.

Other Tools

Sometimes the static tools like the ps (process list) tend to get overlooked in our efforts to observe system performance in as near to real time as we can get. The ps command can produce a static list of processes. It can list all processes, or it can list only the running processes for the user that issues the command. The kill command is used to kill running processes, and it can also send other signals that enable the user or SysAdmin to interact with them.

EXPERIMENT 23-10: EXPLORING OTHER TOOLS

Perform this experiment as the student user. If there are not already some cpuHogs running, start four or five for use in this experiment.

The following command lists currently running processes that belong to the user. This provides an easy way to find the PIDs of running processes that we might be interested in when troubleshooting performance problems:

```
[student@studentvm1 ~]$ ps -r
  PID TTY      STAT    TIME COMMAND
 5036 pts/6    RN+   193:24 /bin/bash ./cpuHog
 8531 pts/7    R<+   192:47 /bin/bash ./cpuHog
 8650 pts/8    R+    187:52 /bin/bash ./cpuHog
 8712 pts/9    R+    189:08 /bin/bash ./cpuHog
 8736 pts/10   R+    189:18 /bin/bash ./cpuHog
23463 pts/12   R+      0:00 ps -r
[student@studentvm1 ~]$
```

---

[7] Glances, Glances, https://Glances.readthedocs.io/en/latest/index.html

I like the next command because it lists all processes whether running or not:

```
[student@studentvm1 ~]$ ps -ef
UID         PID  PPID  C STIME TTY        TIME CMD
root          1     0  0 Feb02 ?      00:00:55 /usr/lib/systemd/systemd
--switched-root --system --deserialize 33
root          2     0  0 Feb02 ?      00:00:00 [kthreadd]
root          3     2  0 Feb02 ?      00:00:00 [rcu_gp]
root          4     2  0 Feb02 ?      00:00:00 [rcu_par_gp]
root          6     2  0 Feb02 ?      00:00:00 [kworker/0:0H-kblockd]
root          8     2  0 Feb02 ?      00:00:00 [mm_percpu_wq]
root          9     2  0 Feb02 ?      00:02:03 [ksoftirqd/0]
root         10     2  0 Feb02 ?      00:03:08 [rcu_sched]
root         11     2  0 Feb02 ?      00:00:00 [rcu_bh]
root         12     2  0 Feb02 ?      00:00:00 [migration/0]
root         14     2  0 Feb02 ?      00:00:00 [cpuhp/0]
root         15     2  0 Feb02 ?      00:00:00 [cpuhp/1]
root         16     2  0 Feb02 ?      00:00:00 [migration/1]
root         17     2  0 Feb02 ?      00:01:33 [ksoftirqd/1]
<snip>
student   25882  1408  0 Feb03 ?      00:00:00 /bin/sh /etc/xdg/xfce4/
xinitrc -- vt
student   25966  4873  0 Feb03 ?      00:00:00 /usr/libexec/
imsettings-daemon
student   25969  4873  0 Feb03 ?      00:00:00 /usr/libexec/gvfsd
student   25976  4873  0 Feb03 ?      00:00:00 /usr/lib64/xfce4/
xfconf/xfconfd
student   26042     1  0 Feb03 ?      00:00:00 /usr/bin/VBoxClient
--clipboard
student   26043 26042  0 Feb03 ?      00:00:00 /usr/bin/VBoxClient
--clipboard
student   26053     1  0 Feb03 ?      00:00:00 /usr/bin/VBoxClient --display
student   26054 26053  0 Feb03 ?      00:00:00 /usr/bin/VBoxClient --display
student   26059     1  0 Feb03 ?      00:00:00 /usr/bin/VBoxClient
--seamless
student   26073 25882  0 Feb03 ?      00:00:01 /usr/bin/ssh-agent /bin/sh -c
exec -l /bin/bash -c "startxfce4"
student   26103 25882  0 Feb03 ?      00:00:01 xfce4-session
```

```
student   26104  4873  0 Feb03 ?          00:00:00 /usr/libexec/at-spi-
bus-launcher
<snip>
```

I can use grep and other commands to locate specific processes using appropriate filters:

```
[root@studentvm1 ~]# ps -ef | grep xfce
student    1311  1283  0 Jul17 ?          00:00:00 /bin/sh /etc/xdg/xfce4/
xinitrc -- vt
student    1399  1290  0 Jul17 ?          00:00:00 /usr/lib64/xfce4/
xfconf/xfconfd
student    1501  1311  0 Jul17 ?          00:00:00 /usr/bin/ssh-agent /bin/sh -c
exec -l /bin/bash -c "startxfce4"
student    1531  1311  0 Jul17 ?          00:00:00 xfce4-session
student    1554     1  0 Jul17 ?          00:00:05 xfce4-panel
student    1584  1531  0 Jul17 ?          00:00:00 /usr/libexec/xfce-polkit
student    1595     1  0 Jul17 ?          00:00:00 xfce4-power-manager
student    1723  1290  0 Jul17 ?          00:00:00 /usr/lib64/xfce4/notifyd/
xfce4-notifyd
student    1944  1554  0 Jul17 ?          00:00:01 /usr/lib64/xfce4/panel/
wrapper-2.0 /usr/lib64/xfce4/panel/plugins/libsystray.so 6 23068680 systray
Notification Area Area where notification icons appear
student    1950  1554  0 Jul17 ?          00:00:00 /usr/lib64/xfce4/panel/
wrapper-2.0 /usr/lib64/xfce4/panel/plugins/libactions.so 2 23068681 actions
Action Buttons Log out, lock or other system actions
student    1951  1554  0 Jul17 ?          00:00:00 /usr/lib64/xfce4/panel/
wrapper-2.0 /usr/lib64/xfce4/panel/plugins/libnotification-plugin.so 18
23068682 notification-plugin Notification Plugin Notification plugin for the
Xfce panel
student    2019     1  0 Jul17 ?          00:00:05 /usr/bin/xfce4-terminal
root       5051 22865  0 12:19 pts/3      00:00:00 grep --color=auto xfce
```

We can display all processes running that belong to the user student. Note that this is not all of the processes that belong to the student user, just the ones that are running when the command is issued. The options are a for all and u for user. Note the interesting syntax that there must not be a space between the u option and the username, student:

```
[student@studentvm1 ~]$ ps -austudent
  PID TTY          TIME CMD
```

```
2272 pts/7      06:23:28 cpuHog
2273 pts/8      06:23:42 cpuHog
2277 pts/11     06:23:14 cpuHog
2278 pts/14     00:00:00 bash
2302 pts/15     00:00:00 bash
2692 pts/16     00:00:00 bash
2845 pts/14     06:17:17 cpuHog
2848 pts/16     06:20:10 cpuHog
4873 ?          00:00:00 systemd
4875 ?          00:00:00 (sd-pam)
4880 ?          00:00:00 pulseaudio
```

What do we do once we have found the process(es) that we are looking for? We usually kill or renice them. You have already used both of these so won't do that again. Let's look at a couple additional useful and interesting commands.

You should have a few cpuHogs still running, and we want to find just those. The pgrep command lists the PID numbers for each process whose name matches the pattern specified as the argument:

```
[student@studentvm1 ~]$ pgrep cpuHog
2272
2273
2277
2845
2848
5096
5162
5285
5314
6006
[student@studentvm1 ~]$
```

That is all — nothing else, just the PIDs. You could use the -i option to ignore case in the names, which would mean not having to be case specific when typing the argument. The -l (lowercase el) is to list the names as well. It might be good to do this if several types of running processes might match the argument:

```
[student@studentvm1 ~]$ pgrep -l cpu
8 mm_percpu_wq
```

```
  14 cpuhp/0
  15 cpuhp/1
2272 cpuHog
2273 cpuHog
2277 cpuHog
2845 cpuHog
2848 cpuHog
5096 cpuHog
5162 cpuHog
5285 cpuHog
5314 cpuHog
6006 cpuHog
[student@studentvm1 ~]$
```

Just be careful that you know what will be killed or altered with some other commands, like this next one:

[student@studentvm1 ~]$ **renice +4 $(pgrep cpuH)**

What do you think that the preceding command does? Use one of the interactive monitors like top or htop to verify this. Here are the results from my VM:

```
2272 (process ID) old priority 0, new priority 4
2273 (process ID) old priority 0, new priority 4
2277 (process ID) old priority 0, new priority 4
2845 (process ID) old priority 0, new priority 4
2848 (process ID) old priority 0, new priority 4
renice: failed to set priority for 5096 (process ID): Permission denied
5162 (process ID) old priority 0, new priority 4
5285 (process ID) old priority 0, new priority 4
5314 (process ID) old priority 0, new priority 4
6006 (process ID) old priority 0, new priority 4
```

I had one cpuHog that was not killed because it was running as root and the student user does not have the authority to kill root or any other user's processes. Note that the pgrep command found all of the cpuHogs, but we could have used the -U option to specify that we only wanted to list those matching processes that were also running as the student user. For this reason it is wise to be very careful when running commands like these as root so that you do not kill processes that belong to a user who does not want or need them terminated.

We have one more interesting command that we can use to kill multiple processes even if the number of them that are running and their PIDs are unknown. The `pkill` utility has the same matching capabilities as `pgrep`, but it simply sends the specified signals to the matching processes. The default is Signal 15, SIGTERM. The following command kills all running processes that match the string "cpuH":

```
[student@studentvm1 ~]$ pkill cpuH
```

At this point there should be no cpuHog instances running that belong to the student user.

The Impact of Measurement

The observer effect[8] is a theory in the scientific discipline of physics that states, "simply observing a situation or phenomenon necessarily changes that phenomenon." This is also true when measuring Linux system performance.

The act of using these monitoring tools alters a system's use of resources including memory and CPU time. top and most of these monitors use perhaps 2% or 3% of a system's CPU time. The Glances utility has much more impact than the others and can use between 10% and 20% of CPU time; I have seen it use as much as 40% of one CPU in my very large and active primary workstation with 32 CPUs. Be sure to consider the observer effect when choosing your tools.

Chapter Summary

As we proceeded through this chapter, you probably observed some things about the processes running on your VM and the total amount of time accrued to each. The cpuHogs together accumulated most of the CPU time, while the kernel threads accumulated very little by comparison. This is because most of the kernel threads do not need to run frequently and take very little time when they do. Other tools that don't accumulate much time, such as LibreOffice, simply spend most of their time waiting for the users to type or select tasks from menus or icon bars.

---

[8] Wikipedia, *Observer effect (physics)*, https://en.m.wikipedia.org/wiki/Observer_effect_(physics)

Be sure to read the man pages for each of the monitors we have experimented with in this chapter because there is a large amount of information about configuring and interacting with them. These tools are the ones I like best for managing processes, but there are more.

These programs can tell you a great deal when you are looking for the root cause of a problem. They can tell you when a process, and which one, is sucking up CPU time, whether there is enough free memory, whether processes are stalled while waiting for I/O such as disk or network access to complete, and much more.

I also highly recommend that you spend time watching these monitoring programs while they run on a system that is functioning normally. This way you will be able to differentiate those things that may be abnormal while you are looking for the cause of a problem. This is one of those tasks that may look to others like you are just sitting there doing nothing but which is an important part of being the lazy SysAdmin.

My favorites are Glances and htop. I also use top when nothing else is available.

Exercises

Complete the following exercises to finish this chapter:

1. There is a specification in the Linux FHS that defines a location for personal executable files that is within your own home directory structure. This allows typing the executable name without a directory path preceding it. What is it?

2. Set up your home directory structure in accordance with the FHS and move the executable files to that location. Test launching the cpuHog script from this new location without using a path.

3. Start an instance of top and set the refresh delay to one second, and then observe the output for a few minutes. How much memory and swap space are free?

4. As both root and the student user, use the nice command to start instances of the cpuHog program with negative numbers. Does it work as you expected?

5. Why are non-root users restricted from lowering the nice numbers of their own processes?

6. What default PID is used by top when you use k to kill or r to renice a process?

7. What is the result of reducing the number of virtual CPUs allocated to the StudentVM1 virtual machine and then rerunning Experiment 23-4?

8. When using atop, what key would you use to freeze the display for longer inspection than the current interval would allow?

9. The htop utility allows filtering the process list so that only those that match the filter specification are displayed. Use that function to display only the running cpuHog instances.

10. Can multiple processes be terminated with a single kill command?

11. Do the accumulated times in the TIME+ columns of top and htop add up to the total uptime? Why?

CHAPTER 24

Special Filesystems

Objectives

In this chapter you will learn

- What constitutes a special filesystem

- Practical uses for two of the special filesystems, /proc and /sys

- The use of some of the tools that allow easy access to view system data in these special filesystems

- How to create and manage swap files

- Using Zram for swap

- Some differing recommendations for swap size

Introduction

In Chapter 23, we looked at some tools like top that allow SysAdmins to look inside the running Linux kernel. We also discussed the observer effect,[1] which is a theory in the scientific discipline of physics that states, "simply observing a situation or phenomenon necessarily changes that phenomenon." This is also true when measuring Linux system performance. The act of using those monitoring tools alters the system's use of resources including memory and CPU time.

---

[1] Wikipedia, *Observer effect (physics)*, https://en.m.wikipedia.org/wiki/Observer_effect_(physics)

© David Both 2023
D. Both, *Using and Administering Linux: Volume 2*, https://doi.org/10.1007/978-1-4842-9615-8_24

Collecting data does not impact the overall performance in a Linux host. The Linux kernel is designed to always collect and store the performance data that is merely accessed and displayed by any and all performance monitoring tools. It is the tools' access of that data to read it and then to manipulate it and display it in a meaningful format that further affects the system performance.

Linux has some special filesystems that it creates in RAM at each boot, two of which are particularly interesting to SysAdmins: the /proc and /sys filesystems. It is in these filesystems that the kernel stores the performance data of the running kernel and much more. The data is always there and it is easy to access. These are virtual filesystems that exist only in RAM while the Linux host is running; they do not exist on any physical disk. Because they exist only in RAM, these filesystems are not persistent like filesystems that are stored on storage devices. They disappear when the computer is turned off and are recreated anew each time Linux starts up.

Unlike /proc and /sys, the swap filesystem does exist on storage devices. Swap space is used to supplement RAM when it gets close to being full, and this allows the host to continue running although with some performance penalty. Swap filesystems are created with specialized tools and are formatted differently than other filesystems.

The /proc, /sys, and swap filesystems are ones with which you will become well acquainted as a SysAdmin, so we are going to explore them in some detail in this chapter. Because we have the most control over the swap filesystems and there are some strong opinions about swap space, we are going to explore this special filesystem in depth.

The /proc Filesystem

The /proc filesystem is defined by the FHS, which we explored in Chapter 19, as the location for Linux to store information about the system, the kernel, and all processes running on the host. It is intended to be a place for the kernel to expose information about itself in order to facilitate access to data about the system. It is also designed to provide access to view kernel configuration parameters and to modify many of them when necessary in order to allow the SysAdmin to tune the running system without needing to perform reboots after making changes.

When used as a window into the state of the operating system and its view of the system and hardware, it provides easy access to virtually every bit of information you might want as a SysAdmin.

EXPERIMENT 24-1: EXPLORING /PROC

For best results with this experiment, it must be performed as root.

Let's first look at the top-level contents of the /proc filesystem of a running Linux host. On your host you may see color coding to differentiate files from directories.

First, look at the numeric entries. The name of these directories is a PID, or process ID, number. Each of those PID directories contains information about the running process that it represents. We will look at these directories in more detail in Experiment 24-2:

```
[root@studentvm1 proc]# cd /proc ; ls
1       124     20      26122   2692    4940    836     946     driver          agetypeinfo
10      1256    21      26141   27      4968    846     95      execdomains     partitions
100     14      22      26143   28      5037    847     950     fb              sched_debug
1007    1408    2278    26153   29      5135    848     96      filesystems     schedstat
1008    14402   23      26158   3       516     849     961     fs              scsi
101     14831   2302    26159   30      5163    851     963     interrupts      self
102     14844   24      26166   31      5230    852     968     iomem           slabinfo
103     15      25      26167   32      5258    874     97      ioports         softirqs
104     16      25882   26171   33      526     875     98      irq             stat
105     17      25966   26174   34      5287    878     987     kallsyms        swaps
1060    17105   25969   26175   35      537     880     99      kcore           sys
107     17517   25976   26179   36      554     899     994     keys            sysrq-trigger
1075    17518   26      26180   386     555     9       995     key-users       sysvipc
109     17559   26042   26186   39      593     900     996     kmsg            thread-self
1090    17607   26043   26189   394     594     901     997     kpagecgroup     timer_list
1092    17649   26053   26191   4       6       902     acpi    kpagecount      tty
1096    17653   26054   26194   40      653     903     asound  kpageflags      uptime
11      17700   26059   26203   450     678     905     buddyinfo  latency_stats version
1105    17704   26060   26205   4868    747     906     bus     loadavg         vmallocinfo
111     17706   26066   26209   4873    765     907     cgroups locks           vmstat
113     17711   26067   26216   4875    767     908     cmdline mdstat          zoneinfo
11594   17712   26073   26220   4880    769     909     consoles meminfo
11598   17779   26103   26228   4881    794     929     cpuinfo misc
117     17780   26104   26282   4882    8       930     crypto  modules
118     18218   26110   26363   4932    833     931     devices mounts
12      19      26116   26415   4938    834     932     diskstats mtrr
```

109

```
1233    2        26121  26483  4939  835   94    dma            net
[root@studentvm1 proc]#
```

Each of the files in the /proc directory contains information about some part of the kernel. Let's take a look at a couple of these files, cpuinfo and meminfo.

The cpuinfo file is mostly static. It contains the specifications for all installed CPUs:

```
[root@studentvm1 proc]# cat cpuinfo
processor       : 0
vendor_id       : GenuineIntel
cpu family      : 6
model           : 58
model name      : Intel(R) Core(TM) i7-3770 CPU @ 3.40GHz
stepping        : 9
microcode       : 0x19
cpu MHz         : 3392.345
cache size      : 8192 KB
physical id     : 0
siblings        : 1
core id         : 0
cpu cores       : 1
apicid          : 0
initial apicid  : 0
fpu             : yes
fpu_exception   : yes
cpuid level     : 13
wp              : yes
flags           : fpu vme de pse tsc msr pae mce cx8 apic sep mtrr pge mca
                  cmov pat pse36 clflush mmx fxsr sse sse2 syscall nx rdtscp
                  lm constant_tsc rep_good nopl xtopology nonstop_tsc cpuid
                  pni pclmulqdq monitor ssse3 cx16 sse4_1 sse4_2 popcnt aes
                  xsave avx rdrand lahf_lm
bugs            :
bogomips        : 6784.69
clflush size    : 64
cache_alignment : 64
address sizes   : 36 bits physical, 48 bits virtual
power management:
<snip>
```

The data from the cpuinfo file includes the processor ID and model, its current speed in MHz, and the flags that can be used to determine the CPU features. Now let's look at memory. First, use cat to view the meminfo file and then use the free command to do a comparison:

```
[root@studentvm1 proc]# cat meminfo
MemTotal:       4044740 kB
MemFree:        2936368 kB
MemAvailable:   3484704 kB
Buffers:         108740 kB
Cached:          615616 kB
SwapCached:           0 kB
Active:          676432 kB
Inactive:        310016 kB
Active(anon):    266916 kB
Inactive(anon):     316 kB
Active(file):    409516 kB
Inactive(file):  309700 kB
Unevictable:       8100 kB
Mlocked:           8100 kB
SwapTotal:      4182012 kB
SwapFree:       4182012 kB
Dirty:                0 kB
Writeback:            0 kB
AnonPages:       270212 kB
Mapped:          148088 kB
Shmem:              988 kB
Slab:             80128 kB
SReclaimable:     64500 kB
SUnreclaim:       15628 kB
KernelStack:       2272 kB
PageTables:       11300 kB
NFS_Unstable:         0 kB
Bounce:               0 kB
WritebackTmp:         0 kB
CommitLimit:    6204380 kB
Committed_AS:    753260 kB
VmallocTotal:  34359738367 kB
VmallocUsed:          0 kB
```

```
VmallocChunk:              0 kB
HardwareCorrupted:         0 kB
AnonHugePages:             0 kB
ShmemHugePages:            0 kB
ShmemPmdMapped:            0 kB
CmaTotal:                  0 kB
CmaFree:                   0 kB
HugePages_Total:           0
HugePages_Free:            0
HugePages_Rsvd:            0
HugePages_Surp:            0
Hugepagesize:           2048 kB
DirectMap4k:           73664 kB
DirectMap2M:         4120576 kB
[root@studentvm1 proc]# free
          total        used         free      shared   buff/cache    available
Mem:    4044740      304492      2935748         988       804500      3484100
Swap:   4182012           0      4182012
```

There is a lot of information in the /proc/meminfo file. A few bits of that data are used by programs like the free command. If you want the complete picture of memory usage, look in /proc/meminfo. The free command, like top, htop, and many other core utilities, gets its data from the /proc filesystem.

Run the cat meminfo command several times in quick succession to see that the /proc/meminfo file is continuously changing. That indicates the file is being updated. You can do this with the watch command:

```
[root@studentvm1 proc]# watch cat meminfo
```

Note   While doing research for this experiment, I discovered that a method I had used before to determine that files were being updated, even when the content had not changed, no longer worked. The command that I used was stat /proc/meminfo, which should have shown continuously changing mtime, atime, and ctime, but which no longer did. This does work correctly in CentOS and Fedora 27 but not Fedora 37 or 29. I reported this problem as bug 1675440 on the Red Hat Bugzilla website. It is very important that we SysAdmins report bugs when we find them. Update: This behavior has not changed up through Fedora 37.

Because the data in /proc is a nearly instantaneous picture of the state of the Linux kernel and the computer hardware, the data may change rapidly. Look at the interrupts file several times in a row.

Spend a little time to compare the data in the /proc/meminfo file against the information you get when using commands like **free** and **top**. Where do you think these utility tools and many others get their information? Right here in the /proc filesystem, that's where.

Let's look a little bit deeper into PID 1. Like all of the process directories, it contains information about the process with that ID. So let's look at some of that information.

```
EXPERIMENT 24-2: VIEWING SYSTEMD
```

Start this experiment as root. Let's enter and look at the contents of the /proc/1 directory. Then view the contents of the cmdline file:

```
[root@studentvm1 proc]# cd /proc/1 ; cat cmdline
/usr/lib/systemd/systemd--switched-root--system--deserialize24
```

We can see from the contents of the cmdline that this is systemd, the mother of all programs. On all older and some current versions of Linux, PID 1 will be the init program.

If there are no cpuHogs running, start one instance in a terminal session as the student user. Use one of the monitoring tools like top to determine the PID of this cpuHog process. On my VM, the PID is 18107, but it will be different on your VM. Be sure to use the correct PID for the cpuHog on your VM.

Make the directory corresponding to the PID of your cpuHog instance the PWD. Then list the contents:

```
[root@studentvm1 18107]# cd /proc/18107 ; ll | less
total 0
dr-xr-xr-x. 2 student student 0 Feb 11 20:29 attr
```

```
--w-------. 1 student student 0 Feb 11 20:29 clear_refs
-r--r--r--. 1 student student 0 Feb 11 20:29 cmdline
-rw-r--r--. 1 student student 0 Feb 11 20:29 comm
-rw-r--r--. 1 student student 0 Feb 11 20:29 coredump_filter
-r--r--r--. 1 student student 0 Feb 11 20:29 cpuset
lrwxrwxrwx. 1 student student 0 Feb 11 20:29 cwd -> /home/student
-r--------. 1 student student 0 Feb 11 20:29 environ
lrwxrwxrwx. 1 student student 0 Feb 11 20:29 exe -> /usr/bin/bash
dr-x------. 2 student student 0 Feb 11 20:29 fd
<snip>
```

Note the entries for cwd and exe. The cwd entry points to the current working directory, a.k.a. the PWD, for the process. The exe entry points to the executable file for the process, which is the Bash shell. But look at the content of the cmdline file:

```
[root@studentvm1 18107]# cat cmdline
/bin/bash./cpuHog
```

This tells us that the program that is running is the cpuHog. It also gives us some insight into the manner in which programs – at least shell scripts – are run in Linux. When starting a shell program, the systemd[2] program first launches a shell, the default being Bash unless otherwise specified, and the shell program, cpuHog, is provided as an argument to the command.

If you are not already using top or htop to monitor the ongoing activities on your VM, start an instance of one now. Look for the COMMAND column, which, as you can see in Figure 24-1, shows the four running instances of the cpuHog.

---

[2] systemd is the program that deals with starting, stopping, and managing all other running processes. We will cover systemd in detail in Chapter 35.

```
top - 09:02:58 up 9 days, 14:54, 16 users,  load average: 5.22, 5.15, 5.10
Tasks: 212 total,   5 running, 207 sleeping,   0 stopped,   0 zombie
%Cpu0  : 36.0 us, 60.0 sy,  0.0 ni,  0.0 id,  0.0 wa,  2.0 hi,  2.0 si,  0.0 st
%Cpu1  : 11.2 us, 74.5 sy,  0.0 ni,  0.0 id,  0.0 wa,  8.2 hi,  6.1 si,  0.0 st
MiB Mem : 21.9/3942.5 [|||||||||||||                                            ]
MiB Swap:  0.0/4096.0 [                                                         ]

  PID USER      PR  NI    VIRT    RES    SHR S  %CPU  %MEM     TIME+ COMMAND
 1105 root      20   0  398352  85676  38904 R   8.9   2.1   7:33.78 Xorg
   17 root      20   0       0      0      0 S   0.0   0.0   6:27.09 ksoftirqd/1
11969 student   20   0  231608   3276   2048 R  29.7   0.1   5:41.53 screen
12019 student   20   0  216336   3188   2940 R  23.8   0.1   5:35.10 bash
11993 student   20   0  216336   1200   1052 R  32.7   0.0   5:32.69 cpuHog
12043 student   20   0  216336   3132   2880 R  22.8   0.1   5:28.42 cpuHog
12070 student   20   0  218500   3000   2720 R  30.7   0.1   5:04.96 ksh
<snip>
```

Figure 24-1. *The top command showing four cpuHogs. They are there but are not easy to identify*

It does show all four instances of the cpuHog, really. It is just not easy to identify two of them. To make it obvious, press the **c** key to display the complete command. The result can be seen in Figure 24-2.

```
top - 09:11:56 up 9 days, 15:03, 16 users,  load average: 5.46, 5.27, 5.14
Tasks: 212 total,   5 running, 207 sleeping,   0 stopped,   0 zombie
%Cpu0  : 47.1 us, 49.0 sy,  0.0 ni,  0.0 id,  0.0 wa,  2.0 hi,  2.0 si,  0.0 st
%Cpu1  : 10.9 us, 74.3 sy,  0.0 ni,  0.0 id,  0.0 wa,  8.9 hi,  5.9 si,  0.0 st
MiB Mem : 21.9/3942.5 [|||||||||||||                                            ]
MiB Swap:  0.0/4096.0 [                                                         ]

  PID USER      PR  NI    VIRT    RES    SHR S  %CPU  %MEM     TIME+ COMMAND
11969 student   20   0  231608   3276   2048 R  26.5   0.1   5:13.00 SCREEN
12019 student   20   0  216336   3188   2940 R  35.3   0.1   5:07.35 bash cpuHog
11993 student   20   0  216336   1200   1052 R  28.4   0.0   5:07.29 /bin/bash ./cpuHog
12043 student   20   0  216336   3132   2880 R  27.5   0.1   5:02.09 /bin/bash ./cpuHog
12070 student   20   0  218500   3000   2720 S  30.4   0.1   4:37.82 ksh ./cpuHog
<snip>
```

Figure 24-2. *After pressing the c key, all four cpuHogs are easy to identify*

The c key toggles display of the complete command line on and off. Now that we can see the command line, it is obvious that the cpuHogs have PIDs of 12019, 11993, 12043, and 12070.

The htop utility displays the command line by default, so start htop if it is not already running and look at the COMMAND column. You can immediately see the four cpuHogs. Be sure to make a note of the four PIDs for the cpuHogs. Now press **F5** to show the process tree, which allows us to see the process hierarchy as in Figure 24-3.

```
<snip>
11969 student   20  0  226M  3276  2048 R 37.4  0.1  4:48.82 ├─ SCREEN
12044 student   20  0  220M  4924  3456 S  0.0  0.1  0:00.03 │  ├─ /bin/bash
12070 student   20  0  213M  3000  2720 R 34.8  0.1  4:15.28 │  │  └─ ksh ./cpuHog
12020 student   20  0  220M  4704  3356 S  0.0  0.1  0:00.05 │  ├─ /bin/bash
12043 student   20  0  211M  3132  2880 R 37.4  0.1  4:38.81 │  │  └─ /bin/bash ./cpuHog
11994 student   20  0  220M  4932  3464 S  0.0  0.1  0:00.07 │  ├─ /bin/bash
12019 student   20  0  211M  3188  2940 R 36.1  0.1  4:43.72 │  │  └─ bash cpuHog
11970 student   20  0  220M  4724  3372 S  0.0  0.1  0:00.02 │  └─ /bin/bash
11993 student   20  0  211M  1200  1052 R 37.4  0.0  4:43.18 │     └─ /bin/bash ./cpuHog
<snip>
```

Figure 24-3. *The htop process tree view clarifies the process hierarchy*

Once again, this helps us understand a bit more about how Linux launches command-line programs. We can see that in all four cases systemd starts a sub-shell and then launches the program within that sub-shell.

Another tool that allows us to view the process tree is the pstree utility. Use the pstree utility to view the process tree:

[root@studentvm1 ~]# **pstree -Acp | less**

Figure 24-4 shows portions of the data stream from the pstree command. Scroll through the output and find the cpuHogs. You should check the man page for pstree to discover the meanings of the options we used for this command.

```
[root@studentvm1 ~]# pstree -Acp | less
systemd(1)-+-ModemManager(899)-+-{ModemManager}(926)
           |                    `-{ModemManager}(962)
           |-NetworkManager(1060)-+-dhclient(1233)
           |                       |-dhclient(1256)
           |                       |-{NetworkManager}(1072)
           |                       `-{NetworkManager}(1074)
           |-VBoxClient(26042)---VBoxClient(26043)---{VBoxClient}(26049)
           |-VBoxClient(26053)---VBoxClient(26054)
<snip>
           |-screen(11969)-+-bash(11970)---cpuHog(11993)
           |               |-bash(11994)---bash(12019)
           |               |-bash(12020)---cpuHog(12043)
           |               `-bash(12044)---ksh(12070)
           |-smartd(929)
<snip>
```

Figure 24-4. *The pstree utility also shows the process tree*

Our real purpose here was to learn the PIDs of the cpuHogs in order to explore them in the /proc filesystem. Now that we know multiple ways to do that, let's get back to our original objective.

Pick one of the cpuHogs and, as root, make /proc/<PID> the PWD. I chose PID 12070, but you should use the PID for an instance of cpuHog on your VM, and then list the contents of the directory:

```
[root@studentvm1 ~]# cd /proc/12070 ; ls
attr            cpuset    latency    mountstats     personality  smaps_
rollup   timerslack_ns
autogroup       cwd       limits     net            projid_map   stack
uid_map
auxv            environ   loginuid   ns             root         stat
wchan
cgroup          exe       map_files  numa_maps      sched        statm
clear_refs      fd        maps       oom_adj        schedstat    status
cmdline         fdinfo    mem        oom_score      sessionid    syscall
comm            gid_map   mountinfo  oom_score_adj  setgroups    task
coredump_filter io        mounts     pagemap        smaps        timers
```

Take some time to explore the content of some of these files and subdirectories. Be sure to view the content of the status, limits, loginuid, and maps files. The maps file is a memory map that lists executable and library locations in virtual memory. The status file contains a great deal of information including some interesting data about virtual memory usage. Also take some time to explore a few of the other files and subdirectories in this and other PID directories.

There is a huge amount of information available in the /proc filesystem, and it can be used to good advantage to solve problems. In fact, the capability to make changes to the running kernel on the fly and without a reboot is a powerful tool. It allows you to make instant changes to the Linux kernel to resolve a problem, enable a function, or tune performance. Let's look at one example.

Linux is very flexible and can do many interesting things. One of those cool things is that any Linux host with multiple network interface cards (NICs) can act as a router. All it takes is a little knowledge, a simple command, and some changes to the firewall.

Routing is a task managed by the kernel. So turning it on (or off) requires that we change a kernel configuration parameter. Fortunately, we do not need to recompile the kernel, and that is one of the benefits of exposing the kernel configuration in the /proc filesystem. We are going to turn on IP forwarding, which provides the kernel's basic routing functionality.

EXPERIMENT 24-3: MODIFY A KERNEL PARAMETER

This little command-line program makes the /proc/sys/net/ipv4 directory the PWD; prints the current state of the ip_forward file, which should be zero (0); sets it to "1"; and then prints its new state, which should be 1. Routing is now turned on. Be sure to enter the command on a single line:

```
[root@studentvm1 ipv4]# cd /proc/sys/net/ipv4 ; cat ip_forward ; echo 1 >
ip_forward ; cat ip_forward
0
1
```

Warning   I intentionally chose to modify a kernel parameter that I am familiar with and that won't cause any harm to your Linux VM. As you explore the /proc filesystem, you should not make any further changes.

Congratulations! You have just altered the configuration of the running kernel.

In order to complete the configuration of a Linux host to fully function as a router, additional changes would need to be made to the iptables firewall, or to whatever firewall software you may be using, and to the routing table. Those changes will define the specifics of the routing such as which packets get routed where. Although beyond the scope of this book, I have written an article[3] with some detail about configuring the routing table to which you can refer if you want more information. I also wrote an article[4]

---

[3] Both, David, "An introduction to Linux network routing," https://opensource.com/business/16/8/introduction-linux-network-routing

[4] Both, David, "Making Your Linux Box Into a Router," www.linux-databook.info/?page_id=697

that briefly covers all of the steps required to turn a Linux host into a router, including making IP forwarding persistent after a reboot.

While you are here in the /proc filesystem, look around some more – follow your own curiosity to explore different areas of this important filesystem.

The /sys Filesystem

The /sys directory is another virtual filesystem that is used by Linux to maintain specific data for use by the kernel and SysAdmins. The /sys directory maintains the list of hardware hierarchically for each bus type in the computer hardware.

A quick look at the /sys filesystem shows us its basic structure.

EXPERIMENT 24-4: EXPLORING THE /SYS FILESYSTEM

In this experiment we look briefly at the contents of the /sys directory and then one of its subdirectories, /sys/block:

```
[root@studentvm1 sys]# cd /sys
[root@studentvm1 sys]# ls
block  bus  class  dev  devices  firmware  fs  hypervisor
kernel  module  power
[root@studentvm1 sys]# ls block
dm-0  dm-1  sda  sr0
```

There are different types of disk (block) devices in /sys/block, and the sda device is one of them. Let's take a quick look at some of the contents of the sda directory:

```
[root@studentvm1 sys]# ls block/sda
alignment_offset   events_async        queue       slaves
bdi                events_poll_msecs   range       stat
capability         ext_range           removable   subsystem
dev                holders             ro          trace
device             inflight            sda1        uevent
discard_alignment  integrity           sda2
events             power               size
[root@studentvm1 sys]# cat block/sda/dev
8:0
```

```
[root@studentvm1 sys]# ls block/sda/device
block                                ncq_prio_enable
bsg                                  power
delete                               queue_depth
device_blocked                       queue_ramp_up_period
device_busy                          queue_type
dh_state                             rescan
driver                               rev
eh_timeout                           scsi_device
evt_capacity_change_reported         scsi_disk
evt_inquiry_change_reported          scsi_generic
evt_lun_change_reported              scsi_level
evt_media_change                     state
evt_mode_parameter_change_reported   subsystem
evt_soft_threshold_reached           sw_activity
generic                              timeout
inquiry                              type
iocounterbits                        uevent
iodone_cnt                           unload_heads
ioerr_cnt                            vendor
iorequest_cnt                        vpd_pg80
modalias                             vpd_pg83
model                                wwid
[root@studentvm1 sys]# cat block/sda/device/model
VBOX HARDDISK
```

For a bit more realistic information from this last command, I also performed this on my own physical hard drive rather than the VM I have been using for these experiments, and that looks like this:

```
[root@myworkstation ~]# cat /sys/block/sda/device/model
ST320DM000-1BD14
```

This information is more like what you would see on one of your own hardware hosts rather than a VM. Now let's use the smartctl command to show that same bit of information and more. I used my physical host for this due to the more realistic data. I have also trimmed a large amount of output from the end of the results:

```
[root@myworkstation proc]# smartctl -x /dev/sda
smartctl 6.5 2016-05-07 r4318 [x86_64-linux-4.13.16-302.fc27.x86_64]
(local build)
Copyright (C) 2002-16, Bruce Allen, Christian Franke, www.smartmontools.org

=== START OF INFORMATION SECTION ===
Model Family:     Seagate Barracuda 7200.14 (AF)
Device Model:     ST320DM000-1BD14C
Serial Number:    Z3TT43ZK
LU WWN Device Id: 5 000c50 065371517
Firmware Version: KC48
User Capacity:    320,072,933,376 bytes [320 GB]
Sector Sizes:     512 bytes logical, 4096 bytes physical
Rotation Rate:    7200 rpm
Device is:        In smartctl database [for details use: -P show]
ATA Version is:   ATA8-ACS T13/1699-D revision 4
SATA Version is:  SATA 3.0, 6.0 Gb/s (current: 6.0 Gb/s)
Local Time is:    Wed Dec 13 13:31:36 2017 EST
SMART support is: Available - device has SMART capability.
SMART support is: Enabled
AAM level is:     208 (intermediate), recommended: 208
APM feature is:   Unavailable
Rd look-ahead is: Enabled
Write cache is:   Enabled
ATA Security is:  Disabled, frozen [SEC2]
Wt Cache Reorder: Enabled

=== START OF READ SMART DATA SECTION ===
SMART overall-health self-assessment test result: PASSED

General SMART Values:
<snip>
```

Had I not cut off the end of the results from this last command, it would also show things like failure indicators and a temperature history, which can be helpful in determining the source of hard drive problems. The data for a virtual hard drive on your VM would be different and significantly less interesting.

The smartctl utility obtains the data it uses from the /sys filesystem, just as other utility programs obtain their data from the /proc filesystem.

The /sys filesystem contains data about the Peripheral Component Interconnect (PCI) and USB system bus hardware and any attached devices. The kernel can use this information to determine which device drivers to use, for one example.

EXPERIMENT 24-5: EXPLORING THE USB

Let's look at some information about one of the buses on the computer, the USB. I am going to skip right to the locations of the devices in the /sys filesystem; you may need to do a little exploring on your own to find the items that interest you:

```
[root@studentvm1 ~]# ls /sys/bus/usb/devices/usb2
2-0:1.0                 bMaxPacketSize0     driver                          quirks
authorized              bMaxPower           ep_00                           removable
authorized_default      bNumConfigurations  idProduct                       remove
avoid_reset_quirk       bNumInterfaces      idVendor                        serial
bcdDevice               busnum              interface_authorized_default    speed
bConfigurationValue     configuration       ltm_capable                     subsystem
bDeviceClass            descriptors         manufacturer                    uevent
bDeviceProtocol         dev                 maxchild                        urbnum
bDeviceSubClass         devnum              power                           version
bmAttributes            devpath             product
```

The preceding results show some of the files and directories that provide data about that particular device. But there is an easier way by using the core utilities so that we don't have to do all that exploration on our own.

If you do not have a usb2 directory or it is empty, that might be because the VirtualBox extensions were not installed. In that case, try this experiment in the **/sys/bus/usb/devices/usb** directory. This is from my own physical workstation:

```
[root@myworkstation ~]# lsusb
Bus 004 Device 001: ID 1d6b:0003 Linux Foundation 3.0 root hub
Bus 003 Device 001: ID 1d6b:0002 Linux Foundation 2.0 root hub
Bus 002 Device 004: ID 045b:0210 Hitachi, Ltd
Bus 002 Device 003: ID 045b:0210 Hitachi, Ltd
```

```
Bus 002 Device 002: ID 0bc2:ab28 Seagate RSS LLC Seagate Backup Plus Portable
5TB SRDOOF1
Bus 002 Device 001: ID 1d6b:0003 Linux Foundation 3.0 root hub
Bus 001 Device 004: ID 04f9:02b0 Brother Industries, Ltd MFC-9340CDW
Bus 001 Device 003: ID 045b:0209 Hitachi, Ltd
Bus 001 Device 002: ID 045b:0209 Hitachi, Ltd
Bus 001 Device 010: ID 1058:070a Western Digital Technologies, Inc. My
Passport Essential (WDBAAA), My Passport for Mac (WDBAAB), My Passport
Essential SE (WDBABM), My Passport SE for Mac (WDBABW
Bus 001 Device 009: ID 14cd:168a Super Top Elecom Co., Ltd MR-K013
Multicard Reader
Bus 001 Device 008: ID 1a40:0201 Terminus Technology Inc. FE 2.1 7-port Hub
Bus 001 Device 007: ID 1b1c:1b49 Corsair CORSAIR K70 RGB MK.2 Mechanical
Gaming Keyboard
Bus 001 Device 006: ID 046d:c52b Logitech, Inc. Unifying Receiver
Bus 001 Device 005: ID 0764:0601 Cyber Power System, Inc. PR1500LCDRT2U UPS
Bus 001 Device 001: ID 1d6b:0002 Linux Foundation 2.0 root hub
```

Go ahead and try the **lspci** command on your own VM.

I sometimes find it helpful to identify specific hardware devices, especially newly added ones. As with the /proc directory, there are some core utilities like lsusb and lspci that make it easy for us to view information about the devices connected to the host.

Storage-Based Swap Space

Swap space is a common aspect of computing today, regardless of the operating system. Linux uses swap space to increase the amount of virtual memory available to a host. It can use one or more dedicated swap partitions or a swap file on a regular filesystem or logical volume.

There are two basic types of memory in a typical computer. Random access memory (RAM) is used to store data and programs while they are being actively used by the computer. Programs and data cannot be used by the computer unless they are stored in RAM. RAM is volatile memory; that is, the data stored in RAM is lost if the computer is turned off.

Storage devices are magnetic or solid-state media used for long-term storage of data and programs. Magnetic and SSD media are nonvolatile; the data stored on a storage[5] device remains even when power is removed from the computer. The CPU cannot directly access the programs and data on the hard drive; they must be copied into RAM first, and that is where the CPU can access its programming instructions and the data to be operated on by those instructions. During the boot process, a computer copies specific operating system programs such as the kernel and init or systemd and data from the hard drive into RAM where it is accessed directly by the computer's processor, the CPU (Central Processing Unit).

Swap space is the second type of memory in modern Linux systems. The primary function of swap space is to substitute disk or SSD storage space for RAM when real RAM fills up and more space is needed. For example, assume you have a computer system with 8GB of RAM. If you start up programs that don't fill that RAM, everything is fine and no swapping is required. But say that a hypothetical very large spreadsheet you are working on grows when you add more rows to it, and that plus everything else you have running now fills all of RAM. Without swap space available, you would have to stop work on the spreadsheet until you could free up some of your limited RAM by closing down some other programs.

The kernel uses a memory management program that locates blocks, a.k.a. pages, of memory in which the contents have not been used recently. The memory management program swaps enough of these relatively infrequently used pages of memory out to a special partition on the hard drive specifically designated for "paging" or swapping. This frees up RAM and makes room for more data to be entered into your spreadsheet. Those pages of memory swapped out to the hard drive are tracked by the kernel's memory management code and can be paged back into RAM if they are needed.

The total amount of memory in a Linux computer is the RAM plus active swap space and is referred to as virtual memory. Linux supports up to 32 swap areas, any or all of which can be online at the same time. A swap area can be a disk partition, a logical volume, or a file in a non-swap partition or volume. Multiple swap areas are usually referred to collectively as "swaps," such as "all active swaps."

---

[5] I use the term "storage" to refer to both spinning storage devices (HDDs) and SSDs.

Types of Linux Swap

Linux provides two types of swap area. By default, most Linux installations create a swap partition or volume, but it is also possible to use a specially configured file as a swap file. A swap partition is just what its name implies – a standard disk partition that is designated as swap space by the mkswap command. A logical volume used as a swap area works just like a standard disk partition for use as a swap area, but its size can be extended like any logical volume.

A swap file can be used if there is no free disk space in which to create a new swap partition or space in a volume group in which a logical volume can be created for swap space. This is just a regular file that is created and preallocated to a specified size. Then the mkswap command is run to configure it as swap space. I don't recommend using a file for swap space unless absolutely necessary. A swap file may be a reasonable choice on systems with a lot of physical memory that never approaches filling up. Disk space is so cheap and plentiful now; there's no reason not to set up a permanent swap partition.

There is also a new swap tool called "Swap on Zram," which uses RAM to temporarily store compressed memory pages. This is faster than any of the storage-based swap spaces.

Thrashing

Thrashing can occur when total virtual memory, both RAM and swap space, becomes nearly full. The system spends so much time paging blocks of memory between swap space and RAM that little time is left for real work.

The typical symptoms of this are fairly obvious; the system becomes completely unresponsive or quite slow, and the hard drive activity light is on almost constantly. If you can manage to issue a command like free that shows CPU load and memory usage, you will see that the CPU load is very high, perhaps as much as 30–40 times the number of CPU cores in the system. Another symptom is that both RAM and swap space are almost completely allocated.

After the fact, looking at SAR (System Activity Reporter) data can also show these symptoms. I install SAR on every system I work on and use it for post-repair forensic analysis. We explored SAR in Volume 1, Chapter 13.

What Is the Right Amount of Storage-Based Swap Space?

Many years ago, the rule of thumb for the amount of storage-based swap space that should be allocated on a hard drive was 2× the amount of RAM installed in the computer. Of course that was when computers typically had RAM amounts measured in KB or MB. So if a computer had 64KB of RAM, a swap partition of 128KB would be an optimum size. This rule of thumb took into account the fact that RAM sizes were typically quite small at that time and the fact that allocating more than 2× RAM for swap space did not improve performance. With more than twice RAM for swap, most systems spent more time thrashing than actually performing useful work.

RAM has become a relatively inexpensive commodity, and most computers these days have amounts of RAM that extend into tens of gigabytes. Most of my newer computers have at least 16GB of RAM; two have 32GB. My main workstation and both of my System76 Oryx Pro laptops have 64GB. My older computers have from 4–8GB of RAM.

When dealing with computers having huge amounts of RAM, the limiting performance factor for swap space is far lower than the 2× multiplier. The Fedora 37 Installation Guide, which can be found online on the Fedora user documentation[6] site, defines current thinking about swap space allocation. I have included in the following some discussion and the table of recommendations from that document.

Figure 24-5 provides the recommended size of a swap partition depending on the amount of RAM in your system and whether you want sufficient memory for your system to hibernate. The recommended swap partition size is established automatically during the Fedora installation. To allow for hibernation, however, you will need to edit the swap space in the custom partitioning stage.

---

[6] Fedora documentation, https://docs.fedoraproject.org/en-US/docs/

Amount of system RAM	Recommended swap space
less than 2 GB	2 times the amount of RAM
2 GB - 8 GB	Equal to the amount of RAM
8 GB - 64 GB	0.5 times the amount of RAM
more than 64 GB	workload dependent

Figure 24-5. *Recommended system swap space in the Fedora 37 documentation*

At the border between each range listed in the preceding table (e.g., a system with 2GB, 8GB, or 64GB of system RAM), discretion can be exercised with regard to chosen swap space and hibernation support. If your system resources allow for it, increasing the swap space may lead to better performance.

Of course most Linux administrators have their own ideas about the appropriate amount of swap space – as well as pretty much everything else. Figure 24-6 contains my own recommendations based on my personal experiences in multiple environments. These may not work for you, but, along with Figure 24-5, they may help you get started determining what does work.

Amount of RAM	Recommended swap space
≤ 2GB	2X RAM
2GB – 8GB	= RAM
>8GB	8GB

Figure 24-6. *Recommended system swap space per the author*

One consideration in both tables is that as the amount of RAM increases, beyond a certain point adding more swap space simply leads to thrashing well before the swap space even comes close to being filled. If you have too little virtual memory while following these recommendations, you should add more RAM, if possible, rather than more swap space. As with all recommendations that affect system performance, you should use what works best for your specific environment. This will take time and effort to experiment and make changes based on the conditions in your Linux environment.

I mentioned that all Linux SysAdmins have their own ideas about swap space. Chris Short, one of my friends and a fellow community moderator at Opensource.com, pointed me to an old article[7] where he recommended using 1GB for swap space. Chris told me that he now recommends zero swap space.

So I got curious and created a poll[8] that was published on Opensource.com. Read the article and especially the comments to more fully understand the range of thought about swap space, but the 2164 votes tallied as of this writing pretty much tell the story. Figure 24-7 shows the raw data from the poll and illustrates the wide range of opinion about the appropriate amount of swap space for today's Linux systems.

---

[7] Short, Chris, "Moving to Linux – Partitioning," https://chrisshort.net/moving-to-linux-partitioning/

[8] Both, David, "What's the right amount of swap space for a modern Linux system?," https://opensource.com/article/19/2/swap-space-poll, Opensource.com

Amount of Swap Space	Votes
Zero	416
<1GB	69
1GB	73
2GB	173
4GB	258
8GB	172
Something similar to Figure 24-5	304
Something similar to Figure 24-6	343
Whatever my distro creates at installation time	198
What is swap space?	38
I don't care	38
Other	85

Figure 24-7. Opensource.com swap space poll results

You can formulate your own opinion about how much swap space is the right amount, but sometimes the amount currently available may not be enough. Let's look at how to add more swap space.

Adding More Swap Space on a Non-LVM Disk Partition

Due to changing requirements for swap space on hosts with Linux already installed, it may become necessary to modify the amount of swap space defined for the system. This procedure can be used for any general case where the amount of swap space needs to be increased. It assumes sufficient available disk space is available. This procedure also assumes that the disks are partitioned in "raw" EXT4 and swap partitions and do not use logical volume management (LVM).

The basic steps to take are simple and a reboot should not be necessary:

1. Turn off the existing swap space.

2. Create a new swap partition of the desired size.

3. Reread the partition table.

4. Configure the partition as swap space.

5. Add the new partition in /etc/fstab.

6. Turn on swap.

For safety's sake, before turning off swap, at the very least you should ensure that no applications are running and that no swap space is in use. The free or top command can tell you whether swap space is in use. To be even more safe, you could revert to the systemd rescue target, which is the same as runlevel 1 under the old SystemV init system.

EXPERIMENT 24-6: ADDING SWAP ON A STORAGE PARTITION

Perform this experiment as root. Although it would be safer in a production environment to reboot the system into rescue mode, it is not necessary in our student virtual machines. Turn off the swap partition with the swapoff command. The -a option turns off all swap space:

[root@studentvm1 ~]# **swapoff -a**

Find the current swap partition and look for a partition in which to create a new swap partition:

```
[root@studentvm1 ~]# lsblk -i
NAME                     MAJ:MIN RM   SIZE RO TYPE MOUNTPOINT
sda                          8:0  0   60G  0 disk
|-sda1                       8:1  0    1M  0 part
|-sda2                       8:2  0    1G  0 part /boot
```

```
|-sda3                            8:3    0    1G  0 part /boot/efi
`-sda4                            8:4    0   58G  0 part
  |-fedora_studentvm1-root 253:0    0    2G  0 lvm  /
  |-fedora_studentvm1-usr  253:1    0   15G  0 lvm  /usr
  |-fedora_studentvm1-tmp  253:3    0    5G  0 lvm  /tmp
  |-fedora_studentvm1-var  253:4    0   10G  0 lvm  /var
  |-fedora_studentvm1-home 253:5    0    4G  0 lvm  /home
  `-fedora_studentvm1-test 253:6    0  500M  0 lvm  /test
sdb                              8:16   0   20G  0 disk
|-sdb1                           8:17   0    2G  0 part
|-sdb2                           8:18   0    2G  0 part
`-sdb3                           8:19   0   16G  0 part
  `-NewVG--01-TestVol1     253:2    0    4G  0 lvm
sdc                              8:32   0    2G  0 disk
`-NewVG--01-TestVol1       253:2    0    4G  0 lvm
sdd                              8:48   0    2G  0 disk
`-sdd1                           8:49   0    2G  0 part
sr0                             11:0    1 1024M  0 rom
zram0                          252:0    0    0B  0 disk
```

The zram0 disk is the default swap space created by the Fedora installation. If no memory pages are stored there and when we turn swap off, it does not show up as swap.

However, we have a couple options for our new swap partition. We used the sdb1 partition for a demonstration of creating new partitions, and it is currently mounted with an entry in /etc/fstab although we are not using it for anything at this time. The sdd1 partition is also available, and it is not mounted nor is there an entry in the fstab. Let's take the easy way and use /dev/sdd1 for our additional swap space.

We first need to change the partition type of sdd1, so start fdisk in interactive mode with the following command. Be sure to use the correct device based on the output from the lsblk command:

```
[root@studentvm1 ~]# fdisk /dev/sdd

Welcome to fdisk (util-linux 2.32.1).
Changes will remain in memory only, until you decide to write them.
Be careful before using the write command.

Command (m for help):
```

The t sub-command allows you to specify the type of partition. So enter t and press Enter. Then type L to get a list of all available partition types supported by Linux. Because there is only one partition in this small virtual drive, fdisk automatically selects partition 1:

```
Command (m for help): t
Selected partition 1
Hex code (type L to list all codes): l
```

00 Empty	27 Hidden NTFS Win	82 Linux swap / So	c1 DRDOS/sec (FAT-
01 FAT12	39 Plan 9	83 Linux	c4 DRDOS/sec (FAT-
02 XENIX root	3c PartitionMagic	84 OS/2 hidden or	c6 DRDOS/sec (FAT-
03 XENIX usr	40 Venix 80286	85 Linux extended	c7 Syrinx
04 FAT16 <32M	41 PPC PReP Boot	86 NTFS volume set	da Non-FS data
05 Extended	42 SFS	87 NTFS volume set	db CP/M / CTOS / .
06 FAT16	4d QNX4.x	88 Linux plaintext	de Dell Utility
07 HPFS/NTFS/exFAT	4e QNX4.x 2nd part	8e Linux LVM	df BootIt
08 AIX	4f QNX4.x 3rd part	93 Amoeba	e1 DOS access
09 AIX bootable	50 OnTrack DM	94 Amoeba BBT	e3 DOS R/O
0a OS/2 Boot Manag	51 OnTrack DM6 Aux	9f BSD/OS	e4 SpeedStor
0b W95 FAT32	52 CP/M	a0 IBM Thinkpad hi	ea Linux extended
0c W95 FAT32 (LBA)	53 OnTrack DM6 Aux	a5 FreeBSD	eb BeOS fs
0e W95 FAT16 (LBA)	54 OnTrackDM6	a6 OpenBSD	ee GPT
0f W95 Ext'd (LBA)	55 EZ-Drive	a7 NeXTSTEP	ef EFI (FAT-12/16/
10 OPUS	56 Golden Bow	a8 Darwin UFS	f0 Linux/PA-RISC b
11 Hidden FAT12	5c Priam Edisk	a9 NetBSD	f1 SpeedStor
12 Compaq diagnost	61 SpeedStor	ab Darwin boot	f4 SpeedStor
14 Hidden FAT16 <3	63 GNU HURD or Sys	af HFS / HFS+	f2 DOS secondary
16 Hidden FAT16	64 Novell Netware	b7 BSDI fs	f8 EBBR protective
17 Hidden HPFS/NTF	65 Novell Netware	b8 BSDI swap	fb VMware VMFS
18 AST SmartSleep	70 DiskSecure Mult	bb Boot Wizard hid	fc VMware VMKCORE
1b Hidden W95 FAT3	75 PC/IX	bc Acronis FAT32 L	fd Linux raid auto
1c Hidden W95 FAT3	80 Old Minix	be Solaris boot	fe LANstep
1e Hidden W95 FAT1	81 Minix / old Lin	bf Solaris	ff BBT
24 NEC DOS			

```
Aliases:
    linux       - 83
    swap        - 82
    extended    - 05
```

```
uefi        - EF
raid        - FD
lvm         - 8E
linuxex     - 85
```

```
Hex code or alias (type L to list all):
```

When it asks for the hex code partition type, type in **82**, which is the Linux swap partition type, and press **Enter**. I then use the p sub-command to list the partitions to ensure that the new partition type is correct:

```
Hex code (type L to list all codes): 82
Changed type of partition 'Linux' to 'Linux swap / Solaris'.
```

```
Command (m for help): p
Disk /dev/sdd: 2 GiB, 2147483648 bytes, 4194304 sectors
Units: sectors of 1 * 512 = 512 bytes
Sector size (logical/physical): 512 bytes / 512 bytes
I/O size (minimum/optimal): 512 bytes / 512 bytes
Disklabel type: dos
Disk identifier: 0xb1f99266
```

```
Device     Boot Start     End Sectors Size Id Type
/dev/sdd1       2048 4194303 4192256   2G 82 Linux swap / Solaris
```

```
Command (m for help):
```

When you are satisfied with the partition you have created, use the w sub-command to write the new partition table to the disk. The fdisk program will exit and return you to the command prompt after it completes writing the revised partition table:

```
Command (m for help): w
The partition table has been altered.
Calling ioctl() to re-read partition table.
Syncing disks.
```

At this point in the real world, you might get an error message that the re-read of the partition table failed. If so, use the partprobe command to force the kernel to re-read the partition table. It is not necessary to perform a reboot to force the kernel to re-read the partition table.

You should now be able to use the command **fdisk -l /dev/sdd** to list the partitions, and the new swap partition should be listed. Be sure that the partition type is "Linux swap."

It is necessary to modify the /etc/fstab file to point to the new swap partition. Add these two new lines to identify and configure the new swap partition:

```
# Adding HDD swap space for chapter 24
/dev/sdd1          swap        swap    defaults        0 0
```

Be sure to use the correct partition number. Now you can perform the final step in creating the swap partition. Use the mkswap command to define the partition as a swap partition:

```
[root@studentvm1 ~]# mkswap /dev/sdd1
mkswap: /dev/sdd1: warning: wiping old ext4 signature.
Setting up swapspace version 1, size = 2 GiB (2146430976 bytes)
no label, UUID=dc4802a7-bb21-4726-a20b-be0fbf906b24
```

The final step is to turn swap on using the swapon command. The -a parameter turns on all swap partitions that are not already turned on:

```
[root@studentvm1 ~]# swapon -a
[root@studentvm1 ~]# lsblk -i
NAME                       MAJ:MIN RM  SIZE RO TYPE MOUNTPOINTS
sda                          8:0    0   60G  0 disk
|-sda1                       8:1    0    1M  0 part
|-sda2                       8:2    0    1G  0 part /boot
|-sda3                       8:3    0    1G  0 part /boot/efi
`-sda4                       8:4    0   58G  0 part
  |-fedora_studentvm1-root 253:0    0    2G  0 lvm  /
  |-fedora_studentvm1-usr  253:1    0   15G  0 lvm  /usr
  |-fedora_studentvm1-tmp  253:3    0    5G  0 lvm  /tmp
  |-fedora_studentvm1-var  253:4    0   10G  0 lvm  /var
  |-fedora_studentvm1-home 253:5    0    4G  0 lvm  /home
  `-fedora_studentvm1-test 253:6    0  500M  0 lvm  /test
sdb                          8:16   0   20G  0 disk
|-sdb1                       8:17   0    2G  0 part
|-sdb2                       8:18   0    2G  0 part
`-sdb3                       8:19   0   16G  0 part
  `-NewVG--01-TestVol1      253:2   0    4G  0 lvm
sdc                          8:32   0    2G  0 disk
`-NewVG--01-TestVol1        253:2   0    4G  0 lvm
sdd                          8:48   0    2G  0 disk
`-sdd1                       8:49   0    2G  0 part [SWAP]
```

```
sr0                     11:0    1 1024M  0 rom
zram0                  252:0    0    8G  0 disk [SWAP]
[root@studentvm1 ~]#
```

This now shows both swap spaces. Using a tool like Glances or htop shows that you now have 10GB of swap space.

Adding Swap to an LVM Disk Environment

If your disk setup uses LVM, adding swap space will be fairly easy. This assumes that space is available in one of the volume groups on the storage devices. By default, the installation procedures for previous versions of Fedora in an LVM environment created the swap partition as a logical volume. That made it easy because we could simply extend the size of the swap volume.

Now, however, we need to create a new space on the storage device for swap.

These are the basic steps required to create new swap space in an LVM environment:

1. Turn off all swap.

2. Add a new hard drive or SSD if necessary.

3. Prepare the new device if one was installed.

4. If necessary and possible, extend the existing volume group.

5. Create a new logical volume that is to be designated for swap.

6. Configure the logical volume as swap space.

7. Add the new swap volume to fstab.

8. Turn on swap.

EXPERIMENT 24-7: ADD SWAP TO AN LVM ENVIRONMENT

This experiment must be performed as root on StudentVM1. In the previous experiment, we ended up with a total of 10GB of swap space, but let's verify the current swap space just because good SysAdmins verify everything.

I have discovered that the best – and possibly the coolest – way to do this is to use the data from /proc/swaps:

```
[root@studentvm1 ~]# cat /proc/swaps
Filename            Type        Size        Used        Priority
/dev/zram0          partition   8388604     0           100
/dev/sdd1           partition   2096124     0           -2
```

We can also use the swapon command:

```
[root@studentvm1 ~]# swapon -s
Filename            Type        Size        Used        Priority
/dev/zram0          partition   8388604     0           100
/dev/sdd1           partition   2096124     0           -2
[root@studentvm1 ~]#
```

Notice the priority settings in the rightmost column. This allows setting priorities for different swaps. For example, you might want the swap on a fast device to be the highest priority so that it gets used before other, slower swaps. Higher priorities are used by the swapping mechanism before the lower priorities. Higher numbers mean higher priority. Also, when creating new swap areas, newer swap areas are always assigned a lower priority than the lowest existing one.

Check to see if there is space available in the volume group to create a new swap volume:

```
[root@studentvm1 ~]# vgs
  VG                 #PV #LV #SN Attr    VSize    VFree
  NewVG-01             3   1   0 wz--n- <19.99g   15.99g
  fedora_studentvm1    1   6   0 wz--n- <58.00g  <21.51g
```

We can see that there is about 21.5GB of space available in the fedora_studentvm1 volume group and about 16GB in the NewVG-01 VG. That is plenty of space to add a 2GB swap volume to either VG, and it still would leave space for extending the other volume if that were ever needed. Look at the existing logical volumes:

```
[root@studentvm1 ~]# lvs
  LV        VG                Attr       LSize  Pool Origin Data% ...
  TestVol1  NewVG-01          -wi-a----- <4.00g
  home      fedora_studentvm1 -wi-ao----  4.00g
  root      fedora_studentvm1 -wi-ao----  2.00g
```

```
test      fedora_studentvm1 -wi-ao---- 500.00m
tmp       fedora_studentvm1 -wi-ao----   5.00g
usr       fedora_studentvm1 -wi-ao----  15.00g
var       fedora_studentvm1 -wi-ao----  10.00g
```

In a real situation, you might choose differently, but I have made an arbitrary decision for us to add the new logical volume to NewVG-01. Give this volume the name of "swap":

```
[root@studentvm1 ~]# lvcreate -L 2G -n swap NewVG-01
  Logical volume "swap" created.
```

Make the volume swap space. It is not necessary to create a partition or a filesystem on the new swap volume:

```
[root@studentvm1 ~]# mkswap /dev/mapper/NewVG--01-swap
Setting up swapspace version 1, size = 2 GiB (2147479552 bytes)
no label, UUID=b6e801d6-fd8f-46d4-a28b-d40d63e28e52
```

Add the following line to the fstab file:

```
/dev/mapper/NewVG--01-swap      swap        swap        defaults      0 0
```

Turn on swap and verify that the new swap volume is active:

```
[root@studentvm1 ~]# swapon -a
[root@studentvm1 ~]# lsblk
NAME                        MAJ:MIN RM  SIZE RO TYPE MOUNTPOINTS
sda                           8:0    0   60G  0 disk
|-sda1                        8:1    0    1M  0 part
|-sda2                        8:2    0    1G  0 part /boot
|-sda3                        8:3    0    1G  0 part /boot/efi
`-sda4                        8:4    0   58G  0 part
  |-fedora_studentvm1-root  253:0    0    2G  0 lvm  /
  |-fedora_studentvm1-usr   253:1    0   15G  0 lvm  /usr
  |-fedora_studentvm1-tmp   253:3    0    5G  0 lvm  /tmp
  |-fedora_studentvm1-var   253:4    0   10G  0 lvm  /var
  |-fedora_studentvm1-home  253:5    0    4G  0 lvm  /home
  `-fedora_studentvm1-test  253:6    0  500M  0 lvm  /test
sdb                           8:16   0   20G  0 disk
|-sdb1                        8:17   0    2G  0 part
|-sdb2                        8:18   0    2G  0 part
`-sdb3                        8:19   0   16G  0 part
```

```
   |-NewVG--01-TestVol1       253:2    0    4G   0 lvm
   `-NewVG--01-swap           253:7    0    2G   0 lvm  [SWAP]
  sdc                          8:32    0    2G   0 disk
  `-NewVG--01-TestVol1        253:2    0    4G   0 lvm
  sdd                          8:48    0    2G   0 disk
  `-sdd1                       8:49    0    2G   0 part [SWAP]
  sr0                         11:0     1 1024M   0 rom
  zram0                       252:0    0    8G   0 disk [SWAP]
```

Use `top`, `htop`, and `Glances` to verify that your total swap space is now 12GB.

Tip   When referring to the swap – or any other volume for that matter – in commands, we can use /dev/dm-X or /dev/mapper/fedora_studentvm1-<LV Name>. We cannot refer to swap volumes or partitions by a mountpoint because they are not mounted like other filesystems.

Before you proceed any further, read the parts on priority in the man pages[9] in both sections 2 and 8 for swapon:

`[root@studentvm1 ~]# man 2 swapon`

and

`[root@studentvm1 ~]# man 8 swapon`

In neither document does it mention priority numbers less than –1, so I am not sure whether the –3 and –2 priorities are bugs or an undocumented extension. Change the swap lines in /etc/fstab to add priorities to the mount options as shown in the following:

```
/dev/mapper/fedora_studentvm1-swap swap swap  pri=5,defaults   0 0
/dev/sdd1                          swap swap  pri=2,defaults   0 0
```

Now stop all swaps and then start all swaps. Verify the new swap priorities.

---

[9] Use the command **man man** to read about the man page sections.

Other Swap Options with LVM

When the need arises to add swap space to an existing system, there may be no available disk space. In such a case, it is necessary to install a new disk device to hold the new swap space. This could be added as an extension of an existing logical volume already being used for a swap volume, or it could be used as a separate volume or partition.

My preference would be to add the new space as a logical volume and make it a higher priority than the existing swap area. This enables you to expand that swap as part of the new volume and eventually deactivate the old swap.

Using Zram for Swap Space

I spend a lot of time playing – I mean working – on my computers and have found a lot of interesting things. One that has most recently come to my attention is the zram0 device. I first noticed Zram[10] when working on one of my Opensource.com articles several months ago. It showed up in the output from the **lsblk** command.

EXPERIMENT 24-8: LOOKING FOR ZRAM

Perform this experiment as root in a Bash terminal session. Use the following command to verify the presence of a Zram device:

```
[root@testvm1 ~]# lsblk
NAME           MAJ:MIN RM    SIZE RO TYPE MOUNTPOINTS
sda              8:0    0 931.5G  0 disk
├─sda1           8:1    0   600M  0 part
<SNIP>
zram0          252:0    0     8G  0 disk [SWAP]
```

You should only see a Zram device, zram0, if you are using Fedora 33 or later.

---

[10] Wikipedia, Zram, https://en.wikipedia.org/wiki/Zram

As you can see, it is identified as swap space, which is what first piqued my curiosity, so I did some exploration. Zram was originally called "compcache," which stands for "compressed cache." It turns out that Zram is a tool for creating in-RAM compressed cache – specifically for use as swap space.

But Why?

When I began researching Zram, all I found was a couple basic articles about using Zram for swap space. At first this seemed a bit counterintuitive to me. After all, if you are running out of RAM and you swap pages into a virtual drive in RAM, what is gained? I then found the Fedora Project wiki page that proposed the use of "Swap on Zram."[11] The proposal says, "Swap is useful, except when it's slow. zram is a RAM drive that uses compression. Create a swap-on-zram during start-up. And no longer use swap partitions by default." The rest of the page is about details, benefits, side effects, and feedback.

Using Zram for swap space is intended to do the same thing as regular partition- or file-based swap space. When memory pressure becomes too great, some of the least recently used data is moved to swap space. On average it is compressed to about 50% of its original size and placed in Zram space in RAM. This is much faster than storing those memory pages on a hard drive and frees up the RAM it was using for other uses.

How Much Swap?

I tried to find revised recommendations for how much traditional swap and/or Zram swap to configure. This led me back to a reassessment of swap and my article, "What's the right amount of swap space for a modern Linux system?"[12] As far as I can tell from the most current documentation for Red Hat Enterprise Linux (RHEL) and Fedora, their recommendations for the amount of swap space have not changed. That documentation still ignores the use of Zram. However, the tables in that previous article still provide a good starting point for swap space allocation when using older releases of Linux that don't use Zram or if Zram has been disabled.

---

[11] Fedora Project, Swap on Zram, `https://fedoraproject.org/wiki/Changes/SwapOnZRAM`
[12] Both, David, Open`https://opensource.com/article/19/2/swap-space-poll`, Opensource.com

The documents I found for the Zram feature are inconsistent in terms of how Zram is allocated with respect to RAM size and the amount of space allocated to Zram swap. Therefore, due to the lack of authoritative documentation, I performed some experiments to empirically determine the algorithm used to allocate Zram swap. I used several of my own physical and virtual systems for this. The results are interesting and do not match any documentation I have so far found.

The default size of Zram is 8GB on all systems large enough to support that but is typically reduced significantly on hosts with small amounts of RAM. On one VM I use for testing, with 4GB of RAM allocated to the VM, the Zram virtual swap space is allocated 3.8GB. One old Dell I have contains 8GB of RAM, and the Zram is set to 7.6GB. When RAM is reduced to 2GB, Zram is reduced to 1.9GB. All of the physical and virtual hosts I have with more than 8GB of RAM show exactly 8GB of Zram, even my primary workstation with 64GB of RAM and other hosts with 16GB or 32GB of RAM.

Based on these few data points, I can draw the conclusion that the current default settings are for 8GB of Zram at most and for Zram to be 95% of RAM on hosts with 8GB or less. I have read a number of articles that mention other sizes for Zram swap, even up to 100% of RAM, but those all seem to be theoretical rather than reality.

The actual Zram swap allocation for Fedora and other Red Hat–related distributions is given in Figure 24-8. Your distribution may be different.

RAM	Zram Swap Size
<= 8GB	= 0.95*RAM
>8GB	= 8GB

Figure 24-8. *Zram swap size is based on RAM size*

Be aware that the Zram swap size algorithm is not based on any recommendations for the "best" swap size for any given real-world system or application. This Zram swap allocation is a rather probabilistic approach to what should work well on a wide range of Linux hosts. However, the fact that the maximum Zram swap size is configured for 8GB and the fact that I have always recommended 8GB as the maximum amount of traditional swap, I think I can say that this documents the optimum sizes for Zram swap.

Managing Zram Swap

The Zram defaults are stored in the /usr/lib/systemd/zram-generator.conf
configuration file.

EXPERIMENT 24-9: EXPLORING ZRAM SWAP

Perform this experiment as the root user. This experiment will familiarize you with some of the
tools that can be used to observe Zram swap.

First, look at the contents of the zram-generator.conf file:

```
[root@testvm1 ~]# cat /usr/lib/systemd/zram-generator.conf
# This config file enables a /dev/zram0 device with the default settings:
# - size - same as available RAM or 8GB, whichever is less
# - compression - most likely lzo-rle
#
# To disable, uninstall zram-generator-defaults or create empty
# /etc/systemd/zram-generator.conf file.
[zram0]
zram-size = min(ram, 8192)
```

You can change the default Zram swap size on the last line of the zram-generator.conf
configuration file. I recommend against doing that unless you can definitively show a reason
for doing so and test your results once you make any changes. Like many other configuration
defaults in Linux, the Zram ones have been well tested and are appropriate for most
use cases.

The `zramctl` utility can be used to view the current state of Zram:

```
[root@testvm1 ~]# zramctl
NAME        ALGORITHM DISKSIZE DATA COMPR TOTAL STREAMS MOUNTPOINT
/dev/zram0 lzo-rle      4.8G   4K   80B   12K      4 [SWAP]
```

The traditional swapon command can also be used to view swap including Zram used
as swap:

```
[root@testvm1 ~]# swapon --show
NAME        TYPE      SIZE USED PRIO
/dev/sdd1 partition   2G   0B    5
```

```
/dev/dm-7   partition   2G   0B    2
/dev/zram0 partition   8G   0B   100
```

One thing to be aware of is that zramctl does not report on Zram if it contains no data, so the results would contain null output. Tools like lsblk, swapon, top, free, htop, and so on do show Zram even if it contains no data.

The **swapoff -a** command turns off Zram swap as well as traditional HDD- or SSD-based storage used as swap. The **swapon -a** command does not show Zram if it is empty. Use **zramctl /dev/zram0** instead.

Note that /dev/zram0 does not show up in these commands as swap space until it is being used for that purpose. This caused me some confusion until my experiments showed it to be the case.

Creating Zram Swap

Zram itself has been around for about 20 years but was only added to the Linux kernel in about 2010. It was introduced as the default swap space implementation in Fedora 33.

The current Linux installation on some or all of your hosts may not have been created with Zram for swap. If that is the case, it can be easily remedied. For Fedora 32, the last release prior to the default use of Zram for swap, it only takes three easy commands.

EXPERIMENT 24-10: ADDING ZRAM SWAP ON OLDER RELEASES OF FEDORA

First, verify the presence of the zram-swap.service file, which is installed as part of the zram RPM package. It should look like this on Fedora 32 and some previous releases. It only means that the Zram swap service used by systemd to control it has been installed:

```
# systemctl status zram-swap
● zram-swap.service - Enable compressed swap in memory using zram
    Loaded: loaded (/usr/lib/systemd/system/zram-swap.service; disabled;
    vendor preset: disabled)
    Active: inactive (dead)
```

Tip The rest of this experiment is irrelevant on Fedora 33 and later because Zram swap is already installed and activated on those later releases. If you are using Fedora 33 or later, you can read the rest of this experiment, but the commands will not work because the commands and tools are different for the later releases. You *should* be using Fedora 37 or later for this course.

Next, install the zram-generator-defaults and zram-generator packages:

```
# dnf install zram-generator-defaults zram-generator
```

Enable and start the zram-swap service.

```
# systemctl enable zram-swap.service
# systemctl start zram-swap.service
```

Verify that zram0 exists and is being used as swap space using the tools you know by now.

That's all there is to it. It was easy with Fedora. Other distributions will likely be just as easy but somewhat different in the details of the commands.

Augmenting Zram Swap

Zram swap can be augmented with standard secondary storage devices. Adding some more traditional swap space can be especially useful on systems with low amounts of RAM. Such augmentation will not normally be useful on hosts with very large amounts of RAM.

If you do choose to augment swap with some type of storage device, hard drives still work but are significantly slower than using SSD in either SATA or m.2 format. However, the flash memory in SSD devices has a more limited life than HDD devices; thus, systems with large amounts of swap activity will significantly reduce the chronological lifespan of the SSD.

Tuning Swap

There is more to tuning swap space than simply allocating a specific amount of swap space. There are other factors that can be used to manage how swap space is used and managed by the system. Swappiness is the primary kernel parameter that can be used to manage swap performance.

I recently wrote an article for Opensource.com, "How I troubleshoot swappiness and startup time on Linux,"[13] in which I discuss the vm.swappiness kernel setting. The short version is that the default setting for how aggressively the Linux kernel forces swapping to begin and to function is 60. Zero (0) is the least aggressive and 100 – or 200 depending upon what you read – is the most aggressive. At that default level, I was experiencing delays when working with very large documents in LibreOffice despite having 64GB of RAM in my primary workstation, much of which was unused.

The resolution to this problem for me is to reduce the vm.swappiness kernel parameter to 13 or lower. This works quite well for my use cases, but you may need to experiment to get it right for your environment.

You can also find more general information about tuning the Linux kernel in an article I wrote for Enable Sysadmin, "How to tune the Linux kernel with the /proc filesystem."[14]

Swap Size Recommendations

At this time I have found no recommendations from any distribution for swap size when using Zram. Based on my personal experience, I have found that having at least a little swap space can be beneficial. Even when you have large amounts of RAM, just the single fact that properly tuned swap for your environment is being used and contains data can indicate that more RAM is needed. The default Zram swap size based on Figure 24-8 is more than sufficient for that purpose. It has worked well so far on all of my Linux hosts.

---

[13] Both, David, "How I troubleshoot swappiness and startup time on Linux," https://opensource.com/article/22/9/swappiness-startup-linux

[14] Both, David, "How to tune the Linux kernel with the /proc filesystem," www.redhat.com/sysadmin/linux-kernel-tuning

In my opinion the ultimate purpose of swap space is to be a small buffer – a red flag – that lets the system administrator know when more RAM is needed in a system. Of course some very old hardware cannot support more than 4 or 8GB of RAM. In such a case a new motherboard is needed – one which will support enough RAM to perform the task at hand.

My recommendation is to do as I have. I set up Zram swap of the default size on every one of my hosts. I then removed all of the existing swap partitions (I don't use swap files), and my hosts have all been running perfectly with that swap setup.

Removing Traditional Swap Partitions and Files

Since I just mentioned removing all of the old swap partitions, I should also mention that the process to do so is not as straightforward as it should be. It is not hard, but it took me some research to figure it out because there is a lot of old and incorrect information out there on the Internet. This procedure works for me on Fedora 36 and higher.

EXPERIMENT 24-11: REMOVING TRADITIONAL SWAP

You should remove the traditional swap partition you created during the Fedora installation as it will no longer be used.

First, turn off swap for the existing swap partitions and files. This can be done using **swapoff /dev/nameofswapdevice**, but it might be easiest to just turn off all swap with the **swapoff -a** command. This command also turns off any existing Zram swap:

```
# swapoff -a
```

Remove the entries for traditional swap partitions or files in the /etc/fstab file. I just commented these out in case of unexpected problems. I deleted those entries later. Zram swap does not require an entry in the /etc/fstab file.

You'd think – at least I did at first – that this would be all that is needed and you could remove the swap partitions or the logical volumes designated as swap. But, no. I did remove the logical volume I had designated as swap space and rebooted to test. The reboot failed and hung very early in the boot process.

Fortunately, I have configured my kernel so that it displays boot and startup messages rather than the graphical boot designed to hide the "scary stuff" from users. As a result I was able to see the error message indicating that the kernel couldn't find the swap volume. To recover from this, I booted from a live Fedora USB drive and created a new swap volume. It is not necessary to do anything else. Then I rebooted and removed the swap entries in kernel line of /etc/defaults/grub. The GRUB (Grand Unified Boot Loader) boot defaults are set in the /etc/default/grub file. Changes are made to this file, and then the grub.cfg file is regenerated.

The default /etc/default/grub configuration file is simple, and we only need concern ourselves with one line:

```
GRUB_TIMEOUT=5
GRUB_DISTRIBUTOR="$(sed 's, release .*$,,g' /etc/system-release)"
GRUB_DEFAULT=saved
GRUB_DISABLE_SUBMENU=true
GRUB_TERMINAL_OUTPUT="console"
GRUB_CMDLINE_LINUX="resume=/dev/mapper/vg01-swap rd.lvm.lv=vg01/root rd.lvm.
lv=vg01/swap rd.lvm.lv=vg01/usr rhgb quiet"
GRUB_DISABLE_RECOVERY="true"
GRUB_ENABLE_BLSCFG=true
```

Change the GRUB_CMDLINE_LINUX line to the following:

```
GRUB_CMDLINE_LINUX="rd.lvm.lv=vg01/root rd.lvm.lv=vg01/usr"
```

Removing "rhgb quiet" causes all of the kernel boot messages and systemd startup messages to be displayed. This can make it easier to quickly locate problems during the boot and startup phases. Removing "resume=/dev/mapper/vg01-swap" and "rd.lvm.lv=vg01/swap" prevents the kernel from looking for the swap volume.

To make these changes take effect, it is necessary to rebuild /boot/grub2/grub.cfg. Make a backup of the current grub.cfg file and then run the following command:

 # grub2-mkconfig > /boot/grub2/grub.cfg

After this I removed the swap partition, ran **swapon -a**, and verified with **swapon --show** and **lsblk**. Rebooting the system gave me a final check to ensure that the system did boot properly and that the only swap is the Zram swap.

Did you notice how easy it is to make changes to the kernel configuration?

Chapter Summary

It is not possible to cover all of the possibilities that exist in these special filesystems. Hopefully, this chapter has at least helped you understand the vast amount of information that is available and the essential openness of Linux as an open source operating system that makes it possible to expose all of its internal data and the ability it gives us to alter the configuration of the running kernel.

Swap space and the philosophies and preferences that have accumulated around it have given rise to a situation in which every SysAdmin you ask will probably have a different answer to questions about how much swap space is the right amount. Many SysAdmins even recommend zero swap space.

My opinion is that regardless of how much RAM is installed in a system, having some minimal amount of swap space is a good idea. It is better to have the system slow down when RAM fills and swapping starts than it is to have a program or the entire system crash. I consider swap as an early warning system that tells me when I need to add more RAM. Of course there are limits on the amount of memory that can be added to even modern Linux hosts.

Zram is a tool that is for creating compressed virtual swap space. The ideal swap configuration depends upon your use case and the amount of physical RAM in your host computer. No matter what combination of Zram, swap partitions, and swap files you use for swap, you should always experiment with your own system loads and verify that your swap configuration works for you. However, using the default Zram swap without any traditional swap partitions or files works as well for me as any other swap configuration I have ever used and better than many.

Exercises

Perform the following exercises to complete this chapter:

1. Where do the utilities that display data about the running Linux system get all of their data?

2. What is the overall function of the /proc filesystem?

3. What type of overhead is incurred by utilities like swap and Glances when they are running?

4. Does the sequence in which swap partitions appear in /etc/fstab affect their priority if no priorities are assigned in fstab?

5. What size of swap space would you use for the StudentVM1 virtual machine based on the recommendations in this chapter?

6. Assume hypothetically that you are installing a new Linux host with 12GB of RAM installed. How much swap space would you create during installation?

7. If no priorities are specified in /etc/fstab for all swaps, does the sequence in which the swaps are started affect their priority?

8. How does the use of Zram for swap space affect these questions?

CHAPTER 25

Regular Expressions

Objectives

In this chapter you will learn

- To define the term "regular expression"

- To describe the purpose of regular expressions and extended regular expressions

- To differentiate between different styles of regular expressions as used by different tools

- To state the difference between basic regular expressions and extended regular expressions

- To identify and use many of the metacharacters and expressions used to build regular expressions for typical administrative tasks

- To use regular expressions and extended regular expressions with tools like grep and sed

Introducing Regular Expressions

In Volume 1 of this course, we explored the use of file name globbing using wildcard characters like * and ? as a means to select specific files or lines of data from a data stream. We have also seen how to use brace expansion and sets to provide more flexibility to match more complex patterns. These tools are powerful, and I use them many times a day. Yet there are things that cannot be done with wildcards.

© David Both 2023

D. Both, *Using and Administering Linux: Volume 2*, https://doi.org/10.1007/978-1-4842-9615-8_25

Regular expressions (REGEXes or REs) provide us with more complex and flexible pattern matching capabilities. Just as certain characters take on special meaning when using file globbing, REs also have special characters. There are two main types of regular expressions (REs), basic regular expressions (BREs) and extended regular expressions (EREs).

The first thing we need are some definitions. There are many definitions for the term "regular expressions," but many are dry and uninformative. Here are mine.

- **Regular expressions** are strings of literal and metacharacters that can be used as patterns by various Linux utilities to match strings of ASCII plain text data in a data stream. When a match occurs, it can be used to extract or eliminate a line of data from the stream or to modify the matched string in some way.

- **Basic regular expressions (BREs)** and **extended regular expressions (EREs)** are not significantly different in terms of functionality.[1] The primary difference is in the syntax used and how metacharacters are specified. In basic regular expressions, the metacharacters "?", "+", "{", "|", "(", and ")" lose their special meaning; instead, it is necessary to use the backslashed versions "\?", "\+", "\{", "\|", "\(", and "\)". The ERE syntax is believed by many users to be easier to use.

Regular expressions (REs)[2] take the concept of using metacharacters to match patterns in data streams much further than file globbing and give us even more control over the items we select from a data stream. REs are used by various tools to parse[3] a data stream to match patterns of characters in order to perform some transformation on the data.

---

[1] See the grep info page in Section 3.6 Basic vs Extended Regular Expressions.

[2] When I talk about regular expressions, in a general sense I usually mean to include both basic and extended regular expressions. If there is a differentiation to be made, I will use the acronym BREs for basic regular expressions or EREs for extended regular expressions.

[3] One general meaning of *parse* is to examine something by studying its component parts. For our purposes we parse a data stream to locate sequences of characters that match a specified pattern.

Regular expressions have a reputation for being obscure and arcane incantations that only those with special wizardly SysAdmin powers use. Figure 25-1 would seem to confirm this. The command pipeline appears to be an intractable sequence of meaningless gibberish to anyone without the knowledge of REGEX. It certainly seemed that way to me the first time I encountered something similar early in my career. As you will see, it is actually relatively simple once it is all explained.

```
cat Experiment_6-1.txt | grep -v Team | grep -v "^\s*$" | sed -e
"s/[Ll]eader//" -e "s/\[//g" -e "s/\]//g" -e "s/)//g" | awk '{print $1"
"$2" <"$3">"}' > addresses.txt
```

Figure 25-1. *A real-world sample of the use of regular expressions. It is actually a single line that I used to transform a file that was sent to me into a usable form*

We can only begin to touch upon all of the possibilities opened to us by regular expressions in a single chapter. There are entire books devoted exclusively to regular expressions, so we will explore the basics in this chapter – just enough to get started with tasks common to SysAdmins.

Getting Started

Now we need a real-world example to use as a learning tool. Here is one I encountered several years ago.

The Mailing List

This example highlights the power and flexibility of the Linux command line, especially regular expressions, for their ability to automate common tasks. I have administered several listservs during my career and still do. People send me lists of email addresses to add to those lists. In more than one case, I have received a list of names and email addresses in a Word format that were to be added to one of the lists.

The list itself was not really very long, but it was very inconsistent in its formatting. An abbreviated version of that list, with name and domain changes, is shown in Figure 25-2. The original list has extra lines, characters like brackets and parentheses that need to be deleted, whitespace such as spaces and tabs, and some empty lines. The format required to add these emails to the list is firstname lastname <email@example.com>. Our task is to transform this list into a format usable by the mailing list software.

```
Team 1 Apr 3
Leader  Virginia Jones  vjones88@example.com
Frank Brown   FBrown398@example.com
Cindy Williams  cinwill@example.com
Marge smith    msmith21@example.com
 [Fred Mack]    edd@example.com

Team 2 March 14
leader  Alice Wonder  Wonder1@example.com
John broth  bros34@example.com
Ray Clarkson  Ray.Clarks@example.com
Kim West     kimwest@example.com
[JoAnne Blank]  jblank@example.com


Team 3 Apr 1
Leader  Steve Jones  sjones23876@example.com
Bullwinkle Moose bmoose@example.com
Rocket Squirrel RJSquirrel@example.com
Julie Lisbon  julielisbon234@example.com
[Mary Lastware) mary@example.com
```

Figure 25-2. *A partial, modified listing of the document of email addresses to add to a listserv*

It was obvious that I needed to manipulate the data in order to mangle it into an acceptable format for inputting to the list. It is possible to use a text editor or a word processor such as LibreOffice Writer to make the necessary changes to this small file. However, people send me files like this quite often, so it becomes a chore to use a word processor to make these changes. Despite the fact that Writer has a good search and replace function, each character or string must be replaced singly, and there is no way to save previous searches. Writer does have a very powerful macro feature, but I am not familiar with either of its two languages, LibreOffice Basic or Python. I do know Bash shell programming.

The First Solution

I did what comes naturally to a SysAdmin – I automated the task. The first thing I did was to copy the address data to a text file so I could work on it using command-line tools. After a few minutes of work, I developed the Bash command-line program in Figure 25-1 that produced the desired output as the file addresses.txt. I used my normal approach to writing command-line programs like this by building up the pipeline one command at a time.

Let's break this pipeline down into its component parts to see how it works and fits together. All of the experiments in this chapter are to be performed as the student user.

Note   The file name Experiment_6-1.txt is correct. The chapters in this edition have been renumbered, but the file name has not.

EXPERIMENT 25-1: INTRODUCING REGULAR EXPRESSIONS

First, download the sample file, Experiment_6-1.txt, from the Apress GitHub website. Let's do all of this work in a new directory, so we will create that too:

[student@studentvm1 ~]$ **mkdir chapter25 ; cd chapter25**

The wget command downloads a file from the URL into the PWD. We are using the simplest form of the command in this experiment:

[student@studentvm1 chapter25]$ **wget https://github.com/Apress/using-and-administering-linux-volume-2/raw/master/Experiment_6-1.txt**

Now we just take a look at the file and see what we need to do:

[student@studentvm1 chapter25]$ **cat Experiment_6-1.txt**
Team 1 Apr 3
Leader Virginia Jones vjones88@example.com
Frank Brown FBrown398@example.com
Cindy Williams cinwill@example.com
Marge smith msmith21@example.com
 [Fred Mack] edd@example.com

```
Team 2  March 14
leader  Alice Wonder  Wonder1@example.com
John broth  bros34@example.com
Ray Clarkson  Ray.Clarks@example.com
Kim West    kimwest@example.com
[JoAnne Blank]  jblank@example.com

Team 3  Apr 1
Leader  Steve Jones  sjones23876@example.com
Bullwinkle Moose bmoose@example.com
Rocket Squirrel RJSquirrel@example.com
Julie Lisbon  julielisbon234@example.com
[Mary Lastware) mary@example.com

[student@studentvm1 chapter25]$
```

The first things I see that can be done are easy ones. Since the team names and dates are on lines by themselves, we can use the following to remove those lines that have the word "Team". I place the end-of-sentence period outside the quotes for clarity to ensure that only the intended string is inside the quotes:

```
[student@studentvm1 chapter25]$ cat Experiment_6-1.txt | grep -v Team
```

I won't reproduce the results of each stage of building this Bash program, but you should be able to see the changes in the data stream as it shows up on STDOUT, the terminal session. We won't save it in a file until the end.

In this first step in transforming the data stream into one that is usable, we use the grep command with a simple literal pattern, "Team". Literals are the most basic type of pattern we can use as a regular expression because there is only a single possible match in the data stream being searched, and that is the string "Team".

We need to discard empty lines, so we can use another grep statement to eliminate them. I find that using double quotes to enclose the regular expression for the second grep command ensures that it gets interpreted properly:

```
[student@studentvm1 chapter25]$ cat Experiment_6-1.txt | grep -v Team | grep
-v "^\s*$"
Leader  Virginia Jones  vjones88@example.com
Frank Brown  FBrown398@example.com
```

```
Cindy Williams  cinwill@example.com
Marge smith    msmith21@example.com
 [Fred Mack]   edd@example.com
leader  Alice Wonder  Wonder1@example.com
John broth  bros34@example.com
Ray Clarkson  Ray.Clarks@example.com
Kim West    kimwest@example.com
[JoAnne Blank]  jblank@example.com
Leader  Steve Jones  sjones23876@example.com
Bullwinkle Moose bmoose@example.com
Rocket Squirrel RJSquirrel@example.com
Julie Lisbon  julielisbon234@example.com
[Mary Lastware) mary@example.com
[student@studentvm1 chapter25]$
```

The expression "^\s*$" illustrates anchors and using the backslash (\) as an escape character to change the meaning of a literal, "s" in this case, to a metacharacter that means any whitespace such as spaces, tabs, or other characters that are unprintable. We cannot see these characters in the file, but it does contain some of them. The asterisk, a.k.a. splat (*), specifies that we are to match zero or more of the whitespace characters. This would match multiple tabs or multiple spaces or any combination of those in an otherwise empty line.

I configured my Vim editor to display whitespace using visible characters. Do this by adding the following line to your own ~.vimrc or the global /etc/vimrc file:

$ echo "set listchars=eol:$,nbsp:_,tab:<->,trail:~,extends:>,space:+" >> ~/.vimrc

Edit the Experiment_6-1.txt file with Vim. Use the : to put Vim in command mode and enter this command:

:set list

The result, before any operation to change the file, is shown in Figure 25-3. Regular spaces are shown as +; tabs are shown as <>, <->, or <--->, which fills the length of the space that the tab covers. The end of line (EOL) character is shown as $.

```
Team+1<>Apr+3~$
Leader++Virginia+Jones++vjones88@example.com<-->$
Frank+Brown++FBrown398@example.com<---->$
Cindy+Williams++cinwill@example.com<--->$
Marge+smith+++msmith21@example.com~$
+[Fred+Mack]+++edd@example.com<>$
$
Team+2<>March+14$
leader++Alice+Wonder++Wonder1@example.com<----->$
John+broth++bros34@example.com<>$
Ray+Clarkson++Ray.Clarks@example.com<-->$

Kim+West++++kimwest@example.com>$
[JoAnne+Blank]++jblank@example.com<---->$
$
Team+3<>Apr+1~$
Leader++Steve+Jones++sjones23876@example.com<-->$
Bullwinkle+Moose+bmoose@example.com<--->$
Rocket+Squirrel+RJSquirrel@example.com<>$
Julie+Lisbon++julielisbon234@example.com<------>$
[Mary+Lastware)+mary@example.com$
```

Figure 25-3. *The Experiment_6-1.txt file showing all of the embedded whitespace*

You can see that there are a lot of whitespace characters that need to be removed from our file. Once you have viewed the whitespace, you can exit from Vim.

We need to get rid of the word "leader" that appears twice and is capitalized once. Let's get rid of "leader" first. This time we will use sed (stream editor) to perform this task by substituting a new string – or a null string in our case – for the pattern it matches. Adding sed -e "s/[Ll]eader//" to the pipeline does this:

[student@studentvm1 chapter25]$ **cat Experiment_6-1.txt | grep -v Team | grep -v "^\s*$" | sed -e "s/[Ll]eader//"**

In this sed command, -e means that the quote-enclosed expression is a script that produces a desired result. In this expression the s means that this is a substitution. The basic form of a substitution is s/REGEX/replacement string/. So /[Ll]eader/ is our search string. The set [Ll] matches L or l, so [Ll]eader matches leader or Leader. In this case the replacement string is null because it looks like this (//), a double forward slash with no characters or whitespace between the two slashes.

Remember that the modified data stream is going to STDOUT and that the original file is not being modified.

Now let's get rid of some of the extraneous characters like []() that will not be needed:

```
[student@studentvm1 chapter25]$ cat Experiment_6-1.txt | grep -v Team | grep
-v "^\s*$" | sed -e "s/[Ll]eader//" -e "s/\[//g" -e "s/]//g" -e "s/)//g" -e
"s/(//g"
```

We have added four new expressions to the sed statement. Each one removes a single character. The first of these additional expressions is a bit different. Because the left square brace [character can mark the beginning of a set, we need to escape it to ensure that sed interprets it correctly as a regular character and not a special one.

We could use sed to remove the leading spaces from some of the lines, but the awk command can do that as well as reorder the fields if necessary and add the <> characters around the email address:

```
[student@studentvm1 chapter25]$ cat Experiment_6-1.txt | grep -v Team | grep
-v "^\s*$" | sed -e "s/[Ll]eader//" -e "s/\[//g" -e "s/]//g" -e "s/)//g" -e
"s/(//g" | awk '{print $1" "$2" <"$3">"}'
```

The awk utility is actually a very powerful programming language that can accept data streams on its STDIN. This makes it extremely useful in command-line programs and scripts.

The awk utility works on data fields, and the default field separator is spaces – any amount of whitespace. The data stream we have created so far has three fields separated by whitespace, first, last, and email. This little program awk '{print $1" "$2" <"$3">"}' takes each of the three fields, $1, $2, and $3, and extracts them without leading or trailing whitespace. It then prints them in sequence adding a single space between each as well as the <> characters needed to enclose the email address.

The last step here would be to redirect the output data stream to a file, but that is trivial so I leave it with you to perform that step. It is not really necessary that you do so.

I saved the Bash program in an executable file, and now I can run this program any time I receive a new list. Some of those lists are fairly short, as is the one in Figure 25-3, but others have been quite long, sometimes containing up to several hundred addresses and many lines of "stuff" that do not contain addresses to be added to the list.

The Second Solution

But now that we have a working solution, one that is a step-by-step exploration of the tools we are using, we can do quite a bit more to perform the same task in a more compact and optimized command-line program.

EXPERIMENT 25-2: A LITTLE SIMPLIFICATION

In this experiment we explore ways in which we can shorten and simplify the command-line program from Experiment 25-1. The final result of that experiment was the following CLI program:

```
cat Experiment_6-1.txt | grep -v Team | grep -v "^\s*$" | sed -e "s/
[Ll]eader//" -e "s/\[//g" -e "s/]//g" -e "s/)//g" -e "s/(//g" | awk '{print
$1" "$2" <"$3">"}'
```

Let's start near the beginning and combine the two grep statements. The result is shorter and more succinct. It also means faster execution because grep only needs to parse the data stream once.

Tip   When the STDOUT from grep is not piped through another utility, and when using a terminal emulator that supports color, the REGEX matches are highlighted in the output data stream. The default for the Xfce4-terminal is a black background, white text, and highlighted text in red.

In the revised grep command, grep -vE "Team|^\s*$", we add the E option, which specifies extended REGEX. According to the grep man page, "In GNU grep there is no difference in available functionality between basic and extended syntaxes." This statement is not strictly true because our new combined expression fails without the E option. Run the following to see the results:

```
[student@studentvm1 chapter25]$ cat Experiment_6-1.txt | grep -vE
"Team|^\s*$"
```

Try it without the E option.

The grep tool can also read data from a file, so we eliminate the cat command:

`[student@studentvm1 chapter25]$ `**`grep -vE "Team|^\s*$" Experiment_6-1.txt`**

This leaves us with the following, somewhat simplified CLI program:

```
grep -vE "Team|^\s*$" Experiment_6-1.txt | sed -e "s/[Ll]eader//" -e "s/\
[//g" -e "s/]//g" -e "s/)//g" -e "s/(//g" | awk '{print $1" "$2" <"$3">"}'
```

We can also simplify the sed command, and we will do so in Experiment 25-6, after we learn more about regular expressions.

It is important to realize that this solution is not the only one. There are different methods in Bash for producing the same output. There are other languages like Python and Perl that can also be used. And, of course, there are always LibreOffice Writer macros. But I can always count on Bash as a part of any Linux distribution. I can perform these tasks using Bash programs on any Linux computer, even one without a GUI desktop or that does not have LibreOffice installed.

grep

Because GNU grep is one of the tools I use the most that provides a more or less standardized implementation of regular expressions, I will use that set of expressions as the basis for the next part of this chapter. We will then look at sed, another tool that uses regular expressions.

If you have been using this series of books as a self-study course, by starting at the beginning and proceeding sequentially through the chapters, you will have already encountered file globs and REGEXes. Along with the previous experiments in this chapter, you should have at least a basic understanding of REGEXes and how they work. However, there are many details that are important to understanding some of the complexity and of REGEX implementations and how they work.

Data Flow

All implementations of regular expressions are line-based. A pattern created by a combination of one or more expressions is compared against each line of a data stream. When a match is made, an action is taken on that line as prescribed by the tool being used. For example, when a pattern match occurs with grep, the usual action is to pass that line on to STDOUT, and lines that do not match the pattern are discarded. As we have seen, the -v option reverses those actions so that the lines with matches are discarded.

Each line of the data stream is evaluated on its own, and the results of matching the expressions in the pattern with the data from previous lines are not carried over. It might be helpful to think of each line of a data stream as a record and that the tools that use REGEXes process one record at a time. When a match is made, an action defined by the tool in use is taken on the line that contains the matching string.

REGEX Building Blocks

Figure 25-4 contains a list of the basic building block expressions and metacharacters implemented by the GNU **grep** command and their descriptions. When used in a pattern, each of these expressions or metacharacters matches a single character in the data stream being parsed.

Expression	Description
Alphanumeric characters Literals A-Z,a-z,0-9	All alphanumeric and some punctuation characters are considered as literals. Thus the letter "a" in a REGEX will always match the letter "a" in the data stream being parsed. There is no ambiguity for these characters. Each literal character matches one and only one character.
. (dot)	The dot (.) metacharacter is the most basic form of expression. It matches any single character in the position it is encountered in a pattern. So the pattern b.g would match big, bigger, bag, baguette, and bog, but not dog, blog, hug, lag, gag, or leg, etc.
Bracket expression [list of characters]	GNU grep calls this a bracket expression and it is the same as a set for the Bash shell. The brackets enclose a list of characters to match for a single character location in the pattern. [abcdABCD] matches the letters a, b, c, or d in either upper or lower case. [a-dA-D] specifies a range of characters that creates the same match. [a-zA-Z] matches the alphabet in upper and lower case.
[:class name:] Character classes	This is a POSIX[4] attempt at REGEX standardization. The class names are supposed to be obvious. For example the [:alnum:] class matches all alphanumeric characters. Other classes are [:digit:] which matches any one digit 0-9, [:alpha:], [:space:], and so on. Note that there may be issues due to differences in the sorting sequences in different locales. Read the grep man page for details.
^ and $ Anchors	These two metacharacters match the beginning and ending of a line, respectively. They are said to anchor the rest of the pattern to either the beginning or ending of a line. The expression ^b.g would only match big, bigger, bag, etc., as shown above, if they occur at the beginning of the line being parsed. The pattern b.g$ would match big or bag only if they occur at the end of the line, but not bigger.

Figure 25-4. *These expressions and metacharacters are implemented by grep and most other REGEX implementations*

---

[4] Wikipedia, POSIX, https://en.wikipedia.org/wiki/POSIX

Let's explore these building blocks before continuing on with some of the modifiers. The text file we will use for Experiment 25-3 is from some lab projects I created for an old Linux class I used to teach. It was originally in a LibreOffice Writer OpenDocument Text (ODT) file, but I saved it to an ASCII text file. Most of the formatting of things like tables was removed, but the result is a long ASCII text file that we can use for this series of experiments.

EXPERIMENT 25-3: REGEX BUILDING BLOCKS

Download the second sample file from the Apress GitHub website. This is a document containing lab projects from which I used to teach. If the directory ~/chapter25 is not the PWD, make it so:

```
[student@studentvm1 chapter25]$ wget https://github.com/Apress/using-and-
administering-linux-volume-2/raw/master/Experiment_6-3.txt
```

To begin, just use the less command to look at and explore the Experiment_6-3.txt file for a few minutes so you have an idea of its content.

Now we will use some simple expressions in grep to extract lines from the input data stream. The Table of Contents (TOC) contains a list of projects and their respective page numbers in the Portable Document Format (PDF) document. Let's extract the TOC starting with lines ending in two digits:

```
[student@studentvm1 chapter25]$ grep [0-9][0-9]$ Experiment_6-3.txt
```

That is not really what we want. It displays all lines that end in two digits and misses TOC entries with only one digit. We will look at how to deal with an expression for one or more digits in a later experiment. Looking at the whole file in less, we could do something like this:

```
[student@studentvm1 chapter25]$ grep "^Lab Project" Experiment_6-3.txt | grep
"[0-9]$"
```

This is much closer to what we want, but it is not quite there. We get some lines from later in the document that also match these expressions. If you study the extra lines and look at those in the complete document, you can see why they match while not being part of the TOC. This also misses TOC entries that do not start with "Lab Project." Sometimes this is the best you can do, but it does give a better look at the TOC than we had before. We will look at how to combine these two grep instances into a single one in a later experiment in this chapter.

Now let's modify this a bit and use the POSIX expression. Notice the double square braces around the POSIX expression. Single braces would generate an error message:

```
[student@studentvm1 chapter25]$ grep "^Lab Project" Experiment_6-3.txt | grep
"[[:digit:]]$"
```

This gives the same results as the previous attempt. Let's look for something different. This lists all occurrences of "systemd" in the file:

```
[student@studentvm1 chapter25]$ grep systemd Experiment_6-3.txt
```

Try using the -i option to ensure that you get all instances including those that start with uppercase.[5] Or you could just change the literal expression to systemd. Count the number of lines with the string systemd contained in them. I always use -i to ensure that all instances of the search expression are found regardless of case:

```
[student@studentvm1 chapter25]$ grep -i systemd Experiment_6-3.txt | wc
     20     478     3098
```

As you can see, I have 20 lines and you should have the same number.

Here is an example of matching a metacharacter, the left bracket ([). First, let's try it without doing anything special:

```
[student@studentvm1 chapter25]$ grep -i "[" Experiment_6-3.txt
grep: Invalid regular expression
```

This occurs because [is interpreted as a metacharacter. We need to "escape" this character with a backslash so that it is interpreted as literal character and not as a metacharacter:

```
[student@studentvm1 chapter25]$ grep -i "\[" Experiment_6-3.txt
```

Most metacharacters lose their special meaning when used inside bracket expressions. To include a literal], place it first in the list. To include a literal ^, place it anywhere but first. To include a literal [, place it last.

Repetition

Regular expressions may be modified using some operators that allow specification of zero, one, or more repetitions of a character or expression. These repetition operators, shown in Figure 25-5, are placed immediately following the literal character or metacharacter used in the pattern.

---

[5] The official form of systemd is all lowercase.

Operator	Description
?	In REGEXes the ? means zero or one occurrence at most of the preceding character. So for example, "drives?" matches drive, and drives but not driver. Using "drive" for the expression would match drive, drives, and driver. This is a bit different from the behavior of ? in a glob.
*	The character preceding the * will be matched zero or more times without limit. In this example, "drives*" matches drive, drives, and drivesss but not driver. Again this is a bit different from the behavior of * in a glob.
+	The character preceding the + will be matched one or more times. The character must exist in the line at least once for a match to occur. As one example, "drives+" matches drives, and drivesss but not drive or driver.
{n}	This operator matches the preceding character exactly n times. The expression "drives{2}" matches drivess but not drive, drives, drivesss, or any number of trailing "s" characters. However, because drivessss contains the string drivess, a match occurs on that string so the line would be a match by grep.
{n,}	This operator matches the preceding character n or more times. The expression "drives{2,}" matches drivess but not drive, drives, drivess, drives, or any number of trailing "s" characters. Because drivessss contains the string drivess, a match occurs.
{,m}	This operator matches the preceding character no more than m times. The expression "drives{,2}" matches drive, drives, and drivess, but not drivesss, or any number of trailing "s" characters. Once again, because drivessss contains the string drivess, a match occurs.
{n,m}	This operator matches the preceding character at least n times but no more than m times. The expression "drives{1,3}" matches drives, drivess, and drivesss, but not drivessss or any number of trailing "s" characters. Once again, because drivessss contains a matching string, a match occurs.

Figure 25-5. *Metacharacter modifiers that specify repetition*

EXPERIMENT 25-4: METACHARACTERS FOR REPETITION

Run each of the following commands and examine the results carefully so that you understand what is happening:

```
[student@studentvm1 chapter25]$ grep -E files? Experiment_6-3.txt
[student@studentvm1 chapter25]$ grep -Ei "drives*" Experiment_6-3.txt
[student@studentvm1 chapter25]$ grep -Ei "drives+" Experiment_6-3.txt
[student@studentvm1 chapter25]$ grep -Ei "drives{2}" Experiment_6-3.txt
[student@studentvm1 chapter25]$ grep -Ei "drives{2,}" Experiment_6-3.txt
[student@studentvm1 chapter25]$ grep -Ei "drives{,2}" Experiment_6-3.txt
[student@studentvm1 chapter25]$ grep -Ei "drives{2,3}" Experiment_6-3.txt
```

Be sure to experiment with these modifiers on other texts in the sample file.

Other Metacharacters

There are still some additional interesting and important modifiers that we need to explore. Figure 25-6 describes these modifers.

Modifier	Description
\<	This special expression matches the empty string at the beginning of a word. The expression "\<fun" would match on " fun" and "Function" but not "refund".
\>	This special expression matches the normal space, or empty " " string at the end of a word as well as punctuation that typically appears in the single character string at the end of a word. So "environment\>" matches "environment", "environment,", and environment." but not environments or environmental.
^	In a character class expression, this operator negates the list of characters. Thus, while the class [a-c] matches a, b , or c, in that position of the pattern, the class [^a-c] matches anything but a, b, or c.
|	When used in a REGEX, the | metacharacter is a logical "or" operator. It is officially called the "infix" or "alternation" operator. We have already encountered this in Experiment 25-2, where we saw that the REGEX "Team|^\s*$" means, "a line with 'Team' or (|) an empty line including one that has zero, one, or more whitespace characters such as spaces, tabs, and other unprintable characters."
(and)	The parentheses (and) allow us to ensure a specific sequence of pattern comparison like might be used for logical comparisons in a programming language.

Figure 25-6. *Metacharacter modifiers*

We now have a way to specify word boundaries with the \< and \> metacharacters. This means we can now be even more explicit with our patterns. We can also use some logic in more complex patterns.

EXPERIMENT 25-5: COMPLEX PATTERN MATCHING

Start with a couple simple patterns. This first one selects all instances of drives but not drive, drivess, or any additional trailing "s" characters:

```
[student@studentvm1 chapter25]$ grep -Ei "\<drives\>" Experiment_6-3.txt
```

Now let's build up a search pattern to locate references to tar, the tape archive command, and related references. The first two iterations display more than just tar-related lines:

```
[student@studentvm1 chapter25]$ grep -Ei "tar" Experiment_6-3.txt
[student@studentvm1 chapter25]$ grep -Ei "\<tar" Experiment_6-3.txt
[student@studentvm1 chapter25]$ grep -Ein "\<tar\>" Experiment_6-3.txt
```

The -n option in the preceding last command displays the line numbers of each line in which a match occurred. This can assist in locating specific instances of the search pattern.

Tip Matching lines of data can extend beyond a single screen, especially when searching a large file. You can pipe the resulting data stream through the less utility and then use the less search facility, which implements REGEXes, too, to highlight the occurrences of matches to the search pattern. The search argument in less is **\<tar\>**.

This next pattern searches for "shell script" or "shell program" or "shell variable" or "shell environment" or "shell prompt" in our test document. The parentheses alter the logical order in which the pattern comparisons are resolved:

```
[student@studentvm1 chapter25]$ grep -Eni "\<shell (script|program|variable|environment|prompt)" Experiment_6-3.txt
```

Remove the parentheses from the preceding command and run it again to see the difference.

Although we have now explored the basic building blocks of regular expressions in grep, there are an infinite variety of ways in which they can be combined to create complex yet elegant search patterns. However, grep is a search tool and does not provide any direct capability to edit or modify the contents of a line of text in the data stream when a match is made.

sed

The sed utility not only allows searching for text that matches a REGEX pattern; it can also modify, delete, or replace the matched text. I use sed at the command line and in Bash shell scripts as a fast and easy way to locate text and alter it in some way. The name sed stands for stream editor because it operates on data streams in the same manner as other tools that can transform a data stream. Most of those changes simply involve selecting specific lines from the data stream and passing them on to another transformer[6] program.

We have already seen sed in action, but now, with an understanding of regular expressions, we can better analyze and understand our earlier usage.

EXPERIMENT 25-6

In Experiment 25-2 we simplified the CLI program we used to transform a list of names and email addresses into a form that could be used as input to a listserv. That CLI program looks like this after some simplification:

```
grep -vE "Team|^\s*$" Experiment_6-1.txt | sed -e "s/[Ll]eader//" -e "s/\
[//g" -e "s/]//g" -e "s/)//g" -e "s/(//g" | awk '{print $1" "$2" <"$3">"}'
```

It is possible to combine four of the five expressions used in the sed command into a single expression. The sed command now has two expressions instead of five:

```
sed -e "s/[Ll]eader//" -e "s/[]()\[]//g"
```

This makes it a bit difficult to understand the more complex expression. Note that no matter how many expressions a single **sed** command contains, the data stream is only parsed once to match all of the expressions.

Let's examine the revised expression, -e "s/[]()\[]//g", more closely. By default, sed interprets all [characters as the beginning of a set and the last] character as the end of that set. In -e "s/[]()\[]//g" the intervening] character is not interpreted as a metacharacter.

---

[6] Many people call tools like grep "filter" programs because they filter unwanted lines out of the data stream. I prefer the term "transformers" because ones such as sed and awk do more than just filter. They can test the content for various string combinations and alter the matching content in many different ways. Tools like sort, head, tail, uniq, fmt, and more all transform the data stream in some way.

Since we need to match [as a literal character in order to remove it from the data stream and sed normally interprets that as a metacharacter, we need to escape it so that it is interpreted as a literal [. So now all of the metacharacters in this expression are highlighted. Let's plug this into the CLI script and test it:

```
[student@studentvm1 chapter25]$ grep -vE "Team|^\s*$" Experiment_6-1.txt |
sed -e "s/[Ll]eader//" -e "s/[]()\[]//g"
```

I know that you are asking, "Why not place the \[after the [that opens the set and before the] character. Try it as I did.

```
[student@studentvm1 chapter25]$ grep -vE "Team|^\s*$" Experiment_6-1.txt |
sed -e "s/[Ll]eader//" -e "s/[\[]()]//g"
```

I thought that should work but it does not. Little unexpected results like this make it clear that we must be careful and test each REGEX carefully to ensure that it actually does what we intend. After some experimentation of my own, I discovered that the escaped left square brace \[works fine in all positions of the expression except for the first one. This behavior is noted in the **grep** man page, which I probably should have read first. However, I find that experimentation reinforces the things I read and I usually discover more interesting things than that for which I was looking.

Adding the last component, the awk statement, our optimized program looks like this, and the results are exactly what we want:

```
[student@studentvm1 chapter25]$ grep -vE "Team|^\s*$" Experiment_6-1.txt |
sed -e "s/[Ll]eader//" -e "s/[]()\[]//g" | awk '{print $1" "$2" <"$3">"}'
```

Other Tools That Implement Regular Expressions

Many Linux tools implement regular expressions. Most of those implementations are very similar to that of awk, grep, and sed so that it should be easy to learn the differences. Although we have not looked in detail at awk, it is a powerful text processing language that also implements REGEXes.

Most of the more advanced text editors use REGEXes. Vim, gVim, Kate, and GNU Emacs are no exceptions. The less utility implements REGEXes as does the search and replace facility of LibreOffice Writer.

Programming languages like Perl, awk, and Python also contain REGEX implementations, which makes them well suited to writing tools for text manipulation.

Resources

I have found some excellent resources for learning about regular expressions. There are more than I have listed here, but these are the ones I have found to be particularly useful.

The grep man page has a good reference but is not appropriate for learning about regular expressions. The O'Reilly book *Mastering Regular Expressions*[7] is a very good tutorial and reference for regular expressions. I recommend it for anyone who is or wants to be a Linux SysAdmin because you will use regular expressions. Another good O'Reilly book is *sed & awk*,[8] which covers both of these powerful tools and also has an excellent discussion of regular expressions.

There are also some good websites that can help you learn about regular expressions and that provide interesting and useful cookbook-style REGEX examples. There are some that ask for money in return for using them. Jason Baker, my technical reviewer for Volumes 1 and 2 of the first edition of this course, suggests `https://regexcrossword.com/` as a good learning tool.

Chapter Summary

This chapter has provided a very brief introduction to the complex world of regular expressions. We have explored the REGEX implementation in the grep utility in just enough depth to give you an idea of some of the amazing things that can be accomplished with REGEXes. We have also looked at several Linux tools and programming languages that also implement REGEXes.

But make no mistake! We have only scratched the surface of these tools and regular expressions. There is much more to learn, and there are some excellent resources for doing so.

---

[7] Friedl, Jeffrey E. F., *Mastering Regular Expressions*, O'Reilly, 2012, Paperback ISBN-13: 978-0596528126

[8] Robbins, Arnold, and Dougherty, Dale, *sed & awk: UNIX Power Tools (Nutshell Handbooks)*, O'Reilly, 2012, ISBN-13: 978-1565922259

Exercises

Perform these exercises to complete this chapter:

1. In Experiment 25-1 we included a sed search for the (character even though there was not one in the Experiment_6-1.txt data file. Why do you think that might be a good idea?

2. Consider the following problem regarding Experiments 25-1 and 25-2. What would happen to the resulting data stream if one or more lines had a different data format such as first, middle, last or if it were last, first?

3. The following REGEX is used in Experiment 25-5: grep -Eni "\<shell (script|program|variable|environment|prompt)" Experiment_6-3.txt. Create a statement of the logic defined by this REGEX. Then create a statement of the logic of this REGEX with the parentheses removed.

4. The grep utility has an option that can be used to specify that only words are to be matched so that the \< and \> metacharacters are not required. In Experiment 25-6, eliminate the word metacharacters using that option and test the result.

5. Use the sed command to replace the grep command in the last iteration of the CLI program in Experiment 25-6: grep -vE "Team|^\s*$" Experiment_6-1.txt | sed -e "s/[Ll]eader//" -e "s/[]()\[]//g" | awk '{print $1" "$2" <"$3">"}'

CHAPTER 26

Printing

Objectives

In this chapter you will learn

- How to install a printer and make it available to the VM

- To describe the flow of a print data stream

- To determine how well a printer is supported by the Common Unix Printing System (CUPS) under Linux

- To select an appropriately well-supported printer for Linux

- To select an appropriate PostScript Printer Description (PPD) file for a printer when an exact match is not available

- To configure a print queue from the command line using CUPS

- To manage print queues, to enable and disable them, and to move print jobs from one queue to another

- To create a print queue that converts printer data streams to PDF format for storage as a file

- To convert ASCII plain text files to PostScript and PDF formats

- To convert PostScript and PDF files to ASCII text format

- To convert data files between Linux/Unix formats, DOS/Windows formats, and Apple formats

© David Both 2023
D. Both, *Using and Administering Linux: Volume 2*, https://doi.org/10.1007/978-1-4842-9615-8_26

Introduction

We have already explored many Linux tools that enable us to do some pretty amazing things. In this chapter we will look at some additional command-line tools that are all designed to manipulate text files and data streams in order to prepare them for printing. Some of these tools can convert data streams from ASCII text to PDF and PostScript and back; some can convert MS Word and LibreOffice Writer documents to ASCII; other tools can convert from Apple or DOS text files to Linux text files.

We also look at command-line tools that enable us to create and manage print queues.

About Printers

Printers are hardware devices that are used to produce images or text on sheets of paper. Well, duh. But it is important to understand that printers build up an image of the page to be printed one line at a time. 3D printers can print objects one layer at a time, but we will stick with printing words and images on paper for this course.

If you have an ink jet printer, you can watch the process as it takes place. The print head travels horizontally across the paper laying down the image of the text or graphic one line at a time. To be very clear, I don't necessarily mean one line of text at a time. I mean that one line of the print image that is as tall as the vertical size of the print head. This may encompass a single line of text, but it also may be the bottom of one line of text and the top of the next line of text or a combination of text and image.

If you try to equate the operation of a modern printer with that of an old dot-matrix printer that printed one line of text at a time, you will not understand today's printers. At least some understanding of how a printer works is important to understanding how Linux prints and the tools used to print documents to paper as well as tools that create images that can be both printed to paper and viewed on a graphical display.

Even when printing text, modern printers, whether ink jet or laser, all print page images of the page or pages being printed. The ink jet printer builds up the image one line at a time directly onto the paper, while the laser printer generates the entire image on a drum inside the printer and then transfers it to the paper an entire page at a time.

Print Languages

To create the images to be printed, applications such as Office suites, web browsers, financial software, and every other bit of software that can print to a printer must generate a data stream that can be interpreted and converted to an image for printing. These data streams are created using one of the common page description languages (PDLs).

The function of these PDLs is to describe the appearance of the page when it is printed. They use commands like draw a box at this location with height and width and background color and center some specified text in it using a specific font face in a specific size and etc. Page description languages are designed to be independent of the hardware, application software, and operating systems on which they are used. This helps standardize the processes and tools used for printing. I won't afflict you with a historical discussion of the vast number of printer drivers that used to be required for each and every application program.

There are many page description languages, at least some of which are listed on Wikipedia,[1] but there are only three that are in common use by most of today's printers:

- **PCL**[2]: Hewlett-Packard's Printer Command Language.

- **PostScript**[3]: Adobe Systems' first page description language.

- **PDF**[4]: Adobe Systems' Portable Document Format. PDF has become a very common format for exchanging documents.

Printers and Linux

If you have access to a physical printer from your virtual machine, you will be able to perform the experiments in this chapter, most of which relate to printing the files or preparing files for printing. I personally use Brother, HP, and Xerox printers because I have always found them to be well supported by Linux. I recommend reading "Choosing

---

[1] Wikipedia, Page Description Language, https://en.wikipedia.org/wiki/Page_description_language

[2] Wikipedia, PCL, https://en.wikipedia.org/wiki/Printer_Command_Language

[3] Wikipedia, PostScript, https://en.wikipedia.org/wiki/PostScript. This page also contains some of the history that explains how the current print architecture came to be.

[4] Wikipedia, PDF, https://en.wikipedia.org/wiki/PDF

a printer for Linux,"[5], and then you can check the OpenPrinting database[6] at the Linux Foundation document wiki. The OpenPrinting database lists printers by manufacturer in four categories that represent their level of compatibility with Linux:

- **Perfectly**: All printer functions work as expected.

- **Mostly**: Some printer features may not work as expected. For example, dual-sided printing or secondary tray paper selection may not work.

- **Partially**: It probably prints some documents, but others will not print correctly and many features don't work as expected.

- **Paperweight**: Not good for anything except being used to hold down documents printed by printers that do work with Linux.

Clearly, printers from one of the first two groups are to be preferred over those in the last two groups. If you need to purchase or recommend a printer for purchase that is compatible with Linux, the OpenPrinting database is the place to start looking.

Just as a point of reference, Jason, my intrepid technical reviewer for the first edition, tested this chapter with an HP Color LaserJet CP2025dn. It's now about 15 years old, and he had to dig it out from a pile because it almost never gets used. It is marked as "Perfect" in the OpenPrinting database.

Most printers are recognized automatically when you plug them into a USB port[7] on a Linux host, but they are not necessarily automatically configured. If possible, locate a printer that is compatible with Linux by searching the OpenPrinting database. Plug that printer into a USB port on the physical host.

If you cannot locate a supported printer, you should skip Experiment 26-1, the second part of Experiment 26-2, and parts of some of the other experiments. Nevertheless, you should at least follow along and read these experiments to better understand the later experiments. Many of the later experiments in this chapter are still accessible to you because it is possible to print to a file, which we will do much of the time anyway in order to save some trees.

---

[5] Watkins, Don, "Choosing a printer for Linux," `https://opensource.com/article/18/11/choosing-printer-linux`, Opensource.com

[6] The Linux Foundation, OpenPrinting database, `www.openprinting.org/printers`

[7] The role of dbus and udev in recognizing devices like printers when they are plugged in will be covered in Chapter 38 of this volume.

EXPERIMENT 26-1: PRINTER SETUP FOR THE VM

Caution   If you do not have a physical printer, you should read this experiment, but there is no part of it that you can perform.

Start by connecting a printer to the physical host and then making it available to your VM.

If the printer is not already set up, do so and plug it into a power source. Using a USB cable, plug the compatible printer into a USB port on the physical host. It is not necessary to configure the printer on the physical host.

In the window for StudentVM1, click **Devices ➤ USB** to view all of the USB devices attached to your physical host as shown in Figure 26-1. Your printer will probably be different, but it should be listed. Put a check in the box for the USB printer. This is all that needs to be done to make the printer available to the VM.

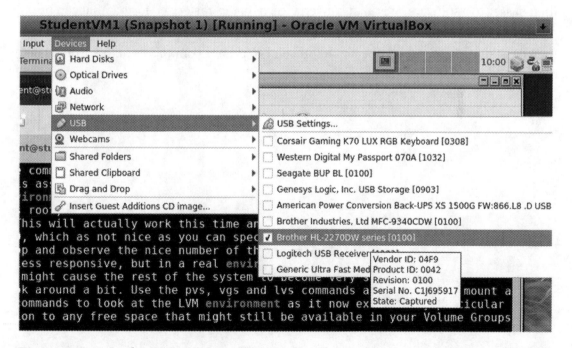

Figure 26-1. *In the USB Settings menu, select the printer connected to the physical host to make it available to the virtual machine*

If by some chance your desktop GUI sees the printer and tries to configure it, ignore that, quit the configuration, and proceed with the manual configuration when you get to Experiment 26-2.

CUPS

CUPS is the Common Unix Printing System.[8] Developed in the late 1990s by Michael Sweet, who was later hired by Apple, CUPS is a modular printing system that makes configuring and printing with most modern printers easy and nearly painless.

CUPS uses PostScript as the final printer data stream. Figure 26-2 illustrates the flow of data from the application programs through the layers of the CUPS subsystem. CUPS accepts input in ASCII text, PDF, HP/GL, and raster image formats and runs them through a filter that transforms the data stream into PostScript. If an incoming data stream is PostScript, no change is required. The data stream, now in PostScript form, then passes to a software layer that converts the data to a rasterized format that can be converted by various drivers to printer-specific language formats. The data stream is then passed to the back-end filters that transfer the printer commands to the printers or other printing devices.

---

[8]Wikipedia, CUPS, https://en.wikipedia.org/wiki/CUPS

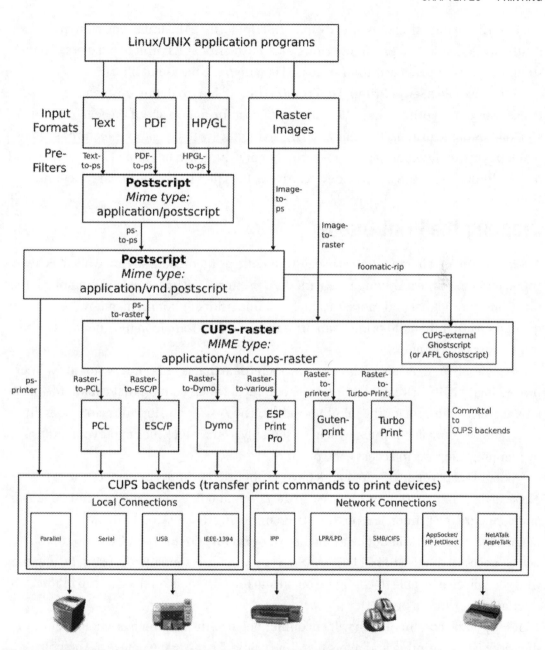

Figure 26-2. *The Common Unix Printing System (CUPS) logical diagram. Glenn Davis (SVG), Ta bu shi da yu (PNG), and Kurt Pfeifle (ASCII) Creative Commons[9] Attribution-ShareAlike 3.0 Unported[10] license*

---

[9] https://en.wikipedia.org/wiki/en:Creative_Commons

[10] https://creativecommons.org/licenses/by-sa/3.0/deed.en

If the input data stream is already in PostScript format, the initial conversion to PostScript is skipped. If the target printer uses PostScript as its print language, the data stream bypasses the rasterization stage and is sent to the back-end filters.

CUPS uses PostScript Printer Description (PPD)[11] files to define the features available in each supported printer. Each PPD file contains information about the features and capabilities of the printer. This allows CUPS to interact with the various features such as paper trays with different paper sizes, print quality, duplex, color or black and white, and more. Although they are not true device drivers, PPD files perform similar functions.

Creating the Print Queue

A print queue is a directory that is used to store the print job data stream while it is being spooled to the printer. Although most modern printers may have internal memory, large print jobs may fill that and more. In a high-volume print environment, many jobs may be queued up faster than the printer can print them, so they remain in the queue until the printer is ready for them.

In general, the /var/spool directory contains data that is temporarily stored for later processing.[12] CUPS has a queue in /var/spool/cups, which contains data about the print jobs as well as the data for the jobs themselves. The /var/spool/lpd/ directory contains a subdirectory for each printer, which is used only to store lock files to prevent multiple overlapping attempts to access each printer.

Skip this experiment if you do not have a supported printer connected to the physical host. In Experiment 26-2 we use the command line to create the print queue and configure the printer. It is possible to do this using the desktop GUI, but there will be times when a GUI will not be available. Many servers do not use a GUI desktop, so it will be necessary to use the CLI. However, when you have configured a printer using the CLI, you will also be able to configure one using the GUI tools on the desktop or the web interface that runs on port 631.

Many of the commands we will encounter begin with "lp", which is a holdover from the early days of printing and refers to a "line printer." Note that what we are actually doing is creating a print queue for the printer.

---

[11] Wikipedia, PostScript Printer Description, `https://en.wikipedia.org/wiki/ PostScript_Printer_Description`

[12] Refer to the Linux Filesystem Hierarchical Standard (FHS), which we explored in Chapter 19.

EXPERIMENT 26-2: CREATING THE PRINT QUEUE

If you do not have a physical printer connected to the virtual machine through the physical host, you can still perform the first part of this experiment. This experiment should be performed as root. We will use the command line to create a print queue for the attached printer.

Identify the Printer

First, let's find the printer on the USB just to verify that it has been recognized. The printer I am using is a Brother HL-2270DW. You will probably have a different printer. If you do not have a physical printer connected to the VM, nothing will show up here:

Tip   Although my Brother printer was listed in the USB devices menu, the VM did not see the printer because it was asleep. Once I woke the printer, it was visible to the system.

```
[root@studentvm1 ~]# lsusb
Bus 002 Device 001: ID 1d6b:0003 Linux Foundation 3.0 root hub
Bus 001 Device 002: ID 04f9:02b0 Brother Industries, Ltd MFC-9340CDW
Bus 001 Device 001: ID 1d6b:0002 Linux Foundation 2.0 root hub
```

And then find the uniform resource identifier (URI) that we will need to create the print queue. The lpinfo -v command is used to list all of the available buses, protocols, and any printers attached to each:

```
[root@studentvm1 ~]# lpinfo -v
file cups-brf:/
network ipps
network https
network http
direct usb://Brother/MFC-9340CDW?serial=U63481A5J631227
network ipp
network lpd
network socket
network beh
network smb
```

The following command provides a more detailed listing and describes the bus or protocol for each possibility. We'll use the direct USB URL to identify the printer's physical location:

```
[root@studentvm1 ~]# lpinfo -lv | less
Device: uri = usb://Brother/MFC-9340CDW?serial=U63481A5J631227
        class = direct
        info = Brother MFC-9340CDW
        make-and-model = Brother MFC-9340CDW
        device-id = MFG:Brother;CMD:PJL,PCL,PCLXL,URF;MDL:MFC-9340CDW;CLS:PRI
        NTER;CID:Brother Color Type4;URF:SRGB24,W8,CP1,IS1-4,MT1-3-4-5-8-11,
        OB10,PQ4-5,RS600,DM1;
        location =
```

We need to find the PostScript Printer Description (PPD) file to use for this printer so we can pass that as an option argument when we create the print queue. First, let's list all of the PPD files located in the printer model directory:

```
[root@studentvm1 ~]# lpinfo -m | less
<SNIP>
gutenprint.5.3://brother-hl-7050n/simple Brother HL-7050N - CUPS+Gutenprint
v5.3.4 Simplified
gutenprint.5.3://brother-mfc-6550mc/expert Brother MFC-6550MC -
CUPS+Gutenprint v5.3.4
gutenprint.5.3://brother-mfc-6550mc/simple Brother MFC-6550MC -
CUPS+Gutenprint v5.3.4 Simplified
gutenprint.5.3://brother-mfc-8300/expert Brother MFC-8300 -
CUPS+Gutenprint v5.3.4
gutenprint.5.3://brother-mfc-8300/simple Brother MFC-8300 - CUPS+Gutenprint
v5.3.4 Simplified
gutenprint.5.3://brother-mfc-9500/expert Brother MFC-9500 -
CUPS+Gutenprint v5.3.4
gutenprint.5.3://brother-mfc-9500/simple Brother MFC-9500 - CUPS+Gutenprint
v5.3.4 Simplified
gutenprint.5.3://brother-mfc-9600/expert Brother MFC-9600 -
CUPS+Gutenprint v5.3.4
gutenprint.5.3://brother-mfc-9600/simple Brother MFC-9600 - CUPS+Gutenprint
v5.3.4 Simplified
gutenprint.5.3://bjc-30/expert Canon BJ-30 - CUPS+Gutenprint v5.3.4
<SNIP>
```

Scroll through these results to get an idea of the printers that are supported by CUPS. There are well over 7,000 – yes, seven thousand – entries in this file, although many of them are intended to support the same printers using different printer languages such as supporting a Xerox WorkCentre 7345 with HP PCL5C, LaserJet 4, LaserJet 4d, or PostScript.

Find the entries for the Brother MFC series of printers and notice that there is no entry for the MFC-9340CDW.

In such a case, I always use a PPD file that seems to come the closest to the attached printer. For my system I am using the PPD file for the Brother MFC-9500:

gutenprint.5.3://brother-mfc-9500/simple Brother MFC-9500

On my physical host, using this PPD and printer combination works fine including all of the functions such as double-sided.

Caution   If you do not have a physical printer attached to your VM, you should read the rest of this experiment, but you should not actually enter these commands.

Create the Print Queue

On the desktop StudentVM1, open the Print Settings using the launcher in the bottom panel so you can watch the print queue appear when we create it using the CLI.

We'll use the information obtained earlier to create the print queue. Add the new print queue using the following options:

- **-p** specifies the name of the printer. This is a text name with no spaces and is how we identify the printer in commands. We'll use MFC-9340CDW. This is just for us to be able to identify the printer when we issue commands or read the results of a command.

- **-E** enables the printer so that it will accept print jobs.

- **-v** specifies the printer URI. This is the target URI to which the data streams for this print queue are sent: usb://Brother/MFC-9340CDW?serial=U6348 1A5J631227.

- **-m** is the name of the standard PostScript Printer Description (PPD) file contained in the model directory. If a PPD file is provided by the vendor and not by the standard CUPS model directory, as is the case with some commercial high-capacity Xerox printers that I have encountered, use the -P (uppercase) option and the fully qualified file name instead of the -m option: gutenprint.5.3://brother-hl-5340d/simple.

Be sure to use the printer name, URI, and PPD file that match the printer connected to your own virtual machine:

Tip   Where the -E flag is in the lpadmin command matters greatly, according to the man page. If you put it at the beginning, you'll encrypt the connection to the printer instead of enabling it.

```
[root@studentvm1 ~]# [root@studentvm1 ~]# lpadmin -p MFC9340CDW -E -v usb://
Brother/MFC-9340CDW?serial=U63481A5J631227  -m gutenprint.5.3://brother-
mfc-9500/simple
lpadmin: Printer drivers are deprecated and will stop working in a future
version of CUPS.
[root@studentvm1 ~]#
```

Tip   Note the warning that printer drivers will be obsolete in the future. Also note that Jason's command uses gutenprint.5.2 because his test was for the first edition and 5.3 has now superseded that.

At this point the print queue should be displayed in the GUI Print Settings. As another point of comparison, Jason's command entry here was

```
lpadmin -p HP-Color-LaserJet-CP2025dn -E -v  usb://HP/Color%20LaserJet%20
CP2025dn?serial=00JPBFR09471 -m gutenprint.5.2://hp-clj_cp2025dn/simple
```

It is okay to verify this, but do not make any changes using the GUI. We can use the lpstat command to verify that the print queue has been created:

```
[root@studentvm1 ~]# lpstat -t
scheduler is running
system default destination: Cups-PDF
device for Brother-HL-2270DW: usb://Brother/MFC-9340CDW?serial=U6348
1A5J631227
device for Cups-PDF: cups-pdf:/
device for DummyPrinter: /dev/null
device for MFC9340CDW: usb://Brother/MFC-9340CDW?serial=U63481A5J631227
Brother-HL-2270DW accepting requests since Thu 02 Mar 2023 02:46:41 PM EST
Cups-PDF accepting requests since Wed 01 Mar 2023 01:49:19 PM EST
DummyPrinter accepting requests since Wed 01 Mar 2023 04:24:02 PM EST
MFC9340CDW accepting requests since Wed 12 Jul 2023 09:40:39 AM EDT
printer Brother-HL-2270DW disabled since Thu 02 Mar 2023 02:46:41 PM EST -
        Paused
printer Cups-PDF is idle.  enabled since Wed 01 Mar 2023 01:49:19 PM EST
printer DummyPrinter disabled since Wed 01 Mar 2023 04:24:02 PM EST -
        Paused
printer MFC9340CDW is idle.  enabled since Wed 12 Jul 2023 09:40:39 AM EDT
```

We can also use the lpstat command to list the names of all print queues and whether the CUPS server is running on our local host. The -e option lists the print queue names, and -r displays the status of the server:

```
[root@studentvm1 ~]# lpstat -er
```

```
Cups-PDF
DummyPrinter
MFC9340CDW
scheduler is running
```

We should test the printer and the newly created queue before we proceed. We can send an ASCII plain text file to the printer as our first test. Be sure to use the printer name exactly as it appears in the output from the lpstat command.

Testing the Printer

Tip   Some printer commands use the -P (uppercase) and some use the -p (lowercase) option to specify the target print queue.

```
[root@studentvm1 ~]# lpr -P MFC9340CDW /etc/fstab
```

A somewhat related part of the SysAdmin's job is to deal with broken and recalcitrant hardware. It's not all about dealing with software. While reviewing this chapter, Jason was delayed for a while by a troublesome bit of hardware. He says, "It also took a while because my jam sensor [on the printer] is overly sensitive and I had to use a piece of tape to fix it, but that's probably out of scope for this [course]."

Actually not so much – it is in the scope of this course. In fact, hardware problems like this are relatively frequent. Many times they can appear to be software problems, and we need to track them down and fix them too. Mechanical devices fail rather too frequently for my liking. Things like fans, storage devices, and printers are all mechanical and have a tendency to fail when it is most inopportune.

This command sets the target printer as the default. Now we can print to the default printer without explicitly specifying the destination. The following command prints the /etc/bashrc file to the default printer:

```
[root@studentvm1 ~]# lpr /etc/bashrc
```

Let's use one of the print options to format a text file for printing. This is the prettyprint option, which prints a small heading on each sheet of paper with the file name, the data and time, and a page number. Setting this option is easy:

```
[root@studentvm1 ~]# lpoptions -p MFC9340CDW -o prettyprint=true
```

It's not necessary to restart CUPS to make this change.

Print the cpuHog file:

```
[student@studentvm1 ~]$ lpr cpuHog
```

Set the Default Printer

If that fails because there is no default printer destination, as the student user, issue the same command you did for root to make the Brother the default printer. This only happened to me once but it can be easily fixed:

```
[student@studentvm1 ~]# lpoptions -d MFC9340CDW
```

Now, again as student, print the /etc/bashrc file. In this case the file does not print in pretty print format as the cpuHog did. Although the man page does not state the reason, a bit of experimentation has led me to the conclusion that only Bash programs that begin with the shebang line, #!/bin/bash, will print in pretty format.

We could add multiple print queues if we have more than one printer, but only one can be the default. All print jobs are sent to the default queue unless a different one is specified.

The lpr and lpoptions commands have a number of options that can be used to set things such as print job priorities so that important jobs are printed first or specify text that describes the location of the printer; the number of copies of a print job to print; how many pages of the print job to print on a sheet of paper, for example, two pages of the print job on a side of each sheet of paper; whether to print in duplex mode, that is, front and back of the paper; banner pages to begin and end print jobs as a way to separate them in high-volume environments; and much more. These are all the same items that can be configured using the GUI Print Settings interface.

Printing to a PDF File

Now since at least some of us do not have a physical printer to use, we will install the cups-pdf RPM package that will allow us to print directly to a PDF file. Many GUI applications allow export to a PDF file, and the GUI print manager interface has an option to print to a file. This package accomplishes the same thing for us for printing from the command line.

Note   Everyone should perform Experiment 26-3 because we will use the PDF print queue to do all further printing for the rest of the experiments in this chapter.

EXPERIMENT 26-3: ADDING THE PDF PRINT QUEUE

Start this experiment as root; we will switch between the root and student users. First, as root, install the cups-pdf RPM package and verify the new print queue has been created:

```
[root@studentvm1 ~]# dnf -y install cups-pdf
<snip>
[root@studentvm1 ~]# lpstat -a
Brother-HL-2270DW accepting requests since Tue 28 Feb 2023 12:25:08 PM EST
Cups-PDF accepting requests since Tue 28 Feb 2023 12:26:35 PM EST
```

Now we make the Cups-PDF queue the default. Do this for both root and the student user:

```
# lpoptions -d Cups-PDF
```

And verify:

```
[root@studentvm1 ~]# lpq
Cups-PDF is ready
no entries
[root@studentvm1 ~]#
```

and

```
[root@studentvm1 ~]# lpstat -d
system default destination: Cups-PDF
```

Unfortunately, cups-pdf has been configured to place the PDF print files in the user's desktop directory, ~/Desktop, which is not what we want and, in my opinion, putting things like files and directories on the desktop is a horrible idea anyway. So we will change this to a new directory that we will create for the student user, ~/chapter26.

As the student user, create the new directory:

```
[student@studentvm1 ~]$ mkdir ~/chapter26
```

We need to change the /etc/cups/cups-pdf.conf file to use this new directory. As root, edit the /etc/cups/cups-pdf.conf file.

Comment out the following line – shown as already commented out here:

```
# Out ${DESKTOP}
```

And add the following line immediately below it:

```
Out ${HOME}/chapter26
```

Restart CUPS:

```
[root@studentvm1 ~]# systemctl restart cups
```

As the student user, print a test file and then verify that it was created in the ~/chapter26 directory. Each file also has the print system job number as part of its name. The job number on your PDF files will probably be different from mine:

```
[student@studentvm1 ~]$ lpr ~/cpuHog
[student@studentvm1 ~]$ ll chapter26
total 12
-rw------- 1 student student 11989 Feb 28 21:46 cpuHog-job_6.pdf
```

The lpr command also accepts data via STDIN, so try this:

```
[student@studentvm1 ~]$ dmesg | lpr
[student@studentvm1 ~]$ ll chapter26
total 148
-rw------- 1 student student  11989 Feb 28 21:46 cpuHog-job_6.pdf
-rw------- 1 student student 135446 Mar  1 11:14 stdin-job_7.pdf
[student@studentvm1 ~]
```

As the student user, open the file manager using the Home icon on the desktop, if it is not already open. Navigate to the ~/chapter26 directory and double-click your cpuHog PDF file. This opens the Evince document viewer and displays the content.

Figure 26-3 shows the two print queues we have created so far. It also shows the cpuHog.pdf file in the ~/chapter26 directory and the Evince document viewer showing the content of the cpuHog print file.

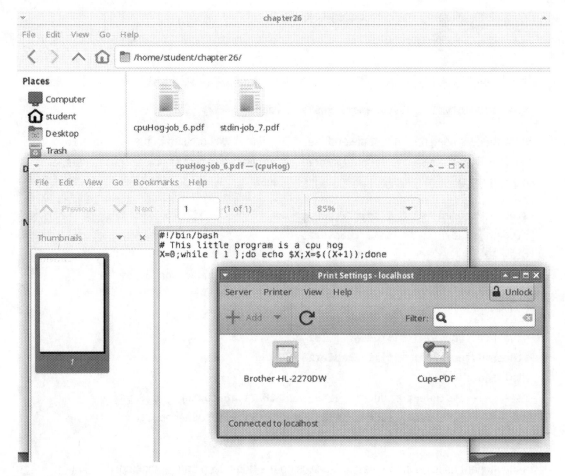

Figure 26-3. *The two print queues created and the Evince document viewer showing the content of the cpuHog.pdf print file*

Note that the default print queue is designated by a heart. A check mark is used on my primary workstation. The difference is in the set of icons you choose for your desktop.

Now, in order to see the status of the print queue for the physical printer, in my case the HL-2270, I need to specify the desired print queue using the -P option:

```
[root@studentvm1 ~]# lpq -P Brother-HL-2270DW
Brother-HL-2270DW is ready
```

All print jobs sent to the default – Cups-PDF – print queue will now be saved as PDF files in the /home/student/chapter26 directory so they can be easily found.

You can disconnect the physical printer from the VM by removing the check from its entry in the list of USB devices. All further printing in this chapter will be done to PDF files. The print queue will not be deleted.

The system-wide printer configuration files are located in the /etc/cups/ directory. This includes the lpoptions file that contains option settings that the root user has made from the command line. The printers.conf file contains the current status information for all defined print queues.

File Conversion Tools

As SysAdmins, we frequently work with ASCII[13] plain text files and text files encoded as UTF-8 or UTF-16. ASCII text files, such as configuration files and those created by editors like Vim, can be printed directly from the command line, but they may not always be formatted well for printing. There are also times when it may be necessary – it has been for me – to convert a word processing document from MS Word or LibreOffice Writer format to ASCII text. In this section we will explore tools that can perform those conversions and more.

Tip   Many non-US users perform operations on UTF-8 or UTF-16 plain text files. That's less of an issue with system files since they will always be encoded as ASCII, but once you get into file conversion and printing, it's something to watch out for. Try copying "Hi ;-)!" into a text file and save it, for example. The **lpr** program won't print the parts in encodings that it doesn't recognize, because PostScript doesn't (natively) support those other encodings.

Let's start by installing a tool that is not installed by default.

---

[13] Wikipedia, ASCII, https://en.wikipedia.org/wiki/ASCII

EXPERIMENT 26-4: INSTALLING THE A2PS TOOL

Perform this experiment and begin as the root user to install one new package. Note that a huge number of packages needed to meet dependencies are also installed – over 400 on my VM:

```
[root@studentvm1 ~]# dnf -y install a2ps
```

This tool and some that are already installed provide us with the ability to manipulate and convert files into various formats. Although there can be many reasons for making these conversions, in this chapter we mostly use them to prepare files for printing. Although plain ASCII text files can be printed directly to a printer, the results are not always aesthetically pleasing because there are no margins, line wrap may be quite random, and some lines may be split with the top half of the characters printed at the bottom of one page and the bottom half printed at the top of the next. This makes reading the file difficult and frustrating so I like to prepare text files a bit so that they print in a more readable format.

a2ps

The a2ps (ASCII to PostScript) utility is my favorite for preparing text files for printing. It converts plain ASCII text files to PostScript files suitable for printing. The resulting PostScript data stream is sent to the default printer. The source file is not altered.

The features I like most about a2ps are the page formatting ones. They allow me great flexibility to define the page format if I do not like the default format. This tool does not require the prettyprint option to be set and is more predictable in its results.

The default format is to print two pages per side of paper and to place a frame around the text. The top area of the frame contains the date the file was last modified, the file name, and the page number with the total number of pages. The bottom area of the frame contains the date the file was printed, the fully qualified file and path, and the sheet number and the total number of sheets.

```
EXPERIMENT 26-5: CONVERTING DATA STREAMS FROM ASCII TO POSTSCRIPT
```

This experiment should be performed as the student user. Be sure that ~/chapter26 is
the PWD.

This command converts the data in the data stream from the /etc/bashrc file to PostScript. The
-o (output file) option sends the resulting PostScript data stream to the file bashrc.ps. The .ps
extension is for PostScript files:

```
[student@studentvm1 chapter26]$ a2ps /etc/bashrc -o bashrc.ps
[/etc/bashrc (plain): 2 pages on 1 sheet]
[Total: 2 pages on 1 sheet] saved into the file `bashrc.ps'
[3 lines wrapped]
```

Now verify the PostScript file was created:

```
[student@studentvm1 chapter26]$ ll
total 172
-rw-r--r-- 1 student student  20926 Mar  1 13:43 bashrc.ps
-rw------- 1 student student  11989 Feb 28 21:46 cpuHog-job_6.pdf
-rw------- 1 student student 135446 Mar  1 11:14 stdin-job_7.pdf
```

The resulting bashrc.ps file can be sent to the printer. Ensure that Cups-PDF is the default print
queue for the student user:

```
[student@studentvm1 chapter26]$ lpoptions -d Cups-PDF
```

Tip   Because we have run the preceding lpoptions command as the student
user, any options set by this command override – for the student user only – the
system-wide option settings for the target printer. The local options are stored
in the ~/.cups/lpoptions configuration file. Each user can have their own printer
option settings. To return to use of the system-wide options, delete this file.

We can now print the PostScript file from the command line:

```
[student@studentvm1 chapter26]$ lpr bashrc.ps
[student@studentvm1 chapter26]$ ll
total 188
```

```
-rw-------  1 student student   16137 Mar   1 13:49 bashrc-job_8.pdf
-rw-r--r--  1 student student   20926 Mar   1 13:43 bashrc.ps
-rw-------  1 student student   11989 Feb 28 21:46 cpuHog-job_6.pdf
-rw-------  1 student student  135446 Mar   1 11:14 stdin-job_7.pdf
```

Use the Thunar GUI file manager to double-click the bashrc.ps and bashrc.pdf files to open the Evince document viewer and look at each of these two documents. They are in different formats, but they should appear identical in the document viewer.

Remember that the Cups-PDF print queue converts files to PDF and we reconfigured it to store them in the /home/student/chapter26 directory. Had we sent the bashrc.ps file to the print queue for the physical printer, it would have been printed.

I suggest reading the a2ps man page in order to understand the full range of its capabilities.

ps2pdf

The ps2pdf utility converts PostScript files to PDF using Ghostscript.[14] Ghostscript is a tool that is typically used to rasterize page description languages into images that can be displayed on a graphical terminal or desktop or printed on a printer.

EXPERIMENT 26-6: CONVERT POSTSCRIPT TO PDF

This experiment should be performed as the student user.

Use the following command to convert the bashrc.ps file to bashrc-2.pdf. Add the -2 to the name because we already have bashrc.pdf in this directory and we do not want to overwrite the existing file:

```
[student@studentvm1 chapter26]$ ps2pdf bashrc.ps bashrc-2.pdf
```

Use the Evince viewer to check the results. You might find it interesting to compare the two files using the cmp (compare) and diff (difference) commands.

---

[14] Wikipedia, Ghostscript, https://en.wikipedia.org/wiki/Ghostscript

pr

The pr utility converts plain ASCII text files into something a little prettier for printing. It simply paginates the text and adds a header to each page of text. The header consists of the date and time the file was run through the pr utility, the name of the file, and a page number. The result is still an ASCII text data stream that can be redirected to a file, sent directly to a printer, or viewed with the less utility.

The pr utility has a few options that can be used to control things like page length, indent (left margin), line width for truncation, and more, but the essential function is still very simple.

EXPERIMENT 26-7: PRETTYPRINT ASCII TEXT FILES

This experiment should be performed as the student user.

The following command does some very basic modification to the /etc/bashrc file to make it print with a little nicer formatting than to just print the raw data stream:

```
[student@studentvm1 ~]$ pr /etc/bashrc | less
```

Page through the data and view the headers and pagination. Print the same file using a bit of left margin:

```
[student@studentvm1 ~]$ pr -o 4 /etc/bashrc | less
```

---

ps2ascii

The ps2ascii is a Ghostscript translator that can extract the ASCII text from PostScript or PDF files. It does not always work very well, sometimes producing no output when there should be some. Most of the time it just extracts the text without regard to any formatting. Still, it can be useful. The output from this tool is in ASCII text to STDOUT.

EXPERIMENT 26-8: CONVERT POSTSCRIPT TO ASCII

Perform this experiment as the student user. This is what the bashrc.ps file looks like after being run through the ps2ascii utility. I have removed much of the data stream to save space:

```
[student@studentvm1 chapter26]$ ps2ascii bashrc.ps
                        1/1
    Page 2/2
  Printed by Student User
    bashrc
    Mar 17, 19 14:55
PATH=$1:$PATH                  fi        esac      }       # By default,
we want umask to get set. This sets it for non-login shell.     #
Current threshold for system reserved uid/gids is 200      # You
could check uidgid reservation validity in     # /usr/share/
doc/setup-*/uidgid file     if [ $UID -gt 199 ] && [ "'id -
gn'" = "'id -un'" ]; then        umask 002     else        umask
022     fi     SHELL=/bin/bash     # Only display echos from profile.d
scripts if we are no login shell     # and interactive - otherwise
just process them to set envvars     for i in /etc/profile.d/*.
sh; do        if [ -r "$i" ]; then           if [ "$PS1" ];
then           . "$i"          else            . "$i" >/
dev/null         fi       fi     done    unset i    unset -f
pathmunge    fifi# vim:ts=4:sw=4
  /etc/bashrc
  Page 1/2
  bashrc
  Mar 17, 19 14:55
    # /etc/bashrc# System wide functions and aliases# Environment stuff
    goes in /etc/profile# It's NOT a good idea to change this file
    unless you know what you# are doing. It's much better to

<snip>

# If you want to do so, just add e.g.    # if [ "$PS1" ]; then    #    PS1="[\
u@\h:\l \W]\\$ "    # fi    # to your custom modification shell script in
/etc/profile.d/ directory   fi  if ! shopt -q login_shell ; then # We're
not a login shell    # Need to redefine pathmunge, it gets undefined
```

```
at the end of /etc/profile    pathmunge () {        case ":${PATH}:"
in            *:"$1":*)                ;;           *)              if
[ "$2" = "after" ] ;
then                  PATH=$PATH:$1                 elseSunday March
17, 2019
```

For obvious reasons, I always keep the original ASCII plain text versions of any files I convert to other formats.

Operating System–Related Conversion Tools

Different operating systems use slightly different non-text codes when storing ASCII text files. For example, DOS and Windows use a carriage-return/line-feed (CR-LF) sequence at the end of each line, whereas Unix and Linux use a single line-feed character, which is called a newline in Unix and Linux. And Apple uses carriage return at the end of a line of text. These characters are not normally displayed using tools like editors and paging tools such as less. Thus, they are called whitespace characters because they are invisible.

We will use the cpuHog program we created earlier for these experiments because it is short.

```
┌─────────────────────────────────────────────────────────────────────┐
│        EXPERIMENT 26-9: EXPLORING FILE CONTENTS                       │
└─────────────────────────────────────────────────────────────────────┘
```

Perform this experiment as the student user. Use the od command to view the cpuHog file as rendered into ASCII characters including whitespace character codes. The newline character is rendered as a \n:

```
[student@studentvm1 chapter26]$ od -c ../cpuHog
0000000   #   !   /   b   i   n   /   b   a   s   h  \n   #       T   h
0000020   i   s       l   i   t   t   l   e       p   r   o   g   r   a
0000040   m       i   s       a       c   p   u       h   o   g  \n   X
0000060   =   0   ;   w   h   i   l   e       [       1       ]   ;   d
0000100   o       e   c   h   o       $   X   ;   X   =   $   (   (   X
0000120   +   1   )   )   ;   d   o   n   e  \n  \n  \n
0000134
```

Notice the \n (newline) characters. Now look at it as hexadecimal (Hex) code. The -x option specifies Hex:

```
[student@studentvm1 chapter26]$ od -x ../cpuHog
0000000 2123 622f 6e69 622f 7361 0a68 2023 6854
0000020 7369 6c20 7469 6c74 2065 7270 676f 6172
0000040 206d 7369 6120 6320 7570 6820 676f 580a
0000060 303d 773b 6968 656c 5b20 3120 5d20 643b
0000100 206f 6365 6f68 2420 3b58 3d58 2824 5828
0000120 312b 2929 643b 6e6f 0a65 0a0a
0000134
```

Can you decode the Hex into ASCII? You could use the tables in the Wikipedia article on ASCII, but a good SysAdmin always has an ASCII table available. You can always find one on the ASCII man page.

Tip   Some tools, such as the printf command that can be used to produce a formatted print in command-line programs and scripts, use ASCII codes like \n for newline and \t for a tab.

---

unix2dos

Now that we can see the newline characters, let's convert this file (without changing the original) to a DOS format.

EXPERIMENT 26-10: CONVERT UNIX FILES TO DOS FORMAT

Perform this experiment as the student user. Convert the cpuHog file into a DOS format without changing the original. The default for the unix2dos utility is to convert the original file to the new format, and this is not what we want for this experiment:

```
[student@studentvm1 ~]$ unix2dos -n cpuHog cpuHog.dos
unix2dos: converting file cpuHog to file cpuHog.dos in DOS format...
[student@studentvm1 ~]$ od -c cpuHog.dos
0000000   #   !   /   b   i   n   /   b   a   s   h  \r  \n   #       T
```

```
0000020    h    i    s         l    i    t    t    l    e         p    r    o    g    r
0000040    a    m         i    s         a         c    p    u         h    o    g   \r
0000060   \n    X    =    0    ;    w    h    i    l    e         [         1         ]
0000100    ;    d    o         e    c    h    o         $    X    ;    X    =    $    (
0000120    (    X    +    1    )    )    ;    d    o    n    e   \r   \n   \r   \n   \r
0000140   \n
0000141
[student@studentvm1 ~]$ od -x cpuHog.dos
0000000 2123 622f 6e69 622f 7361 0d68 230a 5420
0000020 6968 2073 696c 7474 656c 7020 6f72 7267
0000040 6d61 6920 2073 2061 7063 2075 6f68 0d67
0000060 580a 303d 773b 6968 656c 5b20 3120 5d20
0000100 643b 206f 6365 6f68 2420 3b58 3d58 2824
0000120 5828 312b 2929 643b 6e6f 0d65 0d0a 0d0a
0000140 000a
0000141
```

The newline characters have been converted to CR-LF format.

We can use the `diff` command to verify that the files are different. See what the developers did with the name there?

```
[student@studentvm1 ~]$ diff cpuHog cpuHog.dos
1,5c1,5
< #!/bin/bash
< # This little program is a cpu hog
< X=0;while [ 1 ];do echo $X;X=$((X+1));done
<
<
---
> #!/bin/bash
> # This little program is a cpu hog
> X=0;while [ 1 ];do echo $X;X=$((X+1));done
>
>
```

Although this result shows that there is a difference in every line of the files, it does not show the actual differences because they are in the whitespace and cannot be directly displayed by this tool. We can however eliminate whitespace from comparison, which will now show that there are no differences:

```
[student@studentvm1 ~]$ diff -Z cpuHog cpuHog.dos
[student@studentvm1 ~]$
```

This result tells us that the differences in the two files are all in the whitespace.

I find it unusual and somewhat less than helpful that the output data stream from the unix2dos utility cannot be sent to STDOUT and especially so that it does not use STDIO at all. This tool, while useful in a mixed–operating system environment, does not follow the Linux Philosophy.

Refer to the unix2dos man page for details of its capabilities and syntax.

dos2unix

The dos2unix utility performs the reverse of the unix2dos tool by converting DOS text files into ones suitable for Linux.

EXPERIMENT 26-11: CONVERT DOS FILES TO UNIX FORMAT

Perform this experiment as student. The syntax and lack of STDIO capabilities for dos2unix are the same as those of unix2dos:

```
[student@studentvm1 ~]$ dos2unix -n cpuHog.dos cpuHog.Linux
dos2unix: converting file cpuHog.dos to file cpuHog.Linux in Unix format...
```

Now use the od command to view the cpuHog.Linux file in ASCII columnar mode using the -c option and look for the newlines (\n). Note also the sizes of the cpuHog.Linux file and the original cpuHog file compared with the cpuHog.dos file. It is also informative to use the diff command to compare the original cpuHog file and the cpuHog.Linux file after the latter has been through two transitions:

```
[student@studentvm1 ~]$ diff cpuHog cpuHog.Linux
```

You can see that there are no differences.

---

unix2mac and mac2unix

The unix2mac utility does just what its name implies; it converts text files from Linux formats to Apple formats. The mac2unix tool performs the reverse process.

EXPERIMENT 26-12: CONVERT UNIX TO MAC AND BACK

Perform this first part of the experiment as the student user. The syntax of these commands is the same as that for the previous commands. Let's convert the cpuHog file to Apple format and then view the content:

```
[student@studentvm1 ~]$ od -c cpuHog.mac
0000000    #   !   /   b   i   n   /   b   a   s   h  \r   #       T   h
0000020    i   s       l   i   t   t   l   e       p   r   o   g   r   a
0000040    m       i   s       a       c   p   u       h   o   g  \r   X
0000060    =   0   ;   w   h   i   l   e       [       1       ]   ;   d
0000100    o       e   c   h   o       $   X   ;   X   =   $   (   (   X
0000120    +   1   )   )   ;       d   o   n   e  \r  \r  \r
0000134
```

Apple text files use only the carriage return (CR), the \r character at the end of a line of text. There is a little secret here. Let's look at the /usr/bin directory, which is where these binary files are kept.

```
[student@studentvm1 ~]# ll /usr/bin | grep unix
-rwxr-xr-x. 1 root root     55192 Jul 23  2018 dos2unix
lrwxrwxrwx. 1 root root         8 Jul 23  2018 mac2unix -> dos2unix
-rwxr-xr-x. 1 root root     55184 Jul 23  2018 unix2dos
lrwxrwxrwx. 1 root root         8 Jul 23  2018 unix2mac -> unix2dos
```

Think about what that means.

Miscellaneous Tools

There are some additional tools that I have found interesting and useful. Let's look at three of them.

lpmove

The lpmove command can be used to move a print job from one queue to another. This might be necessary if you print a file to a print queue and the printer is out of paper or toner and is not accepting print jobs. The jobs will enter the queue and stay there until the printer is resupplied and once again accepting print jobs.

Moving a print job from one queue to another allows completion of your print job without the need to wait for the original printer to become ready again. To set up this next experiment so that everyone can do it, we will create a dummy printer that sends all print jobs to /dev/null.

A dummy printer can also be useful for testing code that sends a data stream to a printer but where you don't care about the print job itself. You don't want to waste paper on a real printer, and you don't want to clean up a bunch of files that were created during testing. In such an instance, you will test the contents of the print jobs at a different time to verify that they are correct.

EXPERIMENT 26-13: MOVE A PRINT JOB TO A DIFFERENT PRINTER QUEUE

Start this experiment as the root user. Because some of you do not have access to a physical printer, we are going to create a dummy printer that sends all of the print jobs directly to the /dev/null device special file. We explored device special files and /dev/null in Chapter 22 of this volume.

This gives us another queue to work with for this experiment so that everyone can do this. Add the new dummy print queue and verify it:

```
[root@studentvm1 ~]# lpadmin -p DummyPrinter -E -v file:/dev/null
[root@studentvm1 ~]# lpstat -t
scheduler is running
system default destination: Cups-PDF
device for Brother-HL-2270DW: usb://Brother/MFC-9340CDW?serial=U6348
1A5J631227
device for Cups-PDF: cups-pdf:/
device for DummyPrinter: /dev/null
Brother-HL-2270DW accepting requests since Wed 01 Mar 2023 11:31:26 AM EST
Cups-PDF accepting requests since Wed 01 Mar 2023 01:49:19 PM EST
DummyPrinter accepting requests since Wed 01 Mar 2023 04:21:27 PM EST
```

```
printer Brother-HL-2270DW is idle.  enabled since Wed 01 Mar 2023
11:31:26 AM EST
printer Cups-PDF is idle.  enabled since Wed 01 Mar 2023 01:49:19 PM EST
printer DummyPrinter is idle.  enabled since Wed 01 Mar 2023 04:21:27 PM EST
```

Ensure that the student user's home directory is the PWD. Now let's print a test to our dummy printer. Nothing should be printed but we should also get no errors. Do this as the student user:

```
[student@studentvm1 ~]# lpr -P DummyPrinter cpuHog
[student@studentvm1 ~]# lpq -P DummyPrinter
DummyPrinter is ready
no entries
```

Now, as root, let's disable the dummy printer:

```
[root@studentvm1 ~]# cupsdisable DummyPrinter
[root@studentvm1 ~]# lpstat -t
scheduler is running
system default destination: Cups-PDF
device for Brother-HL-2270DW: usb://Brother/MFC-9340CDW?serial=U6348
1A5J631227
device for Cups-PDF: cups-pdf:/
device for DummyPrinter: /dev/null
Brother-HL-2270DW accepting requests since Wed 01 Mar 2023 11:31:26 AM EST
Cups-PDF accepting requests since Wed 01 Mar 2023 01:49:19 PM EST
DummyPrinter accepting requests since Wed 01 Mar 2023 04:24:02 PM EST
printer Brother-HL-2270DW is idle.  enabled since Wed 01 Mar 2023
11:31:26 AM EST
printer Cups-PDF is idle.  enabled since Wed 01 Mar 2023 01:49:19 PM EST
printer DummyPrinter disabled since Wed 01 Mar 2023 04:24:02 PM EST -
        Paused
```

As the student user, send a job to the dummy printer now that it is disabled and then check the queue:

```
[student@studentvm1 ~]$ lpr -P DummyPrinter cpuHog
[student@studentvm1 ~]$ lpq -P DummyPrinter
DummyPrinter is not ready
Rank    Owner   Job     File(s) Total Size
1st     student 10      cpuHog  1024 bytes
```

Our print job is still in the queue belonging to the DummyPrinter. The print job would "print" to /dev/null if we re-enable the DummyPrinter, but we are going to move it to the Cups-PDF queue instead:

```
[student@studentvm1 ~]$ lpmove 10 Cups-PDF
[student@studentvm1 ~]$ lpq
Cups-PDF is ready
no entries
```

Remember that print jobs sent to the Cups-PDF printer are processed and sent as PDF files to ~/chapter26, so we can look there for the resulting "print" document. The date on the cpuHog. pdf file should be only a few seconds old, which tells us that it was just printed. You should delete this file and then do this part of the experiment over just to verify that:

```
[student@studentvm1 ~]$ ll chapter26
total 216
-rw-r--r-- 1 student student  15971 Mar  1 13:54 bashrc-2.pdf
-rw------- 1 student student  16137 Mar  1 13:49 bashrc-job_8.pdf
-rw-r--r-- 1 student student  20926 Mar  1 13:43 bashrc.ps
-rw------- 1 student student  11989 Mar  1 16:28 cpuHog-job_10.pdf
-rw------- 1 student student  11989 Feb 28 21:46 cpuHog-job_6.pdf
-rw------- 1 student student 135446 Mar  1 11:14 stdin-job_7.pdf
```

Look at the Print Settings GUI tool on the desktop. There are now three print queues, and the newest, DummyPrinter, is one of them. Notice that the DummyPrinter print queue is paused because the icon for that queue has a pause symbol (II) superimposed on it. Leave that DummyPrinter disabled.

wvText and odt2txt

The wvText tool can be used to convert MS Word documents to text format, and odt2txt converts LibreOffice documents from OpenDocument Text format to plain ASCII text. I have not used wvText, but I have used odt2txt.

Sometimes I need to determine whether I have discussed a particular topic in a chapter of this book. Each chapter is a separate LibreOffice Writer file. So I do something like that in Figure 26-4 to search all of these chapters for a word or phrase.

```
[dboth@myworkstation RevisionsCompleted]$ for I in `ls *odt`; do echo
"### Working on $I" ; odt2txt $I ; done | grep -Ei "columns|##
Working"
### Working on Chapter-01.odt
### Working on Chapter-02.odt
### Working on Chapter-03.odt
### Working on Chapter-04.odt
on your screen if there are not enough columns in your terminal
your screen if there are not enough columns in your terminal
### Working on Chapter-05.odt
### Working on Chapter-06.odt
### Working on Chapter-07.odt
### Working on Chapter-08.odt
### Working on Chapter-09.odt
### Working on Chapter-10.odt
### Working on Chapter-11.odt
### Working on Chapter-12.odt
### Working on Chapter-13.odt
load the system. It is also interactive and the data columns to
terminal display. The default columns displayed by top are
described below. Several other columns are available and each
any of the displayed columns including CPU and memory usage. By
enough width (columns) the output may be misaligned and
### Working on Chapter-14.odt
is opened. I currently have this adjusted to 130 columns by 65
### Working on Chapter-15.odt
### Working on Chapter-16.odt
### Working on Chapter-17.odt
What is the value of the COLUMNS variable in each of the open
```

Figure 26-4. *Using the odt2txt utility to search for specific words*

By using the echo command to list the chapters as they are converted and scanned, it is easy to identify in which chapter each instance was found. I used the time utility to perform this task to see how long it took. The conversions and content search took less than two seconds of real time. This is much faster than opening each LibreOffice file and using the LibreOffice search tool. Way faster.

Neither of these tools deals with tables well. The data in the tables is converted but the organization is lost.

Chapter Summary

This chapter has explored in some detail the creation and use of print queues and printing from the command line. Although all of this can be accomplished from the GUI and GUI applications, using the command line to perform these tasks fosters a more complete understanding of how printing works in Linux.

We looked at the tools used in this chapter primarily from the standpoint of printing or preparing ASCII plain text files for printing. However, these same tools can be used to manipulate text files in various ways to produce PDF and PostScript files for sending to others as well as long-term retention of text document files in forms that are easy to read and understand. These tools can also be used to allow ASCII text file sharing between operating systems that use somewhat different encoding standards.

Because of the large number of options that the tools we have explored in this chapter can use to control print jobs, it is a good idea to read the man pages for each. There are many possibilities.

Leave the external physical printer connected, if you have one. It will be used in the next chapter.

Exercises

Perform the following exercises to complete this chapter:

1. If you have a physical printer, add some text to the printer queue that describes the printer's physical location.

2. If you have a physical printer, reprint the /etc/bashrc file and format it for two-sided on the long edge and with a double border.

3. Print (to the display) the list of all printer queues on the VM.

4. If you have a physical printer, devise and conduct an experiment that proves that the prettyprint option only works on Bash files with the shebang line.

5. Does prettyprint work when using the Cups-PDF print queue?

6. Can users set different default printers from each other and from the root user?

7. Which Hex character represents a newline?

8. What is the ASCII representation for a tab character and the Hex code for it?

9. In Experiments 26-10 to 26-12, you looked at the unix2dos, unix2mac, dos2unix, and mac2unix executable files. What did you conclude from that observation?

10. What happens to the print queue for a printer when the physical printer is disconnected from the VM?

CHAPTER 27

Hardware Detection

Objectives

In this chapter you will learn to use common Linux tools to detect and identify the hardware installed in a Linux host. This includes the following:

- To determine the motherboard information such as vendor, make, model, and serial number

- To determine the memory type, speed, and size

- To find and list peripheral hardware connected to the system such as printers, mice, keyboards, and more

- To generate a list of the hardware attached to the USB and PCI buses

Introduction

What exactly do I mean by hardware detection? For me, hardware detection is the ability to identify the hardware that's installed in a Linux host and other information such as vendor, model, serial number, memory and hard/SSD drive sizes, and other specific identifying information that might be useful. And I specifically mean without having to take the system apart to do so.

When upgrading memory for a Linux host, for example, I have used the tools we will explore in this chapter to determine the maximum memory supported by a motherboard and what type, as well as how many open memory DIMM slots were available. I could order online or go to my local computer store – a real computer store with people who know what I am talking about, not a big-box monstrosity – and tell them what I want, knowing that it will work when I get home and install it.

© David Both 2023
D. Both, *Using and Administering Linux: Volume 2*, https://doi.org/10.1007/978-1-4842-9615-8_27

In Chapter 26 we saw how to use one of these tools to determine that a printer was installed and what make and model. Another useful purpose for these tools is to use them in automated scripts to document the hardware and software installed in a Linux host. We will look at that application for these tools in the next two chapters.

We have already looked briefly at these tools in Chapter 13 of Volume 1, but we will now explore them in more detail. Although the experimental output from these tools will be for the VM, I will sometimes also include data from one or more of my hardware systems so that you can see the results of these commands on physical hardware.

I mentioned this in Chapter 13 of Volume 1, and it bears repeating here. The lshw (list hardware) and dmidecode (Desktop Management Interface[1] decode) commands both display as much hardware information as is available in SMBIOS.[2] The man page for dmidecode states, "SMBIOS stands for System Management BIOS, while DMI stands for Desktop Management Interface. These two standards are tightly related and were developed by the DMTF (Desktop Management Task Force)."

These two utilities use data stored in SMBIOS, which is a data storage area on system motherboards that allows the BIOS boot process to access data about the system hardware. This hardware data is collected from the SMBIOS and stored in the running system in the /sysfs special filesystem.

Because the task of collecting hardware data is performed by BIOS during the initial BIOS boot, the operating system does not need to probe the hardware directly in order to collect information. The information collected can be used to perform tasks such as determination of which hardware-related kernel modules to load during the Linux kernel portion of the boot and startup process. We will explore this particular usage with udev and dbus in Chapter 38 in this volume.

Much of the data stored in SMBIOS is text data placed there explicitly by the hardware vendors. It is not obtained by actually probing the hardware. The data may be missing some information, or some may even be incorrect. I have not found this to be common but it is possible. Nevertheless, the vendors have good reason to ensure that the essential data is accurate. Other data, the actual hardware information such as CPU, memory, and installed devices, is obtained at each boot and stored in the SMBIOS.

---

[1] Wikipedia, Desktop Management Interface, https://en.wikipedia.org/wiki/Desktop_Management_Interface

[2] Wikipedia, System Management BIOS, https://en.wikipedia.org/wiki/System_Management_BIOS

dmidecode

Let's start our hardware exploration with the dmidecode utility, which can provide us with an amazing amount of hardware information. It does have some limitations as we will see.

One of the limitations of using a virtual machine is that there is little real hardware to return information. Therefore, much of the data you see will be rather limited. To try to overcome that, I will reproduce some of the output from my primary workstation so you can see what the results look like when run on real hardware. Nevertheless, I will still need to significantly reduce the amount of data I show for some of these commands because they can produce prodigious amounts of data.

```
EXPERIMENT 27-1: EXPLORING DMIDECODE
```

Perform this experiment as root.

Starting very simply, we look at the information supplied by dmidecode with no options, which is to say all the information available in SMBIOS:

```
[root@studentvm1 ~]# dmidecode | less
```

There is too much data to reproduce here, so you will need to refer to the results from your VM. As we proceed through this experiment, I will use data from my primary workstation to illustrate data that would be seen on a physical host. You can follow along using data from your VM or from another physical Linux host if you have root access to one.

Let's explore some of the individual DMI types starting with BIOS itself, DMI type 0. You can find the type codes for all hardware types in the dmidecode man page:

```
[root@myworkstation ~]# dmidecode -t 0
# dmidecode 3.2
Getting SMBIOS data from sysfs.
SMBIOS 3.0.0 present.

Handle 0x0000, DMI type 0, 24 bytes
BIOS Information
    Vendor: American Megatrends Inc.
    Version: 0503
    Release Date: 07/11/2017
```

```
      Address: 0xF0000
      Runtime Size: 64 kB
      ROM Size: 16 MB
      Characteristics:
              PCI is supported
              APM is supported
              BIOS is upgradeable
              BIOS shadowing is allowed
              Boot from CD is supported
              Selectable boot is supported
              BIOS ROM is socketed
              EDD is supported
              5.25"/1.2 MB floppy services are supported (int 13h)
              3.5"/720 kB floppy services are supported (int 13h)
              3.5"/2.88 MB floppy services are supported (int 13h)
              Print screen service is supported (int 5h)
              8042 keyboard services are supported (int 9h)
              Serial services are supported (int 14h)
              Printer services are supported (int 17h)
              ACPI is supported
              USB legacy is supported
              BIOS boot specification is supported
              Targeted content distribution is supported
              UEFI is supported
      BIOS Revision: 5.13
```

This information lists the AMI as the BIOS vendor along with the BIOS version number and release date. It can be useful when making a determination of whether a BIOS upgrade is needed along with the information that the BIOS is upgradable.

It lists the device types supported by this BIOS but that are not necessarily installed. For example, various types of floppy diskettes are supported, but I have not installed a floppy drive on any of my system since … Well, I can't remember when because it has been so long.

DMI type 1 contains data about the assembled system. I built my own system, so there is only default data for this type on my workstation. The information on your VM should be similarly limited:

```
[root@myworkstation ~]# dmidecode -t 1
# dmidecode 3.2
Getting SMBIOS data from sysfs.
SMBIOS 3.0.0 present.

Handle 0x0001, DMI type 1, 27 bytes
System Information
     Manufacturer: System manufacturer
     Product Name: System Product Name
     Version: System Version
     Serial Number: System Serial Number
     UUID: 27191c80-d7da-11dd-9360-b06ebf3a431f
     Wake-up Type: Power Switch
     SKU Number: SKU
     Family: To be filled by O.E.M.
```

Type 2 contains data for the motherboard, in this case an ASUSTeK TUF X299:

```
[root@myworkstation ~]# dmidecode -t 2
# dmidecode 3.2
Getting SMBIOS data from sysfs.
SMBIOS 3.0.0 present.

Handle 0x0002, DMI type 2, 15 bytes
Base Board Information
     Manufacturer: ASUSTeK COMPUTER INC.
     Product Name: TUF X299 MARK 2
     Version: Rev 1.xx
     Serial Number: 170807951700403
     Asset Tag: Default string
     Features:
             Board is a hosting board
             Board is replaceable
     Location In Chassis: Default string
     Chassis Handle: 0x0003
     Type: Motherboard
     Contained Object Handles: 0
```

DMI type 4 contains a great deal of information about the processor installed in the host. It has data about the vendor, the CPU flags that help define its functional capabilities, the product version or name, and the current and maximum clock speeds. Most guest systems will show very little data from this command:

```
[root@myworkstation ~]# dmidecode -t 4
# dmidecode 3.2
Getting SMBIOS data from sysfs.
SMBIOS 3.0.0 present.

Handle 0x0057, DMI type 4, 48 bytes
Processor Information
     Socket Designation: LGA 2066 R4
     Type: Central Processor
     Family: Xeon
     Manufacturer: Intel(R) Corporation
     ID: 54 06 05 00 FF FB EB BF
     Signature: Type 0, Family 6, Model 85, Stepping 4
     Flags:
          FPU (Floating-point unit on-chip)
<SNIP>
          HTT (Multi-threading)
          TM (Thermal monitor supported)
          PBE (Pending break enabled)
     Version: Intel(R) Core(TM) i9-7960X CPU @ 2.80GHz
     Voltage: 1.6 V
     External Clock: 100 MHz
     Max Speed: 4000 MHz
     Current Speed: 2800 MHz
     Status: Populated, Enabled
     Upgrade: Other
     L1 Cache Handle: 0x0054
     L2 Cache Handle: 0x0055
     L3 Cache Handle: 0x0056
     Serial Number: Not Specified
     Asset Tag: UNKNOWN
     Part Number: Not Specified
     Core Count: 16
     Core Enabled: 16
```

```
Thread Count: 32
Characteristics:
        64-bit capable
        Multi-Core
        Hardware Thread
        Execute Protection
        Enhanced Virtualization
        Power/Performance Control
```

Even on a physical host, some DMI types are empty. Notice that the dmidecode utility always prints the fact that it is obtaining its SMBIOS data from the /sysfs filesystem:

```
[root@myworkstation ~]# dmidecode -t 5
# dmidecode 3.2
Getting SMBIOS data from sysfs.
SMBIOS 3.0.0 present.
```

As you can see from the dmidecode man page, DMI type 16 contains data for the physical memory array. In the case of my main workstation, it is telling us that there are two physical arrays – sets – of four memory slots for a total of eight DIMM[3] slots.

The maximum capacity stated for each array is 1,536GB for a total of 3,072GB of RAM – three terabytes. However, the official ASUS specification is for eight DIMMs with a capacity of 128GB each for a total of 1,024GB:

```
[root@myworkstation ~]# dmidecode -t 16
# dmidecode 3.2
Getting SMBIOS data from sysfs.
SMBIOS 3.0.0 present.

Handle 0x0044, DMI type 16, 23 bytes
Physical Memory Array
        Location: System Board Or Motherboard
        Use: System Memory
        Error Correction Type: None
        Maximum Capacity: 1536 GB
        Error Information Handle: Not Provided
        Number Of Devices: 4
```

---

[3] Dual Inline Memory Module.

```
Handle 0x004C, DMI type 16, 23 bytes
<SNIP>
```

The ASUS website[4] has a marketing description and pictures of this motherboard in case you want to see what it looks like.

Now let's look at the actual memory that is installed. DMI type 17 contains information about each memory slot, whether it is empty or specific data about the installed DIMM. I won't reproduce all eight sets of slot data here, just the first two that are then duplicated for the rest of the slots:

```
[root@myworkstation ~]# dmidecode -t 17
# dmidecode 3.2
Getting SMBIOS data from sysfs.
SMBIOS 3.0.0 present.

Handle 0x0046, DMI type 17, 40 bytes
Memory Device
        Array Handle: 0x0044
        Error Information Handle: Not Provided
        Total Width: 72 bits
        Data Width: 64 bits
        Size: 16384 MB
        Form Factor: DIMM
        Set: None
        Locator: DIMM_A1
        Bank Locator: NODE 1
        Type: DDR4
        Type Detail: Synchronous
        Speed: 2133 MT/s
        Manufacturer: Corsair
        Serial Number: 00000000
        Asset Tag:
        Part Number: CMK64GX4M4B3600C18
        Rank: 2
        Configured Memory Speed: 2133 MT/s
        Minimum Voltage: 1.2 V
```

---

[4] ASUS, TUF X299 Mark 2 Motherboard, www.asus.com/us/Motherboards/TUF-X299-MARK-2/

```
        Maximum Voltage: 1.2 V
        Configured Voltage: 1.2 V

Handle 0x0048, DMI type 17, 40 bytes
Memory Device
        Array Handle: 0x0044
<SNIP>
```

The bottom line for memory is that I have installed four 16GB DDR4[5] DIMMs and there are four empty memory slots. You can also see the speed of 2133 MT/s (MegaTransfers per second), voltage specs, and a "Locator," which tells us which slot the DIMM is installed in.

We have not looked at all of the DMI types in this experiment that the dmidecode tool exposes to us. You should explore those that we skipped. Of course, the results will be more interesting on a physical host.

Have you figured out the limitations to DMI? It can be hard to see what is missing, so let's continue.

lshw

The lshw utility (list hardware) is similar in function to the dmidecode utility, but it produces output that is a bit more terse.

EXPERIMENT 27-2: USING LSHW TO LIST HARDWARE

Perform this experiment as the root user. Install the lshw package if it is not already:

```
[root@studentvm1 ~]# dnf install -y lshw
```

This program lists data about the motherboard, CPU, and other installed hardware. Run the following command to list the hardware in your host. Look through the data to see all of the (virtual) hardware in your VM. My personal workstation is more interesting, but I won't reproduce it all here. I just have enough so you can see some differences and the similarities.

---

[5] Wikipedia, Double data rate, https://en.wikipedia.org/wiki/Double_data_rate. This article also contains a link to transfer rates (MT/s).

First, note that the lshw utility shows the hostname. SMBIOS does not have that information because that data is scanned for long before the operating system startup sequence sets the hostname:

```
[root@studentvm1 ~]# lshw | less
myworkstation
    description: Desktop Computer
    product: System Product Name (SKU)
    vendor: System manufacturer
    version: System Version
    serial: System Serial Number
    width: 64 bits
    capabilities: smbios-3.0.0 dmi-3.0.0 smp vsyscall32
    configuration: boot=normal chassis=desktop family=To be filled by
O.E.M. sku=SKU uuid=801C1927-DAD7-DD11-
9360-B06EBF3A431F
```

The motherboard and memory information is essentially the same, but lshw has a nice summary of installed RAM:

```
  *-core
       description: Motherboard
       product: TUF X299 MARK 2
       vendor: ASUSTeK COMPUTER INC.
       physical id: 0
       version: Rev 1.xx
       serial: 170807951700403
       slot: Default string
     *-firmware
          description: BIOS
          vendor: American Megatrends Inc.
          physical id: 0
          version: 0503
          date: 07/11/2017
          size: 64KiB
          capacity: 16MiB
          capabilities: pci apm upgrade shadowing cdboot bootselect
          socketedrom edd int13floppy1200 int13flop
```

```
py720 int13floppy2880 int5printscreen int9keyboard int14serial int17printer
acpi usb biosbootspecification ue
fi
   *-memory
         description: System Memory
         physical id: 44
         slot: System board or motherboard
         size: 64GiB
      *-bank:0
            description: DIMM DDR4 Synchronous 2133 MHz (0.5 ns)
            product: CMK64GX4M4B3600C18
            vendor: Corsair
            physical id: 0
            serial: 00000000
            slot: DIMM_A1
            size: 16GiB
            width: 64 bits
            clock: 2133MHz (0.5ns)
      *-bank:1
```

<SNIP>

We also see external devices such as the keyboard …

```
            *-usb:0
                  description: Keyboard
                  product: Corsair Gaming K70 LUX RGB Keyboard
                  vendor: Corsair
                  physical id: 2
                  bus info: usb@1:2
                  version: 3.08
                  serial: 1602B030AF0E98A8596A6476F5001BC6
                  capabilities: usb-2.00
                  configuration: driver=usbfs maxpower=500mA speed=12Mbit/s
```
<SNIP>

…and attached printers that were not shown in the DMI database. I did see the printers on my physical workstation but not the one attached to the VM. So you may see the printer on your VM or not:

```
*-usb:0 UNCLAIMED
        description: Printer
        product: MFC-9340CDW
        vendor: Brother Industries, Ltd
        physical id: 1
        bus info: usb@1:a.1
        version: 1.00
        serial: U63481A5J631227
        capabilities: usb-2.00 bidirectional
        configuration: maxpower=2mA speed=480Mbit/s
*-usb:1
        description: Printer
        product: HL-2270DW series
        vendor: Brother
        physical id: 3
        bus info: usb@1:a.3
        version: 1.00
        serial: C1J695917
        capabilities: usb-2.00 bidirectional
        configuration: driver=usblp maxpower=2mA
        speed=480Mbit/s
```

lsusb

There are some commands available to list devices connected on the Universal Serial Bus[6] (USB). Let's start with lsusb (list USB devices), which lists devices on the USB, including internal and external USB hubs and the devices connected to them.

[6]Wikipedia, USB, https://en.wikipedia.org/wiki/USB

EXPERIMENT 27-3: FINDING USB DEVICES

Perform this experiment as the root user. You won't see much on the VM you are using for this course, just a couple virtual USB hubs and probably a printer if you have one attached to the VM. But here are the results from my workstation:

```
[root@myworkstation ~]# lsusb
Bus 004 Device 001: ID 1d6b:0003 Linux Foundation 3.0 root hub
Bus 003 Device 001: ID 1d6b:0002 Linux Foundation 2.0 root hub
Bus 002 Device 005: ID 0bc2:ab2d Seagate RSS LLC SRD00F1 [Backup Plus
Ultra Slim]
Bus 002 Device 004: ID 045b:0210 Hitachi, Ltd
Bus 002 Device 003: ID 045b:0210 Hitachi, Ltd
Bus 002 Device 002: ID 0bc2:ab28 Seagate RSS LLC Seagate Backup Plus Portable
5TB SRD00F1
Bus 002 Device 001: ID 1d6b:0003 Linux Foundation 3.0 root hub
Bus 001 Device 005: ID 04f9:02b0 Brother Industries, Ltd MFC-9340CDW
Bus 001 Device 003: ID 045b:0209 Hitachi, Ltd
Bus 001 Device 004: ID 0d8c:0012 C-Media Electronics, Inc. USB Audio Device
Bus 001 Device 002: ID 045b:0209 Hitachi, Ltd
Bus 001 Device 012: ID 046d:082d Logitech, Inc. HD Pro Webcam C920
Bus 001 Device 011: ID 1058:070a Western Digital Technologies, Inc. My
Passport Essential (WDBAAA), My Passport for Mac (WDBAAB), My Passport
Essential SE (WDBABM), My Passport SE for Mac (WDBABW
Bus 001 Device 010: ID 14cd:168a Super Top Elecom Co., Ltd MR-K013
Multicard Reader
Bus 001 Device 009: ID 1a40:0201 Terminus Technology Inc. FE 2.1 7-port Hub
Bus 001 Device 008: ID 1b1c:1b49 Corsair CORSAIR K70 RGB MK.2 Mechanical
Gaming Keyboard
Bus 001 Device 007: ID 046d:c52b Logitech, Inc. Unifying Receiver
Bus 001 Device 006: ID 0764:0601 Cyber Power System, Inc. PR1500LCDRT2U UPS
Bus 001 Device 001: ID 1d6b:0002 Linux Foundation 2.0 root hub
```

You can see that there are multiple hubs here, some like the root hubs are internal and others like the Terminus Technology 7-port hub are an external add-on USB 3.0 hub. The APC UPS is listed as are both of my Brother laser printers.

You can also use the -t option to display the output in a tree format:

```
[root@myworkstation ~]# lsusb -t
/:  Bus 04.Port 1: Dev 1, Class=root_hub, Driver=xhci_hcd/2p, 10000M
/:  Bus 03.Port 1: Dev 1, Class=root_hub, Driver=xhci_hcd/2p, 480M
/:  Bus 02.Port 1: Dev 1, Class=root_hub, Driver=xhci_hcd/10p, 5000M
    |__ Port 2: Dev 2, If 0, Class=Mass Storage, Driver=uas, 5000M
    |__ Port 3: Dev 3, If 0, Class=Hub, Driver=hub/4p, 5000M
    |__ Port 4: Dev 4, If 0, Class=Hub, Driver=hub/4p, 5000M
        |__ Port 1: Dev 5, If 0, Class=Mass Storage, Driver=uas, 5000M
/:  Bus 01.Port 1: Dev 1, Class=root_hub, Driver=xhci_hcd/16p, 480M
    |__ Port 3: Dev 2, If 0, Class=Hub, Driver=hub/4p, 480M
        |__ Port 2: Dev 4, If 0, Class=Audio, Driver=snd-usb-audio, 12M
        |__ Port 2: Dev 4, If 1, Class=Audio, Driver=snd-usb-audio, 12M
        |__ Port 2: Dev 4, If 2, Class=Audio, Driver=snd-usb-audio, 12M
        |__ Port 2: Dev 4, If 3, Class=Human Interface Device,
            Driver=usbhid, 12M
    |__ Port 4: Dev 3, If 0, Class=Hub, Driver=hub/4p, 480M
    |__ Port 8: Dev 5, If 0, Class=Printer, Driver=usblp, 480M
<SNIP>
    |__ Port 14: Dev 9, If 0, Class=Hub, Driver=hub/7p, 480M
        |__ Port 2: Dev 10, If 0, Class=Mass Storage, Driver=usb-
            storage, 480M
        |__ Port 6: Dev 11, If 0, Class=Mass Storage, Driver=usb-
            storage, 480M
        |__ Port 7: Dev 12, If 0, Class=Video, Driver=uvcvideo, 480M
        |__ Port 7: Dev 12, If 1, Class=Video, Driver=uvcvideo, 480M
        |__ Port 7: Dev 12, If 2, Class=Audio, Driver=snd-usb-audio, 480M
        |__ Port 7: Dev 12, If 3, Class=Audio, Driver=snd-usb-audio, 480M
```

The physical printer does show up on both my workstation and the VM in this experiment.

This view makes it easier to follow the device connections through multiple hubs and to see which root hub each device is ultimately connected to. This second syntax shows less information about the connected devices, but that can be cross-referenced with the first syntax using the bus, port, and device numbers.

usb-devices

The usb-devices utility performs the same task as lsusb, that of listing devices attached to the bus, but it can provide more information about each device.

EXPERIMENT 27-4: GETTING USB DETAILS

Perform this experiment as root. You will only get two entries – or three if you have a physical printer attached – so I have reproduced some of the output from my workstation because it has some interesting entries you won't see on your VM:

```
[root@myworkstation ~]# usb-devices | less

T:  Bus=01 Lev=00 Prnt=00 Port=00 Cnt=00 Dev#=  1 Spd=480 MxCh=16
D:  Ver= 2.00 Cls=09(hub  ) Sub=00 Prot=01 MxPS=64 #Cfgs=  1
P:  Vendor=1d6b ProdID=0002 Rev=04.20
S:  Manufacturer=Linux 4.20.14-200.fc29.x86_64 xhci-hcd
S:  Product=xHCI Host Controller
S:  SerialNumber=0000:00:14.0
C:  #Ifs= 1 Cfg#= 1 Atr=e0 MxPwr=0mA
I:  If#=0x0 Alt= 0 #EPs= 1 Cls=09(hub  ) Sub=00 Prot=00 Driver=hub

T:  Bus=01 Lev=01 Prnt=01 Port=09 Cnt=01 Dev#=  4 Spd=480 MxCh= 4
D:  Ver= 2.00 Cls=09(hub  ) Sub=00 Prot=02 MxPS=64 #Cfgs=  1
P:  Vendor=050d ProdID=0234 Rev=00.00
C:  #Ifs= 1 Cfg#= 1 Atr=e0 MxPwr=2mA
I:  If#=0x0 Alt= 1 #EPs= 1 Cls=09(hub  ) Sub=00 Prot=02 Driver=hub
<SNIP>
T:  Bus=01 Lev=02 Prnt=04 Port=02 Cnt=02 Dev#= 17 Spd=480 MxCh= 0
D:  Ver= 2.00 Cls=00(>ifc ) Sub=00 Prot=00 MxPS=64 #Cfgs=  1
P:  Vendor=04f9 ProdID=0042 Rev=01.00
S:  Manufacturer=Brother
S:  Product=HL-2270DW series
S:  SerialNumber=C1J695917
C:  #Ifs= 1 Cfg#= 1 Atr=c0 MxPwr=2mA
I:  If#=0x0 Alt= 0 #EPs= 2 Cls=07(print) Sub=01 Prot=02 Driver=usblp

T:  Bus=01 Lev=01 Prnt=01 Port=10 Cnt=02 Dev#=  6 Spd=12  MxCh= 0
D:  Ver= 2.00 Cls=00(>ifc ) Sub=00 Prot=00 MxPS=64 #Cfgs=  1
```

```
P:   Vendor=051d ProdID=0002 Rev=00.90
S:   Manufacturer=American Power Conversion
S:   Product=Back-UPS XS 1500G FW:866.L8 .D USB FW:L8
S:   SerialNumber=3B1551X04045
C:   #Ifs= 1 Cfg#= 1 Atr=e0 MxPwr=2mA
I:   If#=0x0 Alt= 0 #EPs= 1 Cls=03(HID  ) Sub=00 Prot=00 Driver=usbhid
<SNIP>
T:   Bus=01 Lev=03 Prnt=11 Port=00 Cnt=01 Dev#= 13 Spd=480 MxCh= 0
D:   Ver= 2.00 Cls=00(>ifc ) Sub=00 Prot=00 MxPS=64 #Cfgs=  1
P:   Vendor=0424 ProdID=4063 Rev=01.91
S:   Manufacturer=Generic
S:   Product=Ultra Fast Media Reader
S:   SerialNumber=000000264001
C:   #Ifs= 1 Cfg#= 1 Atr=80 MxPwr=96mA
I:   If#=0x0 Alt= 0 #EPs= 2 Cls=08(stor.) Sub=06 Prot=50 Driver=usb-storage
<SNIP>
T:   Bus=01 Lev=01 Prnt=01 Port=01 Cnt=05 Dev#=  2 Spd=12  MxCh= 0
D:   Ver= 2.00 Cls=00(>ifc ) Sub=00 Prot=00 MxPS=64 #Cfgs=  1
P:   Vendor=1b1c ProdID=1b33 Rev=03.08
S:   Manufacturer=Corsair
S:   Product=Corsair Gaming K70 LUX RGB Keyboard
S:   SerialNumber=1602B030AF0E98A8596A6476F5001BC6
C:   #Ifs= 2 Cfg#= 1 Atr=a0 MxPwr=500mA
I:   If#=0x0 Alt= 0 #EPs= 1 Cls=03(HID  ) Sub=01 Prot=01 Driver=usbfs
I:   If#=0x1 Alt= 0 #EPs= 2 Cls=03(HID  ) Sub=00 Prot=00 Driver=usbfs
```

I have removed the entries for most of the USB hubs for my workstation, but this data shows the physical devices such as external USB storage devices, a media reader, and the keyboard.

lspci

The lspci utility lists devices on the Peripheral Component Interconnect[7] (PCI) bus and its extensions, PCI-X and PCI Express (PCIe). This includes many motherboard devices such as memory and bus controllers, as well as devices like audio, Ethernet, SATA, and video devices.

---

[7] Wikipedia, Peripheral Component Interconnect, https://en.wikipedia.org/wiki/Conventional_PCI

EXPERIMENT 27-5: EXPLORING THE PCI BUS

Perform this experiment as root. Without any options, the lspci command provides a list of PCI hardware that starts with the PCI bus address of each device and a simple description. This results in a little more interesting output on the VM, but I have also reproduced a shortened list from my workstation:

```
[root@myworkstation ~]# lspci
00:00.0 Host bridge: Intel Corporation Sky Lake-E DMI3 Registers (rev 04)
00:04.0 System peripheral: Intel Corporation Sky Lake-E CBDMA Registers
(rev 04)
00:04.1 System peripheral: Intel Corporation Sky Lake-E CBDMA Registers
(rev 04)
<SNIP>
00:04.7 System peripheral: Intel Corporation Sky Lake-E CBDMA Registers
(rev 04)
00:05.0 System peripheral: Intel Corporation Sky Lake-E MM/Vt-d Configuration
Registers (rev 04)
00:05.2 System peripheral: Intel Corporation Sky Lake-E RAS (rev 04)
00:05.4 PIC: Intel Corporation Sky Lake-E IOAPIC (rev 04)
00:08.0 System peripheral: Intel Corporation Sky Lake-E Ubox Registers
(rev 04)
00:08.1 Performance counters: Intel Corporation Sky Lake-E Ubox Registers
(rev 04)
00:08.2 System peripheral: Intel Corporation Sky Lake-E Ubox Registers
(rev 04)
00:14.0 USB controller: Intel Corporation 200 Series/Z370 Chipset Family USB
3.0 xHCI Controller
00:14.2 Signal processing controller: Intel Corporation 200 Series PCH
Thermal Subsystem
00:16.0 Communication controller: Intel Corporation 200 Series PCH
CSME HECI #1
00:17.0 SATA controller: Intel Corporation 200 Series PCH SATA controller
[AHCI mode]
00:1c.0 PCI bridge: Intel Corporation 200 Series PCH PCI Express Root Port #1
(rev f0)
<SNIP>
```

```
65:00.0 VGA compatible controller: Advanced Micro Devices, Inc. [AMD/ATI]
Barts XT [Radeon HD 6870]
65:00.1 Audio device: Advanced Micro Devices, Inc. [AMD/ATI] Barts HDMI Audio
[Radeon HD 6790/6850/6870 / 7720 OEM]
<SNIP>
```

Using the -v option for verbose output produces several lines of data for each device. The total output for this command is very long, so you should pipe it through the **less** paging tool. I have only reproduced a few stanzas from my workstation in order to save space:

```
[root@studentvm1 ~]# lspci -v | less
0:00.0 Host bridge: Intel Corporation Sky Lake-E DMI3 Registers (rev 04)
        Subsystem: ASUSTeK Computer Inc. Device 873c
        Flags: fast devsel, NUMA node 0
        Capabilities: [90] Express Root Port (Slot-), MSI 00
        Capabilities: [e0] Power Management version 3
        Capabilities: [100] Vendor Specific Information: ID=0002 Rev=0
        Len=00c <?>
        Capabilities: [144] Vendor Specific Information: ID=0004 Rev=1
        Len=03c <?>
        Capabilities: [1d0] Vendor Specific Information: ID=0003 Rev=1
        Len=00a <?>
        Capabilities: [250] Secondary PCI Express <?>
        Capabilities: [280] Vendor Specific Information: ID=0005 Rev=3
        Len=018 <?>
        Capabilities: [300] Vendor Specific Information: ID=0008 Rev=0
        Len=038 <?>
<SNIP>
00:17.0 SATA controller: Intel Corporation 200 Series PCH SATA controller
[AHCI mode] (prog-if 01 [AHCI 1.0])
        Subsystem: ASUSTeK Computer Inc. Device 873c
        Flags: bus master, 66MHz, medium devsel, latency 0, IRQ 29,
        NUMA node 0
        Memory at 92f68000 (32-bit, non-prefetchable) [size=8K]
        Memory at 92f6c000 (32-bit, non-prefetchable) [size=256]
        I/O ports at 3050 [size=8]
        I/O ports at 3040 [size=4]
        I/O ports at 3020 [size=32]
```

```
        Memory at 92f6b000 (32-bit, non-prefetchable) [size=2K]
        Capabilities: [80] MSI: Enable+ Count=1/1 Maskable- 64bit-
        Capabilities: [70] Power Management version 3
        Capabilities: [a8] SATA HBA v1.0
        Kernel driver in use: ahci
<SNIP>
00:1f.2 Memory controller: Intel Corporation 200 Series/Z370 Chipset Family
Power Management Controller
        Subsystem: ASUSTeK Computer Inc. Device 873c
        Flags: fast devsel, NUMA node 0
        Memory at 92f44000 (32-bit, non-prefetchable) [disabled] [size=16K]
<SNIP>
65:00.0 VGA compatible controller: Advanced Micro Devices, Inc. [AMD/ATI]
Barts XT [Radeon HD 6870] (prog-if
00 [VGA controller])
        Subsystem: Gigabyte Technology Co., Ltd Device 21fa
        Flags: bus master, fast devsel, latency 0, IRQ 42, NUMA node 0
        Memory at c0000000 (64-bit, prefetchable) [size=256M]
        Memory at d8e20000 (64-bit, non-prefetchable) [size=128K]
        I/O ports at b000 [size=256]
        Expansion ROM at 000c0000 [disabled] [size=128K]
        Capabilities: [50] Power Management version 3
        Capabilities: [58] Express Legacy Endpoint, MSI 00
        Capabilities: [a0] MSI: Enable+ Count=1/1 Maskable- 64bit+
        Capabilities: [100] Vendor Specific Information: ID=0001 Rev=1
        Len=010 <?>
        Capabilities: [150] Advanced Error Reporting
        Kernel driver in use: radeon
        Kernel modules: radeon
<SNIP>
```

Now try this to get a tree view:

```
[root@studentvm1 ~]# lspci -tv
```

The motherboard chipset information provided by the lspci tool can be used to determine memory and CPU compatibility. It could also be used to help determine whether to purchase a used computer or explore a new one without having to take it apart.

Cleanup

Let's clean up a little. We no longer need the physical printer, so we can disable it and remove it from the VM.

CLEANUP

Perform this cleanup as root – disable the printer. Be sure to use the correct printer name for your physical printer:

```
[root@studentvm1 spool]# cupsdisable  MFC-9340CDW
```

Refer to Figure 26-1 if necessary and remove the check mark from the printer so that it is no longer associated with the VM.

Chapter Summary

The commands we have explored in this chapter can provide an easy way to examine the hardware components of any computer. It is possible to discover information about a computer that cannot be obtained even by taking it apart. If the computer does not have Linux installed, just boot to a live Linux USB thumb drive and use these tools to examine the hardware in detail not available in any other way. I have used these tools as part of a first look when people have asked me to "fix" their computers or when making a determination of whether I wanted to purchase a specific model that was on display at the local computer store.

All of this information is available using the /proc and /sys filesystems, but these tools make it easier because you don't need to search for it.

Exercises

Perform the following exercises to complete this chapter:

1. What is the motherboard serial number of your VM?

2. What type of device is reported by DMI type 5?

3. Why do you think that external devices like printers, pointing devices, and keyboards show up in the `lshw` data but not in the DMI database?

4. What other devices are missing from the DMI database that appear in the `lshw` output?

5. What make and model of Ethernet controller is virtualized for your VM?

6. What happens to the queue for the physical printer if you disconnect the printer from the VM without first having disabled the queue?

7. What happens if a print job is then sent to an enabled print queue that has no printer?

## CHAPTER 28

Command-Line Programming

Objectives

In this chapter you will learn

- A definition for command-line programs

- To create Bash command-line programs

- To use logical comparisons to alter the execution path of command-line programs

- To use "for" loops to iterate over a code segment of a specified list of items

- To use "while" and "until" to loop over a portion of code a specified number of times

Introduction

We have already used command-line programs in earlier chapters of this course. Those were all fairly simple and straightforward with simple requirements. There are many times when SysAdmins create simple command-line programs to perform a series of tasks. They are a common tool and can save time and effort.

My personal objective when writing CLI programs is to save time and to "be the lazy SysAdmin." CLI programs allow me to accomplish this by listing several commands in a specific sequence so that they will execute one after another. As a result I do not

D. Both, *Using and Administering Linux: Volume 2,* https://doi.org/10.1007/978-1-4842-9615-8_28

need to watch the progress of one command and, when it has finished, type in the next command. I can go do other things and not be concerned about having to continually monitor the progress of each command.

It is not possible to include a complete training course on Bash command-line programming and shell scripts in this course, which is already quite lengthy. This chapter and the next one are intended as an introduction to these concepts and many of the tools available for Bash programming. There are numerous books and courses available that do provide in-depth instruction on Bash usage and programming and, if you are interested, you should use one of those to learn more.

Also, I do not set up some sort of bogus objective to provide a framework for building an application that you will never use. I find that my best learning experiences are when I am working on my own projects. My objective in this chapter is to introduce you to many of the typical forms and structures used in Bash command-line programming and scripts. When you encounter a task that requires CLI programming or a script, you will likely remember that you have seen a method for accomplishing that task and at least know where to start looking for details.

One excellent source is the Bash manual,[1] which can be found at `www.gnu.org` and which is sponsored by the Free Software Foundation (FSF) at `www.fsf.org/`. This free manual is available in many formats and can be downloaded or browsed online.

Definition of a Program

Let's define what we mean by a program. The Free On-line Dictionary of Computing[2] (FOLDOC) defines a program as "the instructions executed by a computer, as opposed to the physical device on which they run." Other sources such as Princeton University's WordNet[3] define a program as "...a sequence of instructions that a computer can interpret and execute ..." Wikipedia also has a good article about computer programs.[4]

---

[1] GNU, `www.gnu.org/software/bash/manual/`

[2] You can install the "dict" package and then use the command dict <word> to look up any word – without the <>. Results are presented from one or more of several online dictionaries including the FOLDOC. Or you can go to `http://foldoc.org/` to look up computing terms. I find it helpful to use the dict command, which enables me to see multiple definitions for many terms.

[3] WordNet, `https://wordnet.princeton.edu/`

[4] Wikipedia, Computer Program, `https://en.wikipedia.org/wiki/Computer_program`

Based on these definitions, a program can consist of one or more instructions that perform a specific related task. A computer program instruction is also called a program statement. For SysAdmins, a program is usually a sequence of shell commands. All of the shells available for Linux, at least the ones with which I am familiar, have at least some basic form of programming capability and Bash, the default shell for most Linux distributions, is no exception. This chapter uses Bash because it is so ubiquitous. You may already prefer or later learn about and come to prefer a different shell. If so, the programming concepts will be the same though the constructs and syntax may differ. Some shells may support some features that others do not. But they all provide some programming capability.

These shell programs can be stored in a file for repeated use, or they may be simply created on an ad hoc basis at the command line as needed. In this chapter we will start working directly at the command line. In Chapter 29, we will discuss storing our simple programs in files for sharing and reuse and more complex and lengthy programs.

Simple CLI Programs

The simplest command-line programs are one or two consecutive program statements, which may be related or not, that are entered on the command line before the Enter key is pressed. For example, the second statement, if there is one, may be dependent upon the actions of the first, but it does not need to be.

There is also one bit of syntactical punctuation that needs to be clearly stated. When entering a single command on the command line, pressing the Enter key terminates the command with an implicit semicolon (;). When used in a CLI shell program entered on the command line, the semicolon must be used to terminate each statement and separate it from the next one. The last statement in a CLI shell program can use an explicit or implicit semicolon.

Some Basic Syntax

Let's look at a couple examples that will clarify this syntax. All of the experiments in this chapter should be performed as the student user.

EXPERIMENT 28-1: BASIC SYNTAX FOR BASH PROGRAMS

For now we will use the explicit semicolon to terminate our program statements. The echo command is used to print data to the screen. This terminology is a legacy of the old teletype machines when all of the output from a program was printed to a roll of paper.

First, ensure that we are in the student user's home directory. Then enter the following program:

```
[student@studentvm1 ~]$ echo "Hello world." ;
Hello world.
```

That may not seem like much of a program, but it is the same first program I have encountered with every new programming language I have ever learned. The syntax may be a bit different for each language, but the result is the same.

Let's expand on this trivial but ubiquitous program a little:

```
[student@studentvm1 ~]$ echo "Hello world." ; ls ;
Hello world.
chapter25    cpuHog.Linux  dmesg2.txt  Downloads  newfile.txt  softlink1  testdir6
chapter26    cpuHog.mac    dmesg3.txt  file005    Pictures     Templates  testdir7
cpuHog       Desktop       dmesg.txt   link3      Public       testdir    Videos
cpuHog.dos   dmesg1.txt    Documents   Music      random.txt   testdir1
```

Okay …that is interesting, but the initial statement is not very meaningful in this context, so let's change it a bit:

```
[student@studentvm1 ~]$ echo "My home directory." ; ls ;
My home directory.
chapter25    cpuHog.Linux  dmesg2.txt  Downloads  newfile.txt  softlink1  testdir6
chapter26    cpuHog.mac    dmesg3.txt  file005    Pictures     Templates  testdir7
cpuHog       Desktop       dmesg.txt   link3      Public       testdir    Videos
cpuHog.dos   dmesg1.txt    Documents   Music      random.txt   testdir1
```

That makes a bit more sense. The results are related, but the individual program statements are independent of each other. Notice that I like spaces before and after the semicolon, which makes the code a bit easier to read. Try this little CLI program again without an explicit semicolon at the end:

```
[student@studentvm1 ~]$ echo "My home directory." ; ls
```

There is no difference in the output data.

Output to the Display

Many CLI programs are intended to produce output of some type. The **echo** command is commonly used in a simple manner as seen in Experiment 28-1. We can use the -e option to enable escape codes that allow us to do a little more complex output. For example, we might want to print multiple lines of output. It is not necessary to use multiple **echo** commands to do this.

EXPERIMENT 28-2: OUTPUT TO THE SCREEN

Enter and run the following single-statement program:

```
[student@studentvm1 ~]$ echo "Twinkle, twinkle, little star How I wonder what
you are Up above the world so high Like a diamond in the sky" ;
Twinkle, twinkle, little star How I wonder what you are Up above the world so
high Like a diamond in the sky
```

We could break it up into four separate **echo** statements to show the structure of the poem, like this:

```
[student@studentvm1 ~]$ echo "Twinkle, twinkle, little star" ; echo "How
I wonder what you are" ; echo "Up above the world so high" ; echo "Like a
diamond in the sky" ;
Twinkle, twinkle, little star
How I wonder what you are
Up above the world so high
Like a diamond in the sky
```

But this next method is, if not easier, at least cleaner:

```
[student@studentvm1 ~]$ echo -e "Twinkle, twinkle, little star\nHow I wonder
what you are\nUp above the world so high\nLike a diamond in the sky\n" ;
Twinkle, twinkle, little star
How I wonder what you are
Up above the world so high
Like a diamond in the sky
```

This method of using a single echo command to print multiple lines can save typing as well so that we can be the lazy SysAdmin. In this case, 19 characters fewer are required. It not only saves typing; it also saves disk space, memory space, and CPU time. One command executes faster than four. I know that these are all relatively cheap commodities these days, but many of us inherit or are gifted with perfectly good, old computers whose specifications are not nearly as generous as newer ones we might purchase.

In my book *The Linux Philosophy for SysAdmins*,[5] I devote a whole chapter to simplicity. One command is always simpler than four commands.

The `printf` (print formatted) command provides even more capabilities because it allows more complex data formatting. It can do the same thing as we did earlier, too, because it recognizes the same escape codes, but without needing an option:

```
[student@studentvm1 ~]$ printf "Twinkle, twinkle, little star\nHow I wonder
what you are\nUp above the world so high\nLike a diamond in the sky\n" ;
Twinkle, twinkle, little star
How I wonder what you are
Up above the world so high
Like a diamond in the sky
```

The printf command can also use all of the C language printf format specifications so that very complex formats such as numerical field widths, decimal precision, and locale formatting can be specified. Those capabilities are beyond the scope of this course, but details can be found using the `man 3 printf` command.

The echo man page contains a complete list of the escape codes that it recognizes.

---

[5] Both, David, *The Linux Philosophy for SysAdmins*, Apress, 2018, Chapter 18

Something About Variables

Like all programming languages, the Bash shell can deal with variables. A variable is a symbolic name that refers to a specific location in memory that contains a value of some sort. The value of a variable is changeable, that is, it is variable.

Bash does not type variables like C and related languages, defining them as integers, floating point, or string types. In Bash, all variables are strings. A string that is an integer can be used in integer arithmetic, which is all that Bash has the capability of doing. If more complex math is required, the bc command can be used in CLI programs and scripts.

Variables are assigned values and can then be used to refer to this values in CLI programs and scripts. The value of a variable is set using its name but not preceded by a $ sign. The assignment VAR=10 sets the value of the variable VAR to 10. To print the value of the variable, we can use the statement echo $VAR. Let's start with text variables, that is, non-numeric.

Bash variables become part of the shell environment until they are unset.

EXPERIMENT 28-3: INTRODUCING VARIABLES

To start, we check the initial value of a variable that has not been assigned. It should be null. Then we will assign a value to the variable and print it to verify its value. We will do all of this in a single CLI program:

Note   The syntax of variable assignment is very strict. There must be no spaces on either side of the equal (=) sign in the assignment statement.

```
[student@studentvm1 ~]$ echo $MyVar ; MyVar="Hello World" ; echo $MyVar ;

Hello World
```

The empty line indicates that the initial value of MyVar is null. Changing the value of a variable is the same as setting it in the first place. In this example we can see both the original and the new value:

```
[student@studentvm1 ~]$ echo $MyVar ; MyVar="Hello World; Welcome to Linux" ;
echo $MyVar ;
```

```
Hello World
Hello World; Welcome to Linux
```

Variables can also be "unset" and returned to a null value:

```
[student@studentvm1 ~]$ unset MyVar ; echo $MyVar ;

[student@studentvm1 ~]$
```

Text string variables can also be combined in various ways:

```
[student@studentvm1 ~]$ Var1="Hello World!" ; Var2="Welcome to Bash CLI
programming." ; printf "$Var1\n$Var2\n" ;
Hello World!
Welcome to Bash CLI programming.
```

Note that these variables remain set in the shell environment until they are unset as we did with $MyVar:

Note   I will no longer use the explicit semicolon (;) at the end of a command-line program and will rely on the one implied by pressing the Enter key at the end of the line.

```
[student@studentvm1 ~]$ echo "$Var1 $Var2"
Hello World! Welcome to Bash CLI programming.
[student@studentvm1 ~]$ set | grep Var
Var1='Hello World!'
Var2='Welcome to Bash CLI programming.'
```

Reliance upon specific variables to already be set in the shell environment from one instance of running a CLI program to the next is poor practice. It is usually a best practice to set those variables needed by a program within the program itself – unless the intent is to check the current value of a shell variable.

Now let's look at doing a bit of math in Bash. As I have mentioned, Bash can only perform integer math, but that can be sufficient for many purposes. In this little program, we reassign $Var1 and $Var2 and then use them in a Bash integer calculation:

```
$ Var1="7" ; Var2="9" ; echo "Result = $((Var1*Var2))"
Result = 63
```

What happens when we perform a math operation that results in a floating point number?

```
$ Var1="7" ; Var2="9" ; echo "Result = $((Var1/Var2))"
Result = 0
$ Var1="7" ; Var2="9" ; echo "Result = $((Var2/Var1))"
Result = 1
```

The result is the nearest integer. Be sure to notice that the calculation was performed as part of the echo statement; no intermediate result is required, but we could have done something like the following if we wanted to keep the result for use more than once in a later part of the program:

```
$ Var1="7" ; Var2="9" ; Result=$((Var1*Var2)) ; echo "Result = $Result"
Result = 63
```

Use variables wherever possible in CLI programs instead of hard-coded values. Even if you think you will only use a particular value once, such as a directory name or a file name, create a variable and use the variable where you would have placed the hard-coded name.

Control Operators

Shell control operators are one of the syntactical operators that allow us to create some interesting command-line programs. We have seen that the simplest form of CLI program is just stringing several commands together in a sequence on the command line:

```
command1 ; command2 ; command3 ; command4 ; . . . ; etc. ;
```

Those commands will all run without a problem so long as no errors occur. But what happens when an error occurs? We can anticipate and allow for errors using the && and || built-in bash control operators. These two control operators provide us with some flow control and enable us to alter the sequence of code execution. The semicolon is also considered to be a bash control operator as is the newline character.

The && operator simply says that if command1 is successful, then run command2. If command1 fails for any reason, then command2 is skipped. That syntax looks like this:

```
command1 && command2
```

Return Codes

The command1 && command2 syntax works because every command sends a return code (RC) to the shell that indicates whether it completed successfully or whether there was some type of failure during execution. By convention, a return code of zero (0) indicates success, and any positive number indicates some type of failure. Some of the tools we use as SysAdmins return only a one (1) to indicate a failure, but many can return other codes as well to further indicate the type of failure that occurred.

The bash shell has a variable, $?, which contains the return code from the last command. This return code can be checked very easily by a script, the next command in a list of commands, or even us SysAdmins.

EXPERIMENT 28-4: RETURN CODES

Let's look at return codes. We can run a simple command and then immediately check the return code. The return code will always be for the last command that was run before we look at it:

```
[student@studentvm1 ~]$ ll ; echo "RC = $?"
total 1264
drwxrwxr-x  2 student student    4096 Mar  2 08:21 chapter25
drwxrwxr-x  2 student student    4096 Mar 21 15:27 chapter26
-rwxr-xr-x  1 student student      92 Mar 20 15:53 cpuHog
<snip>
drwxrwxr-x. 2 student student 663552 Feb 21 14:12 testdir7
drwxr-xr-x. 2 student student   4096 Dec 22 13:15 Videos
RC = 0
[student@studentvm1 ~]$
```

The return code (RC) in this case is zero (0), which means the command completed successfully. Now try the same command on a directory for which we do not have permissions, root's home directory:

```
[student@studentvm1 ~]$ ll /root ; echo "RC = $?"
ls: cannot open directory '/root': Permission denied
RC = 2
[student@studentvm1 ~]$
```

In this case the return code is 2, which specifically means that permission was denied for a non-root user to access a directory to which the user is not permitted access. The control operators use these return codes to enable us to alter the sequence of program execution.

The Operators

Let's try the control operators as they might be used in a command-line program. In this simple case, we want to create a new directory and add a new, empty file to it. We are also using a variable, $Dir, to store the directory name.

EXPERIMENT 28-5: USING CONTROL OPERATORS

Start with something simple. Our objective is to create a new directory and create a file in it. We only want to create the file if the directory has been created successfully:

```
$ Dir=chapter28 ; mkdir $Dir && touch $Dir/testfile1 ; ll $Dir
total 0
drwxr-xr-x  2 student student      4096 Mar  3 06:31 chapter28
```

Everything worked as it should because the chapter28 directory is accessible and writable.

Does the $Dir variable still exist in the environment?

Change the permissions on chapter28 so it is no longer accessible to the student user:

```
$ chmod 076 $Dir ; ls -l | grep $Dir
drwxr-xr-x  2 student student      4096 Mar  3 06:31 chapter28
```

You can see from the listing that the user student no longer has any access to the chapter28 directory. Now let's run some commands that will create a new directory in the chapter28 directory and then – if the new directory creation is successful – will create a new file in that subdirectory. This time we will also use the && control operator:

```
$ mkdir $Dir/subdirectory && touch $Dir/subdirectory/testfile
mkdir: cannot create directory 'chapter28/subdirectory': Permission denied
```

The error seen in the preceding example was emitted by the `mkdir` command. We did not receive an error indicating that the file could not be created because creation of the directory failed. The && control operator sensed the non-zero return code so the `touch` command was skipped. Using the && control operator prevents the `touch` command from running because there was an error in creating the directory. This type of command-line program flow control can prevent errors from compounding and making a real mess of things. Let's get a little more complicated.

The ‖ control operator allows us to add another program statement that executes when the initial program statement returns a code greater than zero. The basic syntax looks like this:

```
command1 || command2
```

This syntax reads, if command1 fails, execute command2. That implies that if command1 succeeds, command2 is skipped. Let's try this with our attempt to create a new directory:

```
$ mkdir $Dir/subdirectory || echo "New directory $Dir was not created."
mkdir: cannot create directory 'chapter28/subdirectory': Permission denied
New directory chapter28 was not created.
```

This is exactly what we expected. Because the new directory could not be created, the first command failed, which resulted in the execution of the second command.

Combining these two operators gives us the best of both. Our control operator syntax using some flow control now takes this general form when we use the && and ‖ control operators:

```
preceding commands ; command1 && command2 || command3 ; following commands
```

This syntax can be stated like so: if command1 exits with a return code of 0, then execute command2; otherwise, execute command3. Let's try it:

```
$ mkdir $Dir/subdirectory && touch $Dir/subdirectory/testfile || echo "New
directory $Dir was not created."
mkdir: cannot create directory 'chapter28/subdirectory': Permission denied
New directory chapter28 was not created.
```

Now reset the permissions on ~/chapter28 to 755 and try this last command again:

```
[student@studentvm1 ~]$ chmod 766 $Dir
[student@studentvm1 ~]$ mkdir $Dir/subdirectory && touch $Dir/subdirectory/
testfile || echo "New directory $Dir was not created."
[student@studentvm1 ~]$ ll $Dir/subdirectory/
```

```
total 0
-rw-r--r-- 1 student student 0 Mar  3 06:41 testfile
[student@studentvm1 ~]$
```

The program using the control operators may be preceded and followed by other commands that can be related to the ones in the flow control section but that are unaffected by the flow control. All of the preceding and following commands will execute without regard to anything that takes place inside the flow control command.

Also, once the $Dir variable was set, it remains in the environment for use by other CLI programs and commands. It will remain there until it is unset or the terminal session is terminated.

These control operators provide us some interesting and powerful capabilities for doing program flow control on the command line, and they can also be used in scripts. I use these operators quite frequently both on the command line and in scripts because …automate everything.

Commands that use these operators for flow control are also called compound commands.

Program Flow Control

Program flow control structure is flexible and can be adjusted to meet needs ranging from very simple to quite complex. Every programming language I have ever used has some form of an "if" flow control structure, and Bash is no exception. The Bash if statement can be used to test whether a condition is true or false in order to determine which execution path to take. This flow control structure is flexible and can be adjusted to meet needs ranging from very simple to quite complex.

We will start with some simple examples and move up in complexity. However, this structure can be less suitable for use in CLI programs as it becomes more complex. So we will keep things fairly simple here.

The logical syntax for this control statement is

```
if condition1; then list1; [ elif condition2; then list2; ] ...
[ else list3; ] fi
```

where "condition" is a list of one or more conditions to be tested and "list" is a list of shell program statements that are to be executed if the condition is true. The elif and else phrases in this construct are optional. I like to read this syntax as: if condition1 is true, then execute the statements in list1, or else if condition2 is true, then execute the statements in list2, or else execute the statements in list3.

The fi statement at the end of the if control statement provides an explicit syntactical ending to the if statement. It is not optional.

Regardless of how many conditional expressions are contained in an if-elif...else compound command, only one list of program statements is executed, the ones associated with the first conditional to return "true."

true and false

Before we get further into the subject of flow control, we need to explicitly define some things that were not always made clear when I was learning Unix and Linux.

First, there is always only one return code that indicates "true" or "success." Zero (0) is always returned when a command or program completes successfully. Any positive integer when used as a return code represents an error, or a failure, with the specific number representing a particular type of error. For logical operations zero (0) is always true and one (1) is always false.

And of course, because Linux is so amazingly cool, it has two commands that can be used for testing or for obtaining specific true or false return code results in a CLI program or a script. What do you think they are? Naturally, they are true and false. The true command always generates a return code of zero (0), which is true, and the false command always generates a return code of one (1), which is false.

EXPERIMENT 28-6: THE TRUE AND FALSE COMMANDS

Let's just look at the return codes from the true and false commands. Remember that the shell variable $? always contains the return code from the last command that was run:

```
[student@studentvm1 ~]$ true ; echo $?
0
[student@studentvm1 ~]$ false ; echo $?
1
```

Now let's use true and false with the control operators with which we are already familiar:

```
[student@studentvm1 ~]$ true && echo "True" || echo "False"
True
[student@studentvm1 ~]$ false && echo "True" || echo "False"
False
```

I frequently use these two simple commands to test the logic of a complex command with control operators when I absolutely need to know whether the RC was true or false.

Logical Operators

Bash has a large set of logical operators that can be used in conditional expressions. The most basic form of the **if** control structure is to test for a condition and then execute a list of program statements if the condition is true. There are three types of operators, file, numeric, and non-numeric operators. Each operator returns true (0) as its return code if the condition is met and false (1) if the condition is not met.

The operators and their descriptions are listed in the following and are taken from the Bash man page. I have added some additional explanations in some instances to help clarify the meanings.

Syntax

The functional syntax of these comparison operators is one or two arguments with an operator that are placed within square braces and then a list of program statements that are executed if the condition is true and an optional list of program statements if the condition is false:

```
if [ arg1 operator arg2 ] ; then list
```

or

```
if [ arg1 operator arg2 ] ; then list ; else list ; fi
```

The spaces in the comparison are required as shown. The single square braces, [and], are the traditional Bash symbols that are equivalent to the **test** command:

```
if test arg1 operator arg2 ; then list
```

There is also a more recent syntax that offers a few advantages and that some SysAdmins prefer. This format is a bit less compatible with different versions of Bash and other shells such as ksh (Korn shell):

```
if [[ arg1 operator arg2 ]] ; then list
```

File Operators

File operators provide easy determination of various file tests. For example, these tests can determine whether a file exists and is empty or contains some data or whether it is a regular file, a link, or a directory. These operators can also be used to detect various attributes such as user and group ID (ownership) and file permissions.

Figure 28-1 lists these file operators.

Operator	Description
-a filename	True if the file exists. It can be empty or have some content but so long as it exists this will be true.
-b filename	True if file exists and is a block special file such as a hard drive like /dev/sda or /dev/sda1.
-c filename	True if the file exists and is a character special file such as a TTY device like /dev/TTY1.
-d filename	This is true if the file exists and is a directory.
-e filename	True if file exists. This is the same as -a, above.
-f filename	True if the file exists and is a regular file as opposed to a directory a device special file or a link, among others.
-g filename	True if the file exists and is set-group-id, SETGID.
-h filename	This is true if file exists and is a symbolic link.
-k filename	True if file exists and its ``sticky'' bit is set.
-p filename	True if file exists and is a named pipe (FIFO).
-r filename	True if file exists and is readable, that is, has its read bit set.
-s filename	True if file exists and has a size greater than zero. A file that exists but that has a size of zero will return false.
-t fd	True if the file descriptor fd is open and refers to a terminal.
-u filename	True if file exists and its set-user-id bit is set.
-w filename	True if file exists and is writable.
-x filename	True if file exists and is executable.
-G filename	True if file exists and is owned by the effective group id.
-L filename	True if file exists and is a symbolic link.
-N filename	True if file exists and has been modified since it was last read.
-O filename	True if file exists and is owned by the effective user id.
-S filename	True if file exists and is a socket.
file1 -ef file2	True if file1 and file2 refer to the same device and iNode numbers.
file1 -nt file2	True if file1 is newer (according to modification date) than file2, or if file1 exists and file2 does not.
file1 -ot file2	True if file1 is older than file2, or if file2 exists and file1 does not.

Figure 28-1. *File operators*

Let's explore a few of these file operators to get an idea for how we might use them in CLI programs and scripts.

EXPERIMENT 28-7: USING FILE OPERATORS

You should already have the files needed for this experiment in your home directory. Make your home directory the PWD.

First, we simply look to see if a file exists:

```
[student@studentvm1 ~]$ File="cpuHog" ; if [ -e $File ] ; then echo "The file
$File exists." ; fi
The file cpuHog exists.
```

or

```
[student@studentvm1 ~]$ File="cpuHog" ; if [[ -e $File ]] ; then echo "The
file $File exists." ; fi
The file cpuHog exists.
```

or

```
[student@studentvm1 ~]$ File="cpuHog" ; if test -e $File ; then echo "The
file $File exists." ; fi
The file cpuHog exists.
```

Now add a bit of code in case the file does not exist. In this case it does exist, so the end result is the same as the previous test:

```
[student@studentvm1 ~]$ File="cpuHog" ; if [ -e $File ] ; then echo "The file
$File exists." ; else echo "The file $File does not exist." ; fi
The file cpuHog exists.
```

But let's change the file name to one that we know does not exist. And note how easy it is to change the value of the $File variable rather than a text string for the file name in multiple locations in this short CLI program:

```
[student@studentvm1 ~]$ File="Non-ExistentFile" ; if [ -e $File ] ; then echo
"The file $File exists." ; else echo "The file $File does not exist." ; fi
The file Non-ExistentFile does not exist.
```

Now let's determine whether a file exists and has a non-zero length, which means it contains data. We will work in the ~/chapter28 directory for this. We have three conditions we want to test for, so we need a more complex set of tests. The three conditions are (1) the file does not exist, (2) the file exists and is empty, and (3) the file exists and contains data. To accomplish this we need to use the elif stanza in the if-elif-else construct to test for all of the conditions. But let's build up the logic a step at a time.

Make chapter28 the PWD. Our first step is to simply see if the file exists or not and print a message to STDOUT if it does:

```
[student@studentvm1 chapter28]$ File="Exp-9-7" ; if [ -s $File ] ; then echo
"$File exists and contains data." ; fi
[student@studentvm1 chapter28]$
```

We get no output because the file does not exist and we have not added an explicit test for that. The other possibility in the real world is that the file exists but does not contain data. But let's create the empty file first and see what happens:

```
[student@studentvm1 chapter28]$ File="Exp-9-7" ; touch $File ; if
[ -s $File ] ; then echo "$File exists and contains data." ; fi
[student@studentvm1 chapter28]$
```

In this case, the file exists but does not contain any data. Let's add some data and try again:

```
[student@studentvm1 chapter28]$ File="Exp-9-7" ; echo "This is file $File" >
$File ; if [ -s $File ] ; then echo "$File exists and contains data." ; fi
Exp-9-7 exists and contains data.
[student@studentvm1 chapter28]$
```

That works, but it is only truly accurate for one specific condition out of the three possible ones we have identified. Let's add an else stanza so we can be somewhat more accurate and delete the file so that we can fully test this new code:

```
[student@studentvm1 chapter28]$ File="Exp-9-7" ; rm $File ; if [ -s $File ] ;
then echo "$File exists and contains data." ; else echo "$File does not exist
or is empty." ; fi
Exp-9-7 does not exist or is empty.
```

Now let's create an empty file to test:

```
[student@studentvm1 chapter28]$ File="Exp-9-7" ; touch $File ; if [ -s $File
] ; then echo "$File exists and contains data." ; else echo "$File does not
exist or is empty." ; fi
Exp-9-7 does not exist or is empty.
[student@studentvm1 chapter28]$
```

Finally, let's add some content to the file and test again:

```
[student@studentvm1 chapter28]$ File="Exp-9-7" ; echo "This is file $File" >
$File ; if [ -s $File ] ; then echo "$File exists and contains data." ; else
echo "$File does not exist or is empty." ; fi
Exp-9-7 exists and contains data.
[student@studentvm1 chapter28]$
```

Now we add the elif stanza to discriminate between a file that does not exist and one that is empty:

```
[student@studentvm1 chapter28]$ File="Exp-9-7" ; rm $File ; touch $File ;
if [ -s $File ] ; then echo "$File exists and contains data." ; elif [ -e
$File ] ; then echo "$File exists and is empty." ; else echo "$File does not
exist." ; fi
Exp-9-7 exists and is empty.
[student@studentvm1 chapter28]$ File="Exp-9-7" ; echo "This is $File" >
$File ; if [ -s $File ] ; then echo "$File exists and contains data." ;
elif [ -e $File ] ; then echo "$File exists and is empty." ; else echo "$File
does not exist." ; fi
Exp-9-7 exists and contains data.
[student@studentvm1 chapter28]$
```

So now we have a Bash CLI program that can test for these three different conditions, but the possibilities are endless.

It is easier to see the logic structure of the more complex compound commands like we used in Experiment 28-7 if we arrange the program statements more like we would in a script that we saved in a file. Figure 28-2 shows how this would look. The indents of the program statements in each stanza of the if-elif-else structure help clarify the logic.

Note that we are not using explicit statement termination with semicolons because we are using ones implicit in a newline at the end of each statement. In this example each program statement is on a line by itself. We also used a variable for the file name because it appears in seven places in this little program.

```
File="Exp-9-7"
echo "This is $File" > $File
if [ -s $File ]
    then
    echo "$File exists and contains data."
elif [ -e $File ]
    then
    echo "$File exists and is empty."
else
    echo "$File does not exist."
fi
```

Figure 28-2. *This line-by-line listing of the Bash CLI program we used in Experiment 28-7 enables us to see the logic more clearly*

Logic of this complexity becomes too lengthy for most CLI programs. Although any Linux or Bash built-in commands may be used in CLI programs, as the CLI programs get longer and more complex, it makes sense to create a script that is stored in a file and that can be executed at any time now or in the future. We will explore scripts in more detail in the next chapter.

String Comparison Operators

String comparison operators enable comparison of alphanumeric strings of characters. There are only a few of these operators, which are listed in Figure 28-3.

Operator	Description
-z string	True if the length of string is zero.
-n string	True if the length of string is non-zero.
string1 == string2 or string1 = string2	True if the strings are equal. = should be used with the test command for POSIX conformance. When used with the [[command, this performs pattern matching as described above (Compound Commands)
string1 != string2	True if the strings are not equal.
string1 < string2	True if string1 sorts before string2 lexicographically[6].
string1 > string2	True if string1 sorts after string2 lexicographically.

Figure 28-3. *Bash string comparison logical operators*

EXPERIMENT 28-8: STRING COMPARISON OPERATORS

It can be useful to know whether a string has a value or is null! – zero length – so let's look at how we can do that. Notice that the quotes around $MyVar in the comparison itself must be there for the comparison to work. The -z option simply looks to see whether the variable is of zero length:

```
[student@studentvm1 ~]$ MyVar="" ; if [ -z $MyVar ] ; then echo "MyVar is
zero length." ; else echo "MyVar contains data" ; fi
MyVar is zero length.
[student@studentvm1 ~]$ MyVar="Random text" ; if [ -z $MyVar ] ; then echo
"MyVar is zero length." ; else echo "MyVar contains data" ; fi
-bash: [: Random: binary operator expected
MyVar contains data
```

---

[6] Refers to locale-specific sorting sequences for all alphanumeric and special characters.

Notice the error in this result even though the logic works as expected. Try the same thing but using the double square braces; we get a correct result without the error:

```
[student@studentvm1 chapter28]$ MyVar="Random text" ; if [[ -z $MyVar ]] ;
then echo "MyVar is zero length." ; else echo "MyVar contains data" ; fi
MyVar contains data
```

We could also do it this way. The -n option is a check for a non-zero length:

```
[student@studentvm1 ~]$ MyVar="Random text" ; if [[ -n "$MyVar" ]] ; then
echo "MyVar contains data." ; else echo "MyVar is zero length" ; fi
MyVar contains data.
[student@studentvm1 ~]$ MyVar="" ; if [[ -n "$MyVar" ]] ; then echo "MyVar
contains data." ; else echo "MyVar is zero length" ; fi
MyVar is zero length
```

Since we are already talking about strings and whether they are zero or non-zero length, it might make sense that we sometimes need to know the exact length. Although this is not a comparison, it is related to them.

Unfortunately there is no simple way to determine the length of a string with Bash. There are a couple ways to do this, but I think using the expr (evaluate expression) is the easiest. Read the man page for expr for more of what it can do. Quotes are required around the string or variable being tested:

```
[student@studentvm1 ~]$ MyVar="" ; expr length "$MyVar"
0
[student@studentvm1 ~]$ MyVar="How long is this?" ; expr length "$MyVar"
17
[student@studentvm1 ~]$ expr length "We can also find the length of a literal
string as well as a variable."
70
```

Back to our comparison operators. I use a lot of testing in my scripts to determine whether two strings are equal, that is, identical. I use the non-POSIX version of this comparison operator:

```
[student@studentvm1 ~]$ Var1="Hello World" ; Var2="Hello World" ; if [
"$Var1" == "$Var2" ] ; then echo "Var1 matches Var2" ; else echo "Var1 and
Var2 do not match." ; fi
Var1 matches Var2
```

Change Var2 to "Hello world":

```
[student@studentvm1 ~]$ Var1="Hello World" ; Var2="Hello world" ; if [
"$Var1" == "$Var2" ] ; then echo "Var1 matches Var2" ; else echo "Var1 and
Var2 do not match." ; fi
Var1 and Var2 do not match.
```

Take some time to experiment with these comparisons.

Numeric Comparison Operators

These logical operators make comparisons between two numeric arguments. Similar to the other operators we have looked at, these can use the result to determine the flow of execution.

Like the other operator classes, most of these are easy to understand.

Operator	Description
arg1 -eq arg2	True if arg1 equals arg2.
arg1 -ne arg	True if arg1 is not equal to arg2.
arg1 -lt arg2	True if arg1 is less than arg2.
arg1 -le arg2	True if arg1 is less than or equal to arg2.
arg1 -gt arg2	True if arg1 is greater than arg2.
arg1 -ge arg2	True if arg1 is greater than or equal to arg2.

Figure 28-4. *Bash numeric comparison logical operators*

EXPERIMENT 28-9: EXPLORING NUMERIC COMPARISON LOGICAL OPERATORS

Let's start with some simple examples in this experiment. In the first instance, we set the variable $X to 1 and then test to see if $X is equal to 1. It is, so the message does get printed. In the second instance, X is set to 0, so the comparison is not true and the message is not printed:

```
[student@studentvm1 ~]$ X=1 ; if [ $X -eq 1 ] ; then echo "X equals 1" ; fi
X equals 1
[student@studentvm1 ~]$ X=0 ; if [ $X -eq 1 ] ; then echo "X equals 1" ; fi
[student@studentvm1 ~]$
```

Let's add an else stanza to this:

```
[student@studentvm1 ~]$ X=1 ; if [ $X -eq 1 ] ; then echo "X equals 1" ; else echo "X does not equal 1" ; fi
X equals 1
```

Change the value of $X to 0 (zero):

```
[student@studentvm1 ~]$ X=0 ; if [ $X -eq 1 ] ; then echo "X equals 1" ; else echo "X does not equal 1" ; fi
X does not equal 1
[student@studentvm1 ~]$
```

We used "-eq," which is a numeric comparison operator. We could have used "==" for a string comparison. The functional result would be the same in this case, but string comparisons can't deal with tests like less than or greater than:

```
[student@studentvm1 ~]$ X=0 ; if [ $X == 1 ] ; then echo "X equals 1" ; else echo "X does not equal 1" ; fi
X does not equal 1
[student@studentvm1 ~]$ X=1 ; if [ $X == 1 ] ; then echo "X equals 1" ; else echo "X does not equal 1" ; fi
X equals 1
[student@studentvm1 ~]$
```

We can also invert the meaning of the comparison using the ! character. We also must change the then and else lists:

```
[student@studentvm1 ~]$ X=0 ; if ! [ $X -eq 1 ] ; then echo "X does not equal
1" ; else echo "X equals 1" ; fi
X does not equal 1
[student@studentvm1 ~]$ X=1 ; if ! [ $X -eq 1 ] ; then echo "X does not equal
1" ; else echo "X equals 1" ; fi
X equals 1
[student@studentvm1 ~]$
```

And we also want to ensure that our logic works for other values of the variable $X as well:

```
[student@studentvm1 ~]$ X=7 ; if ! [ $X -eq 1 ] ; then echo "X does not equal
1" ; else echo "X equals 1" ; fi
X does not equal 1
[student@studentvm1 ~]$
```

Miscellaneous Operators

The miscellaneous operators in Figure 28-5 allow us to see if a shell option is set or a shell variable has a value, but they do not discover the value of the variable, just whether it has one.

Operator	Description
-o optname	True if the shell option optname is enabled. See the list of options under the description of the -o option to the Bash **set** builtin in the Bash man page.
-v varname	True if the shell variable varname is set (has been assigned a value).
-R varname	True if the shell variable varname is set and is a name reference.

Figure 28-5. *Miscellaneous Bash logical operators*

EXPERIMENT 28-10: MISCELLANEOUS LOGICAL OPERATORS

In this experiment we look to see if a variable has been set. Notice the unusual syntax; there are no quotes around Var1, and there is no $ to distinguish it as a variable rather than a fixed string. Just the use of -v and the syntax of the comparison tell Bash that Var1 is a variable:

```
[student@studentvm1 ~]$ Var1="Hello World" ; echo $Var1 ; if [ -v Var1 ] ;
then echo "Var1 has been assigned a value." ; else echo "Var1 does not have a
value." ; fi
Hello World
Var1 has been assigned a value.
[student@studentvm1 ~]$ unset Var1 ; echo $Var1 ; if [ -v Var1 ] ; then
echo "Var1 has been assigned a value." ; else echo "Var1 does not have a
value." ; fi

Var1 does not have a value.
```

The general rule for using the $ character to specify a variable is that it should be used when accessing – reading – the value of the variable. It should not be used when setting the value or when using logical operators.

You should experiment with all of these logical comparison operators, especially the ones not covered explicitly in any of these experiments. However, it is not necessary to memorize all of them along with all of their options and forms. I always find it most beneficial to explore specific operators – and Linux commands in general – while working on a project that requires them. I learn and retain more that way. Over time I have also learned which ones I use frequently and which I almost never use. I see little point in memorizing information that I may never use.

Grouping Program Statements

Sometimes, to get the results you want, it is necessary to group program statements together. For example, I sometimes want to know how much time running a program takes to run on one host so I know what to expect on the rest of the hosts on which I need to run the same program. The time utility shows me the amount of real time, user time, and system time.

Real time is the total amount of clock time used by a program. User time is the amount of time spent by the system to execute the user code that was entered. System (sys) time is the amount of time spent running system code and libraries. But the `time` command only provides the execution times of the single command following. To get the execution time for a series of commands in a command-line program, we must find a way to group the ones we want to time.

EXPERIMENT 28-11: GROUPING PROGRAM STATEMENTS

Let's look first at the `time` utility to see how that works. It can also illustrate a bit about the time delays introduced by input/output (I/O). Do this part as the student user:

```
[student@studentvm1 ~]$ time cat dmesg1.txt
<snip>
[40368.982838] IPv6: ADDRCONF(NETDEV_UP): enpOs3: link is not ready
[40371.049241] e1000: enpOs3 NIC Link is Up 1000 Mbps Full Duplex, Flow
Control: RX
[40371.049584] IPv6: ADDRCONF(NETDEV_CHANGE): enpOs3: link becomes ready

real    0m0.026s
user    0m0.001s
sys     0m0.002s
```

The last three lines show the results from the `time` utility. The result can be interpreted that a total of 0.003 seconds was used in executing code. The rest of the time, 0.023 seconds, was spent waiting for I/O to occur.

If you run this program several times, the amount of real time usually will be significantly reduced due to caching the result of the disk read in memory where it can be accessed faster. I ended up with something like this:

```
real    0m0.007s
user    0m0.001s
sys     0m0.001s
```

However, if I then run this little program and redirect the output to the /dev/null, I get the following results, and you should see something quite similar:

[student@studentvm1 ~]$ **time cat dmesg1.txt > /dev/null**

```
real     0m0.002s
user     0m0.001s
sys      0m0.000s
```

So we can see that sending data to the display screen (I/O activity) takes a relatively large amount of real time. When we send the data to /dev/null instead, the whole thing takes much less time.

Now let's move on to the real purpose of this experiment. Suppose that we want to run multiple program statements and measure the total time that it takes to do so. That might look like Figure 28-6 in which I want to know how much time is used by the pair of commands I normally use to destroy the content of a storage drive and then test it for errors.

Warning!   Do not run the command shown in Figure 28-6 because it will delete all of the data on the sdk storage device if you have one.

```
[root@myworkstation ~]# time ( shred -n 3 -v /dev/sdk ; dd if=/dev/sdk
of=/dev/null )
shred: /dev/sdk: pass 1/3 (random)...
shred: /dev/sdk: pass 1/3 (random)...147MiB/466GiB 0%
shred: /dev/sdk: pass 1/3 (random)...322MiB/466GiB 0%

<snip>

7814037167+0 records in
7814037167+0 records out
4000787029504 bytes (4.0 TB, 3.6 TiB) copied, 39041.5 s, 102 MB/s
real     1986m28.783s
user     85m49.873s
sys      127m49.951s
```

Figure 28-6. *Grouping the* shred *and* dd *commands so that the* time *command measures elapsed time for both commands*

If you have been performing all of the experiments in this course, your VM should have some virtual storage devices we can use for this. Perform the rest of this experiment as the root user. The lsblk command should show that /dev/sdd is 2GB in size and has one partition, /dev/sdd1, that is configured as a swap partition. We can also see this with these two commands.

If you don't see two swap partitions, you may have turned off the one we created in Chapter 24 of this volume. If you did, turn all swap space on and then redo this command:

```
[root@studentvm1 ~]# cat /proc/swaps
Filename                Type            Size            Used    Priority
/dev/zram0              partition       8388604          0      100
/dev/sdd1               partition       2096124          0      5
/dev/dm-3               partition       2097148          0      2
[root@studentvm1 ~]# swapon -s
Filename                Type            Size            Used    Priority
/dev/zram0              partition       8388604          0      100
/dev/sdd1               partition       2096124          0      5
/dev/dm-3               partition       2097148          0      2
```

Where do you think that the swapon -s (-s for summary) command obtains its information?

Turn off /dev/sdd1 as swap and verify that it is off:

```
[root@studentvm1 ~]# swapoff /dev/sdd1 ; swapon -s
Filename        Type            Size            Used            Priority
/dev/zram0      partition       8388604         0               100
/dev/dm-3       partition       2097148         0               2
```

And comment out the following line as shown in /etc/fstab:

```
# /dev/sdd1        swap            swap        defaults        0 0
```

Now the VM won't try to start /dev/sdd1 as swap space when rebooting.

Let's shred the entire storage device, not just the partition. By doing it this way, we also shred the boot record, partition table, and the entire data area of the device. The last command in this CLI program reads the data from the storage device and sends it to /dev/null to test the device for any errors:

```
[root@studentvm1 ~]# time shred -vn 3 /dev/sdd ; dd if=/dev/sdd of=/dev/null
shred: /dev/sdd: pass 1/3 (random)...
```

```
shred: /dev/sdd: pass 1/3 (random)...239MiB/2.0GiB 11%
shred: /dev/sdd: pass 1/3 (random)...514MiB/2.0GiB 25%
<SNIP>
shred: /dev/sdd: pass 3/3 (random)...1.7GiB/2.0GiB 89%
shred: /dev/sdd: pass 3/3 (random)...2.0GiB/2.0GiB 100%

real    1m22.718s
user    0m6.367s
sys     0m1.519s
4194304+0 records in
4194304+0 records out
2147483648 bytes (2.1 GB, 2.0 GiB) copied, 22.8312 s, 94.1 MB/s
```

Notice where the data from the time command appears – between the output from the shred and dd commands. So the time shown is only for the shred command. What result would we get using the following command?

```
shred -vn 3 /dev/sdd ; time dd if=/dev/sdd of=/dev/null
```

We know that won't give us the time for the entire operation. Try it like this, which gives us the total time for both program statements that are enclosed in the parentheses:

```
[root@studentvm1 home]# time ( shred -vn 3 /dev/sdd ; dd if=/dev/sdd of=/
dev/null )
shred: /dev/sdd: pass 1/3 (random)...
shred: /dev/sdd: pass 1/3 (random)...367MiB/2.0GiB 17%
shred: /dev/sdd: pass 1/3 (random)...711MiB/2.0GiB 34%
<SNIP>
shred: /dev/sdd: pass 3/3 (random)...1.6GiB/2.0GiB 82%
shred: /dev/sdd: pass 3/3 (random)...2.0GiB/2.0GiB 100%
4194304+0 records in
4194304+0 records out
2147483648 bytes (2.1 GB, 2.0 GiB) copied, 22.3553 s, 96.1 MB/s

real    1m36.339s
user    0m10.845s
sys     0m10.368s
```

Expansions

Bash supports a number of types of expansions and substitutions, which can be quite useful. According to the Bash man page, Bash has seven (7) forms of expansions. We will look at tilde (~) expansion, arithmetic expansion, and pathname expansion.

Brace Expansion

Brace expansion is a method to use for generating arbitrary strings. We've already discussed brace expansion in Chapter 15, so there is no need to explore that any further here.

Tilde Expansion

Arguably the most common expansion we run into is the tilde (~) expansion. When we use this in a command like `cd ~/Documents`, the Bash shell actually expands that shortcut to the full home directory of the user.

EXPERIMENT 28-12: TILDE EXPANSION

As the student user, use these Bash programs to observe the effects of the tilde expansion:

```
[student@studentvm1 ~]$ echo ~
/home/student
[student@studentvm1 ~]$ echo ~/Documents
/home/student/Documents
[student@studentvm1 ~]$ Var1=~/Documents ; echo $Var1 ; cd $Var1
/home/student/Documents
[student@studentvm1 Documents]$
```

Pathname Expansion

Pathname expansion is a fancy term for expansion of file globbing patterns using the characters ? and * into the full names of directories that match the pattern. As we discussed in Chapter 15, globbing means special pattern characters that allow us significant flexibility in matching file names, directories, and other strings when performing various actions. These special pattern characters allow matching single, multiple, or specific characters in a string.

?: Matches only one of any character in the specified location within the string.

*: Zero or more of any character in the specified location within the string.

In this case we apply this expansion to matching directory names.

EXPERIMENT 28-13

As the student user, let's see how this works. Ensure that your home directory, ~, is the PWD and start with a plain listing:

```
[student@studentvm1 ~]$ ls
chapter25   diskusage.txt   Documents   newfile.txt   testdir1    Videos
chapter26   dmesg1.txt      Downloads   Pictures      testdir6
chapter28   dmesg2.txt      link3       Public        testdir7
cpuHog      dmesg3.txt      Music       Templates     testfile
Desktop     dmesg4.txt      mypipe      testdir       umask.test
```

Now list the directories that start with "Do", ~/Documents and ~/Downloads:

```
[student@studentvm1 ~]$ ls Do*
Documents:
file01  file09  file17  test05  test13  testfile01  testfile09  testfile17
file02  file10  file18  test06  test14  testfile02  testfile10  testfile18
file03  file11  file19  test07  test15  testfile03  testfile11  testfile19
file04  file12  file20  test08  test16  testfile04  testfile12  testfile20
file05  file13  test01  test09  test17  testfile05  testfile13  Test.odt
file06  file14  test02  test10  test18  testfile06  testfile14  Test.pdf
file07  file15  test03  test11  test19  testfile07  testfile15
file08  file16  test04  test12  test20  testfile08  testfile16

Downloads:
[student@studentvm1 ~]$
```

Well, that did not do what we wanted. It listed the contents of the directories that begin with Do. To list only the directories and not their contents, we can use the -d option:

```
[student@studentvm1 ~]$ ls -d Do*
Documents  Downloads
[student@studentvm1 ~]$
```

So what happens here – in both cases – is that the Bash shell expands the Do* pattern into the names of the two directories that match the pattern. But what if there are also files that match the pattern, which there currently are not?

```
[student@studentvm1 ~]$ touch Downtown ; ls -d Do*
Documents  Downloads  Downtown
```

That shows the file too. So any files that match the pattern are also expanded to their full names.

Command Substitution

Command substitution is a form of expansion. Command substitution is a tool that allows the STDOUT data stream of one command to be used as the argument of another command, for example, as a list of items to be processed in a loop. The Bash man page says, "Command substitution allows the output of a command to replace the command name." I find that to be accurate, if a bit obtuse.

There are two forms of this substitution, `command` and $(command). In the older form using backticks (`), a backslash (\) used in the command retains its literal meaning. However, when used in the new parenthetical form, the backslash takes on its meaning as a special character. Note also that the parenthetical form uses only single parentheses to open and close the command statement.

I frequently use this capability in command-line programs and scripts where the results of one command can be used as an argument for another command.

EXPERIMENT 28-14: COMMAND SUBSTITUTION

As the student user, let's start with a very simple example using both forms of this expansion. Ensure that ~ is the PWD:

```
[student@studentvm1 ~]$ echo "Todays date is `date`"
Todays date is Sat Mar  4 04:30:57 PM EST 2023
[student@studentvm1 ~]$ echo "Todays date is $(date)"
Todays date is Sat Mar  4 04:31:25 PM EST 2023
```

We have seen the seq utility previously. It is used to generate a sequence of numbers:

```
[student@studentvm1 ~]$ seq 5
1
2
3
4
5
[student@studentvm1 ~]$ echo `seq 5`
1 2 3 4 5
[student@studentvm1 testdir7]$
```

Notice that by using command substitution, we lose the newlines at the end of each number in the sequence. We have already used this when creating new files for testing in previous experiments. Let's look at it again. Make ~/chapter28 the PWD, and we will create some new files in that directory. The -w option to the seq utility adds leading zeros to the numbers generated to that they are all the same width, that is, number of digits regardless of the value. This makes it easier to sort them in numeric sequence. We have done this before, but this time let's focus on the function of the command substitution:

```
[student@studentvm1 chapter28]$ for I in $(seq -w 5000) ; do touch
file-$I ; done
```

In this usage, the statement seq -w 5000 generates a list of numbers from 1 to 5000. By using command substitution as part of the for statement, the list of numbers is used by the for statement to generate the numerical part of the file names.

List the files in the directory to ensure that they were properly created:

```
[student@studentvm1 chapter28]$ ls | column | less
```

We will explore the use of the for statement just a little further on in this chapter.

Arithmetic Expansion

Bash does integer math, but it is rather cumbersome to do so, as you will soon see. The syntax for arithmetic expansion is $((\text{arithmetic-expression}))$ using double parentheses to open and close the expression.

   Arithmetic expansion works like command substitution in a shell program or script – the value calculated from the expression replaces the expression for further evaluation by the shell.

EXPERIMENT 28-15: ARITHMETIC EXPANSION

Once again we will start with something simple:

```
[student@studentvm1 chapter28]$ echo $((1+1))
2
[student@studentvm1 chapter28]$ Var1=5 ; Var2=7 ; Var3=$((Var1*Var2)) ; echo
"Var 3 = $Var3"
Var 3 = 35
```

The following division results in zero because the result would be a decimal value of less than one:

```
[student@studentvm1 chapter28]$ Var1=5 ; Var2=7 ; Var3=$((Var1/Var2)) ; echo
"Var 3 = $Var3"
Var 3 = 0
```

Here is a simple calculation that I do in a script or CLI program that tells me how much total virtual memory I have in a Linux host. The `free` command does not provide that data:

```
[student@studentvm1 chapter28]$ RAM=`free | grep ^Mem | awk '{print $2}'` ;
Swap=`free | grep ^Swap | awk '{print $2}'` ; echo "RAM = $RAM and Swap =
$Swap" ; echo "Total Virtual memory is $((RAM+Swap))" ;
RAM = 4037080 and Swap = 6291452
Total Virtual memory is 10328532
```

Note that I used the backtick (`) character to delimit the sections of code that were used for command substitution.

I use Bash arithmetic expansion mostly for checking system resource amounts in a script and then choosing a program execution path based on the result.

---

for Loops

Every programming language I have ever used has some version of the `for` command. The Bash implementation of this structure is, in my opinion, a bit more flexible than most because it can handle non-numeric values while the standard C language for loop, for example, can only deal with numeric values.

The basic structure of the Bash version of the `for` command is simple – `for Var in list1 ; do list2 ; done`. This translates to: for each value in list1, set the $Var to that value and then perform the program statements in list2 using that value; when all of the values in list1 have been used, we are done so exit the loop. The values in list1 can be a simple explicit string of values, or it can be the result of a command substitution as we have seen in Experiment 28-14 and many others throughout this course.

As you can see from previous experiments in this course, I use this construct frequently.

EXPERIMENT 28-16: FOR LOOPS

As the student user, ensure that ~/chapter28 is still the PWD. Let's clean up and then look at a trivial example of the `for` loop starting with an explicit list of values. This list is a mix of alphanumeric values, but do not forget that all variables are strings and can be treated as such. We use the path in this command to help ensure that we don't accidentally delete files because we aren't in the correct PWD:

```
$ rm -rf ~/chapter28/*
$ for I in a b c d 1 2 3 4 ; do echo $I ; done
a
b
c
d
1
2
3
4
```

This will be a bit more useful version along with a more meaningful variable name:

```
$ for Dept in "Human Resources" Sales Finance "Information Technology"
Engineering Administration Research ; do echo "Department $Dept" ; done
```

```
Department Human Resources
Department Sales
Department Finance
Department Information Technology
Department Engineering
Department Administration
Department Research
```

Let's make some directories:

```
[student@studentvm1 chapter28]$ for Dept in "Human Resources" Sales Finance
"Information Technology" Engineering Administration Research ; do echo
"Working on Department $Dept" ; mkdir "$Dept"  ; done
Working on Department Human Resources
Working on Department Sales
Working on Department Finance
Working on Department Information Technology
Working on Department Engineering
Working on Department Administration
Working on Department Research
[student@studentvm1 chapter28]$ ll
total 28
drwxrwxr-x 2 student student 4096 Apr  8 15:45  Administration
drwxrwxr-x 2 student student 4096 Apr  8 15:45  Engineering
drwxrwxr-x 2 student student 4096 Apr  8 15:45  Finance
drwxrwxr-x 2 student student 4096 Apr  8 15:45 'Human Resources'
drwxrwxr-x 2 student student 4096 Apr  8 15:45 'Information Technology'
drwxrwxr-x 2 student student 4096 Apr  8 15:45  Research
drwxrwxr-x 2 student student 4096 Apr  8 15:45  Sales
```

Note that it is necessary to enclose $Dept in quotes in the mkdir statement or the two-part department names such as "Information Technology" will be treated as two separate departments. That highlights a best practice that I like to follow, and that is that all file and directory names should be a single word. Although most modern operating systems can deal with spaces in those names, it takes extra work for SysAdmins to ensure that those special cases are considered in scripts and CLI programs. But they almost certainly should be considered, even if they're annoying, because you never know what files you're actually going to have.

So delete everything in ~/chapter28 – again – and let's do this one more time:

```
[student@studentvm1 chapter28]$ rm -rf ~/chapter28/* ; ll
total 0
[student@studentvm1 chapter28]$ for Dept in Human-Resources Sales Finance
Information-Technology Engineering Administration Research ; do echo "Working
on Department $Dept" ; mkdir "$Dept"  ; done
Working on Department Human-Resources
Working on Department Sales
Working on Department Finance
Working on Department Information-Technology
Working on Department Engineering
Working on Department Administration
Working on Department Research
[student@studentvm1 chapter28]$ ll
total 28
drwxrwxr-x 2 student student 4096 Apr  8 15:52 Administration
drwxrwxr-x 2 student student 4096 Apr  8 15:52 Engineering
drwxrwxr-x 2 student student 4096 Apr  8 15:52 Finance
drwxrwxr-x 2 student student 4096 Apr  8 15:52 Human-Resources
drwxrwxr-x 2 student student 4096 Apr  8 15:52 Information-Technology
drwxrwxr-x 2 student student 4096 Apr  8 15:52 Research
drwxrwxr-x 2 student student 4096 Apr  8 15:52 Sales
```

Suppose someone asks for a list of all RPMs on a particular Linux computer and a short description of each. This happened to me while I worked in the state of North Carolina. Since open source was not "approved" for use by state agencies at that time and I only used Linux on my desktop computer, the pointy-haired bosses (PHBs) needed a list of each piece of software that was installed on my computer so that they could "approve" an exception.

How would you approach that? Here is one way, starting with the knowledge that the rpm -qi command provides a complete description of an RPM including the two items we want, the name and a brief summary.

EXPERIMENT 28-17: A REAL-WORLD EXAMPLE

We will build up to the final result one step at a time. This experiment should be performed as the student user. First, we list all RPMs:

```
[student@studentvm1 chapter28]$ rpm -qa
fonts-filesystem-2.0.5-9.fc37.noarch
liberation-fonts-common-2.1.5-3.fc37.noarch
libreport-filesystem-2.17.4-1.fc37.noarch
hyperv-daemons-license-0-0.39.20220731git.fc37.noarch
hunspell-filesystem-1.7.0-21.fc37.x86_64
langpacks-core-font-en-3.0-26.fc37.noarch
abattis-cantarell-fonts-0.301-8.fc37.noarch
<snip>
```

Adding the sort and uniq commands sorts the list and then prints only the unique ones. There is a slight possibility that some RPMs with identical names are installed:

```
[student@studentvm1 chapter28]$ rpm -qa | sort | uniq
a2ps-4.14-51.fc37.x86_64
aajohan-comfortaa-fonts-3.101-5.fc37.noarch
abattis-cantarell-fonts-0.301-8.fc37.noarch
abattis-cantarell-vf-fonts-0.301-8.fc37.noarch
abrt-2.15.1-6.fc37.x86_64
abrt-addon-ccpp-2.15.1-6.fc37.x86_64
abrt-addon-kerneloops-2.15.1-6.fc37.x86_64
abrt-addon-pstoreoops-2.15.1-6.fc37.x86_64
abrt-addon-vmcore-2.15.1-6.fc37.x86_64
abrt-addon-xorg-2.15.1-6.fc37.x86_64
<snip>
```

Since this gives the correct list of RPMs you want to look at, we can use this as the input list to a loop that will print all of the details of each RPM:

```
[student@studentvm1 chapter28]$ for RPM in `rpm -qa | sort | uniq` ;
do rpm -qi $RPM ; done
```

This code produces way more data than was desired. Note that our loop is actually complete. The next step is to extract only the information that was requested. Now we add an egrep command, which is used to select ^Name or ^Summary. Thus, any line with Name or Summary at the beginning of the line (the carat ^ specifies the beginning of the line) is displayed:

```
[student@studentvm1 chapter28]$ for RPM in `rpm -qa | sort | uniq` ; do rpm
-qi $RPM ; done | egrep -i "^Name|^Summary"
Name        : a2ps
Summary     : Converts text and other types of files to PostScript
Name        : aajohan-comfortaa-fonts
Summary     : Modern style true type font
Name        : abattis-cantarell-fonts
Summary     : Humanist sans serif font
Name        : abattis-cantarell-vf-fonts
Summary     : Humanist sans serif font (variable)
Name        : abrt
Summary     : Automatic bug detection and reporting tool
Name        : abrt-addon-ccpp
Summary     : abrt's C/C++ addon
Name        : abrt-addon-kerneloops
Summary     : abrt's kerneloops addon
<snip>
```

You can try grep instead of egrep in the preceding command but it does not work. You could also pipe the output of this command through the less filter so you can explore these results.

The final command sequence looks like this:

```
[student@studentvm1 chapter28]$ for RPM in `rpm -qa | sort | uniq` ;
do rpm -qi $RPM ; done | egrep -i "^Name|^Summary" > RPM-summary.txt
```

It uses pipelines, redirection, and a for loop – all on a single line. It redirects the output of our little CLI program to a file that can be used in an email or as input for other purposes.

This process of building up the program one step at a time allows you to see the results of each step and to ensure that it is working as you expect and provides the desired results.

The PHBs received a list of over 1,900 separate RPM packages. I seriously doubt that anyone actually read that list. But I gave them exactly what they asked for, and I never heard another word from them about this. The VM I use for this book gave me a result of 4,442 lines, which is 2,221 RPM packages. My primary workstation has 3,933 packages installed.

Other Loops

There are two more types of loop structures available in Bash, the while and until structures, which are very similar to each other in both syntax and function. The basic syntax of these loop structures is simple:

```
while [ expression ] ; do list ; done
```

and

```
until [ expression ] ; do list ; done
```

The logic of these reads as follows: "While the expression evaluates as true, execute the list of program statements. When the expression evaluates as false, exit from the loop" and "Until the expression evaluates as true, execute the list of program statements. When the expression evaluates as true, exit from the loop."

while

The while loop is used to execute a series of program statements while (so long as) the logical expression evaluates to true. We used this as a part of the cpuHog programs we wrote in Chapter 13. Let's look at the while loop again in more detail.

EXPERIMENT 28-18: USING WHILE LOOPS

As the student user, make ~ the PWD.

The simplest form of the while loop is one that runs forever. In the following form, we use the true statement to always generate a "true" return code. We could use a simple "1" as we did in the original cpuHog, and that would work just the same, but this illustrates use of the true statement.

```
[student@studentvm1 ~]$ X=0 ; while [ true ] ; do echo $X ; X=$((X+1)) ;
done | head
0
1
2
3
4
5
<snip>
```

This CLI program should make more sense now that we have studied its parts. First, we set $X to zero just in case it had some leftover value from a previous program or CLI command. Then, since the logical expression [true] always evaluates to 1, which is true, the list of program instructions between do and done is executed forever – or until we press Ctrl+C or otherwise send a signal 2 to the program. Those instructions are an arithmetic expansion that prints the current value of $X and then increments it by one.

One of the tenets of "the Linux Philosophy for SysAdmins" is to strive for elegance and that one way to achieve elegance is simplicity. We can simplify this program by using the variable increment operator, ++. In this first instance, the current value of the variable is printed and then the variable is incremented. This is indicated by placing the ++ operator after the variable:

```
[student@studentvm1 ~]$ X=0 ; while [ true ] ; do echo $((X++)) ; done | head
0
1
2
3
4
5
6
<SNIP>
```

Delete | head from the end of the program and run it again.

In this next version, the variable is incremented before its value is printed. This is specified by placing the ++ operator before the variable. Can you see the difference?

```
[student@studentvm1 ~]$ X=0 ; while [ true ] ; do echo $((++X)) ; done | head
1
2
3
4
5
6
<SNIP>
```

We have reduced two statements into a single one that both prints the value of the variable and increments that value. There is also a decrement operator, --.

We need a method for stopping the loop at a specific number. To accomplish that we can change the true expression to an actual numeric evaluation expression. So let's have our program loop to 5 and stop. In Figure 28-4 you can see that -le is the logical numeric operator for "less than or equal to." This means that so long as $X is less than or equal to 5, the loop will continue. When $X increments to 6, the loop terminates:

```
[student@studentvm1 ~]$ X=0 ; while [ $X -le 5 ] ; do echo $((X++)) ; done
0
1
2
3
4
5
[student@studentvm1 ~]$
```

until

The until command is very much like the while command. The difference is that it will continue to loop until the logical expression evaluates to "true."

EXPERIMENT 28-19: USING UNTIL LOOPS

As the student user, make ~ the PWD. As in Experiment 28-18, let's look at the simplest form of this construct:

```
[student@studentvm1 ~]$ X=0 ; until false  ; do echo $((X++)) ; done | head
0
1
2
3
4
5
6
7
8
9
[student@studentvm1 ~]$
```

Now we use a logical comparison to count to a specific value:

```
[student@studentvm1 ~]$ X=0 ; until [ $X -eq 5 ]  ; do echo $((X++)) ; done
0
1
2
3
4
[student@studentvm1 ~]$ X=0 ; until [ $X -eq 5 ]  ; do echo $((++X)) ; done
1
2
3
4
5
[student@studentvm1 ~]$
```

Chapter Summary

We have explored the use of many powerful tools that we can use to build command-line programs and Bash shell scripts. Despite the interesting things we have done in this chapter, Bash command-line programs and shell scripts can do so much more. We have barely scratched the surface.

All we have done here is to inform you of the many possibilities of Bash command-line programming. The rest is up to you. I have discovered over time that the best way to learn Bash programming is to actually do it. Find a simple project that requires multiple Bash commands and make a CLI program out of them. SysAdmins do many tasks that lend themselves to CLI programming this way, so I am sure that you will easily find tasks to automate.

Despite being familiar with other shell languages and Perl, many years ago, I made the decision to use Bash for all of my SysAdmin automation tasks. I have discovered that – perhaps with a bit of searching – I have been able to accomplish everything I need.

Exercises

1. Write a short command-line program to count from 0 to 5000 by increments of 5, and print the resulting data in two columns.

2. What happens when quotes are not used when assigning a value to a variable?

3. How do the variables $PATH and $Path differ?

4. Devise and run an experiment to determine whether the -r file operator returns true if any of the User, Group, or Other ownership for a given file has the read bit set, as opposed to specifically the read bit for User.

5. Create two versions of an "if" compound command that tests if two variables are equal and print "The variables are equal" if they are and "The variables are not equal" if they are not. One version should use the == operator and the other should use the != operator. Use test cases for both versions where the variables are equal and where they are not.

6. Is the CLI program `Var1="7" ; Var2="9" ; echo "Result =`
   `$Var1*$Var2"` valid? What about `Var1="7" ; Var2="9" ; echo`
   `"Result = $Var1*$Var2"`? Why?

7. What happens when you use a decimal such as 5.5 in an
   arithmetic expansion?

8. Which of these works and which does not? Why?

   `RAM=`free | grep ^Mem | awk '{print $2}'` ; echo $RAM`
   `RAM=$((free | grep ^Mem | awk '{print $2}')) ; echo $RAM`

9. Create a CLI program to count down from 10 to 0 and print the
   resulting numbers to the screen.

CHAPTER 29

Automation with Bash Scripts

Objectives

In this chapter you will learn

- The advantages of automation with Bash shell scripts
- Why using shell scripts is a better choice for SysAdmins than compiled languages like C or C++
- To create a set of requirements for new scripts
- To create simple Bash shell scripts from CLI programs
- To use the file ownership and permissions to impose a layer of security on who can run the script
- To further enhance security through the use of the UID of the user running the script
- To use logical comparison tools to provide execution flow control for both command-line programs and scripts
- To use command-line options to control various script functionality
- To create Bash functions that can be called from one or more locations within a script

© David Both 2023
D. Both, *Using and Administering Linux: Volume 2*, https://doi.org/10.1007/978-1-4842-9615-8_29

- Why and how to license your code as open source

- To create a simple test plan

- To test early and test often

Introduction

My question to you is, "What is the function of computers?" In my opinion, the right answer is "to automate mundane tasks in order to allow us humans to concentrate on the tasks that the computers cannot – yet – do." For SysAdmins, those of us who run and manage the computers most closely, we have direct access to the tools that can help us work more efficiently. We should use those tools to maximum benefit.

In this chapter we explore using automation in the form of Bash shell scripts to make our own lives as SysAdmins easier. This chapter is only partly about creating the scripts and making them work. It is also about some of the philosophy of automation and shell scripting.

Why I Use Shell Scripts

In Chapter 9 of my book *The Linux Philosophy for SysAdmins*,[1] I state

> *A SysAdmin is most productive when thinking – thinking about how to solve existing problems and about how to avoid future problems; thinking about how to monitor Linux computers in order to find clues that anticipate and foreshadow those future problems; thinking about how to make [their] job more efficient; thinking about how to automate all of those tasks that need to be performed whether every day or once a year.*

> *SysAdmins are next most productive when creating the shell programs that automate the solutions that they have conceived while appearing to be unproductive. The more automation we have in place the more time we have available to fix real problems when they occur and to contemplate how to automate even more than we already have.*

---

[1] Both, David, *The Linux Philosophy for SysAdmins*, Apress, 2018, 165

Have you ever performed a long and complex task at the command line thinking, "Glad that's done – I never have to worry about it again"? I have – very frequently. I ultimately figured out that almost everything that I ever need to do on a computer, whether mine or one that belongs to an employer or a consulting customer, will need to be done again sometime in the future.

Of course I always think that I will remember how I did the task in question. But the next time I need to do it is far enough out into the future that I sometimes even forget that I have ever done it at all, let alone how to do it. For some tasks I started writing down the steps required on a bit of paper. I thought, "How stupid of me!" So I then transferred those scribbles to a simple notepad-type application on my computer. Suddenly one day I thought again, "How stupid of me!" If I am going to store this data on my computer, I might as well create a shell script and store it in a standard location, /usr/local/bin or ~/bin, so that I can just type the name of the shell program and it does all of the tasks I used to do manually.

For me automation also means that I don't have to remember or recreate the details of how I performed that task in order to do it again. It takes time to remember how to do things and time to type in all of the commands. This can become a significant time sink for tasks that require typing large numbers of long commands. Automating tasks by creating shell scripts reduces the typing necessary to perform my routine tasks.

Shell Scripts

Shell scripts can also be an important aid to newer SysAdmins to enable them to keep things working while the senior SysAdmin – or whoever knows more or has more experience than those who are left, which are usually us – is out on vacation or ill. Figuring out how to do things takes time, even if it's a faster process for the more experienced. Because shell programs are inherently open to view and change, they can be an important tool for less experienced SysAdmins to learn the details of how to perform these tasks when they need to be responsible for them.

Writing shell programs – also known as scripts – provides the best strategy for leveraging my time. Once having written a shell program, it can be rerun as many times as needed. I can update my shell scripts as needed to compensate for changes from one release of Linux to the next. Other factors that might require making these changes are the installation of new hardware and software, changes in what I want or need to accomplish with the script, adding new functions, removing functions that are no longer needed, and fixing the not-so-rare bugs in my scripts. These kinds of changes are just part of the maintenance cycle for any type of code.

Every task performed via the keyboard in a terminal session by entering and executing shell commands can and should be automated. SysAdmins should automate everything we are asked to do or that we decide on our own needs to be done. Many times I have found that doing the automation up front saves time the first time.

One bash script can contain anywhere from a few commands to many thousands. In fact, I have written bash scripts that have only one or two commands in them. Another script I have written contains over 2,700 lines, more than half of which are comments.

Scripts vs. Compiled Programs

When writing programs to automate – well – everything, always use shell scripts. Because shell scripts are stored in ASCII text format, they can be easily viewed and modified by humans just as easily as they can by computers. You can examine a shell program and see exactly what it does and whether there are any obvious errors in the syntax or logic. This is a powerful example of what it means to be open.

I know that some developers tend to consider shell scripts something less than true programming. This marginalization of shell scripts and those who write them seems to be predicated on the idea that the only true programming language is one that must be compiled from source code to produce executable code. I can tell you from experience this is categorically untrue.

I have used many languages including BASIC, C, C++, Pascal, Perl, Tcl/Expect, REXX and some of its variations including Object REXX, and many shell languages including Korn, csh, and Bash and even some assembly language. Every computer language ever devised has had one purpose – to allow humans to tell computers what to do. When you write a program, regardless of the language you choose, you are giving the computer instructions to perform specific tasks in a specific sequence.

Scripts can be written and tested far more quickly than compiled languages. Programs usually must be written quickly by SysAdmins to meet time constraints imposed by circumstances or the PHB. Most of the scripts we write are to fix a problem, to clean up the aftermath of a problem, or to deliver a program that must be operational long before a compiled program could be written and tested.

Writing a program quickly requires shell programming because it allows quick response to the needs of the customer whether that be ourselves or someone else. If there are problems with the logic or bugs in the code, they can be corrected and retested almost immediately. If the original set of requirements was flawed or incomplete, shell scripts can be altered very quickly to meet the new requirements. So, in general, we can say that the need for speed of development in the SysAdmin's job overrides the need to make the program run as fast as possible or to use as little as possible in the way of system resources like RAM.

Most things we do as SysAdmins take longer to figure out how to do than they do to execute. Thus, it might seem counterproductive to create shell scripts for everything we do. Writing the scripts and making them into tools that produce reproducible results and that can be used as many times as necessary takes some time. The time savings come every time we can run the script without having to figure out again how to perform the task.

You may encounter a situation when the execution of a script takes an excessive amount of time or when the problem is so general that it will be done thousands or even millions of times, in which case compiled languages may make more sense. But those are extremely rare cases.

Updates

Most of the time my scripts start with short CLI programs that I use multiple times daily and that morph into more complex forms. So let's take a CLI program we have already used and turn it into a script.

One task I do frequently is to install updates on all of my computers. In fact I have been doing updates this morning. This is a task that requires only a couple decisions and can be easily automated. "But that is so simple. Why automate a task that requires only a command or two?" It turns out that updates are not so simple. Let's think about this for a minute.

About Updates

There are two important things to understand about updates as we enter this programming task. First, installing updates does not preclude using your computer at the same time. With Linux, we can install updates while also performing the other tasks necessary to get our regular work done.

Second, there are times when rebooting after installing updates is a good idea. Linux does not automatically reboot for us – it leaves us to decide when to perform that reboot. Although I usually reboot right after the updates are completed, it is not necessary to do so. But if certain packages are updated, it is a very good idea to reboot soon. The point is that Linux lets us make these choices.

Create a List of Requirements

So what are the requirements for this script? You should always create a set of requirements for every project. I always create a set of requirements for my scripts, even if it is a simple list with only two or three items on it.

First, I must determine whether any updates are available. Then I need to determine whether a package that requires a reboot is being updated, such as the kernel, glibc, or systemd. At this point I can install the update. I then run the mandb utility to update the man pages; if this is not done, new and replacement man pages won't be accessible, and old ones that have been removed will appear to be there even though they are not. Finally, if a reboot is needed, I do that.

That is a nontrivial set of individual tasks and commands that require some decisions. Doing those tasks manually requires paying attention and intervention to enter new commands when the previous ones complete. Because of the need to babysit while waiting to enter the next command, this would take a great deal of my time to monitor each computer as it went through the procedures. There was room for error as I was reminded occasionally when I would enter the wrong command on a host.

Using the statement of requirements I created, because that is what that paragraph really is, it was easy to automate this to eliminate all of those issues. I wrote a script that I call doUpdates.sh. It provides options like help, verbose mode, printing the current version number, and an option to reboot only if the kernel, systemd, or glibc has been updated.

Over half of the lines in this program are comments so I can remember how the program works the next time I need to work on it to fix a bug or add a little more function. I arbitrarily chose this as the program to illustrate creating scripts because it offers many opportunities to expand and implement fun and useful features. It is also illustrative of the process I went through as it grew and became more than a CLI program.

As we work through the series of experiments in this chapter, we will start out very simply. To begin, we will only do the check for updates and some items such as a help facility. Because it may be a few days after doing an actual update that another is needed, we will wait until near the end to actually perform the update. This is, in fact, how I develop my scripts anyway – so that they start out harmless.

The program we will create together in this chapter will be a shorter and more efficient version of the one I have created for myself.

The CLI Program

There are four steps required to actually do the updates in the CLI program. We first do the update, update the man page database, rebuild the GRUB config files, and reboot the host. Refer to Chapter 16 of Volume 1 to review GRUB configuration and why we need to rebuild the GRUB configuration.

Let's make some assumptions for our initial command-line program. We will assume that the man database will always be rebuilt, that a reboot is always required – although we won't always do that in our testing – and that the GRUB configuration file needs to be updated.

EXPERIMENT 29-1: TESTING THE BASIC UPDATE STEPS

As the root user, start with this little CLI program. Remember that we are only checking for updates and not yet doing them. This will leave something for the script to do when it is complete. Enter and run the following CLI program and observe the results:

```
[root@studentvm1 bin]# dnf check-update ; mandb ; reboot
```

It gives us a list of the RPM packages that need to be updated, rebuilds the man database, and then reboots the VM.

Security

Our doUpdates.sh program should only be run by root and should fail if any other user tries to run it. We have looked at security a bit already and seen the effect of using permissions of 750 and 777. We have also looked at using a bit of code to exit from the program if the UID of the account attempting to run the program is not zero, that is, the root user.

Root is the only user that needs access to this program, so let's place it in /root/bin. This also makes it available at all times even if other filesystems are not mounted. Placing it in root's own ~/bin directory makes the program inaccessible to non-root users. Even though /root/bin does not exist by default, this directory is part of root's path. Be sure to check that if you like.

Convert the CLI Program to a Script

We now understand the basic steps required to do the job. That does not seem like a lot, but if you have tens or hundreds of computers to update, it would amount to a lot of typing. So let's create a very minimal script to do these steps.

EXPERIMENT 29-2: DOUPDATES.SH – CONVERT THE CLI PROGRAM TO A BASIC SCRIPT

As the root user, ensure that root's home directory is the PWD. Create a new directory /root/bin to contain executable programs to be used by root and no other users.

Then create a new file named doUpdates.sh in /root/bin and make it executable for root and the root group but with no permissions of any kind for other users.

I follow the standard practice among many SysAdmins to use the .sh extension to help me identify this file as a shell script:

```
[root@studentvm1 ~]# cd ~/bin ; touch doUpdates.sh ; chmod 770
doUpdates.sh ; ll
total 8
-rwxrwx--- 1 root root   0 Apr 10 16:15 doUpdates.sh
```

Use Vim to edit the new file and add the code shown in Figure 29-1 to the file.

```
dnf check-update
mandb
# reboot
```

Figure 29-1. *The first version of our doUpdates.sh script*

We have commented the reboot command so that the program will not reboot every time it is run. This will save time, and it serves as a reminder that we will eventually need to deal with the code that determines whether a reboot is required. We will also handle reboots in a more elegant manner so that we can choose whether or not to do them even when they might be needed.

Without exiting Vim, open another root terminal session and run the program:

[root@studentvm1 bin]# **doUpdates.sh**

In this initial version of our program, we have not started with the shebang (#!), which defines which shell to use to run this program if Bash is not the default shell. So let's add the shebang that defines Bash as the first line of the script. This just ensures that the program is always run in a Bash shell.

Figure 29-2 shows our script now. Run this program again, but the results should be exactly the same.

```
#!/usr/bin/bash
#
dnf check-update
mandb
# reboot
```

Figure 29-2. *Adding the shebang ensures that the script always runs in a Bash shell*

Add Some Logic

The first thing I added to my script was some basic logic that allowed me to skip around certain tasks. For now the actual updates are not actually performed. We will also do the same with rebooting. This will make further testing easier.

EXPERIMENT 29-3: ADDING SOME LOGIC

First, we need to define variables we shall call $Check and $doReboot and then add some logic around the `dnf` and `reboot` commands. We will initially set these variables so that we do the check but not the actual updates and that the reboot is not performed. We should also start adding some comments.

I have also added a message that will print if the reboot is skipped. This helps test the one branch of the logic with some positive feedback. It will also be a nice verification that the logic is working when in actual use.

After adding the new code so that it looks like Figure 29-3, test the program and fix any errors that you might encounter.

```
#!/usr/bin/bash
#
################################################################
# Initialize variables
################################################################
Check=1
doReboot=0


################################################################
# Main body of the program
################################################################
# First we decide whether to do the updates or just check whether
# any are available

if [ $Check == 1 ]
then
    # Check for updates
    dnf check-update
fi

# Update the man database
mandb

# Reboot if necessary
if [ $doReboot == 1 ]
then
    reboot
else
    echo "Not rebooting."
fi
```

Figure 29-3. *We have added some simple logic to control which tasks we want to perform*

For now these settings are built-in, but we will next look at ways to control program flow from the command line. This also does not look at both factors that would initiate a reboot. It only looks at the CLI option -r, but it is fine for now. It doesn't process any command-line options at this point; it only checks the variable.

Limit to Root

This program should be limited to usage by the root user. We can do this partially through ownership and permission settings, but we should also add some code to check for this. Remember that the root user ID (UID) is zero (0) and all other users have UIDs greater than zero.

EXPERIMENT 29-4: YOU MUST BE ROOT

Add the code in Figure 29-4 to our program just below the variable initialization and before the main body of the program. This code checks the UID of the user account attempting to run the program. It only allows the root user to continue and dumps everyone else out with an error.

```
###############################################################
# Check for root
###############################################################
if [ `id -u` != 0 ]
then
    echo "You must be root user to run this program"
    exit
fi
```

Figure 29-4. *Checking for root as the only authorized user*

Now test the program as root, to ensure that it still works for root. Then make a copy of the program in /tmp, and try to run it as the student user. You should first get a permission error:

```
[student@studentvm1 tmp]$ doUpdates.sh
-bash: doUpdates.sh: Permission denied
```

As root, set the permissions for the copy in /tmp to 777 – which is never a good thing in reality. Then try to run it again as the student user:

```
[student@studentvm1 tmp]$ doUpdates.sh
You must be root user to run this program
[student@studentvm1 tmp]$
```

This result is exactly what we want.

Of course a knowledgeable non-root user could modify the code if it is in /tmp with permissions of 777, but every bit of security we can build into our scripts helps deter the casual user from wreaking unexpected havoc.

Add Command-Line Options

We now have some logic in our program but no way to control it other than editing the variable settings in the code itself. That is not very practical, so we need a way to set options at the command line. We also want to determine whether the kernel or glibc[2] is to be updated. It is always a good idea to reboot after one or both of these are updated.

Fortunately, Bash has a couple tools that we can use for this purpose. The `getops` command gets options from the command line and, along with `while` and the `case` structure, allows us to set variables or perform other tasks based on the options read from the command line.

EXPERIMENT 29-5: ADD COMMAND-LINE OPTIONS

First, we need to add some new variables. The revised variables section of our code now looks like Figure 29-5.

The original $doReboot variable will be set to true to cause a reboot if the user enters -r on the command line. The $NeedsReboot variable will be set to true if either the kernel or glibc is to be updated. The system will be rebooted only if both of these variables are true. The $UpdatesAvailable variable will be set to true if one or more updates are available from the Fedora repositories.

---

[2] The glibc package contains the general C libraries that are needed by almost every program that runs as part of the Linux operating system and application programs.

```
###########################################################
# Initialize variables
###########################################################
Check=1
doReboot=0
NeedsReboot=0
UpdatesAvailable=0
```

Figure 29-5. *We added two new variables to enable better control of the doUpdates.sh program*

Now we can add the code that allows us to capture the command options that are input at the command line, evaluate them, and act accordingly. Figure 29-6 shows a very basic version of this. We will add more to this as we proceed.

The getops command gets the list of options the user entered on the command line such as doUpdates.sh -c. It creates a list of options for the while command, which loops until there are no more options left in the list. The case structure evaluates each possible option and executes a list of program statements for each valid option.

The two options we are adding now, -c and -r, are used to set variables in the case structure. If any invalid option is entered at the command line, the last case in the case structure executes. In this case the exit command exits from the program.

Notice that each case ends with a double semicolon. The esac statement ends the case structure, and the done statement closes out the while structure.

Enter the code in Figure 29-6 just below our test for the root user.

```
###############################################################
# Process the input options
###############################################################
# Get the options
while getopts ":cr" option; do
   case $option in
      c) # Check option
            Check=1;;
      r) # Reboot option
            doReboot=1;;
     \?) # incorrect option
            echo "Error: Invalid option."
            exit;;
   esac
done
```

Figure 29-6. *Getting and processing the command-line options*

Before we proceed any further, some testing is needed. Let's first test for an invalid option. The -x is not a valid option, so we should get the error message and the program should exit:

```
[root@studentvm1 bin]# doUpdates.sh -x
Error: Invalid option.
[root@studentvm1 bin]#
```

Because we don't have real logic around the -r option, using it will cause your VM to reboot after doing the check for updates and updating the man pages. At the moment, this is the expected result:

```
[root@studentvm1 bin]# doUpdates.sh -r
```

We now have the ability to control program flow using options on the command line. We will add more options and more logic around these existing options.

Check for Updates

We need to do a real check to see if updates are available and then determine whether a reboot is needed.

EXPERIMENT 29-6: CHECK FOR UPDATES

We need to add the new $UpdatesFile variable in Figure 29-7 and then make some logic changes to check for any available updates.

```
###########################################################
# Initialize variables
###########################################################
Check=1
doReboot=0
NeedsReboot=0
UpdatesAvailable=0
UpdatesFile="/tmp/updates.list"
```

Figure 29-7. *Add the new variable $UpdatesFile*

Delete the following comment line, which is now obsolete:

```
# First we decide whether to do the updates or just check whether any are
available
```

We will also move our logic for the "check" (-c) option into the "else" branch of this new if structure. So we can remove the code fragment in Figure 29-8 from our program.

```
if [ $Check == 1 ]
then
    # Check for updates
    dnf check-update
fi
```

Figure 29-8. *Remove this code from the program*

Add the code in Figure 29-9 immediately after the comment "# Main body of the program." It checks whether updates are available at all while saving a file containing the list of updates that can be parsed for specific packages that require a reboot. This new code will exit the program if no updates are available.

Notice that I have also added a temporary exit command so that we do not need to run any of the code beyond this new section. This saves time by not running code that has not yet been completed with all of the logic necessary. Also note the use of the Bash environment variable $HOSTNAME, which always contains the name of the Linux host.

```bash
################################################################
# Main body of the program
################################################################
################################################################
# Are updates available? Just quit with message if not.
# RC from dnf check-update = 100 if available and 0 if
# none are available. One side effect is to create list
# of updates that can be searched for items that should
# trigger a reboot.
################################################################
dnf check-update > $UpdatesFile
UpdatesAvailable=$?
if [ $UpdatesAvailable == 0 ]
then
    echo "Updates are NOT available for host $HOSTNAME at this time."
    exit
else
    echo "Updates ARE available for host $HOSTNAME."
fi

# Temporary exit
exit
```

Figure 29-9. *Testing to see if any updates are available*

Testing this new bit of code results in the following. We will not be able to test the "then" branch of the new code until we have installed all of the current updates:

```
[root@studentvm1 bin]# doUpdates.sh
Updates ARE available for host studentvm1.
[root@studentvm1 bin]#
```

Is a Reboot Required?

Now that we know that updates are available, we can use the data in the file we created to determine whether any of the packages we have specified as making it a good idea to reboot are in the list. This is easily done.

However, even though a reboot might be a good thing to do, Linux is far more flexible than other operating systems, which force one or more reboots during each update. We can put that Linux reboot off until it is more convenient, such as 02:00 a.m. or over a weekend. To do that we look at two variables, $NeedsReboot, which is determined by looking for the trigger packages that are being updated, and $doReboot, which is set from the command line with the -r option. The -r option is our way of maintaining control over what happens after the update itself is complete.

EXPERIMENT 29-7: CHECK THE NEED FOR A REBOOT

In this experiment we add a series of if statements to determine whether any of the packages that typically need a reboot are being updated. Add the code in Figure 29-10 below the code we added in Experiment 29-6 and just above the temporary exit code.

```
# Does the update include a new kernel
if grep ^kernel $UpdatesFile > /dev/null
then
    NeedsReboot=1
    echo "Kernel update for $HOSTNAME."
fi
# Or is there a new glibc
if grep ^glibc $UpdatesFile > /dev/null
then
    NeedsReboot=1
    echo "glibc update for $HOSTNAME."
fi
# Or is there a new systemd
if grep ^systemd $UpdatesFile > /dev/null
then
    NeedsReboot=1
    echo "systemd update for $HOSTNAME."
fi

if [ $NeedsReboot -eq 1 ]
then
    echo "A reboot will be required for $HOSTNAME."
fi

# Temporary exit
exit
```

Figure 29-10. *Checking for updates to packages that indicate the need for a reboot*

We also need to change the default entry on the -c (check) option from 1 to zero in the variable initialization settings.

After adding the code in Figure 29-10 and changing the initial value of the $Check variable to 0, run some tests to verify that it is correct and working as expected:

```
[root@studentvm1 bin]# doUpdates.sh -c
Updates ARE available for host studentvm1.
Kernel update for studentvm1.
systemd update for studentvm1.
A reboot will be required.
[root@studentvm1 bin]#
```

Change the reboot logic at the bottom of the program to that in Figure 29-11. Note that we have made this fairly verbose, especially in the event of a failure. The "else" entry in the if structure is there in case none of the other expected logical combinations are met.

```
# Reboot if necessary
if [ $NeedsReboot == 0 ]
then
    echo
    echo "####################################################"
    echo "# A reboot is not required."
    echo "####################################################"
    echo
elif [ $doReboot == 1 ] && [ $NeedsReboot == 1 ]
then
    reboot
elif [ $doReboot == 0 ] && [ $NeedsReboot == 1 ]
then
    echo
    echo "####################################################"
    echo "# A reboot is needed."
    echo "# Be sure to reboot at the earliest opportunity."
    echo "####################################################"
    echo
else
    echo
    echo "####################################################"
    echo "# An error has occurred and I cannot determine"
    echo "# whether to reboot or not. Intervention is required."
    echo "####################################################"
    echo
fi
```

Figure 29-11. *Change the reboot logic code to this*

Now a reboot after updates are installed occurs only if the $NeedsReboot and $DoReboot variables are both set to "true," that is, one (1).

We will test this code in later experiments after we remove the temporary exit.

Adding a Help Function

Shell functions are lists of Bash program statements that are stored in the shell environment and that can be executed like any other command, by typing its name at the command line. Shell functions may also be known as procedures or subroutines depending upon which other programming language you might be using.

Functions are called in our scripts or from the CLI by using their names, just as we would for any other command. In a CLI program or a script, the commands in the function are executed when called, and then the sequence of program flow returns to the calling entity and the next series of program statements in that entity is executed.

The syntax of a function is

```
FunctionName(){list}
```

Before we add our Help function, let's explore how functions work.

EXPERIMENT 29-8: INTRODUCING FUNCTIONS

Perform this experiment as the student user. Start by creating a simple function at the CLI. The function is stored in the shell environment for the shell instance in which it is created. We are going to create a function called "hw," which stands for hello world.

Enter the following code at the CLI and press Enter. Then enter hw as you would any other shell command:

```
[student@studentvm1 ~]$ hw(){ echo "Hi there kiddo"; }
[student@studentvm1 ~]$ hw
Hi there kiddo
[student@studentvm1 ~]$
```

Okay, so I am a little tired of the standard "Hello world" we usually start with.

Now let's list all of the currently defined functions. There are a lot of them, so I have shown just the new hw function. It is quite near the end of the list:

```
[student@studentvm1 ~]$ declare -f | less
<snip>
hw ()
```

```
{
    echo "Hi there kiddo"
}
<snip>
```

Now let's remove that function because we do not need it anymore. We can do that with the unset command:

```
[student@studentvm1 ~]$ unset -f hw ; hw
bash: hw: command not found
[student@studentvm1 ~]$
```

Verify that the function has been removed from the environment.

Now that we know a little about how functions work, we can add our help facility.

EXPERIMENT 29-9: ADDING A HELP FUNCTION

As root again, add the function in Figure 29-12 to the doUpdates.sh script. Place it after the shebang line and before the variable initialization section.

```
############################################################
# Help function
############################################################
Help()
{
    echo "doUpdates.sh"
    echo ""
    echo "Installs all available updates from Fedora repositories."
    echo "Can reboot after updates if certain packages are updated."
    echo "Those packages are:"
    echo ""
    echo "1. The kernel"
    echo "2. glibc"
    echo "3. systemd"
    echo ""
    echo "Syntax: doUpdates.sh [-c|h|r]"
    echo "Options:"
    echo "-c   Check whether updates are available and exit."
    echo "-h   Print this Help and exit."
    echo "-r   Reboot if specific trigger packages are updated"
    echo ""
} # end of Help()
```

Figure 29-12. *Add a Help() function*

Now add an option for help to the `case` statement. *Be sure to add the "h" to the* `getops` *option string.* Figure 29-13 shows the revised option processing code that includes the new "h" option.

```
# Get the options
while getopts ":hcr" option; do
   case $option in
      c) # Check option
          Check=1;;
      h) # Help function
          Help
          exit;;
      r) # Reboot option
          doReboot=1;;
     \?) # incorrect option
          echo "Error: Invalid option."
          exit;;
   esac
done
```

Figure 29-13. *Add the Help function to the option processing code*

We now test again and fix any errors we find. I neglected to add the double semicolon (;;) at the end of the Help function processing, so I received the following error:

```
[root@studentvm1 bin]# doUpdates.sh -h
doUpdates.sh: line 55: syntax error near unexpected token `)'
doUpdates.sh: line 55: `        r) # Reboot option'
```

After fixing the problem, I reran the test and the Help function worked as expected:

```
[root@studentvm1 bin]# doUpdates.sh -h
doUpdates.sh

Installs all available updates from Fedora repositories.
Can reboot after updates if certain packages are updated.
Those packages are:

1. The kernel
2. glibc
3. systemd
```

```
Syntax: doUpdates.sh [-c|h|r]
Options:
-c   Check whether updates are available and exit.
-h   Print this Help and exit.
-r   Reboot if specific trigger packages are updated
```

Be sure to test using the -c option to ensure that nothing else is broken. For now we will skip testing the -r (reboot) option for expediency.

Finishing the Script

So there are now only two things we need to do in order to finish this script – at least for now. We need to add the code that actually performs the update and remove the temporary exit. We also need to add some logic to the reboot at the end of the program.

EXPERIMENT 29-10: FINISHING THE SCRIPT

We need to do two things before our program is ready. First, remove the two lines in Figure 29-14.

```
# Temporary exit
exit
```

Figure 29-14. *Remove the temporary exit code ...*

Then add the code in Figure 29-15 to replace what we just deleted.

```
# Perform the update
dnf -y update
```

Figure 29-15. *...and add this code in its place*

```
####################################
# A little cleanup
####################################
rm -f $UpdatesFile

if [ $doReboot = 1 ] && [ $NeedsReboot = 1 ]
then
    # reboot the computer because the kernel or glibc have been updated
    # AND the reboot option was specified.
    Msg="Rebooting $HOSTNAME."
    PrintMsg
    reboot
    # no need to quit here
elif [ $ForceReboot = 1 ]
then
    reboot
elif [ $doReboot = 0 ] && [ $NeedsReboot = 1 ]
then
    Msg="This system, $HOSTNAME, needs rebooted but you did not choose
    the -r option to reboot it."
    PrintMsg
    Msg="You should reboot $HOSTNAME manually at the earliest opportunity."
else
    Msg="NOT rebooting $HOSTNAME."
fi

PrintMsg
Quit
```

So now we are ready to test version 0.1 of our program. But before we do that, let's discuss testing in more detail.

About Testing

There is always one more bug.

—Lubarsky's Law of Cybernetic Entomology

Lubarsky – whoever they might be – is correct. We can never find all of the bugs in our code. For every bug I find, there always seems to be another that crops up, usually at a very inopportune time.

Testing is not just about programs. It is also about verification that problems – whether caused by hardware, software, or the seemingly endless ways that users can find to break things – that we are supposed to have resolved actually have been. These problems can be with application or utility software we wrote, system software, and hardware. Just as importantly, testing is also about ensuring that the code is easy to use and the interface makes sense to the user.

Following a well-defined procedure when writing and testing shell scripts can contribute to consistent and high-quality results. My procedures are simple:

1.   Create a simple test plan.

2.   Start testing right at the beginning of development.

3.   Perform a final test when the code is complete.

4.   Move to production and test more.

You have undoubtedly noticed that we have run multiple tests at every step of creating this program. One of the tenets of *The Linux Philosophy for SysAdmins* is to "Test Early, Test Often."[3]

Testing in Production

Huh, what?

Not until a program has been in production for at least six months will the most harmful error be discovered.

—Troutman's Programming Postulates

---

[3] Op. cit., Chapter 11

Yes, testing in production is now considered normal and desirable. Having been a tester myself, this actually does seem reasonable. "But wait! That's dangerous," you say. My experience is that it is no more dangerous than extensive and rigorous testing in a dedicated test environment. In some cases there is no choice because there *is* no test environment – only production.

SysAdmins are no strangers to the need to test new or revised scripts in production. Any time a script is moved into production, that becomes the ultimate test. The production environment itself constitutes the most critical part of that test. Nothing that can be dreamed up by testers in a test environment can fully replicate the true production environment.

The allegedly new practice of testing in production is just the recognition of what we SysAdmins have known all along. The best test is production – so long as it is not the only test.

Fuzzy Testing

This is another of those buzzwords that caused me to roll my eyes when I first heard it. I learned that its essential meaning is simple – have someone bang on the keys until something happens and see how well the program handles it. But there really is more to it than that.

Fuzzy testing is a bit like the time my son broke the code for a game in less than a minute with his random input. That pretty much ended my attempts to write games for him.

Most test plans utilize very specific input that generates a specific result or output. Regardless of whether the test is for a positive or negative outcome as success, it is still controlled, and the inputs and results are specified and expected, such as a specific error message for a specific failure mode.

Fuzzy testing is about dealing with randomness in all aspects of the test such as starting conditions, very random and unexpected input, random combinations of options selected, low memory, high levels of CPU contention with other programs, multiple instances of the program under test, and any other random conditions that you can think of to be applied to the tests.

I try to do some fuzzy testing right from the beginning. If the Bash script cannot deal with significant randomness in its very early stages, then it is unlikely to get better as we add more code. This is a good time to catch these problems and fix them while the code is relatively simple. A bit of fuzzy testing at each stage of completion is also useful in locating problems before they get masked by even more code.

After the code is completed, I like to do some more extensive fuzzy testing. Always do some fuzzy testing. I have certainly been surprised by some of the results I have encountered. It is easy to test for the expected things, but users do not usually do the expected things with a script.

Testing the Script

```
EXPERIMENT 29-11: TESTING THE SCRIPT
```

Before we start this final test, let's take a snapshot of the StudentVM1 host so that we can return to a known working state in which there are definitely updates to be performed and some that require a reboot. This will give us a good bit of flexibility if we have some fixes to be made to our code. We can boot the snapshot, make the changes, and test again, as many times as necessary to get our script working correctly.

Oh, yes, there are always improvements and functional changes we might want to make that would benefit from having this capability. Hint, hint.

Save the doUpdates.sh program, power off StudentVM1, and make the snapshot. You can refer to Volume 1, Chapter 5, for details of creating the snapshot. I added the following text to the snapshot description: "Near end of Chapter 29. Can be used to roll back to a state where updates are available." Save the snapshot.

Tip   From this point on, when you make changes to the doUpdates.sh script, make a copy of it on an external USB thumb drive or another device. Then you can restart the latest snapshot in which updates are available, copy the latest version of the script into /root, and rerun the test. Using this procedure you can make changes and rerun the test as many times as necessary.

Now reboot, and proceed with the rest of this experiment. We will test but we will not immediately test the update portion of this code. We will start our test using the options that do not lead down that execution path. That way we know those options have not been broken by our latest additions:

```
[root@studentvm1 bin]# doUpdates.sh -c
Updates ARE available for host studentvm1.
[root@studentvm1 bin]# doUpdates.sh -h
doUpdates.sh

Installs all available updates from Fedora repositories. Can reboot
after updates if certain packages are updated. Those packages are:

1. The kernel
2. glibc
3. systemd

Syntax: doUpdates.sh [-c|h|r]
Options:
-c   Check whether updates are available and exit.
-h   Print this Help and exit.
-r   Reboot if specific trigger packages are updated

[root@studentvm1 bin]#
```

It is now time to test the primary function of our script. We will do this first with a manual reboot. We will then reboot StudentVM1 to the last snapshot and run the script again and do a programmatic reboot using the -r option at the command line.

First, run the script with no options:

```
[root@studentvm1 bin]# time doUpdates.sh
```

Depending upon how many packages need to be updated, the speed of your VM, and the speed of your Internet connection, this process may take a long time. On my VM there were 622 packages to update, and it took just over 47 minutes. Jason, my technical reviewer for the first edition of this volume, let me know that it only took 10 minutes for his updates to complete.

Do a manual reboot to verify that the updated VM can still boot. Yes, a reboot can fail after an update though it is a rare occurrence. So test everything. Then power it off.

So we have done one test of our Bash script. We now need to roll back to the last snapshot and retest using the -r option. Let's first do the rollback.

EXPERIMENT 29-12: RESTORING THE SNAPSHOT

This experiment should be performed in the GUI of the host system for the VM. These instructions guide you through reverting to the most recent snapshot.

Open the VirtualBox window and select StudentVM1. Click the menu icon on the right side of the StudentVM1 bar, and then select **Snapshots**. Select the most recent snapshot, which should have been taken earlier in this chapter. Right-click it and then click **Restore**. Uncheck the box "Create a snapshot of the current machine state" and then click Restore.

Hover over the "Current state" line. A little text box opens with the message, "The current state is identical to the state stored in the current snapshot." This is exactly right. Be sure that "Current state" is selected and reboot the VM.

You can check to verify that you have successfully reverted by running dnf check-update to list all of the available updates. You could also run uname -a both before and after rollbacks and compare the release levels.

We can now finish our testing.

EXPERIMENT 29-13: INSTALLING UPDATES WITH A REBOOT

As the root user, run the doUpdates.sh program again, this time using the -r option:

```
[root@studentvm1 bin]# doUpdates.sh -r
```

This should install all of the available updates, rebuild the man database, generate a new GRUB configuration file, and reboot the VM. After the reboot, log in and run some basic tests to verify that the VM is working and responding to simple commands.

Power off, revert to the most recent snapshot, and reboot the VM.

Licensing

One of the best ways I know to give back to the open source community that provides us with all of these incredible programs like the GNU Utilities, the Linux kernel, LibreOffice, WordPress, and thousands more is to open source our own programs and scripts with an appropriate license.

Just because we write a program and we believe in open source and agree that our program should be open source code does not make it so. As SysAdmins we do write a lot of code, but how many of us ever consider the issue of licensing our own code. We must make the choice and explicitly state that the code is open source and under which license it is being distributed. Without this critical step, the code we create is subject to becoming fettered with proprietary licenses so that the community cannot take advantage of our work.

We should include the GPLv2 (or your other preferred) license header statement as a command-line option that would print the license header on the terminal. When distributing code I also recommend that we make it a practice to include a text copy of the entire license with the code – which is a requirement of some licenses.

I find it very interesting that in all of the books I have read and all of the classes I have attended, not once did any of them tell me to be sure to license any code I wrote in my tasks as a SysAdmin. All of these sources completely ignored the fact that SysAdmins write code too. Even in the conference sessions on licensing that I have attended, the focus was on application code, kernel code, or even GNU-type utilities. None of the presentations even so much as hinted at the fact that we SysAdmins write huge amounts of code to automate our work or that we should even consider licensing it in any way. Perhaps you have had a different experience, but this has been mine. At the very least, this frustrates me; at the most it angers me.

We devalue our code when we neglect to license it. Most of us SysAdmins don't even think about licensing, but it is important if we want our code to be available to the entire community. This is neither about credit nor is it about money. This is about ensuring that our code is now and always will be available to others in the best sense of free and open source.

Eric Raymond, author of the 2003 book *The Art of Unix Programming*,[4] writes that in the early days of computer programming and especially in the early life of Unix, sharing code was a way of life. In the beginning this was simply reusing existing code. With the advent of Linux and the open source licensing, this became much easier. It feeds the needs of system administrators to be able to legally share and reuse open source code.

Raymond states, "Software developers want their code to be transparent. Furthermore they don't want to lose their toolkits and their expertise when they change jobs. They get tired of being victims, fed up with being frustrated by blunt tools and intellectual-property fences and having to repeatedly reinvent the wheel."[5] This statement also applies to SysAdmins.

I read an interesting article recently, "The source code is the license,"[6] that helps explain the reasoning behind this.

So let's add a licensing statement to our code that can be displayed with a new option.

EXPERIMENT 29-14: ADD A LICENSING STATEMENT

As root, edit the doUpdates.sh program. First, let's add the function shown in Figure 29-16 immediately after the Help function.

---

[4] Raymond, Eric S., *The Art of Unix Programming*, Addison-Wesley, 2004, 380, ISBN: 0-13-13-142901-9

[5] Ibid

[6] Peterson, Scott K., "The source code is the license," https://opensource.com/article/17/12/source-code-license, Opensource.com

```
#############################################################
# Print the GPL license header                             #
#############################################################
gpl()
{
   echo
   echo "###########################################################################"
   echo "#   Copyright (C) 2019, 2023 David Both                                    #"
   echo "#   http://www.both.org                                                    #"
   echo "#                                                                          #"
   echo "#   This program is free software; you can redistribute it and/or modify   #"
   echo "#   it under the terms of the GNU General Public License as published by   #"
   echo "#   the Free Software Foundation; either version 2 of the License, or      #"
   echo "#   (at your option) any later version.                                    #"
   echo "#                                                                          #"
   echo "#   This program is distributed in the hope that it will be useful,        #"
   echo "#   but WITHOUT ANY WARRANTY; without even the implied warranty of         #"
   echo "#   MERCHANTABILITY or FITNESS FOR A PARTICULAR PURPOSE.  See the          #"
   echo "#   GNU General Public License for more details.                           #"
   echo "#                                                                          #"
   echo "#   You should have received a copy of the GNU General Public License      #"
   echo "#   along with this program; if not, write to the Free Software            #"
   echo "#   Foundation, Inc., 59 Temple Place, Suite 330,                          #"
   echo "#   Boston, MA, 02111-1307 USA                                             #"
   echo "###########################################################################"
   echo
} # End of gpl()
```

Figure 29-16. *Add a function that prints the GPLv2 license header*

Now we need to add an option to the option processing code. Since this is the GPL, I chose "g." Figure 29-17 shows the revised option processing code. I like to place the new case sections in alphabetical order to make them a bit easier to find when performing maintenance.

```
##############################################################
# Process the input options                                  #
##############################################################
# Get the options
while getopts ":cghr" option; do
   case $option in
      c) # Check option
            Check=1;;
      g) # display the GPL header
            gpl
            exit;;
      h) # Help function
            Help
            exit;;
      r) # Reboot option
            doReboot=1;;
     \?) # incorrect option
            echo "Error: Invalid option."
            exit;;
   esac
done
```

Figure 29-17. *Add the g option to the case structure*

Finally, we need to add a line to the Help function. Add the line shown in Figure 29-18 in the option section. I like to try and keep these in alphabetical order, too, but you can place them in any order that makes sense to you.

```
   echo "-g   Print the GPL license notification."
```

Figure 29-18. *Add a line to the Help function that describes the -g option*

Now test this new option and make sure nothing else has been broken.

Make another snapshot.

315

Automated Testing

Testing is important and, if your Bash programs are more than just a few lines, you may want to explore some automated testing tools. Although I have worked as a tester in one of my jobs and used Tcl/Expect to automate our application testing, that type of tool is way overkill for the SysAdmin. We work on tight schedules with little or no time to use complex, and possibly expensive, tools, whether open source or not.

I have found one interesting tool that you might wish to explore. BATS[7] is a tool specifically designed for testing Bash programs. There are undoubtedly other tools that can be useful to testing Bash programs. Most of the time manual testing works just fine for the Bash programs I write so long as I have a test plan.

Additional Levels of Automation

Now I have this incredibly wonderful and useful script. I have copied it to /root/bin on all of my computers. All I have to do now is run it at appropriate times on each of my Linux hosts to do the updates. I can do this by using SSH to log into each host and run the program.

But wait! There's more! Have I told you yet how absolutely cool SSH is?

The **ssh** command is a secure terminal emulator that allows one to log into a remote computer to access a remote shell session and run commands. So I can log into a remote computer and run the doUpdates.sh command on the remote computer as shown in Figure 29-19. The results are displayed in the SSH terminal emulator window on my local host. The Standard Output (STDOUT) from the command is displayed on my terminal window.

For this volume of the course, we do not yet have a second VM to work with, so we cannot do lab projects for this. I will describe the steps, and the CLI programs and scripts will be shown as figures. We will look at SSH in more detail later in this course.

---

[7] Opensource.com, Testing Bash with BATS, https://opensource.com/article/19/2/testing-bash-bats

```
ssh hostname doUpdates.sh -r
```

Figure 29-19. *Using SSH to perform remote updates with the doUpdates.sh script*

That part is trivial and everyone does that. But the next step is a bit more interesting. Rather than maintain a terminal session on the remote computer, I can simply use a command on my local computer such as that in Figure 29-19 to run the command on the remote computer with the results being displayed on the local host. This assumes that SSH public/private key pairs[8] (PPKPs) are in use, and I do not have to enter a password each time I issue a command to the remote host.

So now I run a single command on my local host that sends a command through the SSH tunnel to the remote host. Okay, that is good, but what does it mean?

It means that what I can do for a single computer I can also do for several – or several hundred. The Bash command-line program in Figure 29-20 illustrates the power I now have.

```
for I in host1 host2 host3 ; do ssh $I doUpdates.sh -r ; done
```

Figure 29-20. *Using a simple CLI program to perform remote updates on multiple computers*

This little command-line program is now doing the type of function that advanced tools like Ansible[9] can do. It is important to understand automation with Bash in order to fully understand and appreciate the role and capabilities of advanced tools like Ansible.

Think we're done? No, we are not! The next step is to create a short Bash script of this CLI program so we don't have to retype it every time we want to install updates on our hosts. This does not have to be fancy; the script can be as simple as the one in Figure 29-20.

This script could be named "updates" or something else depending on how you like to name scripts and what you see as its ultimate function. I think we should call this script "`doit`". Now we can just type a single command and run a smart update program

---

[8] How to Forge, `www.howtoforge.com/linux-basics-how-to-install-ssh-keys-on-the-shell`

[9] De La Matta, Jonathan Lozada, "A sysadmin's guide to Ansible: How to simplify tasks," `https://opensource.com/article/18/7/sysadmin-tasks-ansible`, Opensource.com

on as many hosts as we have in the list of the for statement. Our script should be located in the /usr/local/bin directory so it can be easily run from the command line.

Our little doit script looks like it could be the basis for more general application. We could add more code to doit that would enable it to take arguments or options such as the name of a command to run on all of the hosts in the list. This enables us to run any command we want on a list of hosts, and our command to install updates might be doit doUpdates.sh -r or doit myprogram to run "myprogram" on each host.

The next step might be to take the list of hosts out of the program itself and place them in a doit.conf file located in /usr/local/etc – again in compliance with the Linux FHS. That command would look like Figure 29-21 for our simple doit script. Notice the backticks (') that create the list used by the for structure from the results of the cat command.

```
#!/bin/bash
for I in `cat /usr/local/etc/doit.conf` ; do ssh $I doUpdates.sh ; done
```

Figure 29-21. *We have now added a simple external list that contains the hostnames on which the script will run the specified command*

By keeping the list of hosts separate, we can allow non-root users to modify the list of hosts while protecting the program itself against modification. It would also be easy to add an -f option to the doit program so that the users could specify the name of a file containing their own list of hosts on which to run the specified program.

Finally, we might want to set this up as a cron job so that we don't have to remember to run it on whatever schedule we want. Setting up cron jobs is worthy of its own chapter, and that is coming up in Chapter 31.

Cleanup

Let's do a little cleanup to prepare for Chapter 30.

EXPERIMENT 29-15: PREP FOR CHAPTER 30

Power off, revert to the most recent snapshot, and reboot the VM.

Chapter Summary

If you reflect on what we have done in this chapter, you can see that automation is not merely about creating a program to perform every task. It can be about making those programs flexible so that they can be used in multiple ways such as the ability to be called from other scripts and to be called as a cron job.

Computers are designed to automate various mundane tasks, and why should that not also be applied to the SysAdmin's work? We lazy SysAdmins use the capabilities of the computers on which we work to make our jobs easier. Automating everything that we possibly can means that the time we free up by creating that automation can now be used to respond to some real or perceived emergency by others, especially by the PHB. It can also provide us with time to automate even more.

My programs almost always use options to provide flexibility. The `doit` program used in this chapter could easily be expanded to be more general than it is while still remaining quite simple. It could still do one thing well if its objective were to run a specified program on a list of hosts.

My shell scripts did not just spring into existence with hundreds or thousands of lines. In most cases they start as a single ad hoc command-line program. I create a shell script from the ad hoc program. Then another command-line program is added to the short script. Then another. As the short script becomes longer, I add comments, options, and a help feature.

Then, sometimes, it makes sense to make a script more general so that it can handle more cases. In this way the `doit` script becomes capable of "doing it" for more than just a single program that does updates.

As far as this chapter is concerned, this script is complete, and it can be used in production. But as you use it, you will undoubtedly find more refinements you might want to make. Clearly you should feel free to do so.

Exercises

Complete the following exercises to finish this chapter:

1. List at least three advantages to creating and using scripts.

2. There is at least one set of conditions under which we have not
    tested our doUpdates.sh shell program. Devise and implement a
    way to test the doUpdates.sh program in that circumstance. Add
    one line of code to the "incorrect option" case stanza that will
    display the help text before exiting.

3. Add a new option (-u) to the doUpdates.sh program. This option
    should be used to perform the actual updates. If the -u option is
    not present, the updates should not be performed.

CHAPTER 30

Automation with Ansible

Objectives

In this chapter you will learn

- What Ansible can add to your automation strategies
- The Ansible automation strategy
- To install Ansible
- How to perform ad hoc Ansible commands from the command line
- What a playbook is
- To create a simple playbook that performs configuration updates for a single application
- To create a playbook that performs Linux updates

My First Day with Ansible

Getting a new computer, whether physical or virtual, up and running for the first time or the 50th is time-consuming and requires a good deal of work. For many years I used a series of scripts and RPMs that I created to install the packages I needed and to perform many bits of configuration for my favorite tools. This approach has worked well and simplified my work as well as reducing the amount of time I spent actually typing commands.

I am always looking for better ways of doing things and, for several years, I had been hearing and reading about Ansible, which is a powerful tool for automating system configuration and management. Ansible allows the SysAdmin to define a specific state

© David Both 2023
D. Both, *Using and Administering Linux: Volume 2*, https://doi.org/10.1007/978-1-4842-9615-8_30

for each host in one or more playbooks and then performs whatever tasks are necessary to bring the host to that state. This includes installing or deleting various resources such as RPM packages, configuration files and other files, users, groups, and much more.

I had delayed learning how to use it for a long time because …stuff. Until I ran into a problem that I thought Ansible could easily solve for me.

This chapter is not intended to be a complete how-to of getting started with Ansible; it is intended to help you get started using Ansible and to provide you with some insight into some of the issues that I encountered and to provide some information that I found only in some very obscure places. Much of the information I found on various online discussions and Q&A groups about Ansible was incorrect. Errors ranged from information that was really old with no indication of its date or provenance to information that was just wrong. The information in this chapter is known to work – although there might be other ways of accomplishing the same things – and it works with Ansible 2.9.13 and Python 3.8.5 as of this writing.

The Ansible Strategy

Ansible uses a hub strategy for managing hosts. The Ansible software is installed on the host that acts as the hub. Client-side Ansible software does not exist, so none needs to be installed on the remote hosts.

Ansible uses SSH, which is already installed by nearly every Linux distribution, to communicate with remote hosts. Although SysAdmins can choose to use passwords for remote access to hosts, that certainly reduces the efficiency and hands-off nature of a tool like Ansible. So, like most other admins, I use public/private key pairs (PPKPs), which are considered safer than passwords and allow automation of tasks for from one to thousands of remote hosts with no intervention from the administrator.

Ansible sends commands to the remote hosts via SSH and uses the results to determine the success of the command. It can also use those results to determine the next course of action using conditional when statements.

My Problem

All of my best learning experiences start with a problem I need to solve, and this was no exception.

I had been working on a little project to modify the configuration files for Midnight Commander (mc) and push them out to various systems in my network for testing. Although I had a script to automate that, it still required a bit of fussing with a command-line loop to provide the names of the systems to which I wanted to push the new code. The large number of changes I was making to the configuration files made it necessary for me to push the new ones frequently and then, just when I thought I had my new configuration just right, I would find a problem and need to do another push after making the fix.

This environment made it difficult to keep track of which systems had the new files and which did not. I also had a couple hosts that needed to be treated differently. And my little bit of understanding of Ansible suggested that it would probably be able to do all or most of what I needed.

Getting Started

I had previously read a number of good articles and books about Ansible but not in the "I have to get this working NOW!" kind of situation. And now was – well – NOW!

In rereading these documents, I discovered that the books mostly talked about how to install Ansible from GitHub using – wait for it – Ansible. That is cool, but I really just wanted to get started, so I installed it on my Fedora workstation using DNF and the version in the Fedora repository. Easy.

But then I started looking for the file locations and trying to determine which configuration files I needed to modify, where to keep my playbooks, what a playbook even looked like, and what it did. I had lots of unanswered questions running around in my head. So without further descriptions of my tribulations, here are the things I discovered and that got me going.

Installing Ansible

Like the other tools we have installed, Ansible is easy and requires no reboot.

Tip All experiments in this chapter should be performed as the root user unless otherwise directed.

EXPERIMENT 30-1: INSTALLING ANSIBLE

Install Ansible. This installs a few dependencies including some Python modules:

```
[root@studentvm1 ~]# dnf -y install ansible
```

No reboot is required.

Configuration

Ansible's configuration files are kept in /etc/ansible. Makes sense, right – since /etc is where system programs are supposed to keep their configuration files. The two files I needed to work with here are ansible.cfg and hosts.

ansible.cfg

After getting started with some of the exercises I found in the documents and online, I was receiving warning messages about deprecating certain older Python files. I wanted to suppress those warnings, so I modified the ansible.cfg file to accomplish that.

EXPERIMENT 30-2: SUPPRESSING DEPRECATION WARNINGS

Add the following line to the end of ansible.cfg so you won't receive those angry red warning messages:

```
deprecation_warnings = False
```

Those warnings are probably important, so I will revisit them later and figure out what I need to do, but for now they no longer clutter the screen and obfuscate the errors with which I actually need to be concerned. So far I have encountered no problems.

Preparing to Use Ansible

Ansible uses SSH to communicate with all hosts including the hub itself. This ensures a high level of security, but our host is not yet configured to run the SSHD server. We need to configure it before we continue with Ansible.

SSH provides three options when dealing with logins by root. SSH can prevent root from logging in at all, it can allow login with a password, or it can allow root login using public/private key pairs (PPKPs) while blocking password login by root. The default is to block root login.

Ansible needs to have root access in order to perform its tasks. There are two methods for accomplishing that. First, Ansible can log in as a non-root user and use its "become" directive to escalate to root privilege. This is great for Ansible but doesn't allow for scripts to be run remotely as we looked at briefly in Chapter 29.

We'll explore the use of SSH in much more detail in Chapter 45. That will include the use of public/private key pairs for unattended remote login using scripts for automation.

In Experiment 30-3 we'll temporarily allow root to log in using a password with SSH in order to install its public key on the target host and then configure the SSH server to allow only PPKP login by root. After making the needed changes, direct login as root via SSH will be blocked in order to optimize security.

EXPERIMENT 30-3: CONFIGURING THE SSHD SERVER

Begin this experiment as the root user on StudentVM1. Perform a listing of all files (-a) in the root home directory of your student host. You should not find a directory named ~/.ssh in the list. This directory is where local SSH configuration files for the user are located, but it does not get created until the first time the user connects to a remote (or local) host with SSH.

Enable SSHD

We begin by configuring the SSHD server daemon and enabling it so it will start on boot.

We need to make one change to the /etc/ssh/sshd_config configuration file. Edit this file and change the line

```
#PermitRootLogin prohibit-password
```

to

```
PermitRootLogin yes
```

This allows the root user to log into the host directly and to use a password to do so.

Now start and enable the SSHD service:

```
[root@studentvm1 ~]# systemctl start sshd ; systemctl enable sshd
Created symlink /etc/systemd/system/multi-user.target.wants/sshd.service →
/usr/lib/systemd/system/sshd.service.
[root@studentvm1 ~]#
```

Our StudentVM1 host is now ready for us to try out an SSH connection. Because there are no other hosts in the network to which we can connect, we test by connecting to StudentVM1 – the source and target hosts are the same:

Tip   It is common for Linux hosts to communicate with themselves like this. This ability to communicate between different Linux hosts and within a single host using a single set of network protocols prevents the need for two separate protocols – one for internal host communications and one for external network communications to remote hosts.

This is an excellent example of the Linux Philosophy tenet to keep things simple.[1] The local host and all remote hosts are treated exactly the same.

```
[root@studentvm1 ~]# ssh localhost
The authenticity of host 'localhost (::1)' can't be established.
ECDSA key fingerprint is SHA256:NDM/B5L3eRJaalex6IOUdnJsE1smOSiQNWgaI8BwcVs.
Are you sure you want to continue connecting (yes/no)? yes
Warning: Permanently added 'localhost' (ECDSA) to the list of known hosts.
root@localhost's password: <Enter Password>
[root@studentvm1 ~]#
```

The first time an SSH connection is made to any host, the authenticity message is displayed along with the fingerprint of the private key of the remote (in this case local) host. In a very security-conscious environment, we would have already received a copy of the remote host's key fingerprint. This allows comparison so that we know we are connecting to the correct

---

[1] See Chapter 3 in Volume 1 of this course.

remote host. This is not the security key; it is a fingerprint that is unique to that private key. It is impossible to reconstruct the original private key from which the fingerprint was generated.

You must type "**yes**" – the full word – in order for the public key to be transmitted from the remote host to the local one. Then you must enter the password for the remote host.

You should also connect to the local host as the student user via SSH.

Now let's look at the /root/.ssh directory. Then look at the contents of the ~/.ssh/known_hosts file. You should see the public host key for the remote host. This file is created in the local host, the one we are connecting from, and not in the remote host, the one we are connecting to:

```
[root@studentvm1 ~]# cat .ssh/known_hosts
localhost ecdsa-sha2-nistp256 AAAAE2VjZHNhLXNoYTItbmlzdHAyNTYAAAAIbmlzdHA
yNTYAAABBBMDg3AOuakzj1P14aJgeOHCRSJpsxOAlU6fXiVRlc/RwQRvFkMblO5/t7wSFcwOG8
tRSiNaktVs4dxpAoMbrT3c=
```

After accepting this key during the first connection to the remote (in this case local) host, the connections initialize a little faster because the two computers now know each other and can identify themselves via the keys.

Type **exit** to disconnect the SSH connection.

There is one more thing that we need to do before the SSH configuration is complete – generate and set up a public/private key pair (PPKP) for the root user so that passwords won't be required. Create the public/private key pair. Use the following command to create a public/private key pair. The -b 2048 option generates a key that is 2048 bits in length; the minimum allowable length is 1024 bits. By default it will generate an RSA key, but we could also specify other key types. RSA is considered to be very secure so we will use RSA. We will press Enter to respond to all inquiries so as to take all of the defaults:

```
[root@studentvm1 ~]$ ssh-keygen -b 2048
Generating public/private rsa key pair.
Enter file in which to save the key (/root/.ssh/id_rsa): <Enter>
Enter passphrase (empty for no passphrase): <Enter>
Enter same passphrase again: <Enter>
Your identification has been saved in /root/.ssh/id_rsa
Your public key has been saved in /root/.ssh/id_rsa.pub
The key fingerprint is:
SHA256:771Ouc57qPzfGTzCaqLbO+G1xx7iCOKXZ9aYSAH2hSo root@studentvm1
The key's randomart image is:
```

```
+---[RSA 2048]----+
|       o....     |
|       . ..o     |
|         .o      |
|      E .. o +   |
|      S. + * .   |
|       ....=o.   |
|      .+.==o=    |
|      .=.B=o++=  |
|      oo.B*XB=o. |
+----[SHA256]-----+
[root@studentvm1 ~]#
```

The host key's fingerprint and/or the randomart image can be used to verify the validity of a public key for the host. It cannot be used to recreate the original public or private key, and it cannot be used for communication. It is used only to verify the validity of the key.

Now that we have generated our key pair, look again at the contents of the ~/.ssh directory for the root user on StudentVM1. You should see two new files, id_rsa, which is the private key, and id_rsa.pub, which is the public key. The .pub extension kind of gives that away.

Copy the Public Key to the Target Host

It's not necessary to send our public keys via email or another off-network type of delivery. We have a nice tool for that. Do this as the root user on StudentVM1:

```
[root@studentvm1 ~]$ ssh-copy-id studentvm1
/usr/bin/ssh-copy-id: INFO: Source of key(s) to be installed: "/root/.ssh/
id_rsa.pub"
/usr/bin/ssh-copy-id: INFO: attempting to log in with the new key(s), to
filter out any that are already installed
/usr/bin/ssh-copy-id: INFO: 1 key(s) remain to be installed -- if you are
prompted now it is to install the new keys
root@studentvm1's password: <Enter root password>

Number of key(s) added: 1

Now try logging into the machine, with:   "ssh 'studentvm1'"
and check to make sure that only the key(s) you wanted were added.

[root@studentvm1 ~]#
```

As the message at the end of the previous command suggests, let's test this:

```
[root@studentvm1 ~]# ssh studentvm1
Last login: Mon Mar 13 09:43:13 2023 from ::1
[root@studentvm1 ~]#
```

Notice that no password is required.

Exit from all SSH connections if there are more than just the one.

Final SSHD Configuration

We need to make one final adjustment to the SSHD configuration to optimize security.

Change the PermitRootLogin line of the sshd_conf file to

```
PermitRootLogin prohibit-password
```

Testing

Test this final configuration first by ensuring that the student user can't log in as root:

```
[student@studentvm1 ~]$ ssh root@studentvm1
The authenticity of host 'studentvm1 (192.168.56.21)' can't be established.
ED25519 key fingerprint is SHA256:3XJEfAjzJv6S+sBKjt9OyXmeKYxzlWBYXp
2MROWDarU.
This host key is known by the following other names/addresses:
    ~/.ssh/known_hosts:1: localhost
Are you sure you want to continue connecting (yes/no/[fingerprint])? yes
Warning: Permanently added 'studentvm1' (ED25519) to the list of known hosts.
root@studentvm1's password: <Enter root password>
Permission denied, please try again.
root@studentvm1's password: <Enter root password>
Permission denied, please try again.
root@studentvm1's password: <Enter root password>
root@studentvm1: Permission denied (publickey,gssapi-keyex,gssapi-with-
mic,password).
```

Second, ensure that the student user can log in using SSH:

```
[student@studentvm1 ~]$ ssh student@studentvm1
student@studentvm1's password: <Enter student password>
Last login: Thu Jul 13 06:50:50 2023 from 192.168.0.1
[student@studentvm1 ~]$
```

Exit from that login.

Test to ensure that root can log in and not be required to use a password:

```
[root@studentvm1 ~]# ssh studentvm1
Last failed login: Thu Jul 13 06:51:46 EDT 2023 from 192.168.56.21 on
ssh:notty
There were 3 failed login attempts since the last successful login.
Last login: Thu Jul 13 06:37:44 2023 from 192.168.56.21
[root@studentvm1 ~]#
```

For this chapter we used the same host for the originator (client) and the receiver (server) of the SSH connection. This procedure works for remote hosts as well as the local host.

We will explore SSH in more detail in Volume 3, Chapter 45.

Ansible Facts

Most of the books I have read talk about Ansible facts. This information is available in other ways such as lshw, dmidecode, the /proc filesystem, and more, but Ansible generates a JSON file to contain this information. Ansible generates this facts data each time it runs. There is an amazing amount of information in this data stream, all of which is in <"variable-name": "value"> pairs. All of these variables are available for use within an Ansible playbook. The best way to understand the huge amount of information available is to display it for yourself.

EXPERIMENT 30-4: ANSIBLE FACTS

Get the Ansible facts for your StudentVM1 host:

```
[root@studentvm1 ~]# ansible -m setup studentvm1
[WARNING]: provided hosts list is empty, only localhost is available. Note
that the implicit localhost does not match 'all'
[WARNING]: Could not match supplied host pattern, ignoring: studentvm1
```

That failed because we don't have an entry for the Studentvm1 host in the Ansible hosts file. However, the following command does work:

```
[root@studentvm1 ~]# ansible -m setup localhost | less
```

See what I mean? Everything you ever wanted to know about your host hardware and Linux distribution is there and usable in a playbook. I use some of these variables in my Ansible playbooks.

The hosts File

Not the same as the /etc/hosts file, this file is also known as the inventory file, and it lists the hosts in your network. This file allows grouping hosts together in related sets such as servers, workstations, and pretty much any designation you need. This file contains its own help and plenty of examples, so I won't go into boring detail here. However, there are some things to know.

Hosts can be listed outside of any groups, but groups can be helpful in identifying hosts with one or more common characteristics. Groups use the INI format, so a server group looks like this:

```
[servers]
server1
server2
...etc.
```

A hostname must be present in this file for Ansible to work on it. Even though some sub-commands allow you to specify a hostname, the command will fail unless the hostname is in the hosts file. A host can also be listed in multiple groups. So server1 might also be a member of the [webservers] group in addition to the [servers] group and a member of the [fedora] group to differentiate it from other servers that use other distros.

Ansible is smart. If the **all** argument is used for hostname, Ansible scans the file and performs the defined tasks on all hosts listed in the file. Ansible will only attempt to work on each host once no matter how many groups it appears in. This also means that there does not need to be a defined "all" group because Ansible can determine all hostnames in the file and create its own list of unique hostnames.

Another little thing to look out for is multiple entries for a single host. I use CNAME records in my DNS zone file to create aliased names that point to the A records for some of my hosts. That way I can refer to a host as host1 or h1 or myhost. If you use multiple hostnames for the same host in the hosts file, Ansible will try to perform its tasks on all of those hostnames; it has no way of knowing that they refer to the same host. The good news is that this does not affect the overall result; it just takes a bit more time as Ansible works on the secondary hostnames and determines that all of the operations have already been performed.

Creating the hosts File

As we have seen, a hosts file will make running the Ansible playbooks easier. Create the hosts file now. Remember this hosts file is for Ansible. The system /etc/hosts file is used for different purposes and has a different structure.

EXPERIMENT 30-5: CREATING THE HOSTS FILE

Edit the /etc/hosts file as root and add the following content to the bottom:

```
[workstations]
studentvm1
```

Now run the following command to verify that using the hostname works. You can see that Ansible uses SSH to connect to the "remote" host even when it is the local one. Enter "yes" to continue:

```
[root@studentvm1 ~]# ansible -m setup studentvm1
```

Be sure to examine the comments in the Ansible hosts file for guidance when adding entries. It contains a lot of good information.

The Ansible configuration is now complete.

Modules

The previous Ansible command uses the -m option to specify the "setup" module. Ansible has many modules of its own already built-in, so the -m does not need to be used for those. There are also many downloadable modules that can be installed, but for my current projects, the built-ins do everything I have needed so far.

Introduction to Playbooks

Playbooks can be located almost anywhere. Since I need to run my playbooks as root, I placed mine in /root/ansible. As long as this directory is the PWD when I run, Ansible can find my playbook. Of course Ansible also has a runtime option to specify a different playbook and location.

Playbooks can contain comments although I have seen few articles or books that mention this. As a SysAdmin who believes in documenting everything, I find that comments can be very helpful. This is not so much about saying the same things in the comments as I do in the task name, but rather it is about identifying the purpose of groups of tasks and ensuring that I record my reasons for doing certain things in a certain way or order. This can help with debugging problems at a later date when I might have forgotten my original thinking.

Playbooks are simply collections of tasks that define the desired state of a host. A hostname or inventory group is specified at the beginning of the playbook and defines the hosts on which Ansible will run the playbook.

A sample of one of my playbooks looks like Figure 30-1.

```
#############################################################################
# This Ansible playbook updates Midnight commander configuration files.  #
#############################################################################
- name: Update midnight commander configuration files
  hosts: all

  tasks:
  - name: ensure midnight commander is the latest version
    dnf:
      name: mc
      state: present

  - name: create ~/.config/mc directory for root
    file:
      path: /root/.config/mc
      state: directory
      mode: 0755
      owner: root
      group: root

  - name: create ~/.config/mc directory for dboth
    file:
      path: /home/dboth/.config/mc
      state: directory
      mode: 0755
      owner: dboth
      group: dboth
  - name: copy latest personal skin
    copy:
      src: /root/ansible/UpdateMC/files/MidnightCommander/DavidsGoTar.ini
      dest: /usr/share/mc/skins/DavidsGoTar.ini
      mode: 0644
      owner: root
      group: root

  - name: copy latest mc ini file
    copy:
      src: /root/ansible/UpdateMC/files/MidnightCommander/ini
      dest: /root/.config/mc/ini
      mode: 0644
      owner: root
      group: root
<SNIP>
```

Figure 30-1. *A sample portion of an Ansible playbook*

The playbook starts with its own name and the hosts on which it will act, in this case all of the hosts listed in my hosts file. The tasks section lists the specific tasks required to bring the host into compliance with the desired state. In this playbook I start with a task in which the Ansible dnf built-in updates Midnight Commander if it is not the most recent release. The next tasks ensure that the required directories are created if they do not already exist, and the remainder of the tasks copy the files to the proper locations. These file and copy tasks can also set the ownership and file modes for the directories and files.

The details of this playbook are beyond the scope of this chapter, but I used a bit of a brute-force attack on the problem. There are other methods for determining which users need to have the files updated rather than using a task for each file for each user.

Ansible playbooks are written in YAML, which is very strict in its requirement for adherence to a rigid syntax. Even whitespace has meaning in YAML, and the wrong amount of whitespace on a line can cause errors. The "yml" extension stands for YAML. I have seen a couple meanings for that, but my bet is on "Yet Another Markup Language" despite the fact that I have seen some claims that YAML is not a markup language.

Running a playbook is easy. The `ansible-playbook` command is used to run a playbook:

```
# ansible-playbook -f 10 UpdateMC.yml
```

This command runs the playbook I created for updating my Midnight Commander files. The -f option specifies that Ansible should fork up to ten threads in order to perform operations in parallel. This can greatly speed up overall task completion especially when working on multiple hosts.

Output

The output from a running playbook lists each task and the results. An "ok" means that the machine state managed by the task is already defined in the task stanza. Because the state defined in the task is already true, Ansible did not need to perform the actions defined in the task stanza.

A response of "changed" indicates that Ansible performed the task specified in the stanza in order to bring it to the desired state. In this case the machine state defined in the stanza was not true, so the actions defined were performed in order to make it true. On a color-capable terminal, the TASK lines are shown in color. On my host with my amber-on-black terminal color configuration, the TASK lines are shown in amber, changed lines are in brown, and ok lines are shown in green. Error lines are displayed in red.

The output in Figure 30-2 is from a playbook I will eventually use to perform post-install configuration on new hosts.

```
PLAY [Post-installation updates, package installation, and configuration]
TASK [Gathering Facts]
ok: [testvm2]
TASK [Ensure we have connectivity]
ok: [testvm2]
TASK [Install all current updates]
changed: [testvm2]
TASK [Install a few command line tools]
changed: [testvm2]
TASK [copy latest personal Midnight Commander skin to /usr/share]
changed: [testvm2]
TASK [create ~/.config/mc directory for root]
changed: [testvm2]
TASK [Copy the most current Midnight Commander configuration files to
/root/.config/mc]
changed:[testvm2] =>
(item=/root/ansible/PostInstallMain/files/MidnightCommander/DavidsGoTar.ini)
changed: [testvm2] =>
(item=/root/ansible/PostInstallMain/files/MidnightCommander/ini)
changed: [testvm2] =>
(item=/root/ansible/PostInstallMain/files/MidnightCommander/panels.ini)
TASK [create ~/.config/mc directory in /etc/skel]
changed: [testvm2]
<SNIP>
```

Figure 30-2. Typical output from an Ansible playbook run

Files

As with my Midnight Commander task, it is frequently necessary to install and maintain files of various types. There are as many "best practices" defined for creating a directory tree for storing files used in playbooks as there are SysAdmins – or at least the number of authors writing books and articles about Ansible.

I chose a simple structure that makes sense to me as you can see in Figure 30-3.

336

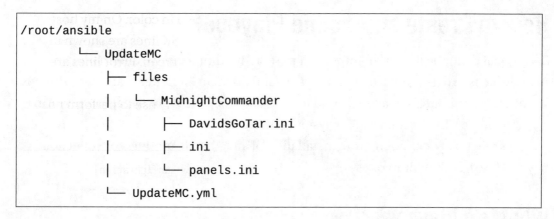

```
/root/ansible
       └── UpdateMC
            ├── files
            |      └── MidnightCommander
            |             ├── DavidsGoTar.ini
            |             ├── ini
            |             └── panels.ini
            └── UpdateMC.yml
```

Figure 30-3. *This is the structure I chose to use for holding the files needed for the Ansible plays*

You should use whatever structure works for you. Just be aware that some other SysAdmin will likely need to work with whatever you set up, so there should be some level of logic to it. When I was using an RPM and Bash scripts to perform my post-install tasks, my file repository was a bit scattered and definitely not structured with any logic. As I work through creating playbooks for many of my administrative tasks, I will be introducing a much more logical structure for managing my files.

Multiple Playbook Runs

It is safe to run a playbook as many times as needed or desired. Each task will only be executed if the state does not match that specified in the task stanza. This makes it easy to recover from errors encountered during previous playbook runs. The playbook stops running when an error is encountered.

While testing my first playbook, I made many mistakes and would then correct them. Each additional run of the playbook – assuming my fix was a good one – would then skip the tasks whose state already matched the specified one and would execute those that were not. When my fix worked, that previously failed task would complete successfully, and any tasks after that one in my playbook would also execute – until another error was encountered.

This makes testing easy. I can add new tasks, and when I run the playbook, only those new tasks are performed because they are the only ones that do not match the desired state of the test host.

How to Create an Ansible Playbook

Scripts will continue to play an important part of my administrative automation, but Ansible looks like it can take over many tasks and do them far better than even complex scripts. It is all about the playbook, and in this section we create one that can perform a system update while accounting for system differences.

This playbook does not require installation of any Ansible modules or collections beyond the default built-in ones.

What Is a Playbook?

As I was writing this chapter, I was also watching some sessions of the year's virtual AnsibleFest. As I watched, I developed my own description of a playbook, one which makes sense to me. This description contains bits of playbook wisdom from several of the presenters as well as some books and blog posts I have read:

An Ansible playbook is a human-created description of the desired state of one or more computers. Ansible reads the playbook and compares the actual state of the computers with the state specified in the playbook and performs the tasks required to bring those computers to conform to the state described in the playbook.

Updates Redux

In Chapter 29 we used a Bash script to automate the installation of updates. Since you are already familiar with the requirements and have already created a simple script to perform this task, we will use Ansible to perform updates as well so that you can compare the two methods.

You should recall that installing updates on modern Linux hosts is a near-constant task, made important by the number of security fixes and feature improvements that come out on a continuous basis. If certain software such as the kernel, glibc, or systemd is updated, the host needs to be rebooted. Some additional tasks also need to be performed such as updating the man page database.

Although the really cool script we created in Chapter 29 does a good job of installing updates and handling reboots and man page updates, some of my hosts need to be treated a little differently than others. For example, I do not want to update my firewall and email/web/DHCP/DNS server at the same time. If the server goes down, the firewall cannot obtain the information it needs to proceed with its own updates, and neither can the other hosts in my network. If the firewall goes down, access to the external Fedora repositories is lost to my server and all other internal hosts. And then there is waiting for these two hosts to reboot before starting updates on the other hosts.

So I used to do those updates by starting the scripts on each host like the firewall and then waiting for it to finish, then moving on to the server, and waiting for it to finish before running a small command-line program to run the update script in sequence on the rest of my hosts. I could have written these dependencies into my scripts, but my first few days with Ansible showed me that it already has those capabilities and many more that would make my task much simpler. Really – MUCH simpler. And faster overall with no intervention from me.

Defining the Requirements

Just like any program, whether written in C, Python, Bash, or any other language, I always start with a set of requirements. You have read my book *The Linux Philosophy for SysAdmins*, haven't you? This is also true for tools like Ansible. I need to define where I am going so I can identify when I have arrived.

These are the requirements for my Ansible playbook:

1. **Play 1**: Ansible hub

    1. First, install updates on the Ansible hub.

    2. Update the man page database.

    3. Reboot if necessary.

    4. Log in after reboot and run the playbook again. Because the hub is already in the desired state, no further actions will be taken in Play 1, and Play 2 will begin.

2. **Play 2**: Servers

    1. Install updates on the firewalls and servers in series, that is, one at a time.

    2. Update the man page database.

    3. Reboot if necessary.

    4. Wait for the first host to reboot if necessary before starting on the next.

3. **Play 3**: Workstations

    1. Do not start updating workstations until servers have completed.

    2. Install updates on each computer running simultaneously in parallel.

    3. Update the man page database.

    4. Reboot if necessary.

There are other ways of doing this. I did think about doing the Ansible hub last so that I do not need to deal with restarting the playbook after the hub reboots. But the way I do things is to do updates on my primary workstation first – which is also my Ansible hub – and then do some testing before updating the rest of the systems, so this strategy works perfectly for that. Your needs will probably differ from mine, so you should use whatever strategy works best for you in the real world. The thing about Ansible is that it is flexible enough to accommodate those different needs.

Now that we have the requirements for a task, we can begin the playbook.

Syntax

Ansible playbooks must conform to the rigid standard YAML syntax and formatting. The most frequent errors I have encountered are my own formatting mistakes. This is usually because I have used or not used leading dashes as required or I have used the wrong indentation.

The play names start in column 1 of the playbook, and each following task is indented by exactly two spaces. Each action in a task is indented by exactly two spaces, and sub-tasks are further indented by exactly two spaces. Any other number of spaces or use of any whitespace other than spaces, such as tabs, will generate a runtime error. Extra white space at the end of a line also generates an error.

You will make formatting errors and will quickly learn to see the problems. There are some tools we can use to assist us in locating these errors before attempting to run playbooks, and they can save a great deal of time in the long run.

Creating the Playbook

Let's create the playbook that will perform those tasks in the required sequence. Playbooks are simply collections of tasks that define the desired state of a host. A hostname or inventory group is specified at the beginning of the playbook and defines the hosts on which Ansible will run the playbook.

My playbook contained three plays, one to handle each type of host I identified in the requirements statement. Each play has a bit different logic but will produce the same end result – one or more hosts with all updates installed. For this course we will create a doUpdates.yml playbook with only one play since there is only one host to consider – for now.

The playbook is located in the /root/ansible/Updates directory, which I created for this project. The Bash program installed by this playbook is located in the /root/ansible/Updates/files directory.

EXPERIMENT 30-6: CREATING AN ANSIBLE PLAYBOOK TO INSTALL UPDATES

I like to start all of my code with some well-structured comments so that the file name and a short description of this playbook are present for myself or some other SysAdmin in the future. Playbooks can contain comments although I have seen few articles or books that mention this.

Starting Comments

As a SysAdmin who believes in documenting everything, I find that comments can be very helpful. This is not so much about saying the same things in the comments as I do in the task name, but rather it is about identifying the purpose of groups of tasks and ensuring that I record my reasons for doing certain things in a certain way or order. This can help with debugging problems at a later date when I might have forgotten my original thinking.

As in Bash, comments begin with a #.

And then, the primary function of this first section is the three dashes (---) that are used to define this as a YAML file. The "yml" extension on the file name stands for YAML. I have seen a couple meanings for that, but my bet is on "Yet Another Markup Language" despite the fact that I have seen some claims that YAML is not one.

Create a new file, /root/ansible/Updates/doUpdates.yml, and add the following code to it:

```
################################################################
#                        doUpdates.yml                         #
#--------------------------------------------------------------#
# This playbook installs all available RPM updates on the      #
# inventory hosts.                                             #
#--------------------------------------------------------------#
#                                                              #
# Change History                                               #
# Date        Name          Version   Description              #
# 2023/03/12  David Both    00.00     Started new code         #
#                                                              #
################################################################
---
```

This next section defines the play in the playbook. Playbooks can have one or more plays.
Ours has only one play for StudentVM1 on which Ansible is run. The one I created for my home
network has one for the Ansible hub, and it also has one for the two servers in my network and
one for the rest of the workstations. Now let's define the play – after all this is a playbook.

Beginning the Play

Notice that the play begins in column 0, and then there is strict indentation of the remaining
lines in the play. There is no statement that defines the beginning of the play. Ansible uses the
strict YAML structure to determine where each play and task begins.

Add this section to the playbook:

```
################################################################
# Play 1 - Do updates for host studentvm1                      #
################################################################
- name: Play 1 - Install updates on studentvm1 - the Ansible hub
  hosts:   studentvm1
  remote_user: root
  vars:
    run: false
    reboot: false
```

We will run into these keywords[2] frequently, so here are some explanations that I wish I had when I started working with Ansible:

- **name:** This line is the name of the play, which is displayed in the STDOUT data stream. This makes it easy to identify each play that runs so that I can keep track as I watch or view the redirected stream later. The keyword is required for each play and task, but the text content is optional.

- **hosts:** This defines the hostnames on which the play will be executed. It can contain a space-separated list of hostnames or the name of a group of hosts. The host group and the names of all listed hosts must appear in the inventory file. By default that is /etc/ansible/hosts but can be another file so long as you use the -i (--inventory) option to specify the alternative file.

- **remote_user:** This line is not a requirement, but it does specify the user that Ansible will act as on the remote host. If the user on the remote host is the same as the user on the local host, this line is not needed. By default Ansible uses the same user ID on the remote host as the user that runs the Ansible playbook. I use it here simply for informational purposes. I run most playbooks as root on the local host, so Ansible logs in to the remote host as root.

- **vars:** This section can be used to define one or more variables, which can be used as in any programming language. In this case I use them in conditional "when" statements later in the playbook to control the execution path.

The "run" variable is set to false for now so that we can perform testing without actually doing the updates. The "reboot" variable is also set to false during development so that testing can be performed without the host rebooting for each test run.

The scope of variables is limited to the section in which they are defined. In this case, they are defined in Play 1 so are limited to that play. If I want to use them in later plays, I will need to set them again in each play in which they are needed. If a variable is set in a task, then it is only available within that task and not in the rest of that play.

Variable values can be overridden at the command line by using the -e (--extra-variables) option to specify a different value. We will see that when it is time to run the playbook.

---

[2] Ansible documents, https://docs.ansible.com/ansible/latest/reference_appendices/ playbooks_keywords.html#playbook-keywords

The Tasks

This is the beginning of the tasks section for Play 1. The tasks keyword is indented by exactly two spaces. Each task must have a name statement even if there is no text for the name. The text does make it easier to follow the playbook logic and is displayed on the screen during execution so that can assist as I follow the progress in real time.

Add this code to the end of the existing playbook:

```
  tasks:
###########################################################################
# Do some preliminary checking                                           #
###########################################################################
    - name: Install the latest version of the doUpdates.sh script
      copy:
        src: /root/ansible/Updates/files/doUpdates.sh
        dest: /root/bin
        mode: 0774
        owner: root
        group: root

    - name: Check for currently available updates
      command: doUpdates.sh -c
      register: check
    - debug: var=check.stdout_lines
```

This section contains three tasks. The first task copies the doUpdates.sh Bash program to the target host. The second runs the program just installed and assigns – registers – the STDOUT data stream from the doUpdates program to the variable "check". The third task prints all of the STDOUT lines in the check variable to the screen. Let's look at the new keywords in a bit more detail:

copy: The copy keyword defines the beginning of a stanza that can be used to copy one or more files from a specified source location to a specified target location. The keywords in this section define various aspects of the copy operation and the final state of the copied file.

src: This is the fully qualified path and name of the file to be copied. In this case we are only going to copy a single file, but it is easy to copy all files in a directory or only those that match a file glob pattern. The source file is usually stored in a location in the Ansible hub directory tree. In this case the fully qualified path to my source file is /root/ansible/Updates/files/doUpdates.

dest: This is the destination path on the target host(s) into which the source file will be copied. In this case we copy the file to /usr/local/bin where it can be used without need for the fully qualified path.

mode: The mode keyword defines the file mode that will be applied to the copied file. Regardless of the file mode of the source file, Ansible will set the file mode to that specified in this statement, for example, rwxr_xr__ or 0754. Be sure to use all 4 bytes when using octal format.

owner: This is the owner account that will be applied to the file.

group: This is the group account that will be applied to the file.

command: Any Linux shell command, shell script, or command-line program along with options and arguments can be used with this keyword. I have used the Bash program that was just installed to obtain some information that is not easily obtainable using the Ansible built-ins such as dnf.

register: The register keyword sets the STDOUT from the command specified into a variable named "check". The content of this variable can be queried by the "when" keyword and used as a conditional to determine whether the task of which it is a part will be performed or not. We will see this in the next section.

debug: Prints the content of the specified variable to the screen. I frequently use this as a debug tool. I find this helpful in debugging. Hint, hint.

The doUpdates.sh Bash program contains some code that determines whether updates are available. It also determines whether the kernel, systemd, or glibc has been updated, any one of which should require a reboot in order to take full effect. My program emits a couple lines to STDOUT that I can use in Ansible as a conditional to decide whether to reboot the target host. I use that in this next section that does the actual updates, and the following one performs a power-off for my main workstation. Similar code performs a reboot on all other hosts as we will see.

The STDOUT from this program used with the -c option looks like Figure 30-4 when updates are available but a reboot is not required. I can use a regular expression to search any of the text in this data stream for key strings, which can be used in a when: conditional to determine whether a specific task is to be performed.

```
####### 48 updates ARE available for host student1.example.com #######
########## Including: ##########
Last metadata expiration check: 1:47:12 ago on Tue 20 Oct 2020 01:50:07 PM
EDT.
Updates Information Summary: available
          3 Security notice(s)
              2 Moderate Security notice(s)
          3 Bugfix notice(s)
          2 Enhancement notice(s)
          2 other notice(s)
### A reboot will NOT be required after these updates are installed. ####
Program terminated normally
```

Figure 30-4. *The output from the doUpdates.sh script is used by the Ansible playbook to determine when a reboot is required*

This next section of the playbook performs the actual updates if all of the conditionals in the when statement are true. This section uses the Ansible DNF package manager built-in:

```
#######################################################################
# Do the updates.                                                     #
#######################################################################
# Install all available updates
   - name: Install all current updates
     dnf:
       name: "*"
       state: latest
     when: (check.stdout | regex_search('updates ARE available')) and run
     == "true"
```

dnf: Calls the Ansible built-in that interfaces with the DNF package manager. Although a bit limited in its capabilities, it can install, remove, and update packages. One of the limitations for the DNF module is that it does not have the check-update function, which is why I continue to use my Bash program to discover the list of packages to be updated and from that determine whether a reboot (or power-off) needs to be performed. Ansible also has YUM and APT built-ins.

name: Provides the name of the package on which to operate. In this case the file glob character * denotes all installed packages.

state: The "latest" value for this keyword indicates that all installed packages are to be brought up to the most recent version. Some of the other options for state are "present," which means that the package is installed but not necessarily the latest version, and "absent," which means to remove the package if it is installed.

when: This conditional phrase specifies the conditions that must be met for this task to run. In this instance the updates will only be installed when the string of text defined in the regular expression is present in the variable "check" that was previously registered and the "run" variable is set to "true".

Now that the updates have been done, we may need to reboot, so let's see how to deal with that. The next task does that for us. Add it to the end of the playbook. Note that the "when" line must be on one line.

```
#######################################################################
# Reboot the host                                                     #
#######################################################################
    - name: Reboot this host if necessary and reboot extra variable is true
      command: reboot
      when: (check.stdout | regex_search('reboot will be required')) and
      reboot == "true" and run == "true"
```

In this task we reboot the computer. Execution of the playbook stops after that reboot so that I need to restart it. This time, because the updates have been installed, the power-off or reboot does not take place, and the next play is run.

Preparing the doUpdates.sh File

One of the tasks we created earlier copies the doUpdates.sh Bash program to the /root/bin directory. We need to make a copy of that file available to our playbook so that it can be copied.

Create the directory /root/ansible/Updates/files and copy the doUpdates.sh file into it.

Testing

There is a tool, yamllint,[3] that we can install to check and verify the syntax of the playbook. This tool can simplify the task of finding those errors before we try to execute the playbook. It can be installed from the Fedora repository:

[root@studentvm1 ~]# **dnf install -y yamllint**

Make /root/ansible/Updates the PWD. First, run yamllint and correct any problems it reports:

$ **yamllint doUpdates.yml**

Run this playbook using this command, which does not perform the updates or reboot. It does give us a way to check the validity of our work, especially the YAML structure. Getting the YAML whitespace just right was the hardest part for me:

```
# ansible-playbook doUpdates.yml
PLAY [Play 1 - Install updates on studentvm1 - the Ansible hub]
*****************************************************************

TASK [Gathering Facts]
*******************************************************************
ok: [studentvm1]

TASK [Install the latest version of the doUpdates.sh script]
******************************************************************
changed: [studentvm1]

TASK [Check for currently available updates]
*******************************************************************
changed: [studentvm1]
```

---

[3] Several languages have "lint" tools. Lint is a reference to lint or bits of fluff on a suit, which the lint programs pick out of the code. Wikipedia, https://en.wikipedia.org/wiki/Lint_(software)

```
TASK [debug]
**********************************************************************

ok: [studentvm1] => {
    "check.stdout_lines": [
        "Updates ARE available for host studentvm1."
    ]
}

TASK [Install all current updates]
**********************************************************************

skipping: [studentvm1]

TASK [Reboot this host if necessary and reboot extra variable is true]
******************************************************************

skipping: [studentvm1]

PLAY RECAP
**********************************************************************
studentvm1 : ok=4 changed=2 unreachable=0 failed=0 skipped=2 rescued=0
ignored=0

[root@studentvm1 Updates]#
```

If that worked correctly, run the following command:

ansible-playbook --extra-vars "run=true reboot=true" doUpdates.yml

We use --extra-vars to specify values for the two "extra variables" defined in each play. In this case setting them both to true allows the updates to be performed and the reboot to take place if it is required. You could use -e instead of the much longer --extra-vars.

I won't reproduce the STDOUT data stream here because it is quite long.

This concludes the first play and the only one required for our single VM in the course.

Ansible for Many Systems

Using Ansible only to perform most tasks on a single system is probably not a good use of your time. However, it does provide a good opportunity to learn how to use Ansible. I have multiple systems and you will too, eventually.

The first play we just created installs updates on the Ansible hub, but in a real-world data center, there will be many Linux hosts, all of which need to be updated. The next two plays are not presented as experiments because you don't yet have multiple hosts to work with. However, it's good to see what a playbook containing plays for multiple systems might look like. In fact, these plays are taken almost unchanged from my home network.

The Second Play

The purpose of this second play as seen in Figure 30-5 is to perform updates on the firewall and server. It also installs the latest doUpdates.sh on the servers.

```
###############################################################################
###############################################################################
# Play 2 - Do servers                                                         #
###############################################################################
###############################################################################
- name: Play 2 - Install updates for servers yorktown and wally
  hosts: all_servers
  serial: 1
  remote_user: root
  vars:
    run: false
    reboot: false

  tasks:
###############################################################################
# Do some preliminary checking                                                #
###############################################################################
    - name: Install the latest version of the doUpdates script
      copy:
        src: /root/ansible/Updates/files/doUpdates.sh
        dest: /root/bin
        mode: 0774
        owner: root
        group: root

    - name: Check for currently available updates
      command: doUpdates.sh -c
      register: check
    - debug: var=check.stdout_lines


###############################################################################
# Do the updates.                                                             #
###############################################################################
# Install all available updates
    - name: Install all current updates
      dnf:
        name: "*"
        state: latest
      when: (check.stdout | regex_search('updates ARE available')) and run == "true"

    - name: Update the man database
      command: mandb
      when: run

    - name: Reboot if necessary and reboot extra variable is true
      reboot:
      when: (check.stdout | regex_search('reboot will be required')) and reboot ==
"true" and run == "true"
```

Figure 30-5. *Play 2 on my primary workstation installs updates on my servers*

The firewall needs to be up and running while the server – and all other hosts – are being updated so they can have access to the Internet in order to download the updated packages. The server needs to run while the firewall and other hosts are being updated in order to provide DHCP and name services. In order to accomplish that, this play updates those two hosts one at a time – in serial mode as defined in the play.

The names for these two hosts are contained in the [all_servers] group in the /etc/ansible/hosts inventory file.

This entire second play is almost the same as the first with the exception of two lines, which I have highlighted in bold:

serial: This additional statement tells Ansible to run this play on one host at a time, that is, serially rather than in parallel. If the all_servers group in the inventory contained ten servers, I could use a bit higher limit such as 2 so that this play would be run against two servers at a time. In this case I need wally, the firewall, to be up and running so that the yorktown server has access to the Internet so that it can download the updated packages. It does not really matter which sequence these two hosts are updated so long as they are not both done at the same time.

reboot: Ansible has a built-in reboot capability, so we can use that in this play instead of the Linux poweroff command. The important feature of the Ansible reboot function is that it performs a verification that the reboot has been successful and the remote host is up and running and SSH communication is once again working. The default timeout for this is ten minutes after which Ansible throws an error.

The Third Play

And Figure 30-6 shows the complete third play. This play updates all of the remaining hosts in my network. It uses the "free" strategy, which allows multiple hosts to be updated simultaneously. The names for these hosts are contained in the [workstations] group of the /etc/ansible/hosts inventory file.

```
###############################################################################
###############################################################################
# Play 3 - Do all workstations except david                                   #
###############################################################################
###############################################################################
- name: Play 3 - Install updates for all other workstations
  hosts: workstations
  strategy: free
  remote_user: root
  vars:
    run: false
    reboot: false
  tasks:
###############################################################################
# Do some preliminary checking                                               #
###############################################################################
    - name: Install the latest version of the doUpdates script
      copy:
        src: /root/ansible/Updates/files/doUpdates
        dest: /root/bin
        mode: 0774
        owner: root
        group: root

    - name: Check for currently available updates
      command: doUpdates -c
      register: check
    - debug: var=check.stdout_lines


###############################################################################
# Do the updates.                                                            #
###############################################################################
# Install all available updates
    - name: Install all current updates
      dnf:
        name: "*"
        state: latest
      when: (check.stdout | regex_search('updates ARE available')) and run == "true"

    - name: Reboot if necessary and reboot extra variable is true
      reboot:
      when: (check.stdout | regex_search('reboot will be required')) and reboot ==
"true" and run == "true"
```

Figure 30-6. *This play updates all the rest of the Linux hosts in my network*

There is only one change in this play other than the list of hosts:

> **strategy:** The free strategy tells Ansible to perform the tasks in this play freely. That is, the tasks in this play are run on each host as quickly as the host can do them. This means that some hosts may finish the last task well before other, slower hosts have completed even the first task in the playbook. It can appear to be sort of a free-for-all as you read the STDOUT data stream.

Each strategy is a separate plugin, and there are a couple other plugins that can be used with this keyword. The default is linear, which performs each task on all hosts before moving on to the next task. The host_pinned plugin performs all tasks in the play on each host before moving on to the next host. The debug plugin runs tasks interactively so that the play can be debugged.

Final Thoughts

Some tasks are not appropriate for Ansible because there are better methods for achieving a specific machine state. The use case that comes to mind is that of returning a VM to an initial state so that it can be used as many times as necessary to perform testing beginning with that known state. It is much easier to get the VM into the desired state – in this case using Ansible is a good method – and then to take a snapshot of the then current machine state. Reverting to that snapshot is usually going to be easier and much faster than using Ansible to return the host to that desired state. This is something I do several times a day when researching articles or testing new code.

After completing the playbook I use for updating Midnight Commander, I started a new playbook that I will use to perform post-installation tasks on newly installed Fedora hosts. I have already made good progress, and the playbook is a bit more sophisticated and less brute-force than my first one.

On my first day of learning Ansible, I created a playbook that solved a problem. I then started a second playbook that I use to solve the very big problem of post-install configuration. And I learned a lot.

Although I really liked using Bash scripts for many of my administrative tasks, I am already finding that Ansible can do almost everything I want and in a way that can maintain the system in the state that I want. After only a single day, I was an Ansible fan.

With a few changes to reflect the details of your own network, this playbook can be used to automate your own update tasks. Performing updates using a playbook similar to mine is a good way to get started using Ansible. Although it uses a number of keywords that can perform complex tasks, this is a relatively simple playbook. I started with just the first play to update my personal workstation, and the rest was mostly copy/paste with a few minor changes to accommodate the needs of the different groups of hosts.

Yes, there are other ways of doing this. I probably could have used different tasks using conditionals within one or two plays instead of three plays. Or I could have used conditionals and blocks to deal with handling certain hosts differently. I personally think that separate plays help separate the logic enough that changing how tasks are handled in one play will not affect the other plays. In my opinion this separation is also more elegant because the overall logic is simpler to write and understand and easier to manage.

Resources

The most complete and useful document I have found is the Ansible User Guide[4] on the Ansible website. This document is intended as a reference and not as a how-to or getting-started document.

Opensource.com has published many articles[5] about Ansible over the years, and I have found most of them very helpful for my needs. The Red Hat Enable Sysadmin website also has a lot of Ansible articles[6] that I have found to be helpful.

There are also some good but somewhat terse man pages available.

Exercises

Perform the following exercises to complete this chapter:

1.   Revise the doUpdates.yml playbook so that you don't need to add the "extra variables" on the command line. The playbook should run and reboot without having those extra variables on the CLI.

---

[4] Ansible User Guide, `https://docs.ansible.com/ansible/latest/user_guide/index.html`

[5] Opensource.com, Ansible articles, `https://opensource.com/sitewide-search?search_api_views_fulltext=Ansible`

[6] Enable Sysadmin, Ansible articles, `www.redhat.com/sysadmin/search?keys=Ansible`

2. Create an Ansible playbook that installs the Konsole, Xfce4-terminal, Tilix, gnome-terminal, cool-retro-term, and terminology terminal emulators and that will also install new versions when they become available. More than one of these terminal emulators may already be installed on your system as defaults or from previous experiments.

3. Run the playbook you just created to test it.

4. How many of the listed terminal emulators were newly installed?

5. Did any of the emulators get updated?

6. Spend a little time having fun with the new emulators that were installed. I had a lot of fun with cool-retro-term.

7. Create a playbook that installs some of your own favorite tools that do not get installed by default on new installations.

CHAPTER 31

Time and Automation

Objectives

In this chapter you will learn

- To use chrony to maintain accurate system time

- To create a crontab file for root using the crontab command

- To add necessary statements to the crontab file that set up the environment for cron jobs

- To interpret the time specifications for cron and configure cron jobs to run at different recurring intervals

- To create cron jobs using crontab

- To create cron jobs for hourly, daily, weekly, and monthly periods

- To use the at command to run scripts or commands once at a specific time in the future

Introduction

In previous chapters we have looked at some examples of using command-line programs and Bash scripts to automate tasks we perform as SysAdmins. All of that is well and good, but what happens when tasks need to be performed at times that are not convenient for us as humans? For example, if we do backups at 01:01 a.m. every morning or run a maintenance script at 03:00 a.m. every Sunday, I do not want to get out of bed to perform those tasks.

D. Both, *Using and Administering Linux: Volume 2*, https://doi.org/10.1007/978-1-4842-9615-8_31

Linux provides multiple tools and ways in which we can use those tools to run those tasks at specified times in the future, repeating as needed or just for a one-time occurrence. However, keeping accurate time is critical to ensuring that scheduled jobs run at the correct times.

This chapter starts by looking at the use of chrony to synchronize the time our computer keeps with a standardized time reference such as an atomic clock. It then covers the use of the traditional Linux tools, `cron` and `at`, to trigger jobs at specific times.

The newer systemd timers will be covered in Chapter 37.

Keeping Time with Chrony

Does anybody really know what time it is? Does anybody really care?

—Chicago, 1969

Perhaps that rock group didn't care what time it was, but our computers really need to know the exact time. In banking, stock markets, and other financial businesses, transactions must be maintained in the proper order, and exact time sequences are critical for that. For SysAdmins and DevOps, following the trail of emails through a series of servers or determining the exact sequence of events using log files on geographically dispersed hosts can be much easier when exact times are kept on the computers in question.

I used to work at one organization that received over 20 million emails per day and that had four servers just to accept and do a basic filter on the incoming flood of emails. From there emails were sent to one of four more servers to perform more complex anti-spam assessments and then deliver the emails to one of several additional servers where the messages were placed in the correct inboxes. At each layer, the emails would be sent to one of the servers at the next level selected only by the randomness of round-robin DNS. Sometimes we needed to trace the arrival of a new message through the system until we could determine where it "got lost," according to the pointy-haired bosses. We had to do this with frightening regularity.

Most of that emails turned out to be spam. Some people actually complained that their [joke, cat pic, recipe, inspirational saying, and a few even more strange emails]-of-the-day was missing and asked us to find it. We did reject those opportunities.

Our email searches, as well as other transactional searches, were all aided by log entries with timestamps that – today – can resolve down to the nanosecond in even the slowest of modern Linux computers. In very-high-volume transaction environments, a few microseconds of difference in the system clocks can mean thousands of transactions to be sorted through in order to find the correct ones.

The NTP Server Hierarchy

NTP is the Network Time Protocol that is used by computers worldwide to synchronize their times with Internet standard reference clocks via a hierarchy of NTP servers. The NTP server hierarchy is built in layers called strata. Each stratum is a layer of NTP servers. The primary servers are at stratum 1, and they are connected directly to various national time services at stratum 0 via satellite, radio, or even modems over phone lines in some cases. Those time services at stratum 0 may be an atomic clock, a radio receiver that is tuned to the signals broadcast by an atomic clock, or a GPS receiver using the highly accurate clock signals broadcast by GPS satellites.

To prevent time requests from time servers lower in the hierarchy, that is, with a higher stratum number, from overwhelming the primary reference servers, there are several thousand public NTP stratum 2 servers that are open and available for all to use. Many users and organizations, myself included, with large numbers of their own hosts that need an NTP server set up their own time servers so that only one local host actually accesses the stratum 2 time servers. The remaining hosts in our networks are all configured to use the local time server, which, in my case, is a stratum 3 server.

NTP Choices

The original NTP daemon, ntpd, has been joined by a newer one, chronyd. Both perform the task of keeping the time of the local host synchronized with the time server. Both services are available, and I have seen nothing to indicate that this will change any time soon.

Chrony has some features that make it the better choice for most environments. Some of the primary advantages of using chrony are shown in this list:

- Chrony can synchronize to the time server much faster than NTP. This is good for laptops or desktops that do not run constantly.

- It can compensate for fluctuating clock frequencies such as when a host hibernates or enters a sleep mode or when the clock speed varies due to frequency stepping that slows clock speeds when loads are low.

- It handles intermittent network connections and bandwidth saturation.

- It adjusts for network delays and latency.

- After the initial time sync is accomplished, chrony never steps the clock. This ensures stable and consistent time intervals for many system services and applications that require that.

- Chrony can work even without a network connection of any type. In this case the local host or server could be updated manually.

Both the ntp and chrony RPM packages are available from standard Fedora repositories. It is possible to install both and switch between them, but modern releases of Fedora, CentOS, and RHEL have moved from NTP to chrony as the default time-keeping implementation. I have found that chrony works well, provides a better interface for the SysAdmin, presents much more information, and increases control. I see no reason to use the old NTP service when chrony is so much better.

So just to make it clear, NTP is a protocol that is implemented with either NTP or chrony. We will explore only chrony for both client and server configuration on a Fedora host. Configuration for current releases of CentOS and RHEL is the same.

Chrony Structure

The chrony daemon, chronyd, runs in the background and monitors the time and status of the time server specified in the chrony.conf file. If the local time needs to be adjusted, chronyd does so smoothly without the programmatic trauma that would occur if the clock were to be instantly reset to a new time.

Chrony also provides the chronyc tool that allows us to monitor the current status of chrony and to make changes if necessary. The chronyc utility can be used as a command that accepts sub-commands, or it can be used as an interactive text-mode program. We will use it both ways in this chapter.

Client Configuration

The NTP client configuration is simple and requires little or no change. The NTP server can be defined by the SysAdmin during the Linux installation, or it can be provided by the DHCP server at boot time. The default /etc/chrony.conf file shown in its entirety in Figure 31-1 requires no alterations to work properly as a client. For Fedora, chrony uses the Fedora NTP pool. CentOS and RHEL also have their own NTP server pools. Like many Red Hat–based distributions, the configuration file is well commented.

```
# Use public servers from the pool.ntp.org project.
# Please consider joining the pool (http://www.pool.ntp.org/join.html).
pool 2.fedora.pool.ntp.org iburst

# Record the rate at which the system clock gains/losses time.
driftfile /var/lib/chrony/drift

# Allow the system clock to be stepped in the first three updates
# if its offset is larger than 1 second.
makestep 1.0 3

# Enable kernel synchronization of the real-time clock (RTC).


# Enable hardware timestamping on all interfaces that support it.
#hwtimestamp *

# Increase the minimum number of selectable sources required to adjust
# the system clock.
#minsources 2

# Allow NTP client access from local network.
#allow 192.168.0.0/16

# Serve time even if not synchronized to a time source.
#local stratum 10

# Specify file containing keys for NTP authentication.
keyfile /etc/chrony.keys

# Get TAI-UTC offset and leap seconds from the system tz database.
leapsectz right/UTC

# Specify directory for log files.
logdir /var/log/chrony

# Select which information is logged.
#log measurements statistics tracking
```

Figure 31-1. *The default chrony.conf configuration file*

Let's look at the current status of NTP on our student virtual machines.

EXPERIMENT 31-1: CHRONY STATUS AND INFORMATION

Perform this experiment as the root user.

When used with the tracking sub-command, the chronyc command provides statistics that tell us how far off the local system is from the reference server:

```
[root@studentvm1 ~]# chronyc tracking
Reference ID    : 9B8AECE1 (ipv4.ntp1.rbauman.com)
Stratum         : 3
Ref time (UTC)  : Tue Mar 14 18:22:34 2023
System time     : 0.000081535 seconds fast of NTP time
Last offset     : +0.000082241 seconds
RMS offset      : 0.010405118 seconds
Frequency       : 0.253 ppm fast
Residual freq   : -0.001 ppm
Skew            : 0.132 ppm
Root delay      : 0.012633221 seconds
Root dispersion : 0.001481692 seconds
Update interval : 1041.9 seconds
Leap status     : Normal
```

The reference ID on the first line of the result is the server to which our host is synchronized. The rest of these lines are described in the chronyc(1) man page. The stratum line indicates which stratum our local VM is at, so the ipv4.ntp1.rbauman.com host is at stratum 3.

The other sub-command I find interesting and useful is sources, which provides information about the time sources configured in chrony.conf:

```
[root@studentvm1 ~]# chronyc sources
MS Name/IP address         Stratum Poll Reach LastRx Last sample
===============================================================================
^- 65-100-46-164.dia.static>  1   10    377    579  -364us[ -280us] +/-    38ms
^- 108.61.73.243              2   10    377    517 -3055us[-2971us] +/-    48ms
^* ipv4.ntp1.rbauman.com      2   10    377    240  -522us[ -440us] +/-  8128us
^- triton.ellipse.net         2   10    377    265  -703us[ -620us] +/-    35ms
```

These four servers were provided by the NTP pool. The "S" column – Source State – indicates that the server with an asterisk (*) on that line is the one to which our host is currently synchronized. This is consistent with the data from the tracking sub-command.

Note that the -v option provides a nice description of the fields in this output:

```
[root@studentvm1 ~]# chronyc sources -v

  .-- Source mode  '^' = server, '=' = peer, '#' = local clock.
 / .- Source state '*' = current best, '+' = combined, '-' = not combined,
 | /            'x' = may be in error, '~' = too variable, '?' = unusable.
 ||                                         .- xxxx [ yyyy ] +/- zzzz
 ||        Reachability register (octal) -.         | xxxx = adjusted offset,
 ||        Log2(Polling interval) --.       |       | yyyy = measured offset,
 ||                               \        |       | zzzz = estimated error.
 ||                               |        |        \
MS Name/IP address            Stratum Poll Reach LastRx Last sample
===============================================================================
^- 65-100-46-164.dia.static>    1   10    377    816   -364us[ -280us] +/-    38ms
^- 108.61.73.243                2   10    377    754  -3055us[-2971us] +/-    48ms
^* ipv4.ntp1.rbauman.com        2   10    377    477   -522us[ -440us] +/-  8128us
^- triton.ellipse.net           2   10    377    502   -703us[ -620us] +/-    35ms
```

If we want a particular server to be the preferred reference time source for this host, even though it may have a slower response time, we could add the following line to the /etc/chrony.conf file. I usually place this line just above the first pool server statement near the top of the file. There is no special reason for this except that I like to keep the server statements together. It would work just as well at the bottom of the file, and I have done that on several hosts. This configuration file is not sequence sensitive:

```
server 108.61.73.243 iburst prefer
```

The "prefer" option marks this as the preferred reference source. As such, this host will always be synchronized with this reference source so long as it is available. You could also use the fully qualified hostname for a remote reference server or the hostname only without the domain name for a local reference time source so long as the search statement is set in the /etc/resolv.conf file. I prefer the IP address to ensure that the time source is accessible even if DNS is not working. In most environments the server name is probably the better option because NTP will continue to work even if the IP address of the server is changed.

You may not have a specific reference source with which you want to synchronize, so it is fine to use the defaults.

chronyc As an Interactive Tool

I mentioned near the beginning of this section that chronyc can be used as an interactive command tool. Let's explore that.

EXPERIMENT 31-2: USING CHRONYC INTERACTIVELY

Perform this experiment as root. Let's look at the `chronyc` command in more detail. Simply run the command without a sub-command, and you get a chronyc command prompt:

```
[root@studentvm1 ~]# chronyc
chrony version 3.4
Copyright (C) 1997-2003, 2007, 2009-2018 Richard P. Curnow and others
chrony comes with ABSOLUTELY NO WARRANTY.  This is free software, and
you are welcome to redistribute it under certain conditions.  See the
GNU General Public License version 2 for details.

chronyc>
```

Now you can enter just the sub-commands. Try using the tracking, ntpdata, and sources sub-commands. The chronyc command line allows command recall and editing for chronyc sub-commands. You can use the help sub-command to get a list of possible commands and their syntax.

One thing I like to do after my client computers have synchronized with the NTP server is to set the system hardware clock from the system (OS) time using the following system command. Note that it is not a chronyc command, so enter this command as root in a separate terminal session:

```
[root@studentvm1 ~]# /sbin/hwclock --systohc
```

This command can be added as a cron job, as a script in cron.daily, or as a systemd timer to keep the hardware clock synced with the system time.

Chrony is a powerful tool for synchronizing the times of client hosts whether they are all in the local network or scattered around the globe. It is easy to configure because, despite the large number of configuration options available, only a few are required in most circumstances.

Chrony and NTP (the old service) both use the same configuration, and the files' contents are interchangeable. The man pages for chronyd, chronyc, and chrony.conf contain an amazing amount of information that can help you get started or learn about some esoteric configuration option.

Using cron for Timely Automation

There are many tasks that need to be performed off-hours when no one is expected to be using the computer or, even more importantly, on a regular basis at specific times. In this chapter we explore the cron service and how to use it.

I use the cron service to schedule obvious things like regular backups that occur every day at 01:01 a.m. I also do a couple less obvious things. All of my many computers have their system times, that is, the operating system time, set using NTP – the Network Time Protocol. Chrony sets the system time; it does not set the hardware time, which can drift and become inaccurate. I use cron to run a command that sets the hardware time using the system time. I also have a bash program I run early every morning that creates a new "message of the day" (MOTD) on each computer that contains information such as disk usage that should be current in order to be useful. Many system processes use cron to schedule tasks as well. Services like logwatch and rkhunter all use the cron service to run programs every day.

The cron Daemon (crond)

The crond is the background service that enables cron functionality. The cron service checks for files in the /var/spool/cron and /etc/cron.d directories and the /etc/anacrontab file. The contents of these files define cron jobs that are to be run at various intervals.

The individual user cron files are located in /var/spool/cron, and system services and applications generally add cron job files in the /etc/cron.d directory. The /etc/anacrontab file is a special case that will be covered a bit further on in this chapter.

crontab

Each user, including root, can have a crontab file. The term *crontab* derives from the Greek word *chronos*, for time, and the term *table*, because the file is a table of tasks set to perform at specific times and days.

Note   The terms *cron file* and *crontab file* are sometimes used interchangeably.

By default no file exists, but using the crontab -e command as shown in Figure 31-2 to edit a crontab file creates them in the /var/spool/cron directory. I strongly recommend that you not use a standard editor such as Vi, Vim, Emacs, Nano, or any of the many other editors that are available. Using the crontab command not only allows you to edit the files; it also restarts crond when you save and exit from the editor. The crontab command uses Vi as its underlying editor because Vi is always present on even the most basic of installations.

All cron files are empty the first time you edit them, so you must create them from scratch. I always add the job definition example in Figure 31-2 to my own cron files just as a quick reference. This help and initial setup section comprises the top part of the crontab file down to the line of "#" characters. The rest of the file consists of the cron jobs I have set up.

Tip   The crontab job definition help is located in the /etc/crontab file so you can copy that to your own crontab.

In Figure 31-2 the first three lines set up a default environment. Setting the environment to that necessary for a given user is required because cron does not provide an environment of any kind. The SHELL variable specifies the shell to use when commands are executed. In this case it specifies the bash shell. The MAILTO variable sets the email address to which cron job results will be sent. These emails can provide the status of backups, updates, or whatever and consist of the output from the programs that you would see if you ran them manually from the command line. The last of these three lines sets up the PATH for this environment. Regardless of the path set here, however, I always like to prepend the fully qualified path to each executable file name.

```
# crontab -e
SHELL=/bin/bash
PATH=/sbin:/bin:/usr/sbin:/usr/bin
MAILTO=root


# For details see man 4 crontabs


# Example of job definition:
# .---------------- minute (0 - 59)
# |  .------------- hour (0 - 23)
# |  |  .---------- day of month (1 - 31)
# |  |  |  .------- month (1 - 12) OR jan,feb,mar,apr ...
# |  |  |  |  .---- day of week (0 - 6) (Sunday=0 or 7) OR
sun,mon,tue,wed,thu,fri,sat
# |  |  |  |  |
# *  *  *  *  * user-name   command to be executed
#########################################################################
# backup using the rsbu program to the internal HDD then the external USB
# HDD
01 01 * * * /usr/local/bin/rsbu -vbd1 ; /usr/local/bin/rsbu -vbd2
# Set the hardware clock to keep it in sync with the more accurate system clock
03 05 * * * /sbin/hwclock --systohc
# Perform monthly updates on the first of the month
25 04 1 * * /usr/local/bin/doUpdates.sh
```

Figure 31-2. *The crontab -e command is used to edit the cron files*

There are several comment lines that detail the syntax required to define a cron job. The entries in the crontab files are checked every minute by the crond. Figure 31-3 defines each of the fields and the values allowed in each.

Interval field	Values allowed	Comments
Minute	0-59	
Hour	0-23	
Day of month	1-31	
Month	0-12 or month abbreviations	Or you can use jan, feb, mar, etc, in lowercase.
Day of the week	0-7 or day abbreviations	Zero (0) and 7 are both Sunday. sun, mon, tue, in lowercase.

Figure 31-3.   The crontab time fields

cron Examples

Each interval field of the crontab entries also supports lists and ranges of values as well as calculated values. For example, suppose we want to run a task on the 1st and 15th of each month at 01:00 a.m. That cron entry would look like this:

```
00 01 * 1,15 * /usr/local/bin/mycronjob.sh
```

We can get more creative using a little math. For example, if we want to run a task every five minutes, the minute field could be set as */5 to denote that. The way this works is that for each minute, the value is divided by 5. If the remainder of the division is zero, that is, the minute is evenly divisible by 5, that is considered a match. Of course the other time intervals must match too. These are called step values:

```
*/5 * * * * /usr/local/bin/mycronjob.sh
```

Suppose that we want to run mycronjob.sh once every three hours on the hour during the day. This specification would run the task at 03:00 a.m., 06:00 a.m., 09:00 a.m., and so on throughout the day:

```
00 */3 * * * /usr/local/bin/mycronjob.sh
```

In a more complex scheduling task, the next example shows one way to run a task on the first Sunday of each month. The logic here is that one and only one Sunday must always fall in the first seven days of the month:

```
00 01 1-7 * sun /usr/local/bin/mycronjob.sh
```

or

```
00 01 1-7 * 0 /usr/local/bin/mycronjob.sh
```

or because Sunday can be either 0 or 7

```
00 01 1-7 * 7 /usr/local/bin/mycronjob.sh
```

Now let's complicate this even more and imagine that we want this cron job to run only in the months of summer, which we designate as June through September:

```
00 01 1-7 jun,jul,aug,sept sun /usr/local/bin/mycronjob.sh
```

or

```
00 01 1-7 6,7,8,9 0 /usr/local/bin/mycronjob.sh
```

or

```
00 01 1-7 6-9 0 /usr/local/bin/mycronjob.sh
```

The crontab(5)[1] man page has a good description of how this all works. It also has some additional examples.

crontab Entries

There are three sample crontab entries in Figure 31-2, so we will explore those now that we know how to interpret them.

The line shown in the following runs one of my bash shell scripts, rsbu, to perform backups of all my systems. This job is kicked off at one minute after 01:00 a.m. every day. The splats/stars/asterisks (*) in positions 3, 4, and 5 of the time specification are like file globs for those time divisions; they match every day of the month, every month, and

---

[1] Use the command form **man 5 crontab**.

every day of the week. This line runs my backups twice: once to back up onto an internal dedicated backup hard drive and once to back up onto an external USB hard drive that I can take to the safe deposit box:

```
01 01 * * * /usr/local/bin/rsbu -vbd1 ; /usr/local/bin/rsbu -vbd2
```

This next cron entry sets the hardware clock on the computer using the system clock as the source of an accurate time. This line is set to run at three minutes after 05:00 a.m. every day:

```
03 05 * * * /sbin/hwclock --systohc
```

The last cron job is the one we are especially interested in. It is used to install Fedora updates at 04:25 a.m. on the first day of each month. The cron service has no option for "the last day of the month," so we use the first day of the following month:

```
25 04 1 * * /usr/local/bin/doUpdates.sh
```

Creating the crontab File

Let's try a couple things to get a feel for using cron for task scheduling using the cron service.

EXPERIMENT 31-3: CREATING A CRONTAB FILE

Perform this experiment as root. Let's look at the crontab file for root using the crontab command. The -l option just prints the current crontab file, while -e edits the cron file:

```
[root@studentvm1 ~]# crontab -l
no crontab for root
```

We can see from this result that there is no crontab file for root. This is also true of all users because there are no crontab files at all. So let's create our own crontab file:

```
[root@studentvm1 ~]# crontab -e
```

This opens the default editor with an empty file. Start by importing the crontab sample help file.

If using Nano, which is the default editor for crontab, do the following:

Ctrl-r

And type in the file name **/etc/crontab** in the field near the bottom of the Nano screen. The cursor will already be there. Note that you can use the Tab key for file name completion.

If you use Vim, it must be in command mode for this, and it is so when it is first launched so we do not need to press Esc to switch to command mode. Of course it never hurts to press Esc to be sure:

:r/etc/crontab

So now we have the beginnings of a crontab file with built-in help. Now we add a simple command to illustrate how cron works with repetitive tasks. I like to use a trivial example for this and repeat it every minute. Add the following two lines to the bottom of the crontab file. This cron job runs the free utility once each minute and stores it in the /tmp/freemem.log file:

```
# Run the free program and store the results in /tmp/freemem.log
*  *  *  *  * /usr/bin/free >> /tmp/freemem.log
```

The crontab file should look like this:

```
SHELL=/bin/bash
PATH=/sbin:/bin:/usr/sbin:/usr/bin
MAILTO=root

# For details see man 4 crontabs

# Example of job definition:
# .---------------- minute (0 - 59)
# |  .------------- hour (0 - 23)
# |  |  .---------- day of month (1 - 31)
# |  |  |  .------- month (1 - 12) OR jan,feb,mar,apr ...
# |  |  |  |  .---- day of week (0 - 6) (Sunday=0 or 7) OR sun,mon,tue,
#                   wed,thu,fri,sat
# |  |  |  |  |
# *  *  *  *  * user-name  command to be executed

# Run the free program and store the results in /tmp/freemem.log
*  *  *  *  * /usr/bin/free >> /tmp/freemem.log
```

Save the data to the disk and exit from the editor to activate the changes. You should receive the message shown next:

```
no crontab for root - using an empty one
crontab: installing new crontab
```

Open a root terminal session and make /tmp the PWD. Use **ls** to check that the file is present, but it will not be until a second or so after the first minute changes to the next. So if you saved the crontab file at 13:54:32, the first entry will be made at about 13:55.01. You can use the stat command to get the exact time precisely.

We can use the **tail -f** command to follow the file. That is, using this command shows the current content of the file, and whenever new lines are added to the file, they are displayed immediately. This makes it unnecessary to use commands like **cat** every minute or so to see the file as it changes:

```
[root@studentvm1 tmp]# tail -f /tmp/freemem.log
              total        used        free      shared  buff/cache   available
Mem:       16367796      315840    14986348       11368     1065608    15748876
Swap:       8388604           0     8388604
              total        used        free      shared  buff/cache   available
Mem:       16367796      315864    14986096       11372     1065836    15748844
Swap:       8388604           0     8388604
              total        used        free      shared  buff/cache   available
Mem:       16367796      316292    14985592       11368     1065912    15748420
Swap:       8388604           0     8388604
<snip>
```

This does not tell us the date or time that the entries were made. We can add another statement to our existing cron job, as shown in the following, to make that happen:

```
# Run the free program and store the results in /tmp/freemem.log
* * * * * /usr/bin/date >> /tmp/freemem.log ; /usr/bin/free >> /tmp/
freemem.log
```

Save the revised crontab and tail the freemem.log file for a few minutes to observe the revised results:

```
[root@studentvm1 tmp]# tail -f freemem.log
              total        used        free      shared  buff/cache
Mem:       16367796      316292    14985592       11368     1065912    15748420
```

```
Swap:       8388604            0      8388604
Thu Mar 16 10:55:01 AM EDT 2023
             total         used         free      shared  buff/cache    available
Mem:      16367796       318124     14983576       11368     1066096     15746564
Swap:      8388604            0      8388604
Thu Mar 16 10:56:01 AM EDT 2023
             total         used         free      shared  buff/cache    available
Mem:      16367796       317948     14983576       11368     1066272     15746748
Swap:      8388604            0      8388604
```

Other Scheduling Options

There are some other options provided by the cron service that we can also use to schedule programs to run on a regular basis.

/etc/cron.hourly

The directory /etc/cron.hourly is where some applications and services install cron files when there are no users under which the programs would run. These cron files have the same format as a user cron file. The crontab files located in the /etc/cron.hourly directory are each run once every hour. The root user can also place crontab files in this directory.

The /etc/cron.d directory should contain one file, the 0hourly crontab file.

EXPERIMENT 31-4: CRON.D

Perform this experiment as root. Make /etc/cron.d the PWD. Then list the contents of the directory and view the contents of 0hourly:

```
[root@studentvm1 ~]# cd /etc/cron.d ; ll ; cat 0hourly
total 12
-rw-r--r--. 1 root root 128 Mar 18 06:56 0hourly
# Run the hourly jobs
SHELL=/bin/bash
PATH=/sbin:/bin:/usr/sbin:/usr/bin
MAILTO=root
01 * * * * root run-parts /etc/cron.hourly
[root@studentvm1 cron.d]#
```

The run-parts command in the 0hourly crontab file runs all of the files in the /etc/cron.hourly directory in alphanumeric sorted sequence beginning at one minute after each hour. We explore the reason for this in the next section.

anacron

The crond service assumes that the host computer runs all the time. What that means is that if the computer is turned off for a period of time and cron jobs were scheduled for that time, they will be ignored and will not run until the next time they are scheduled. This might cause problems if the cron jobs that did not run were critical. So there is another option for running jobs at regular intervals when the computer is not expected to be on all the time.

The anacron program performs the same function as crond, but it adds the ability to run jobs that were skipped if the computer was off or otherwise unable to run the job for one or more cycles. This is very useful for laptops and other computers that get turned off or put in sleep mode.

As soon as the computer is turned on and booted, anacron checks to see whether configured jobs have missed their last scheduled run. If they have, those jobs are run almost immediately, but only once no matter how many cycles have been missed. For example, if a weekly job was not run for three weeks because the system was shut down while you were away on vacation, it would be run soon after you turn the computer on, but it would be run once, not three times.

The anacron program provides some easy options for running regularly scheduled tasks. Just install your scripts in the /etc/cron.[hourly|daily|weekly|monthly] directories, depending on how frequently they need to be run.

How does this work? The sequence is simpler than it first appears. The crond service runs the cron job specified in /etc/cron.d/0hourly as seen in Figure 31-4.

```
# Run the hourly jobs
SHELL=/bin/bash
PATH=/sbin:/bin:/usr/sbin:/usr/bin
MAILTO=root
01 * * * * root run-parts /etc/cron.hourly
```

Figure 31-4. *The contents of /etc/cron.d/0hourly cause the shell scripts located in /etc/cron.hourly to run*

The cron job specified in /etc/cron.d/0hourly runs the run-parts program once per hour. The run-parts program runs all of the scripts located in the /etc/cron.hourly directory. The /etc/cron.hourly directory contains the 0anacron script, which runs the anacron program using the /etc/anacrontab configuration file shown in Figure 31-5.

```
# /etc/anacrontab: configuration file for anacron
# See anacron(8) and anacrontab(5) for details.

SHELL=/bin/sh
PATH=/sbin:/bin:/usr/sbin:/usr/bin
MAILTO=root
# the maximal random delay added to the base delay of the jobs
RANDOM_DELAY=45
# the jobs will be started during the following hours only
START_HOURS_RANGE=3-22

#period in days   delay in minutes   job-identifier    command
1         5         cron.daily              nice run-parts /etc/cron.daily
7        25         cron.weekly             nice run-parts /etc/cron.weekly
@monthly 45         cron.monthly            nice run-parts /etc/cron.monthly
```

Figure 31-5. *The contents of the /etc/anacrontab file run the executable files in the cron.[daily|weekly|monthly] directories at the appropriate times*

The anacron program runs the programs located in /etc/cron.daily once per day, the jobs located in /etc/cron.weekly once per week, and the jobs in cron.monthly once per month. Note the specified delay times on each line that help prevent these jobs from overlapping themselves and other cron jobs.

Files that are located in the /etc/cron.X directories are not executable from the command line unless used with the full path. So instead of placing complete bash programs in the cron.X directories, I install them in the /usr/local/bin directory, which allows me to run them easily from the command line. Then I add a symlink in the appropriate cron directory, such as /etc/cron.daily.

The anacron program is not designed to run programs at specific times. Rather, it is intended to run programs at intervals that begin at the specified times such as 03:00 a.m. (see the START_HOURS_RANGE in Figure 11-5) of each day, on Sunday to begin the week, and the first day of the month. If any one or more cycles are missed, then anacron will run the missed jobs one time as soon as possible.

Thoughts About cron

I use most of these methods for scheduling various tasks to run on my computers. All of those tasks are ones that need to run with root privileges. I have seen only a few times when non-root users had a real need for any type of cron job, one of those, for example, being for a developer to kick off a daily compile in a development lab.

It is important to restrict access to cron functions by non-root users. However, there are circumstances when it may be necessary for a user to set tasks to run at specified times, and cron can allow users to do that when necessary. SysAdmins realize that many users do not understand how to properly configure these tasks using cron and the users make mistakes in the configuration. Some of those mistakes may be harmless, but others can cause problems for themselves and other users. By setting procedural policies that cause users to interact with the SysAdmin, those individual cron jobs are much less likely to interfere with other users and other system functions.

Scheduling Tips

Some of the times I have set in the crontab files for my various systems seem rather random, and to some extent they are. Trying to schedule cron jobs can be challenging especially as the number of jobs increases. I usually only have a few tasks to schedule on each of my own computers, so it is a bit easier than some of the production and lab environments I have worked in.

One system I supported usually had around a dozen cron jobs that needed to run every night and an additional three or four that had to run on weekends or the first of the month. That was a challenge because if too many jobs ran at the same time, especially the backups and compiles, the system would run out of RAM and then nearly fill the swap file, which resulted in system thrashing while performance tanked so that nothing got done. We added more memory and were able to do a better job of scheduling tasks. Adjusting the task list included removing one of the tasks, which was very poorly written and which used large amounts of memory.

Security

Security is always important and that is no different for cron jobs. I recommend that non-root users be prohibited from creating cron jobs. A badly designed script or program that is launched unintentionally multiple times by a cron job can bring a host to a very quick and unexpected stop.

It is considered a best practice to deny use of the cron system to non-root users in order to help eliminate rogue cron jobs. This can be accomplished using the files cron. allow and cron.deny. The logic of these two files is summarized in Figure 31-6. The root user can always use cron.

cron.allow	cron.deny	Effect
Not present	Not present	Only root can use cron.
Present but empty	Not present	Only root can use cron.
Present	Not present	User ID must be listed in cron.allow to use cron.
Not present	Present but empty	All non-root users can use cron.
Not present	Present	Users listed in cron.deny are denied access to cron.

Figure 31-6. Using cron.allow and cron.deny to control access to using cron

All cron jobs should be thoroughly inspected and tested by the root user before being added.

cron Resources

The man pages for cron, crontab, anacron, anacrontab, and run-parts all have excellent information and descriptions of how the cron system works.

at

The tasks we have discussed so far are repetitive and need to occur on a repeating schedule of some type. There are times, however, when the need is to run a job only once at some time in the future. The at command can be used for this.

For example, I have had the need to install updates during a 02:00 a.m. maintenance window for which I did not want to be awake or even on-site. Actually, to be a bit more specific, the updates could be performed during the day, but the reboot required by a new kernel would need to be performed during the maintenance period. This is possible because a Linux system can be updated without an immediate reboot, and that is the default. Additionally, performing the updates does not normally affect the other tasks, so users would not even know that the updates are being installed. The only time a side effect such as slowed response time might be noted is if the host is already running at nearly 100% of CPU capacity. In my case it was totally unnoticeable, so I did the updates during the day. I then set an at job to run during the maintenance window and perform the reboot.

Syntax

The syntax of the at command is simple.

Type at <time specification> and press the Enter key. We look at time specifications immediately in the following. This starts a new line indicated by the prompt, at>. Type in a series of commands to be executed at the specified time, and then press the Ctrl+D key combination to exit and activate the job. As far as I know, this is the only Linux command that uses Ctrl+D to perform a save and exit sequence.

The `atq` command lists the jobs in the queue, and the `atrm <job number>` command allows removal of jobs from the queue.

Time Specifications

The `at` command provides some interesting ways to specify times and dates, both explicit and fuzzy. Some examples of these methods are listed in Figure 31-7. Note that if a time of day (TOD) is specified, but not a specific day, the job will run today if that time is still in today's future. If that time for today has already passed, the job will run the next instance of that time, which would be tomorrow.

We can generalize that any `at` job time specification will execute the first time the specification matches a future time. If the specification matches a time that exists only in the past, it will run as soon as possible, usually within a few minutes.

Time specification	Description
at 05:00	A specific time with no day or date supplied. At 5:00am. Today if the current time is before 5am and tomorrow if the current time is after 5am. 5am and 5:00am also work.
at 5pm	At 5pm today if the current time is before 5pm and tomorrow if the current time is after 5pm.
at 11am tuesday	A time and day of the week is specified. If the current day is Tuesday but the time is after 11am, the job will run on 11am Tuesday in 7 days from now. If today is Monday, the job will run at 11am tomorrow.
at 3pm + 5 days	This job will run at 3pm five days from now regardless of which day today is.
at now + 10 minutes	If the time this job is added to the queue is 11:27am, it will run at 11:37am.
at tomorrow	At this time tomorrow. If the job is entered into the queue at 09:48 today, it will run at 09:48 tomorrow.
at 21:05 January 15	This job will run on a specific month and day at 9:05pm.
at noon	This sets a job to run at the next 12pm (noon), today if the current time is before noon and tomorrow if it is already after noon.
at midnight	This job will run at the next occurrence of midnight, 12:00AM.
At teatime	A job with this specification will run at 4pm.
at 15:35 05/21/2019	This job will be run at the date and time specified of 15:35 (3:35pm) on May 21 of 2019. Acceptable date specification formats are MMDD[CC]YY, MM/DD/[CC]YY, DD.MM.[CC]YY, and [CC]YY-MM-DD.

Figure 31-7. Examples of time/date specifications for the at command

By now you get the idea and should be able to specify time and date for the at command in any number of different ways. I like the flexibility this command provides in the time and date specifications. This is an excellent example of the Linux Philosophy tenet that programs should do one thing and do it well.

EXPERIMENT 31-5: USING THE AT COMMAND

Let's start with something simple and see how it works. Start this experiment as the student user. EOT means end of text, which is issued with the Ctrl+D key combination:

```
[student@studentvm1 ~]$ at now +2 minutes
warning: commands will be executed using /bin/sh
at> free
at> <EOT>
job 1 at Thu May  2 15:06:00 2019
```

Note that the job number is displayed and the date and time the job will be run. We can also use the atq command to see this. The atq command also shows the username that the job belongs to. There is only a single queue for at jobs, and all jobs go into that queue. The atq command shows all at jobs for all users:

```
[student@studentvm1 ~]$ atq
1        Thu May  2 15:06:00 2019 a student
[student@studentvm1 ~]$
```

Now wait until after the runtime shown in the atq results. What happens? Why do we not see anything? Does the job even run? Use the atq command to verify that the queue is now empty.

We can verify the job ran by looking in the cron log. As root, do the following:

```
[root@studentvm1 ~]# tail /var/log/cron
Mar 16 14:01:01 studentvm1 CROND[3972]: (root) CMD (run-parts /etc/
cron.hourly)
Mar 16 14:01:01 studentvm1 run-parts[3972]: (/etc/cron.hourly) starting
0anacron
Mar 16 14:01:01 studentvm1 run-parts[3972]: (/etc/cron.hourly) finished
0anacron
```

```
Mar 16 14:01:01 studentvm1 CROND[3971]: (root) CMDEND (run-parts /etc/
cron.hourly)
Mar 16 15:01:01 studentvm1 CROND[4079]: (root) CMD (run-parts /etc/
cron.hourly)
Mar 16 15:01:01 studentvm1 run-parts[4079]: (/etc/cron.hourly) starting
0anacron
Mar 16 15:01:01 studentvm1 run-parts[4079]: (/etc/cron.hourly) finished
0anacron
Mar 16 15:01:01 studentvm1 CROND[4078]: (root) CMDEND (run-parts /etc/
cron.hourly)
Mar 16 15:05:00 studentvm1 atd[4147]: Starting job 1 (a0000101aafd79) for
user 'root' (0)
Mar 16 15:07:00 studentvm1 atd[4177]: Starting job 2 (a0000201aafd7b) for
user 'student' (1000)
[root@studentvm1 log]#
```

You should see at least one entry indicating that the at job has started. This verifies the job
ran, but what happened to the output? The answer is nowhere. We do not have all of the parts
in place to receive the emails that it would normally send to the user as its default way of
communicating the results. As the root user, check the mail queue, and you will see an email
waiting to be sent to root:

```
[root@studentvm1 ~]# mailq
mail in dir /root/.esmtp_queue/C4kgEDik:
                To: root
1 mails to deliver
```

We need to install Sendmail, which is a mail handling and transfer agent, and mailx, which is a
simple text-mode email client that can be used from the command line.

As root, install these two tools. This may also install a few dependencies on your VM:

```
[root@studentvm1 log]# dnf -y install mailx sendmail
```

Activate Sendmail. We use the systemctl command here to manage the Sendmail server. The
start sub-command obviously starts the server, while the enable sub-command configures it to
start at every system boot. The systemctl command is used to manage system services and
background processes (daemons) and is part of systemd.

We will explore systemd and the systemctl command in Chapter 35 of this volume. We will explore Sendmail and email in general in Volume 3:

```
[root@studentvm1 log]# systemctl status sendmail
● sendmail.service - Sendmail Mail Transport Agent
   Loaded: loaded (/usr/lib/systemd/system/sendmail.service; disabled; vendor
   preset: disabled)
   Active: inactive (dead)
[root@studentvm1 log]# systemctl enable --now sendmail
Created symlink /etc/systemd/system/multi-user.target.wants/sendmail.service
→ /usr/lib/systemd/system/sendmail.service.
Created symlink /etc/systemd/system/multi-user.target.wants/sm-client.service
→ /usr/lib/systemd/system/sm-client.service.
```

Now let's do the same job as before:

```
[student@studentvm1 ~]$ at now + 2 minutes
warning: commands will be executed using /bin/sh
at> free
at> <EOT>
job 7 at Thu May  2 16:23:00 2019
[student@studentvm1 ~]$ atq
7        Thu May  2 16:23:00 2019 a student
```

After two minutes have passed, use **atq** to verify the job queue is now empty. Then type mailx to view the email in your mail queue:

```
[student@studentvm1 ~]$ mailx
Heirloom Mail version 12.5 7/5/10.  Type ? for help.
"/var/spool/mail/student": 1 message 1 new
>N  1 Student User    Thu Mar 16 15:20  19/943  "Output from your job  4"
&
```

The ampersand (&) is the command prompt for mailx. We can see that there is one message in the inbox. It has the number, 1, that we can use to manage it. Type 1 at the prompt and press Enter. The message should look very similar to the following one. It shows the standard email message headers, a subject, and the output from our job:

```
& 1
Message  1:
From student@studentvm1.both.org  Thu Mar 16 15:20:02 2023
Return-Path: <student@studentvm1.both.org>
Date: Thu, 16 Mar 2023 15:20:00 -0400
From: Student User <student@studentvm1.both.org>
Subject: Output from your job          4
To: student@studentvm1.both.org
Status: R

                total        used        free    shared  buff/cache   available
Mem:         16367796      343340    14941192     11456     1083264    15712380
Swap:         8388604           0     8388604

&
```

Type q and press **Enter** to exit from mailx:

```
& q
Held 1 message in /var/spool/mail/student
You have mail in /var/spool/mail/student
[student@studentvm1 ~]$
```

This is a trivial example, but it does show you how the at command works and how to deal with the data stream from the jobs.

Security

The at command uses the files at.allow and at.deny to specify which users have access to the at command. The logic is the same as with cron.allow and cron.deny as discussed previously.

Setting the Hardware Clock

One thing I like to do after my client computers have synchronized with the NTP server is to set the system hardware clock from the system (OS) time. This is useful because it will take longer to synchronize the host to the NTP time if the hardware clock is very far off. The operating system gets its initial time set from the hardware clock located on the motherboard. If that clock is off, the initial system time will be incorrect.

Of course our systems are virtual machines, but they also have virtual hardware clocks, so this experiment works as it should.

EXPERIMENT 31-6: SETTING THE HARDWARE CLOCK

Perform this experiment as root. First, read the current value of and then set the hardware clock from the system (operating system) clock. And then read the hardware clock again:

```
[root@studentvm1 ~]# hwclock -r ; hwclock --systohc --localtime ; hwclock -r
2019-08-25 16:04:56.539023-04:00
2019-08-25 16:04:57.823655-04:00
[root@studentvm1 ~]#
```

The --localtime option ensures that the hardware clock is set to local time rather than UTC. Notice that there was a significant difference in the hardware clock on my instance of StudentVM1. Because the difference was almost exactly four hours, I suspect it was a time zone difference in the hardware clock.

The hwclock command can be added as a cron job or a script in cron.daily to keep the hardware clock synced with the system time.

About Time Zones

Early timekeeping was based on astronomical observation, specifically, when the sun was at the zenith, it was considered to be high noon. This is called local solar time. This was fine until the railroads came into existence. Because their speed enabled them to travel quickly between locations, it became very complex to calculate and define their schedules in terms of local solar times. This is especially true because local and solar times can differ by as much as 15 minutes throughout the year.

The railroads needed more consistency so they, the communications industries, and others worked to create a standardized set of time zones. The function of a time zone is to provide large geographical regions with standard times. Every location within a given time zone uses the same time.

Computers sometimes need to have their time zone changed. The computer might be relocated, or the organization might decide to convert to UTC as they grow. We can do that easily from the command line. The time zone is set in Fedora by a symlink, /etc/localtime, which points to a file in the /usr/share/zoneinfo directory.

```
┌─────────────────────────────────────────────────────────────────────┐
│              EXPERIMENT 31-7: SETTING THE TIME ZONE                    │
└─────────────────────────────────────────────────────────────────────┘
```

Perform this experiment as root on StudentVM1. We will look at the current setting, change the system time zone to UTC, and then change it back to the correct time zone for your locale.

First, do a long listing of the /etc/localtime file:

```
[root@studentvm1 ~]# ll /etc/localtime
lrwxrwxrwx. 1 root root 38 Dec 22  2018 /etc/localtime -> ../usr/share/
zoneinfo/America/New_York
[root@studentvm1 ~]#
```

This tells us a lot about time zone configuration. Primarily we find that /etc/localtime is where the system looks for its time zone configuration file. It also tells us that those files are all located in /usr/share/zoneinfo/ and its subdirectories. By using a symbolic link, we can link to any time zone configuration file in the zoneinfo directory tree.

Spend some time exploring this directory tree to see the many files that are there.

We could look for time zones or change the time zone manually, but we do not need to. Modern Fedora systems that use systemd have a tool that makes this a bit easier. The timedatectl utility allows us to list all available time zones and to change the system time zone. Let's start by listing all time zones. This utility dumps its output to the less utility so we can scroll through the many lines of data:

```
[root@studentvm1 ~]# timedatectl list-timezones
Africa/Abidjan
Africa/Accra
Africa/Addis_Ababa
Africa/Algiers
Africa/Asmara
<snip>
Pacific/Tahiti
Pacific/Tarawa
```

```
Pacific/Tongatapu
Pacific/Wake
Pacific/Wallis
UTC
lines 385-426/426 (END)
```

We can also look at the current time zone settings. This command provides the data in a form readable to the machine if we want to use it in a later command:

```
[root@studentvm1 ~]# timedatectl show
Timezone=America/New_York
LocalRTC=no
CanNTP=yes
NTP=yes
NTPSynchronized=yes
TimeUSec=Fri 2023-04-21 09:01:21 EDT
RTCTimeUSec=Fri 2023-04-21 09:01:21 EDT
[root@studentvm1 ~]#
```

Or this way in more human-readable format:

```
[root@studentvm1 ~]# timedatectl status
               Local time: Fri 2023-04-21 09:02:31 EDT
           Universal time: Fri 2023-04-21 13:02:31 UTC
                 RTC time: Fri 2023-04-21 13:02:31
                Time zone: America/New_York (EDT, -0400)
System clock synchronized: yes
              NTP service: active
          RTC in local TZ: no
```

You might receive an error when using the status sub-command:

```
Warning: The system is configured to read the RTC time in the local time
zone. This mode cannot be fully supported. It will create various problems
with time zone changes and daylight saving time adjustments. The RTC
time is never updated, it relies on external facilities to maintain it. If at
all possible, use RTC in UTC by calling 'timedatectl set-local-rtc 0'.
```

You can safely ignore this in most cases unless you are using the real-time clock (RTC). However, it is best to change the configuration so as to not use the RTC:

```
[root@studentvm1 ~]# timedatectl set-local-rtc 0
```

To change the time zone, use the following command. You can use any time zone in the list you displayed previously:

```
[root@studentvm1 ~]# timedatectl set-timezone Pacific/Tarawa ; date
Sun Aug 25 21:55:27 EDT 2019
[root@studentvm1 ~]#
```

After changing the time zone a few times, be sure to change it back to your home time zone.

Wikipedia has an interesting history of timekeeping in its "Time zone" article.[2]

Cleanup

If you have any cron jobs still active, comment them out. You should also delete the /tmp/freemem.log file.

Chapter Summary

This chapter has explored methods for running tasks at specific times using various repetitive time periods or only a single future time. The ability to run tasks at specified times can make the SysAdmin's job easier by removing the need to be present – or even awake – when the tasks need to be run.

We've explored the use of chrony to maintain accurate times on all of our computers and used that to set the hardware clock.

We looked at how crontab can be used to schedule repetitive tasks at intervals ranging from seconds to years. Scripts can be placed in cron.hourly and cron.daily instead of creating crontab entries for them to make scheduling even easier. We can use the at command to schedule tasks at a single time in the future.

---

[2] Wikipedia, Time zone, https://en.wikipedia.org/wiki/Time_zone

Note that systemd has its own tools called timers that are designed to be used in the same manner as cron and at. Because these timers are so closely integrated with and managed by systemd, we will cover them in Chapter 37.

We looked at time zones, their importance, how they are configured, and how to set your computer to a different time zone. We also learned to set the hardware time from the running system time.

Exercises

Perform the following exercises to complete this chapter:

1. Create a script, /usr/local/bin/mycronjob.sh, that displays the date and time and then uses the df command to display the storage device usage. Then create a crontab entry that runs that new file at 09:00 a.m. and 05:00 p.m. on the 7th and 21st of each month. Be sure to check later to verify that it works.

2. Where are cron files – those created by the crontab command – stored?

3. Describe the difference between cron and anacron.

4. Why are some cron files be stored in /etc/cron.d?

5. When is the first time after a host is booted that the files managed by anacron are executed?

6. As root create a script that generates a listing of the filesystems, their sizes, and how much space is used and/or available. The result should be appended to a file in /tmp. This does not need to be fancy; just a single command can do this. Place the script in /usr/local/bin. Use at least three different cron methods to run this job once per hour. After testing that use three different ways to run it once per day.

7. When entering at jobs and using a specification like now + 5 minutes, assume the time is 09:04 a.m. when the command **at now + 5 minutes** is issued and the time is 09:06 a.m. when **Ctrl+D** is entered to add the job to the queue. At what time does the at job execute?

CHAPTER 32

Networking

Objectives

In this chapter you will learn

- Some basic networking concepts

- To define and describe the TCP/IP five-layer network model

- The structure of IPv4 and IPv6 addresses

- To define and use Classless Inter-Domain Routing (CIDR) network notation

- How to use simple tools to explore network ranges and subnetting

- Basic client-side DHCP network configuration

- How to use Linux CLI tools like `arp`, `ip`, `ping`, `mtr`, and `nmcli` to explore the network and its configuration

- The basics of routing

- To manage firewalls using iptables

Introduction

In 2019, when this course was originally written, and more so today, nearly every electronic device on the planet is connected to the Internet. Devices such as computers, smart TVs, smart phones, and tablets are more or less obvious. But it goes even further because we have thermostats, doorbells, garage door openers, bathroom scales, refrigerators, security systems, and even our cars connected.

© David Both 2023
D. Both, *Using and Administering Linux: Volume 2*, https://doi.org/10.1007/978-1-4842-9615-8_32

Linux-based computers are no exception. At the beginning of this course, you downloaded VirtualBox and the Xfce version of Fedora, and you had to be connected to the Internet to do so. You also configured a virtual network for the virtual machine you created and tested it to ensure that your VM had connectivity to the outside world through that virtual network.

In this chapter we will discuss client-side networking and explore how our VM is configured automatically at boot time. We will look at the functional aspects of routing and firewalls on the client side. We will discuss servers and services such as DHCP, DNS, and routing in more detail from the server side in Volume 3 of this course.

Tip   This second edition no longer uses the deprecated `ifcfg` network commands. We use the newer NetworkManager `nmcli` commands.

About IPv6

We will concentrate on IPv4 (IP version 4) in this course because it is still far more common than IPv6 (IP version 6) at the end user side. Many ISPs use IPv6 for their backbone networks and are slowly progressing with IPv6 to the end user. Very slowly. We will discuss some of the IPv6 concepts but will base our experiments on IPv4.

Basic Networking Concepts

This course is intended to provide a practical approach to Linux and networking. Some important concepts are a necessary foundation on which to build further understanding.

Definitions

Let's start with some important definitions. We will encounter other terms and their definitions as we proceed through this chapter:

- A **node** is any device connected to and accessible in a network including computers, routers, printers, and any other network-attached device.

- A **host** is a node that is specifically a computer attached to the network.

- **IP** stands for Internet Protocol. It is a group of network layer protocols that allow computers to communicate with each other. IP is a best-effort packet-switching protocol used to transmit data packets from one network node to another. It is not considered reliable because data packets can be lost or intentionally dropped for any of a number of reasons.

- **TCP** is Transmission Control Protocol that sits on top of IP. TCP provides reliable communications and flow control including full duplex, which means that communication can go in both directions over the transmission medium at the same time.

- A **network** (of any kind) is a web- or net-like structure of communications systems that allow connected nodes to communicate with each other. There is a good physical model for this. It is inexact but a good starting point for further understanding.

This model is the system of roadways for automobiles and trucks (vehicles) to carry passengers and freight from one location to another. The main end points are the cities and specific homes or businesses in the cities. Each vehicle is analogous to a data packet in a computer network, and the passengers and freight are like the data contained in a packet.

These vehicles start from a location such as a house and travel the roads through surface intersections and large highway interchanges, switching from one route to another as required to get to the final destination. The intersections and interchanges along the way are similar to the routers used to switch data packets from one path on the Internet to another. However, in a computer network, the router makes the decisions, and for these vehicles the driver makes the decisions about where to turn onto another route.

In this model each packet, or vehicle, is transported independently of surrounding packets from source to destination:

- A **NIC** is a network interface controller[1] that is either built-in to a computer motherboard or that can be added as a pluggable device card. A NIC provides the computer with a hardware connection to a network.

---

[1] Wikipedia, Network Interface Controller, http://en.wikipedia.org/wiki/Network_Interface_Controller

- A network **node** is any device connected to a network and that is addressable by other devices such that a connection can be made.

- A **switch** is a hardware device that is used to connect multiple nodes together on a logical network segment. Two or more nodes or hosts have an Ethernet cable connecting them to the switch so that they can communicate with each other. It is possible to connect two computers together using a special crossover cable, but that is unusual and limiting because only two computers can be connected that way. Switches are not visible to the TCP/IP and operate only on the physical layer.

- A **router** is a device that routes data packets between two or more networks based on the destination IP address contained in the data packets. Routers have IP addresses for each network to which they connect and are visible to other devices in those networks.

- At least one router in the network is the **default gateway** to other networks or the rest of the Internet. If a data packet is sent by a host and there are no other routes defined, the default gateway sends the packet to the next router on the way to its final destination.

- A **connection** is a logical link between two nodes in a network. Connections exist at each layer of the TCP/IP stack.

- The term **stack** refers to the stacked layers of the TCP/IP network model. These layers form a stack of hardware and the software protocols that create links between network nodes at each level in the stack.

MAC Address

A **Media Access Control (MAC) address**[2] is a unique hardware address assigned to each network interface card (NIC) that provides the hardware a means of identification. The MAC address is configured permanently in the hardware by the device vendor and cannot be changed. This is called a universally administered address (UAA) and is sometimes referred to as the "burned-in address" or the "hardware address."

---

[2] Wikipedia, MAC address, https://en.wikipedia.org/wiki/MAC_address

There are, however, software methods that can be used to assign different MAC addresses to an interface, but the reasons for doing so are beyond the scope of this book, and I strongly recommend against doing so in any event for wired devices.[3] This is a locally administered address (LAA).

Xerox Network Systems created the original 48-bit Ethernet addressing scheme. The 48-bit address space contains 281,474,976,710,656 (2^{48}) possible MAC addresses.

MAC addresses consist of six two-digit hexadecimal (Hex) numbers separated by colons, such as 08:00:27:01:7d:ad, which is the MAC address of my VM. The first three pairs are the Organizational Unique Identifier (OUI) and can be used to identify the vendor of the NIC.[4] The last three pairs are the hardware ID for that specific NIC. The OUI numbers are assigned to vendors by the Institute of Electrical and Electronics Engineers[5] (IEEE).

EXPERIMENT 32-1: GETTING NETWORK DEVICE INFORMATION

This experiment should be performed as the student user; root access is not required. Identify the installed network interface cards and their MAC and IP addresses:

```
[root@studentvm1 ~] # nmcli
enp0s3: connected to Wired connection 1
        "Intel 82540EM"
        ethernet (e1000), 08:00:27:01:7D:AD, hw, mtu 1500
        ip4 default
        inet4 10.0.2.22/24
        route4 10.0.2.0/24 metric 100
        route4 default via 10.0.2.1 metric 100
        inet6 fe80::b36b:f81c:21ea:75c0/64
        route6 fe80::/64 metric 1024

enp0s9: connected to Wired connection 2
        "Intel 82540EM"
        ethernet (e1000), 08:00:27:FF:C6:4F, hw, mtu 1500
        inet4 192.168.0.181/24
```

---

[3] It is probably a good security practice to alter the MAC address of wireless devices if you want to prevent your device from being tracked.

[4] AJ Arul's utilities, https://aruljohn.com/mac.pl

[5] IEEE, www.ieee.org/

```
            route4 192.168.0.0/24 metric 101
            route4 default via 192.168.0.254 metric 101
            inet6 fe80::6ce0:897c:5b7f:7c62/64
            route6 fe80::/64 metric 1024

lo: unmanaged
            "lo"
            loopback (unknown), 00:00:00:00:00:00, sw, mtu 65536

DNS configuration:
            servers: 192.168.0.52 8.8.8.8 8.8.4.4
            domains: both.org
            interface: enp0s3

            servers: 192.168.0.52 8.8.8.8 8.8.4.4
            domains: both.org
            interface: enp0s9

Use "nmcli device show" to get complete information about known devices and
"nmcli connection show" to get an overview on active connection profiles.

Consult nmcli(1) and nmcli-examples(7) manual pages for complete usage
details.
```

The first entry, enp0s3 (0 = zero), is how Linux sees the first virtual network adapter on a VirtualBox VM. This NIC is connected to the 10.0.2.0/24 virtual network that you created as preparation for this course.

The second entry is the second NIC, which I configured in the VirtualBox Manager for my VM. The link/ether line for this second NIC shows 08:00:27:ff:c6:4f as the MAC address. I connect this NIC to my physical network for my own use to aid in experimenting while I write this book. You will not have this entry – yet. You'll add a second NIC to the server VM that you will create in Volume 3 of this course.

The third entry is the local (lo) interface, which is used by many Linux kernel tasks and applications to communicate within the local host. Every Linux computer has a local interface even if it is not connected to a network or even if it does not have a NIC installed. This interface is an absolute requirement for any Linux (or Unix) computer to function properly.

Finally, the nmcli command shows the DNS configuration. The DNS configuration can be different for each connected network, but is not in this case. The information you get from this command for your VM will be different than this but not completely.

Another application of the nmcli command provides more data in a pretty (-p option) format. This format is easier to read but takes up more screen space:

[student@studentvm1 ~]$ **nmcli -p device show**

Try this command without the -p option for a more compact view.

We are particularly interested in the routing information for each NIC. We can reduce the data stream this way:

[student@studentvm1 ~]$ **nmcli -p device show | grep IP4.ROUTE**

The IP4.ROUTE[1] lines show the mt field, which is the router priority metric. In this case enp0s3 has a metric of 100 and enp0s9 has a metric of 101. The default route is via the connection with the lowest metric, enp0s3.

The MAC address for the installed network devices is found in the GENERAL.HWADDR lines.

All networked devices have a MAC address, and we can see the MAC and IP addresses of the "neighbor" hosts with which our host has communicated. The ip neighbor command shows this information. Recall that I have two virtual NICs configured for my VM and you have only one, so your results will be a bit different:

```
[student@studentvm1 ~]$  ip neighbor
10.0.2.1 dev enp0s3 lladdr 52:54:00:12:35:00 STALE
192.168.0.52 dev enp0s9 lladdr e0:d5:5e:a2:de:a4 DELAY
192.168.0.1 dev enp0s9 lladdr b0:6e:bf:3a:43:1f REACHABLE
10.0.2.3 dev enp0s3 lladdr 08:00:27:aa:93:ef STALE
```

The arp command also displays this information:

```
[student@studentvm1 ~]$  arp
Address             HWtype   HWaddress            Flags Mask      Iface
_gateway            ether    52:54:00:12:35:00    C               enp0s3
yorktown.both.org   ether    e0:d5:5e:a2:de:a4    C               enp0s9
david.both.org      ether    b0:6e:bf:3a:43:1f    C               enp0s9
10.0.2.3            ether    08:00:27:aa:93:ef    C               enp0s3
```

```
[student@studentvm1 ~]$ arp -n
Address              HWtype  HWaddress            Flags Mask        Iface
10.0.2.1             ether   52:54:00:12:35:00    C                 enp0s3
192.168.0.52         ether   e0:d5:5e:a2:de:a4    C                 enp0s9
192.168.0.1          ether   b0:6e:bf:3a:43:1f    C                 enp0s9
10.0.2.3             ether   08:00:27:aa:93:ef    C                 enp0s3
```

You should see the lines for enp0s3 on your VM host as the result of this command. One line should contain the IP address 10.0.2.1, which is for the VirtualBox virtual router, and the other line is 10.0.2.3, which is the virtual DHCP server in the virtual network. If you do not see these lines, use the ping command to ensure that the StudentVM1 host has recently communicated with the router/gateway. Then retry the command.

MAC addresses are limited in scope to the physical network segment on which they reside. They are not routable and cannot be accessed outside the local network segment.

The ip command is designed to replace the ifconfig, arp, and some other network-related commands, so Red Hat has published a very nice IP command cheat sheet[6] that I use frequently. The man page for the arp command contains the following note, "This program is obsolete. For replacement check ip neigh," and the man page for the ifconfig command has a similar note. I still like the arp command as it is simple and easy. For now, these commands are still available, and it may be years before they disappear completely.

IP Address

The IPv4 address[7] is composed of four sets of hexadecimal pairs, called octets because they each contain eight (8) binary bits, for a total of 32 bits. The octets are separated by periods, such as 192.168.25.36. Each octet can have a maximum value of $2^8 - 1$, or 255. Computers and network routing and management equipment deal with the binary forms of IP addresses, but our devices are smart enough to display them to us in a human-readable form.

---

[6] Red Hat, IP Command Cheat Sheet, https://access.redhat.com/sites/default/files/attachments/rh_ip_command_cheatsheet_1214_jcs_print.pdf

[7] Wikipedia, IP Address, https://en.wikipedia.org/wiki/IP_address

Any computer or other device that needs to be accessible in a network or on the Internet must have an IP address assigned to it. IP addresses are routable and can be accessed from other network segments through a router. Some IP address ranges are reserved for internal, private use by organizations. These private IP address ranges are well defined, and we will explore this and more about IP addresses in some detail later in this chapter.

Because the public IPv4 address space was running out of assignable addresses and as a way to implement more efficient routing through the Internet, IPv6 was developed. IPv6 uses 128 bits for addressing, divided into eight sections of four hexadecimal digits. A typical IPv6 address looks like this, `2001:0db8:0000:0000:0000:ff00:0042:8329`, which looks rather daunting, but which can be shortened by omitting leading zeros and eliminating consecutive sections of zeros. The result looks like this, `2001:db8::ff00:42:8329`.

EXPERIMENT 32-2: EXPLORING IP ADDRESSES

Perform this experiment as the student user. Let's use the ip command again, but this time look at the IP addresses it reveals:

```
[root@studentvm1 ~]# ip addr
1: lo: <LOOPBACK,UP,LOWER_UP> mtu 65536 qdisc noqueue state UNKNOWN group
default qlen 1000
    link/loopback 00:00:00:00:00:00 brd 00:00:00:00:00:00
    inet 127.0.0.1/8 scope host lo
       valid_lft forever preferred_lft forever
    inet6 ::1/128 scope host
       valid_lft forever preferred_lft forever
2: enp0s3: <BROADCAST,MULTICAST,UP,LOWER_UP> mtu 1500 qdisc fq_codel state UP
group default qlen 1000
    link/ether 08:00:27:e1:0c:10 brd ff:ff:ff:ff:ff:ff
    inet 10.0.2.7/24 brd 10.0.2.255 scope global dynamic noprefixroute enp0s3
       valid_lft 1099sec preferred_lft 1099sec
    inet6 fe80::b7f2:97cf:36d2:b13e/64 scope link noprefixroute
       valid_lft forever preferred_lft forever
```

The loopback IPv4 address is 127.0.0.1 and, as previously mentioned, this network interface and its IP address are used by many Linux kernel processes and other applications. The IPv6 address is ::1/128. We can ping both addresses. The ping command sends a special ICMP[8] data packet to the target IP address that simply says, "Hi – please respond" and is a way to determine whether another host is in the network and active:

```
[root@studentvm1 ~]# ping -c2 ::1
PING ::1(::1) 56 data bytes
64 bytes from ::1: icmp_seq=1 ttl=64 time=0.067 ms
64 bytes from ::1: icmp_seq=2 ttl=64 time=0.111 ms

--- ::1 ping statistics ---
2 packets transmitted, 2 received, 0% packet loss, time 73ms
rtt min/avg/max/mdev = 0.067/0.089/0.111/0.022 ms
[root@studentvm1 ~]# ping -c2 127.0.0.1
PING 127.0.0.1 (127.0.0.1) 56(84) bytes of data.
64 bytes from 127.0.0.1: icmp_seq=1 ttl=64 time=0.063 ms
64 bytes from 127.0.0.1: icmp_seq=2 ttl=64 time=0.069 ms

--- 127.0.0.1 ping statistics ---
2 packets transmitted, 2 received, 0% packet loss, time 103ms
rtt min/avg/max/mdev = 0.063/0.066/0.069/0.003 ms
```

We can also ping remote hosts. We use the example.com domain, which is a legitimate domain set up specifically for testing. DNS (Domain Name System) converts the human-readable domain name into an IP address, which is then used as the destination address in the ping command:

```
[root@studentvm1 ~]# ping -c2 www.example.com
PING www.example.com (93.184.216.34) 56(84) bytes of data.
64 bytes from 93.184.216.34 (93.184.216.34): icmp_seq=1 ttl=54 time=37.10 ms
64 bytes from 93.184.216.34 (93.184.216.34): icmp_seq=2 ttl=54 time=151 ms

--- www.example.com ping statistics ---
2 packets transmitted, 2 received, 0% packet loss, time 148ms
rtt min/avg/max/mdev = 37.968/94.268/150.568/56.300 ms
```

---

[8] Wikipedia, Internet Control Message Protocol, https://en.wikipedia.org/wiki/internet_Control_Message_Protocol

IP Address Assignments

The Internet Assigned Numbers Authority (IANA)[9] is responsible for the global coordination and management of IP address and Autonomous System (AS) number assignments. This organization coordinates the assignments of IP addresses to large geographical-political entities. Registries within those divisions are responsible for assigning addresses to customers such as ISPs. The IANA website has a great deal of information that you may find useful.

TCP/IP

Before we get into networking any deeper, it helps to understand a little bit about how packets find their way to the correct host in a network. The TCP/IP network model defines a five-layer stack that describes the mechanisms necessary to move data packets from one host to another, whether that host is in the local network or someplace else on the planet.

Tip   Some versions of this model use a four-layer stack in which the bottom two layers, data link and physical, are combined into a single layer. I prefer the five-layer version because I think it provides more clarity.

The TCP/IP Network Model

Each of the five layers in the following description of this model is numbered and also contains the names of the data units that are handled by that layer. The diagram in Figure 32-1 shows each layer and the protocols typically encountered at that layer. This list describes the layers of the stack in vertical order from top to bottom:

1. **Application layer – Message**: This layer consists of the connection protocols required for various network applications to communicate, such as HTTP, DHCP, SSH, FTP, SMTP, IMAP, and others. When you request a web page from a remote website, a

---

[9] Internet Assigned Numbers Authority (IANA), `www.iana.org/`

connection request is sent to the web server, and the response is sent back to your host at this layer, and then your browser displays the web page in its window.

2. **Transport layer – TCP Segment**: The transport layer provides end-to-end data transport and flow management services that are independent of the data and types of protocols being transported. It uses ports such as 80 for HTTP and 25 for SMTP to make connections between the sending host and the remote host.

3. **Internet layer – Packet**: Packet routing is performed on the Internet layer. This layer is responsible for routing packets across two or more different networks in order to reach their final destination. This layer uses IP addresses and the routing table to determine which device to send the packets to next. If sent to a router, each router is responsible for sending the data packets only to the next router in the series and not for mapping out the entire route from the local host to the target host. The Internet layer is mostly about routers talking to routers in order to determine the next router in the chain.

4. **Data link layer – Frame**: The link layer manages the direct connections between hardware hosts in a single, local, logical, physical network. This layer uses the Media Access Control (MAC) addresses embedded in the network interface cards (NICs) to identify the physical devices attached to the local network. This layer cannot access hosts that are not in the local network.

5. **Physical layer – Bits**: This is the hardware layer and consists of the NICs and the physical network (usually Ethernet) cable as well as the hardware-level protocols used to transmit individual bits that make up the data between any two hosts or other network nodes that are locally connected.

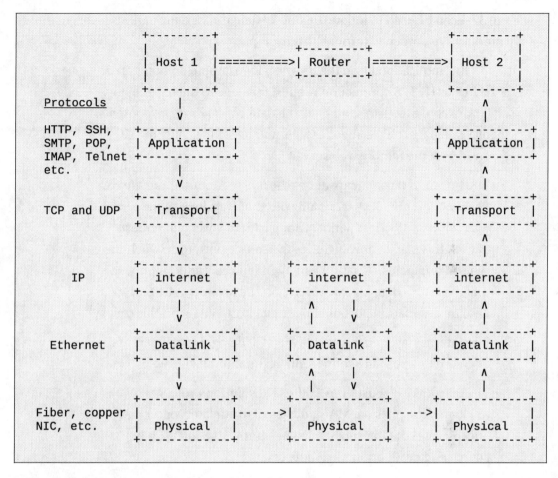

Figure 32-1. *The TCP/IP network model*

A Simple Example

So what does that look like when a host is actually sending data in the network using the TCP/IP network model? Here is my own made-up description of how data is moved from one network to another. In this example my computer is sending a request to a remote server for a web page.

Figure 32-1 can be used to follow the flow of data through the various layers of the TCP/IP model as you proceed through this example:

1. On the application layer, the browser, for example, initiates an HTTP or HTTPS connection request message to the remote host, `www.example.com`, to send back the data comprising the contents of a web page. This is the message, and it includes only the IP address of the remote web server.

2. The transport layer encapsulates the message containing the web page request in a TCP datagram with the IP address of the remote web server as the destination. Along with the original request packet, this packet now includes the source port from which the request originates, usually a very high number random port, so that the return data knows which port the browser is listening on, and the destination port on the remote host, port 80 in this case.

3. The Internet layer encapsulates the TCP datagram in a packet that also contains both the source and destination IP addresses.

4. The data link layer uses the Address Resolution Protocol (ARP) to identify the physical MAC address of the default router and encapsulates the Internet packet in a frame that includes both the source and destination MAC addresses.

5. The frame is sent over the wire – usually CAT5[10] or CAT6[11] – from the NIC on the local host to the NIC on the default router. In a wireless environment, the wireless NIC sends the frame over the air to the receiver in the wireless router. In this case the wireless router is the default, that is, the gateway router.

6. The default router opens the datagram and determines the destination IP address. The router uses its own routing table to identify the IP address of the next router that will take the frame on the next step of its journey. The router then re-encapsulates the

---

[10] Wikipedia, Category 5 cable, `https://en.wikipedia.org/wiki/Category_5_cable`
[11] Wikipedia, Category 6 cable, `https://en.wikipedia.org/wiki/Category_6_cable`

frame in a new datagram that contains its own MAC as the source and the MAC address of the next router and then sends it on through the appropriate interface. The router performs its routing task at layer 3, the Internet layer.

Switches are invisible to all protocols at layers 2 and above, so they do not affect the transmission of data in any logical manner. The function of switches is merely to provide a simple means to connect multiple hosts into a single physical network via lengths of network cable.

There is also an OSI network model, but that is more complex than the TCP/IP model, and that additional complexity adds nothing to our understanding of networking. The OSI model is irrelevant to our needs.

CIDR: Network Notation and Configuration

CIDR stands for Classless Inter-Domain Routing.[12] It defines a notation methodology for network addressing that is used to specify the network portion of an IP address.

Network Classes

Before examining how CIDR actually works, let's first look at the classful network notation that CIDR replaces. Introduced in 1981, the classful methodology defined five network classes to be used for identification and addressing devices on the Internet. The network class is defined by the four high-order bits of the address. Figure 32-2 shows the five network classes defined by classful network addressing, including both the subnet mask and CIDR notation for each class.

---

[12] Wikipedia, Classless Inter-Domain Routing, https://en.wikipedia.org/wiki/Classless_Inter-Domain_Routing

Class	Start	End	Subnet Mask	CIDR	No of Networks	IP Addresses / Networks
A	0.0.0.0	127.255.255.255	255.0.0.0	/8	128	16,177,216 (2^{24})
B	128.0.0.0	191.255.255.255	255.255.0.0	/16	16,384	65,536 (2^{20})
C	192.0.0.0	223.255.255.255	255.255.255.0	/24	2,097,152	256 (2^{8})
D	224.0.0.0	239.255.255.255			Undefined	Undefined
E	240.0.0.0	255.255.255.255			Undefined	Undefined

Figure 32-2. *Classful Internet addressing defines five classes*

Classes A, B, and C are the commonly used unicast address ranges that were assigned to organizations. Unicast means that the data packets are sent to a single target host. Class D was the so-called multicast range of addresses. In this range, data packets would be sent to all hosts in a defined network. This range of IP addresses was essentially unused. The Class E address range was reserved for future expansion but was also never used.

Note that there are only three possible subnet masks that match each class of the classful networks, 255.0.0.0 (8 bits), 255.255.0.0 (16 bits), and 255.255.255.0 (24 bits), divided on the octet boundaries. This is one of the limiting factors in public address allocation due to the relatively limited number of networks that the classes define.

Unfortunately, classful networking assignments led to major waste. Organizations would apply for a number of addresses, but if they needed more than the number of addresses in a class C network, for example, they would apply for and be assigned an entire class B network whether they needed all of the addresses in that network or not. The same is true for class B networks; a few large organizations needed more than a class B network, so they were assigned class A networks. Thus, a few large organizations became assigned very large numbers of IP addresses.[13] See RFC790, "Historic allocation of class A networks,"[14] for the complete list of the assignments of the current /8 blocks and historical class A networks.

---

[13] Wikipedia, List of assigned /8 IPv4 address blocks, https://en.wikipedia.org/wiki/List_of_assigned_/8_IPv4_address_blocks
[14] The Internet Engineering Task Force (IETF), RFC790, Historic allocation of class A networks

The four high-order (leftmost) bits of the address define the class of the network, not the subnet mask or the CIDR equivalent of the subnet mask. In practical terms, this meant that large networks could not be broken down into smaller subnets at the Internet level because the Internet routers could only have a single route to each assigned classful network. Further, although the large, classful networks could be divided into subnets by the organizations that owned them, routing packets to other geographical locations in the same network then required the organization to use private internal networks or public VPNs at a very high cost premium.

For a simple example, imagine a company that has six departments and requires about 400 IP addresses for each. This requires more than a single class C network of 256 IP addresses, a total of 2,400 addresses. The company has a class B network of 65,536 addresses assigned to it. As a result, the remaining 63,136 IP addresses would be wasted because they could not be assigned to other organizations.

Note   For the purposes of these experiments, it is necessary to misuse a portion of the current private 10.0.0.0/8 CIDR block of addresses as if it were a public class B address. This is to protect public addresses that may belong to some real organization.

The **sipcalc** command provides a great deal of information about an IP address, or address ranges. As you will see later, it also has the capability to generate a list of subnets in a given address range given a subnet mask. You may have to install the **sipcalc** program; it was not installed by default on my Fedora system.

```
EXPERIMENT 32-3: EXPLORING IP ADDRESS RANGES
```

First, as the root user, install the `sipcalc` RPM package:

```
[root@studentvm1 ~]# dnf -y install sipcalc
```

Now as the student user, we can use `sipcalc` to explore IP addressing. Use the `sipcalc` command-line program to provide the network data for this randomly selected class B network from our pseudo-public address range:

```
[student@studentvm1 ~]$ sipcalc 10.125.0.0/16
-[IPv4 : 10.125.0.0/16] - 0
```

```
[CIDR]
Host address          - 10.125.0.0
Host address (decimal) - 175964160
Host address (hex)    - A7D0000
Network address       - 10.125.0.0
Network mask          - 255.255.0.0
Network mask (bits)   - 16
Network mask (hex)    - FFFF0000
Broadcast address     - 10.125.255.255
Cisco wildcard        - 0.0.255.255
Addresses in network  - 65536
Network range         - 10.125.0.0 - 10.125.255.255
Usable range          - 10.125.0.1 - 10.125.255.254
```

The output from the sipcalc command shows, among other things, the network address, the netmask, the network address range, as well as the available addresses in that range. The address 10.125.0.0 is the network address, and 10.125.255.254 is the broadcast address for this network. Those two addresses cannot be used for hosts.

Another option would have been to assign multiple class C networks to the company. That would significantly reduce the number of wasted IP addresses, but configuring the routing for this organization would be more complex than it would otherwise need to be with a single network. This option would also reduce the number of class C address blocks available for other organizations.

Along Came CIDR

Classless Inter-Domain Routing[15] (CIDR) notation was introduced in 1993 as a means of extending the lifetime of IPv4,[16] which was running out of assignable addresses. It accomplishes this by making it possible for organizations to more efficiently utilize the public IPv4 address ranges assigned to them and by opening up some previously reserved address ranges.

---

[15] Wikipedia, Classless Inter-Domain Routing, https://en.wikipedia.org/wiki/Classless_Inter-Domain_Routing

[16] Bandel, David A., "CIDR: A Prescription for Shortness of Address Space," www.linuxjournal.com/article/3017, Linux Journal

In 1996, RFC1918[17] enhanced CIDR with the assignments of reserved, externally non-routable networks corresponding to each of the old A, B, and C class ranges. These private networks, shown in Figure 32-3, can be used freely by any organization for their internal networks; no longer is it necessary for every computer to have an assigned public IP address. This feature provides a significant portion of the solution to multiple problems.

CIDR Block	Address Range	No. of IP Addresses
10.0.0.0/8	10.0.0.0 - 10.255.255.255	16,777,216
172.16.0.0/12	172.16.0.0 - 172.31.255.255	1,048,576
192.168.0.0/16	192.168.0.0 - 192.168.255.255	65,536

Figure 32-3. *IPv4 address ranges reserved for use as private internal networks*

The use of these private internal networks allows organizations to be assigned one or possibly a few public IP addresses for access to the outside Internet while providing large private address spaces for internal networks. To be absolutely clear, each of these address ranges can be used by many different organizations because these private network addresses are not routable through the Internet; of course, organizations can route network packets internally between private networks.

Returning to our example company, let's make the assumption that it only requires a single public IP address to connect it to the outside world. The company's Internet provider only assigns minimum blocks of four addresses, two of which are reserved for the network address and the broadcast address, thus leaving two usable addresses. This provides a balance between unusable addresses due to excessive subnetting, wasted addresses, and cost to the customer.

---

[17] The Internet Engineering Task Force (IETF), RFC1918: Address allocation for private internets, https://tools.ietf.org/html/rfc1918

EXPERIMENT 32-4: PICKING AN INTERNAL NETWORK

As the student user, we will now use **sipcalc** to explore using the smallest assignable IP address space to our fictional organization. Assume that the ISP assigns the company a public network address, 10.125.16.32/30. Remember that, for this example, we are using part of the 10.0.0.0/8 private network as if it were public. This assignment provides the company with the following public network, which uses a network mask of 30 bits:

```
[student@studentvm1 ~]$ sipcalc 10.125.16.32/30
-[IPv4 : 10.125.16.32/30] - 0

[CIDR]
Host address              - 10.125.16.32
Host address (decimal)    - 175968288
Host address (hex)        - A7D1020
Network address           - 10.125.16.32
Network mask              - 255.255.255.252
Network mask (bits)       - 30
Network mask (hex)        - FFFFFFFC
Broadcast address         - 10.125.16.35
Cisco wildcard            - 0.0.0.3
Addresses in network      - 4
Network range             - 10.125.16.32 - 10.125.16.35
Usable range              - 10.125.16.33 - 10.125.16.34
```

This provides our organization with four public IP addresses. Two of these addresses are used by the network address and the broadcast address, which leaves two IP addresses for use by our network, 10.125.16.33 and 10.125.16.34.

Our example company is free to choose to use any of the private network ranges for their internal networks. They can use Network Address Translation (NAT) to access the outside world from their internal, private network.

At first glance, the straightforward thing to do might be to choose a network from the private 172.16.0.0/12 range to provide a large enough range for a single internal network. For our example they could choose the 172.16.0.0/12 network, which would provide the following internal network space for them:

```
[student@studentvm1 ~]$ sipcalc 172.16.0.0/12
-[IPv4 : 172.16.0.0/12] - 0

[CIDR]
Host address            - 172.16.0.0
Host address (decimal)  - 2886729728
Host address (hex)      - AC100000
Network address         - 172.16.0.0
Network mask            - 255.240.0.0
Network mask (bits)     - 12
Network mask (hex)      - FFF00000
Broadcast address       - 172.31.255.255
Cisco wildcard          - 0.15.255.255
Addresses in network    - 1048576
Network range           - 172.16.0.0 - 172.31.255.255
Usable range            - 172.16.0.1 - 172.31.255.254
```

Note that this network does not conform to the old B class network as it has fewer network bits in the netmask, thus providing more space for host address bits. The 12 network bits leave 20 bits for hosts, or 1,048,576 hosts. That is far more hosts available than an old class B network would provide for a network. It has also more address space than the organization currently needs for its network.

Variable Length Subnet Masking

CIDR also brings with it a new approach to the old netmask, called Variable Length Subnet Masking, or VLSM. The use of a 12-bit netmask for the private address range defined by the CIDR block in Experiment 32-4 hints at this.

VLSM allows our example company to easily create more manageable subnets from the large private address space available to them by adding bits to the netmask. Using the 12-bit netmask encompasses this entire available private address range, so in order to be more conservative about the address space that the company actually needs, they decide to increase the number of bits in the netmask they will use.

The `sipcalc -s xx` command, where **xx** is the number of bits in the subnet mask, can be used to calculate the subnets in this private address range.

411

EXPERIMENT 32-5: VARIABLE LENGTH SUBNET MASKING

Perform this experiment as the student user. Calculate the subnets of 172.16.0.0/12 that have a 16-bit subnet mask:

```
[student@studentvm1 ~]$ sipcalc 172.16.0.0/12 -s 16
-[IPv4 : 172.16.0.0/12] - 0

[Split network]
Network              - 172.16.0.0      - 172.16.255.255
Network              - 172.17.0.0      - 172.17.255.255
Network              - 172.18.0.0      - 172.18.255.255
Network              - 172.19.0.0      - 172.19.255.255
Network              - 172.20.0.0      - 172.20.255.255
Network              - 172.21.0.0      - 172.21.255.255
Network              - 172.22.0.0      - 172.22.255.255
Network              - 172.23.0.0      - 172.23.255.255
Network              - 172.24.0.0      - 172.24.255.255
Network              - 172.25.0.0      - 172.25.255.255
Network              - 172.26.0.0      - 172.26.255.255
Network              - 172.27.0.0      - 172.27.255.255
Network              - 172.28.0.0      - 172.28.255.255
Network              - 172.29.0.0      - 172.29.255.255
Network              - 172.30.0.0      - 172.30.255.255
Network              - 172.31.0.0      - 172.31.255.255
```

Use **sipcalc** to calculate the number of addresses provided by various numbers of bits in the netmask of the 172.16.0.0/12 network. You should be able to determine and verify the data shown in Figure 32-4.

Bits in netmask	Number of addresses
12	1,048,576
16	65,536
17	32,768
18	16,384
19	8,192
20	4,096

Figure 32-4. *Number of addresses in various subnet ranges for network 172.16.0.0/12*

As mentioned before, the company currently needs about 2,400 IP addresses. To allow plenty of room for growth while reducing the total number of addresses to a manageable level, the company chooses to use a 19-bit netmask that provides 8,192 addresses. They calculate the available 19-bit subnets using sipcalc:

```
[student@studentvm1 ~]$ sipcalc 172.16.0.0/12 -s 19
-[IPv4 : 172.16.0.0/12] - 0

[Split network]
Network            - 172.16.0.0      - 172.16.31.255
Network            - 172.16.32.0     - 172.16.63.255
Network            - 172.16.64.0     - 172.16.95.255
Network            - 172.16.96.0     - 172.16.127.255
Network            - 172.16.128.0    - 172.16.159.255
Network            - 172.16.160.0    - 172.16.191.255
Network            - 172.16.192.0    - 172.16.223.255
Network            - 172.16.224.0    - 172.16.255.255
<snip>
Network            - 172.31.96.0     - 172.31.127.255
Network            - 172.31.128.0    - 172.31.159.255
Network            - 172.31.160.0    - 172.31.191.255
Network            - 172.31.192.0    - 172.31.223.255
Network            - 172.31.224.0    - 172.31.255.255
```

The company randomly chooses to use the 172.30.64.0/19 subnet. Now their network specification can be calculated:

```
[student@studentvm1 ~]$ sipcalc 172.30.64.0/19
-[IPv4 : 172.30.64.0/19] - 0

[CIDR]
Host address          - 172.30.64.0
Host address (decimal) - 2887663616
Host address (hex)    - AC1E4000
Network address       - 172.30.64.0
Network mask          - 255.255.224.0
Network mask (bits)   - 19
Network mask (hex)    - FFFFE000
Broadcast address     - 172.30.95.255
Cisco wildcard        - 0.0.31.255
Addresses in network  - 8192
Network range         - 172.30.64.0 - 172.30.95.255
Usable range          - 172.30.64.1 - 172.30.95.254
```

Of course this is only one possible 19-bit subnet out of 128 in the private address range. The company could have chosen any of the 19-bit subnets calculated previously, any of which would work equally well.

Another option would be to use the 192.168.0.0/16 private address range and select one of the 19-bit subnets available in that range. I leave the task of determining how many and which subnets would be available in that range as an exercise for you.

Using CIDR notation along with the reorganization of previously allocated addresses by CIDR block, as well as the use of VLSM, provides more usable public IP addresses and increased flexibility in the assignment of public addresses. The design of CIDR notation with VLSM respects the old classful networking scheme while providing significantly more flexibility and IP address availability for private internal use by organizations of all sizes. Private address spaces as well as assigned public address spaces can be easily split into subnets by adding bits to the netmask without consideration for network classes.

CIDR notation can be used when referring to classful networks but only as a notational shorthand.

DHCP Client Configuration

Each network interface controller (NIC) on your computer provides a physical connection to your network. Most computers have only one NIC, while others may have several. Laptops usually have a NIC for a wired connection and a NIC for a wireless connection. Some laptops also have a NIC for a cellular network connection. Some Linux desktop or tower computers have multiple wired NICs and are used as inexpensive routers for internal networks; such is the case with a couple of my own systems.

In most instances, as with Fedora, the default is to use Dynamic Host Configuration Protocol[18] (DHCP) configuration for all network interfaces. This requires a DHCP server to be located in the local network. The virtual router in our virtual network provides those DHCP services for our virtual machine.

The DHCP server can provide a large number of network configuration data components, but those in the following list are the only ones that are absolutely required. These are the minimum data required for a host to access the network:

- An IP address

- The IP address of the router/gateway device

- The IP address of at least one name server

Some other configuration data that the DHCP server might provide are but not limited to the following:

- Up to two additional name server IP addresses

- The domain name of the local network so that using a command like ping does not require typing the complete domain name

- The subnet mask

---

[18] Wikipedia, Dynamic Host Configuration Protocol, https://en.wikipedia.org/wiki/ Dynamic_Host_Configuration_Protocol

NIC Naming Conventions

The naming conventions for network interface controllers used to be simple, uncomplicated, and, I thought, easy. Using ethX made sense to me and was easy to type. It also did not require extra steps to figure out what long and obscure name belonged to a NIC. Unfortunately, adding a new NIC could force the renaming of existing ones, causing issues with startup configuration of all the NICs.

That has all changed – more than once. After a short stint with some very long and unintelligible NIC names that apparently made sense to a small group of programmers, we now have a third set of naming conventions, which seemed only marginally better – until I came to understand it better.

How It Works, Sort Of

The udev device manager software that runs in the background of Linux hosts detects when a new device has been added to the system, such as a new NIC, and creates a rule to identify and name it if one does not already exist. The details of how this works have changed in more recent versions of Fedora, CentOS, and RHEL.

During the early part of the startup phase, the Linux kernel via udev identifies connected devices including network interface controllers. At this stage the devices are still known by their traditional names of ethX. A very short time after that, systemd renames the devices according to a series of hierarchical naming schemes.

EXPERIMENT 32-6: NIC RENAMING

Perform this experiment as root. In this experiment I left the information for my second NIC to give you more data to work with:

```
[root@studentvm1 ~]# dmesg | grep eth
[    5.227604] e1000 0000:00:03.0 eth0: (PCI:33MHz:32-bit) 08:00:27:01:7d:ad
[    5.227625] e1000 0000:00:03.0 eth0: Intel(R) PRO/1000 Network Connection
[    5.577171] e1000 0000:00:09.0 eth1: (PCI:33MHz:32-bit) 08:00:27:ff:c6:4f
[    5.577199] e1000 0000:00:09.0 eth1: Intel(R) PRO/1000 Network Connection
[    5.579794] e1000 0000:00:03.0 enp0s3: renamed from eth0
[    5.585332] e1000 0000:00:09.0 enp0s9: renamed from eth1
```

So this shows that at a little over five seconds into the Linux startup sequence, the eth0 and eth1 network devices are located, and less than a second later, eth0 is renamed to enp0s3 and eth1 is renamed enp0s9.

Chapter 11 of the RHEL 7 "Networking Guide" describes how this renaming works. The following is excerpted from that document:

Scheme 1: Names incorporating Firmware or BIOS provided index numbers for on-board devices (example: eno1), are applied if that information from the firmware or BIOS is applicable and available, else falling back to scheme 2.

Scheme 2: Names incorporating Firmware or BIOS provided PCI Express hotplug slot index numbers (example: ens1) are applied if that information from the firmware or BIOS is applicable and available, else falling back to scheme 3.

Scheme 3: Names incorporating physical location of the connector of the hardware (example: enp2s0), are applied if applicable, else falling directly back to scheme 5 in all other cases.

Scheme 4: Names incorporating interface's MAC address (example: enx78e7d1ea46da), is not used by default, but is available if the user chooses.

Scheme 5: The traditional unpredictable kernel naming scheme, is used if all other methods fail (example: eth0).

In scheme 1, eno is used in which the letter "o" means on-board, that is, an integral part of the motherboard. In scheme 2, ens is used and the letter "s" indicates that the device is plugged into a PCI Express slot. Back in Experiment 32-1 we looked at the VM's installed NIC and found that it was named enp0s3. This is consistent with naming scheme 3, which is based on the physical location of the connectors, whether virtual or physical, on the hardware.

The primary function of the revised naming schemes is to provide a consistent set of NIC names so that installing a new NIC or even just a reboot would not cause the NIC names to change. This by itself is well worth the changes. I have had plenty of opportunity to fight with apparently random renaming of several network devices on a single host. That was much less fun than learning the revised naming schemes.

The newest NIC naming conventions are used by RHEL 7 and 8, CentOS 7 and 8, and the current releases of Fedora. The NIC naming conventions for these distributions are described in detail in the RHEL 7 document "Networking Guide"[19] along with a description of how the names are derived. Using the NetworkManager tools to manage networking is covered in the RHEL 8 document "Configuring and Managing Networking[20]" as well as in Chapter 33 of this volume.

Interface Configuration Files: Old Style

All current releases of Fedora default to using DHCP configuration for obtaining network configuration information. No options are provided during the installation of Fedora to configure any aspect of the network interface. Starting with Fedora 29, Linux hosts using DHCP for network configuration no longer require interface configuration files if all of the DHCP default configurations are sufficient. This is likely to be true for most workstations and laptops in a network center using DHCP for network configuration.

However, for Fedora releases up through 35, nonstandard configuration of the NICs for each network connection can still be accomplished with the old-style ifcfg-X interface configuration files in the /etc/sysconfig/network-scripts directory. Each NIC can have an interface configuration file named ifcfg-enp0s3, or something similar, where enp0s3 is the interface name assigned by the udev daemon. Each interface configuration file is bound to a specific physical NIC.

Starting with Fedora 36, the old interface configuration files are no longer supported on new installations, and NetworkManager is used exclusively. We will discuss NetworkManager in more detail in Chapter 33. That will include how it manages wired network connections without interface configuration files and its use of network connection keyfiles for wireless connections. It will also cover how to upgrade to or to create NetworkManager connection keyfiles for wired connections when necessary such as on a server or a system acting as a router where a static IP address is required.

---

[19] Red Hat, Networking Guide, `https://access.redhat.com/documentation/en-us/red_hat_`
`enterprise_linux/7/html/networking_guide/ch-consistent_network_device_naming`
[20] Red Hat, Configuring and Managing Networking, `https://access.redhat.com/`
`documentation/en-us/red_hat_enterprise_linux/8/html/configuring_and_managing_`
`networking/Configuring-Networking-with-nmcli_configuring-and-managing-networking`

When Is an Interface Configuration File Needed?

Never.

Well, at least not with Fedora 36 and later. But there are still a large number of systems around that have not migrated to NetworkManager connection keyfiles, so you should at least know what they look like and be at least minimally familiar with the most common configuration variables.

The Interface Configuration File

Let's look at the contents of a minimal ifcfg file as seen in Figure 32-5.

```
TYPE=Ethernet
PROXY_METHOD=none
BROWSER_ONLY=no
BOOTPROTO=dhcp
DEFROUTE=yes
IPv4_FAILURE_FATAL=no
IPV6INIT=yes
IPV6_AUTOCONF=yes
IPV6_DEFROUTE=yes
IPV6_FAILURE_FATAL=no
IPV6_ADDR_GEN_MODE=stable-privacy
NAME=enp0s3
UUID=4a527023-daa4-4dfb-9775-dbe9fb00fb0b
DEVICE=enp0s3
ONBOOT=yes
```

Figure 32-5. *A typical yet minimal ifcfg file. It was named ifcfg-enp0s3 on one of my test VMs*

Figure 32-6 lists the configuration options shown in the figure and some common ones that aren't in that file we just created, along with some brief explanations for each. Many of the IPv6 options are similar to those of the similarly named IPv4 ones. Note that local configuration variable settings override those provided by a DHCP server.

Configuration variable	Description
TYPE	Type of network such as Ethernet or token ring.
PROXY_METHOD	Proxy configuration method. "none" means no proxy is in use.
BROWSER_ONLY	Whether a proxy configuration is for browsers only.
BOOTPROTO	Options are dhcp, bootp, none, and static.
DEFROUTE	This interface is the default route for this host to the outside world.
IPv4_FAILURE_FATAL	If this is set to "no" failure to obtain an IPv4 connection will not affect any attempt to make an IPv6 connection.
IPv6INIT	Whether to initialize IPv6 or not. The default is yes.
IPv6_AUTOCONF	Yes means use DHCP for configuration of IPv6 on this interface.
IPv6_DEFROUTE	This interface is the IPv6 default route for this host to the outside world.
IPv6_FAILURE_FATAL	If this is set to "no" failure to obtain an IPv6 connection will not affect any attempt to make an IPv4 connection.
IPv6_ADDR_GEN_MODE	Configure IPv6 Stable Privacy addressing.
NAME	The interface name, such as enp0s3.
UUID	A Universally Unique Identifier for the interface. It is created with a hash of the interface name.
DEVICE	The name of the interface to which this configuration file bound.
ONBOOT	If yes, this starts the interface at boot (really startup time. If no, the interface is not started until a user logs in at the GUI or manually starts the inteface. I always set this to yes if it is not already.
HWADDR	The MAC address of the interface.
DNS1, DNS2	Up to two name servers may be specified.
USERCTL	Specifies whether non-privileged users may start and stop this interface. Options are yes/no.

Figure 32-6. *Some of the more common configuration items found in network interface configuration files*

Configuration variable	Description
IPADDR	The IP Address assigned to this NIC
BROADCAST	The broadcast address for this network such as 10.0.2.255
NETMASK	The netmask for this subnet such as 255.255.255.0
NETWORK	The network ID for this subnet such as 10.0.2.0
SEARCH	The DNS domain name to search when doing lookups on unqualified hostnames such as using studentvm1 instead of studentvm1.example.com.
GATEWAY	The network router or default gateway for this subnet, such as 10.0.2.1.
PEERDNS	A value of yes indicates that /etc/resolv.conf is to be modified by inserting the DNS server entries specified by DNS1 and DNS2 options in this file. No means do not alter the resolv.conf file. Yes is the default when DHCP is specified in the BOOTPROTO line.

Figure 32-6. (Continued)

The lines in the interface configuration files are not sequence sensitive and work fine in any order. By convention the option names are in uppercase and the values are in lowercase. Option values can be enclosed in quotes, but that is not necessary unless the value is more than a single word or number.

For more information about configuration files, the file /usr/share/doc/initscripts/ sysconfig.txt contains a list of all the files that can be found in the /etc/sysconfig directory and its subdirectories. This includes the network ifcfg-<interface> files. The descriptions of each file list all of the possible configuration variables and their possible values along with terse explanations.

The networks File

The /etc/networks file is a plain ASCII text file that contains network name information for connected networks that are known to the host. This file only supports class A, B, or C networks. As a result it won't provide accurate information for networks using CIDR notation.

The network File (Deprecated)

There is one old and now deprecated file you might encounter in older installations. The network file usually contained only a single comment line for Fedora, RHEL, and CentOS. It was located in /etc/sysconfig and was used in the past to enable or disable networking. It was also used to set the networking hostname as shown in the following example:

```
NETWORKING=yes
HOSTNAME=host.example.com
```

This file had been present but empty and unused in Fedora since release 19 and was still present in Fedora 30. It is no longer present in current releases. The network hostname is now set in the /etc/hostname file.

The route-<interface> File

The only other network configuration file you might have found in the /etc/sysconfig/ network-scripts directory is the route-<interface> file. This file is no longer used or present.

If you wanted to set up static routes on a multihomed[21] system, you would create a route file for each interface. For example, a file might be named route-enp0s3 and would contain information defining routes to entire networks or specific hosts for that interface. Each interface would have its own route file.

The use of this file was uncommon in Linux clients. However, if you were using the host as a router or had some special routing needs, you would have used this file to configure those complex routes. Therefore, the details of this routing configuration file are beyond the scope of this volume.

Name Services

Surfing the Web is fun and easy, but think what it would be like if you had to type in the IP address of every website you wanted to view. For example, locating a website would look like this when you type it in, https://93.184.216.34, which would be nearly impossible for most of us to remember. Of course using bookmarks would help, but suppose your friend tells you about a cool new website and tells you to go to 93.184.216.34. How would you remember that? Telling someone to go to "example.com" is far easier to remember.

---

[21] A system with multiple NICs, typically used as a router.

The Domain Name System provides the database to be used in the translation from human-readable hostnames, such as `www.example.com`, to IP addresses, like 93.184.216.34, so that your Internet-connected computers and other devices can access them. The primary function of the BIND (Berkeley Internet Name Domain) software is that of a domain name resolver that utilizes that database. There is another name resolver software, but BIND is currently the most widely used DNS software on the Internet. I will use the terms *name server*, *DNS*, and *resolver* pretty much interchangeably throughout this section.

Without these name resolver services, it would be nearly impossible to surf the Web as freely and easily as we do. As humans, we tend to do better with names like example. com, while computers do much better with numbers like 93.184.216.34. So we need a translation service to convert the names that are easy for us to the numbers that are easy for our computers. This process is called name resolution.

In small networks the /etc/hosts file on each host can be used as a name resolver. Maintaining copies of this file on several hosts can become very time-consuming, and errors can cause much confusion and wasted time before they are found. I did this for several years in my own network, and it ultimately became too much trouble to maintain even with the usual 8–12 computers I had operational. So I ultimately converted to running my own name server to resolve both internal and external hostnames.

Most networks of any size require centralized management of this service with name service software such as the Berkeley Internet Name Domain (BIND). BIND is called that because it was developed by the University of California at Berkeley (UCB) in the early 1980s. Hosts use the Domain Name System (DNS) to locate IP addresses from the names given in software such as web browsers, email clients, SSH, FTP, and many other Internet services.

How a Name Search Works

Let's take a look at a simplified example of what happens when a name request for a web page is made by a client service on your computer. For this example, I will use `www.example.com` as the website I want to view in my browser. I also assume that there is a local name server in the network, as is the case with my own network.

1. First, I type in the URL or select a bookmark containing that URL. In this case, the URL is `www.example.com`.

2. The browser client, whether it is Opera, Firefox, Chrome, Lynx, Links, or any other browser, sends the request to the operating system.

3. The operating system first checks the /etc/hosts file to see if the URL or hostname is there. If so, the IP address of that entry is returned to the browser. If not, we proceed to the next step. In this case we assume that it is not.

4. The URL is then sent to the first name server specified in /etc/resolv.conf. In this case the IP address of the first name server is my own internal name server. For this example, my name server does not have the IP address for `www.example.com` cached and must look further afield. So we go on to the next step.

5. The local name server sends the request to a remote name server. This can be one of two destination types, one of which is a forwarder. A forwarder is simply another name server such as the ones at your ISP or a public name server such as Google at 8.8.8.8 or 8.8.4.4. The other destination type is that of the top-level root name servers. The root servers don't usually respond with the desired target IP address of `www.example.com`; they respond with the authoritative name server for that domain. The authoritative name servers are the only ones that have the authority to maintain and modify name data for a domain.

6. The local name server is configured to use the root name servers, so the root name server for the .com top-level domain returns the IP address of the authoritative name server for example.com. That IP address could be for any one of the two (at the time of this writing) name servers, a.iana-servers.net or b.iana-servers.net.

7. The local name server then sends the query to the authoritative name server, which returns the IP address for `www.example.com`.

8. The browser uses the IP address for `www.example.com` to send a request for a web page, which is downloaded to my browser.

One of the important side effects of this name search is that the results are cached for a period of time by my local name server. That means that the next time I, or anyone in my network, wants to access example.com, the IP address is probably already stored locally, which prevents the need to perform a remote lookup.

Using the /etc/hosts File

Most computers need little configuration to enable them to access name services. That usually consists of adding the IP addresses of one to three name servers to the /etc/resolv.conf file. And that is typically performed at boot time on most home and laptop computers because they are configured using the DHCP in which a DHCP server provides them with their IP address, gateway address, and the IP addresses of the name servers. In general, the DHCP server is provided in the router provided by your ISP.

For hosts that are configured statically, the /etc/resolv.conf file is usually generated during installation from information entered by the SysAdmin during installation.

Adding entries to the /etc/hosts file can make accessing remote hosts by name possible in the absence of centralized name services. This can work well for single systems or small networks. So let's look at the default version of the file and add some hosts to it.

EXPERIMENT 32-7: USING /ETC/HOSTS

Perform this experiment as root. Start by examining the default version of the /etc/hosts file. It has only four active lines, and those are for the local host for both IPv4 and IPv6:

```
[root@studentvm1 ~]# cd /etc ; cat hosts
# Loopback entries; do not change.
# For historical reasons, localhost precedes localhost.localdomain:
127.0.0.1   localhost localhost.localdomain localhost4 localhost4.
localdomain4
::1         localhost localhost.localdomain localhost6 localhost6.
localdomain6
# See hosts(5) for proper format and other examples:
# 192.168.1.10 foo.mydomain.org foo
# 192.168.1.13 bar.mydomain.org bar
```

These entries allow us to address commands using the names for the local host. This first command uses IPv6 by default:

```
[root@studentvm1 etc]# ping -c2 localhost
PING localhost(localhost (::1)) 56 data bytes
64 bytes from localhost (::1): icmp_seq=1 ttl=64 time=0.076 ms
64 bytes from localhost (::1): icmp_seq=2 ttl=64 time=0.077 ms
```

```
--- localhost ping statistics ---
2 packets transmitted, 2 received, 0% packet loss, time 43ms
rtt min/avg/max/mdev = 0.076/0.076/0.077/0.008 ms
```

This command explicitly uses the IPv4 hostname:

```
[root@studentvm1 etc]# ping -c2 localhost4
PING localhost (127.0.0.1) 56(84) bytes of data.
64 bytes from localhost (127.0.0.1): icmp_seq=1 ttl=64 time=0.046 ms
64 bytes from localhost (127.0.0.1): icmp_seq=2 ttl=64 time=0.074 ms
```

This command explicitly uses the IPv6 hostname:

```
--- localhost ping statistics ---
2 packets transmitted, 2 received, 0% packet loss, time 31ms
rtt min/avg/max/mdev = 0.046/0.060/0.074/0.014 ms
[root@studentvm1 etc]# ping -c2 localhost6
PING localhost6(localhost (::1)) 56 data bytes
64 bytes from localhost (::1): icmp_seq=1 ttl=64 time=0.066 ms
64 bytes from localhost (::1): icmp_seq=2 ttl=64 time=0.083 ms

--- localhost6 ping statistics ---
2 packets transmitted, 2 received, 0% packet loss, time 66ms
rtt min/avg/max/mdev = 0.066/0.074/0.083/0.012 ms
```

That works, but suppose we want to ping the local host by its actual hostname. For this we will use the current IP address of enp0s3 rather than the loopback address. This IP address may change in the future – and will in Volume 3 of this course.

First, verify the current IP address:

```
[root@studentvm1 ~]# ip addr show enp0s3
2: enp0s3: <BROADCAST,MULTICAST,UP,LOWER_UP> mtu 1500 qdisc fq_codel state UP
group default qlen 1000
    link/ether 08:00:27:01:7d:ad brd ff:ff:ff:ff:ff:ff
    inet 10.0.2.22/24 brd 10.0.2.255 scope global dynamic
noprefixroute enp0s3
       valid_lft 499sec preferred_lft 499sec
    inet6 fe80::b36b:f81c:21ea:75c0/64 scope link noprefixroute
       valid_lft forever preferred_lft forever
```

This shows the IP address for StudentVM1 as 10.0.2.22/24. Your IP address may be different from the one I have on my VM, but that would be unlikely if you have been performing all of the experiments as directed.

Using your preferred editor, add the following two lines to the end of the /etc/hosts file. I use comments like I do in Bash scripts, so I know what I did and why at later times and for other SysAdmins who will take over my job in the future. Be sure to use the IP address for your own VM because it can be different:

```
# Added the following lines for testing
10.0.2.22          studentvm1 svm1 vm1 s1
```

Note that you can have multiple hostnames for each IP address. This makes it possible to use both the full hostname and any nicknames you may have for a particular host. Notice that the /etc/hosts file is generally not used to provide services for Fully Qualified Domain Names (FQDNs) such as studentvm1.example.com; rather, only the unqualified hostnames themselves are typically used:

```
[root@studentvm1 ~]# ping -c2 studentvm1
PING studentvm1 (10.0.2.7) 56(84) bytes of data.
64 bytes from studentvm1 (10.0.2.7): icmp_seq=1 ttl=64 time=0.069 ms
64 bytes from studentvm1 (10.0.2.7): icmp_seq=2 ttl=64 time=0.088 ms

--- studentvm1 ping statistics ---
2 packets transmitted, 2 received, 0% packet loss, time 60ms
rtt min/avg/max/mdev = 0.069/0.078/0.088/0.013 ms
[root@studentvm1 ~]# ping -c2 svm1
PING studentvm1 (10.0.2.7) 56(84) bytes of data.
64 bytes from studentvm1 (10.0.2.7): icmp_seq=1 ttl=64 time=0.081 ms
64 bytes from studentvm1 (10.0.2.7): icmp_seq=2 ttl=64 time=0.098 ms

--- studentvm1 ping statistics ---
2 packets transmitted, 2 received, 0% packet loss, time 35ms
rtt min/avg/max/mdev = 0.081/0.089/0.098/0.012 ms
[root@studentvm1 ~]# ping -c2 vm1
PING studentvm1 (10.0.2.7) 56(84) bytes of data.
64 bytes from studentvm1 (10.0.2.7): icmp_seq=1 ttl=64 time=0.085 ms
64 bytes from studentvm1 (10.0.2.7): icmp_seq=2 ttl=64 time=0.079 ms

--- studentvm1 ping statistics ---
```

```
2 packets transmitted, 2 received, 0% packet loss, time 11ms
rtt min/avg/max/mdev = 0.079/0.082/0.085/0.003 ms
```

Now let's add an entry for the virtual router. Add the following line to the bottom of the /etc/hosts file:

```
10.0.2.1            router gateway
```

Now ping the router:

```
[root@studentvm1 ~]# ping -c2 router
PING router (10.0.2.1) 56(84) bytes of data.
64 bytes from router (10.0.2.1): icmp_seq=1 ttl=255 time=0.254 ms
64 bytes from router (10.0.2.1): icmp_seq=2 ttl=255 time=0.266 ms

--- router ping statistics ---
2 packets transmitted, 2 received, 0% packet loss, time 31ms
rtt min/avg/max/mdev = 0.254/0.260/0.266/0.006 ms
[root@studentvm1 ~]# ping -c2 gateway
PING router (10.0.2.1) 56(84) bytes of data.
64 bytes from router (10.0.2.1): icmp_seq=1 ttl=255 time=0.246 ms
64 bytes from router (10.0.2.1): icmp_seq=2 ttl=255 time=0.253 ms

--- router ping statistics ---
2 packets transmitted, 2 received, 0% packet loss, time 33ms
rtt min/avg/max/mdev = 0.246/0.249/0.253/0.016 ms
```

I am highly against adding entries for any hosts outside the local network. It can be done, but that links an IP address to the external hostname on our local systems. The actual IP address may change at a later time, and you will not be able to access the host. It can be difficult to troubleshoot such a problem unless you remember that an entry exists in the local hosts file. Yes, I have done this, and it took a couple hours for me to find and resolve this problem.

Close the editor session, leaving the changes to /etc/hosts in place.

Introduction to Network Routing

Every computer attached to a network requires some type of routing instructions for network TCP/IP packets when they leave the local host. This is usually very straightforward because many network environments are very simple and there are only two options for departing packets. All packets are sent either to a device in the local network or to some other, remote network.

Let's be sure to define the "local" network as the logical, and usually also the physical, network in which the local host resides. Logically that means the local subnet in which the host is assigned one of the ranges of the local subnet's IP addresses. Physically that means the host is physically connected to one or more switches that are also connected to the rest of the local network.

All packets not addressed to a host or another node like a printer that are located in the local network are sent to the default router – no exception.

The Routing Table

All network devices, whether they are hosts, routers, or other types of network nodes such as network-attached printers, need to make decisions about where to route TCP/IP data packets. Each host has a routing table that provides the configuration information required to make those decisions. The routing table for any host in the network is used to determine whether to send packets to a host in the local network or to the default gateway router.

For hosts connected to the network using DHCP, the DHCP server provides that configuration information for the default route along with DNS, the hosts' IP address, and possibly other information such as the IP address for a NTP server.

EXPERIMENT 32-8: ROUTING

Perform this experiment as the student user. Root privileges are not required.

The `route -n` command lists the routing table; the -n option displays the results as IP addresses only and does not attempt to perform a DNS lookup, which would replace the IP addresses with hostnames if they are available:

```
[student@studentvm1 ~]$ route -n
```

```
Kernel IP routing table
Destination     Gateway         Genmask          Flags Metric Ref    Use Iface
0.0.0.0         10.0.2.1        0.0.0.0          UG    100    0        0 enp0s3
10.0.2.0        0.0.0.0         255.255.255.0    U     100    0        0 enp0s3
```

The netstat -rn command produces very similar results except for the Metric column, which helps us understand multihomed systems such as routers or simply hosts that must be connected to multiple networks as is the StudentVM1 host on my personal workstation.

The example in Figure 32-7 is from the StudentVM1 host on my workstation, and it is connected to two networks. It shows that each network to which a host is connected has a gateway.

```
[student@studentvm1 ~]$ route -n
Kernel IP routing table
Destination     Gateway         Genmask          Flags Metric Ref    Use Iface
0.0.0.0         45.20.209.46    0.0.0.0          UG    102    0        0 enp4s0
45.20.209.40    0.0.0.0         255.255.255.248  U     102    0        0 enp4s0
192.168.0.0     0.0.0.0         255.255.255.0    U     100    0        0 enp2s0
192.168.10.0    0.0.0.0         255.255.255.0    U     101    0        0 enp1s0
```

Figure 32-7. *The StudentVM1 host on my personal workstation is connected to two networks*

The Iface (Interface) column in the output from the route command is the name of the outbound NIC, in this case, enp0s3 or enp0s9. For hosts that are acting as routers, there will likely be at least two and sometimes more NICs used. Each NIC used as a route will be connected to a different physical and logical network. The flags in the Flags column indicate that the route is Up (U) and which is the default Gateway (G). Other flags may also be present.

My VM is not a router; it is just a Linux host connected to multiple networks. However, it would take very little to turn it into a router. We will explore how to configure a Linux host as a router in the third volume in this series.

Figure 32-8 shows the results for the physical Fedora host in my home network that I use as a router. Besides routing packets between my network and the outside world via my ISP, it also routes to another internal network that I use for wireless and wired guests in my home. This little extra bit of security prevents guests from having direct access to the other hosts in my network while allowing them full access to the Internet.

```
[root@wally ~]# route -n
Kernel IP routing table
Destination     Gateway         Genmask           Flags Metric Ref    Use Iface
0.0.0.0         45.20.209.46    0.0.0.0           UG    102    0        0 enp4s0
45.20.209.40    0.0.0.0         255.255.255.248   U     102    0        0 enp4s0
192.168.0.0     0.0.0.0         255.255.255.0     U     100    0        0 enp2s0
192.168.10.0    0.0.0.0         255.255.255.0     U     101    0        0 enp1s0
```

Figure 32-8. *My home router is a Fedora host connected to three different networks*

In Figure 32-8 the Flags column contains a "G," which stands for "Gateway." Gateway is synonymous with "default route" in this context. The default route is always shown with the destination 0.0.0.0 when the -n option is used. If -n is not used, the word "Default" appears in the Destination column of the output. The IP address in the Gateway column is that of the outbound gateway router. The Genmask of 0.0.0.0 for the default gateway means that any packet not addressed to the local network or another outbound router by additional entries in the routing table is to be sent to the default gateway.

What does this mean for my own StudentVM1 host in Figure 32-7 since it has two entries that appear to be the default router? Each interface is in a different network, which assigns the default gateway via DHCP, and each network has a default gateway, so each assigns a different default gateway to the VM.

```
[student@studentvm1 ~]$ ip route
default via 10.0.2.1 dev enp0s3 proto dhcp src 10.0.2.22 metric 100
default via 192.168.0.254 dev enp0s9 proto dhcp src 192.168.0.181 metric 101
10.0.2.0/24 dev enp0s3 proto kernel scope link src 10.0.2.22 metric 100
192.168.0.0/24 dev enp0s9 proto kernel scope link src 192.168.0.181
metric 101
```

This has all the information needed to describe the routing table. The true default route has the lowest (highest priority) metric. We can use the traceroute tool to view the complete route our packets will take to a remote host. This will allow us to verify the true default gateway in Figure 32-7:

```
[student@studentvm1 ~]# traceroute www.example.org
traceroute to www.example.org (93.184.216.34), 30 hops max, 60 byte packets
 1   studentvm2.example.com (192.168.56.1)  0.323 ms  0.796 ms  0.744 ms
 2   10.0.2.1 (10.0.2.1)  1.106 ms  1.089 ms  1.063 ms
 3   * * *
 4   * * *
 5   * * *
 6   * * *
 7   * * *
 8   * * *
 9   * * *
10   * * *
11   * * *
12   * * *
13   * *^C
```

Many of the nodes intentionally don't respond to TCP packets, but it does show the true default
route, which is 10.0.2.1 – the virtual router in the virtual network. This tool used to work very
nicely and it is not deprecated, so I think it should work better than this.

We can force it to use ICMP with the -I option instead of TCP. This seems to work better, and
it shows both the node name of routers that have one in DNS and the IP address of each
responding node:

```
[student@studentvm1 ~]$ traceroute -I www.example.org
traceroute to www.example.org (93.184.216.34), 30 hops max, 60 byte packets
 1   _gateway (10.0.2.1)  0.461 ms  0.389 ms  0.368 ms
 2   _gateway (192.168.0.254)  0.617 ms  0.600 ms  0.571 ms
 3   45-20-209-46.lightspeed.rlghnc.sbcglobal.net (45.20.209.46)   1.256
ms  1.139 ms  *
 4   * * *
 5   99.173.76.162 (99.173.76.162)  2.614 ms * *
 6   99.134.77.90 (99.134.77.90)  2.346 ms * *
 7   * * *
 8   * * *
 9   * * *
10   * * *
11   32.130.16.19 (32.130.16.19)  14.824 ms * *
12   att-gw.atl.edgecast.com (192.205.32.102)  13.391 ms *  12.549 ms
```

```
13  ae-71.core1.agb.edgecastcdn.net (152.195.80.141)  12.616 ms  12.564
ms  12.543 ms
14  93.184.216.34 (93.184.216.34)  12.302 ms  12.272 ms  11.831 ms
```

My preferred tool for this is `mtr`. This tool started out as Matt's traceroute because Matt wrote it. It was designed as a dynamic replacement for the old `traceroute` tool. Because Matt no longer maintains this and someone else has taken over, it is now referred to as "my traceroute."

In the following example, the -c2 (Count) option causes `mtr` to only run two cycles to the target host instead of running continuously, which is the default. The -n option means use numeric IP addresses and don't do DNS name lookups. The -r option puts it into report mode in which it displays the data all at once after all cycles are run. This mode has a bit prettier output for use in documents and books:

```
[root@studentvm1 etc]# mtr -c2 -n -r example.com
Start: 2023-03-18T21:43:27-0400
HOST: studentvm1            Loss%  Snt   Last   Avg  Best  Wrst StDev
  1.|-- 10.0.2.1             0.0%    2    0.7   0.7   0.7   0.7   0.0
  2.|-- 192.168.0.254        0.0%    2    1.2   1.2   1.1   1.2   0.1
  3.|-- 45.20.209.46         0.0%    2    1.7   1.9   1.7   2.0   0.2
  4.|-- ???                100.0     2    0.0   0.0   0.0   0.0   0.0
  5.|-- 99.173.76.162        0.0%    2    3.6   3.8   3.6   3.9   0.2
  6.|-- 99.134.77.90         0.0%    2    3.7   3.7   3.7   3.7   0.0
  7.|-- 12.83.103.9          0.0%    2    8.9   8.5   8.2   8.9   0.5
  8.|-- 12.123.138.102       0.0%    2   15.4  15.2  14.9  15.4   0.4
  9.|-- ???                100.0     2    0.0   0.0   0.0   0.0   0.0
 10.|-- ???                100.0     2    0.0   0.0   0.0   0.0   0.0
 11.|-- 32.130.16.19         0.0%    2   14.9  15.8  14.9  16.8   1.3
 12.|-- 192.205.32.102       0.0%    2   13.3  13.6  13.3  13.8   0.4
 13.|-- 152.195.80.141       0.0%    2   13.5  13.4  13.4  13.5   0.1
 14.|-- 93.184.216.34        0.0%    2   12.8  12.8  12.8  12.8   0.0
```

This provides good results and shows us the path that our data packets are taking to the remote host. Some routers still don't respond, but we don't really need that information for this experiment.

The routers shown in your results will be different from my results until the last few hops, as it gets closer to the target host.

When used without the Count option, it keeps checking the route until you press q to quit. Because of this, `mtr` can display statistics for each hop along the way to the destination including response times and packet loss at each intermediate router along the way – with the exception of those nonresponsive routers.

Another thing you might see for any given hop number (the sequential numbers down the left side of the display) is multiple routers indicating that the path to the remote host is not always through the same sequence of routers.

We can use another tool to learn more about who owns that IP address. Sometimes communicating with the abuse contact for the remote network can be useful in tracking down and stopping some types of attacks. Some contacts will go out of their way to help, but in some areas of the world, don't expect any help:

```
[student@studentvm1 ~]$ whois 93.184.216.34
[Querying whois.ripe.net]
[whois.ripe.net]
% This is the RIPE Database query service.
% The objects are in RPSL format.
%
% The RIPE Database is subject to Terms and Conditions.
% See http://www.ripe.net/db/support/db-terms-conditions.pdf

% Note: this output has been filtered.
%       To receive output for a database update, use the "-B" flag.

% Information related to '93.184.216.0 - 93.184.216.255'

% Abuse contact for '93.184.216.0 - 93.184.216.255' is 'abuse@
verizondigitalmedia.com'

inetnum:        93.184.216.0 - 93.184.216.255
netname:        EDGECAST-NETBLK-03
descr:          NETBLK-03-EU-93-184-216-0-24
country:        EU
admin-c:        DS7892-RIPE
tech-c:         DS7892-RIPE
status:         ASSIGNED PA
mnt-by:         MNT-EDGECAST
created:        2012-06-22T21:48:41Z
last-modified:  2012-06-22T21:48:41Z
```

```
source:         RIPE # Filtered

person:         Derrick Sawyer
address:        13031 W Jefferson Blvd #900, Los Angeles, CA 90094
phone:          +18773343236
nic-hdl:        DS7892-RIPE
created:        2010-08-25T18:44:19Z
last-modified:  2017-03-03T09:06:18Z
source:         RIPE
mnt-by:         MNT-EDGECAST

% This query was served by the RIPE Database Query Service version
1.94 (WAGYU)
```

Routing decisions are fairly simple for most hosts:

1. If the destination host is in the local network, send the data directly to the destination host.

2. If the destination host is in a remote network that is reachable via a local gateway listed in the routing table, send it to the explicitly defined gateway.

3. If the destination host is in a remote network and there is no other entry that defines a route to that host, send the data to the default gateway.

These rules simply mean that if all else fails because there is no match, send the packet to the default gateway.

iptraf-ng

In troubleshooting network connection problems, it can be helpful to use a tool such as **iptraf-ng** (IP traffic next generation) to monitor the network traffic on one or more interfaces. This is an easy tool to use, and it employs a text-mode menu-style interface.

This is probably not a tool that anyone who has been a SysAdmin for a short time would be likely to use on a regular basis. In order to interpret the results in a meaningful way, it would be necessary to understand networking in far more depth than we cover here. However, I think that it is an interesting tool, and knowing that it exists can be helpful. I found that just watching the traffic helped me learn about networking and it became easier to see when a host was not responding. This is a tool that takes some time to build experience with.

EXPERIMENT 32-9: USING IPTRAF-NG

Perform this experiment as the root user. The **iptraf-ng** program will not run when launched by a non-root user. Install iptraf-ng if it is not already installed:

```
[root@studentvm1 ~]# dnf -y install iptraf-ng
```

In one terminal, ping the router. Do not limit the ping count as we want this to continue until we have completed this experiment. Notice that we are using the name we assigned to the router in /etc/hosts:

```
[student@studentvm1 ~]$ ping www.example.com
PING www.example.com (93.184.216.34) 56(84) bytes of data.
64 bytes from 93.184.216.34: icmp_seq=1 ttl=50 time=12.4 ms
64 bytes from 93.184.216.34: icmp_seq=2 ttl=50 time=12.6 ms
64 bytes from 93.184.216.34: icmp_seq=3 ttl=50 time=12.9 ms
64 bytes from 93.184.216.34: icmp_seq=4 ttl=50 time=12.4 ms
64 bytes from 93.184.216.34: icmp_seq=5 ttl=50 time=12.5 ms
64 bytes from 93.184.216.34: icmp_seq=6 ttl=50 time=12.5 ms
64 bytes from 93.184.216.34: icmp_seq=7 ttl=50 time=14.1 ms
64 bytes from 93.184.216.34: icmp_seq=8 ttl=50 time=12.6 ms
64 bytes from 93.184.216.34: icmp_seq=9 ttl=50 time=12.4 ms
<snip>
```

In another terminal session, start **iptraf-ng**:

```
[root@studentvm1 ~]# iptraf-ng
```

This command launches the menu-driven interface shown in Figure 32-9, which allows selection of various options. Highlight the "IP traffic monitor" line and press the Enter key. Then select the enp0s3 interface to monitor and press Enter.

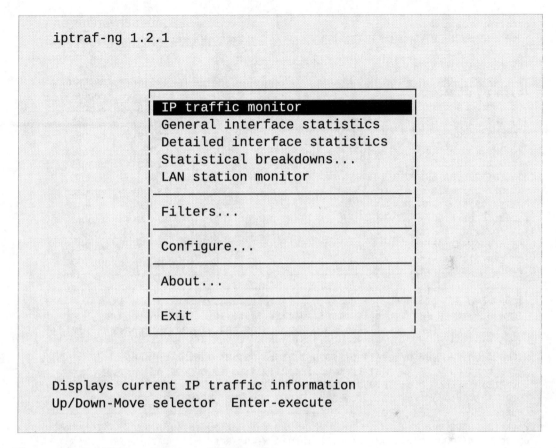

```
iptraf-ng 1.2.1


            ┌─────────────────────────────────────┐
            │ IP traffic monitor                  │
            │ General interface statistics        │
            │ Detailed interface statistics       │
            │ Statistical breakdowns...           │
            │ LAN station monitor                 │
            ├─────────────────────────────────────┤
            │ Filters...                          │
            ├─────────────────────────────────────┤
            │ Configure...                        │
            ├─────────────────────────────────────┤
            │ About...                            │
            ├─────────────────────────────────────┤
            │ Exit                                │
            └─────────────────────────────────────┘



 Displays current IP traffic information
 Up/Down-Move selector  Enter-execute
```

Figure 32-9. *The main menu of* **iptraf-ng**

After selecting the enp0s3 interface, the bottom portion of the resulting screen contains a
continuous display of the ICMP packets and the responses from the router. Figure 32-10
shows the total number of ICMP packets.

```
iptraf-ng 1.2.1
┌ TCP Connections (Source Host:Port) ─────── Packets ─── Bytes Flag  Iface ──┐
│┌10.0.2.22:42818                          =        2        124 S---  enpOs3 |
│└93.184.216.34:5355                       =        0          0 ----  enpOs3 |
│┌10.0.2.22:42830                          =        2        124 S---  enpOs3 |
│└93.184.216.34:5355                       =        0          0 ----  enpOs3 |
│┌10.0.2.22:34154                          =        2        124 S---  enpOs3 |
│└93.184.216.34:5355                       =        0          0 ----  enpOs3 |
│┌10.0.2.22:34166                          =        2        124 S---  enpOs3 |
│└93.184.216.34:5355                       =        0          0 ----  enpOs3 |
│┌10.0.2.22:34168                          =        2        124 S---  enpOs3 |
│└93.184.216.34:5355                       =        0          0 ----  enpOs3 |
│┌10.0.2.22:34172                          =        2        124 S---  enpOs3 |
│└93.184.216.34:5355                       =        0          0 ----  enpOs3 |
│┌10.0.2.22:34180                          =        2        124 S---  enpOs3 |
│└93.184.216.34:5355                       =        0          0 ----  enpOs3 |
│┌10.0.2.22:34194                          =        2        124 S---  enpOs3 |
│└93.184.216.34:5355                       =        0          0 ----  enpOs3 |
└ TCP:      21 entries ──────────────────────────────────────── Active ─┘
┌──────────────────────────────────────────────────────────────────────────┐
| ICMP echo req (84 bytes) from 10.0.2.22 to 93.184.216.34 on enpOs3        |
| ICMP echo rply (84 bytes) from 93.184.216.34 to 10.0.2.22 on enpOs3       |
| ICMP echo req (84 bytes) from 10.0.2.22 to 93.184.216.34 on enpOs3        |
| ICMP echo rply (84 bytes) from 93.184.216.34 to 10.0.2.22 on enpOs3       |
| ICMP echo req (84 bytes) from 10.0.2.22 to 93.184.216.34 on enpOs3        |
| ICMP echo rply (84 bytes) from 93.184.216.34 to 10.0.2.22 on enpOs3       |
| UDP (316 bytes) from 10.0.2.22:68 to 10.0.2.3:67 on enpOs3                |
| UDP (576 bytes) from 10.0.2.3:67 to 10.0.2.22:68 on enpOs3                |
└ Bottom ─────── Time:   0:01 ─────────── Drops:    0 ─────────────────────┘
 Packets captured:                    91 | TCP flow rate:        0.00 kbps
 Up/Dn/PgUp/PgDn-scroll  M-more TCP info   W-chg actv win  S-sort TCP  X-exit
```

Figure 32-10. *The ICMP traffic resulting from the ping command*

But that really does not show us very much. Leave **iptraf-ng** and **ping** running as they are. On the desktop as the student user, open the browser and go to my web page at www.both. org or the example.com website. Or, to be horrified, go to your local newspaper or TV station's homepage and watch all of the ad and tracking connections pile up. While doing so, watch the iptraf-ng session. Figure 32-11 shows a sample of the results you might expect.

Port 80 is the HTTP port used by web servers. On the first line of the output in the TCP Connections section of iptraf-ng, you can see the source address and port of the request from the host VM as 10.0.2.7:60868. The next line is the destination IP address and port number, which is 23.45.181.162:80. So we are sending a request to port 80 (HTTP) at IP address 23.45.181.162.

You can see other conversations taking place with other servers as the embedded images and links are accessed by the browser.

```
iptraf-ng 1.2.1
┌ TCP Connections (Source Host:Port) ──────── Packets ──── Bytes Flag Iface ─┐
│ ┌10.0.2.7:60868                        =       6        556 --A- enp0s3    │
│ └23.45.181.162:80                      =       4        562 --A- enp0s3    │
│ ┌10.0.2.7:43760                        =      10       1448 --A- enp0s3    │
│ └52.18.148.152:443                     =       7       3930 --A- enp0s3    │
│ ┌10.0.2.7:33940                        =      14       2854 --A- enp0s3    │
│ └72.21.91.29:80                        =       8       5059 -PA- enp0s3    │
│ ┌10.0.2.7:57806                        =     213      12020 --A- enp0s3    │
│ └104.16.41.2:443                       =     207     288665 -PA- enp0s3    │
│ ┌10.0.2.7:40886                        =      10       1730 --A- enp0s3    │
│ └54.186.120.41:443                     =       8       4925 --A- enp0s3    │
│ ┌10.0.2.7:45864                        =      27       2499 --A- enp0s3    │
│ └8.43.85.67:443                        =      27      31059 -PA- enp0s3    │
│ ┌67.219.144.68:443                     >       1         46 --A- enp0s3    │
│ └10.0.2.7:41160                        =       0          0 ---- enp0s3    │
│ ┌10.0.2.7:44138                        =      20       1863 --A- enp0s3    │
│ └85.236.55.6:443                       =      21      23215 -PA- enp0s3    │
│ ┌10.0.2.7:53256                        =      11       1478 -PA- enp0s3    │
│ └209.132.181.15:443                    =      11      11209 --A- enp0s3    │
│ ┌10.0.2.7:33262                        =      11       1468 --A- enp0s3    │
└ TCP:      36 entries ─────────────────────────────────────────── Active ─┘
┌──────────────────────────────────────────────────────────────────────────┐
│ UDP (58 bytes) from 10.0.2.7:37096 to 10.0.2.1:53 on enp0s3               │
│ UDP (113 bytes) from 10.0.2.1:53 to 10.0.2.7:37096 on enp0s3              │
│ UDP (108 bytes) from 10.0.2.1:53 to 10.0.2.7:37096 on enp0s3              │
│ ICMP echo req (84 bytes) from 10.0.2.7 to 10.0.2.1 on enp0s3              │
│ ICMP echo rply (84 bytes) from 10.0.2.1 to 10.0.2.7 on enp0s3            │
│ UDP (70 bytes) from 10.0.2.7:51486 to 10.0.2.1:53 on enp0s3              │
│ UDP (70 bytes) from 10.0.2.7:51486 to 10.0.2.1:53 on enp0s3              │
<snip>
```

Figure 32-11. *The results get more interesting when other activity is taking place, in this case using the web browser*

The UDP entries in the bottom section are name service (DNS) requests on port 53 looking for the IP addresses of other web servers to supply the linked content.

Press **x** twice to exit from iptraf-ng.

There are plenty of GUI tools available for performing these types of analysis, such as Wireshark, but iptraf-ng will work without a GUI while providing a lot of valuable information.

Chapter Summary

In this chapter we have explored some of the basics of networking and been introduced to some common tools that enable exploration of networking on a Linux host.

We have explored basic network configuration of the client host in a DHCP environment and created an interface configuration file that allows us to turn a connection on and off. We have explored name services, CIDR notation, a bit about IPv6, and routing. We have also used a simple tool, **sipcalc**, to explore CIDR notation and how to use it to determine the variable data for a network, such as the number of usable IP addresses, the network address, and more.

We have just scratched the surface, and there is much more to learn. More of networking will be covered in the next volume in this series, *Using and Administering Linux: Volume 3 – Zero to SysAdmin: Network Services.*

Exercises

1. Name the layers of the TCP/IP network model and list the protocols used in each.

2. Describe the flow of data from one network host to another using the TCP/IP model.

3. How many usable network addresses are available to the 10.125.16.32/31 network?

4. What is the function of name services?

5. Describe how you could use the /etc/hosts file to provide name services for a small network.

6. Describe the function of the default route.

7. Determine the route from your host to `www.example.com`. Is there any packet loss?

8. Is the route from your StudentVM1 host to `www.example.com` always the same over a period of several days?

9. Geographically, where is the server for `www.example.com` located?

CHAPTER 33

NetworkManager

In this chapter you will learn

- More about the functions of NetworkManager

- Where NetworkManager fits in the series of tools that have been used to manage network connections

- How to use the **nmcli** command-line tool to view and manage network interfaces

- How NetworkManager configures network interfaces

- How to migrate from the old ifcfg files to the new NetworkManager keyfiles

- Multiple methods for creating new keyfiles from scratch

Introduction

In Chapter 32 of this volume, you used some basic commands including the NetworkManager nmcli command to explore network hardware and logical structures and to perform some tests that can be used for simple network troubleshooting.

NetworkManager[1] is a tool designed to simplify and automate network configuration and connections, especially wireless connections. The intent is to prevent the user from having to manually configure each new network before using it – especially wireless ones.

---

[1] Wikipedia, NetworkManager, https://en.wikipedia.org/wiki/NetworkManager

© David Both 2023
D. Both, *Using and Administering Linux: Volume 2*, https://doi.org/10.1007/978-1-4842-9615-8_33

We discuss NetworkManager in this chapter. This includes how it manages both wired and wireless network connections, its use of network connection files for wireless connections, and how to create NetworkManager connection files when necessary. We look at NetworkManager commands in more detail to enable you to directly manage your network hardware and connections.

Network Startup

With the advent of gazillions of mobile devices and tens of thousands of wireless networks, reconfiguring the network interfaces for each new wireless network could be very complicated and time-consuming, which is not a good thing for people who are not technical.

Something new was needed in order to simplify connecting Linux devices to networks whether wired or wireless.

The NetworkManager Service

Red Hat introduced NetworkManager in 2004 as a way to simplify and automate network configuration and connections, especially wireless connections. The intent is to prevent the user from having to manually configure each new wireless network before using it.

NetworkManager starts the network services during Linux startup and provides a management interface while the host is running. NetworkManager works for both wired and wireless networks, so it can make setting up a home or small business network much easier in addition to its ability to making Internet connections easy and fast at your favorite coffee shop.

The NetworkManager service makes network management better and easier for non-technical users because it integrates well with udev and dbus to deal with pluggable devices and various wireless networks. Both udev and dbus are covered in this chapter, but you will explore them in more detail in Chapter 38.

Our primary interface with NetworkManager is the family of `nmcli` commands. We can also use `nmtui`, the NetworkManager Text User Interface, a menu-driven interface that I find cumbersome compared with the command line. Others, like Jason, technical reviewer for the first edition of this book, find it to be "awesome." You can try it yourself, but for this course we will stick to the command line.

What NetworkManager Replaces

NetworkManager is a replacement for previous network management tools. The original interface configuration command, **ifconfig**, and its interface configuration files are obsolete. You can see this in the ifconfig man pages, which contain a note stating just that.

The **ip** command temporarily replaced **ifconfig** and performs essentially the same tasks. Both commands have co-existed for some time now, so SysAdmins could use either one, and any scripts that depended upon the ifconfig command would still work. Although its man pages do not yet indicate that the **ip** command is obsolete, NetworkManager has made many of its functions obsolete in fact.

Red Hat Enterprise Linux (RHEL) and Fedora currently use NetworkManager as the default network management tool and, as of Fedora 36, the tools required for NetworkManager to utilize the deprecated interface configuration (ifcfg) files are no longer installed by default.

What NetworkManager Does

NetworkManager is run as a systemd service and is enabled by default. NetworkManager[2] works with D-Bus[3] to detect and configure network interfaces as they are plugged into the Linux computer. This plug-and-play management of network interfaces makes dealing with plugging into new networks – both wired and wireless – trivially easy for the user. As previously installed network interfaces are detected during Linux startup,[4] they are treated exactly like a device that is plugged in after the system is already up and running. This treatment of all devices as all plug and play all the time makes handling those devices easier for the operating system since there is only one code base to deal with both sets of circumstances.

---

[2] GNOME Developer, NetworkManager Reference Manual, `https://developer.gnome.org/ NetworkManager/stable/`

[3] See Chapter 38 for a discussion of D-Bus.

[4] Chapter 16, Volume 1

The udev daemon creates an entry for each NIC installed in the system in the network rules file. NetworkManager uses these entries to initialize each NIC. Most distributions including Fedora keep their network connection files in the /etc/NetworkManager/system-connections directory, with the name of the network as the file name. For example, my System76 laptop uses Fedora, and the /etc/NetworkManager/system-connections directory on that laptop contains files for each of the wireless networks I have connected with. The structure of these files is different from the ifcfg files, but they are in ASCII plain text format and are readable and easily understandable.

D-Bus signals the presence of a new network device – wired or wireless. NetworkManager listens to the traffic on D-Bus and responds by creating a configuration for this new device. Every device is considered "new" at startup time or when it is plugged in, for example, a USB network interface card (NIC). Such a configuration is stored only in RAM and is not permanent. It must be created every time the computer is booted.

NetworkManager uses the ifcfg-rh plugin to allow the use of the legacy interface configuration files for backward compatibility. If the plugin is installed, NetworkManager first checks for the existence of network interface configuration files (ifcfg-*) in the /etc/sysconfig/network-scripts directory.

Second, NetworkManager looks for its own interface connection files, which would be located in the /etc/NetworkManager/system-connections directory.

If there are no network connection files, NetworkManager attempts to obtain a configuration for each network interface card (NIC) using DHCP. The DHCP server provides all of the data required for NetworkManager to generate a configuration for that NIC on the fly. In this situation, interface configuration files are neither needed nor created.

This is all sequence sensitive. The first set of configuration files found is used. If no configuration files are found, NetworkManager generates a configuration using the data from a DHCP server. If no configuration files or DHCP server is found, no network connection is possible.

Using the NetworkManager tools is covered in some detail in the RHEL 9 document "Configuring and Managing Networking."[5]

---

[5] Red Hat, Configuring and Managing Networking, https://access.redhat.com/documentation/en-us/red_hat_enterprise_linux/9/html-single/configuring_and_managing_networking/index

Viewing Interface Configuration

The NetworkManager command-line interface program, **nmcli**, provides a number of options that can be used to determine the current state of any and all network interface hardware installed in the host as well as currently active connections. The nmcli program can be used to manage networking on any host whether it uses a GUI or not, so it can also be used to manage remote hosts via an SSH[6] connection. It works on both wired and wireless connections.

Let's start with getting some basic information for using the nmcli tool. Note that I am performing the experiments on a Fedora system I have set up as a router because that is much more interesting with multiple network interfaces than on a simple workstation VM host with only a single or even a double network interface. You should follow along and use the commands as shown in the experiments, but your results will be different and much simpler than mine.

This and other experiments in this chapter will show some of the deprecated interface configuration files, which you won't have on your student VM. However, you will undoubtedly run into them in your work as a SysAdmin because there are most certainly a large number of systems out there that still use them. The experiments in this chapter will provide you a method for migrating from the old ifcfg files to the new NetworkManager keyfiles. It will also show you multiple methods for creating new keyfiles from scratch.

EXPERIMENT 33-1: USING NMCLI TO EXPLORE THE NETWORK HARDWARE

Let's start with the easiest command, **nmcli** with no options. This simple command shows information similar to the obsolete ifconfig command including the name and model of the NIC, MAC address, IP address, and which NIC is configured as the default gateway. It also shows the DNS configuration for each interface:

```
[root@wally network-scripts]# nmcli
enp4s0: connected to enp4s0
        "Realtek RTL8111/8168/8411"
        ethernet (r8169), 84:16:F9:04:44:03, hw, mtu 1500
        ip4 default, ip6 default
```

---

[6] Chapter 42, Volume 3

```
        inet4 45.20.209.41/29
        route4 0.0.0.0/0
        route4 45.20.209.40/29

    enp1s0: connected to enp1s0
        "Realtek RTL8111/8168/8411"
        ethernet (r8169), 84:16:F9:03:E9:89, hw, mtu 1500
        inet4 192.168.10.1/24
        route4 192.168.10.0/24

    enp2s0: connected to enp2s0
        "Realtek RTL8111/8168/8411"
        ethernet (r8169), 84:16:F9:03:FD:85, hw, mtu 1500
        inet4 192.168.0.254/24
        route4 192.168.0.0/24

    eno1: unavailable
        "Intel I219-V"
        ethernet (e1000e), 04:D9:F5:1C:D5:C5, hw, mtu 1500

    lo: unmanaged
        "lo"
        loopback (unknown), 00:00:00:00:00:00, sw, mtu 65536

    DNS configuration:
        servers: 192.168.0.52 8.8.8.8 8.8.4.4
        interface: enp4s0

        servers: 192.168.0.52 8.8.8.8
        interface: enp1s0

        servers: 192.168.0.52 8.8.8.8
        interface: enp2s0

Use "nmcli device show" to get complete information about known devices and
<SNIP>
```

Issue the following help command as the root user to view the basic top-level nmcli commands:

```
[root@wally ~]# nmcli -h
Usage: nmcli [OPTIONS] OBJECT { COMMAND | help }
```

OPTIONS
```
  -a, --ask                            ask for missing parameters
  -c, --colors auto|yes|no             whether to use colors in output
  -e, --escape yes|no                  escape columns separators in values
  -f, --fields <field,...>|all|common  specify fields to output
  -g, --get-values <field,...>|all|common  shortcut for -m tabular -t -f
  -h, --help                           print this help
  -m, --mode tabular|multiline         output mode
  -o, --overview                       overview mode
  -p, --pretty                         pretty output
  -s, --show-secrets                   allow displaying passwords
  -t, --terse                          terse output
  -v, --version                        show program version
  -w, --wait <seconds>                 set timeout waiting for finishing
                                       operations
```

OBJECT
```
  g[eneral]      NetworkManager's general status and operations
  n[etworking]   overall networking control
  r[adio]        NetworkManager radio switches
  c[onnection]   NetworkManager's connections
  d[evice]       devices managed by NetworkManager
  a[gent]        NetworkManager secret agent or polkit agent
  m[onitor]      monitor NetworkManager changes
```
```
[root@wally ~]#
```

Note that the objects can be spelled out or abbreviated down to the first character. Fortunately, these objects are all unique, so only the first character is required to specify any single object.

Try a simple command to view the general status:

```
[root@wally ~]# nmcli g
STATE        CONNECTIVITY WIFI-HW  WIFI     WWAN-HW  WWAN
connected    full         enabled  enabled  missing  enabled
[root@wally ~]#
```

That really does not show very much. I also know that the host, wally, has no Wi-Fi hardware so this result shows that. However, a couple better object[7] commands are c (connection) and d (device), which are the ones I use most frequently:

```
[root@wally ~]# nmcli c
NAME            UUID                                   TYPE      DEVICE
enp4s0          b325fd44-30b3-c744-3fc9-e154b78e8c82   ethernet  enp4s0
enp1s0          c0ab6b8c-0eac-a1b4-1c47-efe4b2d1191f   ethernet  enp1s0
enp2s0          8c6fd7b1-ab62-a383-5b96-46e083e04bb1   ethernet  enp2s0
enp0s20f0u7     0f5427bb-f8b1-5d51-8f74-ac246b0b00c5   ethernet  --
enp1s0          abf4c85b-57cc-4484-4fa9-b4a71689c359   ethernet  --

[root@wally ~]# nmcli d
DEVICE  TYPE      STATE        CONNECTION
enp4s0  ethernet  connected    enp4s0
enp1s0  ethernet  connected    enp1s0
enp2s0  ethernet  connected    enp2s0
eno1    ethernet  unavailable  --
lo      loopback  unmanaged    --
[root@wally ~]#
```

There is a lot of really interesting information here that I could not have recreated on the VM used for the experiments in this course. Notice that the last two entries using the [c]onnection object have no entries in the DEVICE column. This could mean that they are not active or do not exist and could mean that there are one or more configuration errors.

The additional information we get using the [d]evice object command does not even show the enp0s20f0u7 device, and it shows device eno1 (a motherboard device) that was not displayed using the [c]onnection object command.

The output on your VM should look more like this. The device name[8] might be different, and it will depend upon the specific location on the virtual PCI bus to which the NIC is connected:

```
[root@testvm1 ~]# nmcli c
NAME               UUID                                   TYPE      DEVICE
Wired connection 1 6e6f63b9-6d9e-3d13-a3cd-d54b4ca2c3d2   ethernet  enp0s3
[root@testvm1 ~]# nmcli d
```

---

[7] I have no idea why these are called object commands.

[8] NIC naming conventions are covered in Chapter 32.

```
DEVICE   TYPE      STATE       CONNECTION
enp0s3   ethernet  connected   Wired connection 1
lo       loopback  unmanaged   --
[root@testvm1 ~]#
```

Did you notice the problems in the output? I certainly did not expect to find them – yet there they are.

Fixing the Found Problems

That is the end of the experiment because your hosts don't have the problems I discovered while experimenting with nmcli. However, I have included a discussion in the following of the rest of the steps I took to resolve the anomalies I discovered because it makes a good case study for network problem solving.

First, I wanted to know what enp0s20f0u7 was. Since NetworkManager did not recognize this device in the nmcli d output, there was probably a network configuration file in /etc/sysconfig/network-scripts. I checked that directory and found the following. You won't find anything in that directory except the readme-ifcfg-rh.txt file. You would only find ifcfg files here on some Fedora hosts that were previously installed and then upgraded to Fedora 36 or higher as was the case with my firewall/router:

```
[root@wally network-scripts]# ll
total 20
-rw-r--r-- 1 root root 352 Jan  2 2021 ifcfg-eno1
-rw-r--r-- 1 root root 419 Jan  5 2021 ifcfg-enp0s20f0u7
-rw-r--r-- 1 root root 381 Jan 11 2021 ifcfg-enp1s0
-rw-r--r-- 1 root root 507 Jul 27 2020 ifcfg-enp2s0
-rw-r--r-- 1 root root 453 Jul 27 2020 ifcfg-enp4s0
[root@wally network-scripts]# cat ifcfg-enp0s20f0u7
# Interface configuration file for ifcfg-enp0s20f0u7
# This is a USB Gb Ethernet dongle
# Correct as of 20210105
TYPE="Ethernet"
BOOTPROTO="static"
NM_CONTROLLED="yes"
DEFROUTE="no"
```

```
NAME=enp0s20f0u7
# UUID="fa2117dd-6c7a-44e0-9c9d-9c662716a352"
ONBOOT="yes"
HWADDR=8c:ae:4c:ff:8b:3a
IPADDR=192.168.10.1
PREFIX=24
DNS1=192.168.0.52
DNS2=8.8.8.8
[root@wally network-scripts]#
```

After looking at this, I recalled that I had used a dongle for a while because the NIC on that motherboard had failed. That was a quick fix, and I later installed a new NIC on the motherboard PCIe bus. Therefore, I could remove this interface configuration file, so I did. I did not delete it; I moved it to the /root directory in case I'd ever need it again.

The second anomaly is why the entry for enp1s0 appeared twice. This can only occur when the NIC name is specified in more than one interface configuration file. So I did the following, and sure enough, enp1s0 erroneously appeared in the ifcfg-eno1 configuration file as well as where it should be, in the ifcfg-enp1s0 file:

```
[root@wally network-scripts]# grep enp1s0 *
ifcfg-eno1:NAME=enp1s0
ifcfg-enp1s0:# Interface configuration file for enp1s0 / 192.168.10.1
ifcfg-enp1s0:NAME=enp1s0
[root@wally network-scripts]#
```

I changed the ifcfg-eno1 file to show the correct name. Later I also deleted the file from this directory. The changes in the interface configuration files are not activated until the NetworkManager is restarted:

```
[root@wally network-scripts]# systemctl restart NetworkManager
[root@wally network-scripts]# nmcli d
DEVICE   TYPE       STATE        CONNECTION
enp4s0   ethernet   connected    enp4s0
enp1s0   ethernet   connected    enp1s0
enp2s0   ethernet   connected    enp2s0
eno1     ethernet   unavailable  --
lo       loopback   unmanaged    --
```

```
[root@wally network-scripts]# nmcli c
NAME    UUID                                   TYPE      DEVICE
enp4s0  b325fd44-30b3-c744-3fc9-e154b78e8c82   ethernet  enp4s0
enp1s0  c0ab6b8c-0eac-a1b4-1c47-efe4b2d1191f   ethernet  enp1s0
enp2s0  8c6fd7b1-ab62-a383-5b96-46e083e04bb1   ethernet  enp2s0
eno1    abf4c85b-57cc-4484-4fa9-b4a71689c359   ethernet  --
[root@wally network-scripts]#
```

Another option is to show only the active connections. This is a good option, but it can also mask other problems if you use it exclusively:

```
[root@wally network-scripts]# nmcli connection show --active
NAME    UUID                                   TYPE      DEVICE
enp4s0  b325fd44-30b3-c744-3fc9-e154b78e8c82   ethernet  enp4s0
enp1s0  c0ab6b8c-0eac-a1b4-1c47-efe4b2d1191f   ethernet  enp1s0
enp2s0  8c6fd7b1-ab62-a383-5b96-46e083e04bb1   ethernet  enp2s0
[root@wally network-scripts]#
```

Having changed the device name in the ifcfg-eno1 file to the correct one, I tried to see whether the motherboard NIC, eno1, would work again. It did not, so I moved the ifcfg-enp1s0 file to /root and configured the host's UEFI BIOS to disable the on-board NIC.

Activate and Deactivate Network Connections

After viewing the current status of a network connection, some of the other tasks that can be performed are activating and deactivating network connections. Many SysAdmins call this turning the connection up or down. That makes sense since the command uses those words.

EXPERIMENT 33-2

Turn down the network connection on the StudentVM1 host. I don't always remember the exact syntax of these commands, so I use tab completion to provide me with the help I need to know which objects and verbs come next.

Don't forget that my VM has two network connections and yours should have only one:

```
[root@studentvm1 ~]# nmcli connection <Tab><Tab>
add       clone    delete   down     edit     export   help     import   load
migrate  modify   monitor  reload   show     up
[root@studentvm1 ~]# nmcli connection down  <Tab><Tab>
apath        enpOs3              filename            help
id           path                uuid                Wired\ connection\ 1
[root@studentvm1 ~]# nmcli connection down Wired\ connection\ 1
Connection 'enpOs3' successfully deactivated (D-Bus active path: /org/
freedesktop/NetworkManager/ActiveConnection/1)
```

The backslashes in the preceding command "escape" the blanks in the name of the connection so that it appears to the nmcli command as a single entry. You could also enter it this way, which makes that a bit more obvious:

```
# nmcli connection down "Wired connection 1"
```

Now look at the connection status:

```
[root@studentvm1 ~]# nmcli
enpOs9: connected to Wired connection 1
        "Intel 82540EM"
        ethernet (e1000), 08:00:27:CA:1F:16, hw, mtu 1500
        ip4 default
        inet4 192.168.0.181/24
        route4 192.168.0.0/24 metric 101
        route4 default via 192.168.0.254 metric 101
        inet6 fe80::ed7:4603:dd8:1c8c/64
        route6 fe80::/64 metric 1024

enpOs3: disconnected
        "Intel 82540EM"
        1 connection available
        ethernet (e1000), 08:00:27:99:5A:29, hw, mtu 1500

lo: unmanaged
        "lo"
        loopback (unknown), 00:00:00:00:00:00, sw, mtu 65536
```

DNS configuration:
        servers: 192.168.0.52 8.8.8.8 8.8.4.4
        domains: both.org
        interface: enpOs9

<snip>
[root@studentvm1 ~]#

And then we will usually want to activate the connection again:

[root@studentvm1 ~]# **nmcli connection up "Wired connection 1"**
Connection successfully activated (D-Bus active path: /org/freedesktop/
NetworkManager/ActiveConnection/3)
[root@studentvm1 system-connections]# nmcli
enpOs9: connected to Wired connection 1
        "Intel 82540EM"
        ethernet (e1000), 08:00:27:CA:1F:16, hw, mtu 1500
        ip4 default
        inet4 192.168.0.181/24
        route4 192.168.0.0/24 metric 101
        route4 default via 192.168.0.254 metric 101
        inet6 fe80::ed7:4603:dd8:1c8c/64
        route6 fe80::/64 metric 1024

enpOs3: connected to enpOs3
        "Intel 82540EM"
        ethernet (e1000), 08:00:27:99:5A:29, hw, mtu 1500
        inet4 10.0.2.35/24
        route4 10.0.2.0/24 metric 102
        route4 default via 10.0.2.1 metric 102
        inet6 fe80::a00:27ff:fe99:5a29/64
        route6 fe80::/64 metric 256

lo: unmanaged
        "lo"
        loopback (unknown), 00:00:00:00:00:00, sw, mtu 65536

DNS configuration:
        servers: 192.168.0.52 8.8.8.8 8.8.4.4
        domains: both.org
        interface: enpOs9

```
        servers: 10.0.2.1 8.8.8.8 8.8.4.4
        domains: both.org
        interface: enp0s3
```

`<snip>`

These are pretty simple commands, but you can also see in the tab completion results that there are plenty of other arguments that can be used.

Because the network connections created by NetworkManager on your VM are created on the fly using configuration information supplied by the virtual network's DHCP server, there are no configuration files of any kind necessary. This means that NetworkManager generates the connection IDs in the format "Wired connection X." I like shorter names, and I particularly like names that reflect the device name like "enp0s3." This makes typing the names easier and helps me relate the connection to the hardware itself, which helps me when I am problem solving.

One of the things we can do with NetworkManager keyfiles is to specify the connection ID along with other things like a static IP address and up to three name servers. Let's look at how to do that.

NetworkManager Keyfiles

NetworkManager is intended to make network configuration more flexible and dynamic. The old SystemV startup shell scripts, of which the old interface configuration files were part, were incapable of handling Wi-Fi, wired, VPNs, broadband modems, and more – at least not quickly or efficiently. Most of the restrictions lay in the structure – or lack thereof – in the ifcfg files. NetworkManager introduced the new network connection keyfiles to overcome those issues. But it still recognized the old ifcfg configuration files.

Support for those deprecated ifcfg files is no longer provided by default for new installations beginning with Fedora 36. Therefore, it's not a good idea at this late stage to depend upon deprecated ifcfg configuration files. So in this section we will explore migrating existing interface configuration files to the NetworkManager keyfiles using the command-line tool provided. I also look at use of both command-line and GUI tools to create new keyfiles from scratch.

The migration is considerably easier than it sounds. I used the `nmcli connection migrate` command on the two systems I needed to migrate, one with a single network interface card (NIC) and one, my router/firewall, with three NICs. After some extensive testing on a VM, it also worked perfectly the first time on both production hosts. Yes, that's it. No other commands, options, or arguments required. And it is fast, taking much less than one second on both hosts.

But let's look at the details.

Why Should I Migrate My Files?

Things have changed significantly with the release of Fedora 36. NetworkManager will no longer create or support ifcfg files for new installations. It will continue to use them on systems that have been upgraded from earlier versions of Fedora to release 36 – at least for a while longer.

I experimented with NetworkManager on a new Fedora 36 installation and was unable to convince it to use newly created ifcfg files. It continued to treat the interfaces as DHCP and to obtain its configuration values from the DHCP server. The reason the ifcfg files are no longer supported on new installations is that the NetworkManager-initscripts-ifcfg-rh package is no longer installed. That package contains the tools needed to use the ifcfg files.

Hosts upgraded from older releases of Fedora will still have the NetworkManager-initscripts-ifcfg-rh package installed, so it will – for the time being at least – be upgraded along with the rest of the installation to Fedora 36. This also may not be true in the future.

If you are using DHCP configuration for your network hosts, there is no need to migrate any ifcfg files you have. In fact you can simply delete them, if they still exist, and NetworkManager will deal with managing the network connections. Personally, I move deprecated files like these to an archive subdirectory in /root so that I can find them later – just in case.

All hosts with static connections should be migrated. This usually includes servers, firewalls, and other hosts that may need to perform their network functions without the DHCP server being active.

I have two hosts like this, my main server and my firewall/router.

Migration Experiments

When NetworkManager officially deprecated the interface configuration files located in the /etc/sysconfig/network-scripts directory, it did not immediately stop using them, but the update procedure did drop in a readme file, /etc/sysconfig/network-scripts/readme-ifcfg-rh.txt. This short file states explicitly that the ifcfg-style files are deprecated. It also provides a simple command that performs the migration for us.

You can perform Experiment 33-3 on your Fedora student VM so that you can see how the old interface configuration files work and how to migrate them to the new NetworkManager keyfiles.

EXPERIMENT 33-3: MIGRATING TO NETWORKMANAGER KEYFILES

In this experiment we look at how to migrate from the deprecated interface configuration files to the NetworkManager keyfiles for network connection configuration.

In this experiment because you will create an interface configuration file, ensure that works, and then do the migration. If you ever do run into an older host that still uses them, this procedure can be used to migrate to the NetworkManager keyfiles. It's really simple.

Before I started making changes, I displayed the connection data to get the current state of the network connection:

```
[root@studentvm1 ~]# nmcli
enp0s9: connected to Wired connection 2
        "Intel 82540EM"
        ethernet (e1000), 08:00:27:FF:C6:4F, hw, mtu 1500
        ip4 default
        inet4 192.168.0.181/24
        route4 192.168.0.0/24 metric 101
        route4 default via 192.168.0.254 metric 101
        inet6 fe80::6ce0:897c:5b7f:7c62/64
        route6 fe80::/64 metric 1024

enp0s3: connected to Wired connection 1
        "Intel 82540EM"
        ethernet (e1000), 08:00:27:01:7D:AD, hw, mtu 1500
        inet4 10.0.2.22/24
```

```
        route4 10.0.2.0/24 metric 102
        route4 default via 10.0.2.1 metric 102
        inet6 fe80::b36b:f81c:21ea:75c0/64
        route6 fe80::/64 metric 1024

lo: unmanaged
        "lo"
        loopback (unknown), 00:00:00:00:00:00, sw, mtu 65536

DNS configuration:
        servers: 192.168.0.52 8.8.8.8 8.8.4.4
        domains: both.org
        interface: enp0s9

        servers: 192.168.0.52 8.8.8.8 8.8.4.4
        domains: both.org
        interface: enp0s3
<SNIP>
```

The connection enp0s9 is a back door that lets me work via SSH from my primary workstation. I do this so that I can still access the VM while the enp0s3 connection is being worked on, that is, down, and to make it a bit easier to do copy/paste from the VM to this document.

First, I created the /etc/sysconfig/network-scripts directory, which did not exist for new installations of Fedora 36 and a couple higher releases. You don't need to create this directory because it is now created during installation and contains only a Red Hat readme file that explains how to migrate interface configuration files to NetworkManager keyfile format. Read the /etc/sysconfig/network-scripts/readme-ifcfg-rh.txt file before continuing.

Then I created the /etc/sysconfig/network-scripts/ifcfg-enp0s3 file with the content shown in Figure 33-1. When you create this file, be sure to use the hardware address of the enp0s3 network interface on your VM. I also used a different IP address, IPADDR=10.0.2.25, than the interface received from the DHCP server in the virtual network gateway to help me verify that the configuration was really from the interface configuration file instead of the DHCP server.

```
HWADDR=08:00:27:01:7D:AD
TYPE=Ethernet
PROXY_METHOD=none
BROWSER_ONLY=no
BOOTPROTO=static
DEFROUTE=yes
IPADDR=10.0.2.25
PREFIX=24
GATEWAY=10.0.2.1
DOMAIN=both.org
IPV6INIT=no
NAME="System eth0"
DNS1=10.0.2.1
DNS2=8.8.8.8
DNS3=8.8.4.4
IPV4_FAILURE_FATAL=no
IPV6INIT=no
NAME=enp0s3
ONBOOT=yes
AUTOCONNECT_PRIORITY=-999
DEVICE=enp0s3
```

Figure 33-1. *Create the /etc/sysconfig/network-scripts/ifcfg-enp0s3 file with the content shown*

This file does not need to be executable. The permissions for this file should already be set to 644.

I commented out the hardware (MAC) address in the ifcfg-enp0s3 file on my VM because it did not seem necessary. I tried it both ways, and it worked just as well either way – once I finally got it working at all. NetworkManager completely ignored the contents of this file until I installed the NetworkManager-initscripts-ifcfg-rh package. After that, NetworkManager was able to set the network configuration from this ifcfg-enp0s3 file.

I installed the NetworkManager-initscripts-ifcfg-rh package:

```
[root@studentvm1 ~]# dnf -y install NetworkManager-initscripts-ifcfg-rh
```

A restart of NetworkManager activates the values stored in the interface configuration file. There is a nmcli connection reload command that does not work – at least not with these interface configuration files. So the restart of NetworkManager is necessary, but a reboot is not required:

[root@studentvm1 ~]# **systemctl restart NetworkManager**

I used the **nmcli** command and pinged example.com to verify that the changes had been made and the network was working as expected. Note the new IP address:

```
[root@studentvm1 network-scripts]# nmcli
enpOs3: connected to enpOs3
        "Intel 82540EM"
        ethernet (e1000), 08:00:27:01:7D:AD, hw, mtu 1500
        ip4 default
        inet4 10.0.2.25/24
        route4 10.0.2.0/24 metric 100
        route4 default via 10.0.2.1 metric 100
        inet6 fe80::a00:27ff:fe01:7dad/64
        route6 fe80::/64 metric 256

enpOs9: connected to Wired connection 2
        "Intel 82540EM"
        ethernet (e1000), 08:00:27:FF:C6:4F, hw, mtu 1500
        inet4 192.168.0.181/24
        route4 default via 192.168.0.254 metric 101
        route4 192.168.0.0/24 metric 101
        inet6 fe80::6ce0:897c:5b7f:7c62/64
        route6 fe80::/64 metric 1024

lo: unmanaged
        "lo"
        loopback (unknown), 00:00:00:00:00:00, sw, mtu 65536

DNS configuration:
        servers: 192.168.0.52 8.8.8.8 8.8.4.4
        domains: both.org
        interface: enpOs9
```

```
      servers: 10.0.2.1 8.8.8.8 8.8.4.4
      domains: both.org
      interface: enp0s3
<SNIP>
```

Be sure to verify the new name for the connection and that the default route is still 10.0.2.1. I also used the `mtr` command to verify that the route to example.com was via the 10.0.2.1 virtual router.

Then it was time to try the migration tool. I ran the **nmcli connection migrate** to migrate the ifcfg file to a keyfile. I then checked /etc/sysconfig/network-scripts to verify that the old ifcfg file had been deleted, which it was. I also checked the /etc/NetworkManager/system-connections directory to verify that the new enp0s3.nmconnection file had been created:

```
[root@studentvm1 network-scripts]# nmcli connection migrate
Connection 'enp0s3' (3c36b8c2-334b-57c7-91b6-4401f3489c69) successfully
migrated.
Connection 'Wired connection 1' (9803fd55-04f7-3245-a67d-f10697dc40d6)
successfully migrated.
[root@studentvm1 network-scripts]# ll
total 4
-rw-r--r--. 1 root root 1244 May 30 08:27 readme-ifcfg-rh.txt
[root@studentvm1 network-scripts]# cd /etc/NetworkManager/system-connections/
[root@studentvm1 system-connections]# ll
total 4
-rw-------. 1 root root 324 Jul 27 10:43 enp0s3.nmconnection
[root@studentvm1 system-connections]#
```

I checked the contents of the enp0s3.nmconnection file to see if it looked reasonable:

```
[root@studentvm1 system-connections]# cat enp0s3.nmconnection
[connection]
id=enp0s3
uuid=3c36b8c2-334b-57c7-91b6-4401f3489c69
type=ethernet
autoconnect-priority=-999
interface-name=enp0s3

[ethernet]
mac-address=08:00:27:01:7D:AD
```

```
[ipv4]
address1=10.0.2.25/24,10.0.2.1
dns=10.0.2.1;8.8.8.8;8.8.4.4;
dns-search=both.org;
method=manual

[ipv6]
addr-gen-mode=eui64
method=ignore

[proxy]
[root@studentvm1 system-connections]#
```

This command took less than a second. It created the new keyfile and then deleted the ifcfg file. So I suggest making a copy of the original ifcfg file before running this migration tool. It created the /etc/NetworkManager/system-connections/enp0s3.nmconnection file for my host.

Without specifying a particular interface, the command shown earlier will migrate all of the ifcfg files located in /etc/sysconfig/network-scripts. If a host has multiple NICs and corresponding ifcfg files, only some of which you want to migrate, you can specify a list of connections to migrate.

I restarted the NetworkManager and verified that the connection data was still correct.

Although a reboot is not necessary to actually make the change, I did perform a reboot to verify that the network configuration remained as it was intended after a reboot. Kind of a worst-case test and I am all about testing after making changes like this; I want no surprises when I do something like this in production.

The keyfiles can be modified using your favorite editor. I tried this by changing the IPADDR entry and restarting NetworkManager just to make sure it did work. The nmcli connection reload command did not work for me. Making changes directly to the keyfiles using an editor is not recommended, but it does work. Most of us …uumm …experienced …SysAdmins really prefer editing ASCII text configuration files directly so – recommended or not – that is how I do things most of the time. We like to know what is actually in those files so we can recognize when something is wrong with them. It helps with solving configuration problems.

What If I Don't Have ifcfg Files?

New installations of Fedora don't create any type of network interface configuration files. The default is for NetworkManager to handle network interfaces as DHCP connections. So you really don't need to do anything for hosts that use DHCP to obtain their network configuration information.

However, you may need to create a static configuration for some new hosts even when you don't have a deprecated ifcfg file to migrate.

Reverting to DHCP

Reversion to the use of DHCP is easy. Just remove the keyfile for the desired connection from /etc/NetworkManager/system-connections/ and restart NetworkManager. "Remove" can mean to move the file somewhere else or to just delete it.

In preparation for this next series of experiments in creating new keyfiles, I moved the enp0s3.nmconnection keyfile to /root and restarted NetworkManager.

Creating New Keyfiles

And although the old `ip` command can still be used to modify network interface settings in a live environment, those changes are not persistent after a reboot. Changes made using the NetworkManager tools such as `nmcli`, `nmtui`, and the GUI NetworkManager connection editor (nm-connection-editor) and your favorite text editor are persistent. The connection editor is available for Fedora on the system tray for each of the desktops that I tried, Xfce, Cinnamon, LXDE, and KDE Plasma, and probably most of the desktops I haven't yet tried.

Text Editor

It is always possible – assuming you are familiar with the keyfile structure, syntax, and variables – to create (or modify) keyfiles from scratch with just a plain text editor. As much as I appreciate and use that capability, it is usually so much more simple to use one of the three tools provided.

Using nmtui

This nmtui (NetworkManager Text User Interface) tool is my second choice for a tool in this trio. I find the interface cumbersome, unattractive, and not intuitive. This tool is not installed by default, and I probably would not have installed it if I were not writing this book.

However, it does work, and it created a keyfile for me that was essentially identical to the one created by the GUI Connection Manager that I discuss in the following. The only differences I found – using the **diff** command of course – were the timestamp field in the file and one different selection I intentionally made when I configured the connection. The interface does provide some clues about the data you need to provide to create a working keyfile.

EXPERIMENT 33-4: USING NMTUI

Start this tool by entering the command **nmtui** on the command line. In general, the arrow keys allow movement between the fields on the displayed pages, and the Enter key selects an item to modify or add. The Page Up/Page Down keys scroll the page. Select **Edit a connection** as shown in Figure 33-2 and press **Enter** to create a new keyfile and press **Enter**.

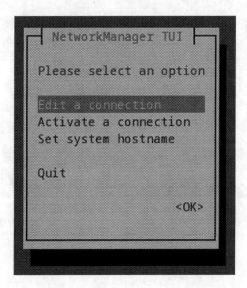

*Figure 33-2. Using nmtui, select **Edit a connection** to create a new keyfile*

After wending your way through the interface, you will arrive at the Edit Connection page seen in Figure 33-3. It was not clear to me from this interface that the CIDR prefix should be appended to the IP address, but I did that anyway and it worked.

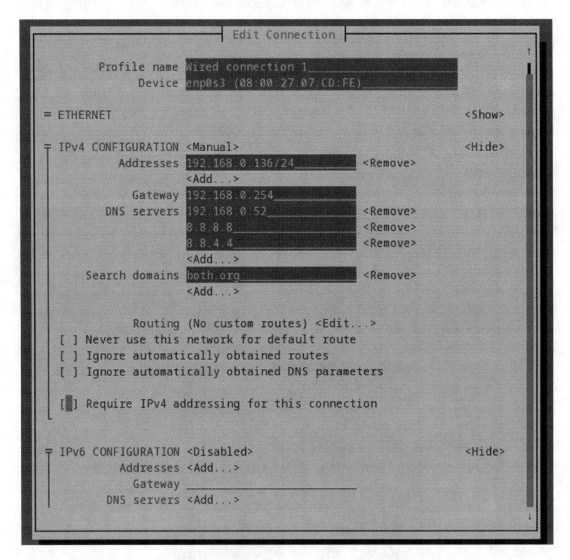

Figure 33-3. *Fill in the appropriate data on this page to configure the interface*

Fill in the appropriate data on this page to configure the interface. Notice that I have disabled IPv6 and you should too.

Then scroll down to the bottom of the page using the keyboard and press **OK** to save the keyfile. The keyfile is saved immediately, but NetworkManager must be restarted to activate this file whether new or changed.

This is not my favorite interface for creating and managing NetworkManager keyfiles.

Using nmcli

I have used the **nmcli** (Network Manager command-line interface) tool to configure an interface, and this tool works very well. I dislike it the most of these three tools because it requires the most typing and reading of the man page and online references. Executing the command immediately creates the interface configuration file in the /etc/ NetworkManager/system-connections/ directory.

EXPERIMENT 33-5: ADDING A CONNECTION KEYFILE WITH NMCLI

Delete the keyfile created in the previous experiment to prepare for this one. This command adds the needed keyfile, just like the other tools:

```
[root@studentvm1 system-connections]# nmcli connection add con-name enp0s3-
Wired ifname enp0s3 type ethernet ipv4.addresses 192.168.0.136/24 ipv4.
gateway 192.168.0.254 ipv4.dns 192.168.0.254,8.8.8.8,8.8.4.4 ipv4.dns-search
both.org ipv6.method disabled
Connection 'ethernet-enp0s3' (67d3a3c1-3d08-474b-ae91-a1005f323459)
successfully added.
[root@studentvm1 system-connections]# cat enp0s3-Wired.nmconnection
[connection]
id=ethernet-enp0s3
uuid=67d3a3c1-3d08-474b-ae91-a1005f323459
type=ethernet
interface-name=enp0s3
```

```
[ethernet]

[ipv4]
address1=192.168.0.136/32,192.168.0.254
dns=192.168.0.52;8.8.8.8;8.8.4.4;
dns-search=both.org;
method=manual

[ipv6]
addr-gen-mode=stable-privacy
method=disabled

[proxy]
[root@studentvm1 system-connections]#
```

One of the assistance tools available while using **nmcli connection add** is the Bash tab completion sequence that shows the available sub-commands. However, there are a lot of choices at nearly every sub-command step, and it can still take a long time to determine the correct command.

I eventually got the command correct by referring to the example in the manual page, nmcli-examples(7).

I typically prefer the command line for most tasks. However, the complexity of getting the syntax and options of this command correct means that I must always use the man page and research the command before I issue it. That takes time. And it still complained about things I missed or got incorrect. Even when it did not throw an error, it created keyfiles that worked poorly if at all. One example was that the connection worked when I would SSH out from the test VM but I could not SSH into the test VM. I am still not sure what the problem was, but that keyfile had the wrong CIDR prefix for the IP address. When nmcli is the only available method, I can do this, but it is my least preferred tool.

Using the GUI NetworkManager Connection Editor

I used one of my laptops for parts of this section in order to show both wired and wireless connections. Despite the fact that I typically prefer command-line tools, I like this GUI NetworkManager connection editor tool best of all the three available tool options. It is easy to use and intuitive, provides fast access to any configuration item that would ever be needed, and is directly available itself on the desktop system tray of all the desktops I have tried.

EXPERIMENT 33-6: USING THE GUI CONNECTION EDITOR

Just right-click the network icon, the one that looks like a pair of computers, on the system tray. Then choose **Configure Connections**, or **Edit Connections**, depending upon which desktop you are using, as shown in Figure 33-4.

Figure 33-4. *Select "Edit (or Configure) Connections…" to configure a network interface*

This opens the connection editing window seen in Figure 33-5. Double-click the desired connection from the connection list – usually **Wired Connection 1** or a Wi-Fi SSID. Figure 33-5 shows both wired and wireless connections open for editing on one of my laptops. I have never needed to edit a wireless connection because the ones I connect to always use DHCP for configuration. It is possible to require static addressing for wireless connections, but I have never encountered that.

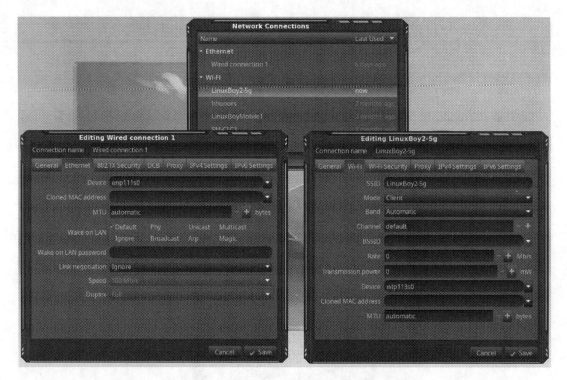

Figure 33-5. *Both wired and wireless connections can be viewed and edited using the GUI connection editor*

The **Ethernet** tab of the **Editing Wired connection 1** dialog window shows the device name enp111s0 for my personal laptop. In most cases nothing on this page needs to be changed.

Back on my own student VM, in Figure 33-6 I have changed the **Method** field from **Automatic (DHCP)** to **Manual**. I added the IP address, the CIDR prefix, and the default route (gateway) I wanted for this host. I also added three DNS servers and the search domain. These are the minimum configuration variables that are needed for a network connection. They are also the same ones that were defined in the interface configuration files and the previous keyfiles. The device name for this NIC is enp0s3.

Figure 33-6. *The configuration for the wired connection using the GUI
NetworkManager connection editor tool*

Another option available for the **Method** field is **Disabled**. I set that on IPv6 since I don't
use IPv6.

After setting these values, clicking the **Save** button immediately creates the new keyfile.
Making changes to existing keyfiles is just as easy. However, NetworkManager must be
restarted for these configuration changes to take effect.

In terms of the amount of time and work involved in creating new NetworkManager
keyfiles, the GUI connection editor is far better than the other options. It provides an
easy-to-use interface with enough information about the data that is required to be
helpful. I like it the best when it is available, but you must be working directly on the host
and not remotely.

How to Manage Wireless Networks Using the Command Line

All laptop computers and many desktop and tower computers have Wi-Fi capabilities. NetworkManager is used to manage those connections as well, with both GUI and CLI tools.

The experiments in this section require the use of a wireless (Wi-Fi) adapter in your physical host. You may already have a wireless device in your computer, especially if it is a laptop. If there is no wireless adapter in your physical computer, you can obtain an inexpensive USB Wi-Fi adapter and plug that into your physical computer.

EXPERIMENT 33-7: CONFIGURING WIRELESS NETWORKS USING THE COMMAND LINE

Insert a USB wireless adapter to your physical computer. You'll need to capture it in the StudentVM1 virtual machine. Use the VirtualBox menu as shown in Figure 33-7 to capture the USB Wi-Fi adapter, **Devices ➤ USB ➤ <Wi-Fi device>**. Note that the name of the USB Wi-Fi device will depend upon the vendor, model, and revision of the device. So, yes, it will be different from the one shown.

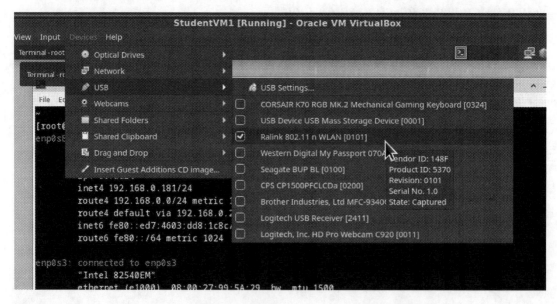

Figure 33-7. *Capture the USB Wi-Fi device so it can be used by the virtual machine*

In a terminal session on your VM, do two things to establish the current status of the Wi-Fi device. First, use nmcli to verify that the device is recognized by the VM and then use the ll command to verify that there is *not* a keyfile for this Wi-Fi device in the system-connections directory:

```
[root@studentvm1 system-connections]# nmcli
enpOs9: connected to Wired connection 1
        "Intel 82540EM"
        ethernet (e1000), 08:00:27:CA:1F:16, hw, mtu 1500
        ip4 default
        inet4 192.168.0.181/24
        route4 192.168.0.0/24 metric 101
        route4 default via 192.168.0.254 metric 101
        inet6 fe80::ed7:4603:dd8:1c8c/64
        route6 fe80::/64 metric 1024

enpOs3: connected to enpOs3
        "Intel 82540EM"
        ethernet (e1000), 08:00:27:99:5A:29, hw, mtu 1500
        inet4 10.0.2.35/24
        route4 10.0.2.0/24 metric 102
        route4 default via 10.0.2.1 metric 102
        inet6 fe80::a00:27ff:fe99:5a29/64
        route6 fe80::/64 metric 256

wlpOs12u1: disconnected
        "Ralink RT5370"
        wifi (rt2800usb), 9A:75:2F:B0:D6:75, hw, mtu 1500

lo: unmanaged
        "lo"
        loopback (unknown), 00:00:00:00:00:00, sw, mtu 65536

<SNIP>

[root@studentvm1 ~]# ll /etc/NetworkManager/system-connections/
total 4
-rw------- 1 root root 304 Mar 28 13:10 enpOs3.nmconnection
```

The Wi-Fi device should appear in the display of connections generated by the **nmcli** command. Although the device name will be different for your VM, Wi-Fi device names always start with "wl."

Next, display more data about the Wi-Fi device:

```
[root@studentvm1 system-connections]# nmcli device show wlp0s12u1
GENERAL.DEVICE:                    wlp0s12u1
GENERAL.TYPE:                      wifi
GENERAL.HWADDR:                    9A:75:2F:B0:D6:75
GENERAL.MTU:                       1500
GENERAL.STATE:                     30 (disconnected)
GENERAL.CONNECTION:                --
GENERAL.CON-PATH:                  --
IP4.GATEWAY:                       --
IP6.GATEWAY:                       --
[root@studentvm1 system-connections]#
```

Although the wlp0s12u1 device in my example is not yet connected, we can still list the available Wi-Fi signals:

```
[root@studentvm1 system-connections]# nmcli device wifi list
IN-USE  BSSID              SSID                           MODE   CHAN
RATE         SIGNAL  BARS     SECURITY
        18:A6:F7:B2:0E:83  LinuxBoy2                      Infra  1
195 Mbit/s  100     ▂▄▆█    WPA1 WPA2
        1E:A6:F7:B2:0E:84  LinuxBoy2-Guest                Infra  1
195 Mbit/s  100     ▂▄▆█    WPA1 WPA2
        D8:07:B6:D9:65:B8  LinuxBoy3                      Infra  4
405 Mbit/s  92      ▂▄▆█    WPA1 WPA2
        DE:07:B6:D9:65:B9  LinuBoy3_Guest_65B9            Infra  4
405 Mbit/s  89      ▂▄▆█    WPA1 WPA2
        C8:D3:FF:14:22:49  DIRECT-48-HP ENVY 5640 series  Infra  8
65 Mbit/s   89      ▂▄▆█    WPA2
        54:A0:50:D9:B1:10  BigE                           Infra  8
195 Mbit/s  82      ▂▄▆█    WPA2
```

Whether viewing the available Wi-Fi signals via nmcli or the GUI network tool on the system tray, NetworkManager displays the signals sorted by signal strength. This result from the USB Wi-Fi device also tells me that the USB device is not nearly as sensitive to weaker signals as the built-in wireless devices in my System76 Oryx Pro laptops. For example, my older Oryx Pro 4 laptop gives the following result, and it is located only about two feet from the USB device used with the VM:

```
root@voyager ~]# nmcli device wifi list
IN-USE  BSSID                  SSID                        MODE   CHAN
RATE         SIGNAL  BARS  SECURITY
        18:A6:F7:B2:0E:83  LinuxBoy2                   Infra  1
195 Mbit/s   100         ▃▅▇  WPA2
        1E:A6:F7:B2:0E:84  LinuxBoy2-Guest             Infra  1
195 Mbit/s   100         ▃▅▇  WPA1 WPA2
*       18:A6:F7:B2:0E:82  LinuxBoy2-5g                Infra  36
405 Mbit/s   87          ▃▅▇  WPA2
        1E:A6:F7:B2:0E:83  LinuxBoy2-Guest-5G          Infra  36
405 Mbit/s   87          ▃▅▇  WPA2
        C8:D3:FF:14:22:49  DIRECT-48-HP ENVY 5640 series  Infra  8
65 Mbit/s    84          ▃▅▇  WPA2
        54:A0:50:D9:B1:10  BigE                        Infra  8
195 Mbit/s   70          ▃▅_  WPA2
        D8:07:B6:D9:65:B7  LinuxBoy3-5G_2              Infra  149
405 Mbit/s   59          ▃▅_  WPA2
        DE:07:B6:D9:65:B7  LinuxBoy3_Guest_65B9_5G_1   Infra  44
405 Mbit/s   47          ▃__  WPA2
        44:D4:53:71:98:AE  Lynmedlin                   Infra  6
195 Mbit/s   39          ▃__  WPA2
        E8:9F:80:12:AE:80  BigE_2G_Ext                 Infra  157
540 Mbit/s   35          ▃__  WPA2
        C0:3C:04:A5:46:7E  SpectrumSetup-78            Infra  6
540 Mbit/s   32          ▃__  WPA2
        88:96:4E:1F:71:C0  ATTEY6Q3Pi                  Infra  1
195 Mbit/s   29          ▃__  WPA2
        B0:98:2B:48:E4:BC  GoodeTimes2022_2G           Infra  1
195 Mbit/s   29          ▃__  WPA2
[root@voyager ~]#
```

Find a strong Wi-Fi signal for which you have the password and use the following command to connect to it. Note that I placed the password in quotes because it has spaces in it. Be sure to use your own Wi-Fi SSID and password in the command:

```
# nmcli device wifi connect LinuxBoy2 password "My Password"
Device 'wlp0s12u1' successfully activated with '80589678-b07d-4bf2-
a65a-6dd23c4cad4b'.
```

Now check the contents of the /etc/Network-Manager/system-connections directory. You should see a new keyfile for the wireless connection you made. This file contains the details of the connection similar to those for the wired connections. It also contains the password for the Wi-Fi connection:

```
[root@studentvm1 system-connections]# ll
total 8
-rw-------. 1 root root 324 Jul 27 10:43 enp0s3.nmconnection
-rw-------. 1 root root 289 Jul 31 21:31 LinuxBoy2.nmconnection
```

The keyfiles for wireless connections are not deleted. After connecting with other wireless routers over time, you will build up a number of NetworkManager keyfiles, one for each Wi-Fi network. Check the contents of the Wi-Fi connection keyfile to see what it contains.

It is possible to use the `nmcli wifi` command to set up a Wi-Fi hotspot using your computer. The nmcli man page contains the details for that.

Now let's look at something else. You can find some very interesting things by looking at the list of Wi-Fi connections. Here is a listing from my other laptop, which is in a different portion of the house. Can you see a possible problem here? Or two?

```
[root@voyager2 ~]# nmcli device wifi list
IN-USE  BSSID                   SSID                          MODE
CHAN   RATE         SIGNAL  BARS  SECURITY
        D8:07:B6:D9:65:B8  LinuxBoy3                      Infra  4    405
Mbit/s  87          ▂▄▆   WPA2
        DE:07:B6:D9:65:B9  LinuBoy3_Guest_65B9            Infra  4    405
Mbit/s  87          ▂▄▆   WPA2
*       D8:07:B6:D9:65:B6  LinuxBoy3-5G_1                 Infra  44   405
Mbit/s  79          ▂▄▆_  WPA2
```

DE:07:B6:D9:65:B7	LinuxBoy3_Guest_65B9_5G_1	Infra	44	405 Mbit/s	79 ▃▃▂ WPA2
D8:07:B6:D9:65:B7	LinuxBoy3-5G_2	Infra	149	405 Mbit/s	79 ▃▃▂ WPA2
18:A6:F7:B2:0E:83	LinuxBoy2	Infra	1	195 Mbit/s	65 ▃▃▂ WPA2
1E:A6:F7:B2:0E:84	LinuxBoy2-Guest	Infra	1	195 Mbit/s	65 ▃▃▂ WPA1 WPA2
18:A6:F7:B2:0E:82	LinuxBoy2-5g	Infra	36	405 Mbit/s	45 ▃▂_ WPA2
1E:A6:F7:B2:0E:83	LinuxBoy2-Guest-5G	Infra	36	405 Mbit/s	45 ▃▂_ WPA2
C8:9E:43:5D:07:EE	canes	Infra	9	270 Mbit/s	40 ▃▂_ WPA2
4E:BA:D7:B1:34:5A	[LG_Oven]345a	Infra	11	65 Mbit/s	35 ▂▃_ WPA2
54:A0:50:D9:B1:10	BigE	Infra	8	195 Mbit/s	29 ▂__ WPA2
D8:0F:99:B3:D1:F4	lucydog001	Infra	11	195 Mbit/s	27 ▂__ WPA2
C8:D3:FF:14:22:49	DIRECT-48-HP ENVY 5640 series	Infra	8	65 Mbit/s	25 ▂__ WPA2
EC:A9:40:20:04:00	Eat More Fiber	Infra	1	195 Mbit/s	24 ▂__ WPA2
3C:84:6A:BC:55:56	killthemoonlight	Infra	11	195 Mbit/s	22 ▂__ WPA1 WPA2
C0:3C:04:A5:46:7E	SpectrumSetup-78	Infra	6	540 Mbit/s	20 ▂__ WPA2
88:96:4E:1F:71:C0	ATTEY6Q3Pi	Infra	1	195 Mbit/s	15 ▂__ WPA2

Yes, the LG oven is a Wi-Fi hotspot. It is not mine! Many appliances and household devices are available with Wi-Fi, so they can be monitored and managed remotely. The web page for that oven includes being able to turn it on and monitor it from work or the next room. It works with Alexa or any Android or iOS device. All of those devices, including the so-called "smart" appliances like ovens and refrigerators, can be hacked. I have received spam from a few of those "smart appliances.

Also, the HP Envy is a printer at one of my neighbors' houses. I don't know whose. But some cracker could also attack that device in any number of ways.

Remember that the Internet of Things (IoT), like home wireless routers, appliances, and computer-related devices, can be easily cracked if the administrative ID and passwords are not changed. Of course they also need to be good, hard-to-crack passwords.

EXPERIMENT 33-8: DISCONNECTING A WIRELESS CONNECTION

It's easy to terminate a wireless connection:

```
root@studentvm1 system-connections]# nmcli connection down LinuxBoy2
Connection 'LinuxBoy2' successfully deactivated (D-Bus active path: /org/
freedesktop/NetworkManager/ActiveConnection/5)
[root@studentvm1 system-connections]#
```

Verify that the connection has been terminated. You can then release the wireless device from the VM.

Chapter Summary

Fedora 36 changes the equation for using the old-style, deprecated interface configuration files. For new installations of Fedora 36, those files will not work unless the NetworkManager-initscripts-ifcfg-rh package is explicitly installed. This is a warning that all support for those deprecated ifcfg scripts will be completely ignored in the future.

Fortunately, the migration from any existing ifcfg scripts is trivially easy, and creating new ones is not much more difficult using one of the three tools available – well, mostly. I prefer the GUI NetworkManager connection editor tool because it is clear and easy. I can use the **nmtui** tool, which does the same thing as the GUI version but has a little clunkier user interface. I try not to use the **nmcli** tool for creating keyfiles if I can help it. It does work but is cumbersome and takes a lot of reading and experimentation to get the correct command syntax and all of the right arguments to create a fully usable keyfile.

However, **nmcli** is a powerful tool for viewing and managing both wired and wireless network interfaces. I use it frequently to verify the correct configuration of the network interfaces on my hosts and to make changes as necessary. It can be a big help in network problem determination.

CHAPTER 34

BtrFS

Objectives

In this chapter you will learn

- What the B-Tree Filesystem (BtrFS) is.

- BtrFS is the default filesystem beginning with Fedora 33.

- Red Hat's current lack of support for BtrFS.

- Some advantages of the B-Tree Filesystem over EXT4.

- What happens to LVM/EXT4 filesystems during Fedora version upgrades.

- How to create and use BtrFS volumes.

- What subvolumes and snapshots are and how they can be used.

- How to create subvolumes

- How to use subvolumes.

- Why BtrFS should only be used in certain limited circumstances.

Author's note   Due to the issues with BtrFS I discovered as I wrote this chapter, and the fact that Red Hat no longer supports it, I don't recommend using it. However, you may encounter it already installed, and it is the filesystem used when taking the defaults during installation of Fedora. I think it's important to be familiar with it for those reasons. You can skip this chapter for now and return to it later if you encounter BtrFS in your capacity as a SysAdmin.

© David Both 2023
D. Both, *Using and Administering Linux: Volume 2*, https://doi.org/10.1007/978-1-4842-9615-8_34

Introduction

Over the more than 25 years I have been using Linux, the default filesystem for Red Hat Linux (not RHEL) and Fedora has evolved considerably. EXT2, the second extended filesystem, was the default when I started using Linux, and it had many drawbacks including but not the least of which was that it took hours and sometimes days to recover from an improper shutdown such as a power failure. Now at EXT4, the extended filesystem can recover from many types of occurrences such as that in only seconds. It is fast and works very well in concert with logical volume management (LVM) to provide a flexible and powerful filesystem structure that works well in many storage environments.

BtrFS[1] or the B-Tree Filesystem is a relatively new filesystem that employs a Copy-on-Write[2] (CoW) strategy. Copy-on-Write differs significantly from the EXT4 journaling strategy for committing data to the storage device medium. The next two paragraphs are extremely simplified, conceptual summaries of how they work:

- With a journaling filesystem, new or revised data is stored in the fixed-size journal, and when all of the data has been committed to the journal, it is then written to the main data space of the storage device, either into newly allocated blocks or to replace modified blocks. The journal is marked as having been committed when the write operation is completed.

- In a BtrFS Copy-on-Write filesystem, the original data is not touched. New or revised data is written to a completely new location on the storage device. When the data has been completely written to the storage device, the pointer to the now old data is simply changed to point to the new data in an atomic operation that minimizes the possibility of data corruption. The storage space containing the old data is then released for reuse.

BtrFS is also designed to be fault tolerant, and it is self-healing in case errors occur. It is intended to be easy to maintain. It has built-in volume management, which means the separate logical volume management (LVM) tool used to provide that functionality behind the EXT4 filesystem is not needed.

---

[1] Wikipedia, BtrFS, https://en.wikipedia.org/wiki/BtrFS

[2] Wkipedia, Copy-on-Write, https://en.wikipedia.org/wiki/Copy-on-write

BtrFS is the default Fedora filesystem starting with Fedora 33,[3] but this can be easily overridden during the installation procedure.

Tip   BtrFS is usually pronounced as "butterfs."

Based on a 2007 paper by IBM researcher Ohad Rodeh, BtrFS was designed at Oracle Corporation for use in their version of Linux. In addition to being a general-purpose filesystem, it was intended to address a different and more specific set of problems from the EXT filesystem. BtrFS is designed to accommodate huge storage devices with capacities that don't exist even yet and large amounts of data, especially massively large databases in highly transactional environments.

You created a small BtrFS filesystem in Chapter 19 of Volume 1, but we didn't explore any of the reasons it is an important filesystem in Fedora. We look at those reasons in this chapter and take some time to explore BtrFS in more detail.

A very complete set of BtrFS documentation is available from the BtrFS project website.[4]

Caution   Red Hat does not support BtrFS.

Red Hat has removed all support for BtrFS in RHEL 9, and that is an implicit statement that it does not trust this filesystem. The fact that BtrFS supersedes EXT4 as the default filesystem for Fedora – despite its removal from RHEL – means that we need to know more than just a little about it. But there are some important problems to consider, and I will cover those as we proceed through this chapter.

Tip   When upgrading Fedora from one release version to another, such as from Fedora 37 to Fedora 38, the procedure does not convert existing EXT filesystems to BtrFS. This is a good thing as you will see.

---

[3] Murphy, Chris, "Btrfs Coming to Fedora 33," `https://fedoramagazine.org/btrfs-coming-to-fedora-33/`, 08/24/2020, Fedora Magazine

[4] BtrFS documentation, `https://BtrFS.readthedocs.io/en/latest/index.html`

BtrFS vs. EXT4

We looked at the EXT4 filesystem in some detail in Chapter 19 of Volume 1 and in Chapter 20 of this volume. In this section we explore the similarities between the EXT4 and BtrFS filesystems as well as the differences.

Although BtrFS has many interesting features, I think the best way to describe the functional differences from the standpoint of the SysAdmin is that BtrFS combines the functions of a journaling filesystem (EXT4) with the volume management capabilities of LVM. Many of its other features are designed for large commercial use cases and provide little benefit over EXT4 to smaller businesses, individual users, or even larger users unless they have some specific requirements that call for the use of BtrFS.

BtrFS uses a different strategy for space allocation than EXT4, but it maintains some of the same meta-structures such as inodes and directories.

BtrFS Advantages

BtrFS has a number of advantages over the EXT4 filesystem:

- In a pooled storage system like BtrFS, the available storage space gets assigned to a subvolume only when it is needed. This makes storage allocation invisible to the user, and there is no need to preallocate volume size as there is in an EXT filesystem. It is an extremely efficient way in which to deal with storage allocation.

- BtrFS is a Copy-on-Write (CoW) filesystem that was designed for high-capacity and high-performance storage servers.

- BtrFS uses its own logical volume manager. This means that it can easily configure multiple physical devices and partitions into a single logical storage space. Although this can also be done on EXT filesystems, it requires the separate LVM system that we have already seen.

- BtrFS has integral support for creating software-based RAID systems.

- BtrFS has an integral system for performing compression on individual files or directories or even an entire filesystem.

- EXT4 can grow a filesystem while it is online but it cannot shrink one. BtrFS can perform online resizing of filesystems to both expand and shrink the filesystem.

- BtrFS supports block sub-allocation and tail packing, which is also called inline extents. For most files, the last block of the file does not occupy the entire block. This last block is called the tail block. This is also true with many small files because they don't occupy the entire block. Both of these situations waste a lot of disk space. These are strategies that store the tail parts of other files or complete small files in the tail block of one file, thus saving disk space.

BtrFS and EXT4 Similarities

BtrFS and EXT4 share some important attributes:

- Both the EXT4 and BtrFS filesystems are extent-based filesystems. In Chapter 19 of Volume 1, we explored the structure of the EXT4 filesystem including extents. An extent is a contiguous area of the storage device that is allocated to a file. When possible extent-based filesystems store complete files in a contiguous storage area. This improves filesystem performance in hard drives with rotating disks, by improving read/write times. It makes little difference for SSDs.

- Both EXT4 and BtrFS filesystems support allocate-on-flush. Data is not written directly to the storage device. It is stored in a RAM buffer. Only when the buffer is full does the data get written to the storage device. This strategy reduces CPU and I/O usage, speeds up disk writes, and helps reduce disk fragmentation.

- Both EXT4 and BtrFS support TRIM for SSD storage devices. When a file is deleted from an SSD, the data blocks that were assigned to it are marked as deleted but not usable. Similarly, when a data block is "overwritten," a new data block is allocated to the file, and the old one is marked as not usable. This strategy speeds data write operations while helping ensure the integrity of the data on the SSD. The TRIM command is necessary to locate all of those "unusable" data blocks, delete the data in them, and mark them as available.

EXT4 Advantages

The EXT4 filesystem still has some important advantages:

- The EXT4 filesystem is mature, well known, and understood, and in addition it is very stable. It is the default filesystem in many popular Linux distributions such as Ubuntu and Debian-related ones. It was the default filesystem in Fedora up through release 33.

- As a journaling filesystem, the EXT4 filesystem is safe during power failures and other problems that can cause your system to crash.

- It is reliable.

Filesystem Structure with BtrFS

The BtrFS metadata structure and data allocation strategies on the storage device are much different from those of EXT4 on LVM. For this reason partitioning a storage device on a new system during initial installation works differently. Some things we used to do with LVM/EXT are no longer available, and other things are a bit ...strange compared with my previous experience. Different tools show this in different ways.

The first time I installed a new VM using BtrFS, I took the default storage partitioning option, not really knowing what to expect. Figure 34-1 illustrates the result after a default installation on a 120GB (virtual) storage device. The -T option displays the filesystem type. The root (/) and /home partitions are both located on /dev/sda3, which is a BtrFS partition, and both appear to have 119G of space available.

```
# df -Th
Filesystem       Type       Size   Used  Avail Use% Mounted on
devtmpfs         devtmpfs   4.0M      0   4.0M   0% /dev
tmpfs            tmpfs      7.9G      0   7.9G   0% /dev/shm
tmpfs            tmpfs      3.2G   1.1M   3.2G   1% /run
/dev/sda3        BtrFS      119G   2.8G   115G   3% /
tmpfs            tmpfs      7.9G   4.0K   7.9G   1% /tmp
/dev/sda3        BtrFS      119G   2.8G   115G   3% /home
/dev/sda2        EXT4       974M   189M   718M  21% /boot
tmpfs            tmpfs      1.6G    72K   1.6G   1% /run/user/984
tmpfs            tmpfs      1.6G    64K   1.6G   1% /run/user/0
```

Figure 34-1. *Storage configuration after a default installation of Fedora 37*

486

Using fdisk, the partitions look like Figure 34-2, which is helpful in terms of understanding the actual disk usage and partitioning.

```
Device       Start       End    Sectors   Size Type
/dev/sda1     2048      4095       2048    1M BIOS boot
/dev/sda2     4096   2101247    2097152    1G Linux filesystem
/dev/sda3  2101248 251656191  249554944  119G Linux filesystem
```

Figure 34-2. *The disk partitioning scheme for a default Fedora installation with BtrFS*

You can see that the lsblk command in Figure 34-3 shows both the / and /home partitions as part of /dev/sda3, thus making it clear that both filesystems are located on the same partition. The -f option displays additional information about the filesystems.

```
# lsblk -f
NAME    FSTYPE FSVER LABEL          UUID                      FSAVAIL
FSUSE% MOUNTPOINTS
sda
├─sda1
├─sda2 EXT4   1.0                   3cdf9efd-<snip>dbe03  717.6M   19% /boot
└─sda3 BtrFS         fedora_testvm3 f5daf918-<snip>62aee  114.7G    2% /home
                                                                        /

sr0
zram0
[SWAP]
```

Figure 34-3. *The lsblk command shows both / and /home filesystems located on the /dev/sda3 partition*

How It Works

So how is it that the /dev/sda3 partition that is 119GB in size can support two filesystems, each of which is 119GB in size?

Well, it doesn't. Not really.

The / and /home filesystems are called subvolumes on BtrFS.[5] The /dev/sda3 partition is used as a storage location for those subvolumes, and the storage space in that partition is used as a pool of available storage for any and all subvolumes created on that partition. When additional space is needed to store a new file or an expansion of an existing file on one of the subvolumes, the space is assigned to that subvolume and removed from the available storage pool.

Creating BtrFS Filesystems

Although you have already created and used a small BtrFS partition in Chapter 19, there was nothing in Experiment 19-11 to illustrate managing BtrFS including things such as subvolumes. It's time to do so in this chapter.

You will start by creating a new BtrFS filesystem using three storage devices that have already been created for your VM. You will then learn about mounting a BtrFS filesystem, which can be a little different than mounting other filesystems. You will be introduced to creating subvolumes and get to experience first-hand how they differ from other filesystems like EXT4, ZFS, and others.

EXPERIMENT 34-1: CREATING A BTRFS FILESYSTEM FROM THREE STORAGE DEVICES

This experiment will create a BtrFS filesystem from three different storage devices. You have already created the devices you will use to create this filesystem. You repurposed the /dev/sdb2 BtrFS partition you created in Chapter 19, so it won't show up in this command, which tells us that there are no BtrFS filesystems currently extant on our VM:

```
[root@studentvm1 ~]# btrfs filesystem show
[root@studentvm1 ~]#
```

There are three (virtual) storage devices that are not currently in use, so we can repurpose them for the experiments in this chapter. That's a good place to start in any event – creating a new BtrFS volume that consists of multiple storage devices.

---

[5] Notice the two meanings of "filesystem" in this sentence.

A quick look shows those devices as not mounted:

```
[root@studentvm1 ~]# lsblk -i
NAME                        MAJ:MIN RM   SIZE RO TYPE MOUNTPOINTS
sda                             8:0   0   60G  0 disk
|-sda1                          8:1   0    1M  0 part
|-sda2                          8:2   0    1G  0 part /boot
|-sda3                          8:3   0    1G  0 part /boot/efi
`-sda4                          8:4   0   58G  0 part
  |-fedora_studentvm1-root 253:0   0    2G  0 lvm  /
  |-fedora_studentvm1-usr  253:1   0   15G  0 lvm  /usr
  |-fedora_studentvm1-tmp  253:4   0    5G  0 lvm  /tmp
  |-fedora_studentvm1-var  253:5   0   10G  0 lvm  /var
  |-fedora_studentvm1-home 253:6   0    4G  0 lvm  /home
  `-fedora_studentvm1-test 253:7   0  500M  0 lvm  /test
sdb                            8:16   0   20G  0 disk
|-sdb1                         8:17   0    2G  0 part
|-sdb2                         8:18   0    2G  0 part
`-sdb3                         8:19   0   16G  0 part
  |-NewVG--01-TestVol1      253:2   0    4G  0 lvm
  `-NewVG--01-swap          253:3   0    2G  0 lvm
sdc                            8:32   0    2G  0 disk
`-NewVG--01-TestVol1        253:2   0    4G  0 lvm
sdd                            8:48   0    2G  0 disk
sr0                           11:0    1 1024M  0 rom
zram0                        252:0   0    8G  0 disk [SWAP]
```

The devices we want to use to create our new BtrFS filesystem are /dev/sdb, /dev/sdc, and /dev/sdd. Check /etc/fstab and comment out all lines that refer to any of these three devices. Then remove the NewVG-01 volume group. Leaving it in place results in an error message indicating that the sdb device is in use. This command removes the volume group from sdb and sdc:

```
[root@studentvm1 ~]# vgremove NewVG-01
```

The existing partition tables – even when no partitions are present – need to be overwritten using the -f option to force creation of BtrFS:

```
[root@studentvm1 ~]# mkfs -t btrfs -f /dev/sdb /dev/sdc /dev/sdd
BtrFS-progs v6.2.1
See http://BtrFS.wiki.kernel.org for more information.

NOTE: several default settings have changed in version 5.15, please make sure
      this does not affect your deployments:
        - DUP for metadata (-m dup)
        - enabled no-holes (-O no-holes)
        - enabled free-space-tree (-R free-space-tree)

Label:              (null)
UUID:               bf283fe5-7f2a-45a6-9ab6-153582672578
Node size:          16384
Sector size:        4096
Filesystem size:    24.00GiB
Block group profiles:
  Data:             single              8.00MiB
  Metadata:         RAID1               256.00MiB
  System:           RAID1               8.00MiB
SSD detected:       no
Zoned device:       no
Incompat features:  extref, skinny-metadata, no-holes
Runtime features:   free-space-tree
Checksum:           crc32c
Number of devices:  3
Devices:
   ID        SIZE  PATH
    1    20.00GiB  /dev/sdb
    2     2.00GiB  /dev/sdc
    3     2.00GiB  /dev/sdd
```

All three devices are now part of the single 24GB filesystem, and the BtrFS tools will show us the information about the BtrFS volumes:

```
[root@studentvm1 ~]# btrfs filesystem show
Label: none   uuid: 498ea267-40aa-4dca-a723-5140aae8b093
        Total devices 3 FS bytes used 144.00KiB
        devid    1 size 20.00GiB used 8.00MiB path /dev/sdb
        devid    2 size 2.00GiB used 264.00MiB path /dev/sdc
        devid    3 size 2.00GiB used 264.00MiB path /dev/sdd
```

You can also use `lsblk -f` to display filesystem information including the filesystem type and UUID.

BtrFS RAID Structure

You probably noticed in the filesystem data displayed in the previous experiment that the multiple storage devices are configured into a RAID1 array. RAID1 is a configuration in which the data is mirrored (duplicated) across multiple devices. RAID type 0 or 1 is the default when the BtrFS filesystem is created without specifying a particular type of RAID structure. RAID type 0 or 1 is determined at BtrFS creation time and depends upon the size and configuration of the storage devices that are included in the BtrFS volume.

Certain other RAID types are supported but not all. Use `man 5 BtrFS` for a discussion of BtrFS and how it utilizes RAID.

Mounting BtrFS Filesystems

BtrFS filesystems can be mounted much the same way as the EXT4 filesystem we have already explored in some detail. In fact, in Chapter 19 you mounted the small BtrFS filesystem using the device special file /dev/sdb2 just like you would with an EXT4 filesystem. They can also be mounted using labels and the UUID just as with EXT4 filesystems.

The difference with BtrFS is when there are multiple devices like in this case, /dev/sdb, /dev/sdc, and /dev/sdd. If you have the need, desire, or procedure that says that all filesystems will be mounted by device special file name, that can be done too. Just select any one of the device special files and use that one.

```
┌──────────────────────────────────────────────────────────────────────┐
│           EXPERIMENT 34-2: MOUNTING BTRFS FILESYSTEMS                  │
└──────────────────────────────────────────────────────────────────────┘
```

This experiment explores the different mounting methods for BtrFS filesystems. We will start
by mounting the filesystem on /mnt and using the device special files:

```
[root@studentvm1 ~]# mount /dev/sdb /mnt
[root@studentvm1 ~]# df -h
Filesystem                        Size  Used Avail Use% Mounted on
<SNIP>
/dev/sdb                          24G   3.8M  24G   1% /mnt

[root@studentvm1 ~]# lsblk -f
NAME        FSTYPE   FSVER    LABEL    UUID        FSAVAIL FSUSE% MOUNTPOINTS
sda
├─sda1
├─sda2      ext4     1.0      boot     498ea267-<SNIP>
<SNIP>
sdb         BtrFS             498ea267<snip> 23.5G    0% /mnt
sdc         BtrFS             498ea267<snip>
sdd         BtrFS             498ea267<snip>
<SNIP>
```

I find that the lsblk command can sometimes fail to display the most accurate filesystem
size, so I tend to rely on the df -h command to verify the correct size data. However, the
lsblk -f command does show the devices that make up the BtrFS filesystem.

Unmount the BtrFS filesystem and mount it again on /mnt using /dev/sdc and /dev/sdd as the
device special files to be mounted. Then view the results as you did previously and see what
you notice.

You can see that no matter which device special file used in the mount command, only the
/dev/sdb device special file ever shows as being mounted. All three of the device special files
have the same UUID, which means they are part of the same filesystem.

Unmount the filesystem:

```
[root@studentvm1 ~]# umount /mnt
```

Next, mount the BtrFS filesystem using the UUID. The following command uses the UUID of the VM I am using, so be sure to substitute the UUID for your BtrFS filesystem in the command you use on your VM:

```
[root@studentvm1 ~]# mount UUID=498ea267-40aa-4dca-a723-5140aae8b093 /mnt
```

Use the df and lsblk commands as you did previously to verify that the filesystem has been mounted on /mnt.

Unmount the filesystem again.

BtrFS filesystems can be mounted using labels just like EXT4 filesystems. Also like the EXT4 filesystem, we need to create the label for our BtrFS filesystem. We could have specified a label when we created the filesystem, but we can also do it after as in this experiment.

The label can be created using the device special file name (/dev/sdb) if the filesystem is unmounted or the mountpoint (/mnt) if the filesystem is mounted. In this case we will use the device special file name since the filesystem has already been unmounted.

The first command adds the label to the filesystem, overwriting any existing label. The second command displays the label. Null is displayed if no label is present:

```
[root@studentvm1 ~]# btrfs filesystem label /mnt BtrFS-test
[root@studentvm1 ~]# btrfs filesystem label /mnt
BtrFS-test
[root@studentvm1 ~]#
```

We could create a new mountpoint for the BtrFS filesystem, but the /TestFS mountpoint is still there and no longer used by anything else, so we can use that. The filesystem can now be mounted manually using the label:

```
[root@studentvm1 ~]# mount LABEL=BtrFS-test /TestFS
```

Verify that the filesystem is mounted.

Now unmount /TestFS and add the following line to the /etc/fstab so that this BtrFS filesystem will mount automatically when the system boots. There is another line with "/TestFS" in it. Verify that it is commented out:

```
LABEL=BtrFS-test      /TestFS        btrfs    auto,defaults   1 2
```

Run the following to force the system to reload fstab. You would receive an error message telling you to do this if you skip it:

```
[root@studentvm1 ~]# systemctl daemon-reload
```

Now remount the filesystem:

```
[root@studentvm1 ~]# mount /TestFS
```

Set the permissions of the mountpoint so that everyone has access to it. That way we can perform more of these experiments as a non-root user:

```
[root@studentvm1 ~]# chmod 777 /TestFS/
```

Verify that the filesystem is mounted.

As a last test of your work, reboot the VM and verify that the BtrFS filesystem mounts properly, has 777 permissions, and contains the correct devices.

Exploring the BtrFS Volume

Having created a BtrFS filesystem and gotten it mounted, let's explore it and then store some data on it. In Experiment 34-3 we use the btrfs filesystem command group that works on the whole filesystem. Use man 8 btrfs-filesystem for more details about this command group including descriptions of the data fields displayed by the sub-commands in this group. I suggest you read this man page as it contains some very interesting information.

EXPERIMENT 34-3: EXPLORING THE BTRFS VOLUME

We start our exploration of the new BtrFS filesystem using some of the tools we have already learned about to provide us with the metadata unique to BtrFS filesystems. This first command displays the basic information we need to understand the structural components of the filesystem:

```
[root@studentvm1 ~]# btrfs filesystem show
Label: 'BtrFS-test'  uuid: 498ea267-40aa-4dca-a723-5140aae8b093
        Total devices 3 FS bytes used 144.00KiB
```

```
devid    1 size 20.00GiB used 8.00MiB path /dev/sdb
devid    2 size 2.00GiB used 264.00MiB path /dev/sdc
devid    3 size 2.00GiB used 264.00MiB path /dev/sdd
```

This next command provides us with information about the metadata that makes up the filesystem as well as the amounts of space that is allocated and unallocated. This is a good view into the filesystem and is one of the more useful tools I have found. There isn't any user data on this filesystem yet, but we'll explore that soon:

```
[root@studentvm1 ~]# btrfs filesystem usage /TestFS
Overall:
    Device size:               24.00GiB
    Device allocated:          536.00MiB
    Device unallocated:        23.48GiB
    Device missing:             0.00B
    Device slack:               0.00B
    Used:                      288.00KiB
    Free (estimated):          23.48GiB        (min: 11.75GiB)
    Free (statfs, df):         23.48GiB
    Data ratio:                 1.00
    Metadata ratio:             2.00
    Global reserve:            3.50MiB         (used: 0.00B)
    Multiple profiles:            no

Data,single: Size:8.00MiB, Used:0.00B (0.00%)
   /dev/sdb        8.00MiB

Metadata,RAID1: Size:256.00MiB, Used:128.00KiB (0.05%)
   /dev/sdc       256.00MiB
   /dev/sdd       256.00MiB

System,RAID1: Size:8.00MiB, Used:16.00KiB (0.20%)
   /dev/sdc        8.00MiB
   /dev/sdd        8.00MiB

Unallocated:
   /dev/sdb       19.99GiB
   /dev/sdc        1.74GiB
   /dev/sdd        1.74GiB
[root@studentvm1 ~]#
```

Now that we have some knowledge about the BtrFS filesystem, let's store some data on it. We want enough to make the next couple experiments interesting, but we don't want to fill it up entirely. I used the file extension .rand to indicate explicitly that these files contain random data. The following CLI program creates 50,000 files each containing 50KB of random data:

```
[student@studentvm1 ~]$ cd /TestFS/
[student@studentvm1 TestFS]$ for X in `seq -w 1 50000` ; do echo "Working on $X" ; dd if=/dev/urandom of=TestFile-$X.rand bs=2048 count=25; done
```

This operation will take a little time, the exact amount of which will depend upon the overall speed of the physical host that your VM is running on. It took 2 minutes and 28 seconds on my VM.

Verify that the /TestFS directory contains 50,000 non-empty files and that at least a random sampling of them contains 50KB of data.

At this point the BtrFS volume is ready and can be used to store data like any other filesystem. However, the use of subvolumes allows access to the more interesting aspects and features of BtrFS. We will get to that after this short side trip.

Notes on an Edge-Case BtrFS Failure

While I was creating Experiment 34-3, I inadvertently managed to create an edge case[6] in which a failure of the BtrFS filesystem occurred. In part the failure was apparently due to the unusual makeup of the BtrFS filesystem with two small 2GB storage devices and one large 20GB device. I wanted to create 1.5 million small files for testing, and that failed about 90% or so of the way through the process. I knew there was a problem when it took more than 2.5 hours on the VM on my primary workstation and never completed because the metadata structures filled up, leaving no room to create new files even though there was still data space available.

The metadata structures, having been relegated to the RAID1 array consisting of the two 2GB devices, did not contain enough space to allow creation of 1.5 million files. In a more normal use case, this would not have occurred.

---

[6] "Edge case" is a term used in testing that means when one condition exceeds an extreme maximum or minimum value. In this case the number 1.5 million files exceeded the capacity of the available metadata space. Wikipedia, Edge Case, https://en.wikipedia.org/wiki/Edge_case

It was difficult to tell how many files were actually created because the filesystem failed in such a way that the kernel – as it is supposed to do – placed it into read-only mode as a means of protecting the filesystem from further damage. However, the `BtrFS filesystem usage /TestFS` showed that approximately 1.35 million files had been created.

Although it should have been possible to use the `-o remount` option of the `mount` program to atomically remount the filesystem, that also failed. Unmounting and then mounting as separate operations also failed. Only a reboot worked to remount the BtrFS filesystem properly in read/write mode.

I tried to delete the files that had already been created using `rm -f *` as root, but that just hung with no apparent effect. After a long wait, it finally displayed an error message to the effect that there were too many arguments. This means that there were too many files for the `rm` command to deal with using the file glob, *.

I then tried a different approach with the command `for X in ` + "`ls`" + ` ; do echo "Working on $X" ; rm -f $X ; done`, and that worked for a while but eventually ended in another hang and with the filesystem in read-only mode again.

To shorten a long story, after some additional testing, I decided to recreate the BtrFS volume and to reduce the number of files to be created to 50,000 while increasing their size to take up more space. This works well as you have seen in the resulting experiment.

However, one lesson I learned is that strange and unexpected failures can still occur. Therefore, it's important for us to understand the technologies that are used in our devices so that we can be effective in finding and fixing or circumventing the root causes of the problems we encounter.

And, yes, I did test this edge case in an EXT4/LVM setup by converting those three devices on my StudentVM1 VM to EXT4 on LVM. It worked much faster and created 1.5 million files without any problems. However, after exploring the number of inodes remaining in the EXT4 filesystem after creating 1.5 million files, I discovered that the EXT4 filesystem could only have held about 38,000 additional files before it, too, failed. All filesystems have limits.

Although this situation is an extremely unusual edge case, I still plan to continue using LVM+EXT4 on my personal systems. This decision is due not to the edge case itself but rather to the fact that the entire filesystem became unusable after the problem. That is not a situation I want to encounter in a production environment, whether my home office or a huge organization.

Another factor in my decision to remain with LVM+EXT4 filesystems is an article published on Ars Technica by Jim Salter, "Examining btrfs, Linux's perpetually half-finished filesystem."[7] In this article Salter describes some of the interesting features of BtrFS but covers in some detail the problems extant in the filesystem concluding with the following statement:

> *Btrfs' refusal to mount degraded, automatic mounting of stale disks, and lack of automatic stale disk repair/recovery do not add up to a sane way to manage a "redundant" storage system.*

The final factor I considered is the fact that Red Hat has removed all support for BtrFS from its RHEL flagship operating system. This is not comforting at all.

Simplification

Because we have an unstable BtrFS configuration set up, let's simplify it before we go any further. To do that we will attempt to use an interesting command that should allow us to remove devices from a BtrFS volume.

EXPERIMENT 34-4: SIMPLIFY THE BTRFS VOLUME

Before removing devices from a BtrFS volume, verify which devices to remove. We are going to remove the two smallest ones from the following list:

```
[root@studentvm1 ~]# btrfs filesystem show /TestFS/
Label: 'BtrFS-test'  uuid: 498ea267-40aa-4dca-a723-5140aae8b093
        Total devices 3 FS bytes used 2.51GiB
        devid    1 size 20.00GiB used 3.00GiB path /dev/sdb
        devid    2 size 2.00GiB used 264.00MiB path /dev/sdc
        devid    3 size 2.00GiB used 264.00MiB path /dev/sdd
```

Let's begin by removing one device:

```
[root@studentvm1 ~]# btrfs device delete /dev/sdc /TestFS/
```

---

[7] Salter, Jim, "Examining btrfs, Linux's perpetually half-finished filesystem," https://arstechnica.com/gadgets/2021/09/examining-btrfs-linuxs-perpetually-half-finished-filesystem/, Ars Technica, 2021

That took about nine seconds, and a quick check showed the data to be intact.

[root@studentvm1 ~]# **btrfs device delete /dev/sdd /TestFS/**
ERROR: error removing device '/dev/sdd': unable to go below two devices
on raid1

That didn't work, but the man page did actually say that a RAID1 BtrFS volume can't have fewer than two devices. Some additional reading indicated that there is a way to circumvent that but it appears truly ugly, and I had no desire to spend more time heading down that wormhole.

So I decided to brute-force it by using fdisk to delete the BtrFS signature from both remaining devices. First, unmount the BtrFS volume and then make the changes. The -w always option means to always wipe the existing signature data when exiting fdisk with a write command. So just issue the command and then use w to exit, and that removes the BtrFS signature:

[root@studentvm1 ~]# **fdisk -w always /dev/sdb**

Welcome to fdisk (util-linux 2.38.1).
Changes will remain in memory only, until you decide to write them.
Be careful before using the write command.

The device contains 'btrfs' signature and it will be removed by a write
command. See fdisk(8) man page and --wipe option for more details.

Device does not contain a recognized partition table.
Created a new DOS disklabel with disk identifier 0xdddf783c.

Command (m for help): **w**
The partition table has been altered.
Calling ioctl() to re-read partition table.
Syncing disks.

Do this for /dev/sdc and /dev/sdd. The /dev/sdc device has already been removed from the BtrFS volume, so it will no longer have the BtrFS signature.

Now create a new BtrFS volume using only the /dev/sdb device, which has 20GB of space on it:

[root@studentvm1 ~]# **mkfs -t btrfs -f /dev/sdb**
btrfs-progs v6.2.1
See http://btrfs.wiki.kernel.org for more information.

NOTE: several default settings have changed in version 5.15, please make sure
      this does not affect your deployments:
      - DUP for metadata (-m dup)
      - enabled no-holes (-O no-holes)
      - enabled free-space-tree (-R free-space-tree)

```
Label:               (null)
UUID:                2c101d21-6053-44bb-b70d-c3347cb0fa86
Node size:           16384
Sector size:         4096
Filesystem size:     20.00GiB
Block group profiles:
   Data:             single              8.00MiB
   Metadata:         DUP               256.00MiB
   System:           DUP                 8.00MiB
SSD detected:        no
Zoned device:        no
Incompat features:   extref, skinny-metadata, no-holes
Runtime features:    free-space-tree
Checksum:            crc32c
Number of devices:   1
Devices:
   ID         SIZE  PATH
    1     20.00GiB  /dev/sdb

[root@studentvm1 ~]#
```

Add a label to the new volume. We use the same label as the previous volume so that we don't need to change the entry in the /etc/fstab file. This is one of the advantages of using the label:

```
[root@studentvm1 ~]# btrfs filesystem label /dev/sdb BtrFS-test
[root@studentvm1 ~]# btrfs filesystem label /dev/sdb
BtrFS-test
```

Mount the filesystem on the existing mountpoint:

```
[root@studentvm1 ~]# mount /TestFS/
```

Finally, verify that the filesystem is mounted and that you can create a file or two on it.
The BtrFS volume is now ready for the next experiment with subvolumes and should not be susceptible to the problems associated with multidisk configurations.

What Is a Subvolume?

A subvolume is a logical subdivision of a BtrFS volume such as the volume you created in Experiment 34-4. Subvolumes are dedicated file B-trees, not separate filesystems. They're more complex than a directory but less complex than a filesystem. Each subvolume has its own 2^64 inode pool, and the inode numbers repeat. Subvolumes can be treated exactly as regular directories if you choose, but they have capabilities that can have significant impact on things like filesystem management, snapshots, and more. Subvolumes can also be treated as mountable filesystems.

Each BtrFS volume or subvolume can support multiple subvolumes. All subvolumes share the resources of the top-level BtrFS volume. It's the use of subvolumes that provides many of the advanced features and advantages of BtrFS.

Snapshots – images of the subvolume at a moment in time – can be created and used as backups or rollback images that can be easily rolled back. The BtrFS documentation describes an interesting use case:

> There are two ways how the system root directory and subvolume layout could be organized. The interesting use case for root is to allow rollbacks to previous version, as one atomic step. If the entire filesystem hierarchy starting in "/" is in one subvolume, taking snapshot will encompass all files. This is easy for the snapshotting[sic] part but has undesirable consequences for rollback. For example, log files would get rolled back too, or any data that are stored on the root filesystem but are not meant to be rolled back either (database files, VM images, …).

This is one of the features that drives subvolume strategies. For another example you may want to create snapshots of specific directories such as a shared directory that is a part of a larger directory structure in /var but not make snapshots of the entire /var directory. So if /var is a BtrFS volume or subvolume, you could create /var/shared as a subvolume and set up a strategy for creating regular snapshots.

Using BtrFS Subvolumes

Subvolumes provide the basis for many of the more interesting capabilities BtrFS offers. In this section you will create and use a pair of subvolumes to the /TestFS volume.

EXPERIMENT 34-5: BTRFS SUBVOLUMES

Start by creating a subvolume on the existing /TestFS volume. Note that this command does not take a list of subvolumes to create; rather, only one subvolume can be created for each invocation of the command:

```
[root@studentvm1 ~]# btrfs subvolume create /TestFS/SubVol1
Create subvolume '/TestFS/SubVol1'
```

Verify the existence of the new subvolume:

```
[root@studentvm1 ~]# btrfs subvolume list /TestFS
ID 256 gen 12 top level 5 path SubVol1
```

Subvolumes are created as subdirectories of the primary volume.

```
[root@studentvm1 ~]# ll /TestFS | grep ^d
drwxr-xr-x 1 root root 0 Apr 12 09:10 SubVol1
```

This subvolume could be used just as it is, but mounting it is more interesting. We will mount it on the /mnt temporary mountpoint although a permanent mountpoint and an entry in /etc/fstab would be used in a production environment.

First, we need to know the device special file of the new subvolume so we can use that to perform the mount:

```
[root@studentvm1 TestFS]# findmnt -vno SOURCE /TestFS
/dev/sdb
```

The standard mount command works to mount this subvolume using the subvol=SubVol1 option:

```
[root@studentvm1 TestFS]# mount -o subvol=SubVol1 /dev/sdb /mnt
[root@studentvm1 TestFS]# lsblk
NAME                     MAJ:MIN RM  SIZE RO TYPE MOUNTPOINTS
sda                          8:0  0   60G  0 disk
|-sda1                       8:1  0    1M  0 part
<SNIP>
  `-fedora_studentvm1-test 253:5  0  500M  0 lvm  /test
```

```
sdb                            8:16   0   20G  0 disk /mnt
                                                      /TestFS
sdc                            8:32   0    2G  0 disk
sdd                            8:48   0    2G  0 disk
sr0                           11:0    1 1024M  0 rom
zram0                        252:0    0    8G  0 disk [SWAP]
[root@studentvm1 TestFS]# df -h
Filesystem                         Size  Used Avail Use% Mounted on
<SNIP>
/dev/mapper/fedora_studentvm1-root  2.0G  633M  1.2G  35% /
/dev/mapper/fedora_studentvm1-usr    15G  6.8G  7.2G  49% /usr
/dev/mapper/fedora_studentvm1-tmp   4.9G  116K  4.6G   1% /tmp
/dev/mapper/fedora_studentvm1-home  3.9G  1.4G  2.4G  37% /home
/dev/mapper/fedora_studentvm1-var   9.8G  1.2G  8.1G  13% /var
/dev/mapper/fedora_studentvm1-test  459M  1.1M  429M   1% /test
/dev/sda2                          974M  277M  631M  31% /boot
/dev/sda3                         1022M   18M 1005M   2% /boot/efi
<SNIP>
/dev/sdb                            20G  3.9M   20G   1% /TestFS
/dev/sdb                            20G  3.9M   20G   1% /mnt
```

Now let's add some data to /mnt:

```
[root@studentvm1 TestFS]# cd /mnt
[root@studentvm1 mnt]# for X in `seq -w 1 5000` ; do dmesg > File-$X.
txt ; done
```

Now look at the disk usage:

```
[root@studentvm1 mnt]# df
Filesystem                 1K-blocks     Used Available Use% Mounted on
<SNIP>
/dev/sdb                    20971520   316736  20123840   2% /TestFS
/dev/sdb                    20971520   316736  20123840   2% /mnt
```

Both the BtrFS volume and the subvolume, identified by their mountpoints, show exactly the same usage and free space. This is because they both use storage space from the same pool, the top-level volume.

Spend a bit of time to experiment with this subvolume configuration.

Converting from EXT to BtrFS

Converting from EXT filesystems 2, 3, and 4 as well as the Reiser filesystem to BtrFS is possible, and there is a BtrFS tool to perform that task. The btrfs-convert tool is used for this purpose.

However, given the issues I encountered, the things I have seen written, Red Hat's removal of BtrFS from RHEL 9, and the opinions of knowledgeable people whom I trust, I strongly recommend against converting to BtrFS.

Using BtrFS as Swap

A BtrFS filesystem can be used as swap if necessary though you need to use the BtrFS `filesystem mkswap` command instead of the EXT4 `mkswap` command. However, as you have already seen in Chapter 24, for most environments the default 8GB of Zram swap is the optimal choice for swap.

Cleanup

Perform just a bit of cleanup by unmounting the subvolume from /mnt and the volume from /TestFS.

OpenZFS: An Alternative

The EXT4 filesystem is an excellent filesystem for the majority of users. However, for users with needs such as those that BtrFS was designed to meet, there is OpenZFS.[8]

Having never used OpenZFS, I can only say that it is well respected in the open source community and has none of the problems found in BtrFS. It has many but not quite all of the features that BtrFS is supposed to. If your use case requires huge quantities of extremely large files, OpenZFS will be the best candidate for a data storage filesystem.

---

[8] Wikipedia, ZFS, https://en.wikipedia.org/wiki/ZFS

Chapter Summary

The only reason I include this chapter is that BtrFS has become the default filesystem for Fedora, so you do need some knowledge of it.

BtrFS can be used to hide the complexities of traditional Linux filesystem structures for relatively non-technical users such as individuals or businesses who just want to get their work done. BtrFS is the default filesystem on Fedora and other distributions in part because of its apparent simplicity from the viewpoint of the non-technical user.

The edge-case failure I experienced while developing Experiment 34-3 serves to illustrate that BtrFS is still not ready for use except in the simplest of environments where a single BtrFS volume is the filesystem for a single storage device. The lack of accurate documentation caused me to spend hours of time researching commands and their syntax. Additionally, my experiments with performance show that BtrFS is much slower at certain tasks such as creating large numbers of files very rapidly.

Although the BtrFS development team's response to a query I submitted indicated that concentrating on edge cases can be misleading, I can't ignore the fact that it was so easy to randomly create a test case for this chapter that failed.

I strongly recommend using LVM+EXT4 and will continue to do so myself for the foreseeable future. That is the primary reason this course is based upon the LVM+EXT4 combination for its filesystems rather than BtrFS. Stay away from multidisk BtrFS volumes at all cost.

## CHAPTER 35

Getting Started with systemd

Objectives

In this chapter you will learn

- To describe the functions of systemd

- About the controversy surrounding SystemV vs. systemd

- Why systemd is an improvement over SystemV startup and init services

- To understand and troubleshoot Linux systemd startup

- To list and define the systemd startup targets

- How to manage startup

- What a systemd unit is

Introduction

We have briefly explored systemd in the context of the Linux startup in Chapter 16, and one might be tempted to think that we have covered the greater part of systemd and that there is no reason for a full chapter about it. That would be incorrect.

© David Both 2023
D. Both, *Using and Administering Linux: Volume 2*, https://doi.org/10.1007/978-1-4842-9615-8_35

There is much left to explore including much more about Linux startup. Because the volume of this material about systemd is so great, it has been split into three chapters. In these chapters we will explore the functions of systemd, both those of startup and those that begin after startup is completed.

systemd[1,2] is the mother of all processes, and it is responsible for bringing the Linux host up to a state in which productive work can be done. Some of the functions assumed by systemd, which are far more extensive than the old SystemV start scripts and the init program, are to manage many aspects of a running Linux host, including mounting filesystems, managing hardware, and starting and managing system services required to have a productive Linux host. In this chapter we explore those functions of systemd that pertain to system startup.

Learning to Love systemd

systemd – yes, all in lowercase even at the beginning of a sentence – is the modern replacement for init and SystemV init scripts. It is also much more.

Like most SysAdmins I think of Linux startup and also shutdown when I think of the obsolete init program and SystemV and not really much else such as managing services once they are up and running. Like init, systemd is the mother of all processes, and it is responsible for bringing the Linux host up to a state in which productive work can be done. Some of the functions assumed by systemd, which are far more extensive than the old init program, are to manage many aspects of a running Linux host, including mounting filesystems, managing hardware, handling timers, and starting and managing system services required to have a productive Linux host.

Linux Boot

The complete process that takes a Linux host from an off state to a running state is complex, but it is open and knowable. Before we get into the details, a quick overview of the time the host hardware is turned on until the system is ready for a user to log in will

---

[1] Wikipedia, systemd, `https://en.wikipedia.org/wiki/Systemd`

[2] Yes, systemd should always be spelled like this without any uppercase even at the beginning of a sentence. The documentation for systemd is very clear about this.

help orient us. Most of the time we hear about "the boot process" as a single entity, but it is not. There are, in fact, three major parts to the complete boot and startup process:

- Hardware boot, which initializes the system hardware

- Linux boot, which loads the Linux kernel and then systemd

- Linux startup in which systemd prepares the host for productive work

Just to ensure that we are all on the same page here, the Linux startup sequence begins after the kernel has loaded systemd. The systemd programs start and manage all the other processes, also known as the mother of all processes.

It is important to separate the hardware boot from the Linux boot process from the Linux startup and to explicitly define the demarcation points between them. Understanding these differences and what part each plays in getting a Linux system to a state where it can be productive makes it possible to manage these processes and to better determine the portion in which a problem is occurring during what most people refer to as "boot."

Controversy

The name *systemd* can evoke a wide range of reactions from system administrators and others closely associated with keeping Linux systems up and running. The fact that systemd is taking over so many tasks in many Linux systems has engendered push-back and discord among certain groups of developers and system administrators.

SystemV and systemd are two different methods of performing the Linux startup sequence. SystemV start scripts and the init program are the old method, and systemd using targets is the new method. Although most modern Linux distributions use the newer systemd for startup, shutdown, and process management, there are still some that do not. One reason for this is that some distribution maintainers and some SysAdmins prefer the older SystemV method over the newer systemd.

I think both have their advantages, so let me explain my reasoning.

Why I Prefer SystemV

I prefer SystemV because it is more flexible. Startup is accomplished using bash scripts. After the kernel starts the init program, which is a compiled binary, init launches the rc.sysinit script, which performs many system initialization tasks. After rc.sysinit has completed, init launches the /etc/rc.d/rc script, which in turn starts the various services as defined by the SystemV start scripts in the /etc/rc.d/rcX.d, where "X" is the number of the runlevel that is being started.

Except for the init program itself, all these programs are open and easily knowable scripts. It is possible to read through these scripts and learn exactly what is taking place during the entire startup process; I don't think that many SysAdmins actually do that, however. Each start script is numbered so that it starts the service for which it is intended in a specific sequence. Services are started serially, and only one service is started at a time.

systemd, developed by Red Hat's Lennart Poettering and Kay Sievers, is a complex system of large compiled binary executables that are not understandable without access to the source code. It is open source, so "access to the source code" isn't hard, just less convenient. systemd appears to represent a significant refutation of multiple tenets of the Linux Philosophy. As a binary, systemd is not directly open to view or easy to change by the SysAdmin. systemd tries to do everything such as managing running services while providing significantly more status information than SystemV. It also manages hardware, processes and groups of processes, filesystem mounts, and much more. systemd is present in almost every aspect of the modern Linux host, making it the one-stop tool for system management. All of this is a clear violation of the tenets that programs should be small and that each program should do one thing and do it well.

Why I Prefer systemd

I prefer systemd as my startup mechanism because it starts as many services as possible in parallel, depending upon the current stage in the startup process. This speeds the overall startup and gets the host system to a login screen faster than SystemV.

systemd manages almost every aspect of a running Linux system. It can manage running services while providing significantly more status information than SystemV. It also manages hardware, processes and groups of processes, filesystem mounts, and much more. systemd is present in almost every aspect of the modern Linux operating system, making it the one-stop tool for system management. Does this sound familiar?

The systemd suite of tools are compiled binaries, but they are open because all the configuration files are ASCII text files. Startup configuration can be modified through various GUI and command-line tools, as well as adding or modifying various configuration files to suit the needs of the specific local computing environment.

The Real Issue

Did you think I could not like both startup systems? I do and I can work with either one.

In my opinion, the real issue and the root cause of most of the controversy between SystemV and systemd is that there is no choice on the SysAdmin level. The choice of whether to use SystemV or systemd has already been made by the developers, maintainers, and packagers of the various distributions. However, this is with good reason. Scooping out and replacing an init system, by its extreme, invasive nature, has a lot of consequences that would be hard to tackle outside the distribution design process.

Despite the fact that this particular choice has been made for us, our Linux hosts boot up and work, which is what I usually care the most about. As an end user and even as a SysAdmin, my primary concern is whether I can get my work done, work such as writing my books and this series, installing updates, and writing scripts to automate everything. So long as I can do my work, I don't really care about the start sequence used on my distro.

I do care when there is a problem during startup or service management. Regardless of which startup system is used on any host, I know enough and am able to follow the sequence of events to find the failure and fix it.

Despite the fact that most Linux developers agree that replacing the old SystemV startup is a good idea, many developers and SysAdmins dislike systemd for that. Rather than rehash all the so-called issues that people have – or had – with systemd, I will refer you to two good, if somewhat old, articles that should cover most everything. Linus Torvalds, creator of the Linux kernel, seems disinterested. In a 2014 ZDNet article "Linus Torvalds and others on Linux's systemd,"[3] Linus is clear about his feelings:

> *I don't actually have any particularly strong opinions on systemd itself. I've had issues with some of the core developers that I think are much too cavalier about bugs and compatibility, and I think some of the design details are insane (I dislike the binary logs, for example), but those are details, not big issues.*

---

[3] Torvalds, Linus, "Linus Torvalds and others on Linux's systemd," `www.zdnet.com/article/linus-torvalds-and-others-on-linuxs-systemd/`, ZDNet, 2013

For those of you who don't know much about Torvalds, if he does not like something, he is very outspoken, explicit, and quite clear about that dislike. He has become more socially acceptable in his manner of addressing his dislike about things.

In 2013, Poettering wrote a long blog post in which he debunks the myths about systemd[4] while providing insight into some of the reasons for creating systemd. This is a very good read and I highly recommend it.

Previous Work

There have been previous attempts at replacing SystemV with something a bit more modern. For about two releases, Fedora used Upstart, which was originally used in Ubuntu to replace the aging SystemV, but it did not replace init and provided no changes that were noticeable to me. Because Upstart provided no significant changes to the issues surrounding SystemV, efforts in this direction were quickly dropped in favor of systemd.

The systemd Plan to Take Over the World

Over the years I have read a lot of articles and posts on the Internet about how systemd is replacing everything and trying to take over everything in Linux. And I agree; it is taking over pretty much everything.

But really not "everything-everything." Just everything in that middle ground of services that lies between the kernel itself and things like the GNU core utilities, GUI desktops, and user applications.

Let's start to explore that by examining the structure of our favorite operating system. Figure 35-1 shows the three basic software layers found in Linux. The bottom is the Linux kernel. The middle layer consists of services that may perform startup tasks such as launching various other services like NTP, DHCP, DNS, SSH, device management, login services, GETTYs, NetworkManager, journal and log management, logical volume management, printing, kernel module management, local and remote filesystems, sound and video, display management, swap space, system statistics collection, and much more.

---

[4] Poettering, Lennart, "The Biggest Myths [about systemd]," http://0pointer.de/blog/projects/the-biggest-myths.html, blog post, 2013

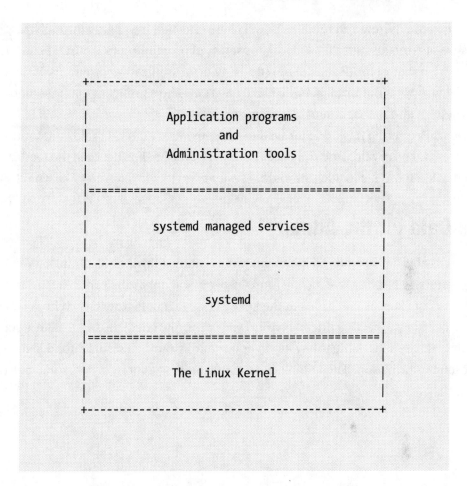

```
+------------------------------------------------+
|                                                |
|            Application programs                |
|                   and                          |
|            Administration tools                |
|                                                |
|================================================|
|                                                |
|            systemd managed services            |
|                                                |
|------------------------------------------------|
|                                                |
|                  systemd                        |
|                                                |
|================================================|
|                                                |
|               The Linux Kernel                 |
|                                                |
+------------------------------------------------+
```

Figure 35-1. *A simple conceptual diagram of systemd and the services it manages with respect to the kernel and application programs such as tools used by the SysAdmin*

It is clear from Figure 35-1 as well as the collective experience as SysAdmins over the last several years that systemd is indeed intended to completely replace the old SystemV init system. But I also know that it significantly extends the capabilities of the init system.

It is also important to recognize that, although Linus Torvalds rewrote the Unix kernel as a hobby – an exercise – he did nothing to change the middle layer of system services and simply recompiled SystemV init to work with his completely new kernel. SystemV is much older than Linux itself and has been much in need of a complete change to something totally new for decades.

So the kernel is new and remains new as it is refreshed frequently through the leadership of Torvalds and the work of thousands of programmers around the planet. There are also tens of thousands of new and powerful application programs at the top layer of Figure 35-1. But until recently there have been no significant enhancements to the init system and management of system services.

Lennart Poettering has done for system services what Linus Torvalds did for the kernel itself. Like Torvalds and the Linux kernel, Poettering has become the leader and arbiter of what happens inside this middle system services layer. And I like what I see.

More Data for the Admin

The new capabilities of systemd include far more status information about services whether running or not. I like having more information about the services I am trying to monitor. For example, let's look at the DHCPD service in Figure 35-2. Where I use the SystemV command, service dhcpd status, I would simply get a message that the service is running or stopped. Using the systemd command, systemctl status dhcpd, I get much more useful information. The following data is from the server in my personal network.

```
[root@yorktown ~]# systemctl status dhcpd
● dhcpd.service - DHCPv4 Server Daemon
     Loaded: loaded (/usr/lib/systemd/system/dhcpd.service; enabled; vendor
preset: disabled)
     Active: active (running) since Fri 2021-04-09 21:43:41 EDT; 4 days ago
       Docs: man:dhcpd(8)
             man:dhcpd.conf(5)
   Main PID: 1385 (dhcpd)
     Status: "Dispatching packets..."
      Tasks: 1 (limit: 9382)
     Memory: 3.6M
        CPU: 240ms
     CGroup: /system.slice/dhcpd.service
             └─1385 /usr/sbin/dhcpd -f -cf /etc/dhcp/dhcpd.conf -user dhcpd
-group dhcpd --no-pid

Apr 14 20:51:01 yorktown.both.org dhcpd[1385]: DHCPREQUEST for 192.168.0.7
from e0:d5:5e:a2:de:a4 via eno1
Apr 14 20:51:01 yorktown.both.org dhcpd[1385]: DHCPACK on 192.168.0.7 to
e0:d5:5e:a2:de:a4 via eno1
Apr 14 20:51:14 yorktown.both.org dhcpd[1385]: DHCPREQUEST for 192.168.0.8
from e8:40:f2:3d:0e:a8 via eno1
Apr 14 20:51:14 yorktown.both.org dhcpd[1385]: DHCPACK on 192.168.0.8 to
e8:40:f2:3d:0e:a8 via eno1
<SNIP>
```

Figure 35-2. *systemd displays significantly more information about services than the old SystemV*

Having all of this information available in a single command is empowering and simplifies the problem determination process for me. I get more information right at the start. I not only see that the service is up and running but some of the most recent log entries as well. The information supplied by this command gives me a more complete picture of how this particular service is faring.

systemd Standardizes Configuration

One of the problems I have had over the years is that, even though "Linux is Linux," not all distributions stored their configuration files in the same places or used the same names or even formats. With the huge numbers of Linux hosts in the world these days, that lack of standardization is a problem. I have also encountered horrible config files and SystemV startup files created by developers who were trying to jump on the Linux bandwagon and had no idea how to create software for Linux and especially not for services that required inclusion in the Linux startup sequence.

The systemd unit files standardize configuration and enforce a startup methodology and organization that provides a level of safety from poorly written SystemV start scripts. They also provide tools the SysAdmin can use to monitor and manage services.

Lennart Poettering wrote a short blog post describing the systemd standard names and locations for common critical configuration files.[5] This standardization makes the SysAdmin's job easier, and it also makes automating administrative tasks easier in environments with multiple Linux distributions. Developers benefit from this standardization as well.

Sometimes, the Pain

All undertakings as massive as replacing and extending an entire init system cause some levels of pain during the transition. I don't mind learning the new commands and how to create configuration files of various types such as targets, timers, and so on. It does take some work, but I think the results are well worth the effort.

New configuration files and changes in the sub-systems that own and manage them can also seem daunting at first. Not to mention the fact that sometimes new tools such as systemd-resolvd can break the way things have worked for a long time as I point out in my article, "Resolve systemd-resolved name-service failures with Ansible."[6]

It is tools like scripts and Ansible that can mitigate the pain while we wait for the changes to arrive that resolve the pain.

---

[5] Poettering, Lennart, `http://0pointer.de/blog/projects/the-new-configuration-files`

[6] Both, David, "Resolve systemd-resolved name-service failures with Ansible," `https://opensource.com/article/21/4/systemd-resolved`

Because this wholesale replacement is such a massive undertaking, the developers of systemd have been working in stages for several years and replacing various parts of the init system as well as services and tools that were not parts of the init system but that should have been. Many of the new capabilities of systemd are made possible only by the tight integration of systemd with the services and other tools used to manage modern Linux systems.

Although there has been some pain along the way, and there will undoubtedly be more, I think the long-term plan and goals are good ones. The advantages of systemd that I have experienced for myself are quite significant.

There is no nefarious plan to take over the world, just one to bring service management into the twenty-first century.

systemd Tasks

Let's look at what systemd actually consists of. Depending upon the options used during the compile process – which we will not consider in this series – it can have as many as 69 binary executables that perform the following tasks, among others:

- The systemd program runs as PID 1 and provides system startup of as many services in parallel as possible, which, as a side effect, speeds overall startup times. It also manages the shutdown sequence.

- The systemctl program provides a user interface for service management.

- Support for SystemV and LSB start scripts for backward compatibility.

- Service management and reporting that provides more service status data than SystemV.

- Tools for basic system configuration, such as hostname, date, locale, maintaining a list of logged-in users and running containers and virtual machines, system accounts, runtime directories and settings, and daemons to manage simple network configuration, network time synchronization, log forwarding, and name resolution.

- Socket management.

- System timers that provide advanced cron-like capabilities to include running a script at times relative to system boot, systemd startup, the last time the timer itself was started, and more.

- A tool to analyze dates and times used in timer expressions.

- Mounting and unmounting of filesystems with hierarchical awareness that allows safer cascading of mounted filesystems.

- Positive creation and management of temporary files including deletion.

- Interface to D-Bus that provides the ability to run scripts when devices are plugged in or removed. This allows all devices, whether pluggable or not, to be treated as plug and play, which considerably simplifies device handling.

- A tool to analyze the startup sequence that can be used in locating those services that take the most time.

- Journals for storing system log messages and tools for managing the journals.

Architecture

Those tasks and more are supported by a number of daemons, control programs, and configuration files. In Figure 35-3 we can see many of the components belonging to systemd. This is a simplified diagram designed to provide a high-level overview, so it does not include all of the individual programs or files. Nor does it provide any insight into data flow, which is so complex as to be a useless exercise within the context of this course.

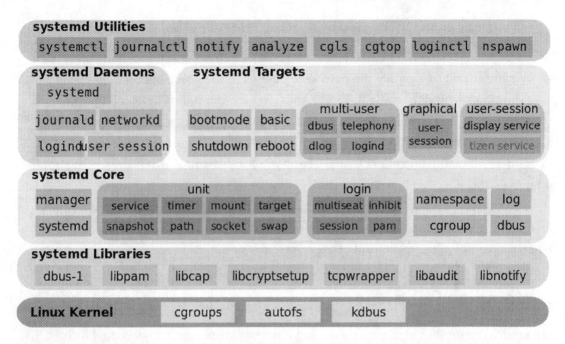

Figure 35-3. *"Architecture of systemd" by Shmuel Csaba Otto Traian, licensed under Creative Commons Attribution-ShareAlike 3.0 Unported,* `https://creativecommons.org/licenses/by-sa/3.0/deed.en`

A full exposition of systemd would take a book all on its own. We do not need to understand all of the details of how the systemd components shown in Figure 35-3 fit together, so our explorations will consist of those programs and components that enable us to manage various Linux services and to deal with log files and journals. But we can see that systemd is not the monolithic monstrosity it is purported to be by some of its critics.

Linux Startup with systemd

The complete process that takes a Linux host from an off state to a running state is complex, but it is open and knowable. Before we get into the details, a quick overview of the time the host hardware is turned on until the system is ready for a user to log in will help orient us. Most of the time we hear about "the boot process" as a single entity, but it is not. There are, in fact, three parts to the complete boot and startup process:

- Hardware boot, which initializes the system hardware

- Linux boot, which loads the Linux kernel and systemd

- Linux startup in which systemd makes the host ready for productive work

It is important to separate the hardware boot from the Linux boot process from the Linux startup and to explicitly define the demarcation points between them. Understanding these differences and what part each plays in getting a Linux system to a state where it can be productive makes it possible to manage these processes and to better determine the portion in which a problem is occurring during what most people refer to as "boot."

The startup process follows the boot process and brings the Linux computer up to an operational state in which it is usable for productive work. The startup process begins when the kernel transfers control of the host to systemd.

systemd as PID 1

systemd is the mother of all processes, and it is responsible for bringing the Linux host up to a state in which productive work can be done. systemd is PID 1. Some of its functions, which are far more extensive than the old SystemV init program, are to manage many aspects of a running Linux host, including mounting filesystems and starting and managing system services required to have a productive Linux host. Any of systemd's tasks that are not related to the startup sequence are outside the scope of this chapter, but we will explore some of them in later chapters of this series.

First, systemd mounts the filesystems as defined by /etc/fstab, including any swap files or partitions. At this point it can access the configuration files located in /etc, including its own. It uses its configuration link, /etc/systemd/system/default.target, to determine which state or target into which it should boot the host. The default.target file is a symbolic link to the true target file. For a desktop workstation, this is typically going to be the graphical.target, which is equivalent to runlevel 5 in SystemV. For a server, the default is more likely to be the multi-user.target, which is most likely runlevel 3 in SystemV. The emergency.target is similar to single-user mode. Targets and services are systemd units.

Figure 35-4 is a comparison of the systemd targets with the old SystemV startup runlevels. The systemd target aliases are provided by systemd for backward compatibility. The target aliases allow scripts – and many SysAdmins – to use SystemV commands like init 3 to change runlevels. The SystemV commands are forwarded to systemd for interpretation and execution.

systemd targets	run level	target aliases	Description
default.target			This target is always aliased with a symbolic link to either multi-user.target or graphical.target. systemd always uses the default.target to start the system. The default.target should never be aliased to halt.target, poweroff.target, or reboot.target.
graphical.target	5	runlevel5.target	Multi-user.target with a GUI.
	4	runlevel4.target	Unused. Runlevel 4 was identical to runlevel 3 in the SystemV world. This target could be created and customized to start local services without changing the default multi-user.target.
multi-user.target	3	runlevel3.target	All services running but command line interface (CLI) only.
	2	runlevel2.target	Multiuser, without NFS but all other non-GUI services running.
rescue.target	1	runlevel1.target	A basic system including mounting the filesystems with only the most basic services running and a rescue shell on the main console.
emergency.target	S		Single user mode. No services are running; filesystems are not mounted. This is the most basic level of operation with only an emergency shell running on the main console for the user to interact with the system.
halt.target			Halts the system without powering it down.
reboot.target	6	runlevel6.target	Reboot
poweroff.target	0	runlevel0.target	Halts the system and turns the power off.

Figure 35-4. *Comparison of SystemV runlevels with systemd targets and some target aliases*

Each target has a set of dependencies described in its configuration file. systemd starts the required dependencies. These dependencies are the services required to run the Linux host at a specific level of functionality. When all of the dependencies listed in the target configuration file are loaded and running, the system is running at that target level. Figure 35-4 shows targets with the least functionality toward the bottom of the table and those with the most functionality at the top of the table.

systemd also looks at the legacy SystemV init directories to see if any startup files exist there. If so, systemd used those as configuration files to start the services described by the files.

Figure 35-5 is copied directly from the bootup man page. It shows a map of the general sequence of events during systemd startup and the basic ordering requirements to ensure a successful startup.

The sysinit.target and basic.target targets can be considered as checkpoints in the startup process. Although systemd has as one of its design goals to start system services in parallel, there are still certain services and functional targets that must be started before other services and targets can be started. These checkpoints cannot be passed until all of the services and targets required by that checkpoint are fulfilled.

The sysinit.target is reached when all of the units on which it depends are completed. All of those units, mounting filesystems, setting up swap files, starting udev, setting the random generator seed, initiating low-level services, and setting up cryptographic services if one or more filesystems are encrypted, must be completed, but within the sysinit.target those tasks can be performed in parallel.

The sysinit.target starts up all of the low-level services and units required for the system to be marginally functional and that are required to enable moving on to the basic.target.

After the sysinit.target is fulfilled, systemd next starts all the units required to fulfill the next target. The basic target provides some additional functionality by starting units that are required for all of the next targets. These include setting up things like paths to various executable directories, communication sockets, and timers.

Finally, the user-level targets, multi-user.target or graphical.target, can be initialized. The multi-user.target must be reached before the graphical target dependencies can be met. The underlined targets in Figure 35-5 are the usual startup targets. When one of these targets is reached, then startup has completed. If the multi-user.target is the default, then you should see a text-mode login on the console. If graphical.target is the default, then you should see a graphical login; the specific GUI login screen you see will depend upon the default display manager.

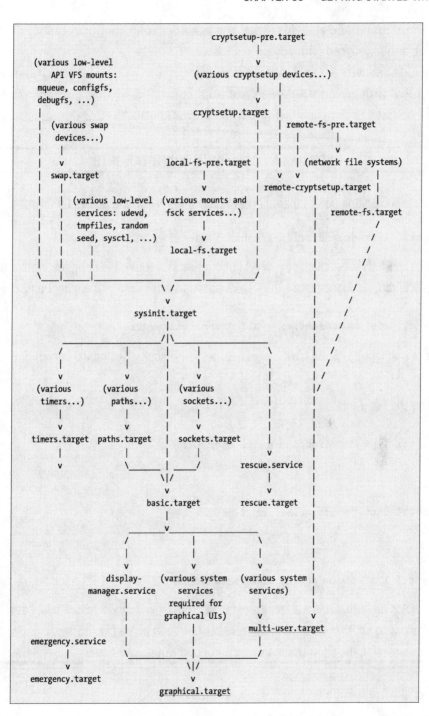

Figure 35-5. *The systemd startup map*

The bootup man page also describes and provides maps of the boot into the initial RAM disk and the systemd shutdown process.

systemd also provides a tool that list dependencies of a complete startup or for a specified unit. A unit is a controllable systemd resource entity that can range from a specific service such as httpd or sshd to timers, mounts, sockets, and more.

EXPERIMENT 35-1: EXPLORING TARGETS

Try the following commands as the root user and scroll through the results for each:

 # systemctl list-dependencies graphical.target

Notice that this fully expands the top-level target units list required to bring the system up to the graphical target run mode. Use the --all option to expand all of the other units as well:

 # systemctl list-dependencies --all graphical.target

You can search for strings such as "target," "slice," and "socket" using the search tools of the less command.

So now try the following:

 # systemctl list-dependencies multi-user.target

and

 # systemctl list-dependencies local-fs.target

and

 # systemctl list-dependencies dbus.service

This tool helps me visualize the specifics of the startup dependencies for the host I am currently working on. I am sure that your curiosity has been piqued, so go ahead and spend some time exploring the startup tree for one or more of your Linux hosts.

Be careful – the systemctl man page contains this note:

Note that this command [systemctl] only lists units currently loaded into memory by the service manager. In particular, this command is not suitable to get a comprehensive list at all reverse dependencies on a specific unit, as it won't list the dependencies declared by units currently not loaded.

Even before we have gotten very deep into systemd, we have already discovered that it is both powerful and complex. It is also starting to be apparent that systemd is not a single huge monolithic binary executable file. Rather, we can see that it is composed of many smaller components and sub-commands that are designed to perform specific tasks.

Exploring Startup

In this section we begin to explore the files and tools that are used to manage the Linux startup sequence. We directly explore the systemd startup sequence, how to change the default startup target (runlevel in SystemV terms), and how to manually switch to a different target without going through a reboot. We begin to familiarize ourselves with two important systemd tools. The first is the systemctl command, which is our primary means of interacting with systemd and sending it commands. The second is journalctl, which provides us access to the systemd journals which that huge amounts of system history data such as kernel and service messages both informational and errors.

GRUB

Before we can observe the startup sequence, we need to do a couple things to make the boot and startup sequences open and visible. Normally most distributions use a startup animation or splash screen to hide the detailed messages that can be displayed during startup and shutdown of a modern Linux host. This is called the Plymouth boot screen for Red Hat–based distros. Those hidden messages can provide a great deal of information about startup and shutdown to a SysAdmin looking for information to troubleshoot a bug or to just learn about the startup sequence. We can change this using the GRUB (Grand Unified Boot Loader) configuration.

The main GRUB configuration file is /boot/grub2/grub.cfg, but we do not change that file because it can get overwritten when the kernel is updated to a new version. Instead, we make modifications to the /etc/default/grub local configuration file. The contents of this file are used to modify the default settings of grub.cfg.

EXPERIMENT 35-2: LOOKING AT /ETC/DEFAULT/GRUB

Start by looking at the current unmodified version of the /etc/default/grub file:

```
[root@studentvm1 ~]# cd /etc/default ; cat grub
GRUB_TIMEOUT=5
GRUB_DISTRIBUTOR="$(sed 's, release .*$,,g' /etc/system-release)"
GRUB_DEFAULT=saved
GRUB_DISABLE_SUBMENU=true
GRUB_TERMINAL_OUTPUT="console"
GRUB_CMDLINE_LINUX="resume=/dev/mapper/fedora_studentvm1-swap rd.lvm.
lv=fedora_studentvm1/root rd.lvm.lv=fedora_studentvm1/swap rd.lvm.lv=fedora_
studentvm1/usr rhgb quiet"
GRUB_DISABLE_RECOVERY="true"
[root@studentvm1 default]#
```

Your GRUB file should look like this. It can be easily changed, but don't make any just yet.

Chapter 6 of the GRUB documentation[7] contains a complete listing of all the possible entries in the /etc/default/grub file, but there are a couple that we should look at here. I always change GRUB_TIMEOUT, the number of seconds for the GRUB menu countdown, from five to ten, which gives a bit more time to respond to the GRUB menu before the countdown hits zero.

The GRUB_CMDLINE_LINUX line can be changed too. This line lists the command-line parameters that are passed to the kernel at boot time. I usually delete the last two parameters on this line. The rhgb parameter stands for Red Hat Graphical Boot, and it causes the little graphical animation of the Fedora icon to display during the kernel initialization instead of showing boot-time messages. The quiet parameter prevents the display of the startup messages that document the progress of the startup and any errors that might occur.

---

[7] Gnu.org, GRUB, www.gnu.org/software/grub/manual/grub

EXPERIMENT 35-3: CHANGE THE GRUB CONFIGURATION

Use the text editor to delete both "rhgb" and "quiet" because SysAdmins need to be able
to see these messages. If something goes wrong during boot, the messages displayed on the
screen can point us to the cause of the problem.

Change these two lines as described so that your GRUB file looks like this:

```
[root@studentvm1 default]# cat grub
GRUB_TIMEOUT=10
GRUB_DISTRIBUTOR="$(sed 's, release .*$,,g' /etc/system-release)"
GRUB_DEFAULT=saved
GRUB_DISABLE_SUBMENU=true
GRUB_TERMINAL_OUTPUT="console"
GRUB_CMDLINE_LINUX="resume=/dev/mapper/fedora_studentvm1-swap rd.lvm.
lv=fedora_studentvm1/root rd.lvm.lv=fedora_studentvm1/swap rd.lvm.lv=fedora_
studentvm1/usr"
GRUB_DISABLE_RECOVERY="false"
[root@studentvm1 default]#
```

The GRUB_CMDLINE_LINUX= line is wrapped in the preceding code and may be in your
terminal session, but it is a single line in the file.

The grub2-mkconfig program is used to generate the grub.cfg configuration file using the
contents of the /etc/default/grub file to modify some of the default GRUB settings. The grub2-
mkconfig program sends its output to STDOUT. It has a -o option that allows you to specify
a file to send the data stream to, but it is just as easy to use redirection. Run the following
command to update the /boot/grub2/grub.cfg configuration file:

```
[root@studentvm1 grub2]# grub2-mkconfig > /boot/grub2/grub.cfg
Generating grub configuration file ...
Found linux image: /boot/vmlinuz-4.18.9-200.fc28.x86_64
Found initrd image: /boot/initramfs-4.18.9-200.fc28.x86_64.img
Found linux image: /boot/vmlinuz-4.17.14-202.fc28.x86_64
Found initrd image: /boot/initramfs-4.17.14-202.fc28.x86_64.img
Found linux image: /boot/vmlinuz-4.16.3-301.fc28.x86_64
Found initrd image: /boot/initramfs-4.16.3-301.fc28.x86_64.img
Found linux image: /boot/vmlinuz-0-rescue-7f12524278bd40e9b10a085bc82dc504
```

Found initrd image: /boot/initramfs-0-rescue-7f12524278bd40e9b10a085bc82
dc504.img
done
[root@studentvm1 grub2]#

Now reboot your VM to view the startup messages that would otherwise be hidden behind the
Plymouth boot animation.

But what if you need to view the startup messages and have not disabled the Plymouth boot
animation or if you have but the messages stream by too fast to read? Which they do.

There are a couple options and both involve log files and systemd journals, which are your
friends. You can use the less command to view the contents of the /var/log/messages file.
This file contains boot and startup messages as well as messages generated by the operating
system during normal operation. You can also use the journalctl command without any options
to view the systemd journal, which contains essentially the same information:

```
[root@studentvm1 grub2]# journalctl
-- Logs begin at Sat 2020-01-11 21:48:08 EST, end at Fri 2020-04-03
08:54:30 EDT. --
Jan 11 21:48:08 f31vm.both.org kernel: Linux version 5.3.7-301.fc31.x86_64
(mockbuild@bkernel03.phx2.fedoraproject.org) (gcc version 9.2.1 20190827
(Red Hat 9.2.1-1) (GCC)) #1 SMP Mon Oct >
Jan 11 21:48:08 f31vm.both.org kernel: Command line: BOOT_IMAGE=(hd0,msdos1)/
vmlinuz-5.3.7-301.fc31.x86_64 root=/dev/mapper/VG01-root ro resume=/dev/
mapper/VG01-swap rd.lvm.lv=VG01/root rd>
Jan 11 21:48:08 f31vm.both.org kernel: x86/fpu: Supporting XSAVE feature
0x001: 'x87 floating point registers'
Jan 11 21:48:08 f31vm.both.org kernel: x86/fpu: Supporting XSAVE feature
0x002: 'SSE registers'
Jan 11 21:48:08 f31vm.both.org kernel: x86/fpu: Supporting XSAVE feature
0x004: 'AVX registers'
Jan 11 21:48:08 f31vm.both.org kernel: x86/fpu: xstate_offset[2]:   576,
xstate_sizes[2]:   256
Jan 11 21:48:08 f31vm.both.org kernel: x86/fpu: Enabled xstate features 0x7,
context size is 832 bytes, using 'standard' format.
Jan 11 21:48:08 f31vm.both.org kernel: BIOS-provided physical RAM map:
Jan 11 21:48:08 f31vm.both.org kernel: BIOS-e820: [mem 0x0000000000000000-0
x000000000009fbff] usable
```

```
Jan 11 21:48:08 f31vm.both.org kernel: BIOS-e820: [mem 0x000000000009fc00-0
x000000000009ffff] reserved
Jan 11 21:48:08 f31vm.both.org kernel: BIOS-e820: [mem 0x00000000000f0000-0
x00000000000fffff] reserved
<SNIP>
```

I have truncated this data stream because it can be hundreds of thousands or even millions of lines long. The journal listing on my primary workstation is 1,188,482 lines long as I write this, and my StudentVM1 host has 262,778 lines.

You can navigate with the arrow and Page Up/Down keys. Uppercase "G" takes you to the end of the data stream.

Explore this journal data because there is a lot of information that can be very useful when performing problem determination. Knowing what this data looks like for a normal boot and startup can help you locate problems when they do occur.

We will discuss systemd journals, the journalctl command, and how to sort through all of that data to find what you want in more detail in Chapter 36.

After the kernel is loaded into memory by GRUB, it must first extract itself from the compressed version of the file before it can perform any useful work. After the kernel has extracted itself and started running, it loads systemd and turns control over to it.

This is the end of the boot process. At this point, the Linux kernel and systemd are running but unable to perform any productive tasks for the end user because nothing else is running, no shell to provide a command line, no background processes to manage the network or other communication links, and nothing that enables the computer to perform any productive function.

It is now the function of systemd to load the functional units required to bring the system up to a selected target run state.

Targets

A systemd target represents the current or desired run state of a Linux system. Targets define the services that must be present for the system to be running and active in that state. Figure 35-4 shows the possible run state targets of a Linux system using systemd. As we saw in Figure 35-5 and in the systemd bootup man page (man bootup), there are other, intermediate targets that are required to enable various necessary services. These can include swap.target, timers.target, local-fs.target, and more. Some targets, like the basic.target, are used as checkpoints to ensure that all the required services are up and running before moving on to the next higher-level target.

Unless otherwise changed at boot time by using the GRUB menu, systemd always starts the default.target. The default.target file is a symbolic link to the true target file. For a desktop workstation, this is typically going to be the graphical.target, which is equivalent to runlevel 5 in SystemV. For a server, the default is more likely to be the multi-user.target, which is like runlevel 3 in SystemV. The emergency.target is similar to single-user mode. Targets and services are systemd units.

Each target has a set of dependencies described in its configuration file. systemd starts the required dependencies. These dependencies are the services required to run the Linux host at a specific level of functionality. When all of the dependencies listed in the target configuration file are loaded and running, the system is running at that target level.

About the Current Target

Many Linux distributions default to installing a GUI desktop interface so that the installed systems can be used as workstations. I always install from a Fedora live boot USB drive with either Xfce or LXDE desktops. Even when installing a server or another infrastructure type of host such as ones I use for routers and firewalls, I use one of these installations that installs a GUI desktop.

It is possible to install a server without a desktop and that would be typical for data centers, but that does not meet my needs. That is not because I need the GUI desktop so much as that the LXDE installation includes many of the other tools I use that are not present in a default server installation. This means less work for me after the initial installation.

However, even having a GUI desktop installed does not mean it makes sense to always use it. I have a 16-port KVM that I can use to access the KVM interface of most of my Linux systems, but the vast majority of my interaction with them is via a remote SSH connection from my primary workstation. This way is more secure and uses fewer system resources to run the multi-user.target compared with the graphical.target.

EXPERIMENT 35-4: EXPLORING TARGETS AND RUNLEVELS

First, let's check the default target to verify that it is the graphical.target:

```
[root@studentvm1 ~]# systemctl get-default
graphical.target
[root@studentvm1 ~]#
```

Now let's verify the currently running target. It should be the same as the default target. We can still use the old method, which displays the old SystemV runlevels. Note that the previous runlevel is on the left and is N, which means None indicating that the runlevel has not been changed since the host was booted. The number 5 indicates the current target as defined in the old SystemV terminology:

```
[root@studentvm1 ~]# runlevel
N 5
[root@studentvm1 ~]#
```

The man page for runlevel indicates that runlevels are obsolete and provides a conversion table. We can also use the systemd method. There is no one-line answer here, but it does provide the answer in systemd terms:

```
[root@studentvm1 ~]# systemctl list-units --type target
UNIT                     LOAD   ACTIVE SUB    DESCRIPTION
basic.target             loaded active active Basic System
cryptsetup.target        loaded active active Local Encrypted Volumes
getty.target             loaded active active Login Prompts
graphical.target         loaded active active Graphical Interface
local-fs-pre.target      loaded active active Local File Systems (Pre)
local-fs.target          loaded active active Local File Systems
multi-user.target        loaded active active Multi-User System
network-online.target    loaded active active Network is Online
network.target           loaded active active Network
nfs-client.target        loaded active active NFS client services
nss-user-lookup.target   loaded active active User and Group Name Lookups
paths.target             loaded active active Paths
remote-fs-pre.target     loaded active active Remote File Systems (Pre)
remote-fs.target         loaded active active Remote File Systems
rpc_pipefs.target        loaded active active rpc_pipefs.target
```

```
slices.target          loaded active active Slices
sockets.target         loaded active active Sockets
sshd-keygen.target     loaded active active sshd-keygen.target
swap.target            loaded active active Swap
sysinit.target         loaded active active System Initialization
timers.target          loaded active active Timers

LOAD   = Reflects whether the unit definition was properly loaded.
ACTIVE = The high-level unit activation state, i.e. generalization of SUB.
SUB    = The low-level unit activation state, values depend on unit type.

21 loaded units listed. Pass --all to see loaded but inactive units, too.
To show all installed unit files use 'systemctl list-unit-files'.
[root@studentvm1 ~]#
```

This shows all of the currently loaded and active targets. We can also see the graphical.target and the multi-user.target. The multi-user.target is required before the graphical.target can be loaded. In this example the graphical.target is active.

Switching to a Different Target

Making the switch to the multi-user.target is easy:

```
[root@studentvm1 ~]# systemctl isolate multi-user.target
```

The display should now change from the GUI desktop or login screen to a virtual console login. Log in and list the currently active systemd units to verify that the graphical.target is no longer running:

```
[root@studentvm1 ~]# systemctl list-units --type target
```

Be sure to use the runlevel command to verify that it shows both previous and current "runlevels":

```
[root@studentvm1 ~]# runlevel
5 3
```

Changing the Default Target

Now let's change the default target to multi-user.target so that it will always boot into the multi-user.target for a console command-line interface rather than a GUI desktop interface. As the root user on your test host, change to the directory in which systemd configuration is maintained and do a quick listing:

```
[root@studentvm1 ~]# cd /etc/systemd/system/ ; ll
drwxr-xr-x. 2 root root 4096 Apr 25  2018  basic.target.wants
<SNIP>
lrwxrwxrwx. 1 root root   36 Aug 13 16:23  default.target -> /lib/systemd/
system/graphical.target
lrwxrwxrwx. 1 root root   39 Apr 25  2018  display-manager.service -> /usr/
lib/systemd/system/lightdm.service
drwxr-xr-x. 2 root root 4096 Apr 25  2018  getty.target.wants
drwxr-xr-x. 2 root root 4096 Aug 18 10:16  graphical.target.wants
drwxr-xr-x. 2 root root 4096 Apr 25  2018  local-fs.target.wants
drwxr-xr-x. 2 root root 4096 Oct 30 16:54  multi-user.target.wants
<SNIP>
[root@studentvm1 system]#
```

I have shortened this listing to highlight a few important things that will help us understand how systemd manages the boot process. You should be able to see the entire list of directories and links on your VM.

The default.target entry is a symbolic link (symlink, soft link) to the directory /lib/systemd/system/graphical.target. List that directory to see what else is there:

```
[root@studentvm1 system]# ll /lib/systemd/system/ | less
```

You should see files, directories, and more links in this listing, but look specifically for multi-user.target and graphical.target. Now display the contents of default.target, which is a link to /lib/systemd/system/graphical.target:

```
[root@studentvm1 system]# cat default.target
#  SPDX-License-Identifier: LGPL-2.1+
#
#  This file is part of systemd.
#
#  systemd is free software; you can redistribute it and/or modify it
#  under the terms of the GNU Lesser General Public License as published by
#  the Free Software Foundation; either version 2.1 of the License, or
#  (at your option) any later version.

[Unit]
Description=Graphical Interface
Documentation=man:systemd.special(7)
```

```
Requires=multi-user.target
Wants=display-manager.service
Conflicts=rescue.service rescue.target
After=multi-user.target rescue.service rescue.target display-manager.service
AllowIsolate=yes
[root@studentvm1 system]#
```

This link to the graphical.target file describes all of the prerequisites and needs that the graphical user interface requires. We will explore at least some of these options in the next chapter in this series.

To enable the host to boot to multiuser mode, we need to delete the existing link and then create a new one that points to the correct target. Make /etc/systemd/system the PWD if it is not already:

```
[root@studentvm1 system]# rm -f default.target
[root@studentvm1 system]# ln -s /lib/systemd/system/multi-user.target
default.target
```

List the default.target link to verify that it links to the correct file:

```
[root@studentvm1 system]# ll default.target
lrwxrwxrwx 1 root root 37 Nov 28 16:08 default.target -> /lib/systemd/system/
multi-user.target
[root@studentvm1 system]#
```

If your link does not look exactly like that, delete it and try again. List the content of the default.target link:

```
[root@studentvm1 system]# cat default.target
#  SPDX-License-Identifier: LGPL-2.1+
#
#  This file is part of systemd.
#
#  systemd is free software; you can redistribute it and/or modify it
#  under the terms of the GNU Lesser General Public License as published by
#  the Free Software Foundation; either version 2.1 of the License, or
#  (at your option) any later version.

[Unit]
Description=Multi-User System
```

```
Documentation=man:systemd.special(7)
Requires=basic.target
Conflicts=rescue.service rescue.target
After=basic.target rescue.service rescue.target
AllowIsolate=yes
[root@studentvm1 system]#
```

The default.target – which is really a link to the multi-user.target at this point – now has different requirements in the [Unit] section. It does not require the graphical display manager.

Reboot.

Your VM should boot to the console login for virtual console 1, which is identified on the display as tty1. Now that you know what is necessary to change the default target, change it back to the graphical.target using a command designed for the purpose. Let's first check the current default target:

```
[root@studentvm1 ~]# systemctl get-default
multi-user.target
[root@studentvm1 ~]# systemctl set-default graphical.target
Removed /etc/systemd/system/default.target.
Created symlink /etc/systemd/system/default.target → /usr/lib/systemd/
system/graphical.target.
[root@studentvm1 ~]#
```

Enter the following command to go directly to the graphical.target and the display manager login page without having to reboot:

```
[root@studentvm1 system]# systemctl isolate default.target
```

Log into the GUI desktop and verify that it is working as it should.

I am unsure why the term "isolate" was chosen for this sub-command by the developers of systemd. My current research indicates that it may refer to running the specified target but "isolating" and terminating all other targets that are not required to support this target. However, the effect is to switch targets from one run target to another, in this case from the multi-user target to the graphical target. The preceding command is equivalent to the old init 5 command in the days of SystemV start scripts and the init program.

Using systemd Units

In this section we will look at systemd units in more detail and the use of the systemctl command to explore and manage units. You will learn how to stop and disable units, and you will create a new systemd mount unit to mount a new filesystem and enable it to initiate during startup.

All of the experiments in this section should be performed as the root user unless otherwise specified. Some of the commands that simply list various systemd units can be performed by non-root users, but those that make changes cannot.

To prepare for one of the experiments in this section, install the sysstat package. The sysstat RPM installs several statistical tools that can be used for problem determination including SAR, or System Activity Reporter. This tool records many system performance data points at regular intervals, ten minutes by default. Rather than run as a daemon in the background, the sysstat package installs two systemd timers. One of the timers runs every ten minutes to collect data, and the other timer runs once a day to aggregate the daily data. We will look briefly at these timers, and then you will create your own timer in the section of Chapter 37 dedicated to systemd timers.

EXPERIMENT 35-5: INSTALLING SYSSTAT

Install the sysstat package with the following command:

```
[root@studentvm1 ~]# dnf -y install sysstat
```

The systemd Suite

systemd is more than just a single program. It is a large suite of programs all designed to work together in order to manage nearly every aspect of a running Linux system. A full exposition of systemd would take a book all on its own. We do not need to understand all of the details of how all systemd components fit together, so our explorations will consist of those programs and components that enable us to manage various Linux services and to deal with log files and journals.

Unit Files

The structure of systemd – outside of its executable files – is contained in its many configuration files. Although these files have different names and identifier extensions, they are all called "unit" files. The basis of everything systemd is units.

Unit files are ASCII plain text files that are accessible and that can be modified or created by the SysAdmin. There are a number of unit file types, each of which has its own man page. Figure 35-6 lists some of these unit file types by their file name extensions along with a short description of each.

systemd Unit	Description
.automount	The .automount units are used to implement on-demand, i.e., plug and play, and mounting of filesystem units in parallel during startup.
.device	The .device unit files define hardware and virtual devices that are exposed to the SysAdmin in the /dev/directory. Not all devices have unit files, Typically block devices such as hard drives, and network devices have unit files, as well as some others.
.mount	The .mount unit defines a mount point on the Linux filesystem directory structure.
.scope	This unit defines and manages a set of system processes. This unit is not configured using unit files, but is created programmatically. Per the systemd.scope man page, "The main purpose of scope units is grouping worker processes of a system service for organization and for managing resources."
.service	.service unit files define processes that are managed by systemd. These include service such as crond cups (Common Unix Printing System), IPTables, multiple logical volume management (LVM) services, NetworkManager, and more.
.slice	The .slice unit defines a "slice," which is a conceptual division of system resources that are related to a group of processes. You can think of all system resources as a pie and this subset of resources as a "slice" out of that pie.
.socket	.socket units define inter-process communication sockets such as network sockets.
.swap	Defines swap devices or files.
.target	.target units define groups of unit files that define startup synchronization points, runlevels, and services. Target units define the services and other units that must be active in order to start successfully.
.timer	This unit defines timers that can initiate program execution at specified times.

Figure 35-6. *A list of systemd unit file types*

We have already looked at targets from a functional point of view, and now we will explore other unit types, specifically service and mount units. In Chapter 36, we will look at timer units.

systemctl

Having already looked at its startup functions in a previous chapter, we start further exploration of systemd with its service management functions. systemd provides the systemctl command that is used to start and stop services, configure them to launch – or not – at system startup, and to monitor the current status of running services.

EXPERIMENT 35-6: GETTING FAMILIAR WITH SYSTEMCTL

In a terminal session as the root user, ensure that root's home directory (~) is the PWD. Let's start by just looking at units in various ways. List all of the loaded and active systemd units. systemctl automatically pipes its STDOUT data stream through the less pager so we do not need to do so:

```
[root@studentvm1 ~]# systemctl
  UNIT                                                        LOAD   ACTIVE SUB     DESCRIPTION >
  proc-sys-fs-binfmt_misc.automount                           loaded active running Arbitrary Ex>
  sys-devices-pci0000:00-0000:00:01.1-ata6-host5-target5:0:0-5:0:0:0-block-sr0.device  loaded
  active plugged    VBOX_CD-ROM
  sys-devices-pci0000:00-0000:00:02.0-drm-card0.device        loaded active plugged /sys/devices>
  sys-devices-pci0000:00-0000:00:03.0-net-enpos3.device       loaded active plugged 82540EM Giga>
  sys-devices-pci0000:00-0000:00:09.0-net-enpos9.device
<SNIP>
  sys-devices-platform-serial8250-tty-ttyS0.device            loaded active plugged /sys/devices>
  sys-devices-platform-serial8250-tty-ttyS1.device            loaded active plugged /sys/devices>
  sys-devices-platform-serial8250-tty-ttyS10.device           loaded active plugged /sys/devices>
  sys-devices-platform-serial8250-tty-ttyS11.device           loaded active plugged /sys/devices>
  sys-devices-platform-serial8250-tty-ttyS12.device           loaded active plugged /sys/devices>
  sys-devices-platform-serial8250-tty-ttyS13.device           loaded active plugged /sys/devices>
  sys-devices-platform-serial8250-tty-ttyS14.device           loaded active plugged /sys/devices>
<SNIP>
  -.mount                                                     loaded active mounted Root Mo>
  boot-efi.mount                                              loaded active mounted /boot/e>
  boot.mount                                                  loaded active mounted /boot
```

539

```
  dev-hugepages.mount                              loaded active mounted     Huge Pa>
  dev-mqueue.mount                                 loaded active mounted     POSIX M>
  home.mount                                       loaded active mounted     /home
  <SNIP>
  test.mount                                       loaded active mounted     /test
  tmp.mount                                        loaded active mounted     /tmp
  usr.mount                                        loaded active mounted     /usr
  var-lib-nfs-rpc_pipefs.mount                     loaded active mounted     RPC Pip>
  var.mount                                        loaded active mounted     /var   >
<SNIP - removed lots of lines of data from here>
  dnf-makecache.timer                              loaded active waiting     dnf mak>
  fstrim.timer                                     loaded active waiting     Discard>
  logrotate.timer                                  loaded active waiting     Daily r>
  plocate-updatedb.timer                           loaded active waiting     Update >
  raid-check.timer                                 loaded active waiting     Weekly >
  sysstat-collect.timer                            loaded active waiting     Run sys>
  sysstat-summary.timer                            loaded active waiting     Generat>
  systemd-tmpfiles-clean.timer                     loaded active waiting     Daily C>

LOAD   = Reflects whether the unit definition was properly loaded.
ACTIVE = The high-level unit activation state, i.e. generalization of SUB.
SUB    = The low-level unit activation state, values depend on unit type.

206 loaded units listed. Pass --all to see loaded but inactive units, too.
To show all installed unit files use 'systemctl list-unit-files'.
```

As you scroll through the data in your terminal session, look for some specific things. The first section lists devices such as hard drives, sound cards, network interface cards, and TTY devices. Another section shows the filesystem mountpoints. Other sections include various services and a list of all loaded and active targets.

The sysstat timers at the very bottom of the output are used to collect and generate daily system activity summaries for SAR, the System Activity Reporter. I covered SAR in Chapter 13 of Volume 1.

Near the very bottom, three lines describe the meanings of the status, loaded, active, and sub. Press q to exit from the pager.

Use the following command, as suggested by the last line of the preceding output, to see all units that are installed, whether they are loaded or not. I won't reproduce the output here, because you can scroll through them on your own. The systemctl program has an excellent tab completion facility that makes it easy to enter complex commands without the need to memorize each of the many options:

```
[root@studentvm1 ~]# systemctl list-unit-files
```

You will see that some units are disabled. Table 1 in the man page for systemctl lists and provides short descriptions of the entries you might see in this listing. Let's use the -t (type) option to view only the timer units:

```
[root@studentvm1 ~]# systemctl list-unit-files -t timer
UNIT FILE                        STATE
chrony-dnssrv@.timer             disabled
dnf-makecache.timer              enabled
fstrim.timer                     disabled
logrotate.timer                  disabled
logwatch.timer                   disabled
mdadm-last-resort@.timer         static
mlocate-updatedb.timer           enabled
sysstat-collect.timer            enabled
sysstat-summary.timer            enabled
systemd-tmpfiles-clean.timer static
unbound-anchor.timer             enabled
```

Or we could do the same thing like this, which provides considerably more detail:

```
[root@studentvm1 ~]# systemctl list-timers
```

We can list the mountpoints. There is no option to do systemctl list-mounts, but we can list the mountpoint unit files:

```
[root@studentvm1 ~]# systemctl list-unit-files -t mount
UNIT FILE                        STATE      PRESET
-.mount                          generated  -
boot-efi.mount                   generated  -
boot.mount                       generated  -
dev-hugepages.mount              static     -
dev-mqueue.mount                 static     -
home.mount                       generated  -
```

```
proc-fs-nfsd.mount                static    -
proc-sys-fs-binfmt_misc.mount disabled  disabled
run-vmblock\x2dfuse.mount         disabled  disabled
sys-fs-fuse-connections.mount static    -
sys-kernel-config.mount           static    -
sys-kernel-debug.mount            static    -
sys-kernel-tracing.mount          static    -
test.mount                        generated -
TestFS.mount                      generated -
tmp.mount                         generated -
usr.mount                         generated -
var-lib-nfs-rpc_pipefs.mount static    -
var.mount                         generated -

19 unit files listed
[root@studentvm1 ~]#
```

The STATE column in this data stream is interesting and requires a bit of explanation. The "generated" states indicate that the mount unit was generated on the fly during startup using the information in /etc/fstab. The program that generates these mount units is /lib/systemd/system-generators/systemd-fstab-generator along with other tools that generate a number of other unit types. The "static" mount units are for filesystems like /proc and /sys, and the files for these are located in the /usr/lib/systemd/system directory.

Now let's look at the service units. This command will show all services installed on the host whether they are active or not:

```
[root@studentvm1 ~]# systemctl --all -t service
```

At the bottom of this listing of service units, it displays 179 as the total number of loaded units on my host. Your number will very probably be different from that.

Unit files do not have a file name extension such as .unit to help identify them. Rather, we can generalize that most configuration files belonging to systemd are unit files of one type or another. The few remaining files are mostly .conf files located in /etc/systemd.

Unit files are stored in the /usr/lib/systemd directory and its subdirectories, while the /etc/systemd/ directory and its subdirectories contain symbolic links to the unit files necessary to the local configuration of this host. Let's explore this.

Make /etc/systemd the PWD and list its contents. Then make /etc/systemd/system the PWD and list its contents. Also list the contents of at least a couple of the subdirectories of the current PWD.

Let's explore one unit file. The default.target file determines which runlevel target to which the system will boot. In section "About the Current Target" of this chapter, we discussed how to change the default target from the GUI (graphical.target) to the command-line-only (multiuser) target. The default.target file on my test VM is simply a symlink to /usr/lib/systemd/system/graphical.target.

Examine the contents of the /etc/systemd/system/default.target file:

```
[root@studentvm1 system]# cat default.target
#   SPDX-License-Identifier: LGPL-2.1+
#
#   This file is part of systemd.
#
#   systemd is free software; you can redistribute it and/or modify it
#   under the terms of the GNU Lesser General Public License as published by
#   the Free Software Foundation; either version 2.1 of the License, or
#   (at your option) any later version.

[Unit]
Description=Graphical Interface
Documentation=man:systemd.special(7)
Requires=multi-user.target
Wants=display-manager.service
Conflicts=rescue.service rescue.target
After=multi-user.target rescue.service rescue.target display-manager.service
AllowIsolate=yes
```

Notice that it requires the multi-user.target. The graphical.target cannot be started if the multi-user.target is not already up and running. It also says it "wants" the display-manager.service unit. A "want" does not need to be fulfilled in order for the unit to be started successfully. If the "want" cannot be fulfilled, it will be ignored by systemd, and the rest of the target will be started regardless.

The subdirectories in /etc/systemd/system are lists of wants for various targets. Take a few minutes to explore the files and their contents in the /etc/systemd/system/graphical.target. wants directory.

The systemd.unit man page contains much good information about unit files, their structure, the sections into which they can be divided, and lists of the options that can be used. It also lists many of the unit types, all of which have man pages of their own. If you want to interpret a unit file, this would be one good place to start.

Service Units

Now that we know a bit about unit files and targets, let's explore some other units. Much of the time a Fedora installation installs and enables services that are not needed for normal operation for a particular host or, conversely, other services may need to be installed, enabled, and started. Services that are not needed for the Linux host to function as desired but that are installed and possibly running represent a security risk and should be stopped and disabled at the least and at best uninstalled.

EXPERIMENT 35-7: MANAGING SYSTEMD UNITS

The systemctl command is used to manage systemd units including services, targets, mounts, and more. Let's take a closer look at the list of services because we can easily find services that will never be used:

```
[root@studentvm1 ~]# systemctl --all -t service
UNIT                        LOAD       ACTIVE SUB      DESCRIPTION
<SNIP>
chronyd.service             loaded     active running NTP client/server
crond.service               loaded     active running Command Scheduler
cups.service                loaded     active running CUPS Scheduler
dbus-daemon.service         loaded     active running D-Bus System
Message Bus
<SNIP>
● ip6tables.service         not-found inactive dead   ip6tables.service
● ipset.service             not-found inactive dead   ipset.service
● iptables.service          not-found inactive dead   iptables.service
<SNIP>
firewalld.service           loaded     active   running firewalld -
dynamic firewall daemon
<SNIP>
```

● ntpd.service	not-found	inactive	dead	ntpd.service
● ntpdate.service	not-found	inactive	dead	ntpdate.service
pcscd.service	loaded	active	running	PC/SC Smart Card Daemon

I have pruned out all but a few lines of output from the command to save space. The services that show as "loaded active running" are obvious. The "not-found" services are ones of which systemd is aware but that are not installed on the Linux host. If you want to run those services, the packages that contain them must be installed first.

The pcscd.service unit is the PC/SC smart card daemon. Its function is to communicate with smart card readers. Many Linux hosts – including our virtual machines – have no need for such a reader or the service that is loaded and taking up memory and CPU resources. We can stop this service and also disable it so it will not start again on the next boot. First, we will simply check its status:

```
[root@studentvm1 ~]# systemctl status pcscd.service
● pcscd.service - PC/SC Smart Card Daemon
   Loaded: loaded (/usr/lib/systemd/system/pcscd.service; indirect; vendor
   preset: disabled)
   Active: active (running) since Fri 2019-05-10 11:28:42 EDT; 3 days ago
     Docs: man:pcscd(8)
 Main PID: 24706 (pcscd)
    Tasks: 6 (limit: 4694)
   Memory: 1.6M
   CGroup: /system.slice/pcscd.service
           └─24706 /usr/sbin/pcscd --foreground --auto-exit

May 10 11:28:42 studentvm1 systemd[1]: Started PC/SC Smart Card Daemon.
```

This data illustrates what I mean about the additional information provided by systemd; SystemV would tell us only that the service was running or not. Note that specifying the .service unit type is optional. Now stop and disable the service. Then recheck its status:

```
[root@studentvm1 ~]# systemctl stop pcscd ; systemctl disable pcscd
Warning: Stopping pcscd.service, but it can still be activated by:
  pcscd.socket
Removed /etc/systemd/system/sockets.target.wants/pcscd.socket.
[root@studentvm1 ~]# systemctl status pcscd
```

- pcscd.service - PC/SC Smart Card Daemon
    Loaded: loaded (/usr/lib/systemd/system/pcscd.service; indirect; vendor
    preset: disabled)
    Active: failed (Result: exit-code) since Mon 2019-05-13 15:23:15
    EDT; 48s ago
      Docs: man:pcscd(8)
 Main PID: 24706 (code=exited, status=1/FAILURE)

May 10 11:28:42 studentvm1 systemd[1]: Started PC/SC Smart Card Daemon.
May 13 15:23:15 studentvm1 systemd[1]: Stopping PC/SC Smart Card Daemon...
May 13 15:23:15 studentvm1 systemd[1]: pcscd.service: Main process exited,
code=exited, status=1/FAIL>
May 13 15:23:15 studentvm1 systemd[1]: pcscd.service: Failed with result
'exit-code'.
May 13 15:23:15 studentvm1 systemd[1]: Stopped PC/SC Smart Card Daemon.

The short log entry display for most services prevents us having to search through various log files to locate this type of information. Check the status of the system runlevel targets. Notice that specifying the "target" unit type is required for this:

[root@studentvm1 ~]# **systemctl status multi-user.target**
- multi-user.target - Multi-User System
    Loaded: loaded (/usr/lib/systemd/system/multi-user.target; static; vendor
    preset: disabled)
    Active: active since Thu 2019-05-09 13:27:22 EDT; 4 days ago
      Docs: man:systemd.special(7)

May 09 13:27:22 studentvm1 systemd[1]: Reached target Multi-User System.
[root@studentvm1 ~]# **systemctl status graphical.target**
- graphical.target - Graphical Interface
    Loaded: loaded (/usr/lib/systemd/system/graphical.target; indirect; vendor
    preset: disabled)
    Active: active since Thu 2019-05-09 13:27:22 EDT; 4 days ago
      Docs: man:systemd.special(7)

May 09 13:27:22 studentvm1 systemd[1]: Reached target Graphical Interface.
[root@studentvm1 ~]# **systemctl status default.target**
- graphical.target - Graphical Interface
    Loaded: loaded (/usr/lib/systemd/system/graphical.target; indirect; vendor
    preset: disabled)

```
    Active: active since Thu 2019-05-09 13:27:22 EDT; 4 days ago
      Docs: man:systemd.special(7)

May 09 13:27:22 studentvm1 systemd[1]: Reached target Graphical Interface.
```

Note that the default target is the graphical target. The status of any unit can be checked in this way.

Mounts the Old Way

A mount unit is one that defines all of the parameters required to mount a filesystem on a designated mountpoint. systemd can manage mount units with more flexibility while still using the /etc/fstab file for filesystem configuration and mounting purposes. systemd uses the systemd-fstab-generator tool to create transient mount units from the data in the fstab file.

Let's explore using a traditional mount setup and then convert that mount to a systemd mount unit. You have already done much of the work with previously created mountpoints and logical volumes, so we will use those.

EXPERIMENT 35-8: TRADITIONAL MOUNTS

There are already a mountpoint (/TestFS) and logical volumes left over from previous storage experimentation. We will use some of those for this experiment.

First, comment out any existing line for /TestFS in /etc/fstab. I have found anomalous results when doing this part of the experiment with an entry that does not target to the correct mountpoint.

Identify an available storage volume:

```
[root@studentvm1 ~]# lsblk -i
NAME                       MAJ:MIN RM  SIZE RO TYPE MOUNTPOINTS
sda                            8:0   0   60G  0 disk
|-sda1                         8:1   0    1M  0 part
|-sda2                         8:2   0    1G  0 part /boot
|-sda3                         8:3   0    1G  0 part /boot/efi
`-sda4                         8:4   0   58G  0 part
  |-fedora_studentvm1-root 253:0   0    2G  0 lvm  /
```

```
  |-fedora_studentvm1-usr  253:1   0   15G  0 lvm  /usr
  |-fedora_studentvm1-tmp  253:4   0    5G  0 lvm  /tmp
  |-fedora_studentvm1-var  253:5   0   10G  0 lvm  /var
  |-fedora_studentvm1-home 253:6   0    4G  0 lvm  /home
  `-fedora_studentvm1-test 253:7   0  500M  0 lvm  /test
sdb                          8:16   0   20G  0 disk
|-sdb1                       8:17   0    2G  0 part
|-sdb2                       8:18   0    2G  0 part
`-sdb3                       8:19   0   16G  0 part
  |-NewVG--01-TestVol1     253:2   0    4G  0 lvm
  `-NewVG--01-swap         253:3   0    2G  0 lvm
sdc                          8:32   0    2G  0 disk
`-NewVG--01-TestVol1       253:2   0    4G  0 lvm
sdd                          8:48   0    2G  0 disk
sr0                         11:0   1 1024M  0 rom
zram0                      252:0   0    8G  0 disk [SWAP
```

Let's use NewVG--01-TestVol1 for this experiment. Mount the filesystem manually. This overrides the entry for /TestFS in /etc/fstab:

```
[root@studentvm1 ~]# mount /dev/mapper/NewVG--01-TestVol1 /TestFS/
```

If you get the following message ...

```
mount: (hint) your fstab has been modified, but systemd still uses
       the old version; use 'systemctl daemon-reload' to reload.
```

...run the command as suggested:

```
[root@studentvm1 ~]# systemctl daemon-reload
```

Then view the results of your mount command:

```
[root@studentvm1 ~]# lsblk -i
NAME                     MAJ:MIN RM  SIZE RO TYPE MOUNTPOINTS
sda                          8:0    0   60G  0 disk
|-sda1                       8:1    0    1M  0 part
<SNIP>
sdb                          8:16   0   20G  0 disk
|-sdb1                       8:17   0    2G  0 part
|-sdb2                       8:18   0    2G  0 part
`-sdb3                       8:19   0   16G  0 part
```

```
  |-NewVG--01-TestVol1    253:2   0    4G  0 lvm  /TestFS
   `-NewVG--01-swap       253:3   0    2G  0 lvm
sdc                        8:32   0    2G  0 disk
`-NewVG--01-TestVol1      253:2   0    4G  0 lvm  /TestFS
sdd                        8:48   0    2G  0 disk
sr0                       11:0    1 1024M  0 rom
zram0                     252:0   0    8G  0 disk [SWAP]
[root@studentvm1 ~]#
```

We can see that the new filesystem is mounted in the proper location. List the mount unit files:

```
[root@studentvm1 ~]# systemctl list-unit-files -t mount
```

The result shows a generated entry for the /TestFS filesystem because a .mount file does not exist for it. The command systemctl status TestFS.mount does not display any information about our new filesystem either. We can also try this using wildcards with the systemctl status command:

```
[root@studentvm1 ~]# systemctl status *mount
● home.mount - /home
    Loaded: loaded (/etc/fstab; generated)
    Active: active (mounted) since Fri 2023-04-14 05:46:12 EDT; 3 days ago
     Where: /home
      What: /dev/mapper/fedora_studentvm1-home
      Docs: man:fstab(5)
            man:systemd-fstab-generator(8)
     Tasks: 0 (limit: 19130)
    Memory: 156.0K
       CPU: 6ms
    CGroup: /system.slice/home.mount

Apr 14 05:46:11 studentvm1 systemd[1]: Mounting home.mount - /home...
Apr 14 05:46:12 studentvm1 systemd[1]: Mounted home.mount - /home.

<SNIP>

● TestFS.mount - /TestFS
    Loaded: loaded (/proc/self/mountinfo)
    Active: active (mounted) since Mon 2023-04-17 12:21:28 EDT; 10s ago
     Where: /TestFS
      What: /dev/mapper/NewVG--01-TestVol1
```

The last command provides some very interesting information about the mounts on our system, and our new filesystem does show up. Filesystems like /home, /var, and /usr are identified as being generated from /etc/fstab, while our new filesystem simply shows that it is loaded and the location of the info file in the /proc/self/mountinfo file.

Now let's automate this mount. We will start by doing this the old-fashioned way and add an entry in /etc/fstab, and then we will do it the new way, which will allow us to learn about creating units and integrating them into the startup sequence.

Unmount the /TestFS filesystem. There is already an entry in /etc/fstab for the /TestFS mountpoint, so modify that entry to look like this:

```
/dev/mapper/NewVG--01-TestVol1   /TestFS        ext4    defaults        1 2
```

Now reload the systemd config and mount the filesystem with the simpler mount command and list the mount units again:

```
[root@studentvm1 ~]# systemctl daemon-reload
[root@studentvm1 ~]# mount /TestFS
[root@studentvm1 ~]# systemctl status TestFS.mount
● TestFS.mount - /TestFS
     Loaded: loaded (/etc/fstab; generated)
     Active: active (mounted) since Mon 2023-04-17 14:35:42 EDT; 17s ago
      Where: /TestFS
       What: /dev/mapper/NewVG--01-TestVol1
       Docs: man:fstab(5)
             man:systemd-fstab-generator(8)
```

Using other tools, verify that the filesystem is mounted and working properly.

Creating a Mount Unit

Mount units may be configured either with the traditional /etc/fstab file or with systemd units. Fedora uses the fstab file as it is created during the installation. However, systemd uses the systemd-fstab-generator program to translate the fstab file into systemd units for each entry in the fstab file. Now that we know we can use systemd .mount unit files for filesystem mounting, let's try that out. We will create a mount unit for this filesystem.

EXPERIMENT 35-9: CREATING A SYSTEMD MOUNT UNIT

In this experiment you will create a systemd mount unit for the filesystem and unmount /TestFS. Edit the /etc/fstab file and delete or comment out the TestFS line. Create a new file with the name TestFS.mount in the /etc/systemd/system directory. Edit it to contain the following configuration data. It is required that the unit file name and the name of the mountpoint be identical, or the mount will fail.

The Description line in the [Unit] section is for us humans, and it provides the name we see when we list mount units with `systemctl -t mount`. The data in the [Mount] section of this file contains essentially the same data that would be found in the fstab file:

```
# This mount unit is for the TestFS filesystem
# By David Both
# Licensed under GPL V2
# This file should be located in the /etc/systemd/system directory

[Unit]
Description=TestFS Mount

[Mount]
What=/dev/mapper/VG01-TestFS
Where=/TestFS
Type=ext4
Options=defaults

[Install]
WantedBy=multi-user.target
```

Enable the mount unit with this command:

```
[root@studentvm1 etc]# systemctl enable TestFS.mount
Created symlink /etc/systemd/system/multi-user.target.wants/TestFS.mount →
/etc/systemd/system/TestFS.mount.
```

This creates the symlink in the /etc/systemd/system directory, which will cause this mount unit to be mounted on all subsequent boots. The filesystem has not yet been mounted, so we need to "start" it in order to do so:

```
[root@studentvm1 ~]# systemctl start TestFS.mount
```

Now verify that the filesystem has been mounted:

```
[root@studentvm1 ~]# systemctl status TestFS.mount
● TestFS.mount - TestFS Mount
   Loaded: loaded (/etc/systemd/system/TestFS.mount; enabled; vendor preset:
   disabled)
   Active: active (mounted) since Sat 2020-04-18 09:59:53 EDT; 14s ago
    Where: /TestFS
     What: /dev/mapper/VG01-TestFS
    Tasks: 0 (limit: 19166)
   Memory: 76.0K
      CPU: 3ms
   CGroup: /system.slice/TestFS.mount

Apr 18 09:59:53 studentvm1 systemd[1]: Mounting TestFS Mount...
Apr 18 09:59:53 studentvm1 systemd[1]: Mounted TestFS Mount.
```

This experiment has been specifically about creating a unit file for a mount, but it can be applied to other types of unit files as well. The details will be different but the concepts are the same. Yes, I know it is still easier to add a line to the /etc/fstab file than it is to create this mount unit. But I use this as a good example of how to create a unit file because systemd does not have generators for every type of unit.

Chapter Summary

In this chapter we started with an overview of systemd, what it does, and why there is some controversy surrounding it. We saw that systemd provides more information for the SysAdmin and provides a greater level of standardization than SystemV. We also briefly explored the architecture of systemd.

We have explored the Linux systemd startup sequence enough to have a decent understanding and begun to learn about two important systemd tools, systemctl and journalctl. We have switched from one target to another and have changed the default target. We have looked at systemd units in more detail and the use of the systemctl command to explore systemd units. We also created a new systemd mount unit to mount a new filesystem and enabled it to initiate during startup.

But there is more to come in the next two chapters.

Exercises

Complete the following exercises to complete this chapter:

1. What was the impetus to replace SystemV and init as the startup program?

2. What function does systemd play during Linux startup?

3. What advantages does systemd have for the SysAdmin?

4. When does system boot end, and when does Linux startup begin?

5. What does GRUB do?

6. What function does the /etc/systemd/system/default.target perform, and how does that work?

7. What targets are currently loaded and active on your StudentVM1 host?

## CHAPTER 36

Advanced systemd Functions

Objectives

In this chapter you will learn

- To analyze systemd calendar and time spans

- How to use systemd journals for exploring and problem solving

- How to analyze systemd startup and configuration using analytic graphs and tools

- How to manage systemd startup

- To use systemd timers to launch programs in a manner similar to using cron

systemd Calendar and Time Spans

In our past encounters with systemd, we have seen that it uses calendar time, specifying one or more moments in time to trigger events such as a backup program and the manner in which entries in the journal are timestamped. systemd can also use time spans, which define the amount of time between two events but which are not directly tied to specific calendar times.

In this chapter we will look in more detail at the way in which time and date are used and specified. Because two slightly different, noncompatible formats can be used, it is important to identify these and how and when they can be used. We will also use time

© David Both 2023
D. Both, *Using and Administering Linux: Volume 2*, https://doi.org/10.1007/978-1-4842-9615-8_36

and the systemd journals to explore and manage Linux startup in detail. All of this is very dependent upon time and our understanding of how to read and specify it in the commands we use. So that's where we will start.

Definitions

Time-related commands in systemd use some terms that we need to understand more fully, so let's start with some definitions. The systemd.time(7) man page has a complete description of time and date expressions that can be used in timers and other systemd tools.

Absolute Timestamp

A single unambiguous and unique point in time as defined in the format YYYY-MM-DD HH:MM:SS. The timestamp format is used to specify points in time at which events are triggered by timers. An absolute timestamp can represent only a single point in time, such as 2025-04-15 13:21:05.

Accuracy

The quality of closeness to the true time – how close to the specified calendar time an event is triggered by a timer. The default accuracy for systemd timers is defined as the one-minute time span starting at the defined calendar time. An event specified to occur at the OnCalendar time of 09:52:17 might actually be triggered at any time between that and 09:53:17.

Calendar Event

One or more specific times specified by a systemd timestamp format YYYY-MM-DD HH:MM:SS. These can be a single point in time or a series of points that are well defined and for which the exact times can be calculated. Timestamps are also used by the systemd journals to mark each event with the exact time it occurred.

An exact moment in time as specified in systemd in the timestamp format YYYY-MM-DD HH:MM:SS. When only the YYYY-MM-DD portion is specified, the time defaults to 00:00:00. When only the HH:MM:SS portion is specified, the date is arbitrarily defined to be that of the next calendar instance of that time. If the time specified is before the current time today, the next instance will be tomorrow, and if the specified time is later than the current time, the next instance will be today. This is the format used for expression of the OnCalendar times in a systemd timer.

Recurring calendar events can be specified using special characters and formats to represent fields that have multiple value matches. For example, 2026-08-15..25 12:15:00 represents 12:15 p.m. of the 15th through the 25th of August 2026 and would trigger eleven matches. Calendar events can also be specified with an absolute timestamp.

Time Span

The amount of time between two events, the duration of something such as an event, or the time between two events. Time spans can be used in specifying the desired accuracy with which an event should be triggered by a timer as well as in defining the time to elapse between events. The following units are recognized:

- usec, us, μs
- msec, ms
- seconds, second, sec, s
- minutes, minute, min, m
- hours, hour, hr, h
- days, day, d
- weeks, week, w
- months, month, M (defined as 30.44 days)
- years, year, y (defined as 365.25 days)

Calendar Event Expressions

Calendar event expressions are a key component of tasks such as specifying time ranges for journal searches and triggering timers at desired repetitive times. systemd itself and its timers use a different style for time and date expressions than the format used in crontab. It is more flexible than crontab and allows fuzzy dates and times in the manner of the at command. It should also be familiar enough that it will be easy to understand.

The format for calendar event expressions using OnCalendar= is DOW YYYY-MM-DD HH:MM:SS. The DOW (day of week) is optional, and other fields can use an asterisk (*) to match any value for that position. If the time is not specified, it is assumed to be 00:00:00. If the date is not specified but the time is, the next match may be today or tomorrow depending upon the current time. All of the various calendar time expression formats are converted to a normalized form for use. The systemd-analyze calendar command shows the normalized form of the time expression.

systemd provides us with an excellent tool for validating and examining calendar events that are to be used in an expression. The systemd-analyze calendar tool will parse a calendar time event expression and provide the normalized form as well as other interesting information such as the date and time of the next "elapse," that is, match, and the approximate amount of time before the trigger time is reached.

The commands used in this section can be performed by non-root users, but the data displayed for some commands will not be as complete as for the root user. So I suggest you perform all of the experiments in this chapter as the root user.

Tip   The times for "Next elapse" and "UTC" will differ based on your local time zone.

Exploring systemd Time Syntax

Let's start with the syntax used with the systemd-analyze calendar command.

EXPERIMENT 36-1: SYSTEMD TIME SYNTAX

Start with a date in the future without a time. Because all of the date unit fields are explicitly specified, this is a one-time event:

```
[root@studentvm1 ~]$ systemd-analyze calendar 2030-06-17
   Original form: 2030-06-17
Normalized form: 2030-06-17 00:00:00
     Next elapse: Mon 2030-06-17 00:00:00 EDT
        (in UTC): Mon 2030-06-17 04:00:00 UTC
        From now: 7 years 1 month left
```

Now let's add a time. In this example the date and time are analyzed separately as nonrelated entities:

```
[root@studentvm1 system]# systemd-analyze calendar 2030-06-17 15:21:16
   Original form: 2030-06-17
Normalized form: 2030-06-17 00:00:00
    Next elapse: Mon 2030-06-17 00:00:00 EDT
       (in UTC): Mon 2030-06-17 04:00:00 UTC
       From now: 7 years 1 month left

   Original form: 15:21:16
Normalized form: *-*-* 15:21:16
    Next elapse: Tue 2023-04-25 15:21:16 EDT
       (in UTC): Tue 2023-04-25 19:21:16 UTC
       From now: 1h 40min left
[root@studentvm1 ~]$
```

To analyze the date and time as a single entity, enclose them together in quotes:

```
[root@studentvm1 system]# systemd-analyze calendar "2030-06-17 15:21:16"
Normalized form: 2030-06-17 15:21:16
    Next elapse: Mon 2030-06-17 15:21:16 EDT
       (in UTC): Mon 2030-06-17 19:21:16 UTC
       From now: 7 years 1 month left
```

Now specify a time earlier than the current time and one later. In this case the current time is 16:16 on 2019-05-15:

```
[root@studentvm1 ~]$ systemd-analyze calendar 15:21:16 22:15
   Original form: 15:21:16
Normalized form: *-*-* 15:21:16
    Next elapse: Fri 2019-05-17 15:21:16 EDT
       (in UTC): Fri 2019-05-17 19:21:16 UTC
       From now: 23h left

   Original form: 22:15
Normalized form: *-*-* 22:15:00
    Next elapse: Thu 2019-05-16 22:15:00 EDT
       (in UTC): Fri 2019-05-17 02:15:00 UTC
       From now: 5h 59min left
```

The `systemd-analyze calendar` tool does not work on timestamps. So things like "tomorrow" or "today" will cause errors when used with the calendar sub-command because they are timestamps rather than OnCalendar time formats:

```
[root@studentvm1 ~]$ systemd-analyze calendar "tomorrow"
Failed to parse calendar expression 'tomorrow': Invalid argument
Hint: this expression is a valid timestamp. Use 'systemd-analyze timestamp
"tomorrow"' instead?
```

The term "tomorrow" will always resolve to tomorrow's date and a time of 00:00:00. You must use the normalized expression format, "YYYY-MM-DD HH:MM:SS," for this tool to work in calendar mode. Despite this, the `systemd-analyze calendar` tool can still help you understand the structure of the calendar time expressions used by systemd timers. I recommend reading the systemd.time(7) man page for a more complete understanding of the time formats that can be used with systemd timers.

Timestamps

Whereas calendar times can be used to match single or multiple points in time, timestamps unambiguously represent a single point in time. For example, timestamps in the systemd journal refer to a precise moment in time when each logged event occurred:

```
[root@studentvm1 ~]$ journalctl -S today
Hint: You are currently not seeing messages from other users and the system.
      Users in groups 'adm', 'systemd-journal', 'wheel' can see all messages.
      Pass -q to turn off this notice.
Apr 25 13:40:11 studentvm1 systemd[1813]: Queued start job for default target
default.target.
Apr 25 13:40:11 studentvm1 systemd[1813]: Created slice app.slice - User
Application Slice.
Apr 25 13:40:11 studentvm1 systemd[1813]: Started grub-boot-success.timer -
Mark boot as successful after the user session has run 2 minutes.
Apr 25 13:40:11 studentvm1 systemd[1813]: Started systemd-tmpfiles-clean.
timer - Daily Cleanup of User's Temporary Directories.
Apr 25 13:40:11 studentvm1 systemd[1813]: Reached target paths.
target - Paths.
Apr 25 13:40:11 studentvm1 systemd[1813]: Reached target timers.
target - Timers.
```

```
Apr 25 13:40:11 studentvm1 systemd[1813]: Starting dbus.socket - D-Bus User
Message Bus Socket...
Apr 25 13:40:11 studentvm1 systemd[1813]: Listening on pipewire-pulse.
socket - PipeWire PulseAudio.
<SNIP>
Apr 25 13:45:26 studentvm1 systemd[1813]: Starting systemd-tmpfiles-clean.
service - Cleanup of User's Temporary Files and Directories...
Apr 25 13:45:26 studentvm1 systemd[1813]: Finished systemd-tmpfiles-clean.
service - Cleanup of User's Temporary Files and Directories.
```

The `systemd-analyze timestamp` command can be used to analyze timestamp expressions in the same manner that we analyzed calendar expressions. Let's look at one of these times from the journal data stream and one from a couple years in the past:

```
[root@studentvm1 ~]$ systemd-analyze timestamp "Apr 25 13:40:11"
  Original form: Apr 25 13:40:11
Normalized form: Tue 2023-04-25 13:40:11 EDT
       (in UTC): Tue 2023-04-25 17:40:11 UTC
   UNIX seconds: @1682444411
       From now: 3h 13min ago
[root@studentvm1 ~]$ systemd-analyze timestamp "Wed 2020-06-17 10:08:41"
  Original form: Wed 2020-06-17 10:08:41
Normalized form: Wed 2020-06-17 10:08:41 EDT
       (in UTC): Wed 2020-06-17 14:08:41 UTC
   UNIX seconds: @1592402921
       From now: 2 years 10 months ago
[root@studentvm1 ~]$
```

These two timestamps are formatted differently, but any unambiguously expressed time, such as "2020-06-17 10:08:41," is a timestamp because it can only occur once. A timestamp that will occur in the future can also be used in a systemd timer, and that timer will only trigger its defined action once.

A time expressed somewhat more ambiguously, such as "2025-*-* 22:15:00," can only be a calendar time to be used in the OnCalendar statement in a timer unit file. This expression will trigger an event every day in the year 2025 at 22:15:00 (10:15:00 p.m.).

The `journalctl` command tool has some options that can display the timestamps in a format that we can easily use with the systemd-analyze tool:

```
[root@studentvm1 ~]# journalctl -o short-full
<SNIP>
Tue 2023-01-17 09:46:25 EST studentvm1 systemd[1625]: Queued start job for
default target default.target.
Tue 2023-01-17 09:46:25 EST studentvm1 systemd[1625]: Created slice app.
slice - User Application Slice.
Tue 2023-01-17 09:46:25 EST studentvm1 systemd[1625]: Started grub-boot-
success.timer - Mark boot as successful after the user session has run 2
minutes.
Tue 2023-01-17 09:46:25 EST studentvm1 systemd[1625]: Started systemd-
tmpfiles-clean.timer - Daily Cleanup of User's Temporary Directories.
Tue 2023-01-17 09:46:25 EST studentvm1 systemd[1625]: Reached target paths.
target - Paths.
Tue 2023-01-17 09:46:25 EST studentvm1 systemd[1625]: Reached target timers.
target - Timers.
Tue 2023-01-17 09:46:25 EST studentvm1 systemd[1625]: Starting dbus.socket -
D-Bus User Message Bus Socket...
Tue 2023-01-17 09:46:25 EST studentvm1 systemd[1625]: Listening on pipewire-
pulse.socket - PipeWire PulseAudio.
Tue 2023-01-17 09:46:25 EST studentvm1 systemd[1625]: Listening on pipewire.
socket - PipeWire Multimedia System Socket.
Tue 2023-01-17 09:46:25 EST studentvm1 systemd[1625]: Starting systemd-
tmpfiles-setup.service - Create User's Volatile Files and Directories...
Tue 2023-01-17 09:46:25 EST studentvm1 systemd[1625]: Finished systemd-
tmpfiles-setup.service - Create User's Volatile Files and Directories.
<SNIP>
```

We can also display the journal timestamps in a monotonic format, which shows the number of seconds since startup:

```
[root@studentvm1 ~]# journalctl -S today -o short-monotonic
[    0.000000] studentvm1 kernel: Linux version 6.1.18-200.fc37.x86_64
    (mockbuild@bkernel01.iad2.fedoraproject.org) (gcc (GCC) 12.2.1 20221121
    (Red Hat 12.2.1-4), GNU ld version 2>
[    0.000000] studentvm1 kernel: Command line: BOOT_IMAGE=(hd0,gpt2)/
    vmlinuz-6.1.18-200.fc37.x86_64 root=/dev/mapper/fedora_studentvm1-root
    ro rd.lvm.lv=fedora_studentvm1/root rd>
[    0.000000] studentvm1 kernel: x86/fpu: Supporting XSAVE feature 0x001:
    'x87 floating point registers'
```

```
[    0.000000] studentvm1 kernel: x86/fpu: Supporting XSAVE feature 0x002:
    'SSE registers'
<SNIP>
[35220.697475] studentvm1 audit[1]: SERVICE_START pid=1 uid=0 auid=4294967295
ses=4294967295 subj=kernel msg='unit=sysstat-collect comm="systemd" exe="/
usr/lib/systemd/systemd" ho>
[35220.697747] studentvm1 audit[1]: SERVICE_STOP pid=1 uid=0 auid=4294967295
ses=4294967295 subj=kernel msg='unit=sysstat-collect comm="systemd" exe="/
usr/lib/systemd/systemd" hos>
[35220.697863] studentvm1 systemd[1]: sysstat-collect.service: Deactivated
successfully.
[35220.698048] studentvm1 systemd[1]: Finished sysstat-collect.service -
system activity accounting tool.
[35235.078746] studentvm1 CROND[2544]: (root) CMD (run-parts /etc/
cron.hourly)
[35235.088435] studentvm1 run-parts[2547]: (/etc/cron.hourly) starting
0anacron
[35235.098777] studentvm1 run-parts[2553]: (/etc/cron.hourly) finished
0anacron
[35235.100165] studentvm1 CROND[2543]: (root) CMDEND (run-parts /etc/
cron.hourly)
<SNIP>
```

Be sure to read the journalctl man page for, among other things, a complete list of the timestamp format options.

Time Spans

Time spans are primarily used in systemd timers to define a specific span of time between events. This could be used to trigger events so that they occur a specified amount of time after system startup or after a previous instance of the same event. A sample expression to trigger an event 32 minutes after system startup would look like this in the timer unit file:

```
OnStartupSec=32m
```

The default accuracy for triggering systemd timers is a time window starting at the specified time and lasting for one minute. You can specify a greater trigger time span accuracy to within a microsecond by adding a statement like the following one to the Timer section of the timer unit file:

```
AccuracySec=1us
```

EXPERIMENT 36-2: TIME SPANS

The `systemd-analyze timespan` command can help ensure that you are using a valid time span in the unit file. The following samples will get you started:

```
[root@studentvm1 ~]$ systemd-analyze timespan 15days
Original: 15days
      μs: 1296000000000
   Human: 2w 1d
[root@studentvm1 ~]$ systemd-analyze timespan "15days 6h 32m"
Original: 15days 6h 32m
      μs: 1319520000000
   Human: 2w 1d 6h 32min
```

Experiment with these and some of your own:

- "255days 6h 31m"

- "255days 6h 31m 24.568ms"

Time spans are used to schedule timer events a specified interval after a defined event such as startup. Calendar timestamps can be used to schedule timer events on specific calendar days and times either as one-offs or repeating. Timestamps are also used on systemd journal entries although not in a default format that can be used directly in tools like systemd-analyze.

This was all more than just a little confusing to me when I first started working with systemd timers and creating calendar and timestamp expressions that would trigger events. That was partly because of the similar but not quite identical formats used for specifying timestamps and calendar event trigger times.

Using systemd Journals

Problem determination can be as much an art as it can a science. Sometimes it seems even a little magic can be useful. We have all encountered situations where a reported failure could not be reproduced, and that is always frustrating for the user as well as the system administrator. Even home appliances and automobiles can be obstinate and refuse to fail when the service person shows up.

Anthropomorphism aside, we system administrators have some tools that can show us what has been happening in our Linux computers with varying degrees of granularity. We have tools like top, htop, glances, sar, iotop, tcpdump, traceroute, mtr, iptraf-ng, df, du, and many more, all of which can display the current state of a host and several of which can produce logs of various levels of detail.

While these tools can be used to locate ongoing problems, they are not particularly helpful for transient problems and those that have no symptoms that are directly observable by the user – at least until some major and possibly catastrophic problem occurs.

One important tool I have used for problem determination are the system logs – and now with systemd, the systemd journals. The systemd journal is always one of my first tools when solving a problem, especially those that don't seem to happen when I am watching. It took me a long time at the beginning of my SysAdmin career to realize the wealth of information in the log files, and it improved the speed at which I could resolve problems once I finally did.

You have already seen some uses of the journalctl command earlier in this chapter. Let's explore some of the details of the systemd journal and how it works as well as some additional ways for SysAdmins to use journalctl to use the resulting journals to locate and identify problems.

The Journal

The objective of any log or journal is to maintain a time-sequenced history of the normal activities of the various services and programs that run on a host and to record any errors and warning messages that might occur. The log messages used to be maintained in separate files in /var/log, usually one for the kernel and separate ones for most of the services running on the host. Unfortunately, the large number of log files could delay discovery of the root cause of the problem by spreading out needed information. This could be especially time-consuming while trying to determine what was taking place in the system when the error occurred.

The old /var/log/dmesg file was usually for the kernel, but that file was discontinued several years ago in favor of using the dmesg command to display the same information and integrating those messages and more into the /var/log/messages file. This merger of other logs into the messages file did help speed up problem determination by keeping much of the data in one file, but there were still many services that had not integrated their logs into the more central messages file.

The systemd journal is designed to collect all messages into a single, unified structure that can show a complete picture of everything that happened in a system at and around a specific time or event. Because all of the events, regardless of the source, are in one place in time sequence order, it is possible to see at a glance everything that was happening at a specific point or range of times. In my opinion, this is one of the main benefits of systemd journaling.

The systemd Journal Service

The systemd journaling service is implemented by the systemd-journald daemon. According to the man page

> *systemd-journald is a system service that collects and stores logging data. It creates and maintains structured, indexed journals based on logging information that is received from a variety of sources:*
>
> * *Kernel log messages*
>
> * *Simple system log messages*
>
> * *Structured system log messages*
>
> * *Standard output and standard error of service units*
>
> * *Audit records, originating from the kernel audit subsystem*
>
> *The daemon will implicitly collect numerous metadata fields for each log messages in a secure manner that can't be faked. See systemd.journal-fields(7) for more information about the collected metadata.*
>
> *Log data collected by the journal is primarily text-based but can also include binary data where necessary. Individual fields making up a log record stored in the journal may be up to 2^{64}-1 bytes in size.*

Configuration

The systemd journal daemon can be configured using the /etc/systemd/journald.conf file. For many hosts this file needs no changes because the defaults are quite reasonable. You should look at the journald.conf file now if you have not already.

The most common configuration changes you might encounter are those that specify the maximum journal file size, the number of older journal files, and the maximum file retention times. The primary reason for making those changes would be to reduce the storage space used by the journal if you have a small storage device. In a mission-critical environment, you may also want to reduce the amount of time in syncing journal data stored in RAM to the storage device.

The journald.conf man page has more details.

About That Binary Data Format…

One of the controversies surrounding systemd is the binary format in which the journal contents are stored. Some arguments against systemd are based on the systemd journal being stored in a binary format. This would seem to be contrary to the Unix/Linux Philosophy to use ASCII text for data. Those who dislike systemd use arguments like the following to support their viewpoints.

Doug McIlroy, the inventor of the pipes, says this, as quoted in Eric S. Raymond's book *The Art of Unix Programming*:

> *This is the Unix Philosophy: Write programs that do one thing well. Write programs to work together. Write programs to handle text streams, because that is a universal interface.*

However, these arguments seem to be based on at least a partial misconception because the man page clearly states that the data "is primarily text-based" although it does allow for binary data forms.

EXPERIMENT 36-3: ARE THE JOURNAL FILES IN BINARY?

The systemd journal files are stored in one or more subdirectories of /var/log/journal. Log into a test system for which you have root access and make /var/log/journal the PWD. List the subdirectories here, choose one, and make it the PWD. I looked at these files in a number of ways. I started with the stat command. The journal file names on your host will be different from the ones on mine:

```
[root@studentvm1 d1fbbe41229942289e5ed31a256200fb]# stat system@34a336922
9c84735810ef3687e3ea888-0000000000000001-0005f69cf1afdc92.journal
  File: system@34a3369229c84735810ef3687e3ea888-0000000000000001-0005f69cf1a
  fdc92.journal
```

```
 Size: 7143400         Blocks: 13960      IO Block: 4096     regular file
Device: 253,5   Inode: 524435      Links: 1
Access: (0640/-rw-r-----)  Uid: (    0/    root)  Gid: (  190/
systemd-journal)
Access: 2023-04-27 06:14:20.645000073 -0400
Modify: 2023-03-12 11:43:29.527817022 -0400
Change: 2023-03-12 11:43:29.527817022 -0400
 Birth: 2023-03-11 05:00:33.278000717 -0500
[root@studentvm1 d1fbbe41229942289e5ed31a256200fb]#
```

The journal file is identified as a "regular" file, which is not especially helpful. The file command identifies it as a "journal" file, but we already know that. But let's look a little inside the file with the dd command. The following command sends the output data stream to STDOUT; you may want to pipe it through the less pager:

```
[root@studentvm1 d1fbbe41229942289e5ed31a256200fb]# dd if=system@34a336922
9c84735810ef3687e3ea888-0000000000000001-0005f69cf1afdc92.journal | less
<SNIP>
AGE=pam_unix(systemd-user:session): session opened for user student(uid=1000)
by (uid=0)^@^@^@^@^A^@^@^@^@^@^@^@k^@^@^@^@^@^@^@eQ<99><FD><A1>'^O<AF
>^@^@^@^@^@^@^@^@<F8><F2>l^@^@^@^^@^@x<F7>l^@^@^@^@^@^@^@^@^@^@^@^@^@^@
^A^@^@^@^@^@^@^@_SOURCE_REALTIME_TIMESTAMP=1678635805628867^@^@^@^@^@^C^@^@^
@^@^@^@^@<C0>^A^@^@^@^@^@^@<96>^L^@^@^@^@^@^@<D4><D9><E6>j<F6>^E^@^K<95>w<B8>
^T^@^@^@7<CE><CF>aU$J^^<9A><A3><EE>^N^<B5><B0>^]j<92>^WS<FF><B2><9F>^F^@<8B>
7^@^@^@^@^@<94>_<BD>^B<F4>/W<BF><A0><8B>7^@^@^@^@^@<C5>O ^@^@^@^@^@<B6>8.^__
<C7><E1><FC>^H]P^@^@^@^@^@VhZ<94>^Y*^]<E1>8_P^@^@^@^@^@<EA><E3><CB><F9><A3>
<FF><CB>^TX<A3>l^@^@^@^@^@<FF>Rl<A1>#<CD>^E<CB>^P<E3>l^@^@^@^@^@/<87>´<85><82
><F5><88>`<E3>l^@^@^@^@^@<9A>r<E<E7>=<E8>^D<BA>`<E0><E3>l^@^@^@^@^@^G}<8B><F
D>J^\^U<FD>l^@^@^@^@^@^@^@^@^@^@^@^@^@^A^@^@^@^^^@^@^@^@_SOURCE_REALTIME_TIME
STAMP=1678635805627000^@^@^@^@^@^A^@^@^@^@^@^@^@^@^@M^@^@^@^@^@^@^@<E9>+{AU<EA><
DB>s^@^@^@^@^@^@^@X<EF>l^@^@^@^@^@ <FD>l^@^@^@^@^@^@^@^@^@^@^@^@^@^A^@^@^^
@^@^@^@^@_AUDIT_ID=671^@^@^@^A^@^@^@^@^@^@^@g^A^@^@^@^@^@^@^@v<E5><D2>^\'c^X<
8D>^@^@^@^@^@^@^@^@h<F6>l^@^@^@^@^@
<SNIP>
```

The data stream from the dd command, of which I only reproduced a minuscule amount, shows an interesting mixture of ASCII text and binary data. Another useful tool is the strings command, which simply displays all of the ASCII text strings contained in a file and ignores the binary data:

```
[root@studentvm1 d1fbbe41229942289e5ed31a256200fb]# strings system@34a336922
9c84735810ef3687e3ea888-0000000000000001-0005f69cf1afdc92.journal | less
```

This data can be interpreted by humans, and this particular segment looks very similar to the output data stream from the dmesg command. I leave you to further explore on your own, but my conclusion is that the journal files are clearly a mix of binary and ASCII text. That mixture makes it cumbersome at best to use the traditional text-based Linux tools to extract usable data.

There is a better way that provides us with many possibilities for extracting and viewing journal data.

Using journalctl

The journalctl command is designed to extract usable information from the systemd journals using powerful and flexible criteria for identifying the desired data. Let's explore this powerful command in depth.

EXPERIMENT 36-4: USING JOURNALCTL

You can use the journalctl command without any options or arguments to view the systemd journal that contains all journal and log information starting with the oldest. This amounted to about three months' worth of data for me. As we proceed through this experiment, I will show you various ways to select only the data in which you are interested:

```
[root@studentvm1 ~]# journalctl
```

I'm not even going to try to reproduce the data stream here because there is so much. Scroll through this data using the less pager's movement keys.

You can also explicitly show the same data as the dmesg command you encountered in Chapter 7 of Volume 1. Open two terminal sessions next to each other and issue the **dmesg** command in one and the following command in the other:

```
[root@studentvm1 ~]# journalctl --dmesg
```

The only difference you should find is the time format. The dmesg command is in a monotonic format that shows the number of seconds since the system boot. The journalctl output is in a date and time format. The short-monotonic option displays the time since boot, starting with the first boot:

```
[root@studentvm1 ~]# journalctl --dmesg -o short-monotonic
```

The journalctl command has many options including the -o (output) option with several sub-options that allow you to select from several time and date formats that meet different sets of requirements. I have listed most of these in Figure 36-1 along with a short description of each that I have expanded upon or modified a bit from the journalctl man page. Note that the primary difference among most of these is the format of the date and time, while the other information remains the same.

Format name	Description

short	This is the default format and generates an output that is most closely like the formatting of classic syslog files, showing one line per journal entry. This option shows journal metadata including the monotonic time since boot, the fully qualified host name, and the unit name, such as the kernel, DHCP, etc.
	
	`Jul 20 08:43:01 testvm1.both.org kernel: Inode-cache hash`
	`table entries: 1048576 (order: 11, 8388608 bytes, linear)`

short-full	This format is very similar to the default, but shows timestamps in the format that the --since= and --until= options accept. Unlike the timestamp information shown in short output mode this mode includes weekday, year and timezone information in the output, and is locale-independent.
	
	`Mon   2020-06-08   07:47:20   EDT   testvm1.both.org   kernel:`
	`x86/fpu: Supporting XSAVE feature 0x004: 'AVX registers'`

short-iso	The short-iso format is very similar to the default, but shows ISO 8601 wallclock timestamps.
	
	`2020-06-08T07:47:20-0400   testvm1.both.org   kernel:   kvm-`
	`clock: Using msrs 4b564d01 and 4b564d00`

short-iso-precise	This format is the same as short-iso, above, but includes full microsecond precision.
	
	`2020-06-08T07:47:20.223738-0400   testvm1.both.org   kernel:`
	`Booting paravirtualized kernel on KVM`

short-monotonic	Very similar to the default, short-full, but shows monotonic timestamps instead of wallclock timestamps. I find this most useful for
	`[     2.091107] testvm1.both.org kernel: ata1.00: ATA-6:`
	`VBOX HARDDISK, 1.0, max UDMA/133`

Figure 36-1. *journalctl time and date formats*

short-precise	This format is also similar to the default, but shows classic syslog timestamps with full microsecond precision. `Jun 08 07:47:20.223052 testvm1.both.org kernel: BIOS-e820: [mem 0x000000000009fc00-0x000000000009ffff] reserved`
short-unix	Like the default but shows seconds passed since January 1st 1970 UTC instead of wallclock timestamps ("UNIX time"). The time is shown with microsecond accuracy. `1591616840.232165          testvm1.both.org          kernel: tcp_listen_portaddr_hash hash table entries: 8192`
cat	Generates a very terse output, only showing the actual message of each journal entry with no metadata, not even a timestamp. `ohci-pci 0000:00:06.0: irq 22, io mem 0xf0804000`
verbose	This format shows the full data structure for all of the entry items with all fields. This is the format option that is most different from all of the others. `Mon          2020-06-08          07:47:20.222969          EDT [s=d52ddc9f3e8f434b9b9411be2ea50b1e;i=1;b=dcb6dcc0658e4a8d 8c781c21a2c6360d;m=242d7f;t=5a7912c6148f9;x=8f>` `_SOURCE_MONOTONIC_TIMESTAMP=0` `_TRANSPORT=kernel` `PRIORITY=5` `SYSLOG_FACILITY=0` `SYSLOG_IDENTIFIER=kernel` `MESSAGE=Linux   version   5.6.6-300.fc32.x86_64 (mockbuild@bkernel03.phx2.fedoraproject.org)  (gcc  version 10.0.1 20200328 (Red Hat 10.0.1-0>` `_BOOT_ID=dcb6dcc0658e4a8d8c781c21a2c6360d` `_MACHINE_ID=3bccd1140fca488187f8a1439c832f07` `_HOSTNAME=testvm1.both.org`

Figure 36-1. *(continued)*

There are other choices available with the -o option that provide for exporting the data in various formats such as binary or JSON. I also find the -x option illuminating because it can show additional explanatory messages for some journal entries. If you try this option, be aware that it can greatly increase the volume of the output data stream, for one useful example, the additional information for an entry like the following:

```
[root@studentvm1 ~]# journalctl -x -S today -o short-monotonic
[121206.308026] studentvm1 systemd[1]: Starting unbound-anchor.service -
update of the root trust anchor for DNSSEC validation in unbound...
░░ Subject: A start job for unit unbound-anchor.service has begun execution
░░ Defined-By: systemd
░░ Support: https://lists.freedesktop.org/mailman/listinfo/systemd-devel
░░
░░ A start job for unit unbound-anchor.service has begun execution.
░░
░░ The job identifier is 39813.
[121206.308374] studentvm1 rsyslogd[975]: [origin software="rsyslogd"
swVersion="8.2204.0-3.fc37" x-pid="975" x-info="https://www.rsyslog.com"]
rsyslogd w>
[121206.308919] studentvm1 systemd[1]: Starting logrotate.service - Rotate
log files...
░░ Subject: A start job for unit logrotate.service has begun execution
░░ Defined-By: systemd
░░ Support: https://lists.freedesktop.org/mailman/listinfo/systemd-devel
░░
░░ A start job for unit logrotate.service has begun execution.
░░
░░ The job identifier is 39491.
<SNIP>
```

There is some new information here, but I think the main benefit is that the available information is contextualized to provide some clarification of the original terse messages.

Narrowing the Search

Most of the time it is not necessary or desirable to list all of the journal entries and manually search through them. Sometimes I look for entries related to a specific service and sometimes entries that took place at specific times. The journalctl command provides powerful options that allow us to see only those data in which we have an interest.

Tip   Be sure to use boot offsets and UIDs as well as dates and times for your situation as the ones shown here are for my time and date.

Let's start with the --list-boots option, which lists all of the boots that took place during the time period for which journal entries exist. Note that the journalctl.conf file may specify that journal entries be discarded after they reach a certain age or after the storage device (HDD/SSD) space taken by the journals reaches a specified maximum amount:

```
[root@studentvm1 ~]# journalctl --list-boots
IDX BOOT ID                          FIRST ENTRY               LAST ENTRY
-79 93b506c4ef654d6c85da03a9e3436894 Tue 2023-01-17 02:53:26 EST Wed
2023-01-18 07:55:16 EST
-78 85bacafb6f11433089b0036374865ad9 Fri 2023-01-20 06:11:11 EST Fri
2023-01-20 11:15:44 EST
-77 39ac25ab4bfa43a8ae3de0c6fe8c1987 Fri 2023-01-20 11:18:40 EST Fri
2023-01-20 11:21:13 EST
-76 61b9a620bfaa4e39ba1151ea87702360 Fri 2023-01-20 11:25:15 EST Fri
2023-01-20 11:30:57 EST
<SNIP>
 -3 2624601ee2464c68abc633fe432876e5 Tue 2023-04-25 09:20:47 EDT Tue
2023-04-25 10:27:57 EDT
 -2 74796c22509344849f4cacb57278151d Tue 2023-04-25 10:28:28 EDT Wed
2023-04-26 07:40:51 EDT
 -1 a60f595794bf4789b04bbe50371147a8 Thu 2023-04-27 02:13:49 EDT Fri
2023-04-28 05:49:54 EDT
  0 920a397a6fc742899bb4e0576cfe7a70 Fri 2023-04-28 10:20:14 EDT Fri
  2023-04-28 20:50:16 EDT
```

The most recent boot ID appears at the bottom and is the long, random Hex number. Now we can use this data to view the journals for a specific boot. This can be specified using the boot offset number in the leftmost column or the UID in the second column. This command displays the journal for the boot instance with the offset of -2 – the second previous boot from the current one:

```
[root@studentvm1 ~]# journalctl -b -2
```

```
Apr 25 10:28:28 studentvm1 kernel: Linux version 6.1.18-200.fc37.x86_64
(mockbuild@bkernel01.iad2.fedoraproject.org) (gcc (GCC) 12.2.1 20221121
(Red Hat 1>
Apr 25 10:28:28 studentvm1 kernel: Command line: BOOT_IMAGE=(hd0,gpt2)/
vmlinuz-6.1.18-200.fc37.x86_64 root=/dev/mapper/fedora_studentvm1-root ro
rd.lvm.lv>
Apr 25 10:28:28 studentvm1 kernel: x86/fpu: Supporting XSAVE feature 0x001:
'x87 floating point registers'
Apr 25 10:28:28 studentvm1 kernel: x86/fpu: Supporting XSAVE feature 0x002:
'SSE registers'
<SNIP>
```

Or you could use the UID for the desired boot. The offset numbers change after each boot, but the UID does not. In this example I am using the UID for the 76th previous boot. The UIDs for the boots on your VM will be different, but choose one and use it in the following command:

```
[root@studentvm1 ~]# journalctl -b 61b9a620bfaa4e39ba1151ea87702360
```

The -u option allows selection of specific units to examine. You can use a unit name or a pattern for matching and can use this option multiple times to match multiple units or patterns. In this example I used it in combination with -b to show chronyd journal entries for the current boot:

```
[root@studentvm1 ~]# journalctl -u chronyd -b
Apr 28 10:20:41 studentvm1 systemd[1]: Starting chronyd.service - NTP client/
server...
Apr 28 10:20:43 studentvm1 chronyd[1045]: chronyd version 4.3 starting
(+CMDMON +NTP +REFCLOCK +RTC +PRIVDROP +SCFILTER +SIGND +ASYNCDNS +NTS
+SECHASH +IP>
Apr 28 10:20:43 studentvm1 chronyd[1045]: Frequency 15369.953 +/- 0.034 ppm
read from /var/lib/chrony/drift
Apr 28 10:20:43 studentvm1 chronyd[1045]: Using right/UTC timezone to obtain
leap second data
Apr 28 10:20:43 studentvm1 chronyd[1045]: Loaded seccomp filter (level 2)
Apr 28 10:20:43 studentvm1 systemd[1]: Started chronyd.service - NTP
client/server.
Apr 28 14:20:58 studentvm1 chronyd[1045]: Forward time jump detected!
Apr 28 14:21:16 studentvm1 chronyd[1045]: Selected source 192.168.0.52
```

```
Apr 28 14:21:16 studentvm1 chronyd[1045]: System clock TAI offset set to
37 seconds
Apr 28 14:24:32 studentvm1 chronyd[1045]: Selected source 138.236.128.36
(2.fedora.pool.ntp.org)
```

Suppose we want to look at events that were recorded between two arbitrary times. We can use -S (--since) and -U (--until) to specify the beginning and ending times as well. The following command displays journal entries starting at 15:36:00 on March 24, 2023, up through the current time:

```
[root@studentvm1 ~]# journalctl -S "2023-03-24 15:36:00"
```

And this command displays all journal entries starting at 15:36:00 on March 24, 2023, and up until 16:00:00 on March 30:

```
[root@studentvm1 ~]# journalctl -S "2023-03-24 15:36:00" -U "2023-03-30
16:00:00"
```

The next command combines -S, -U, and -u to give us the journal entries for the NetworkManager service unit starting at 15:36:00 on July 24, 2020, and up until 16:00:00 on July 25:

```
[root@studentvm1 ~]# journalctl -S "2023-03-24 15:36:00" -U "2023-03-30
16:00:00" -u NetworkManager
```

Some syslog facilities such as cron, auth, mail, daemon, user, and more can be viewed with the --facility option. You can use --facility=help to list the available facilities. In this example the mail facility is not the Sendmail service that would be used for an email service but the local client used by Linux to send emails to root as event notifications. Sendmail actually has two parts: the server, which, for Fedora and related distributions, is not installed by default, and the client, which is always installed so that it can be used to deliver system emails to local recipients, especially root. There were no entries in the mail facility on my VM, so I listed the facilities and then picked the user facility:

```
[root@studentvm1 ~]# journalctl --facility=help
Available facilities:
kern
user
mail
<SNIP>
[root@studentvm1 ~]# journalctl --facility=user
```

The table in Figure 36-2 summarizes some of the options that I use most frequently. Most of these options can be used in various combinations to further narrow down the search. Be sure to refer to section "systemd Calendar and Time Spans" for details of creating and testing timestamps as well as important tips like using quotes around timestamps.

Option	Description
`--list-boots`	Displays a list of boots. That information can be used to specify that only journal entries for a selected boot be shown.
`-b [offset|boot ID]`	Used to specify which boot to display information for. This includes all journal entries from that boot through shutdown or reboot.
`--facility=[facility name]`	Used to specify the facility names as known to syslog. Use --facility=help to list the valid facility names.
`-k, --dmesg`	Displays only kernel messages. This is equivalent to using the dmesg command.
`-S, --since [timestamp]`	Shows all journal entries since (after) the specified time. Can be used with --until to display an arbitrary range of time. Fuzzy times such as "yesterday" and "2 hours ago" – with quotes – are also allowed.
`-u [unit name]`	The -u option allows selection of specific units to examine. You can use a unit name or a pattern for matching. This option can be used multiple times to match multiple units or patterns.
`-U, --until [timestamp]`	Shows all journal entries until (prior to) the specified time. Can be used with --since to display an arbitrary range of time. Fuzzy times such as "yesterday" and "2 hours ago" – with quotes – are also allowed.

Figure 36-2. *Some options used to narrow searches of the journal*

The journalctl man page lists all of the options that can be used to narrow searches to the specific data we need.

Other Interesting Options

The `journalctl` program offers other interesting options, some of which are listed in Figure 36-3. These options are useful for refining the data search, how the journal data is displayed, and managing the journal files themselves.

Option	Description
-f, --follow	This **journalctl** option is similar to using the **tail -f** command. It shows the most recent entries in the journal that match whatever other options have been specified and also displays new entries as they occur. This can be useful when watching for events and when testing changes.
-e, --pager-end	The -e option displays the end of the data stream instead of the beginning. This does not reverse the order of the data stream, rather it causes the pager to jump to the end.
--file [journal filename]	Specify the name of a specific journal file in /var/log/journal/<journal subdirectory>
-r, --reverse	This option reverses the order of the journal entries in the pager so that the newest are at the top rather than the bottom.
-n, --lines=[X]	Shows the most recent X number lines from the journal.
--utc	Displays the times in UTC rather than local time.
-g, --grep=[REGEX]	I like the -g option because it enables me to search for specific patterns in the journal data stream. This is just like piping a text data stream through the **grep** command. This option uses Perl-compatible regular expressions.
--disk-usage	This option displays the amount of disk storage used by the current and archived journals. It might not be as much as you think.
--flush	Journal data stored in the virtual filesystem /run/log/journal/ which is volatile storage is written to /var/log/journal/ which is persistent storage.
--sync	Writes all unwritten journal entries (still in RAM but apparently not in /run/log/journal) to the persistent filesystem. All journal entries known to the journaling system at the time the command is entered are moved to persistent storage.
--vacuum-size= --vacuum-time= --vacuum-files=	These can be used singly or in combination to remove the oldest archived journal files until the specified condition is met. These options only consider the archived files and not active files so the result might not be exactly what was specified.

Figure 36-3. *Some additional interesting journalctl options*

More options can be found in the journalctl man page. We explore some of the entries in Figure 36-3 in the next sections.

Journal Files

If you have not already done so, be sure to list the files in the journal directory on your host. Remember that the directory containing the journal files has a long random number as a name. This directory contains multiple active and archived journal files including some for users:

```
[root@studentvm1 ~]# cd /var/log/journal/
[root@studentvm1 journal]# ll
total 8
drwxr-sr-x+ 2 root systemd-journal 4096 Apr 25 13:40
d1fbbe41229942289e5ed31a256200fb
[root@studentvm1 journal]# cd d1fbbe41229942289e5ed31a256200fb
[root@studentvm1 d1fbbe41229942289e5ed31a256200fb]# ll
<SNIP>
-rw-r-----+ 1 root systemd-journal  4360720 Mar 14 10:15 user-1000@81e2499fc0
df4505b251bf3c342e2d88-000000000000cfe6-0005f6b5daebaab2.journal
-rw-r-----+ 1 root systemd-journal  4246952 Apr 25 09:17 user-1000@81e2499fc0
df4505b251bf3c342e2d88-000000000000f148-0005f74376644013.journal
-rw-r-----+ 1 root systemd-journal  8388608 Apr 28 05:49 user-1000.journal
-rw-r-----+ 1 root systemd-journal  3692360 Mar 12 11:43 user-1001@1c165b49f1
1f42399380c5d449c7e7e1-0000000000005151-0005f4fc6561390c.journal
[root@studentvm1 d1fbbe41229942289e5ed31a256200fb]#
```

You can see the user files in this listing for the UID 1000, which is our Linux login account. The --files option allows us to see the content of specified files including the user files:

```
[root@studentvm1 ad8f29ed<SNIP>]# journalctl --file user-1000.journal
```

This output shows, among other things, the temporary file cleanup for the user with UID1000. Data relating to individual users may be helpful in locating the root cause of problems originating in user space. I found a number of interesting entries here. Try it on your VM and see what you find.

After experimenting with this for a while, make root's home directory the PWD.

Adding Your Own Journal Entries

It can be useful to add your own entries to the journal. This is accomplished with the systemd-cat program, which allows us to pipe the STDOUT of a command or program to the journal. This command can be used as a part of a pipeline on the command line or in a script:

```
[root@studentvm1 ~]# echo "Hello world" | systemd-cat -p info -t myprog
```

The -p option specifies a priority, "emerg," "alert," "crit," "err," "warning," "notice," "info," or "debug," or a value between 0 and 7 that represents each of those named levels. These priority values are the same as defined by syslog(3). The default is "info." The -t option is an identifier that can be any arbitrary short string such as a program or script name. This string can be used for searches by the journalctl command.

The next command lists the most recent five entries in the journal:

```
[root@studentvm1 ~]# journalctl -n 5
Apr 30 15:20:16 studentvm1 audit[1]: SERVICE_STOP pid=1 uid=0 auid=4294967295
ses=4294967295 subj=kernel msg='unit=sysstat-collect comm="systemd" exe="/us>
Apr 30 15:20:16 studentvm1 systemd[1]: sysstat-collect.service: Deactivated
successfully.
Apr 30 15:20:16 studentvm1 systemd[1]: Finished sysstat-collect.service -
system activity accounting tool.
Apr 30 15:21:10 studentvm1 NetworkManager[1117]: <info>  [1682882470.4523]
dhcp4 (enp0s9): state changed new lease, address=192.168.0.181
Apr 30 15:24:49 studentvm1 myprog[6265]: Hello world
lines 1-5/5 (END)
```

There is not a lot happening on our VMs, so the last line is the journal entry we created. We can also use the string "myprog" to search for the entry:

```
[root@studentvm1 ~]# journalctl -t myprog
Apr 30 15:24:49 studentvm1 myprog[6265]: Hello world
[root@studentvm1 ~]#
```

This can be a powerful tool to embed in the Bash programs we use for automation. We can use it to create records of when and what our programs do in case problems occur.

Journal Storage Usage

Journal files take up storage space, so it is necessary to monitor them. That way we can rotate them and delete old ones when necessary in order to free up storage space. In this context rotation means to stop adding data to the currently active journal (or log) file and to start a new file and add all future data to that one. Old, inactive files are maintained for some arbitrary time span and deleted when that time expires.

The journalctl command provides methods for us to see how much storage space is being used by the journals as well as configuration of the parameters used to trigger rotation. It also allows us to initiate rotation manually on demand.

EXPERIMENT 36-5: JOURNAL STORAGE AND ROTATION

Start by determining how much storage space is used by the journals:

```
[root@studentvm1 ~]# journalctl --disk-usage
Archived and active journals take up 551.2M in the file system.
[root@studentvm1 ~]#
```

The result on my primary workstation is 3.5GB. Journal sizes depend greatly on the use to which a host is put and daily runtime. My physical hosts all run 24 × 7.

The /etc/systemd/journald.conf file can be used to configure the journal file sizes and rotation and retention times to meet any needs not met by the default settings. You can also configure the journal storage location; you can specify the directory on the storage device or whether to store everything in RAM – volatile storage. If the journals are stored in RAM, they will not be persistent between boots.

The default time unit in the journald.conf file is seconds, but that can be overridden using the suffixes "year", "month", "week", "day", "h", or "m".

Suppose you want to limit the total amount of storage space allocated to journal files to 1GB, store all journal entries in persistent storage, keep a maximum of ten files, and delete any journal archive files that are more than one month old. You can configure this in /etc/systemd/journald.conf using the following entries:

```
SystemMaxUse=1G
Storage=persistent
SystemMaxFiles=10
MaxRetentionSec=1month
```

By default the SystemMaxUse is 10% of available disk space. All of the default settings have been fine for the various systems I work with, and I have had no need to change any of them. The journald.conf man page also states that the time-based settings that can be used to determine the length of time to store journal entries in a single file or to retain older files are normally not necessary. This is because the file number and size configurations usually force rotation and deletion of old files before any time settings might come into effect.

The SystemKeepFree option can be used to ensure that a specific amount of space is kept free for other data. Many databases and application programs use the /var filesystem to store data, so ensuring enough storage space is available can be critical in systems with smaller hard drives and a minimum amount of space allocated to /var.

If you do make changes to this configuration, be sure to monitor the results carefully for an appropriate period of time to ensure that they are performing as expected.

Journal File Rotation

The journal files are typically rotated automatically based upon the configuration in the /etc/systemd/journald.conf file. Files are rotated whenever one of the specified conditions is met. So if, for one example, the amount of space allocated to journal files is exceeded, the oldest file or files are deleted, the active file is made into an archive, and a new active file is created.

Journal files can also be rotated manually. I suggest using the --flush option first to ensure that all current data is moved to persistent storage to ensure that it is all rotated and the new journal files start empty. This option is listed in Figure 36-3 but can also be found in the option section of the `journalctl` man page.

It is also possible to purge old journal files without performing a file rotation. The vacuum-size=, vacuum-files=, and vacuum-time= commands are tools that can be used to delete old archive files down to a specified total size, number of files, or time prior to the present. The option values consider only the archive files and not the active ones, so the resulting reduction in total file size might be somewhat less than expected unless you flush all data from volatile storage to persistent storage.

```
┌─────────────────────────────────────────────────────────────────┐
│           EXPERIMENT 36-6: JOURNAL FILE MANAGEMENT                │
└─────────────────────────────────────────────────────────────────┘
```

Before starting this experiment, we need to set some conditions to make it work properly. As I discovered when creating this experiment, there was not enough data to cause a rotation even when performed manually.

There were 39 files that took up about 497M on my VM.

Open a terminal session and escalate your privileges to root. Make /var/log/journal/<Your-Journal-Directory> the PWD and look at the files in the journal directory. I have only a single journal directory on my VM, but the files it contains go back about three months:

```
[root@studentvm1 ~]# cd  /var/log/journal/d1fbbe41229942289e5ed31a256200fb
[root@studentvm1 d1fbbe41229942289e5ed31a256200fb]# ls
system@0005f2b035b5ec5c-a8d2b8b6d3f7b880.journal~
system@0005f2b04d5b1e40-350154cf9aedf8d0.journal~
system@0005f2b0d952b50f-9a23264d3adef5f5.journal~
system@0005f2b0fa23a6f4-376b000f611d8ac3.journal~
system@0005f2b13b66495c-2888d80cf01e1793.journal~
system@0005f2b8d01f6b1b-36122a575e54d385.journal~
system@0005f2b8eaf61ac9-3071861fcecbcb11.journal~
system@0005f2b90329031c-bd4bef8a7bdce927.journal~
system@0005f2ff9e4c5cdc-e1f2ef3a72fc7675.journal~
system@0005f301c088fb9c-789178eb0f4ea0fd.journal~
system@0005f32735d4452f-4f5917137c44c9fd.journal~
system@0005f404e4026118-048976ba41c03dc2.journal~
system@0005f41ea1668b3d-cc6c81aed5f935f1.journal~
system@0005f42ea3e53fc5-ce69998ea6a38a3f.journal~
system@0005f431322b92b4-831c6756317a6dd1.journal~
system@0005f453110b09e4-6c80463d876ae956.journal~
system@0005f4d7e9ca1d4a-80c25a84c8aec6d1.journal~
system@0005f56bd926461d-f89a91e4425992ef.journal~
system@0005f5b08a161a8f-309c9fceb66b753c.journal~
system@0005f5b3b6ea5881-a8dc0539c4ab3197.journal~
system@0005f5fe836012c6-d6ce03272713f47b.journal~
system@0005f637ce5e849a-330fd866eb58a62e.journal~
system@0005f69cf2da4392-3e38a13f8e0bc669.journal~
system@0005f6c9e94576a2-f314d048307ac935.journal~
```

```
system@0005f6ca18260e8b-8c793b1d198593b6.journal~
system@0005f6ca2587111d-ea8996c255b04c5f.journal~
system@0005f7401797df22-5ecb9901d0977a51.journal~
system@0005f764896fe3c2-672a972fa95262ce.journal~
system@0005f8071a1af6a7-97ce48062602e8ed.journal~
system@34a3369229c84735810ef3687e3ea888-0000000000000001-0005f69cf1af
dc92.journal
system@a4c3fe82821e4894a5b2155fe84a1bb0-0000000000000001-0005f6ca24
00d3f8.journal
system@cd7e3b29fb8e45bdb65d728e1b69e29e-0000000000000001-0005f8071
9125411.journal
system.journal
user-1000@0005f43566ce0a41-96c83a31073b4c54.journal~
user-1000@81e2499fc0df4505b251bf3c342e2d88-000000000000068a-0005f43566ce
084c.journal
user-1000@81e2499fc0df4505b251bf3c342e2d88-000000000000cfe6-0005f6b5daeb
aab2.journal
user-1000@81e2499fc0df4505b251bf3c342e2d88-000000000000f148-0005f743
76644013.journal
user-1001@1c165b49f11f42399380c5d449c7e7e1-0000000000005151-0005f4fc6561
390c.journal
[root@studentvm1 d1fbbe41229942289e5ed31a256200fb]# journalctl --disk-usage
Archived and active journals take up 496.8M in the file system.
[root@studentvm1 d1fbbe41229942289e5ed31a256200fb]# ll | wc -l
39
[root@studentvm1 d1fbbe41229942289e5ed31a256200fb]#
```

Make a long listing of the files in this directory so you will have something to compare with the results of the commands we are going to be experimenting with.

Power off the VM and take a new snapshot of your StudentVM1. Add the following text in the "Description" field:

"Taken at the beginning of Experiment 36-6: Journal File Management. This allows restoring this snapshot in order to see the different effects of journal rotation and vacuum on the same set of starting journal data."

You will restore this snapshot multiple times during this experiment. Then boot the VM.

The most simple approach to journal file management is a simple rotation:

```
[root@studentvm1 ~]# journalctl --rotate
```

View the files in the journal directory. They haven't changed much – not at all, really. I don't know why as the `journalctl` man page indicates that this command should stop adding data to the existing files and start new ones. Because this did not work as the man page said it should, I reported the failure on Red Hat's Bugzilla web page.

The following command does work, and it purges old archive files so that only ones that are less than one month old are left. You can use the "s", "m", "h", "days", "months", "weeks", and "years" suffixes:

```
[root@studentvm1 ~]# journalctl --vacuum-time=1month
Deleted archived journal /var/log/journal/d1fbbe41229942289e5ed31a256200fb/
system@0005f2b035b5ec5c-a8d2b8b6d3f7b880.journal~ (16.0M).
Deleted archived journal /var/log/journal/d1fbbe41229942289e5ed31a256200fb/us
er-1000@0005f43566ce0a41-96c83a31073b4c54.journal~ (8.0M).
Deleted archived journal /var/log/journal/d1fbbe41229942289e5ed31a256200fb/sy
stem@0005f2b04d5b1e40-350154cf9aedf8d0.journal~ (8.0M).
<SNIP>
Vacuuming done, freed 488.8M of archived journals from /var/log/journal/
d1fbbe41229942289e5ed31a256200fb.
Vacuuming done, freed 0B of archived journals from /run/log/journal.
Vacuuming done, freed 0B of archived journals from /var/log/journal.
```

Check the disk usage.

Power off the VM and restore the last snapshot. You did create that snapshot, right? Verify that the expected number of files and data are present.

This command deletes all archive files except for the four most recent ones. If there are fewer than four archive files, nothing will be done, and the original number of files will remain:

```
[root@studentvm1 d1fbbe41229942289e5ed31a256200fb]# journalctl
--vacuum-files=4
Deleted archived journal /var/log/journal/d1fbbe41229942289e5ed31a256200fb/
system@0005f2b035b5ec5c-a8d2b8b6d3f7b880.journal~ (16.0M).
Deleted archived journal /var/log/journal/d1fbbe41229942289e5ed31a256200fb/us
er-1000@0005f43566ce0a41-96c83a31073b4c54.journal~ (8.0M).
Deleted archived journal /var/log/journal/d1fbbe41229942289e5ed31a256200fb/sy
stem@0005f2b04d5b1e40-350154cf9aedf8d0.journal~ (8.0M).
<snip>
```

Deleted archived journal /var/log/journal/d1fbbe41229942289e5ed31a256200fb/sy
stem@0005f764896fe3c2-672a972fa95262ce.journal~ (16.0M).
Vacuuming done, freed 459.1M of archived journals from /var/log/journal/
d1fbbe41229942289e5ed31a256200fb.
Vacuuming done, freed 0B of archived journals from /run/log/journal.
Vacuuming done, freed 0B of archived journals from /var/log/journal.
Check the disk usage after this vacuum.

Power off and restore the last snapshot again. Verify that the expected number of files and
data are present.

This last vacuum command deletes archive files until only 200MB or less of archive files
are left:

[root@studentvm1 ~]# **journalctl --vacuum-size=200M**
Vacuuming done, freed 0B of archived journals from /var/log/journal.
Vacuuming done, freed 0B of archived journals from /run/log/journal.
Deleted archived journal /var/log/journal/d1fbbe41229942289e5ed31a256200fb/
system@0005f2b035b5ec5c-a8d2b8b6d3f7b880.journal~ (16.0M).
Deleted archived journal /var/log/journal/d1fbbe41229942289e5ed31a256200fb/us
er-1000@0005f43566ce0a41-96c83a31073b4c54.journal~ (8.0M).
<snip>
Deleted archived journal /var/log/journal/d1fbbe41229942289e5ed31a256200fb/sy
stem@0005f4d7e9ca1d4a-80c25a84c8aec6d1.journal~ (24.0M).
Deleted archived journal /var/log/journal/d1fbbe41229942289e5ed31a256200fb/
system@0005f56bd926461d-f89a91e4425992ef.journal~ (24.0M).
Deleted archived journal /var/log/journal/d1fbbe41229942289e5ed31a256200fb/us
er-1001@1c165b49f11f42399380c5d449c7e7e1-0000000000005151-0005f4fc6561390c.
journal (3.5M).
Deleted archived journal /var/log/journal/d1fbbe41229942289e5ed31a256200fb/sy
stem@0005f5b08a161a8f-309c9fceb66b753c.journal~ (16.0M).
Vacuuming done, freed 305.5M of archived journals from /var/log/journal/
d1fbbe41229942289e5ed31a256200fb.

Check the disk usage again.

Only complete files are deleted. The vacuum commands do not truncate archive files to meet
the specification. They also only work on archive files, not active ones. But they do work and
do what they are supposed to.

Analyzing systemd Startup and Configuration

One of our jobs as SysAdmins is to analyze the performance of the systems we support and to find and resolve problems that cause poor performance and long startup times. We also need to check other aspects of systemd configuration and usage.

The systemd system provides the systemd-analyze tool that can help us discover performance and other important systemd information. We have already used systemd-analyze earlier in this chapter to analyze timestamps and time spans for use in systemd timers, but it has other interesting and valuable uses as well. We will explore some of those uses in this section.

Startup Overview

The Linux startup sequence is a good place to begin our explorations because many of the functions provided by the systemd-analyze tool are targeted at startup. Before we begin, however, it is important to understand the difference between boot and startup, so I will say it again here. The boot sequence starts with the BIOS power-on self-test (POST) and ends when the kernel is finished loading and takes control of the host system, which is the beginning of startup and the point at which the systemd journal begins.

The results in this section are all from my primary workstation, which are much more interesting than those from a virtual machine. This workstation consists of an ASUS TUF X299 Mark 2 motherboard, an Intel i9-7960X CPU with 16 cores and 32 CPUs (threads), and 64GB of RAM.

There are several options we can use to examine the startup sequence. The simplest form of the systemd-analyze command displays a simple overview of the amount of time spent in each of the main sections of startup, the kernel startup, loading and running initrd that is a temporary system image that is used to initialize some hardware and mount the / (root) filesystem, and user space in which all of the programs and daemons required to bring the host up to a usable state are loaded. If no sub-command is passed to the command, systemd-analyze time is implied.

EXPERIMENT 36-7: USING SYSTEMD-ANALYZE

As mentioned previously, I performed this experiment on my primary workstation, which provides a more realistic view of a physical host. However, you should perform this experiment on your VM.

Basic Analysis

This command performs a very basic analysis that looks at the overall times for each stage of boot and startup:

```
[root@david ~]# systemd-analyze
Startup finished in 53.951s (firmware) + 6.606s (loader) + 2.061s (kernel) +
5.956s (initrd) + 8.883s (userspace) = 1min 17.458s
graphical.target reached after 8.850s in userspace.
[root@david ~]#
```

The most notable data in this output is the amount of time spent in firmware (BIOS) at almost 54 seconds. This is an extraordinarily long amount of time, and none of my other physical systems take anywhere near as long to get through BIOS.

My System76 Oryx Pro laptop only spends 7.216 seconds in BIOS, and all of my home-built systems take a bit less than 10 seconds. After some online searches, I found that this ASUS motherboard is known for its inordinately long BIOS boot time.

This is exactly the type of information that tools like this are intended to provide.

Be aware that the firmware data is not shown for all hosts. I have a 13-year-old Dell OptiPlex 755 for which `systemd-analyze` does not display BIOS times. My unscientific experiments led me to the hypothesis that BIOS data is shown only for Intel processors at gen 9 or above. But that could be incorrect.

This overview of the boot startup process is interesting and provides good though limited information, but there is much more information available about startup itself.

Assigning Blame

We can use `systemd-analyze blame` to discover which systemd units take the most time to initialize. This provides much more detail and enables us to see what portions of the startup process take the most time.

The results are displayed in order by the amount of time they took to initialize from highest to lowest:

```
[root@david ~]$ systemd-analyze blame
      2min 30.408s fstrim.service
   33.971s vboxdrv.service
   5.832s dev-disk-by\x2dpartuuid-4212eea1\x2d96d0\x2dc341\x2da698\
   x2d18a0752f034f.device
   5.832s dev-disk-by\x2ddiskseq-1\x2dpart1.device
   5.832s dev-sda1.device
<SNIP - removed lots of entries with increasingly small times>
```

Because many of these services start in parallel, the numbers from this command may add up to equal significantly more than the total given by systemd-analyze time for everything that comes after the BIOS. The number of units that can truly start in parallel is determined by the number of CPUs in your host.

The data from this command can provide indicators of which services we might look at to improve boot times. Service that are not used can be disabled. The fstrim and vboxdrv services take a large amount of time during the startup sequence on my workstation. You will see somewhat different results for your VMs. If you have access to a physical host that runs a Linux distribution with systemd, try this to see what that looks like.

Critical Chain

Like the critical path in project management, the critical chain shows the time-critical chain of events that took place during startup. These are the systemd units you want to look at if the startup is slow – they are the ones that would be causing the delays. This tool does not display all units that started, only those in this critical chain of events.

Tip   On a terminal that supports color – which the terminal emulators used in this course do – the units that cause delays are highlighted in red.

I have used this tool on two of my physical hosts and on my own StudentVM1 host so we can compare them. This first is from my primary workstation:

```
[root@david ~]# systemd-analyze critical-chain
```

The time when unit became active or started is printed after the "@" character.
The time the unit took to start is printed after the "+" character.

```
graphical.target @8.850s
└─multi-user.target @8.849s
  └─vboxweb-service.service @8.798s +38ms
    └─network-online.target @8.776s
      └─NetworkManager-wait-online.service @4.932s +3.843s
        └─NetworkManager.service @4.868s +39ms
          └─network-pre.target @4.850s
            └─dkms.service @3.438s +1.411s
              └─basic.target @3.409s
                └─dbus-broker.service @3.348s +55ms
                  └─dbus.socket @3.309s
                    └─sysinit.target @3.267s
                      └─systemd-binfmt.service @2.814s +452ms
                        └─proc-sys-fs-binfmt_misc.mount @3.232s +21ms
                          └─proc-sys-fs-binfmt_misc.automount @967ms
```

The numbers with "@" preceding them show the absolute number of seconds since startup began at which the unit becomes active. The numbers preceded by "+" show the amount of time it takes for the unit to start.

Among others, the vboxweb-service.service was highlighted as a blockage on my workstation. If it were not needed, I could disable it and speed up the overall start time. However, that doesn't mean that another service won't take its place with a startup that is only slightly faster. I live with it because I need VirtualBox so I can run the VMs I use to create the experiments for this course and other testing.

Here are the results from my System76 Oryx Pro laptop:

```
[root@voyager ~]# systemd-analyze critical-chain
The time when unit became active or started is printed after the "@"
character.
The time the unit took to start is printed after the "+" character.

graphical.target @36.899s
└─multi-user.target @36.899s
  └─vboxweb-service.service @36.859s +38ms
    └─vboxdrv.service @2.865s +33.971s
```

```
          └─basic.target @2.647s
            └─dbus-broker.service @2.584s +60ms
              └─dbus.socket @2.564s
                └─sysinit.target @2.544s
                  └─systemd-resolved.service @2.384s +158ms
                    └─systemd-tmpfiles-setup.service @2.290s +51ms
                      └─systemd-journal-flush.service @2.071s +193ms
                        └─var.mount @1.960s +52ms
                          └─systemd-fsck@dev-mapper-vg01\x2dvar.service
                            @1.680s +171ms
                            └─dev-mapper-vg01\x2dvar.device @1.645s
```

In this example the vboxdrv.service and vboxweb-service.service both take a good bit of startup time.

This next example is for my StudentVM1 host. Compare this output to your VM and see how much it differs:

```
[root@studentvm1 ~]# systemd-analyze critical-chain
The time when unit became active or started is printed after the "@"
character.
The time the unit took to start is printed after the "+" character.

graphical.target @56.173s
└─multi-user.target @56.173s
  └─plymouth-quit-wait.service @51.543s +4.628s
    └─systemd-user-sessions.service @51.364s +93ms
      └─remote-fs.target @51.347s
        └─remote-fs-pre.target @51.347s
          └─nfs-client.target @42.954s
            └─gssproxy.service @41.430s +1.522s
              └─network.target @41.414s
                └─NetworkManager.service @40.803s +609ms
                  └─network-pre.target @40.793s
                    └─firewalld.service @24.867s +15.925s
                      └─polkit.service @19.081s +5.568s
                        └─basic.target @18.909s
                          └─dbus-broker.service @17.886s +1.015s
                            └─dbus.socket @17.871s
                              └─sysinit.target @17.852s
```

```
        └─systemd-resolved.service @16.872s +978ms
          └─systemd-tmpfiles-setup.service
            @16.265s +272ms
            └─systemd-journal-flush.service
              @13.764s +2.493s
              └─var.mount @13.013s +593ms
                └─systemd-fsck@dev-mapper-
                  fedora_studentvm1\x2dvar.service
                  @11.077s +1.885s
                  └─local-fs-pre.target @11.056s
                    └─lvm2-monitor.service
                      @5.803s +5.252s
                      └─dm-event.socket @5.749s
                        └─system.slice
                          └─.slice
```

I was surprised at the long chain here, but it's probably because there was no single service that took up a lot of time, like VirtualBox, and that hid the others, thus removing them from the critical chain.

System State

You may sometimes need to determine the current state of the system. The `systemd-analyze dump` command really does dump a massive amount of data about the current system state. This starts with a list of the primary boot timestamps and a list of each systemd unit and a complete description of the state of each:

```
[root@david ~]# systemd-analyze dump
Manager: systemd 253 (253.2-1.fc38)
Features: +PAM +AUDIT +SELINUX -APPARMOR +IMA +SMACK +SECCOMP -GCRYPT +GNUTLS
+OPENSSL +ACL +BLKID +CURL +ELFUTILS +FIDO2 +IDN2 -IDN ->
Timestamp firmware: 1min 557.292ms
Timestamp loader: 6.606226s
Timestamp kernel: Sun 2023-04-30 17:09:49 EDT
Timestamp initrd: Sun 2023-04-30 17:09:51 EDT
Timestamp userspace: Sun 2023-04-30 17:09:57 EDT
Timestamp finish: Sun 2023-04-30 21:10:06 EDT
Timestamp security-start: Sun 2023-04-30 17:09:57 EDT
Timestamp security-finish: Sun 2023-04-30 17:09:57 EDT
```

```
Timestamp generators-start: Sun 2023-04-30 21:09:57 EDT
Timestamp generators-finish: Sun 2023-04-30 21:09:57 EDT
Timestamp units-load-start: Sun 2023-04-30 21:09:57 EDT
Timestamp units-load-finish: Sun 2023-04-30 21:09:58 EDT
Timestamp units-load: Tue 2023-05-02 13:30:41 EDT
Timestamp initrd-security-start: Sun 2023-04-30 17:09:51 EDT
Timestamp initrd-security-finish: Sun 2023-04-30 17:09:51 EDT
Timestamp initrd-generators-start: Sun 2023-04-30 17:09:51 EDT
Timestamp initrd-generators-finish: Sun 2023-04-30 17:09:51 EDT
Timestamp initrd-units-load-start: Sun 2023-04-30 17:09:51 EDT
Timestamp initrd-units-load-finish: Sun 2023-04-30 17:09:51 EDT
-> Unit logwatch.service:
        Description: Log analyzer and reporter
        Instance: n/a
        Unit Load State: loaded
        Unit Active State: inactive
        State Change Timestamp: Wed 2023-05-03 00:00:20 EDT
        Inactive Exit Timestamp: Wed 2023-05-03 00:00:05 EDT
        Active Enter Timestamp: n/a
        Active Exit Timestamp: n/a
<SNIP - Deleted a bazillion lines of output>
```

On my main workstation, this command generated a stream of 59,859 lines and about 1.75MB. This command is very fast, so you don't need to wait for the results. It does call the default pager so you can page through the data. I do like the wealth of detail provided for the various connected devices such as storage. Each systemd unit has a section with details such as modes for various runtime, cache, and log directories, the command line used to start the unit, the PID, and the start timestamp, as well as memory and file limits.

Note   The man page for systemd-analyze shows an option `systemd-analyze --user` dump that is intended to display information about the internal state of the user manager. This fails for me, and Internet searches indicate that there may be a problem with this option. systemd user instances are instances of systemd that are used to manage and control the resources for the hierarchy of processes belonging to each user. The processes for each user are part of a control group.

Analytic Graphs

Most pointy-haired-bosses (PHBs) and many good managers find pretty graphs easy to read and easier to understand than the text-based system performance data I usually prefer to work with. Sometimes even I like a good graph, and `systemd-analyze` provides the capability to display boot and startup data in an *.svg vector graphics chart.

The following command generates a vector graphics file that displays the events that take place during boot and startup. It takes a few seconds to generate this file:

```
[root@david ~]# systemd-analyze plot > /tmp/bootup.svg
```

The svg file created by the preceding command is a text file that defines a series of graphic vectors that are used by a number of applications to generate a graph. The svg files created by this command can be processed to create an image by a number of svg-capable applications such as Image Viewer, Ristretto, Okular, Eye of MATE, LibreOffice Draw, and others.

I used LibreOffice Draw to render the graph. In this case the graph is huge, and you need to zoom in considerably to make out any detail. Figure 36-4 shows a small portion of the resulting graph.

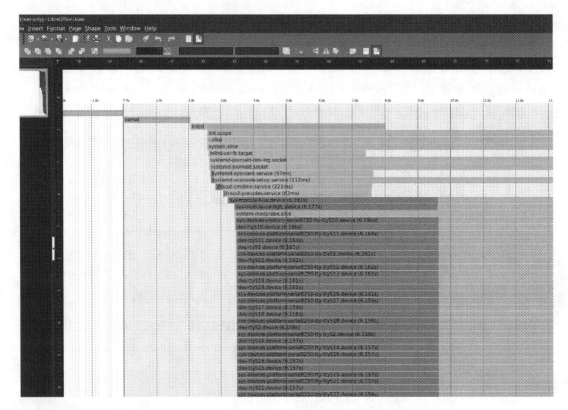

Figure 36-4. *The bootup.svg file displayed in LibreOffice Draw*

The bootup sequence is to the left of the zero (0) point on the timeline in the graph, and the startup sequence is to the right of the zero. This small portion shows the kernel and initrd and the processes started by initrd.

This graph shows at a glance what started when, how long it took to start up, and the major dependencies. The critical path is highlighted in red.

Another command that generates graphical output is systemd-analyze plot, which generates textual dependency graph descriptions in dot format. The resulting data stream is then piped through the dot utility, which is a part of a family of programs that can be used to generate vector graphic files from various types of data. The resulting svg file can be viewed by the same svg tools listed previously.

First, generate the file. This took almost nine minutes on my primary workstation:

```
[root@david ~]# time systemd-analyze dot | dot -Tsvg > /tmp/test.svg
  Color legend: black     = Requires
```

```
            dark blue = Requisite
            dark grey = Wants
            red       = Conflicts
            green     = After

real    8m37.544s
user    8m35.375s
sys     0m0.070s
[root@david ~]#
```

I won't reproduce the displayed output here because the resulting graph is pretty much spaghetti. But you should definitely try this and view the result yourself to see what I mean.

Conditionals

One of the more interesting yet somewhat generic capabilities I discovered while reading the man page for systemd-analyze(1) is the condition sub-command. (Yes – I do read the man pages, and it is amazing what I have learned that way!) This condition sub-command can be used to test the various conditions and asserts that can be used in systemd unit files.

This command can also be used in scripts to evaluate one or more conditions and return a zero (0) if all are met or a 1 if any condition is not met. In either case it also spews text indicating its findings.

The example in the man page is a bit complex, but the one I have concocted for this experiment is less so. It is testing for a kernel version greater than 5.1 and that the host is running on AC power. I have added the echo $? statement to print the return code:

```
[root@david ~]# systemd-analyze condition 'ConditionACPower=|true'
'ConditionKernelVersion = >=5.1' ; echo $?
test.service: ConditionKernelVersion=>=5.1 succeeded.
test.service: ConditionACPower=|true succeeded.
Conditions succeeded.
0
[root@david ~]#
```

The return code of zero (0) indicates that all conditions that were tested for were met. The list of conditions and asserts can be found starting on about line 600 on the systemd.unit(5) man page.

Listing Configuration Files

The systemd-analyze tool provides us with a means of sending the contents of various configuration files to STDOUT as shown here. The base directory is /etc/:

```
[root@david ~]# systemd-analyze cat-config systemd/system/display-
manager.service
# /etc/systemd/system/display-manager.service
[Unit]
Description=LXDM (Lightweight X11 Display Manager)
#Documentation=man:lxdm(8)
Conflicts=getty@tty1.service
After=systemd-user-sessions.service getty@tty1.service plymouth-quit.service
livesys-late.service
#Conflicts=plymouth-quit.service

[Service]
ExecStart=/usr/sbin/lxdm
Restart=always
IgnoreSIGPIPE=no
#BusName=org.freedesktop.lxdm

[Install]
Alias=display-manager.service
[root@david ~]#
```

I find that to be a lot of typing to do nothing more than a standard cat command. The command I do find a tiny bit helpful is this next one. It can at least search out all of the files with the specified pattern within the standard systemd locations:

```
[root@david ~]# systemctl cat basic*
# /usr/lib/systemd/system/basic.target
#   SPDX-License-Identifier: LGPL-2.1-or-later
#
#  This file is part of systemd.
#
#  systemd is free software; you can redistribute it and/or modify it
#  under the terms of the GNU Lesser General Public License as published by
#  the Free Software Foundation; either version 2.1 of the License, or
#  (at your option) any later version.
```

```
[Unit]
Description=Basic System
Documentation=man:systemd.special(7)
Requires=sysinit.target
Wants=sockets.target timers.target paths.target slices.target
After=sysinit.target sockets.target paths.target slices.target tmp.mount

# We support /var, /tmp, /var/tmp, being on NFS, but we don't pull in
# remote-fs.target by default, hence pull them in explicitly here.
Note that we
# require /var and /var/tmp, but only add a Wants= type dependency on
/tmp, as
# we support that unit being masked, and this should not be considered
an error.
RequiresMountsFor=/var /var/tmp
Wants=tmp.mount
```

Both of these commands preface the contents of each file with a comment line containing the full path and name of the file.

Unit File Verification

After creating a new unit file, it can be helpful to verify that it is at least syntactically correct. That is what the verify sub-command does. It can list directives that are spelled incorrectly and call out missing service units. The backup.service unit is one that I created, so it won't be present on your VM hosts. Yet.

We will cover backups in Chapter 47. That will include creating a script, a service unit, and a timer to run the backup program every night.

For now, just know that this command works as it is supposed to:

```
[root@david ~]# systemd-analyze verify /etc/systemd/system/backup.service
[root@david ~]#
```

Adhering to the Linux Philosophy tenet "silence is golden," a lack of output messages means that there are no errors in the scanned file.

Security

The security sub-command checks the security level of specified services. It only works on service units and not on other types of unit files. So let's check:

```
[root@david ~]# systemd-analyze security NetworkManager.service
  NAME                                        DESCRIPTION
✗ RootDirectory=/RootImage=          Service runs within the host's root directory
  SupplementaryGroups=                Service runs as root, option does not matter
  RemoveIPC=                          Service runs as root, option does not apply
✗ User=/DynamicUser=                 Service runs as root user
✗ CapabilityBoundingSet=~CAP_SYS_TIME Service processes may change the system clock
✗ NoNewPrivileges=                   Service processes may acquire new privileges
<SNIP>
→ Overall exposure level for sshd.service: 9.6 UNSAFE ☹
lines 40-83/83 (END)
```

Yes, the emoji is part of the output. I ran this program against several services including my own backup service, and the results may differ but the bottom line seems to be mostly the same – UNSAFE. But, of course, most services need pretty much complete access to everything in order to perform their work.

This tool would be very useful for checking and fixing user space service units in security-critical environments. Developers will find it useful in identifying the areas that they should concentrate on when securing services as much as possible. I don't think it has much to offer for most of us who work as SysAdmins.

Managing Startup with systemd

It's important to understand how systemd deals with managing the startup sequence, especially determining the order in which services can be started in what is an essentially parallel system. I am specifically interested in exploration of how to ensure that the dependencies for services and other units are up and running before those dependent services and units are started.

We have already seen how to create a mount unit file. In this section we will create a service unit file that will run a program for us at startup. We can change various configuration settings in the unit file and use the systemd journal to view how the location of the message changes in the startup sequence.

EXPERIMENT 36-8: CREATING A SERVICE UNIT

In this experiment you will create a service unit to run during startup and that will display a message on the terminal as well as in the systemd journal.

Preparation

Make sure that you have removed `rhgb` and `quiet` from the GRUB_CMDLINE_LINUX= line in the /etc/default/grub file. You should have done this in Chapter 35. If you have not already done so, you should do it now because you will perform some experiments in this chapter that require you to observe the Linux startup message stream.

Our objective is to create a simple program that will enable is to observe a message both during the startup on the console and later in the systemd journal.

Creating a Program

Create the shell program /usr/local/bin/hello.sh and add the following content. We want to ensure that the result is visible during startup and that we can easily find it when looking through the systemd journal. We will use a version of the "Hello world" program with some bars around it so that it stands out. Make sure the file is executable and has user and group ownership by root with 700 permissions for security:

```
#!/usr/bin/bash
# Simple program to use for testing startup configurations
# with systemd.
# By David Both
# Licensed under GPL V2
#
echo "#############################"
echo "######### Hello World! ########"
echo "#############################"
```

Run this program from the command line to verify that it works correctly:

```
[root@studentvm1 ~]# hello.sh
#############################
######### Hello World! ########
#############################
[root@studentvm1 ~]#
```

601

This is just like any other program that could be created in any scripting or compiled language. The hello.sh program could also be located in other places based on the Linux Filesystem Hierarchical Structure (FHS). I place it in the /usr/local/bin directory so that it can be easily run from the command line without having to prepend a path when I type the command. I find that many of the shell programs I create need to be run from the command line as well as by other tools such as systemd.

Create the Service Unit File

Create the service unit file /etc/systemd/system/hello.service with the following content. This file does not need to be executable, but for security it does need user and group ownership by root and 644 permissions:

```
# Simple service unit file to use for testing
# startup configurations with systemd.
# By David Both
# Licensed under GPL V2
#

[Unit]
Description=My hello shell script

[Service]
Type=oneshot
ExecStart=/usr/local/bin/hello.sh

[Install]
WantedBy=multi-user.target
```

Now verify that the service unit file performs as expected by viewing the status of the service. Any syntactical errors will show up here:

```
[root@studentvm1 ~]# systemctl status hello.service
● hello.service - My hello shell script
    Loaded: loaded (/etc/systemd/system/hello.service; disabled; vendor
    preset: disabled)
    Active: inactive (dead)
[root@studentvm1 ~]#
```

You can run this oneshot service type more than once with no problem. The "oneshot" type is intended for services in which the program launched by the service unit file is the main process but that process must complete before systemd starts any dependent process.

There are seven service types and, along with the other parts of a service unit file, an explanation of each can be found in the manual page systemd.service(5). You can find more information in the man pages and the other resources listed in the Bibliography.

As curious as I am, I wanted to see what an error might look like. I deleted the "o" from the Type=oneshot line so it looked like "Type=neshot" and ran the previous command again:

```
[root@studentvm1 ~]# systemctl status hello.service
● hello.service - My hello shell script
    Loaded: loaded (/etc/systemd/system/hello.service; disabled; vendor
    preset: disabled)
    Active: inactive (dead)

May 06 08:50:09 testvm1.both.org systemd[1]: /etc/systemd/system/hello.
service:12: Failed to parse service type, ignoring: neshot
[root@studentvm1 ~]#
```

These results told me precisely where the error was and made it very easy to resolve the problem.

Just be aware that even after you restore the hello.service file to its original form, the error persists. Although a reboot will clear this error, that should not be required. So I went looking for a method for clearing out persistent errors such as this one. I had previously encountered service errors that required the command systemctl daemon-reload to reset an error condition, but that did not work in this case. The error messages that can be fixed with this command always seem to have a statement to that effect, so you will know when to run it.

It is recommended to run **systemctl daemon-reload** after changing a unit file or creating a new one. This notifies systemd that the changes have been made and can prevent certain types of problems with managing the altered services or units. Go ahead and run this command now.

After correcting the misspelling in the service unit file, a simple systemctl restart hello.service cleared the error. You should experiment a bit by introducing some other errors into the hello. service file to see what kinds of results you get.

Although you probably did a restart in the previous section, we are now ready to start the new service, and we can then check the status to see the result. We can start or restart a oneshot service as many times as we want since it runs only once and then exits.

Go ahead and start the service as shown here and then check the status. Depending upon how much you experimented with errors, the exact results you see may be different from mine:

```
[root@studentvm1 ~]# systemctl start hello.service
[root@studentvm1 system]# systemctl status hello.service
○ hello.service - My hello shell script
    Loaded: loaded (/etc/systemd/system/hello.service; disabled; preset:
    disabled)
    Active: inactive (dead)

May 03 14:53:19 studentvm1 systemd[1]: Starting hello.service - My hello
shell script...
May 03 14:53:19 studentvm1 systemd[1]: hello.service: Deactivated
successfully.
May 03 14:53:19 studentvm1 hello.sh[3904]: ##############################
May 03 14:53:19 studentvm1 hello.sh[3904]: ######### Hello World! ########
May 03 14:53:19 studentvm1 hello.sh[3904]: ##############################
May 03 14:53:19 studentvm1 systemd[1]: Finished hello.service - My hello
shell script.
[root@studentvm1 system]#
```

Be sure to notice in the output from the status command that the systemd messages indicate that the hello.sh script started and that the service completed. We can also see the output from the script itself. This display is generated from the journal entries of the most recent invocations of the service. Try starting the service several times and then run the status command again to see what I mean.

We can also look at the journal contents directly, and there are at least a couple ways to do this. First, we can specify the record type identifier, in this case the name of the shell script. This shows the journal entries for previous reboots as well as the current session:

```
[root@studentvm1 ~]# journalctl -t hello.sh
May 03 14:52:21 studentvm1 hello.sh[3863]: ############################
May 03 14:52:21 studentvm1 hello.sh[3863]: ######### Hello World! ########
May 03 14:52:21 studentvm1 hello.sh[3863]: ############################
May 03 14:53:19 studentvm1 hello.sh[3904]: ############################
May 03 14:53:19 studentvm1 hello.sh[3904]: ######### Hello World! ########
May 03 14:53:19 studentvm1 hello.sh[3904]: ############################
<SNIP>
[root@studentvm1 ~]#
```

To locate the systemd records for the hello.service unit, we can search on systemd. We can use **G<Enter>** to page to the end of the journal entries and then scroll back to locate the ones in which we are interested. Use the -b option here to show only the entries for this most recent startup:

```
[root@studentvm1 ~]# journalctl -b -t systemd
```

This command spews all of the journal lines pertaining to systemd – a total of 109,183 lines at the time I wrote this. So that is a lot of data to sort through. You could use the search facility of the pager, which is usually less, or we can use the built-in grep feature. The -g (or --grep=) option uses Perl-compatible regular expressions:

```
[root@studentvm1 ~]# journalctl -b -t systemd -g "hello"
-- Logs begin at Tue 2020-05-05 18:11:49 EDT, end at Sun 2020-05-10
11:01:01 EDT. --
May 10 10:37:49 testvm1.both.org systemd[1]: Starting My hello shell
script...
May 10 10:37:49 testvm1.both.org systemd[1]: hello.service: Succeeded.
May 10 10:37:49 testvm1.both.org systemd[1]: Finished My hello shell script.
May 10 10:54:45 testvm1.both.org systemd[1]: Starting My hello shell
script...
May 10 10:54:45 testvm1.both.org systemd[1]: hello.service: Succeeded.
May 10 10:54:45 testvm1.both.org systemd[1]: Finished My hello shell script.

[root@studentvm1 ~]#
```

We could have used the standard GNU grep command, but that would not show the log metadata on the first line.

If you want to see not just the journal entries pertaining to our hello service, we can narrow things down a bit by specifying a time range. For now, let's just start with the start time of the preceding entries. Note that the --since= option must be enclosed in quotes and that this option can also be expressed as -S "<time expression>".

We will explore systemd time and time expressions just a bit later in this chapter.

The date and time will be different on your host, so be sure to use the timestamps that work with the times in your own journals:

```
[root@studentvm1 ~]# journalctl --since="2023-04-24 15:35"
Apr 24 15:35:09 studentvm1 systemd[1]: Configuration file /etc/systemd/
system/hello.service is marked world-inaccessible. This has no effect as
configuration data is accessible vi>
Apr 24 15:35:09 studentvm1 systemd[1]: Starting hello.service - My hello
shell script...
Apr 24 15:35:09 studentvm1 hello.sh[14639]: ##############################
Apr 24 15:35:09 studentvm1 hello.sh[14639]: ######### Hello World! ########
Apr 24 15:35:09 studentvm1 hello.sh[14639]: ##############################
Apr 24 15:35:09 studentvm1 systemd[1]: hello.service: Deactivated
successfully.
Apr 24 15:35:09 studentvm1 systemd[1]: Finished hello.service - My hello
shell script.
Apr 24 15:35:09 studentvm1 audit[1]: SERVICE_START pid=1 uid=0
auid=4294967295 ses=4294967295 subj=kernel msg='unit=hello comm="systemd"
exe="/usr/lib/systemd/systemd" hostname=? >
Apr 24 15:35:09 studentvm1 audit[1]: SERVICE_STOP pid=1 uid=0 auid=4294967295
ses=4294967295 subj=kernel msg='unit=hello comm="systemd" exe="/usr/lib/
systemd/systemd" hostname=? a>
Apr 24 15:35:31 studentvm1 systemd[1]: Reloading.
Apr 24 15:35:31 studentvm1 systemd-sysv-generator[14665]: SysV service '/
etc/rc.d/init.d/livesys' lacks a native systemd unit file. Automatically
generating a unit file for compat>
Apr 24 15:35:31 studentvm1 systemd-sysv-generator[14665]: SysV service '/etc/
rc.d/init.d/livesys-late' lacks a native systemd unit file. Automatically
generating a unit file for c>
Apr 24 15:35:32 studentvm1 audit: BPF prog-id=116 op=LOAD
Apr 24 15:35:32 studentvm1 audit: BPF prog-id=59 op=UNLOAD
Apr 24 15:35:32 studentvm1 audit: BPF prog-id=117 op=LOAD
```

```
Apr 24 15:35:32 studentvm1 audit: BPF prog-id=118 op=LOAD
<snip>
Apr 24 15:35:42 studentvm1 systemd[1]: Starting hello.service - My hello
shell script...
Apr 24 15:35:42 studentvm1 hello.sh[14677]: ##############################
Apr 24 15:35:42 studentvm1 hello.sh[14677]: ######### Hello World! ########
Apr 24 15:35:42 studentvm1 hello.sh[14677]: ##############################
Apr 24 15:35:42 studentvm1 systemd[1]: hello.service: Deactivated
successfully.
Apr 24 15:35:42 studentvm1 systemd[1]: Finished hello.service - My hello
shell script.
Apr 24 15:35:42 studentvm1 audit[1]: SERVICE_START pid=1 uid=0
auid=4294967295 ses=4294967295 subj=kernel msg='unit=hello comm="systemd"
exe="/usr/lib/systemd/systemd" hostname=? >
Apr 24 15:35:42 studentvm1 audit[1]: SERVICE_STOP pid=1 uid=0 auid=4294967295
ses=4294967295 subj=kernel msg='unit=hello comm="systemd" exe="/usr/lib/
systemd/systemd" hostname=? a>
Apr 24 15:35:43 studentvm1 systemd[1]: Configuration file /etc/systemd/
system/hello.service is marked world-inaccessible. This has no effect as
configuration data is accessible vi>
Apr 24 15:35:43 studentvm1 systemd[1]: Starting hello.service - My hello
shell script...
Apr 24 15:35:43 studentvm1 hello.sh[14681]: ##############################
Apr 24 15:35:43 studentvm1 hello.sh[14681]: ######### Hello World! ########
Apr 24 15:35:43 studentvm1 hello.sh[14681]: ##############################
Apr 24 15:35:43 studentvm1 systemd[1]: hello.service: Deactivated
successfully.
Apr 24 15:35:43 studentvm1 systemd[1]: Finished hello.service - My hello
shell script.
<snip>
```

The "since" expression skips all of the entries before that time, but we still have a lot of entries that we do not need after that time. So we can also use the "until" option to trim off the entries that come a bit after the time in which we are interested. In this case I want the entire minute in which the event occurred and nothing more:

```
[root@studentvm1 ~]# journalctl --since="2023-04-24 15:35"
--until="2023-04-24 15:36"
```

We can also narrow down the resulting data stream further using a combination of these options:

```
[root@studentvm1 system]# journalctl --since="2023-04-24 15:35"
--until="2023-04-24 15:36" -t "hello.sh"
Apr 24 15:35:09 studentvm1 hello.sh[14639]: ##############################
Apr 24 15:35:09 studentvm1 hello.sh[14639]: ######### Hello World! ########
Apr 24 15:35:09 studentvm1 hello.sh[14639]: ##############################
Apr 24 15:35:42 studentvm1 hello.sh[14677]: ##############################
Apr 24 15:35:42 studentvm1 hello.sh[14677]: ######### Hello World! ########
Apr 24 15:35:42 studentvm1 hello.sh[14677]: ##############################
Apr 24 15:35:43 studentvm1 hello.sh[14681]: ##############################
Apr 24 15:35:43 studentvm1 hello.sh[14681]: ######### Hello World! ########
Apr 24 15:35:43 studentvm1 hello.sh[14681]: ##############################
Apr 24 15:35:44 studentvm1 hello.sh[14684]: ##############################
Apr 24 15:35:44 studentvm1 hello.sh[14684]: ######### Hello World! ########
Apr 24 15:35:44 studentvm1 hello.sh[14684]: ##############################
[root@studentvm1 system]#
```

You should see results similar to mine. We can see from this series of little experiments that the service was properly executed during that time.

Reboot – Finally

So far we have not rebooted the host on which we have installed our service. So let's do that now because, after all, this is about running some program at startup. First, we need to enable the service to launch during the startup sequence:

```
[root@studentvm1 system]# systemctl enable hello.service
Created symlink /etc/systemd/system/multi-user.target.wants/hello.service →
/etc/systemd/system/hello.service.
[root@studentvm1 system]#
```

Notice that the link was created in the /etc/systemd/system/multi-user.target.wants directory. This is because the service unit file specifies that the service is "wanted" by the multi-user.target.

Go ahead and reboot now. Be sure to watch the data stream during the startup sequence to see the "Hello World!" message. Wait … You did not see it? Well, neither did I because it is not there.

But let's look at the journal since the latest system boot:

```
[root@studentvm1 ~]# journalctl -b
May 03 16:27:54 studentvm1 systemd[1]: Starting hello.service - My hello
shell script...
May 03 16:27:54 studentvm1 hello.sh[968]: ##############################
May 03 16:27:54 studentvm1 hello.sh[968]: ######### Hello World! ########
May 03 16:27:54 studentvm1 hello.sh[968]: ##############################
```

This shows the entire sequence of events since the most recent boot. Scroll down until you can see that systemd started our hello.service unit, which ran the hello.sh shell script. If you were able to catch it during the actual boot, you also would have seen the systemd message indicating that it was starting the script and the one indicating that the service succeeded. Look at the first systemd message in the preceding data stream. We can see that systemd started our service very soon after reaching the basic system target.

Using the -t option shows only those systemd entries that relate to our new service unit:

```
[root@studentvm1 ~]# journalctl -b -t "hello.sh"
May 03 16:35:29 studentvm1 hello.sh[969]: ##############################
May 03 16:35:29 studentvm1 hello.sh[969]: ######### Hello World! ########
May 03 16:35:29 studentvm1 hello.sh[969]: ##############################
[root@studentvm1 ~]#
```

I would like to see the message displayed at startup time as well. There is a way to make that happen. Add the following line to the [Service] section of the hello.service file:

```
StandardOutput=journal+console
```

Our hello.service file now looks like this:

```
# Simple service unit file to use for testing
# startup configurations with systemd.
# By David Both
# Licensed under GPL V2
#

[Unit]
Description=My hello shell script

[Service]
Type=oneshot
```

```
ExecStart=/usr/local/bin/hello.sh
StandardOutput=journal+console

[Install]
WantedBy=multi-user.target
```

After adding this line, reboot the system and be sure to watch the data stream as it scrolls up the display during the boot process. You should easily see the message in its little box. After the startup sequence completes, you can view the journal for the most recent boot and locate the entries for our new service:

```
[root@studentvm1 ~]# journalctl -b -u hello.service -o short-monotonic
[   29.607375] studentvm1 systemd[1]: Starting hello.service - My hello shell
    script...
[   29.619302] studentvm1 hello.sh[969]: ##############################
[   29.619302] studentvm1 hello.sh[969]: ######### Hello World! ########
[   29.619302] studentvm1 hello.sh[969]: ##############################
[   31.355272] studentvm1 systemd[1]: hello.service: Deactivated
    successfully.
[   31.357765] studentvm1 systemd[1]: Finished hello.service - My hello
    shell script.
```

Changing the Sequence

Now that the hello.service is working, we can look at where it starts in the startup sequence and experiment with changing it. It is important to remember that the intent of systemd is to start as many services and other unit types in parallel within each of the major targets, basic. target, multi-user.target, and graphical.target. You have just viewed the journal entries for the most recent boot. It should look similar to my journal as seen in the preceding output.

Notice that systemd started our hello.service soon after it reached the target basic system. This is what we specified in the service unit file on the WantedBy line, so it is correct. Before we change anything, list the contents of the /etc/systemd/system/multi-user.target.wants directory, and you will see a symbolic (soft) link to the service unit file. The [Install] section of the service unit file specifies which target will start the service, and running the systemctl enable hello.service command created the link in the appropriate target wants directory:

```
hello.service -> /etc/systemd/system/hello.service
```

Certain services need to start during the basic.target, and others don't need to be started unless the system is starting up to the graphical.target. Let's assume we do not need our service to start until the graphical.target. So change the WantedBy line to the following:

```
WantedBy=graphical.target
```

Be sure to disable the hello.service and re-enable it in order to delete the old link and add the new one in the graphical.targets.wants directory. I have noticed that if I forget to disable the service before changing the target that wants it, I can run the systemctl disable command, and the links will be removed from both target wants directories:

```
[root@studentvm1 ~]# systemctl disable hello.service
Removed "/etc/systemd/system/multi-user.target.wants/hello.service".
[root@studentvm1 ~]# systemctl enable hello.service
Created symlink /etc/systemd/system/graphical.target.wants/hello.service →
/etc/systemd/system/hello.service.
[root@studentvm1 ~]#
```

Then reboot.

Tip   One concern with starting services in the graphical.target is that if the host boots to multi-user.target, this service will not start automatically. That may be what you want if the service is not required for the multi-user.target, but it may not be what you want.

Let's look at the journal entries for the graphical.target and the multi-user.target using the -o short-monotonic option, which displays seconds after kernel startup with nanosecond precision. The first entry looks at the second most recent boot in which our service started as part of the multi-user.target. The -b option offset of -1 is used for this. The second entry is for the most recent boot in which the service starts as part of the graphical.target:

```
[root@studentvm1 ~]# journalctl -b -1 -t "hello.sh" -o short-monotonic
[   29.619302] studentvm1 hello.sh[969]: ##############################
[   29.619302] studentvm1 hello.sh[969]: ######### Hello World! ########
[   29.619302] studentvm1 hello.sh[969]: ##############################
[root@studentvm1 ~]# journalctl -b -t "hello.sh" -o short-monotonic
```

```
[   30.535586] studentvm1 hello.sh[968]: ###############################
[   30.535586] studentvm1 hello.sh[968]: ########## Hello World! ########
[   30.535586] studentvm1 hello.sh[968]: ###############################
```

The hello.service unit starts at almost the same time as after startup begins. Although a second or two is a long time for computers, it's not really much in real time. After experimenting with this multiple times, I found that the time the hello.service unit started was always between about 29 and 37 seconds regardless of whether it was started by the multi-user.target or the graphical.target.

So what does this mean?

Look at the /etc/systemd/system/default.target link. The contents of that file show that systemd first starts the default target, graphical.target, which in turn pulls in the multi-user.target:

```
[root@studentvm1 system]# cat /etc/systemd/system/default.target
#   SPDX-License-Identifier: LGPL-2.1-or-later
#
#  This file is part of systemd.
#
#  systemd is free software; you can redistribute it and/or modify it
#  under the terms of the GNU Lesser General Public License as published by
#  the Free Software Foundation; either version 2.1 of the License, or
#  (at your option) any later version.

[Unit]
Description=Graphical Interface
Documentation=man:systemd.special(7)
Requires=multi-user.target
Wants=display-manager.service
Conflicts=rescue.service rescue.target
After=multi-user.target rescue.service rescue.target display-manager.service
AllowIsolate=yes
```

I have found that, whether starting our service with the graphical.target or the multi-user.target, the hello.service unit runs at about the same amount of time into startup. So based on this and what I see in the journal results, especially the ones using the monotonic output, both of these targets are starting in parallel. Look at one more thing from the journal output from the last three reboots:

```
[root@studentvm1 ~]# journalctl -S today -g "Reached target" -o short-
monotonic
<SNIP>
[    56.229204] studentvm1 systemd[1]: Reached target multi-user.target -
    Multi-User System.
[    56.229356] studentvm1 systemd[1]: Reached target graphical.target -
    Graphical Interface.
<SNIP>
[    61.739340] studentvm1 systemd[1]: Reached target multi-user.target -
    Multi-User System.
[    61.739496] studentvm1 systemd[1]: Reached target graphical.target -
    Graphical Interface.
<SNIP>
[    64.001235] studentvm1 systemd[1]: Reached target multi-user.target -
    Multi-User System.
[    64.001427] studentvm1 systemd[1]: Reached target graphical.target -
    Graphical Interface.
```

Both targets finish at almost the same time. This is consistent because the graphical.target pulls in the multi-user.target and cannot finish until the multi-user.target is reached, that is, finished. But our service finishes much earlier than this.

What all this really means is that these two targets start up pretty much in parallel. If you explore the journal entries, you will see various targets and services from each of those primary targets starting in parallel. It is clear that the multi-user.target does not need to complete before the graphical.target is started. Therefore, simply using these primary targets to sequence the startup does not work very well although it can be useful for ensuring that units are started only when they are needed for the graphical.target.

Before continuing, revert the hello.service unit file to WantedBy=multi-user.target.

Ensure a Service Is Started After the Network Is Running

One of the more common startup sequence needs is to ensure that a unit starts after the network is up and running. The freedesktop.org website article "Running Services After the Network is up"[1] discusses the fact that there is no real consensus on when the network can

---

[1] freedesktop.org [sic], "Running Services After the Network is up," www.freedesktop.org/wiki/Software/systemd/NetworkTarget/, last edited on Wednesday, May 18, 09:46:20 2022

be considered to be "up," but it provides three options, and the one that meets our needs of a fully operational network is the network-online.target. Just be aware that the network. target is used during shutdown rather than startup, so it will not do us any good when trying to sequence the startup.

Before making any additional changes, be sure to examine the journal and verify that the hello.service unit starts well before the network. You can look for the network-online.target to locate that.

Our service does not really require the network service, but we will simply use it as an avatar for one that does.

Because setting WantedBy=graphical.target does not ensure that our service will be started after the network is up and running, we need another way to ensure that it is. Fortunately, there is an easy way to do this. Add the following two lines to the [Unit] section of the hello. service unit file:

```
After=network-online.target
Wants=network-online.target
```

Both of these entries are required to make this work. Reboot the host and look for the location of entries for our service in the journals:

```
<SNIP>
[   53.450983] studentvm1 systemd[1]: Reached target network-online.target -
    Network is Online.
<SNIP>
[   53.455470] studentvm1 systemd[1]: Starting hello.service - My hello shell
    script...
[   53.521378] studentvm1 hello.sh[1298]: #############################
[   53.521378] studentvm1 hello.sh[1298]: ######### Hello World! ########
[   53.521959] studentvm1 hello.sh[1298]: #############################
[   53.841829] studentvm1 systemd[1]: hello.service: Deactivated
    successfully.
[   53.850192] studentvm1 systemd[1]: Finished hello.service - My hello
    shell script.
<SNIP>
[   60.358890] studentvm1 systemd[1]: Reached target multi-user.target -
    Multi-User System.
[   60.359111] studentvm1 systemd[1]: Reached target graphical.target -
    Graphical Interface.
```

This tells us that our hello.service unit started very soon after the network-online.target was reached. This is exactly what we wanted. You may also have been able to view the "Hello World!" message as it passed by during the startup.

Chapter Summary

We have explored Linux startup with systemd in more detail in this chapter and learned more about unit files and the systemd journals. We also discovered what happens when errors are introduced into the service file. As a SysAdmin I find that this type of experimentation helps me learn the behaviors of any program or service when it breaks. Breaking things intentionally provides us with a good way to learn in a safe environment.

We learned from the experiments that just adding a service unit to either the multi-user.target or the graphical.target does not provide a method for defining its place in the start sequence. All that is good for is to determine whether a particular unit starts as a part of a graphical environment or not. The reality is that both of our startup targets, multi-user.target and graphical.target, and all of their wants and requires start up pretty much in parallel. The best way to ensure that a unit starts in a specific order is to determine the unit on which it is dependent and configure the new unit to "Want" and "After" the unit upon which it is dependent.

In this chapter we have looked at the use of the `journalctl` command to extract data of various types from the systemd journal in different formats. We have also explored management of the journal files and how to add entries to the log from commands and scripts.

The systemd journal system provides a significant amount of metadata and context for its entries than the old syslogd program. This additional data and the context that includes all other journal entries around the times of specific incidents can help the SysAdmin locate and resolve problems much faster than when having to search multiple syslog files.

You should now have enough information to enable you to use the systemd journal more effectively. There is more than I have covered here, and much of it can be found in the man pages for journalctl and systemd-cat.

Exercises

Complete the following exercises to complete this chapter:

1. Why would using a statement like OnCalendar=tomorrow fail when used in a timer?

2. Do the startup times for systemd services vary from one bootup to the next? Or are they all constant?

3. Which services in the critical chain were highlighted in red on your VM?

4. What happens if (assuming you have CPUs available) you assign additional ones to the VM and reboot?

5. Use systemd-analyze to determine the total amount of time it took for startup at the last boot.

6. What does avahi do?

7. How long did avahi take to start?

8. Terminate avahi and disable it.

9. Are there any emergency-level entries in the systemd journal?

CHAPTER 37

systemd Finale

Objectives

In this chapter you will learn

- To create a systemd timer that runs a Bash script at regular intervals

- To create systemd timers that run once at specified times

- To apply systemd security to the /home directory and its contents

- How to use systemd cgroups for resource management

Introduction

We are not quite done with coverage of systemd. This chapter is the last one that is exclusively about systemd.

We will do a quick review of calendar event expressions and the timers in which you will use them. We will look at how to add another layer of security to your /home directory by using systemd. Finally, we will explore resource management using systemd cgroups.

All of the experiments in this chapter must be performed as the root user.

Calendar Event Expression Review

Calendar event expressions are a key part of triggering timers at desired times. We have already looked at calendar event expressions, but let's do a quick review with an emphasis on using them with timers.

© David Both 2023

D. Both, *Using and Administering Linux: Volume 2*, https://doi.org/10.1007/978-1-4842-9615-8_37

systemd itself and its timers use a different style for time and date expressions than the format used in crontab. It is more flexible than crontab and allows fuzzy dates and times in the manner of the at command. It should also be familiar enough that it will be easy to understand.

The basic format for systemd timers using OnCalendar= is DOW YYYY-MM-DD HH:MM:SS. The DOW (day of week) is optional, and other fields can use an asterisk (*) to match any value for that position. All of the various calendar time forms are converted to a normalized form for use. If the time is not specified, it is assumed to be 00:00:00. If the date is not specified but the time is, the next match may be today or tomorrow depending upon the current time. Names or numbers can be used for the month and day of the week. Comma-separated lists of each unit can be specified. Unit ranges can be specified with ".." between the beginning and ending values.

There are a couple interesting options for specifying dates. The tilde (~) can be used to specify the last day of the month or a specified number of days prior to the last day of the month. The "/" can be used to specify a day of the week as a modifier.

Figure 37-1 shows examples of some typical time expressions as used in the OnCalendar statements along with their meanings.

Calendar event timestamp	Description
`"DOW YYYY-MM-DD HH:MM:SS"`	
`"*-*-* 00:15:30"`	Every day of every month of every year at 15 minutes and 30 seconds after midnight.
`Weekly`	Every Monday at 00:00:00.
`"Mon *-*-* 00:00:00"`	Same as Weekly.
`Mon`	Same as Weekly.
`"Wed 2020-*-*"`	Every Wednesday in 2020 at 00:00:00.
`"Mon..Fri 2021-*-*"`	Every weekday in 2021 at 00:00:00.
`"2028-6,7,8-1,15 01:15:00"`	The 1st and 15th of June, July, and August of 2028 at 01:15:00am.
`"Mon *-05~03"`	The next occurrence of a Monday in May of any year which is also the 3rd day from the end of the month.
`"Mon..Fri *-8~4"`	The 4th day preceding the end of August for any years in which it also falls on a weekday.
`*-05~03/2`	The 3rd day from the end of the month of May and then again two days later. Note that this expression uses the Tilde (~). Repeats every year.
`*-05-03/2`	The third day of the month of may and then every 2nd day for the rest of May. Repeats every year.

Figure 37-1. Sample OnCalendar event expressions

Remember that, by default, the `systemd-analyze calendar` tool only shows the next time elapse for each timestamp. You can also use --iterations=X as a modifier to display the next X iterations of elapses for the given expression.

systemd Timers

I am in the process of converting my cron jobs to systemd timers. I have used timers for a few years now, but I usually only explored enough to perform whatever task on which I was then working. While researching systemd for a series of articles and this book, I have found that systemd timers have some very interesting capabilities.

As with cron jobs, systemd timers can trigger events – shell scripts and programs – at specified time intervals such as once a day, a specific day of the month, perhaps only if it is a Monday, or every 15 minutes during business hours from 08:00 a.m. to 06:00 p.m. Timers can also do some things that cron jobs cannot. For example, a timer can trigger a script or program a specific amount of time after an event such as boot, startup, completion of a previous task, or even the previous completion of the service unit called by the timer and many more.

When Fedora, or any systemd-based distribution, is installed on a new system, the installation procedure creates several timers that are part of the system maintenance procedures that take place in the background of any Linux host. These timers trigger events that are used to perform common maintenance tasks such as updating system databases, cleaning temporary directories, rotating log files, and more.

EXPERIMENT 37-1: SYSTEMD TIMERS ON A FEDORA HOST

Let's look at some of the ones I see on my own primary workstation. Use the systemctl status *timer command as shown here to list all of the timers for your host. The star/splat/asterisk works the same as it does when used for file globbing, so this command lists all systemd timer units:

```
[root@studentvm1 ~]# systemctl status *timer
● systemd-tmpfiles-clean.timer - Daily Cleanup of Temporary Directories
    Loaded: loaded (/usr/lib/systemd/system/systemd-tmpfiles-clean.
    timer; static)
    Active: active (waiting) since Thu 2023-05-04 08:21:53 EDT; 4h 53min ago
```

```
   Trigger: Fri 2023-05-05 08:37:15 EDT; 19h left
  Triggers: ● systemd-tmpfiles-clean.service
      Docs: man:tmpfiles.d(5)
            man:systemd-tmpfiles(8)
```

May 04 08:21:53 studentvm1 systemd[1]: Started systemd-tmpfiles-clean.timer - Daily Cleanup of Temporary Directories.

```
● fstrim.timer - Discard unused blocks once a week
    Loaded: loaded (/usr/lib/systemd/system/fstrim.timer; enabled; preset:
    enabled)
    Active: active (waiting) since Thu 2023-05-04 08:21:53 EDT; 4h 53min ago
   Trigger: Mon 2023-05-08 00:33:58 EDT; 3 days left
  Triggers: ● fstrim.service
      Docs: man:fstrim
```

May 04 08:21:53 studentvm1 systemd[1]: Started fstrim.timer - Discard unused blocks once a week.

```
● sysstat-collect.timer - Run system activity accounting tool every
10 minutes
    Loaded: loaded (/usr/lib/systemd/system/sysstat-collect.timer; enabled;
    preset: enabled)
    Active: active (waiting) since Thu 2023-05-04 08:21:53 EDT; 4h 53min ago
   Trigger: Thu 2023-05-04 13:20:00 EDT; 4min 53s left
  Triggers: ● sysstat-collect.service
```

May 04 08:21:53 studentvm1 systemd[1]: Started sysstat-collect.timer - Run system activity accounting tool every 10 minutes.

```
● raid-check.timer - Weekly RAID setup health check
    Loaded: loaded (/usr/lib/systemd/system/raid-check.timer; enabled;
    preset: enabled)
    Active: active (waiting) since Thu 2023-05-04 08:21:53 EDT; 4h 53min ago
   Trigger: Sun 2023-05-07 01:00:00 EDT; 2 days left
  Triggers: ● raid-check.service
```

May 04 08:21:53 studentvm1 systemd[1]: Started raid-check.timer - Weekly RAID setup health check.

```
● sysstat-summary.timer - Generate summary of yesterday's process accounting
```

```
   Loaded: loaded (/usr/lib/systemd/system/sysstat-summary.timer; enabled;
   preset: enabled)
   Active: active (waiting) since Thu 2023-05-04 08:21:53 EDT; 4h 53min ago
  Trigger: Fri 2023-05-05 00:07:00 EDT; 10h left
 Triggers: ● sysstat-summary.service
```

May 04 08:21:53 studentvm1 systemd[1]: Started sysstat-summary.timer -
Generate summary of yesterday's process accounting.

```
● dnf-makecache.timer - dnf makecache --timer
   Loaded: loaded (/usr/lib/systemd/system/dnf-makecache.timer; enabled;
   preset: enabled)
   Active: active (waiting) since Thu 2023-05-04 08:21:53 EDT; 4h 53min ago
  Trigger: Thu 2023-05-04 13:16:04 EDT; 58s left
 Triggers: ● dnf-makecache.service
```

May 04 08:21:53 studentvm1 systemd[1]: Started dnf-makecache.timer - dnf
makecache --timer.

```
● unbound-anchor.timer - daily update of the root trust anchor for DNSSEC
   Loaded: loaded (/usr/lib/systemd/system/unbound-anchor.timer; enabled;
   preset: enabled)
   Active: active (waiting) since Thu 2023-05-04 08:21:53 EDT; 4h 53min ago
  Trigger: Fri 2023-05-05 00:00:00 EDT; 10h left
 Triggers: ● unbound-anchor.service
     Docs: man:unbound-anchor(8)
```

May 04 08:21:53 studentvm1 systemd[1]: Started unbound-anchor.timer - daily
update of the root trust anchor for DNSSEC.

```
● plocate-updatedb.timer - Update the plocate database daily
   Loaded: loaded (/usr/lib/systemd/system/plocate-updatedb.timer; enabled;
   preset: enabled)
   Active: active (waiting) since Thu 2023-05-04 08:21:53 EDT; 4h 53min ago
  Trigger: Fri 2023-05-05 11:36:13 EDT; 22h left
 Triggers: ● plocate-updatedb.service
```

May 04 08:21:53 studentvm1 systemd[1]: Started plocate-updatedb.timer -
Update the plocate database daily.

```
● logrotate.timer - Daily rotation of log files
     Loaded: loaded (/usr/lib/systemd/system/logrotate.timer; enabled;
     preset: enabled)
     Active: active (waiting) since Thu 2023-05-04 08:21:53 EDT; 4h 53min ago
    Trigger: Fri 2023-05-05 00:00:00 EDT; 10h left
   Triggers: ● logrotate.service
       Docs: man:logrotate(8)
             man:logrotate.conf(5)
```

```
May 04 08:21:53 studentvm1 systemd[1]: Started logrotate.timer - Daily
rotation of log files.
```

Each timer has at least six lines of information associated with it. The first line for each timer has its file name and a short description of its purpose. The second line displays status of the timer, whether it is loaded or not, the full path to the timer unit file, and the vendor preset. The third line indicates its active status, which includes the date and time the timer became active.

Line 4 of the data for each timer contains the date and time that the timer is next triggered and an approximate time until the trigger occurs. The fifth line shows the name of the event, the service, that is triggered by the timer.

Some systemd unit files have pointers to the relevant documentation. That is true of some but not all. Three of the timers in the output from my VM have pointers to documentation. This is a nice but optional bit of data.

The final line of this output for each timer is the journal entry for the most recent instance of the service triggered by the timer.

I suggest that you read the details of the timers on your host. You can see the timers that perform SAR data collection and daily aggregation, the weekly fstrim for SSD storage devices, log rotation, and more.

Creating a Timer

Although we can deconstruct one or more of the existing timers to learn how they work, let's create our own service unit and a timer unit to trigger it. We will use a fairly trivial example in order to keep this simple. After we have finished this, it will be easier to understand how the other timers work and to determine what they are doing.

```
EXPERIMENT 37-2: CREATE A TIMER
```

First, create a simple service that will run something basic such as the free command. For example, we may want to monitor free memory at regular intervals. Create the following myMonitor.service unit file in the /etc/systemd/system directory. It does not need to be executable:

```
# This service unit is for testing timer units
# By David Both
# Licensed under GPL V2
#

[Unit]
Description=Logs system statistics to the systemd journal
Wants=myMonitor.timer

[Service]
Type=oneshot
ExecStart=/usr/bin/free

[Install]
WantedBy=multi-user.target
```

This is about the simplest service unit that we can create. Now let's look at the status and test our service unit to ensure that it works as we expect it to:

```
[root@studentvm1 system]# systemctl status myMonitor.service
● myMonitor.service - Logs system statistics to the systemd journal
     Loaded: loaded (/etc/systemd/system/myMonitor.service; disabled; vendor
     preset: disabled)
     Active: inactive (dead)
[root@studentvm1 system]# systemctl start myMonitor.service
[root@studentvm1 system]#
```

So where does the output go? By default the standard output (STDOUT) from programs run by systemd service units is sent to the systemd journal, which leaves a record we can view now or in the future:

```
[root@studentvm1 system]# systemctl status myMonitor.service
```

○ myMonitor.service - Logs system statistics to the systemd journal
     Loaded: loaded (/etc/systemd/system/myMonitor.service; disabled; preset:
     disabled)
     Active: inactive (dead)

```
May 04 16:04:09 studentvm1 systemd[1]: Starting myMonitor.service - Logs
system statistics to the systemd journal...
May 04 16:04:09 studentvm1
free[2338]:                    total        used        free       shared
buff/cache    available
May 04 16:04:09 studentvm1 free[2338]:
Mem:        16367772      302556     15190668         7124      874548
15786704
May 04 16:04:09 studentvm1 free[2338]: Swap:             8388604
0      8388604
May 04 16:04:09 studentvm1 systemd[1]: myMonitor.service: Deactivated
successfully.

May 04 16:04:09 studentvm1 systemd[1]: Finished myMonitor.service - Logs
system statistics to the systemd journal.
[root@studentvm1 system]#
```

Look at the journal, specifically for our service unit. The -S option, which is the short version of --since, allows us to specify the period of time that the journalctl tool should search for entries. This is not just because we don't care about previous results – in our case there won't be any – it is to shorten the time spent searching in the event your host has been running for a long time and accumulated a large number of entries in the journal.

This command shows the same data that we see previously using the systemctl status command. That previous command will only show a limited amount of historical data, while the following one can show as much as we need:

```
[root@studentvm1 system]# journalctl -S today -u myMonitor.service
May 04 16:04:09 studentvm1 systemd[1]: Starting myMonitor.service - Logs
system statistics to the systemd journal...
May 04 16:04:09 studentvm1
free[2338]:                    total        used        free       shared  buff/
cache    available
```

```
May 04 16:04:09 studentvm1 free[2338]:
Mem:          16367772        302556      15190668        7124       874548
15786704
May 04 16:04:09 studentvm1 free[2338]: Swap:          8388604            0
8388604
May 04 16:04:09 studentvm1 systemd[1]: myMonitor.service: Deactivated
successfully.
May 04 16:04:09 studentvm1 systemd[1]: Finished myMonitor.service - Logs
system statistics to the systemd journal.
[root@studentvm1 system]#
```

The task triggered by a service can be a single program as we have seen, a series of programs, or a script written in any scripting language. Let's add another task to the service. Add the following line to the end of the [Service] section of the myMonitor.service unit file. It should now look like this:

```
# This service unit is for testing timer units
# By David Both
# Licensed under GPL V2
#

[Unit]
Description=Logs system statistics to the systemd journal
Wants=myMonitor.timer

[Service]
Type=oneshot
ExecStart=/usr/bin/free
ExecStart=/usr/bin/lsblk -i

[Install]
WantedBy=multi-user.target
```

Start the service again and check the journal for the results, which should look like this. You should see the results from both commands in the journal:

```
[root@studentvm1 system]# journalctl -S today -u myMonitor.service
May 04 16:21:33 studentvm1 systemd[1]: Starting myMonitor.service - Logs
system statistics to the systemd journal...
May 04 16:21:33 studentvm1 free[2436]:                total        used
free      shared  buff/cache    available
```

```
May 04 16:21:33 studentvm1 free[2436]: Mem:        16367772        318188
15168016        7120        881568        15770784
May 04 16:21:33 studentvm1 free[2436]: Swap:        8388604          0
8388604
May 04 16:21:33 studentvm1 lsblk[2437]: NAME                      MAJ:MIN RM
SIZE RO TYPE MOUNTPOINTS
May 04 16:21:33 studentvm1 lsblk[2437]: sda                          8:0
0    60G  0 disk
May 04 16:21:33 studentvm1 lsblk[2437]: |-sda1                       8:1
0    1M  0 part
May 04 16:21:33 studentvm1 lsblk[2437]: |-sda2                       8:2
0    1G  0 part /boot
May 04 16:21:33 studentvm1 lsblk[2437]: |-sda3                       8:3
0    1G  0 part /boot/efi
May 04 16:21:33 studentvm1 lsblk[2437]: `-sda4                       8:4
0    58G  0 part
May 04 16:21:33 studentvm1 lsblk[2437]:    |-fedora_studentvm1-root 253:0
0    2G  0 lvm  /
May 04 16:21:33 studentvm1 lsblk[2437]:    |-fedora_studentvm1-usr  253:1
0    15G  0 lvm  /usr
May 04 16:21:33 studentvm1 lsblk[2437]:    |-fedora_studentvm1-tmp  253:2
0    5G  0 lvm  /tmp
May 04 16:21:33 studentvm1 lsblk[2437]:    |-fedora_studentvm1-var  253:3
0    10G  0 lvm  /var
May 04 16:21:33 studentvm1 lsblk[2437]:    |-fedora_studentvm1-home 253:4
0    4G  0 lvm  /home
May 04 16:21:33 studentvm1 lsblk[2437]:    `-fedora_studentvm1-test 253:5
0    500M 0 lvm  /test
May 04 16:21:33 studentvm1 lsblk[2437]: sdb                          8:16
0    20G  0 disk
May 04 16:21:33 studentvm1 lsblk[2437]: |-sdb1                       8:17
0    2G  0 part
May 04 16:21:33 studentvm1 lsblk[2437]: |-sdb2                       8:18
0    2G  0 part
May 04 16:21:33 studentvm1 lsblk[2437]: `-sdb3                       8:19
0    16G  0 part
May 04 16:21:33 studentvm1 lsblk[2437]:    |-NewVG--01-TestVol1     253:6
0    4G  0 lvm  /TestFS
```

```
May 04 16:21:33 studentvm1 lsblk[2437]:    `-NewVG--01-swap         253:7
0    2G  0 lvm
May 04 16:21:33 studentvm1 lsblk[2437]: sdc                          8:32
0    2G  0 disk
May 04 16:21:33 studentvm1 lsblk[2437]: `-NewVG--01-
TestVol1        253:6     0    4G  0 lvm  /TestFS
May 04 16:21:33 studentvm1 lsblk[2437]: sdd                          8:48
0    2G  0 disk
May 04 16:21:33 studentvm1 lsblk[2437]: sr0                          11:0
1 1024M  0 rom
May 04 16:21:33 studentvm1 lsblk[2437]:
zram0                         252:0     0    8G  0 disk [SWAP]
May 04 16:21:33 studentvm1 systemd[1]: myMonitor.service: Deactivated
successfully.
May 04 16:21:33 studentvm1 systemd[1]: Finished myMonitor.service - Logs
system statistics to the systemd journal.
```

Now that we know our service works as expected, create the timer unit file, myMonitor.timer, in /etc/systemd/system and add the following contents:

```
# This timer unit is for testing
# By David Both
# Licensed under GPL V2
#

[Unit]
Description=Logs some system statistics to the systemd journal
Requires=myMonitor.service

[Timer]
Unit=myMonitor.service
OnCalendar=*-*-* *:*:00

[Install]
WantedBy=timers.target
```

The OnCalendar time expression in the myMonitor.timer file should trigger the timer to execute the myMonitor.service unit every minute.

We want to observe any journal entries pertaining to the running of our service when it is triggered by the timer. We could also follow the timer, but following the service allows us to see the results in near real time. Run journalctl with the -f (follow) option:

```
[root@studentvm1 system]# journalctl -S today -f -u myMonitor.service
```

Now let's start but not enable the timer and see what happens when it runs for a while:

```
[root@studentvm1 ~]# systemctl start myMonitor.timer
```

We get one result right away and the next ones at – sort of – one-minute intervals. Watch the journal for a few minutes and see if you notice the same things I did.

Check the status of both the timer and the service.

Like me, you probably noticed at least two things in the journal. First, we do not need to do anything special to cause the STDOUT from the ExecStart triggers in the myMonitor.service unit to be stored in the journal. That is all part of using systemd for running services. However, it does mean that you should be careful about running scripts from a service unit and how much STDOUT they generate.

The second thing I noticed was that the timer does not trigger exactly on the minute at :00 seconds or even exactly one minute from the previous instance. This is intentional, but it can be overridden if necessary or if it just offends your sensibilities as a SysAdmin.

The reason for this is to prevent multiple services from triggering at exactly the same time. For example, as you will see in the following, you can use time expressions such as "Weekly," "Daily," and more. These shortcuts are all defined to trigger at 00:00:00 hours on the day they are triggered. With multiple timers specified this way, there is a strong likelihood that they would attempt to start simultaneously.

systemd timers are intentionally designed to trigger somewhat randomly around the specified times to try to prevent simultaneous triggers. Timers trigger semi-randomly within a time window that starts with the specified trigger time as earliest and the specified time plus one minute at the latest. This trigger time is maintained at a stable position with respect to all other defined timer units, according to the systemd. timer man page. You can see by the preceding journal entries that the timer triggered immediately upon being started and then at about 46 or 47 seconds after each minute.

Most of the time, such probabilistic trigger times are fine. When scheduling tasks such as backups to run, so long as they run during off-hours, there will be no problems. A deterministic starting time such as 01:05:00 in a typical cron job expression is selected by the SysAdmin to not conflict with other tasks, but there is a large range of time values that will accomplish that. A one-minute bit of randomness in such a start time is usually irrelevant.

For some tasks, exact trigger times are not just preferable but an absolute requirement. For those tasks, we can specify a greater trigger time span accuracy to within a microsecond by adding a statement like the following one to the Timer section of the timer unit file:

AccuracySec=1us

Time spans can be used in specifying the desired accuracy as well as in defining repeating or one-time events. The following units are recognized:

- usec, us, μs
- msec, ms
- seconds, second, sec, s
- minutes, minute, min, m
- hours, hour, hr, h
- days, day, d
- weeks, week, w
- months, month, M (defined as 30.44 days)
- years, year, y (defined as 365.25 days)

All of the default timers located in /usr/lib/systemd/system specify a much larger range for accuracy because exact times are not critical. Let's check it out.

EXPERIMENT 37-3: EXPLORING TIMER UNIT FILES

Look at some of the expressions in the system-created timers:

```
[root@studentvm1 system]# grep Accur /usr/lib/systemd/system/*timer
```

```
/usr/lib/systemd/system/fstrim.timer:AccuracySec=1h
/usr/lib/systemd/system/logrotate.timer:AccuracySec=1h
/usr/lib/systemd/system/plocate-updatedb.timer:AccuracySec=20min
/usr/lib/systemd/system/raid-check.timer:AccuracySec=24h
/usr/lib/systemd/system/unbound-anchor.timer:AccuracySec=24h
[root@studentvm1 system]#
```

These accuracy settings range from 20 minutes to 24 hours, which is quite a range. This value depends upon the degree of timeliness required for each program launched by the timer. Some are far more critical than others.

View the complete contents of some of the timer unit files in the /usr/lib/systemd/system directory to see how they are constructed.

It is not necessary to enable the timer in our experiment so that it is activated at boot time, but the command to do so would be this – but don't do it:

```
[root@studentvm1 system]# systemctl enable myMonitor.timer
```

The unit files we created do not need to be executable. We also did not enable the service unit because it is triggered by the timer. We can still trigger the service unit manually from the command line should we want to do so. Try that and observe the journal.

Now stop the timer:

```
[root@studentvm1 ~]# systemctl stop myMonitor.timer
[root@studentvm1 ~]# systemctl status myMonitor.timer
○ myMonitor.timer - Logs some system statistics to the systemd journal
    Loaded: loaded (/etc/systemd/system/myMonitor.timer; disabled; preset:
    disabled)
    Active: inactive (dead)
   Trigger: n/a
  Triggers: ● myMonitor.service

May 04 16:30:10 studentvm1 systemd[1]: Started myMonitor.timer - Logs some
system statistics to the systemd journal.
May 04 16:42:43 studentvm1 systemd[1]: myMonitor.timer: Deactivated
successfully.
May 04 16:42:43 studentvm1 systemd[1]: Stopped myMonitor.timer - Logs some
system statistics to the systemd journal.
```

See the man pages for systemd.timer and systemd.time for more information
about timer accuracy, event time expressions, and trigger events.

Timer Types

systemd timers have additional capabilities that are not present with cron, which
only triggers on specific repetitive real-time dates and times. systemd timers can be
configured to trigger based on the status changes of other systemd units. For example,
a timer might be configured to trigger a specific elapsed time after system boot, after
startup, or after activation of a defined service unit. These are called monotonic timers.
Monotonic refers to a count or sequence that continually increases. These timers are not
persistent because they reset after each boot.

Figure 37-2 lists the monotonic timers along with a short definition of each, as well as
the onCalendar timer – which is not monotonic and which is used to specify particular
times in the future, which may or may not be repetitive. This information is derived from
the systemd.timer man page with a few minor changes.

Timer	Monotonic	Definition
OnActiveSec=	X	Defines a timer relative to the moment the timer itself is activated.
OnBootSec=	X	Defines a timer relative to when the machine was booted up.
OnStartupSec=	X	Defines a timer relative to when the service manager was first started. For system timer units this is very similar to OnBootSec= as the system service manager is generally started very early at boot. It's primarily useful when configured in units running in the per-user service manager, as the user service manager is generally started on first login only, not already during boot.
OnUnitActiveSec=	X	Defines a timer relative to when the timer that is to be activated was last activated.
OnUnitInactiveSec =	X	Defines a timer relative to when the unit the timer that is being activated was last deactivated.
OnCalendar=		Defines realtime (i.e. wallclock) timers with calendar event expressions. See systemd.time(7) for more information on the syntax of calendar event expressions. Otherwise, the semantics are similar to OnActiveSec= and related settings. This timer is the one most like those used with the cron service.

Figure 37-2. *A list of systemd timer definitions*

The monotonic timers can use the same shortcut names for their time spans as the AccuracySec statement previously discussed, but systemd normalizes those names to seconds. For example, you might want to specify a timer that triggers an event for one time five days after the system was booted, and that might look like this: OnBootSec=5d. If the host was booted at 2020-06-15 09:45:27, the timer would trigger at 2020-06-20 09:45:27 or within one minute after.

Home Directory Security with systemd-homed

One relatively new service, systemd-homed, extends the reach of systemd into management of users' home directories, that is, human users only and not system users in the user ID (UID) range between 0 and 999.

What Is It?

The systemd-homed service is intended to support user account portability that is independent of the underlying computer system. A practical example would be to carry around your home directory on a USB thumb drive and be able to plug it into any system that would automatically recognize and mount it. According to Lennart Poettering, lead developer of systemd, access to a user's home directory should not be allowed to anyone unless the user is logged in. The systemd-homed service is designed as a security enhancement especially for mobile devices such as laptops. It also seems like a tool that might be useful with containers.

This objective can only be achieved if all of the user metadata is self-contained in the home directory. User account information is stored in an identity file, ~/.identity, on your home directory, which is only accessible to systemd-homed when the password is entered. All of the account metadata is stored in this file, including everything Linux needs to know about you, so that the home directory can be portable to any Linux host that uses systemd-homed. This prevents the need to have an account with a stored password on every system you might need to use.

The home directory can also be encrypted using your password, which under systemd-homed is stored in your home directory with all of your user metadata. Your encrypted password is not stored anywhere else and thus cannot be accessed by anyone.

Although the methods used to encrypt and store passwords for modern Linux systems are considered to be unbreakable, the best safeguard is to prevent its being accessed in the first place. Assumptions about the invulnerability of their security have led many to ruin.

This service is primarily intended for use with portable devices such as laptops. Poettering states, "Homed is intended primarily for client machines, that is, laptops and thus machines you typically ssh from a lot more than ssh to if you follow what I mean." It is not intended for use on servers or workstations that are tethered to a single location by cables or locked into a server room.

The systemd-homed service is enabled on new installations – at least for Fedora, which is the distro that I use – and is started by default. This is by design and I don't expect that to change. On systems with existing filesystems, upgrades or reinstallations that keep the existing partitions, logical volumes, and user accounts are not affected or changed in any way.

Creating Controlled Users

Use of the traditional tools such as useradd creates accounts and home directories that are not managed by systemd-homed. Therefore, if you continue to use the traditional user management tools, your home directories will not be managed by systemd-homed. This is still the case with the non-root user account created during a new installation.

The homectl Command

The homectl command is used to create user accounts that are managed by systemd-homed. Simply using the homectl command to create a new account generates the metadata needed to make the home directory portable.

The homectl command man page has a good explanation of the objectives and function of the systemd-homed service. However, reading the homectl man page is quite interesting, especially the Example section. Of the five examples given, three show how to create user accounts with specific limits imposed, such as a maximum number of concurrent processes or a maximum amount of disk space.

In a non-homectl setup, these limits are imposed using the /etc/security/limits. conf file. The only advantage I can see to this is that it makes it possible to add a user and apply limits with a single command. With the traditional method, the limits.conf file must be configured manually by the SysAdmin.

635

Limitations

The only significant limitation of which I am aware is that it is not possible to remotely access a user home directory using OpenSSH. This limitation is due to the current inability of PAM to provide access to a home directory managed by homectl. Poettering seems doubtful that this can be overcome. This limitation would prevent me from using systemd-homed for my home directory on my primary workstation or even my laptop. I typically log into both computers remotely several times per day using SSH, so this is a showstopper for me.

The other limitation I can see is that you still need a Linux computer for use with a USB thumb drive with your home directory on it, and that computer needs to have systemd-homed running.

But I Don't Want It!

You don't have to use it, then. I'm not using it, and I do not intend to any time soon. I will almost certainly never use it. I plan to continue to do what I have been all along, using the traditional tools for user management. The default for the few distros with which I have some little knowledge, including Fedora, which is what I use, is for the systemd-homed service to be enabled and running. You can disable and stop the systemd-homed service with no impact on traditional user accounts, and I have done that.

Resource Management with systemd

There is little more frustrating to me as a SysAdmin than unexpectedly running out of some computing resource. On more than one occasion, I have filled all available disk space in a partition, run out of RAM, and not had enough CPU time to perform the tasks at hand in a reasonable period of time. Resource management is one of the most important tasks performed by SysAdmins.

The point of resource management is to ensure that all processes have relatively equal access to the system resources they need. Resource management also involves ensuring that RAM, hard drive space, and CPU capacity are added when necessary or rationed when that is not possible. Users who hog system resources, whether intentionally or accidentally, should also be prevented from doing so.

We have tools that enable us to monitor and manage various system resources. Tools such as top and many similar tools allow us to monitor the use of memory, I/O, storage (disk, SSD, etc.), network, swap space, CPU usage, and more. These tools, particularly those that are CPU-centric, are mostly based on the paradigm that the running process is the unit of control. At best they provide a way to adjust the nice number – and through that the priority – or to kill a running process.

Other tools based on traditional resource management in a SystemV environment are the /etc/security/limits.conf file and the local configuration files located in the /etc/security/limits.d directory. Resources can be limited in a fairly crude but useful manner by user or group. Resources that can be managed include various aspects of RAM, total CPU time per day, total amount of data, priority, nice number, number of concurrent logins, number of processes, maximum file size, and more.

Using cgroups for Process Management

One major difference between systemd and SystemV is the way in which they handle processes. SystemV treats each process as an entity unto itself. systemd collects related processes into control groups called cgroups and manages system resources for the cgroup as a whole. This means that resources can be managed per application rather than the individual processes that make up an application.

The control units for cgroups are slice units. Slices are a conceptualization that allows systemd to order processes in a tree format for ease of management. I found the following description in an article[1] by Steve Ovens of Red Hat that provides an excellent example of how cgroups are used by the system itself:

As you may or may not know, the Linux kernel is responsible for all of the hardware interacting reliably on a system. That means, aside from just the bits of code (drivers) that enable the operating system (OS) to understand the hardware, it also sets limits on how many resources a particular program can demand from the system. This is most easily understood when talking about the amount of memory (RAM) a system has to divide up amongst all of the applications your computer may execute. In its most basic form, a Linux system is allowed to run most applications without restriction. This can be great for general computing if all applications play

---

[1] Ovens, Steve, "A Linux sysadmin's introduction to cgroups," www.redhat.com/sysadmin/cgroups-part-one, Enable Sysadmin, 2020

nicely together. But what happens if there is a bug in a program, and it starts to consume all of the available memory? The kernel has a facility called the Out Of Memory (OOM) Killer. Its job is to halt applications in order to free up enough RAM so that the OS may continue to function without crashing.

That's great, you say, but what does this have to do with cgroups? Well, the OOM process acts as a last line of defense before your system comes crashing down around you. It's useful to a point, but since the kernel can control which processes must survive the OOM, it can also determine which applications cannot consume too much RAM in the first place.

Cgroups are, therefore, a facility built into the kernel that allow the administrator to set resource utilization limits on any process on the system. In general, cgroups control:

- *The number of CPU shares per process.*

- *The limits on memory per process.*

- *Block Device I/O per process.*

- *Which network packets are identified as the same type so that another application can enforce network traffic rules.*

There are more facets than just these, but those are the major categories that most administrators care about.

EXPERIMENT 37-4: VIEWING CGROUPS

Let's start with some commands that allow us to view various types of information about cgroups. The systemctl status <service> command displays slice information about a specified service including its slice. This example shows the at daemon:

```
[root@studentvm1 ~]# systemctl status atd.service
● atd.service - Deferred execution scheduler
     Loaded: loaded (/usr/lib/systemd/system/atd.service; enabled; preset:
     enabled)
     Active: active (running) since Thu 2023-05-04 08:22:16 EDT; 13h ago
       Docs: man:atd(8)
   Main PID: 1324 (atd)
      Tasks: 1 (limit: 19130)
```

```
   Memory: 252.0K
      CPU: 4ms
   CGroup: /system.slice/atd.service
           └─1324 /usr/sbin/atd -f
```

May 04 08:22:16 studentvm1 systemd[1]: Started atd.service - Deferred execution scheduler.

This is an excellent example of one reason that I find systemd more usable than SystemV and the old init program; there is so much more information here that SystemV was able to provide. The cgroup entry includes the hierarchical structure where the system.slice is systemd (PID 1) and the atd.service is one level below and is part of the system.slice. The second line of the cgroup entry also shows the process ID (PID) and the command used to start the daemon.

The systemctl command allows us to see multiple cgroup entries. The --all option shows all slices including those that are not currently active:

```
[root@studentvm1 ~]# systemctl -t slice --all
UNIT                                      LOAD   ACTIVE SUB    DESCRIPTION
-.slice                                   loaded active active Root Slice
system-getty.slice                        loaded active active Slice /
                                                              system/getty
system-lvm2\x2dpvscan.slice               loaded active active Slice /system/
                                                              lvm2-pvscan
system-modprobe.slice                     loaded active active Slice /system/
                                                              modprobe
system-sshd\x2dkeygen.slice               loaded active active Slice /system/
                                                              sshd-keygen
system-systemd\x2dfsck.slice              loaded active active Slice /system/
                                                              systemd-fsck
system-systemd\x2dzram\x2dsetup.slice     loaded active active Slice /system/
                                                              systemd-zram-setup
system.slice                              loaded active active System Slice
user-0.slice                              loaded active active User Slice
                                                              of UID 0
user-1000.slice                           loaded active active User Slice of
                                                              UID 1000
```

```
user-984.slice                             loaded active active User Slice
                                           of UID 984
user.slice                                 loaded active active User and
                                           Session Slice

LOAD   = Reflects whether the unit definition was properly loaded.
ACTIVE = The high-level unit activation state, i.e. generalization of SUB.
SUB    = The low-level unit activation state, values depend on unit type.
12 loaded units listed.
To show all installed unit files use 'systemctl list-unit-files'.
```

The first thing to notice about the preceding data is that it shows user slices for UIDs 0 (root) and 1000, which is my user login. This shows only the slices and not the services that are part of each slice. So it becomes obvious from this data that a slice is created for each user at the time they log in. This can provide a means to manage all of the tasks for that user as a single cgroup entity.

Exploring the cgroup Hierarchy

All well and good so far, but cgroups are hierarchical, and all of the service units run as members of one of these cgroups. Viewing that hierarchy is easy and uses one old command and one new one that is part of systemd.

EXPERIMENT 37-5: CGROUPS

The ps command can be used to map the processes and their locations in the cgroup hierarchy. Note that it is necessary to specify the desired data columns when using the ps command. I have significantly reduced the volume of output from this command but have tried to leave enough so that you can get a feel for what you might find on your own systems:

```
[root@studentvm1 ~]# ps xawf -eo pid,user,cgroup,args
    PID USER     CGROUP                      COMMAND
      2 root     -                           [kthreadd]
      3 root     -                            \_ [rcu_gp]
      4 root     -                            \_ [rcu_par_gp]
      5 root     -                            \_ [slub_flushwq]
<SNIP>
```

```
1154 root      0::/system.slice/gssproxy.s /usr/sbin/gssproxy -D
1175 root      0::/system.slice/sshd.servi sshd: /usr/sbin/sshd -D
               [listener] 0 of 10-100 startups
1442 root      0::/user.slice/user-0.slice \_ sshd: root [priv]
1454 root      0::/user.slice/user-0.slice  |   \_ sshd: root@pts/0
1455 root      0::/user.slice/user-0.slice  |      \_ -bash
1489 root      0::/user.slice/user-0.slice  |         \_ screen
1490 root      0::/user.slice/user-0.slice  |            \_ SCREEN
1494 root      0::/user.slice/user-0.slice  |              \_ /
               bin/bash
4097 root      0::/user.slice/user-0.slice  |                   |  \_ ps
               xawf -eo pid,user,cgroup,args
4098 root      0::/user.slice/user-0.slice  |                   |  \_ less
2359 root      0::/user.slice/user-0.slice  |                   \_ /
               bin/bash
2454 root      0::/user.slice/user-0.slice \_ sshd: root [priv]
2456 root      0::/user.slice/user-0.slice  |   \_ sshd: root@pts/3
2457 root      0::/user.slice/user-0.slice  |      \_ -bash
3014 root      0::/user.slice/user-1000.sl \_ sshd: student [priv]
3027 student   0::/user.slice/user-1000.sl    \_ sshd: student@pts/4
3028 student   0::/user.slice/user-1000.sl       \_ -bash
1195 colord    0::/system.slice/colord.ser /usr/libexec/colord
<SNIP>
```

We can view the entire hierarchy with the systemd-cgls command, which is a bit simpler because it requires no complex options.

I have shortened this tree view considerably too. This was done on StudentVM1 and is about 230 lines long; the amount of data from my primary workstation is about 400 lines:

```
[root@studentvm1 ~]# systemd-cgls
Control group /:
-.slice
├─user.slice (#1323)
│ → user.invocation_id: 05085df18c6244679e0a8e31a9d7d6ce
│ → trusted.invocation_id: 05085df18c6244679e0a8e31a9d7d6ce
│ ├─user-0.slice (#6141)
│ │ → user.invocation_id: 6535078b3c70486496ccbca02a735139
│ │ → trusted.invocation_id: 6535078b3c70486496ccbca02a735139
```

```
│   │   ├─session-2.scope (#6421)
│   │   │ → user.invocation_id: 4ce76f4810e04e2fa2f166971241030c
│   │   │ → trusted.invocation_id: 4ce76f4810e04e2fa2f166971241030c
│   │   │ ├─1442 sshd: root [priv]
│   │   │ ├─1454 sshd: root@pts/0
│   │   │ ├─1455 -bash
│   │   │ ├─1489 screen
│   │   │ ├─1490 SCREEN
│   │   │ ├─1494 /bin/bash
│   │   │ ├─2359 /bin/bash
│   │   │ ├─4119 systemd-cgls
│   │   │ └─4120 less
│ <SNIP>
│   └─user-1000.slice (#10941)
│     → user.invocation_id: 2b5f1a03abfc4afca295e003494b73b2
│     → trusted.invocation_id: 2b5f1a03abfc4afca295e003494b73b2
│     ├─user@1000.service … (#11021)
│     │ → user.delegate: 1
│     │ → trusted.delegate: 1
│     │ → user.invocation_id: cfd09d6c3cd641d898ddc23e22916195
│     │ → trusted.invocation_id: cfd09d6c3cd641d898ddc23e22916195
│     │ └─init.scope (#11061)
│     │   ├─3017 /usr/lib/systemd/systemd --user
│     │   └─3019 (sd-pam)
│     └─session-5.scope (#11221)
│       → user.invocation_id: a8749076931f425d851c59fd956c4652
│       → trusted.invocation_id: a8749076931f425d851c59fd956c4652
│       ├─3014 sshd: student [priv]
│       ├─3027 sshd: student@pts/4
│ <SNIP>
│     ├─session-7.scope (#14461)
│     │ → user.invocation_id: f3e31059e0904df08d6b44856aac639b
│     │ → trusted.invocation_id: f3e31059e0904df08d6b44856aac639b
│     │ ├─1429 lightdm --session-child 13 20
│     │ ├─4133 /usr/bin/gnome-keyring-daemon --daemonize --login
│     │ ├─4136 xfce4-session
│     │ ├─4300 /usr/bin/VBoxClient --clipboard
│     │ ├─4301 /usr/bin/VBoxClient --clipboard
```

```
│   │   ├─4315 /usr/bin/VBoxClient --seamless
│   │   ├─4316 /usr/bin/VBoxClient --seamless
│   │   ├─4321 /usr/bin/VBoxClient --draganddrop
│   │   ├─4326 /usr/bin/VBoxClient --draganddrop
│   │   ├─4328 /usr/bin/VBoxClient --vmsvga-session
│   │   ├─4329 /usr/bin/VBoxClient --vmsvga-session
│   │   ├─4340 /usr/bin/ssh-agent /bin/sh -c exec -l /bin/bash -c
│   │           "startxfce4"
│   │   ├─4395 /usr/bin/gpg-agent --sh --daemon
│   │   ├─4396 xfwm4 --display :0.0 --sm-client-id 2e79712f7-299e-4c6f-
│   │           a503-2f64940ab467
│   │   ├─4409 xfsettingsd --display :0.0 --sm-client-id 288d2bcfd-3264-4caf-
│   │           ac93-2bf552b14688
│   │   ├─4412 xfce4-panel --display :0.0 --sm-client-id 2f57b404c-
│   │           e176-4440-9830-4472e6757db0
│   │   ├─4416 Thunar --sm-client-id 21b424243-7aed-4e9e-9fc5-
│   │           c3b1421df3fa –daemon
<SNIP>
```

This tree view shows all of the user and system slices and the services and programs running in each cgroup. Notice that within the user-1000.slice in the preceding listing are the units called "scopes", which group related programs together into a manageable unit. The user-1000.slice/session-7.scope cgroup contains the GUI desktop program hierarchy starting with the LXDM display manager session and all of its sub-tasks including things like the Bash shell and the Thunar GUI file manager.

Scope units are not defined in configuration files but are generated programmatically as the result of starting groups of one or more related programs. Scope units do not create or start the processes running as part of that cgroup. All processes within the scope are equal, and there is no internal hierarchy. The life of a scope begins when the first process is created and ends when the last process is destroyed.

Open several windows on your desktop such as terminal emulators, LibreOffice, or whatever you want, and then switch to an available virtual console and start something like top or Midnight Commander. Run the systemd-cgls command on your host and take note of the overall hierarchy and the scope units.

The `systemd-cgls` command provides the most complete representation of the cgroup hierarchy and details of the units that make it up of any other command that I have found. I prefer its cleaner representation of the tree than that provided by the ps command.

Managing cgroups with systemd

I thought about writing this section myself but found a series of four articles by Steve Ovens on Red Hat's Enable Sysadmin website. I have found this information helpful in what I have written already, but since it covers the subject so well and goes beyond the scope of this course, I decided to list the articles here and let you read them for yourself:

1. "A Linux sysadmin's introduction to cgroups"[2]

2. "How to manage cgroups with CPUShares"[3]

3. "Managing cgroups the hard way – manually"[4]

4. "Managing cgroups with systemd"[5]

Although some SysAdmins may need to manage system resources using cgroups, many others will not. If you do, the best way to get started is with the series of articles listed.

Chapter Summary

We started this final chapter about systemd by creating a timer that triggered every minute and produced output in the systemd journal. Using the journalctl tool, we looked at various ways to extract that and other data from the journal.

---

[2] Ovens, Steve, "A Linux sysadmin's introduction to cgroups," `www.redhat.com/sysadmin/cgroups-part-one`, Enable Sysadmin, 2020

[3] Ovens, Steve, "How to manage cgroups with CPUShares," `www.redhat.com/sysadmin/cgroups-part-two`, , Enable Sysadmin, 2020

[4] Ovens, Steve, "Managing cgroups the hard way – manually," `www.redhat.com/sysadmin/cgroups-part-three`, Enable Sysadmin, 2020

[5] Ovens, Steve, "Managing cgroups with systemd," `www.redhat.com/sysadmin/cgroups-part-four`, , Enable Sysadmin, 2020

The systemd-homed service can be used for a secure form of management of roaming users' home directories. It is useful on portable devices like laptops but can be especially useful for users who carry a thumb drive with only their own home directories on it and just plug it into any convenient Linux computer.

The primary limitation to using systemd-homed is that it is not possible to log in remotely using SSH. And even though the systemd-homed is enabled by default, it does not affect home directories that were created with the useradd command. I do need to point out that – like many systemd tools – systemd-homed is optional. So I just stopped and disabled the service.

We also looked at cgroups and how they can be used for managing system resources such as RAM and CPU. Because actual resource management using cgroups is beyond the scope of this course, I have provided links to some excellent materials by Steve Ovens that provide enough information to get you started.

Exercises

Complete the following exercises to finish this chapter:

1. What unit files are required to implement a timer?

2. Create a timer unit that triggers within ten minutes of 04:00 a.m. the last day of every month. It should do nothing more than add a string of text of your choosing to the systemd journal.

3. Why are cgroups important for resource management?

4. Add a controlled user to the system. Who can access that user's home directory. What about the root user?

CHAPTER 38

D-Bus and udev

Objectives

In this chapter you will learn

- How Linux treats all devices as plug and play
- What D-Bus and udev are
- How D-Bus and udev work together to make device access easy
- How to write rules for udev

/dev Chaos

The /dev directory has always been the location for the device special files in all Unix and Linux operating systems. Note that device special files are not the same as device drivers. Each device file represents one actual or potential physical device connected to the host.

In the past the device files were created at the time the operating system was created. This meant that all possible devices that might ever be used on a system needed to be created in advance. In fact, tens of thousands of device files needed to be created to handle all of the possibilities. It became very difficult to determine which device file actually related to a specific physical device.

The development of two very important tools, D-Bus and udev, has provided Linux with the ability to create many of the device files only when they are needed by a device that is already installed or one that is hot-plugged into the running system.

© David Both 2023
D. Both, *Using and Administering Linux: Volume 2*, https://doi.org/10.1007/978-1-4842-9615-8_38

About D-Bus

D-Bus[1] is a Linux software interface used for inter-process communications (IPC). It was first released in 2006. We looked at one form of IPC in Volume 1, Chapter 13, the named pipe, in which one program would push data into the named pipe and another program would extract the data.

D-Bus is a system-wide and more complex form of IPC that allows many kernel and system-level processes to send messages to the logical message bus. Other processes listen to the messages on the bus and may choose to react to those messages or not.

About udev

The udev[2] daemon is designed to simplify the chaos that had overtaken the /dev directory with huge numbers of mostly unneeded devices. At startup, udev creates entries in /dev only for those devices that actually currently exist or that have a high probability of actually existing on the host. This significantly reduces the number of device files required.

In addition to detecting devices, udev assigns names to those devices when they are plugged into the system, such as USB storage and printers and other non-USB types of devices as well. In fact, udev treats all devices as plug and play, even at boot time. This makes dealing with devices consistent at all times. udev also moves device naming out of kernel space and into user space.

Greg Kroah-Hartman, one of the authors of udev, wrote an interesting and informative article[3] for *Linux Journal*. It provides insight into the details of udev and how it is supposed to work. That article discusses udev, a program that replaces and improves upon the functionality of the old devfs. It provides /dev entries for devices in the system at any moment in time. It also provides features previously unavailable through devfs alone, such as persistent naming for devices when they move around the device tree, a flexible device naming scheme, notification of external systems of device changes, and moving all naming policy out of the kernel.

---

[1] Wikipedia, D-Bus, https://en.wikipedia.org/wiki/D-Bus

[2] Wikipedia, udev, https://en.wikipedia.org/wiki/Udev

[3] Kroah-Hartman, Greg, "Kernel Korner – udev – Persistent Device Naming in User Space," www.linuxjournal.com/article/7316, Linux Journal, 2004

Note that udev has matured since the article was written and some things have changed, such as the udev rule location and structure, but the overall objectives and architecture are the same.

One of the main consequences of using udev for persistent plug-and-play naming is that it makes things much easier for the average non-technical user. This is a good thing in the long run; however, there have been migration problems.

EXPERIMENT 38-1: UDEV IN ACTION

Perform this experiment as the student user on the GUI desktop. This experiment assumes that the USB stick is formatted and has one partition.

Open the Thunar file manager and ensure that the side panel is visible. It does not matter whether it is in Shortcuts or Tree mode because the storage devices are visible in both.

Plug a USB thumb drive that is known to be working into the physical host. Then, on the VirtualBox window for StudentVM1, use the menu bar to open Devices ➤ USB and, while watching the Thunar window, place a check mark next to the USB device you just plugged in. The device will now be available to the VM, and it will be shown in the Thunar side panel.

Verify that the new device special file has been created in /dev/:

```
[root@studentvm1 ~]# ll /dev | grep sd
brw-rw----  1 root     disk      8,   0 May 17 11:35 sda
brw-rw----  1 root     disk      8,   1 May 17 11:35 sda1
brw-rw----  1 root     disk      8,   2 May 17 11:35 sda2
brw-rw----  1 root     disk      8,  16 May 17 11:35 sdb
brw-rw----  1 root     disk      8,  17 May 17 11:35 sdb1
brw-rw----  1 root     disk      8,  18 May 17 11:35 sdb2
brw-rw----  1 root     disk      8,  32 May 17 11:35 sdc
brw-rw----  1 root     disk      8,  48 May 17 11:35 sdd
brw-rw----  1 root     disk      8,  64 May 20 08:29 sde
brw-rw----  1 root     disk      8,  65 May 20 08:29 sde1
```

You should see that the new devices, /dev/sde and /dev/sde1, have been created within the last couple minutes or so. One device special file was created for the entire device, /dev/sde, and one was created for the partition on the device, /dev/sde1. The device name may be different on your VM depending upon how closely you have been performing the experiments in the preceding chapters of this course.

The D-Bus and udev services work together to make this happen.

Here is a simplified version of what takes place when a new device is connected to the host. I stipulate here that the host system is already booted and running at multi-user.target (runlevel 3) or graphical.target (runlevel 5):

1. The user plugs in a new device, usually into an external USB, SATA, or eSATA connector.

2. The kernel detects this and sends a message on D-Bus to announce the new device.

3. udev reads the message proffered on D-Bus.

4. Based on the device properties and its location in the hardware bus tree, udev creates a name for the new device if one does not already exist.

5. The udev system creates the device special file in /dev.

6. If a new device driver is required, it is loaded.

7. The device is initialized.

8. udev may send a notification to the desktop so that the desktop may display an icon for the new device to the user.

The process of hot-plugging a new hardware device into a running Linux system and making it ready is very complex – for the operating system. It is very simple for the user who just wants to plug in a new device and have it work. This simplifies things immensely for the end user. For USB and SATA storage devices, USB thumb drives, keyboards, mice, printers, displays, and nearly anything else, all that a user needs to do is to plug the device into the appropriate USB or SATA port and it will work.

Naming Rules

udev stores its default naming rules in files in the /usr/lib/udev/rules.d directory and its local configuration files in the /etc/udev/rules.d directory. Each file contains a set of rules for a specific device type. These rules should not be changed.

In earlier versions of udev, there were many local rule sets created, including a set for NIC naming. As each NIC was discovered by the kernel and renamed by udev for the very first time, a rule was added to the rule set for the network device type. This was initially done to ensure consistency before names had changed from "ethX" to more consistent ones.

Now that udev has multiple consistent default rules for determining device names, especially for NICs, storing the specific rules for each device in local configuration files is not required to maintain that consistency.

EXPERIMENT 38-2: NIC RENAMING BY UDEV

Perform this experiment as the student user. We can look at dmesg for our VM and see where the NIC names were changed by udev. You may also encounter some other messages that match the search pattern:

```
[student@studentvm1 ~]$ dmesg | grep -i eth
[    7.739484] e1000 0000:00:03.0 eth0: (PCI:33MHz:32-bit) 08:00:27:01:7d:ad
[    7.739524] e1000 0000:00:03.0 eth0: Intel(R) PRO/1000 Network Connection
[    8.142361] e1000 0000:00:09.0 eth1: (PCI:33MHz:32-bit) 08:00:27:ff:c6:4f
[    8.142398] e1000 0000:00:09.0 eth1: Intel(R) PRO/1000 Network Connection
[    8.145736] e1000 0000:00:09.0 enp0s9: renamed from eth1
[    8.149176] e1000 0000:00:03.0 enp0s3: renamed from eth0
```

This result is from my VM, which has two NICs so there are lines for both. You should have only a single NIC so only one set of entries in the **dmesg** data stream.

The first line for eth0 shows when the NIC was "discovered," at 5.014594 seconds after startup. The second line shows the ID of the device as an (virtual) Intel network device. The last line for eth0 records the renaming from eth0 to enp0s3.

Making udev Work

udev is the sub-system in Linux that supplies your computer with information about device events. In plain English, that means it's the code that detects when you have things plugged into your computer, like a network card, external storage devices (including USB thumb drives), mice, keyboards, joysticks and gamepads, DVD-ROM drives, and so on. That makes it a potentially useful utility, and it's well-enough exposed to a standard user such that you can manually script it to, for instance, perform certain tasks when a certain hard drive is plugged in.

This section teaches you how to create a udev script triggered by some udev event, such as plugging in a specific thumb drive. Once you understand the process for working with udev, you can use it to do all manner of things, like loading a specific driver when a gamepad is attached or performing an automatic backup when your backup drive is attached.

A Basic Script

The best way to work with udev is in small chunks. Don't write the entire script up front, but instead start with something that simply confirms that udev does indeed trigger some custom event.

Depending on the ultimate goal of your script, you won't be able to guarantee that you will ever see the results of a script with your own eyes, so make your script log that it was successfully triggered. The usual place for log files is in the /var directory, but that's mostly the root user's domain, so for testing, use /tmp, which is accessible by normal users and also usually gets cleaned out every so often.

EXPERIMENT 38-3: USING UDEV TO TRIGGER A SCRIPT

Open your favorite text editor as root and enter this simple script. Place it in /usr/local/bin and name it trigger.sh:

```
#!/usr/bin/bash
/usr/bin/date >> /tmp/udev.log
```

Make it executable with chmod +x:

```
[root@studentvm1 bin]# chmod +x /usr/local/bin/trigger.sh
```

This script has nothing to do with udev. When this script is executed, this script places a timestamp in the file /tmp/udev.log. Test the script yourself:

```
[root@studentvm1 ~]# trigger.sh ; cat /tmp/udev.log
Sun May  7 03:15:03 PM EDT 2023
```

After getting at least one line in the log file, use the following command in a separate terminal session to follow the file as we add more entries:

```
[root@studentvm1 ~]# tail -f /tmp/udev.log
Sun May  7 03:15:03 PM EDT 2023
Sun May  7 03:15:05 PM EDT 2023
```

In the original terminal session, run the `trigger.sh` program again a couple times and verify that the new entries show up immediately.

The next step is to make udev, rather than yourself, trigger the script.

Unique Device Identification

In order for your script to be triggered by a device event, udev must know under what conditions it should call the script. In real life, you can identify a thumb drive by its color, the manufacturer, and the fact that you just plugged it into your computer. Your computer, however, obviously needs a different set of criteria.

udev identifies devices by serial numbers, manufacturers, and even vendor ID and product ID numbers. Since this is early in the life span of your udev script, be as broad, nonspecific, and all-inclusive as possible. In other words, you want first to catch nearly any valid udev event to trigger your script.

With the udevadm monitor command, you can tap into udev in real time and see what it sees when you plug in different devices. Try it as root:

```
[root@studentvm1 ~]# udevadm monitor
The monitor function prints received events for:
```

- UDEV: the event which udev sends out after rule processing

- KERNEL: the kernel uevent

With udevadm monitor running, connect a thumb drive to the VM and watch as all kinds of information are spewed out onto your screen. Notice, particularly, that the type of event is an

ADD event. That's a good way of identifying what type of event you want. The following is a partial listing of the data stream generated by the event:

```
KERNEL[24806.003207] add      /devices/pci0000:00/0000:00:0c.0/usb1/1-1 (usb)
KERNEL[24806.007600] add      /devices/pci0000:00/0000:00:0c.0/
                              usb1/1-1/1-1:1.0 (usb)
KERNEL[24806.008133] add     /devices/virtual/workqueue/scsi_tmf_7 (workqueue)
KERNEL[24806.009826] add      /devices/pci0000:00/0000:00:0c.0/usb1/1-1
                              /1-1:1.0/host7 (scsi)
KERNEL[24806.009882] add      /devices/pci0000:00/0000:00:0c.0/usb1/1-1
                              /1-1:1.0/host7/scsi_host/host7 (scsi_host)
KERNEL[24806.009953] bind     /devices/pci0000:00/0000:00:0c.0/usb1/1-1
                              /1-1:1.0 (usb)
KERNEL[24806.010031] bind     /devices/pci0000:00/0000:00:0c.0/usb1/1-1 (usb)
UDEV   [24806.019294] add      /devices/virtual/workqueue/scsi_tmf_7
                              (workqueue)
UDEV   [24806.024541] add      /devices/pci0000:00/0000:00:0c.0/usb1/1-1 (usb)
UDEV   [24806.029305] add     /devices/pci0000:00/0000:00:0c.0/usb1/1-1/1-1:1.0 (usb)
UDEV   [24806.032781] add      /devices/pci0000:00/0000:00:0c.0/usb1/1-1
                              /1-1:1.0/host7 (scsi)
UDEV   [24806.036195] add      /devices/pci0000:00/0000:00:0c.0/usb1/1-1
                              /1-1:1.0/host7/scsi_host/host7 (scsi_host)
UDEV   [24806.038410] bind     /devices/pci0000:00/0000:00:0c.0/usb1/1-1
                              /1-1:1.0 (usb)
UDEV   [24806.051152] bind     /devices/pci0000:00/0000:00:0c.0/usb1/1-1 (usb)
KERNEL[24807.047146] add      /devices/pci0000:00/0000:00:0c.0/usb1/1-1
                              /1-1:1.0/host7/target7:0:0 (scsi)
KERNEL[24807.047255] add      /devices/pci0000:00/0000:00:0c.0/usb1/1-1
                              /1-1:1.0/host7/target7:0:0/7:0:0:0 (scsi)
KERNEL[24807.047303] add      /devices/pci0000:00/0000:00:0c.0/usb1/1-1
                              /1-1:1.0/host7/target7:0:0/7:0:0:0/scsi_
                              device/7:0:0:0 (scsi_device)
KERNEL[24807.048012] add      /devices/pci0000:00/0000:00:0c.0/usb1/1-1
                              /1-1:1.0/host7/target7:0:0/7:0:0:0/scsi_
                              disk/7:0:0:0 (scsi_disk)
KERNEL[24807.048128] add      /devices/pci0000:00/0000:00:0c.0/usb1/1-1
                              /1-1:1.0/host7/target7:0:0/7:0:0:0/scsi_
                              generic/sg5 (scsi_generic)
```

```
KERNEL[24807.048338] add      /devices/pci0000:00/0000:00:0c.0/usb1/1-1
                              /1-1:1.0/host7/target7:0:0/7:0:0:0/
                              bsg/7:0:0:0 (bsg)
UDEV   [24807.053770] add     /devices/pci0000:00/0000:00:0c.0/usb1/1-1
                              /1-1:1.0/host7/target7:0:0 (scsi)
KERNEL[24807.055003] add      /devices/virtual/bdi/8:64 (bdi)
UDEV   [24807.062903] add     /devices/pci0000:00/0000:00:0c.0/usb1/1-1
                              /1-1:1.0/host7/target7:0:0/7:0:0:0 (scsi)
KERNEL[24807.064836] add      /devices/pci0000:00/0000:00:0c.0/usb1/1-1
                              /1-1:1.0/host7/target7:0:0/7:0:0:0/block/
                              sde (block)
KERNEL[24807.064954] add      /devices/pci0000:00/0000:00:0c.0/usb1/1-1
                              /1-1:1.0/host7/target7:0:0/7:0:0:0/block/sde/
                              sde1 (block)
KERNEL[24807.065022] bind     /devices/pci0000:00/0000:00:0c.0/usb1/1-1
                              /1-1:1.0/host7/target7:0:0/7:0:0:0 (scsi)
<SNIP>
```

The udevadm monitor command provides a lot of good info, but you can see it with prettier formatting with the command udevadm info, assuming you know where your thumb drive is currently located in your /dev tree. If not, unplug and then plug your thumb drive back in and then immediately issue this command:

```
[root@studentvm1 ~]# dmesg | tail | grep -i sd*
[24312.124701] usb 1-1: new high-speed USB device number 3 using xhci_hcd
[24312.412680] usb 1-1: New USB device found, idVendor=abcd, idProduct=1234,
bcdDevice= 1.00
[24312.412695] usb 1-1: New USB device strings: Mfr=1, Product=2,
SerialNumber=3
[24312.412701] usb 1-1: Product: UDisk
[24312.412707] usb 1-1: Manufacturer: General
[24312.412711] usb 1-1: SerialNumber: 14041419271202224970300
[24312.417465] usb-storage 1-1:1.0: USB Mass Storage device detected
[24312.419358] scsi host7: usb-storage 1-1:1.0
[24313.436048] scsi 7:0:0:0: Direct-Access     General  UDisk
5.00 PQ: 0 ANSI: 2
[24313.436968] sd 7:0:0:0: Attached scsi generic sg5 type 0
[24313.440749] sd 7:0:0:0: [sde] 15974400 512-byte logical blocks: (8.18
GB/7.62 GiB)
```

```
[24313.442362] sd 7:0:0:0: [sde] Write Protect is off
[24313.442372] sd 7:0:0:0: [sde] Mode Sense: 0b 00 00 08
[24313.443367] sd 7:0:0:0: [sde] No Caching mode page found
[24313.443376] sd 7:0:0:0: [sde] Assuming drive cache: write through
[24313.453063]  sde: sde1
[24313.453672] sd 7:0:0:0: [sde] Attached SCSI removable disk
```

Assuming that command returned sde: sde1, for instance, then your thumb drive is being assigned the sde label by the kernel. Alternately, you can use the lsblk command to see all drives, including sizes and partitions, attached to your system. I also like the lshw (list hardware) command, which can also generate a huge amount of data about all installed hardware devices. I have left a large amount of the data stream regarding the USB device tree intact so you can get an idea what it will look like.

Search the output (type /usb) to find the USB device listing:

```
[root@studentvm1 ~]# lshw | less
studentvm1
    description: Computer
    product: VirtualBox
    vendor: innotek GmbH
    version: 1.2
    serial: 0
    width: 64 bits
    capabilities: smbios-2.5 dmi-2.5 smp vsyscall32
    configuration: family=Virtual Machine uuid=8DDC4A2F-
    F39F-5344-816C-76A8189CD7BD
  *-core
      description: Motherboard
      product: VirtualBox
      vendor: Oracle Corporation
      physical id: 0
      version: 1.2
      serial: 0
    *-firmware
        description: BIOS
        vendor: innotek GmbH
<SNIP>
          *-usbhost:0
              product: xHCI Host Controller
```

```
    vendor: Linux 6.1.18-200.fc37.x86_64 xhci-hcd
    physical id: 0
    bus info: usb@1
    logical name: usb1
    version: 6.01
    capabilities: usb-2.00
    configuration: driver=hub slots=8 speed=480Mbit/s
*-usb
    description: Mass storage device
    product: UDisk
    vendor: General
    physical id: 1
    bus info: usb@1:1
    logical name: scsi7
    version: 1.00
    serial: 1404141927120224970300
    capabilities: usb-2.00 scsi emulated scsi-host
    configuration: driver=usb-storage maxpower=100mA
    speed=480Mbit/s
  *-disk
      description: SCSI Disk
      product: UDisk
      vendor: General
      physical id: 0.0.0
      bus info: scsi@7:0.0.0
      logical name: /dev/sde
      version: 5.00
      size: 7800MiB (8178MB)
      capabilities: removable
      configuration: ansiversion=2 logicalsectorsize=512
      sectorsize=512
    *-medium
        physical id: 0
        logical name: /dev/sde
        size: 7800MiB (8178MB)
        capabilities: partitioned partitioned:dos
        configuration: signature=00227f4c
      *-volume
```

```
                            description: Windows FAT volume
                            vendor: MSDOS5.0
                            physical id: 1
                            logical name: /dev/sde1
                            version: FAT32
                            serial: 4c29-7788
                            size: 7799MiB
                            capacity: 7799MiB
                            capabilities: primary bootable fat initialized
                            configuration: FATs=2 filesystem=fat
```

Tip   The lshw command is one of the very few commands that use a single dash (-) for options that are more than a single character. Most use two dashes (--) for those long option names. A single dash (-) is typically used for options that are a single character, such as -h or --help for help.

The amount of data can be significantly reduced by using the -short option, but you get much less information about the individual devices:

```
[root@studentvm1 ~]# lshw -short
H/W path                 Device       Class      Description
============================================================
                                      system     VirtualBox
/0                                    bus        VirtualBox
/0/0                                  memory     128KiB BIOS
/0/1                                  memory     16GiB System memory
/0/2                                  processor  Intel(R) Core(TM) i9-7960X CPU
                                                 @ 2.80GHz
/0/100                                bridge     440FX - 82441FX PMC [Natoma]
/0/100/1                              bridge     82371SB PIIX3 ISA [Natoma/
                                                 Triton II]
/0/100/1.1               scsi5        storage    82371AB/EB/MB PIIX4 IDE
/0/100/1.1/0.0.0         /dev/cdrom   disk       CD-ROM
/0/100/2                              display    SVGA II Adapter
/0/100/3                 enp0s3       network    82540EM Gigabit Ethernet
                                                 Controller
/0/100/4                              generic    VirtualBox Guest Service
```

/0/100/7		bridge	82371AB/EB/MB PIIX4 ACPI
/0/100/9	enp0s9	network	82540EM Gigabit Ethernet Controller
/0/100/c		bus	7 Series/C210 Series Chipset Family USB xHCI Host Controller
/0/100/c/0	usb1	bus	xHCI Host Controller
/0/100/c/0/1	scsi7	storage	UDisk
/0/100/c/0/1/0.0.0	/dev/sde	disk	8178MB UDisk
/0/100/c/0/1/0.0.0/0	/dev/sde	disk	8178MB
/0/100/c/0/1/0.0.0/0/1	/dev/sde1	volume	7799MiB Windows FAT volume
/0/100/c/1	usb2	bus	xHCI Host Controller
/0/100/d	scsi0	storage	82801HM/HEM (ICH8M/ICH8M-E) SATA Controller [AHCI mode]
/0/100/d/0	/dev/sda	disk	64GB VBOX HARDDISK
/0/100/d/0/1	/dev/sda1	volume	1023KiB BIOS Boot partition
/0/100/d/0/2	/dev/sda2	volume	1GiB EXT4 volume
/0/100/d/0/3	/dev/sda3	volume	1023MiB Windows FAT volume
/0/100/d/0/4	/dev/sda4	volume	57GiB LVM Physical Volume
/0/100/d/1	/dev/sdb	disk	21GB VBOX HARDDISK
/0/100/d/1/1	/dev/sdb1	volume	2GiB EXT4 volume
/0/100/d/1/2	/dev/sdb2	volume	2GiB Linux filesystem partition
/0/100/d/1/3	/dev/sdb3	volume	15GiB Linux filesystem partition
/0/100/d/2	/dev/sdc	volume	2GiB VBOX HARDDISK
/0/100/d/3	/dev/sdd	disk	2147MB VBOX HARDDISK
/0/3		input	PnP device PNP0303
/0/4		input	PnP device PNP0f03

Now that you have established where your drive is currently located in your filesystem, you can view udev information about that device:

```
[root@studentvm1 ~]# udevadm info -a -n /dev/sde | less
Udevadm info starts with the device specified by the devpath and then
walks up the chain of parent devices. It prints for every device
found, all possible attributes in the udev rules key format.
A rule to match, can be composed by the attributes of the device
and the attributes from one single parent device.

  looking at device '/devices/pci0000:00/0000:00:0c.0/usb1/1-1/1-1:1.0/host7/
  target7:0:0/7:0:0:0/block/sde':
    KERNEL=="sde"
```

```
    SUBSYSTEM=="block"
    DRIVER==""
    ATTR{alignment_offset}=="0"
    ATTR{capability}=="1"
    ATTR{discard_alignment}=="0"
    ATTR{diskseq}=="17"
    ATTR{events}=="media_change"
    ATTR{events_async}==""
    ATTR{events_poll_msecs}=="-1"
    ATTR{ext_range}=="256"
<SNIP>
```

This returns a lot of information. Focus on the first block of info for now. Your job is to pick out parts of udev's report about a device that are most unique to that device and then tell udev to trigger your script when those unique attributes are detected.

What's happening on a technical level is that the `udevadm info` process reports on a device (specified by the device path) and then "walks" up the chain of parent devices. For every device found, it prints all possible attributes, using a key-value format. You can compose a rule to match according to the attributes of a device plus attributes from one single parent device. A udev rule must contain one attribute from one single parent device.

Parent attributes are things that describe a device from the most basic level, such as that it's something that has been plugged into a physical port or it is something with a size or this is a removable device. Since the KERNEL label of sde can change depending upon how many other drives you happen to have plugged in before you plug that thumb drive in, that's not the optimal parent attribute for a udev rule. However, it works for a proof of concept, so you could use it.

An even better candidate is the SUBSYSTEM attribute, which identifies that this is a "block" system device (which is why the lsblk command lists the device). Using the "block" attribute means that this rule will trigger when *any* new block device, that is, storage device like HDD or SSD, is inserted.

Create a new file called 80-local.rules in /etc/udev/rules.d and add this content:

```
SUBSYSTEM=="block", ACTION=="add", RUN+="/usr/local/bin/trigger.sh"
```

Save the file, disconnect your test thumb drive from the VM, and then reboot the VM.

Wait, reboot on a Linux machine?

Theoretically, you can just issue **udevadm control --reload**, which should load all rules, but at this stage in the game, it's best to eliminate all variables. udev is complex enough without wondering if that rule didn't work because of a syntax error or if you just should have rebooted. So reboot regardless of what your POSIX pride tells you.

Tip   Although rebooting your StudentVM1 host at this juncture is still a very good idea, I did try using the **udevadm control --reload** command, and the trigger.sh script did trigger as expected, leaving a new entry in /tmp/udev.log.

When your system is back online, switch to a text console (with Ctrl+Alt+F3 or similar) and plug your thumb drive in. If you are running a recent kernel, you will probably see a bunch of output on your console when you plug the drive in. If you see an error message such as *Could not execute /usr/local/bin/trigger.sh*, then you probably forgot to make the script executable. Otherwise, hopefully all you see is that a device was plugged in and that it got some kind of kernel device assignment and so on. Now, the moment of truth as we check the results in the terminal session in which we are following the file udev.log. You should see something like this:

```
[root@studentvm1 tmp]# cat udev.log
Sun May  7 03:15:03 PM EDT 2023
Sun May  7 03:15:05 PM EDT 2023
Sun May  7 15:39:52 EDT 2023
Sun May  7 15:39:53 EDT 2023
```

So this worked for me, but I see two entries for the moment when I connected the USB device to the VM. Why do I see two entries? Well, that's one entry for each new device, one for the whole device, /dev/sde, and one for the partition, sde1.

Refining the Rule into Something Useful

The problem with the rule right now is that it's very generic. Plugging in a mouse, a thumb drive, or someone else's thumb drive will all indiscriminately trigger your script. Now is the time to start focusing in on the exact thumb drive you want to trigger your script.

One way to do this is with the vendor ID and product ID.

EXPERIMENT 38-4: TRIGGER ON A SPECIFIC DEVICE

To get the vendor and product ID numbers, you can use the lsusb command:

```
[root@studentvm1 rules.d]# lsusb
Bus 002 Device 001: ID 1d6b:0003 Linux Foundation 3.0 root hub
Bus 001 Device 002: ID abcd:1234 LogiLink UDisk flash drive
Bus 001 Device 001: ID 1d6b:0002 Linux Foundation 2.0 root hub
```

Tip   I have a large number of USB thumb drives of different types and with different company imprints, such as DataOcean or iPromo, that all have the same ID, abcd:1234. This is typical of many inexpensive USB thumb drives because they come from the same manufacturer. Some drives have serial numbers that can be viewed using dmesg, but others do not or they have a trivial serial number. So we just will work with what we have for the rest of this experiment.

In this example, the abcd:1234 before "LogiLink UDisk flash drive" denotes the idVendor and idProduct attributes. You can now include these attributes in your rule. Be sure to use the IDs for your device and not the ones for my device:

```
SUBSYSTEM=="block", ATTRS{idVendor}=="abcd", ACTION=="add", RUN+="/usr/local/
bin/trigger.sh"
```

Test this (yes, you should still reboot, just to make sure you're getting fresh reactions from udev), and it should work the same as before, only now if you plug in, say, a thumb drive manufactured by a different company (therefore with a different idVendor) or a mouse or a printer, the script is not triggered.

Keep adding in new attributes to further focus in on that one unique thumb drive that you actually want to have trigger your script. Using udevadm info -a -n /dev/sde, you can find out things like the vendor name or sometimes a serial number or the product name and so on.

For your own sanity, be sure to add only one new attribute at a time. Most mistakes I have made and have seen other people make are to throw a bunch of attributes into the udev rule and wonder why the thing no longer works. Testing attributes one by one is the safest way to ensure udev can identify your device successfully.

Security

This brings up the security concerns of writing udev rules to automatically do something when a drive is plugged in. On my machines, I don't even have auto-mount turned on, and yet this chapter proposes scripts and rules that execute commands just by having something plugged in.

There are two things to bear in mind here.

Focus your udev rules once you have them working so that they only trigger scripts when you really want them to. Executing a script that blindly copies data to or from your computer is a bad idea if anyone who happens to be carrying a thumb drive of the same brand as yours comes along and plugs it into your box. Do not write your udev rule and scripts and then forget about them. Know which computers have udev rules on them, and those boxes should be personal computers rather than the laptops that you take around to conferences or have in your office at work. The more "social" a computer is, the less likely it should be to get a udev rule on it that could potentially result in your data ending up on someone else's device or someone else's data or malware on your device.

In other words, as with so much of the power that a GNU system provides you, it is your job to be mindful of how you are wielding that power. If you abuse it or fail to treat it with respect, then it very well could go horribly wrong.

udev in the Real World

Now that you can confirm that your script is triggered by udev, you can turn your attention to the function of the script. Right now, it is useless, doing nothing more than logging the fact that it has been executed.

You could add code to the trigger.sh script to mount the USB devices when they are inserted. Or the script could perform backups or delete all the files on them. However, udev can grab lots of other things, like gamepads (this is useful on systems that aren't set to load the xboxdrv module when a gamepad is attached) and cameras and microphones (useful to set inputs when a specific mic is attached), so don't think that dealing with USB devices is all it's good for.

udev is a very flexible system and enables you to define rules and functions in ways that few other systems dare provide users. Learn it and use it, and enjoy its power.

Chapter Summary

In this chapter we have explored how D-Bus and udev work together to enable a very powerful and flexible plug-and-play feature for Linux. We have looked at how udev works to provide names for newly plugged-in devices and how it creates device special files in the /dev directory.

We have also created custom udev rules of our own that are used to trigger events of various types. This capability enables us to exercise control over what happens when a device is plugged into our Linux hosts to a degree that is impossible in most other PC operating systems.

This chapter once again merely provides a very brief experience with D-Bus and udev. There is much more that can be done using udev rules, but you should now at least be aware of some of the possibilities.

Exercises

Perform the following exercises to complete this chapter:

1. Describe the relationship between D-Bus and udev when a new hardware device is plugged into a Linux host.

2. List the steps taken by D-Bus and udev from when a USB thumb drive is plugged into a host until the device icon appears on the desktop.

3. Given that the udev action when a device like the USB drive used in this chapter is unplugged from the host is "removed," write a udev rule that adds a timestamp to the /tmp/udev.log file when the USB thumb drive is removed. Test to verify that this new rule works as expected.

CHAPTER 39

Using Traditional Logs

Objectives

In this chapter you will learn

- To use traditional log files to monitor system performance and events

- To configure and use logrotate to manage log files

- To configure and use logwatch to provide a daily summary of log and journal entries for use in problem determination

- To install and use the Sendmail mail transfer agent (MTA) and the mailx text-mode email client to test logwatch

About Traditional Logs

Traditional logs are no longer needed because of the systemd journal we have already covered fairly extensively throughout large parts of this course. However, Fedora and some other Linux distributions still maintain traditional log files in addition to the systemd journal. This is accomplished in Fedora by also installing the traditional rsyslog package.

The log files are traditionally located in /var/log and can be accessed either directly or with simple commands. The most current of each type of log file has no date as part of its name, while names of older log files have dates to differentiate them.

© David Both 2023
D. Both, *Using and Administering Linux: Volume 2*, https://doi.org/10.1007/978-1-4842-9615-8_39

EXPERIMENT 39-1: INTRODUCING TRADITIONAL LOGS

Open a terminal session and become root. Make /var/log the PWD. List the files in this directory. I have pruned a lot of this data but left a few to use for discussion:

```
[root@studentvm1 log]# ls
<SNIP>
drwxr-xr-x  2 root     root               4096 Jul 21  2022 iptraf-ng
drwxr-sr-x+ 3 root     systemd-journal    4096 Jan 17 02:53 journal
-rw-rw-r--. 1 root     utmp             292876 May  8 08:11 lastlog
drwxr-xr-x. 2 lightdm  lightdm            4096 May  8 08:11 lightdm
-rw-r-----  1 root     root               2088 Feb  7 16:18 lxdm.log
-rw-r-----  1 root     root               2107 Feb  5 16:46 lxdm.log.old
-rw-------  1 root     root                  0 May  7 00:00 maillog
-rw-------  1 root     root                  0 Mar 28 11:48 maillog-20230414
-rw-------  1 root     root                  0 Apr 14 09:46 maillog-20230416
-rw-------  1 root     root                  0 Apr 16 00:00 maillog-20230502
-rw-------  1 root     root                  0 May  2 15:07 maillog-20230507
-rw-------  1 root     root             932518 May  8 09:20 messages
-rw-------  1 root     root             592863 Apr 14 09:46 messages-20230414
-rw-------  1 root     root             317229 Apr 15 23:50 messages-20230416
<SNIP>
lrwxrwxrwx. 1 root     root                 39 Nov  5  2022 README -> ../../
usr/share/doc/systemd/README.logs
drwxr-xr-x. 2 root     root               4096 May  8 04:11 sa
<SNIP>
```

The systemd journal directory is located in /var/log. You will also see a number of log files and subdirectories. Using wc I counted 74 entries in the /var/log directory. I have 108 on my primary workstation, but that is because of the many additional services I have on it.

The total space taken by log (and journal) files on my StudentVM1 is about 273MB, which is rather trivial:

```
[root@studentvm1 log]# du . -sm
273     .
```

My primary workstation has about 3.75GB of data in logs and journals, while the host I use as my firewall/router has about 4.2GB. Both of those are very much working systems and run 24 × 7.

Let's look at the README file:

```
[root@david log]# cat README
```

You are looking for the traditional text log files in /var/log, and they are

gone?

Here's an explanation on what's going on:

You are running a systemd-based OS where traditional syslog has been replaced

with the Journal. The journal stores the same (and more) information
as classic

syslog. To make use of the journal and access the collected log data simply

invoke "journalctl", which will output the logs in the identical text-based

format the syslog files in /var/log used to be. For further details, please

refer to journalctl(1).

Alternatively, consider installing one of the traditional syslog

implementations available for your distribution, which will generate the

classic log files for you. Syslog implementations such as syslog-ng or rsyslog

may be installed side-by-side with the journal and will continue to function

the way they always did.

Thank you!

Further reading:
        man:journalctl(1)
        man:systemd-journald.service(8)
        man:journald.conf(5)
        http://0pointer.de/blog/projects/the-journal.html
```
[root@david log]#
```

That explains the overall situation. The last entry in the "Further reading" list has a complete description of the problems that the systemd journal is designed to rectify and the thinking behind it.

You can also see by the list of files in the PWD that the log files are maintained for a period of one month with each log file containing one week of data. If the amount of data in a file passes a pre-configured threshold, the file may be rotated when it reaches that threshold rather than waiting for the full seven-day time period to pass. The logrotate facility manages log file rotation and deletion.

logrotate

Before we examine other log files, we need to explore the logrotate facility. Many system services and programs dump log entries into log files, which enable us as SysAdmins to view them and locate the causes of some types of system problems. That is a good thing.

But what if those log files were to grow to many gigabytes in size and perhaps ultimately fill up the /var filesystem? That would not be so good. I have had that happen and many errors are generated, but they cannot be stored in the log files because there is no more room on the filesystem for them. Other symptoms include programs refusing to start because there is no room to create their PID files on /var or running programs being unable to perform certain tasks because they cannot open files due to being unable to create lock files on /var. It gets messy very quickly.

The logrotate facility is designed to prevent these potential problems. It accomplishes this by rotating the logs on a regular basis, as its name implies. Log rotation can be triggered by time parameters such as weekly or monthly, as well as by log file size.

The task of log rotation consists of renaming a file such as messages by appending the date the file was "closed" to further additions, such as messages-20190501, and starting a new messages file. The maximum number of older files to be retained is defined in the configuration files for each service, and if the creation of the new log file results in more than the maximum specified number, the oldest file is deleted.

By default, Fedora specifies four as the maximum number of older files to keep. The system defaults for logrotate are defined in /etc/logrotate.conf. Individual services can override the defaults.

EXPERIMENT 39-2: EXPLORING LOGROTATE CONFIGURATION

This experiment should be performed as the root user. However, we will not be making any changes to the logrotate configuration, just exploring it.

First, cat the /etc/logrotate.conf file. This file is not long, so it should fit in your terminal session:

```
[root@studentvm1 log]# cat /etc/logrotate.conf
# see "man logrotate" for details

# global options do not affect preceding include directives

# rotate log files weekly
weekly

# keep 4 weeks worth of backlogs
rotate 4

# create new (empty) log files after rotating old ones
create

# use date as a suffix of the rotated file
dateext

# uncomment this if you want your log files compressed
#compress

# packages drop log rotation information into this directory
include /etc/logrotate.d

# system-specific logs may also be configured here.
[root@studentvm1 log]#
```

This file is well commented so it should be self-explanatory. One of the options is that of compression. I do not typically compress my log files, so I leave this option commented out.

Make /etc/logrotate.d the PWD. List the contents of this directory, and you can see the configuration files for several different services. Several services do not have separate files in this directory, but they are all aggregated into the single file, rsyslog. The syslog service is the system logger and is responsible for logging messages that are sorted into the appropriate log files listed in the beginning of the configuration file.

Look at the contents of the rsyslog file:

```
[student@studentvm1 logrotate.d]$ cat rsyslog
/var/log/cron
/var/log/maillog
/var/log/messages
/var/log/secure
/var/log/spooler
{
    missingok
    sharedscripts
    postrotate
        /usr/bin/systemctl kill -s HUP rsyslog.service >/dev/null 2>&1 || true
    endscript
}
```

First, we have a list of the log files for which this is the defined configuration file and then a list of directives contained within curly braces {}. The man page for logrotate lists over 60 directives, but we will only look at the most common ones:

- **missingok**: This means to simply ignore the fact that any log file is missing and to not throw an error message. logrotate is to continue with the next file.

- **sharedscripts**: Instead of running the script that is contained between the postrotate and endscript directives once for each log that is rotated, the script is run once. If there are no scripts that need rotating, the script is not run.

- **postrotate**: Designates that the following script is to be run after the log files are rotated.

- **endscript**: Defines the end of the script.

- **create mode owner group**: Specifies the file mode and ownership of the new log file when it is created.

- **nocreate**: Prevents new log files from being created. The /etc/logrotate.d/chrony file uses this directive to prevent logrotate from creating a new log file. The chronyc program uses its own cyclelogs directive in the script to generate its own new log files.

- **compress**: Specifies that the rotated log file is to be compressed. The current log file is not compressed.

- **delaycompress**: This delays compression of the newly rotated log file until the next rotation cycle so that not only the current log file but also the most recently rotated one are uncompressed and can be easily viewed without having to be decompressed.

- **notifempty**: Do not rotate the log if the file is empty.

- **rotate X**: Defines the number, specified by X, of old log files to keep.

- **size Y**: Rotates a log based on a specified size (Y) if that size is exceeded before the specified rotation time is reached. Thus, if a log file is to be rotated weekly but it reaches the size, Y, before the week is complete, the log is rotated anyway.

- Time-related options such as **hourly**, **daily**, **weekly**, **monthly**, and **yearly** define the time intervals at which the logs are to be rotated. Be sure to check the man page for special considerations if a log needs to be rotated hourly.

View the contents of the dnf file in the logrotate.d directory. It manages several dnf-related log files, but each has its own stanza despite the fact that they are all configured identically.

Now let's look at the log files themselves. Make /var/log the PWD and list the contents of the directory again.

This shows the log files with the file name extension .log-YYYYMMDD or just the date. These are the older, rotated log files. Some of these entries are directories, and that should be obvious on your terminal session.

The logrotate man page has a description of all the options available for use in the configuration files.

Log File Content

Let's look at the content of some of the log files I have found most useful in the past. Some of those files don't yet exist because they are for services we have not installed on this VM. We will look at those server services and log files in Volume 3.

messages

The /var/log/messages log files contain kernel and other system-level messages of various types and are another of the files I frequently use to assist me with problem determination. The entries found in the messages logs are not usually performance related and are more informational.

Entries from the kernel, systemd, the DHCP client, and many of the running services are logged here. Each log entry begins with the date and time to make it easy to determine the sequence of events and to locate entries made at specific times in the log file. The messages log files are full of interesting and useful information:

- User logins and logouts

- DHCP client requests for network configuration

- The resulting DHCP configuration information as shown by NetworkManager

- Data logged by systemd during startup and shutdown

- Kernel data about things such as USB memory devices when they are plugged in

- USB hub information

- And much more

The messages file is usually the first place I look when working on non-performance issues. It can also be useful for performance issues, but I start with SAR for that.

Because it is so important, let's take a quick look at the messages file.

EXPERIMENT 39-3: VIEWING THE MESSAGES LOG

Perform this experiment as the root user. Make /var/log the PWD. Use the less command to view the messages log:

```
[root@studentvm1 ~]# less messages
<snip>
May  7 00:00:43 studentvm1 systemd[1]: unbound-anchor.service: Deactivated
successfully.
```

```
May  7 00:00:43 studentvm1 systemd[1]: Finished unbound-anchor.service -
update of the root trust anchor for DNSSEC validation in unbound.
May  7 00:00:43 studentvm1 audit[1]: SERVICE_START pid=1 uid=0
auid=4294967295 ses=4294967295 subj=kernel msg='unit=unbound-anchor
comm="systemd" exe="/usr
/lib/systemd/systemd" hostname=? addr=? terminal=? res=success'
May  7 00:00:43 studentvm1 audit[1]: SERVICE_STOP pid=1 uid=0 auid=4294967295
ses=4294967295 subj=kernel msg='unit=unbound-anchor comm="systemd" exe="/usr/
lib/systemd/systemd" hostname=? addr=? terminal=? res=success'
May  7 00:00:43 studentvm1 systemd[1]: rsyslog.service: Sent signal SIGHUP to
main process 977 (rsyslogd) on client request.
May  7 00:00:43 studentvm1 rsyslogd[977]: [origin software="rsyslogd"
swVersion="8.2204.0-3.fc37" x-pid="977" x-info="https://www.rsyslog.com"]
rsyslogd wa
s HUPed
May  7 00:00:43 studentvm1 systemd[1]: logrotate.service: Deactivated
successfully.
May  7 00:00:43 studentvm1 systemd[1]: Finished logrotate.service - Rotate
log files.
May  7 00:00:43 studentvm1 audit[1]: SERVICE_START pid=1 uid=0
auid=4294967295 ses=4294967295 subj=kernel msg='unit=logrotate comm="systemd"
exe="/usr/lib/
systemd/systemd" hostname=? addr=? terminal=? res=success'
May  7 00:00:43 studentvm1 audit[1]: SERVICE_STOP pid=1 uid=0 auid=4294967295
ses=4294967295 subj=kernel msg='unit=logrotate comm="systemd" exe="/usr/lib/s
ystemd/systemd" hostname=? addr=? terminal=? res=success'
May  7 00:00:43 studentvm1 audit: BPF prog-id=97 op=UNLOAD
May  7 00:07:41 studentvm1 systemd[1]: Starting sysstat-summary.service -
Generate a daily summary of process accounting...
May  7 00:07:42 studentvm1 systemd[1]: sysstat-summary.service: Deactivated
successfully.
May  7 00:07:42 studentvm1 audit[1]: SERVICE_START pid=1 uid=0
auid=4294967295 ses=4294967295 subj=kernel msg='unit=sysstat-summary
comm="systemd" exe="/us
r/lib/systemd/systemd" hostname=? addr=? terminal=? res=success'
<snip>
```

This tiny bit of the data stream from the messages log is just to give you an idea of what it looks like. Locate and view NetworkManager and USB device messages to view some specific entries. Is this more or less difficult than finding the same information using journalctl?

Browse through the contents of the messages file to get a feel for the types of messages you will typically encounter. Use **Ctrl+C** to terminate less.

View some of the other non-empty log files.

secure

The /var/log/secure log file contains security-related entries. This includes information about successful and unsuccessful attempts to log into the system. Let's look at some of the entries you might see in this file.

EXPERIMENT 39-4: THE SECURE LOG

This experiment must be performed as root. Use the **less** command to view the contents of the secure log file. Ensure that /var/log is the PWD:

```
[root@studentvm1 log]# less secure
May 19 22:23:30 studentvm1 lightdm[1335]: pam_unix(lightdm-greeter:session):
session closed for user lightdm
May 19 22:23:30 studentvm1 systemd[16438]: pam_unix(systemd-user:session):
session opened for user student by (uid=0)
May 19 22:23:31 studentvm1 lightdm[1477]: pam_unix(lightdm:session): session
opened for user student by (uid=0)
May 19 22:23:34 studentvm1 polkitd[990]: Registered Authentication Agent for
unix-session:4 (system bus name :1.1357 [/usr/libexec/xfce-polkit], object
path /org/freedesktop/PolicyKit1/AuthenticationAgent, locale en_US.utf8)
May 20 11:18:54 studentvm1 sshd[29938]: Accepted password for student from
192.168.0.1 port 52652 ssh2
May 20 11:18:54 studentvm1 sshd[29938]: pam_unix(sshd:session): session
opened for user student by (uid=0)
May 20 17:08:52 studentvm1 sshd[3380]: Accepted publickey for root from
192.168.0.1 port 56306 ssh2: RSA SHA256:4UDdGg3FP5sITB8ydfCb5JDg2QCIrsW4c
foNgFxhC5A
```

May 20 17:08:52 studentvm1 sshd[3380]: pam_unix(sshd:session): session opened for user root by (uid=0)
May 21 07:49:05 studentvm1 sshd[3382]: Received disconnect from 192.168.0.1 port 56306:11: disconnected by user
May 21 07:49:05 studentvm1 sshd[3382]: Disconnected from user root 192.168.0.1 port 56306
May 21 07:49:05 studentvm1 sshd[3380]: pam_unix(sshd:session): session closed for user root
May 21 08:17:15 studentvm1 login[18310]: pam_unix(login:auth): authentication failure; logname=LOGIN uid=0 euid=0 tty=tty2 ruser= rhost= user=root
May 21 08:17:15 studentvm1 login[18310]: pam_succeed_if(login:auth): requirement "uid >= 1000" not met by user "root"
May 21 08:17:17 studentvm1 login[18310]: FAILED LOGIN 1 FROM tty2 FOR root, Authentication failure
May 21 08:17:23 studentvm1 login[18310]: pam_unix(login:session): session opened for user root by LOGIN(uid=0)
May 21 08:17:23 studentvm1 login[18310]: ROOT LOGIN ON tty2
May 21 13:31:16 studentvm1 sshd[24111]: Accepted password for student from 192.168.0.1 port 54202 ssh2
May 21 13:31:16 studentvm1 sshd[24111]: pam_unix(sshd:session): session opened for user student by (uid=0)

Most of the data in /var/log/secure pertains to records of user logins and logouts and information about whether a password or public key was used for authentication.

This log also contains failed password attempts.

My primary use for the secure log file is to identify break-in attempts from hackers. But I don't even do that – I use automation tools for that, too, in this case the logwatch tool, which we will explore a bit later in this chapter.

dmesg

dmesg is not a log file; it is a command. At one time in the past there was a log file, /var/
log/dmesg, which contained all of the messages generated by the kernel during boot
and most messages generated during startup. The startup process begins when the boot
process ends, when init or systemd takes control of the host.

The **dmesg** command displays all of the messages generated by the kernel including
data about the hardware it discovers during the boot process. I like to start with this
command when looking for bootup problems and hardware issues.

Tip   Much of the hardware data found in the output from dmesg can be found in
the /proc filesystem.

Let's look at a bit of the output from the dmesg command.

EXPERIMENT 39-5: DMESG OUTPUT

This experiment can be performed as either the root or the student user:

```
[root@studentvm1 log]# dmesg | less
[    0.000000] Linux version 6.1.18-200.fc37.x86_64 (mockbuild@bkernel01.
iad2.fedoraproject.org) (gcc (GCC) 12.2.1 20221121 (Red Hat 12.2.1-4), GNU ld
version 2.38-25.fc37) #1 SMP PREEMPT_DYNAMIC Sat Mar 11 16:09:14 UTC 2023
[    0.000000] Command line: BOOT_IMAGE=(hd0,gpt2)/vmlinuz-6.1.18-200.
fc37.x86_64 root=/dev/mapper/fedora_studentvm1-root ro rd.lvm.lv=fedora_
studentvm1/root rd.lvm.lv=fedora_studentvm1/usr
[    0.000000] x86/fpu: Supporting XSAVE feature 0x001: 'x87 floating point
registers'
[    0.000000] x86/fpu: Supporting XSAVE feature 0x002: 'SSE registers'
[    0.000000] x86/fpu: Supporting XSAVE feature 0x004: 'AVX registers'
[    0.000000] x86/fpu: xstate_offset[2]:  576, xstate_sizes[2]:  256
[    0.000000] x86/fpu: Enabled xstate features 0x7, context size is 832
bytes, using 'standard' format.
[    0.000000] signal: max sigframe size: 1776
[    0.000000] BIOS-provided physical RAM map:
[    0.000000] BIOS-e820: [mem 0x0000000000000000-0x000000000009fbff] usable
```

```
[    0.000000] BIOS-e820: [mem 0x000000000009fc00-0x000000000009ffff]
reserved
<snip>
[   33.366463] 08:11:07.772577 main      VBoxDRMClient: already running,
exiting
[   33.368108] 08:11:07.774116 main      vbglR3GuestCtrlDetectPeekGetCancel
Support: Supported (#1)
[   36.078908] NET: Registered PF_QIPCRTR protocol family
[   43.217157] 12:11:20.118964 timesync vgsvcTimeSyncWorker: Radical guest
time change: 14 412 339 974 000ns (GuestNow=1 683 547 880 118 883 0
[   49.492308] e1000: enp0s3 NIC Link is Up 1000 Mbps Full Duplex, Flow
Control: RX
[   49.496250] IPv6: ADDRCONF(NETDEV_CHANGE): enp0s3: link becomes ready
[   49.508642] e1000: enp0s9 NIC Link is Up 1000 Mbps Full Duplex, Flow
Control: RX
[   49.510085] IPv6: ADDRCONF(NETDEV_CHANGE): enp0s9: link becomes ready
[   59.502839] 12:11:36.781151 main      VBoxService 7.0.6_Fedora r155176
(verbosity: 0) linux.amd64 (Jan 30 2023 00:00:00) release log
               12:11:3
[   59.503389] 12:11:36.782652 main      OS Product: Linux
[   59.507114] 12:11:36.786248 main      OS Release: 6.1.18-200.fc37.x86_64
[   59.508742] 12:11:36.787614 main      OS Version: #1 SMP PREEMPT_DYNAMIC
Sat Mar 11 16:09:14 UTC 2023
<snip>
```

Each line of data starts with a timestamp accurate to within a microsecond. The timestamp represents the time since the kernel started. The data in this stream can be used to determine whether the kernel recognizes certain devices.

For one example, when a new USB device is plugged in, a number of lines are added to the dmesg data buffer. You should see something similar to that in the following from at or near the end of the dmesg data. This data shows the sequence of events as the kernel detects the new device and the kernel, D-Bus, and udev determine what type of device it is and assign a device name to it. Search for "USB device" in this data stream to locate similar entries for your VM:

```
[23045.357352] usb 1-1: new high-speed USB device number 2 using xhci_hcd
[23045.676233] usb 1-1: New USB device found, idVendor=0781, idProduct=5575,
bcdDevice= 1.27
```

```
[23045.676249] usb 1-1: New USB device strings: Mfr=1, Product=2,
SerialNumber=3
[23045.676256] usb 1-1: Product: Cruzer Glide
[23045.676261] usb 1-1: Manufacturer: SanDisk
[23045.676266] usb 1-1: SerialNumber: 4C530000860108102424
[23046.478699] usb-storage 1-1:1.0: USB Mass Storage device detected
[23046.479135] scsi host7: usb-storage 1-1:1.0
[23046.479273] usbcore: registered new interface driver usb-storage
[23046.492360] usbcore: registered new interface driver uas
[23047.499671] scsi 7:0:0:0: Direct-Access     SanDisk  Cruzer Glide     1.27
PQ: 0 ANSI: 6
[23047.500261] sd 7:0:0:0: Attached scsi generic sg5 type 0
[23047.502164] sd 7:0:0:0: [sde] 15633408 512-byte logical blocks: (8.00
GB/7.45 GiB)
[23047.504135] sd 7:0:0:0: [sde] Write Protect is off
[23047.504145] sd 7:0:0:0: [sde] Mode Sense: 43 00 00 00
[23047.505530] sd 7:0:0:0: [sde] Write cache: disabled, read cache: enabled,
doesn't support DPO or FUA
[23047.515120]  sde: sde1 sde2 sde3
[23047.515407] sd 7:0:0:0: [sde] Attached SCSI removable disk
```

The device in this data snippet is a SanDisk Cruzer Glide with meaningful vendor and product IDs as well as a serial number that could be used in the dbus rule set you created in Chapter 38.

Scroll through the data to familiarize yourself with the many different types of data to be found here.

The data displayed by the dmesg command is located in RAM rather than on the hard drive. No matter how much RAM you have in your host, the space allocated to the dmesg buffer is limited. When it fills up, the oldest data is discarded as newer data is added.

Following Log Files

Searching through log files can be a time-consuming and cumbersome task even when using tools like grep to help isolate the desired lines. Many times while troubleshooting it can be helpful to continuously view the contents of a text-format log file especially to see the newest entries as they arrive. Using cat or grep to view log files displays the contents at the moment in time the command was entered.

I like to use the tail command to view the end of the file, but it can be time-consuming and disruptive to my problem determination process to rerun the tail command to see new lines. Using tail -f enables the tail command to "follow" the file and immediately display new lines of data as they are added to the end of the log file.

EXPERIMENT 39-6: FOLLOWING LOG FILES

Perform this experiment as root. You will need two terminal sessions with root logins. These terminal sessions should be in separate windows and arranged so you can see both of them at the same time. If your terminal emulator supports multiple panes, like Tilix and Konsole do, use two panes for this experiment. In one root terminal session, make /var/log the PWD and then follow the messages file:

```
[root@studentvm1 ~]# cd /var/log
[root@studentvm1 log]# tail -f messages
May  8 14:56:16 studentvm1 audit[1]: SERVICE_START pid=1 uid=0
auid=4294967295 ses=4294967295 subj=kernel msg='unit=systemd-hostnamed
comm="systemd" exe="/usr/lib/systemd/systemd" hostname=? addr=? terminal=?
res=success'
May  8 14:56:16 studentvm1 systemd-logind[1029]: New session 6 of user root.
May  8 14:56:16 studentvm1 systemd[1]: Started session-6.scope - Session 6 of
User root.
May  8 14:56:16 studentvm1 systemd[1]: Starting systemd-hostnamed.service -
Hostname Service...
May  8 14:56:16 studentvm1 systemd[1]: Started systemd-hostnamed.service -
Hostname Service.
May  8 14:56:45 studentvm1 systemd[1]: systemd-hostnamed.service: Deactivated
successfully.
May  8 14:56:45 studentvm1 audit[1]: SERVICE_STOP pid=1 uid=0 auid=4294967295
ses=4294967295 subj=kernel msg='unit=systemd-hostnamed comm="systemd"
exe="/usr/lib/systemd/systemd" hostname=? addr=? terminal=? res=success'
May  8 14:56:45 studentvm1 audit: BPF prog-id=98 op=UNLOAD
May  8 14:56:45 studentvm1 audit: BPF prog-id=97 op=UNLOAD
May  8 14:56:45 studentvm1 audit: BPF prog-id=96 op=UNLOAD
```

tail displays the last ten lines of the log file and then waits for more data to be appended. Let's make some log entries appear. There are several ways to do this, but the easiest is to use the logger command. In the second window, enter this command as root to log a new entry to the messages file:

```
[root@studentvm1 ~]# logger "This is test message 1."
```

The following line should have appeared in the other terminal at the end of the messages log file:

```
May  8 14:58:25 studentvm1 root[3314]: This is test message 1.
```

We can also use STDIO for this:

```
[root@studentvm1 ~]# echo "This is test message 2." | logger
```

And the results are the same – the message appears in the messages log file:

```
May  8 14:59:22 studentvm1 root[3320]: This is test message 2.
```

In a terminal session as the student user, add another line to the messages file:

```
[student@studentvm1 ~]$ logger "This is test message 3."
```

And view the result in the other terminal:

```
May  8 15:03:37 studentvm1 student[3384]: This is test message 3.
```

Note that your VM may pop additional messages on this log file while you are performing this experiment; in real life log messages are added to these files quite frequently. Use Ctrl+C to terminate following the log file.

logwatch

Using tools like grep and tail to view a few lines from a log file while working on a problem is fine. But what if you need to search through a large number of log files? That can be tedious even when using those tools.

logwatch is a tool that can analyze the system log files and detect anomalous entries that the SysAdmin should look at. It generates a report every night around 03:30 a.m. that is triggered by a shell script in /etc/cron.daily. logwatch condenses thousands of lines of log files into a report that can be scanned by the SysAdmin to more easily locate those entries that may constitute a problem.

The default configuration is for logwatch to email a report of what it finds in the log files to root. There are various methods for ensuring that the email gets sent to someone and someplace other than root on the local host. One option is to set the mailto address in the local configuration file in the /etc/logwatch directory. The default configuration files are located in /usr/share/logwatch.

logwatch can also be run from the command line, and the data is sent to STDOUT and is displayed in the terminal session by the Bash shell.

EXPERIMENT 39-7: LOGWATCH

This experiment must be performed as root. Our objective is to run logwatch from the command line and view the results. First, we need to install it:

```
[root@studentvm1 log]# dnf -y install logwatch
```

I have used output from logwatch on my personal workstation because there is more to see than there is on my instance of StudentVM1. Note that logwatch always scans the previous day's log entries by default although other dates can be specified.

In this command we specify a detail level of 10, which provides the most detail. I have once again removed a few pages and some empty lines of data to save space:

```
[root@myworkstation ~]# logwatch --detail 10 | less

 ################## Logwatch 7.8 (01/22/23) ###################
         Processing Initiated: Tue May  9 09:54:06 2023
         Date Range Processed: yesterday
                             ( 2023-May-08 )
                             Period is day.
         Detail Level of Output: 10
         Type of Output/Format: stdout / text
         Logfiles for Host: studentvm1
 ##############################################################
```

```
-------------------- Kernel Audit Begin ------------------------

  Number of audit daemon starts: 1

  Number of audit initializations: 1

**Unmatched Entries**
    audit: PROCTITLE proctitle="/sbin/auditd": 2 Time(s)
    audit: CONFIG_CHANGE op=set audit_enabled=1 old=1 auid=4294967295
    ses=4294967295 subj=kernel res=1: 2 T ime(s)
    audit: BPF prog-id=73 op=UNLOAD: 1 Time(s)
    audit[3325]: USER_START pid=3325 uid=0 auid=1000 ses=7 subj=kernel
    msg='op=PAM:session_open grantors=pa
    m_selinux,pam_loginuid,pam_selinux,pam_namespace,pam_keyinit,pam_keyinit,
    pam_limits,pam_systemd,pam_unix,pa
    m_umask,pam_lastlog acct="student" exe="/usr/sbin/sshd"
    hostname=192.168.0.1 addr=192.168.0.1 terminal=ssh
res=success': 1 Time(s)
    audit: BPF prog-id=41 op=UNLOAD: 1 Time(s)
    audit: type=1334 audit(1683533450.005:95): prog-id=29 op=UNLOAD:
    1 Time(s)
    audit: BPF prog-id=101 op=LOAD: 1 Time(s)
    audit: BPF prog-id=96 op=UNLOAD: 1 Time(s
<SNIP>
  ---------------------- Kernel Audit End ------------------------
-------------------- Cron Begin ------------------------
  Commands Run:
    User root:
        /sbin/hwclock --systohc --localtime: 1 Time(s)
        run-parts /etc/cron.hourly: 24 Time(s)
        systemctl try-restart atop: 1 Time(s)
        time /usr/local/bin/rsbu -vbd1 ; time /usr/local/bin/rsbu -vbd2:
        1 Time(s)
--------------------- Cron End ------------------------
-------------------- SSHD Begin ------------------------

  SSHD Started: 2 Times

  Users logging in through sshd:
```

```
root:
    192.168.0.1 (david.both.org): 2 Times
student:
    192.168.0.1 (david.both.org): 1 Time

-------------------- SSHD End -----------------------

-------------------- Systemd Begin ----------------------

Condition check resulted in the following being skipped:
        abrt-vmcore.service - Harvest vmcores for ABRT: 1 Time(s)
        auth-rpcgss-module.service - Kernel Module supporting RPCSEC_GSS:
        1 Time(s)
        bluetooth.service - Bluetooth service: 1 Time(s)
        dev-block-8:18.device - VBOX_HARDDISK 2: 1 Time(s)
        dev-block-8:19.device - VBOX_HARDDISK 3: 1 Time(s)
        dev-block-8:32.device - VBOX_HARDDISK: 1 Time(s)
        dev-block-8:4.device - VBOX_HARDDISK 4: 1 Time(s
<snip>
-------------------- Systemd End -----------------------

-------------------- Disk Space Begin ----------------------

Filesystem                       Size  Used Avail Use% Mounted on
/dev/mapper/fedora_studentvm1-root  2.0G  633M  1.2G  35% /
/dev/mapper/fedora_studentvm1-usr   15G  6.8G  7.2G  49% /usr
/dev/mapper/NewVG--01-TestVol1      3.9G   24K  3.7G   1% /TestFS
/dev/sda2                          974M  277M  631M  31% /boot
/dev/mapper/fedora_studentvm1-test  459M  1.1M  429M   1% /test
/dev/mapper/fedora_studentvm1-tmp   4.9G  152K  4.6G   1% /tmp
/dev/mapper/fedora_studentvm1-var   9.8G  934M  8.4G  10% /var
/dev/mapper/fedora_studentvm1-home  3.9G  1.4G  2.4G  37% /home
/dev/sda3                         1022M   18M 1005M   2% /boot/efi

-------------------- Disk Space End -----------------------

-------------------- lm_sensors output Begin ----------------------

No sensors found!
Make sure you loaded all the kernel drivers you need.
Try sensors-detect to find out which these are.
```

```
-------------------- lm_sensors output End ------------------------

##################### Logwatch End ##########################
```

Page through the data produced by logwatch and be sure to look for the Kernel, Cron, Disk Space, and systemd sections. If you have a physical host on which to run this experiment, and if the lm_sensors package is installed, you will also see a section showing temperatures in various parts of the hardware, including that for each CPU.

We can use options to cause logwatch to display the log data from previous days and for specific services. Note that using ALL when specifying the services to scan results in significantly more results than when no service is specified. The list of valid services is located in the default configuration tree for logwatch, /usr/share/logwatch/scripts/services.

Try this with the following commands:

```
[root@studentvm1 ~]# logwatch --service systemd | less
[root@studentvm1 ~]# logwatch --service systemd --detail high | less
[root@studentvm1 ~]# logwatch --detail high | less
[root@studentvm1 ~]# logwatch --detail 1 | less
[root@studentvm1 ~]# logwatch --service ALL --detail high | less
```

We can also tell logwatch to report on log entries for all of the stored logs and not just for yesterday. This one took a couple minutes for me but may be less for your VM:

```
[root@studentvm1 ~]# logwatch --service ALL --range All | less
```

The ALL specifications are not case sensitive. This is an anomaly in the usually lowercase world of Linux.

Or you can try a day or a range of days in the past. The --range option takes fuzzy entries like the following list. These should all be self-explanatory, but check the logwatch man page in case you have questions:

- --range today

- --range yesterday

- --range "4 hours ago for that hour"

- --range "-3 days"

- --range "since 2 hours ago for those hours"

- --range "between -10 days and -2 days"

- --range "Apr 15, 2005"

- --range "first Monday in May"

- --range "between 4/23/2005 and 4/30/2005"

- --range "2005/05/03 10:24:17 for that second"

```
[root@studentvm1 ~]# logwatch --detail high --range "-3 days" | less
```

All of these options allow us to easily search for log entries using various criteria. Try some differing combinations of your own devising.

The sections that appear in the logwatch output depend upon the software packages you have installed on your Linux computer. So if you are looking at the output from logwatch for a basic installation rather than a primary workstation or even a server, you will see far fewer entries.

Since 2014 logwatch has been able to search the journald database for log entries.[1] This compatibility with the systemd logging facility ensures that a major source of log entries is not ignored.

logwatch runs once daily and is triggered by a Bash shell script in /etc/cron.daily. This script sets the output of the logwatch command to email, which, by the default Linux email configuration, is sent to root. The /etc/aliases file defines where email addressed to root is sent.

EXPERIMENT 39-8: LOGWATCH DETAIL LEVEL

Perform this experiment as root. Make /etc/cron.daily the PWD and then look at the contents of the file 0logwatch. The zero at the beginning of the name ensures that this shell script is run before any other scripts in this directory. The scripts are run in alphanumeric sorted order:

```
[root@studentvm1 ~]# cd /etc/cron.daily/ ; ll ; cat 0logwatch
total 8
-rwxr-xr-x  1 root root 486 Jan 28 06:22 0logwatch
-rwxr-xr-x. 1 root root 193 Jan  4  2018 logrotate
#!/usr/bin/sh
```

---

[1] SourceForge, Logwatch repository, https://sourceforge.net/p/logwatch/patches/34/

```
#Set logwatch executable location
LOGWATCH_SCRIPT="/usr/sbin/logwatch"

# Add options to the OPTIONS variable. Most options should be defined in
# the file /etc/logwatch/conf/logwatch.conf, but some are only for the
# nightly cron run such as "--output mail" and should be set here.
# Other options to consider might be "--format html" or "--encode base64".
# See 'man logwatch' for more details.
OPTIONS="--output mail"

#Call logwatch
$LOGWATCH_SCRIPT $OPTIONS

exit 0
```

This script scans the log files using the default detail level of 5 where the range is from 0 to 10. We want to change that to the highest setting of 10. Although you can use text equivalents where low = 0, med = 5, and high = 10, I prefer to use the numeric value of 10 when setting the detail level. Edit the 0logwatch file and change the $OPTIONS variable to the following to set the detail level:

```
OPTIONS="--output mail --detail 10"
```

Save the file and make root's home the PWD. The next run of logwatch triggered by the script located in cron.daily will run at the highest level of detail.

Because logwatch will not be triggered by cron.daily until about 03:30 a.m., you could wait until tomorrow to perform Experiment 39-9. Or we can force to do this from the command line. However, we need to install two packages to support sending and reading emails on our VMs.

We need to install a mail transfer agent (MTA) to accept emails from tools like logwatch and send them to the correct recipient, root, on the local host. We will use Sendmail. These emails don't get sent anywhere outside the host, so we don't yet need to configure Sendmail for that. Sendmail is one of the first MTAs if not the first.

We also need a text-based email client. The mailx client does this nicely. The mailx email client has been around for many years and is well known and stable.

We'll look at both of these tools and how email works more extensively in Volume 3, when we look at servers. For now let's get them installed and see what emails from logwatch look like.

EXPERIMENT 39-9: USE MAILX TO VIEW LOGWATCH REPORTS

In this experiment we install the Sendmail MTA and the mailx email client. Perform this experiment as root. In a terminal session, install the mailx and sendmail packages:

```
[root@studentvm1 ~]# dnf -y install mailx sendmail
```

Start and enable Sendmail. No emails can be sent inside or outside your local host unless Sendmail is running:

```
[root@studentvm1 ~]# systemctl start sendmail
[root@studentvm1 ~]# systemctl enable sendmail
Created symlink /etc/systemd/system/multi-user.target.wants/sendmail.service
→ /usr/lib/systemd/system/sendmail.service.
Created symlink /etc/systemd/system/multi-user.target.wants/sm-client.service
→ /usr/lib/systemd/system/sm-client.service.
[root@studentvm1 ~]# systemctl status sendmail
● sendmail.service - Sendmail Mail Transport Agent
    Loaded: loaded (/usr/lib/systemd/system/sendmail.service; enabled;
    preset: disabled)
    Active: active (running) since Tue 2023-05-09 11:43:06 EDT; 10s ago
  Main PID: 9486 (sendmail)
     Tasks: 1 (limit: 19130)
    Memory: 3.8M
       CPU: 190ms
    CGroup: /system.slice/sendmail.service
            └─9486 "sendmail: accepting connections"

May 09 11:43:06 studentvm1 systemd[1]: Starting sendmail.service - Sendmail
Mail Transport Agent...
May 09 11:43:06 studentvm1 sendmail[9486]: starting daemon (8.17.1):
SMTP+queueing@01:00:00
May 09 11:43:06 studentvm1 systemd[1]: sendmail.service: Can't open PID file
/run/sendmail.pid (yet?) afte>
May 09 11:43:06 studentvm1 systemd[1]: Started sendmail.service - Sendmail
Mail Transport Agent.
```

Let's test mailx first. It can be used to send emails directly from the command line as well as from within shell scripts, so it is perfect for our needs.

So start by sending a test email to root. The -s parameter to the mailx command allows entry of a subject for the email and the last entry is the "To:" address, in this case root, without a domain name as part of the address:

```
[root@studentvm1 ~]# echo "Hello World" | mailx -s "Test 1" root
```

Start the mailx email client. If you start mailx and no emails are in root's inbox, it prints a message to the terminal, "No mail for root," and returns to the command line:

```
[root@studentvm1 ~]# mailx
Heirloom Mail version 12.5 7/5/10.  Type ? for help.
"/var/spool/mail/root": 1 message 1 new
>N  1 root                  Tue May  9 12:24  21/826   "Test 1"
&
```

View the email by pressing the Enter key or entering its number at the ampersand (&) prompt. If your mail queue is longer than just the single message, be sure to use the correct number for the email with "Test 1" in the subject:

```
& 1
Message  1:
From root@studentvm1.both.org  Tue May  9 12:24:00 2023
Return-Path: <root@studentvm1.both.org>
From: root <root@studentvm1.both.org>
Date: Tue, 09 May 2023 12:23:57 -0400
To: root@studentvm1.both.org
Subject: Test 1
User-Agent: Heirloom mailx 12.5 7/5/10
Content-Type: text/plain; charset=us-ascii
Status: R

Hello World

&
```

Now we know that email is working as it should. We can now see how logwatch works with email. The following command runs logwatch on yesterday's log data and emails the resulting data to the root user. Since you are already in the mailx interface, use a different root terminal session to enter the command:

```
[root@studentvm1 ~]# logwatch --output mail

& h
>   1 root                   Tue May  9 12:24  22/837   "Test 1"
& h
>   1 root                   Tue May  9 12:24  22/837   "Test 1"
New mail has arrived.
Loaded 1 new message
 N  3 logwatch@studentvm1.  Tue May  9 13:45 124/4673  "Logwatch for
studentvm1 (Linux)"
& 3
Message  3:
From root@studentvm1.both.org  Tue May  9 13:45:11 2023
Return-Path: <root@studentvm1.both.org>
Date: Tue, 9 May 2023 13:45:07 -0400
To: root@studentvm1.both.org
From: logwatch@studentvm1.both.org
Subject: Logwatch for studentvm1 (Linux)
Auto-Submitted: auto-generated
Precedence: bulk
Content-Type: text/plain; charset="UTF-8"
Status: R

 ################### Logwatch 7.8 (01/22/23) ###################
        Processing Initiated: Tue May  9 13:45:07 2023
        Date Range Processed: yesterday
                             ( 2023-May-08 )
                             Period is day.
        Detail Level of Output: 0
        Type of Output/Format: mail / text
        Logfiles for Host: studentvm1
 ##############################################################

 -------------------- Kernel Begin -----------------------

WARNING:  Kernel Errors Present
    12:11:36.918413 main     Error: Failed to becom ...:  1 Time(s)
    12:11:36.922180 main     Error: Service 'contro ...:  1 Time(s)
    18:53:34.575206 main     VBoxClient VMSVGA: Error: Service ended w
    ...:  1 Time(s)
```

```
    WARNING: Spectre v2 mitigation leaves CPU vulner ...:  1 Time(s)
    [drm:vmw_host_printf [vmwgfx]] *ERROR* Failed to send  ...:  1 Time(s)

 --------------------- Kernel End ------------------------
<SNIP>
```

Yes, there was a message 2 due to my testing, but your message from logwatch should be number 2, unless you were experimenting too.

Scroll through the email from logwatch, which should be the same as what you saw when we just ran it from the command line without sending it to email.

Exit the email message with **q**. Then you can press **d** to delete the email. Or you can keep it, if you choose. Then exit from mailx using **q** again.

Emails will be renumbered sequentially the next time you start `mailx`.

Chapter Summary

Logs and journals are a rich source of information for SysAdmins as we work to resolve problems of many kinds. Despite knowing this, I sometimes forget to use them, and that has prevented me from solving those problems as quickly as I could. When I remember to go to the logs, the answers come quickly.

We have looked at some traditional text logs and explored how to access and search these logs. We also used logwatch to assist us in locating log entries that might indicate a problem.

A side benefit of this chapter is that we also installed Sendmail and mailx as tools for testing logwatch. This is an excellent example of using tools that "...do one thing and do it well" to test other tools that do the same. You will experience much more of this as you finish this course and experience the real world of Linux.

Exercises

Perform the following exercises to complete this chapter:

1. Use SAR to view disk activity for two days ago, displaying the device names like sda rather than the block device IDs like dev8-16.

2. What tools besides SAR can be used to view and analyze historical performance and event data?

3. What is the default data collection interval for SAR?

4. What caused these security log entries?

   ```
   May 23 12:54:29 studentvm1 login[18310]: pam_
   unix(login:session): session closed for user root
   May 23 12:54:35 studentvm1 login[20004]: pam_
   unix(login:auth): check pass; user unknown
   May 23 12:54:35 studentvm1 login[20004]: pam_
   unix(login:auth): authentication failure; logname=LOGIN
   uid=0 euid=0 tty=tty2 ruser= rhost=
   May 23 12:54:37 studentvm1 login[20004]: FAILED LOGIN 1
   FROM tty2 FOR (unknown), User not known to the underlying
   authentication module
   May 23 12:54:49 studentvm1 login[20004]: pam_
   unix(login:auth): check pass; user unknown
   May 23 12:54:49 studentvm1 login[20004]: pam_
   unix(login:auth): authentication failure; logname=LOGIN
   uid=0 euid=0 tty=tty2 ruser= rhost=
   May 23 12:54:52 studentvm1 login[20004]: FAILED LOGIN 2
   FROM tty2 FOR (unknown), User not known to the underlying
   authentication module
   May 23 12:56:04 studentvm1 login[20147]: pam_
   unix(login:auth): authentication failure; logname=LOGIN
   uid=0 euid=0 tty=tty2 ruser= rhost=  user=root
   ```

```
May 23 12:56:04 studentvm1 login[20147]: pam_succeed_
if(login:auth): requirement "uid >= 1000" not met by
user "root"
May 23 12:56:05 studentvm1 login[20147]: FAILED LOGIN 1
FROM tty2 FOR root, Authentication failure
```

5. Do messages added using the logger command show up in both the systemd journal and the /var/log/messages file?

6. Use logwatch from the CLI to search for all logical volume management (LVM) entries. Did you have any?

7. What minimum detail level must be specified when using logwatch in order to obtain non-null output for the systemd service?

CHAPTER 40

Managing Users

Objectives

In this chapter you will learn

- How user accounts and groups are used to provide access and security

- The function and structures of the passwd, group, and shadow files in /etc

- To add and delete user accounts using basic useradd and userdel commands

- To create user-level configurations that replicate for new users

- To lock a user account

Introduction

You are probably asking why I waited so long to talk about managing users. The answer is that many Linux systems today are essentially single-user systems. Very seldom do we see multiple users needing simultaneous access to a Linux computer, but it does happen. In most cases we find that one of several users of a Linux system will login and su - to root in order to perform some sort of administrative task. In other environments, several users may log in remotely as non-privileged users to a single system to perform normal work – whatever that might be.

Even if you are the only human with access rights to a particular Linux host, you are still dealing with at least two user accounts, root and your own user account. There are also a number of user accounts that belong to various services and programs on a Linux host.

693

© David Both 2023
D. Both, *Using and Administering Linux: Volume 2*, https://doi.org/10.1007/978-1-4842-9615-8_40

Much of this chapter is about creating and managing user accounts. We will spend a significant amount of time on the files used to manage user accounts, passwords, and security.

The Root Account

Your Linux computer has many accounts even if no other human actually uses your computer on a regular basis. Most of those accounts are used by Linux when it performs particular functions.

One of the special accounts is that of root. The root account is present on all Linux computers, and it allows the person logged in as root to read, change, and delete any file on the computer regardless of who owns the file. The root account is restricted by file permissions, but root can change the permissions of any file on the computer. The root account can do anything and everything on a Linux computer even changing the password of any user or locking out users. To protect the integrity of the system, the only person who should have the root password to a Linux computer is the system administrator.

We explored "working as root" in Chapter 11 of Volume 1, including reasons not to use sudo. In this chapter we are more interested in using the root account to manage other users.

Your User Account

By virtue of logging in using your account ID and password, you are granted access to read and write files that are located in your home directory because you are the owner of those files. You can create new files and directories in your home directory and modify them as you see fit.

Your account does not provide you enough rights to access other users' home directories, let alone view or modify the files located there. Your account does not have sufficient rights to alter any important system files, although you may be able to see some of them and view the contents of some.

There is a common practice to create account names using the first letter of your first name and your last name. Thus, the person Jo User would have an account name of juser. Notice that it is also common practice for the account name to be all lowercase. Case is important in Linux, so the account name JUser is not the same as juser.

Your Home Directory

Your home directory is where files that belong to you are stored. Another word for directory is folder.

When you create files in your home directory or in any of the subdirectories in your home directory, they are created with the appropriate ownership and permissions to allow you to read and write them. This should allow you to create new documents and spreadsheets and so on and then to be able to modify them as needed and store them back to the disk after they have been modified.

You can also use the file browser to change the permissions of the files in your home directory, but we recommend that you do not do so unless you have a very good reason to do so and know exactly why you are doing it.

User Accounts and Groups

User accounts and groups are the first line of security on your Linux computer. Knowledge of user accounts and file permissions will make it much less frustrating for you as you do your work.

The root account is always UID 0 and the root group is always GID 0.

Historically, all system-level users were assigned a UID and GID between 1 and 99. Convention defined the specific user and group IDs for various programs and services. For a time, Red Hat, and therefore Fedora, recommended starting human user and group IDs at UID 500 and GID 500. That was inconsistent with other Linux distributions and caused some issues.

Today, because of a proliferation of services and system-level account needs, all of the newer standard Linux system- and application-level users are located in the UID range between 100 and 999, which is now reserved for this purpose.[1] All application-level users – those required by installed services and applications – should be added in the UID range between 101 and 999. All regular (human) users should be added starting at UID 1000 and above.

---

[1] RHEL 7, "System Administrator's Guide," Red Hat, 2018, 44

The RHEL 7 "System Administrator's Guide" goes further and recommends starting human user IDs at 5000[2] to allow for future expansion of the system IDs. However, the current RHEL and Fedora implementations still begin at UID/GID 1000 for human users. The guide does explain how to make this change so that new users are automatically assigned IDs in the recommended range.

Group ID assignments should follow the same practices as UIDs to help ensure consistency and to make troubleshooting easier.

There are some interesting historical anomalies within this structure. For example, GID 100 is reserved for the "Users" group. In some environments it is common for all regular users to be added to this group, but this is not recommended as it constitutes a security risk that would allow users to have access to one another's files.

For regular users the UID and GID should be identical, that is, a user with UID 1001 should have a GID of 1001 as well. Since each user belongs to its own group, security is enhanced because files are not automatically shared between users. By default, users should not all belong to a single common primary group such as the Users group (GID 100).

Making files available to other users should be accomplished by using secondary group memberships to which the sharing users all belong and a directory where shared files can be stored and that has group ownership by the common group. Group membership should be limited to those who have a specific need to share related files. This allows for more granular management of shared files. We experimented with how to do this in Chapter 18 of Volume 1.

When adding group IDs for things like shared directories and files, I like to choose numbers starting at 5000 and above, as we did in Chapter 18. This allows space for 4000 users with identical UID and GID numbers. That should be more than enough for most Linux installations. Your needs may differ so you should adapt as necessary.

Figure 40-1 shows the conventional and currently common usage assignments for UID and GID ranges. The range 0–999 and the ID 65534 should be considered as completely unusable for use or assignment by the SysAdmin. The range between 1000 and 65533 can be considered flexible and can be used according to local requirements.

---

[2] Ibid., 44

696

Description	User ID range	Group ID range
root	0	0
Historical Linux system level accounts. These are all documented and assigned by convention.	1 - 99	1 - 99
Accounts used by services and applications. This has changed over the years, but this range is now consistent with Unix and other Linux distributions.	100 - 999	100 – 999
Accounts used by regular (Human) users.	1000 – 4999	1000-4999
Miscellaneous – Shared directory and file GIDs, for example.	5000 - 9999	5000 - 9999
Open – not assigned or otherwise designated for any use. Can be used as desired for local needs.	10000 - 65533	10000 - 65533
nfsnobody – an anonymous NFS (Network File System) user that is used for access to remote files.	65534	65534

Figure 40-1. *Recommended UID and GID numeric ranges*

User and group ID data are stored in the files /etc/passwd, /etc/shadow, and /etc/group.

The /etc/passwd File

We will start by looking at the user and group information located in the /etc/passwd file. While here we will also look at the other information stored in this file.

EXPERIMENT 40-1: EXPLORING /ETC/PASSWD

Much of this experiment should be performed as root. As the root user, the **id** command shows us information about our ID:

```
[root@studentvm1 ~]# id
uid=0(root) gid=0(root) groups=0(root)
[root@studentvm1 ~]#
```

This shows that the UID and GID for root are both 0 (zero) and that the root user is a member of the root group with a GID of 0.

Now, as the root user, let's look at the information for the student user:

```
[root@studentvm1 ~]# id 1000
uid=1000(student) gid=1000(student) groups=1000(student),5000(dev)
```

The student user has both UID and GID set as 1000. The student user also has group membership in the dev group. This membership allows the student user to share files with other users. Look at the student1 user, which also has membership in this shared group:

```
[root@studentvm1 ~]# id 1001
uid=1001(student1) gid=1001(student1) groups=1001(student1),5000(dev)
```

Now let's look at the file that defines and contains user information. Enter the following command as root:

```
[root@studentvm1 ~]# cat /etc/passwd
```

The result is not sorted in any meaningful way, so let's make it a bit easier by sorting on the UID. This number is located in the third field of each user. The -t option specifies the field delimiter character, and -k specifies starting the sort at field 3, the first character. The -g option specifies the use of a general numeric sort. This results in a data stream that is much easier to read:

```
[root@studentvm1 etc]# cat /etc/passwd | sort -t: -k3.1 -g
root:x:0:0:root:/root:/bin/bash
bin:x:1:1:bin:/bin:/sbin/nologin
daemon:x:2:2:daemon:/sbin:/sbin/nologin
adm:x:3:4:adm:/var/adm:/sbin/nologin
lp:x:4:7:lp:/var/spool/lpd:/sbin/nologin
```

```
sync:x:5:0:sync:/sbin:/bin/sync
shutdown:x:6:0:shutdown:/sbin:/sbin/shutdown
halt:x:7:0:halt:/sbin:/sbin/halt
mail:x:8:12:mail:/var/spool/mail:/sbin/nologin
operator:x:11:0:operator:/root:/sbin/nologin
games:x:12:100:games:/usr/games:/sbin/nologin
ftp:x:14:50:FTP User:/var/ftp:/sbin/nologin
rpcuser:x:29:29:RPC Service User:/var/lib/nfs:/sbin/nologin
rpc:x:32:32:Rpcbind Daemon:/var/lib/rpcbind:/sbin/nologin
mailnull:x:47:47::/var/spool/mqueue:/sbin/nologin
smmsp:x:51:51::/var/spool/mqueue:/sbin/nologin
tss:x:59:59:Account used for TPM access:/:/sbin/nologin
avahi:x:70:70:Avahi mDNS/DNS-SD Stack:/var/run/avahi-daemon:/sbin/nologin
tcpdump:x:72:72:tcpdump:/:/sbin/nologin
sshd:x:74:74:Privilege-separated SSH:/usr/share/empty.sshd:/sbin/nologin
dbus:x:81:81:System Message Bus:/:/usr/sbin/nologin
rtkit:x:172:172:RealtimeKit:/proc:/sbin/nologin
abrt:x:173:173::/etc/abrt:/sbin/nologin
systemd-network:x:192:192:systemd Network Management:/:/usr/sbin/nologin
systemd-resolve:x:193:193:systemd Resolver:/:/usr/sbin/nologin
saslauth:x:978:76:Saslauthd user:/run/saslauthd:/sbin/nologin
systemd-timesync:x:979:979:systemd Time Synchronization:/:/usr/sbin/nologin
systemd-coredump:x:980:980:systemd Core Dumper:/:/usr/sbin/nologin
dnsmasq:x:982:981:Dnsmasq DHCP and DNS server:/var/lib/dnsmasq:/usr/
sbin/nologin
vboxadd:x:983:1::/var/run/vboxadd:/sbin/nologin
lightdm:x:984:983::/var/lib/lightdm:/sbin/nologin
sstpc:x:985:984:Secure Socket Tunneling Protocol(SSTP) Client:/var/run/
sstpc:/sbin/nologin
flatpak:x:986:985:Flatpak system helper:/:/usr/sbin/nologin
setroubleshoot:x:987:986:SELinux troubleshoot server:/var/lib/
setroubleshoot:/sbin/nologin
pipewire:x:988:987:PipeWire System Daemon:/var/run/pipewire:/sbin/nologin
unbound:x:989:988:Unbound DNS resolver:/etc/unbound:/sbin/nologin
nm-openconnect:x:990:989:NetworkManager user for OpenConnect:/:/sbin/nologin
nm-openvpn:x:991:990:Default user for running openvpn spawned by
NetworkManager:/:/sbin/nologin
openvpn:x:992:991:OpenVPN:/etc/openvpn:/sbin/nologin
```

```
colord:x:993:992:User for colord:/var/lib/colord:/sbin/nologin
chrony:x:994:993:chrony system user:/var/lib/chrony:/sbin/nologin
nm-fortisslvpn:x:995:994:Default user for running openfortivpn spawned by
NetworkManager:/:/sbin/nologin
geoclue:x:996:995:User for geoclue:/var/lib/geoclue:/sbin/nologin
polkitd:x:997:996:User for polkitd:/:/sbin/nologin
systemd-oom:x:998:998:systemd Userspace OOM Killer:/:/usr/sbin/nologin
student:x:1000:1000:Student User:/home/student:/bin/bash
student1:x:1001:1001:Student user 1:/home/student1:/bin/bash
student2:x:1002:1002:Student User 2:/home/student2:/bin/bash
nobody:x:65534:65534:Kernel Overflow User:/:/sbin/nologin
```

Let's deconstruct the line for the student account, UID 1000, shown in Figure 40-2. The field separator for this file is the colon (:).

			`student:x:1000:1000:Student User:/home/student:/bin/bash`
Field	**Field name**	**Value**	**Description**
1	Account name	student	The user login name for the account
2	Password	x	No longer used to store passwords. This field is retained for backward compatibility.
3	User ID (UID)	1000	The User ID number for this account.
4	Group ID (GID)	1000	The primary Group ID number for this account. This is the default and many times the only group to which a user belongs.
5	GECOS	student	This is a text field that can contain multiple words for a description of the account. GECOS stands for General Electric Comprehensive Operating System. Yes, *that* GE[3].
6	Home directory	/home/student	The home directories for users may differ depending upon the organizational needs, specifications, and historical usage.
7	Shell	/bin/bash	The default shell for this user. Bash is the default shell for most Linux distributions. Users can change their default shell.

Figure 40-2. Deconstructing the /etc/passwd entry for the student user

---

[3] During the 1960s, GE designed and built computers of their own and participated in the doomed-by-committee Multics project, which was the forerunner of Unix.

The password field in account entries is no longer used. Storing a password in this file is a security issue because the file needs to be accessible by all user accounts. Reading a password from this file, even an encrypted password, constitutes a serious security issue. For this reason passwords have long ago been moved to the /etc/shadow file, which is not universally readable and thus is more secure.

nologin Shells

Many of the system users in the /etc/passwd file have a nologin shell, /sbin/nologin. This type of shell is a small shell that does not allow a login of any type. This is a security feature as it prevents crackers from accessing a Linux host system by escalating privileges to or beyond these accounts.

The /etc/shadow File

As mentioned previously, the password location for user accounts has been moved from /etc/passwd to /etc/shadow. The shadow file is more secure because it is readable only by root and by system processes that run with the root user ID.

EXPERIMENT 40-2: THE /ETC/SHADOW FILE

Perform this experiment as the root user. We now look at the /etc/shadow file. Your root terminal session should still have /etc as the PWD.

View the content of the /etc/shadow file. I have removed a number of lines to save space:

```
[root@studentvm1 etc]# cat shadow
root:$y$j9T$FVKiIj5u3CRbWDyO4lsfxt7e$Evlxg6k/
xSYNVNeUoWAGtf9BwAI4U6p6PK3RRnbt60C::0:99999:7:::
bin:*:19196:0:99999:7:::
daemon:*:19196:0:99999:7:::
adm:*:19196:0:99999:7:::
lp:*:19196:0:99999:7:::
sync:*:19196:0:99999:7:::
shutdown:*:19196:0:99999:7:::
halt:*:19196:0:99999:7:::
mail:*:19196:0:99999:7:::
```

```
operator:*:19196:0:99999:7:::
games:*:19196:0:99999:7:::
ftp:*:19196:0:99999:7:::
nobody:*:19196:0:99999:7:::
dbus:!!:19301::::::
tss:!!:19301::::::
systemd-network:!*:19301::::::
systemd-oom:!*:19301::::::
<SNIP>
lightdm:!!:19301::::::
rpcuser:!!:19301::::::
vboxadd:!!:19301::::::
sshd:!!:19301::::::
dnsmasq:!!:19301::::::
tcpdump:!!:19301::::::
systemd-coredump:!*:19301::::::
systemd-timesync:!*:19301::::::
student:$y$j9T$F1bU1XyjGrsx9vj8DY/W1X1j$nfvhi6yhEKMMRHDAEBuiwnbwGK.wFuLGc2mH/
xaqqV3::0:99999:7:::
student1:$y$j9T$PU8zFAELrJQ4TPrKA8U1f.$WmZXnLiocJkQpaDIOfkLg48fce06e0ouRK
YLBzMOu9.:19397:0:99999:7:::
student2:$y$j9T$1Ch.293dasUtkOlUTOJ4r1$ZaJI.XzZMGmuAnOaJuThXgLWpxF5nelG28wN5.
0iAT6:19398:0:99999:7:::
saslauth:!!:19486::::::
mailnull:!!:19486::::::
smmsp:!!:19486::::::
```

Note that only root and other human user accounts have passwords.

Let's deconstruct the shadow file entry in Figure 40-3 for the student user. The entries for this file contain nine colon (:)-separated fields.

```
student:$y$j9T$F1bU1XyjG<SNIP>c2mH/xaqqV3::0:99999:7:::
```

Field	Field name	Value	Description
1	Account name	student	The user login name for the account
2	Password	yj9T$F1bU1XyjG<SNIP>	The encrypted password, also called a hash, and truncated here for brevity. If this field starts with an exclamation point (!) the account is locked.
3	Date of the last password change.	Empty	The date of the last password change in days since Jan 1, 1970 00:00 UTC. If this field is empty, the password has never been changed. If this field is 0, then the password must be changed at the next login.
4	Minimum password age.	0	If this number is non-zero the user must wait that number of days before changing the password again. This prevents users from doing a required change and then immediately changing the password back to their "favorite" password.

Figure 40-3. *Deconstructing the /etc/shadow entry for the student user*

```
student:$y$j9T$F1bU1XyjG<SNIP>c2mH/xaqqV3::0:99999:7:::
```

Field	Field name	Value	Description
5	Maximum password age.	99999	The number of days that the password will remain valid. The value of 99999 is interpreted as the password will never expire.
6	Password warning period.	7	The number of days left until the password expires during which the user will be warned each day.
7	Password inactivity period.	Empty	The number of days after password expiration during which the old password will be accepted and the user required to create a new password.
8	Account expiration date.	Empty	The number of days since Jan 1, 1970 00:00 UTC at which the account will expire. The user will not be allowed to login to an expired account. If this field is empty the account will never expire. This is different from the password expiration.
9	Reserved	Empty	Reserved for future use.

Figure 40-3. *(continued)*

Fields 4 through 8 are typically used to implement password security policies by forcing users to change their passwords on a regular basis. Notice that the student user has not changed their password.

EXPERIMENT 40-3: EXPLORING PASSWORD CHANGES

Perform this experiment as the student user. Change the student user's password from the command line. Let's start with a bad password to see what happens:

```
[student@studentvm1 ~]$ passwd
Changing password for user student.
Current password: <Enter the current password>
New password: mypassword
BAD PASSWORD: The password fails the dictionary check - it is based on a
dictionary word
passwd: Authentication token manipulation error
```

So entering a password that contains a dictionary word or a string of characters that are typically substituted in dictionary words causes an error and does not allow the password to be changed. Try this – the 0 is a zero:

```
[student@studentvm1 ~]$ passwd
Changing password for user student.
Current password: <Enter the current password>
New password: myp@ssw0rd
BAD PASSWORD: The password fails the dictionary check - it is based on a
dictionary word
passwd: Authentication token manipulation error
```

A non-root user is not allowed to create passwords that do not pass certain minimum criteria. The root user can set any password for any user although the same messages will be displayed as a reminder. But root can do anything.

Let's change the password for real:

```
[student@studentvm1 ~]$ passwd
Changing password for user student.
Current password: <Enter the current password>
New password: Yu2iyief
Retype new password: Yu2iyief
passwd: all authentication tokens updated successfully.
```

This works because the password is not too short – it must be at least eight characters in length – and it is a series of random letters, upper- and lowercase, as well as a numeric digit. Now let's see what happens when root changes the student user's password with a dictionary word:

```
[root@studentvm1 etc]# passwd student
Changing password for user student.
New password: myp@sswOrd
BAD PASSWORD: The password is shorter than 8 characters
Retype new password: myp@sswOrd
passwd: all authentication tokens updated successfully.
You have new mail in /var/spool/mail/root
```

Root does not need to enter the current password and, although the bad password message is displayed, the password is changed anyway.

Tip   Root has mail in the previous example. This is the daily logwatch email report. Depending upon how fast you are working through this course, you may have seen this already, or you may not see it until later.

Now look at the shadow file entry for the student user:

```
[root@studentvm1 etc]# grep student shadow
student:$6$.9B/OvGhNwsdf.cc$X/Ed1<snip>dD/:18041:0:99999:7:::
<snip>
```
The third field, the date of the last password change, now has a number in it, 18041 on my host. Your number will be different.

Change the password to something you choose.

Note that for a non-root user changing their own password, they must also enter that existing password before they can change it. This is a simple security procedure that can prevent passersby from changing a user's password. Remember, root can do anything, including changing the password of any user without the need to know the old password.

The /etc/group File

The /etc/group file contains a list of all of the groups on the local host. This includes the standard system groups as well as groups created by the system administrator for specific local use.

We created two groups in Chapter 18 of Volume 1, dev and shared, to allow users to have a place to share files and to work cooperatively. Having already looked at the group file there and earlier in this chapter, there is no need to explore it more.

The /etc/login.defs File

The /etc/login.defs file is used to set certain default configuration items that are incorporated when adding new users. The values in this file include the starting and maximum UIDs and GIDs for new users, the default mail directory location, and the default password expiration options.

EXPERIMENT 40-4: THE LOGIN.DEFS FILE

Perform this experiment as the root user. View the contents of the /etc/login.defs file. You can read the comments in that file to understand it a bit, but there are two lines that need some discussion.

PASS_MIN_LEN: The minimum length for a password is specified as five characters. This should be set to a minimum of eight to ensure a reasonable amount of security.

PASS_MAX_DAYS: This line is set to 99999 so that the passwords never expire. In a real-world environment, passwords should be set to expire no less frequently than every 30 days.

Remember that, although the root user will still see password warnings, root can ignore them. Non-root users are not able to ignore the warnings and must create a password that meets the length policy set in this file.

Account Configuration Files

As you have already seen in Volume 1, there are several configuration files that are present in a new account home directory. All user shell configuration files that are located in the /etc/skel directory, such as ~/.bash_profile and ~/.bashrc, are copied into the new account home directory when each new user account is created.

If you have local configuration files that should be in the users' home directories instead of in one of the system-wide configuration files found in /etc/profile.d, you can place them in /etc/skel, and the files will be copied to the new home directory. One reason to place them in the account home directory is so that the user can alter them as needed.

Password Security

It is advisable as a good security precaution to change your password about once a month. This prevents other people from using your password for very long even if they happen to discover it. Once you have changed it, they can no longer use your previous password to access the system. You never know when or how someone might obtain or guess your password, so even if you do not think it has been compromised, you should change your password regularly. Of course a password should be changed immediately if you suspect that it has been compromised.

Passwords should be protected and never written down. If a password is stolen, it can be used to access your computer and the network if your computer is so connected and thus compromise your data.

Linux requires passwords to be a specified minimum length. The default is five characters but that can be changed. I recommend that you use a longer password to increase the difficulty of someone guessing your password. Passwords should never be dates, initials, acronyms, words, or easy-to-remember sequences such as "ASDFG" from the left of the middle row of the keyboard. Passwords should be composed of upper- and lowercase alphabetic characters as well as numbers and special characters.

My personal calculations show that an automated attack of 500 access attempts per second on a host with a five-character password can crack in anywhere from 6 hours to 21 days depending upon whether the password contains only lowercase alpha or upper- and lowercase alpha as well as numbers. The time to crack a really good randomly generated password that includes special characters (#, $, %, ^, etc.) rises to 152 days.

This should be set to a minimum of eight to ensure a reasonable amount of security. The time to crack an eight-character password rises to from 13 years to over 325,000 years, once again depending upon using upper- and lowercase alpha, numbers, and special characters.

Crackers – bad hackers, people who want to get into your computer – have dictionaries of words, common acronyms, and key sequences that they can try to attempt to crack into your system. They also try easy-to-guess sequences that are available to anyone with a little persistence such as birthdays; anniversaries; the names of spouses, children, pets, or significant others; Social Security numbers; and other possible passwords of this type. The point is that when you change your password, you should choose one that is not based on a dictionary word or one that will be easy to guess or deduce from your personal information. Passwords based on any of these non-random sources will likely be cracked in seconds.

There is a significant downside of changing passwords frequently and setting strict policies that require them to be excessively long and not easily memorized. Such policies will almost certainly result in users who write their passwords on Post-it notes and stick them on the display or under the keyboard. There is a fine line between workable security and self-defeating security.

Password Encryption

Passwords cannot be safely stored on the hard drive in plain text format as this would leave them open to incredibly easy hacking. In order to ensure that the user accounts are secure, passwords are encrypted using the OpenSSL encryption libraries. The `openssl` command-line tool can be used to access the encryption libraries from the command line so that we can explore a bit about password encryption.

EXPERIMENT 40-5: PASSWORD ENCRYPTION

Perform this experiment as the student user. The `openssl passwd` command-line utility allows encryption of a plain text string into an encrypted password that can be used when creating a new account. It also lets us explore the structure of the passwords in the /etc/shadow file.

Starting with a simple example and without specifying a specific encryption method, the password is truncated to eight characters and encrypted with the crypt algorithm, which is not particularly secure. For most of the examples in this experiment, we will use the string "mypassword" for the password to be encrypted:

```
[student@studentvm1 ~]$ openssl passwd mypassword
$1$6HSQkhNO$7Bj5BFzgf1RC9IIirucU41
```

Compare the password generated to that of the student1 password in the /etc/shadow file, which looks like that in the following. This password hash is much longer than what we got from using the default settings:

```
student:$y$j9T$8wWmtQ9YBTBduOab1uP1b1$OovMpOq3iNs6P4um..iiU/
zSC8jlKEkjFczMaYYyqf/:19487:0:99999:7:::
```

I have highlighted the first three characters of the password because they tell us – and the system password and login utilities – the encryption algorithm used to create the password. 6 means that the SHA512 bit algorithm was used to create this password. We can specify the SHA512 algorithm with the -6 option:

```
[student@studentvm1 ~]$ openssl passwd -6 mypassword
$6$d97oQ/z8flJUPO5p$fhCJDLFEwl89bb9Ucp9DVfQNvuUgParsq/NasrYqw91zOKfj.
W5rHHFw8VUY9M2kyoOaqAmVAT/xYDeFjKOFX1
```

Note the 6 characters at the beginning of this password indicating that it is SHA512. Now do the same with the SHA256 option:

```
[student@studentvm1 ~]$ openssl passwd -5 mypassword
$5$TIXlQaYbLX.buCu5$r7Kb4hN/mEORRYgfibgT54/daIJOXlfKEXJrkTKyeq3
```

Notice the first three characters are now 5, and the password is shorter.

Open the openssl-passwd man page (man openssl-passwd) and view the other encryption options available. Create password hashes using crypt, MD5, apr1, SHA256 (-5), and SHA512 (-6) algorithms.

Let's get back to the SHA512 algorithm. Run the command several times in sequence:

```
[student@studentvm1 ~]$ openssl passwd -6 mypassword
```

Notice that the password hash is always different despite the fact that the password string is the same. This is because the password encryption algorithms use a different random seed for every iteration. This is called the "salt,"[4] presumably because it spices things up a bit. Normally, the salt is taken from the /dev/urandom data stream. This adds a bit of randomness into the algorithm and produces a different result for every iteration.

We also can specify a salt to use with the algorithm instead of using a random one, using the -salt option. Execute the following command several times; it will always produce the same result:

```
[student@studentvm1 ~]$ openssl passwd -salt 123456 -6 mypassword
$6$123456$KKcK3jDXxN5TVYNLbMdEIjnfRjaSlbqj5X9bBgryaa4qLDO4lrM9kswCpAZL27/
WXlbsDQcJ8kBxPjcpips781
```

Notice that the salt string is included after the algorithm specifier, $6$123456$. Using the same salt string removes the randomness from the algorithm to always produce the same result, given the same password. Using a different string for the salt creates a new password hash.

Go back and look at some of the passwords you created without the salt option and locate the random string.

Theoretically, the well-known algorithms used to generate password hashes do so in such a way that there is no known algorithm that can reverse the process and generate the plain text password from the password hash. However, if a cracker has access to the hash – which also contains the salt string – a brute-force attack could conceivably eventually find the plain text that generated the hash. This would not take long if the password was based on dictionary words, but could take years if good passwords were used.

Generating Good Passwords

Creating good passwords is a challenge. It can take some thought and effort. Linux has at least one tool that provides us with suggestions for good passwords.

---

[4] The Free On-line Dictionary of Computing (FOLDOC) defines salt as "a tiny bit of near-random data inserted where too much regularity would be undesirable ..."

The pwgen utility gives us the ability to specify the number and length of passwords we want to generate as well as to make them relatively easy or impossible to remember. By default, when used without the -s (secure) and -y (use special characters) options, the resulting passwords are alleged to be easy for humans to memorize. My experience is that some are and others not so much.

EXPERIMENT 40-6: GENERATING GOOD PASSWORDS

This experiment can be performed as the student user. We explore the pwgen utility to learn how it can help us create reasonably secure passwords.

Start by using pwgen with no options, which, when STDOUT is to a terminal, generates a list of 160 random eight-character passwords using uppercase, lowercase, and numeric characters. I can choose one of the passwords from the list to use:

```
[student@studentvm1 ~]$ pwgen
Iiqu4ahY Eeshu1ei raeZoo8o ahj6Sei3 Moo5ohTu ieGh6eit Is0Eisae eiVo5Ohv
Gooqu5ji ieX9VoN5 aiy3kiSo Iphaex4e Vait1thu oi5ruaPh eL7Mohch iel2Aih6
Elu5Fiqu eeZ4aeje Ienooj6v iFie2aiN ruu7ohSh foo4Chie Wai5Ap1N ohRae1lu
urahn2Oo eal6Zuey GuX3cho0 iesh1Oot eepha1Ai oe6Chaij ISaeb3ch OK7Iuchu
aeNgee6O Iequit9U OoNgi2oo cohY4Xei Ziengi3E quohTei4 eefe2ieC eong8Qui
Vo5aip8m EishiOei Xith9eil aongu4Ai paiFe1zo gaiPh5Ko Be7ieYu2 Fathah9h
Gu7UcePh lee7aiSh aj4AuChe Zo3caeR1 Yo8jei5x maeChe5a IdObaigh Fu4tei4e
geiLeid7 quaeK4Ro ohVoe5iZ AY2Noodi nem0tahJ ahPiw1oh gah6baeH Aa5pohCh
ahShai1h uQu3Hah1 Eth3coo5 EChoboc9 Iey0ahCh Mee3iewu Iek6oMai aePoo2ei
aeVoM8Sh IeR0hohr Duew9ogh toh8AeXu Nohgh0me ain4Ooph ooyuKoh1 huth1Mei
si4ohCao ahthaeOI ohquah5F chohpe9G yoiM2noh iePh9iej aij7uXu7 Phoophi8
Bei5iLah uR3aicer oagh2OVo uThox9Xa Gu4reeOv shohNe2a weReth7A Vae4ga3b
Jee9jieX kohjoR6o Zimaish2 ut9mahJ8 ephu8Ray Iep0eiTh ooB3joom Rai1ohzu
em0Eeruv Tu7Phoh1 bohOIFee roh6Phae tauT3ohh LieFiu0a Voo9uvah pahpuiJ1
ohSiaN9a ooBahnu9 Uo2DahS0 oor6Huwe ahs6Och3 aeCai1oo ahw2Lawi oCaeboo8
oshahB8e Xu3iyohx NoX4ohCi oa5aiLih uLah7noo Thopie2a ua6iuQuo ooYab5ai
Gae5ahsh Eech1re7 feeDah4v wou7Oek4 iefoo9AJ zei4ahVi uMiel7sh jae3eiVo
zahC3Tue Eiphei6E ke6GiaJ8 oquieBaO chi8Ohba ooZ9OC3e deiV7pae sieCho6W
nu1oba1D aiYoh2oo OoluaZ7u Ahg5pee7 Teepha6E oochOMod ThaiPui5 Ehui9ioF
ekuina3Z Oafaivi1 Pusuef9g aChoh2Eb Cio7aebe eoPOiepu seGh2kie fiax4Cha
```

Pipe the data stream through the sort command. The result is a single password. Whenever the data stream of pwgen with no options is sent through a pipe, only a single password is generated. This is ideal for automation scripts:

```
[student@studentvm1 ~]$ pwgen | sort
Eaphui7K
```

This behavior can be overridden using the -N option to specify the desired number of passwords:

```
[student@studentvm1 ~]$ pwgen -N 6 | sort
boot6Ahr
Die2thah
nohSoh1T
reob9eiR
shahXoL6
Wai6aiph
```

pwgen recognizes two arguments in the syntax, pwgen pw_length number_of_passwds:

```
[student@studentvm1 ~]$ pwgen 20 10
huo7ooz5shoom2eg9Sha PahJein4oRohleiOphu4 Air2ahxu4AeLae7dee7G
mug2feingooT6thoo7mo eeshipicoosh8Cahfil8 KaeniuM3aic2eiZo9yiO
Uze9aejoh6og1thaTh1e Noitongeiri7goh9XeeN ZohxeejiewaeKaeth1vo
kohngoh7Nienughai5oo
```

Now use the -s and -y options in various combinations:

```
[student@studentvm1 ~]$ pwgen -s
[student@studentvm1 ~]$ pwgen -y
[student@studentvm1 ~]$ pwgen -sy
[student@studentvm1 ~]$ pwgen -s 25 90
```

Read the man page for pwgen and check out some of its other options. Of particular interest is the option to remove ambiguous characters, those that can be confused for each other such as I (eye) and 1 (one) or 0 (zero) and O (oh).

Password Quality

There is a configuration file that is used to define the quality requirements of new passwords, /etc/security/pwquality.conf. The system defaults are defined to us humans as commented lines in this file. Lines that need to be changed to improve security can be uncommented and the default value for the variable changed to whatever is desired.

For one example, you might wish to change the default password length from 8 to 10. So uncomment the # minlen = 8 line and change 8 to 10.

One trick many users try when required to change their passwords is to simply change one character in the existing one. So they change the old password, password3, to password4. The default setting of the "difference OK" variable to difok = 1 allows this, but it is a bad idea.

EXPERIMENT 40-7: PASSWORD QUALITY

This experiment will be performed partly as root and partly as the student1 user. First, read the man page for pwquality.conf to get an idea of the variables available that can be changed. Then as root, set the password for student1 to "password1234". Log in to the student1 account using that password.

As student1, change the password to "password9876".

Edit the /etc/security/pwquality.conf file and change the line

```
# difok = 1
```

to

```
difok = 5
```

Now try to change the password for student1 to "password4567". Note that a reboot is not required. These changes are activated immediately:

```
[student1@studentvm1 ~]$ passwd
Changing password for user student1.
Current password: password9876
New password: password4567
BAD PASSWORD: The password is too similar to the old one
passwd: Authentication token manipulation error
```

Another trick users try is to use all one class of characters for their passwords, such as all lowercase or all numbers. The minclass = 0 can be changed to require as many as four classes of characters, uppercase, lowercase, numbers, and special characters. It is a good practice to require at least three different classes of characters.

Change minclass to 3 and try to change the password for student1 to one with one or two classes of characters. Then change the password to one with three classes. This setting does not specify which character classes are required.

Change the altered lines back to their original values and set the password for student1 to your preferred one.

Managing User Accounts

Managing user accounts is a very common task for system administrators in many environments. This can include adding new accounts, deleting accounts that are no longer needed, and modifying existing accounts.

There are at least three methods that can be used to create, delete, and modify user accounts. Most desktop environments have some form of GUI tool. There are command-line tools useradd and adduser; the latter is simply a symlink to useradd but is retained for backward compatibility. There are also commands to delete and to modify user accounts. And there is also the very retro method of editing the required files by hand.

In the next few experiments, we will manage user accounts using the command line and by manually editing the various files. I liked editing these files by hand when I was first learning because it provided me with knowledge of what the commands actually do as well as all of the files required and their structures.

Creating New Accounts

Creating new accounts is easy no matter which method is used. Let's start with the useradd command.

The useradd Command

We start with the easy method. The useradd command is flexible and can allow the SysAdmin to just take the defaults for things like password expiration, the default shell, and more.

EXPERIMENT 40-8: ADDING NEW USERS WITH USERADD

Perform this experiment as the root user.

Start by checking one of the files that defines some defaults for new users, /etc/defaults/ useradd. These can be set permanently here or overridden at the command line:

```
[root@studentvm1 ~]# cat /etc/default/useradd
# useradd defaults file
GROUP=100
HOME=/home
INACTIVE=-1
EXPIRE=
SHELL=/bin/bash
SKEL=/etc/skel
CREATE_MAIL_SPOOL=yes
```

Now add a user using the default settings. The -c (comment) option adds the text in quotes to the GECOS comment field in /etc/passwd:

```
[root@studentvm1 ~]# useradd -c "Test User 1" tuser1
```

Set a password for this new user:

```
[root@studentvm1 ~]# passwd tuser1
Changing password for user tuser1.
New password: <Enter new password>
BAD PASSWORD: The password is shorter than 8 characters
Retype new password: <Enter new password>
passwd: all authentication tokens updated successfully.
[root@studentvm1 ~]#
```

Then look at the lines for this user in /etc/passwd, /etc/shadow, and /etc/group. Look at the contents of the home directory for tuser1, including hidden files.

Now let's create a user account with a different shell, zsh, and home directory location, /TestFS/tuser2. We added a number of different shells in Chapter 7 of Volume 1, so the ZShell should already be installed. The -d option specifies the complete path of the home directory. If the base directory, in this case /TestFS, does not exist, neither it nor the home directory will be created. The -s option specifies the user's default shell:

```
[root@studentvm1 etc]# useradd -c "Test User 2" -d /TestFS/tuser2 -s /usr/
bin/zsh tuser2
```

Set the password for this user. Check the lines that were added to the passwd, shadow, and group files. Log in or **su -** as this user to verify that zsh is the default shell. The command prompt will be a bit different. Notice the difference in command-line editing and the lack of tab completion. Log out from this user account.

Let's add a user with a password expiration date of today. The -e option specifies the expiration data in YYYY-MM-DD format and does the conversion to days elapsed since January 1, 1970, 00:00 UTC. Note that "today" for you will be different from "today" as I write this, so be sure to use your today:

```
[root@studentvm1 etc]# useradd -c "Test User 3" -e 2019-05-28 tuser3
```

Set a password for tuser3. As the student user, use su to log in as tuser3 from a terminal session. You could also use a virtual console to log in as tuser3:

```
[student@studentvm1 ~]$ su - tuser3
Password: <Enter password for tuser3>
Your account has expired; please contact your system administrator
su: User account has expired
```

Now let's use the usermod command to set the expiration date to a few days in the future – your future:

```
[root@studentvm1 etc]# usermod -e 2023-06-05 tuser3
```

As the student user again, use su to log in as tuser3:

```
[student@studentvm1 ~]$ su - tuser3
Password: <Enter password for tuser3>
[tuser3@studentvm1 ~]$
```

Setting the account expiration date is not tied to the password expiration date. For example, you might hire a contractor to work on a project that will take six months. So you can set the account expiration date to six months while the password expiration is set to 30 days. The password will expire every 30 days during that six months, but the account will expire at the specified future date. Even if the password has not expired, the user will not be able to log into an expired account.

Log out of the tuser3 session.

Although the password expiration date can be set using the -K option of the useradd command, these should be system-wide settings and belong in the /etc/login.defs file to ensure consistency in its application.

It is possible to set an initial password, already encrypted, while adding a new account. We can use the openssl command to encrypt the password into a string called a hash and then use the result as an option in the useradd command.

Now we will add a new user with an encrypted password.

EXPERIMENT 40-9: ADDING A NEW USER WITH A PASSWORD

Perform this experiment as the root user. Add a new user using a password hash to set the password with the useradd command. Enter this command all on one line. Be sure to place the backticks (`) around the openssl passwd command as shown:

```
[root@studentvm1 ~]# useradd -c "Test User 4" -p `openssl passwd -salt 123456
-6 mypassword` tuser4
```

Now look at the shadow file and verify that it looks like this. Because we used the same salt and the same password to generate the password hash, the resulting hash should be identical:

```
tuser4:$6$123456$KKcK3jDXxN5TVYNLbMdEIjnfRjaSlbqj5X9bBgryaa4qLDO4lrM9ksw
CpAZL27/WXlbsDQcJ8kBxPjcpips781:18044:0:99999:7:::
```

Now log in as tuser4 using the password "mypassword" to verify that this has produced the desired result. Log out of the tuser4 account.

Creating New Accounts by Editing the Files

Although it is a bit more involved and takes a little more time than using the **useradd** command, editing the files to add a new user can be a helpful learning experience. It is really not all that difficult. It just takes time and knowledge.

Although we would never expect to add a new user in this way, I have had the need to repair a user account. Knowing all of the files involved and how to edit them safely has been useful to me. So this experiment is more about gaining a knowledge of the files that comprise a user account rather than a need to ever add a new user using this method.

EXPERIMENT 40-10: ADDING NEW ACCOUNTS WITH A TEXT EDITOR

This experiment must be performed as the root user. We will add a new user, Test User 5, tuser5, by editing the appropriate configuration files and creating a home directory.

Start by adding the following line to the /etc/passwd file. I used the Vim editor to copy the line for tuser4 and made the appropriate changes. The account for tuser4 is UID and GID 1006, so the UID and GID for tuser5 will be 1007:

```
tuser5:x:1007:1007:Test User 5:/home/tuser5:/bin/bash
```

Edit the /etc/group file by adding the following line. Once again I just copied the line for tuser4 and made the needed changes:

```
tuser5:x:1007:
```

Edit the /etc/shadow file and add the following line. Again, I just copied the line for tuser4 and changed the user account name to tuser5. This results in tuser5 having the same password as tuser4:

```
tuser5:$6$123456$KKcK3jDXxN5TVYNLbMdEIjnfRjaSlbqj5X9bBgryaa4qLDO4lrM9ksw
CpAZL27/WXlbsDQcJ8kBxPjcpips781:18044:0:99999:7:::
```

Note that when you attempt to save this change, Vim displays an error, "E45: 'readonly' option is set (add ! to override)". So instead of simply using :wq, you need to add an exclamation mark (!) to force Vim to save the changes, **:wq!**.

Create the new home directory and set its permissions to 700:

```
[root@studentvm1 home]# cd /home ; mkdir tuser5 ; ll
total 52
drwxrws---    2 root     dev        4096 Apr  2 09:19 dev
drwx------.   2 root     root      16384 Dec 22 11:01 lost+found
drwxrws---    2 root     dev        4096 Apr  2 12:34 shared
drwx------.  27 student  student    4096 May 28 16:09 student
drwx------    4 student1 student1   4096 Apr  2 09:20 student1
drwx------    3 student2 student2   4096 Apr  1 10:41 student2
drwx------    3 tuser1   tuser1     4096 May 27 21:48 tuser1
drwx------    3 tuser3   tuser3     4096 May 28 08:27 tuser3
drwx------    3 tuser4   tuser4     4096 May 28 17:35 tuser4
drwxr-xr-x    2 root     root       4096 May 28 21:50 tuser5
[root@studentvm1 home]# chmod 700 tuser5 ; ll
total 60
<snip>
drwx------    2 root     root      12288 May 28 21:53 tuser5
```

Copy the files from /etc/skel into the new home directory:

```
[root@studentvm1 home]# cp -r /etc/skel/.[a-z]* /home/tuser5 ; ll -a tuser5
total 40
drwx------    3 root root 12288 May 29 07:45 .
drwxr-xr-x. 12 root root  4096 May 28 21:50 ..
-rw-r--r--   1 root root    18 May 29 07:45 .bash_logout
-rw-r--r--   1 root root   141 May 29 07:45 .bash_profile
-rw-r--r--   1 root root   376 May 29 07:45 .bashrc
-rw-r--r--   1 root root   172 May 29 07:45 .kshrc
drwxr-xr-x   4 root root  4096 May 29 07:45 .mozilla
-rw-r--r--   1 root root   658 May 29 07:45 .zshrc
```

Set the ownership of the directory and its contents to the new user:

```
[root@studentvm1 home]# chown -R tuser5.tuser5 tuser5 ; ll -a tuser5
total 32
drwx------    3 tuser5 tuser5 4096 May 29 07:51 .
drwxr-xr-x. 12 root   root   4096 May 29 07:50 ..
-rw-r--r--   1 tuser5 tuser5   18 May 29 07:51 .bash_logout
-rw-r--r--   1 tuser5 tuser5  141 May 29 07:51 .bash_profile
```

```
-rw-r--r--   1 tuser5 tuser5  376 May 29 07:51 .bashrc
-rw-r--r--   1 tuser5 tuser5  172 May 29 07:51 .kshrc
drwxr-xr-x   4 tuser5 tuser5 4096 May 29 07:51 .mozilla
-rw-r--r--   1 tuser5 tuser5  658 May 29 07:51 .zshrc
```

To test this new user with a login, you can use either a virtual console or use **su – tuser5** from a student user terminal session. Or do both. Remember that tuser5 has the same password as tuser4, mypassword:

```
[student@studentvm1 ~]$ su - tuser5
Password: mypassword
Running /etc/profile
Running /etc/profile.d/myBashConfig.sh
Running /etc/bashrc
Running /etc/bashrc
[tuser5@studentvm1 ~]$
```

That was fairly easy, but using the useradd command is even easier most of the time. Log out of the tuser5 account.

You have now performed all of the steps necessary and modified all of the files involved in creating a new user. This knowledge has been useful in my SysAdmin work. I have sometimes found it easier to simply edit a group or passwd file than to use an appropriate CLI command like **usermod**. It is also easier to spot a damaged entry in one of these files having edited them by hand.

Locking a User Account

Is one of your users going on extended vacation? Or is a user leaving the organization or transferring to another location? Sometimes you want to secure an account so that no one – except for you, the SysAdmin, as root – has access, but you do not want to delete it. The need to do this could also be for forensic reasons.

A locked password prevents the user – or anyone else – from logging into the account, but it does not change the password hash. The password can be easily unlocked when necessary. The user can then log in with the original password.

EXPERIMENT 40-11: LOCKING A USER ACCOUNT

Parts of this experiment will be performed as root and parts as tuser5. Be sure to log out of the tuser5 account. Now lock the tuser5 account. The -l (lowercase ell) option locks the account:

```
[root@studentvm1 ~]# passwd -l tuser5
Locking password for user tuser5.
passwd: Success
```

Look at the line for tuser5 in the /etc/shadow file:

```
[root@studentvm1 ~]# grep tuser5 /etc/shadow
tuser5:!!$y$j93jN5TVYNLbMdEIjnfRj<SNIP>QcJ8kBxPjcpips781:18044:0:99999:7:::
```

Notice the two exclamation points (!!) at the beginning of the password hash. Now log in to the tuser5 account from a virtual console or using **su** from a student account terminal session:

```
[student@studentvm1 ~]$ su - tuser5
Password:
su: Authentication failure
```

Now unlock the account:

```
[root@studentvm1 ~]# passwd -u tuser5
Unlocking password for user tuser5.
passwd: Success
```

Log in to it again to verify that it is unlocked.

We could also have used Vim to edit the /etc/shadow file to add and remove the "!!" from the beginning of the password field.

Deleting User Accounts

User accounts are very easy to delete. Depending upon the reason for deletion, you may wish to retain the user's home directory or to delete it along with the rest of the account.

EXPERIMENT 40-12: DELETING USER ACCOUNTS

Perform this experiment as the root user. Use the **userdel** command to delete tuser3 but leave the home directory:

```
[root@studentvm1 ~]# userdel tuser3 ; ll /home
total 52
drwxrws---  2 root     dev       4096 Apr  2 09:19 dev
drwx------. 2 root     root     16384 Dec 22 11:01 lost+found
drwxrws---  2 root     dev       4096 Apr  2 12:34 shared
drwx------. 27 student  student   4096 May 28 16:09 student
drwx------  4 student1 student1  4096 Apr  2 09:20 student1
drwx------  3 student2 student2  4096 Apr  1 10:41 student2
drwx------  3 tuser1   tuser1    4096 May 27 21:48 tuser1
drwx------  3    1005     1005   4096 May 29 07:53 tuser3
drwx------  3 tuser4   tuser4    4096 May 28 17:35 tuser4
drwx------  3 tuser5   tuser5    4096 May 29 07:53 tuser5
```

Because the tuser3 account no longer exists, the account name is no longer shown in the long listing of the /home directory. The directory and its contents still have UID and GID of 1005, and that is what we see here.

Now delete the account for tuser4 along with its home directory. The -r option removes the home directory for an account:

```
[root@studentvm1 ~]# userdel -r tuser4 ; ll /home
total 48
drwxrws---  2 root     dev       4096 Apr  2 09:19 dev
drwx------. 2 root     root     16384 Dec 22 11:01 lost+found
drwxrws---  2 root     dev       4096 Apr  2 12:34 shared
drwx------. 27 student  student   4096 May 28 16:09 student
drwx------  4 student1 student1  4096 Apr  2 09:20 student1
drwx------  3 student2 student2  4096 Apr  1 10:41 student2
drwx------  3 tuser1   tuser1    4096 May 27 21:48 tuser1
drwx------  3    1005     1005   4096 May 29 07:53 tuser3
drwx------  3 tuser5   tuser5    4096 May 29 07:53 tuser5
```

Remove the home directory for tuser3:

```
[root@studentvm1 ~]# rm -rf /home/tuser3
[root@studentvm1 ~]# ll /home
total 40
drwxrws---   2 root     dev       4096 Feb 12 09:06 dev
drwx------.  2 root     root     16384 Jan 17 07:29 lost+found
drwx------. 25 student  student   4096 May  8 14:53 student
drwx------   4 student1 student1  4096 Feb 10 13:45 student1
drwx------   4 student2 student2  4096 Feb 11 09:41 student2
drwx------   3 tuser1   tuser1    4096 May 10 09:13 tuser1
drwx------   4 tuser5   tuser5    4096 May 11 08:37 tuser5
```

It is also possible to delete user accounts by editing the appropriate files to remove the lines pertaining to the account we want to remove.

Forcing Account Logoff

Sometimes it may become necessary to force a user account to log off. This may be required because a user has left for the day and the system needs to be updated with no users logged in, the user has left the organization, or there may be one or more runaway processes.

Whatever the reason, there is no "logout other user" command, but there is a simple way to deal with this need to force the termination of all processes belonging to a user. This is, in fact, even more effective than simply forcing a logout.

EXPERIMENT 40-13: FORCE AN ACCOUNT LOGOFF

This experiment will be performed as root and the student1 user. First, let's see if the student1 user is logged in. The pgrep command can be used as root to locate the PIDs of running processes that belong to a specific user account:

```
[root@studentvm1 ~]# pgrep -U student1
[root@studentvm1 ~]#
```

In this case the student1 user is not logged in. If you find that there are no processes belonging to the student1 user or you find only three or four processes, open a terminal session on your desktop and su to the student1 user:

```
[student@studentvm1 ~]$ su - student1
Password: <Enter Password for student1>
[student1@studentvm1 ~]$
```

Also log in at a virtual console as student1. As root, look for processes belonging to student1. The specific PIDs you see will be different from those listed here from my VM:

```
[root@studentvm1 ~]# pgrep -U student1
30774
30775
30780
30781
30785
30831
30840
```

Now we can kill all of these processes to force the user off the system. This is not a logout; it kills all of the user's processes, even ones that might be left running in the background after a logout:

```
[root@studentvm1 ~]# pkill -KILL -U student1
[root@studentvm1 ~]# pgrep -U student1
[root@studentvm1 ~]#
```

This will also show "Killed" in the terminal window you had opened.

Setting Resource Limits

You might think that with huge amounts of disk space, high CPU counts and speeds, gigabytes of RAM, and terabytes of disk space that modern Linux hosts do not have limited resources. That is not true, and I have seen huge systems overburdened by programs in test or even fully released programs that were poorly written. More frequently, I have caused myself problems where a shell script I have written sucks up most or all of some critical resource. You saw how easy that was when we did it intentionally earlier in this course. It seems to be even easier when it is unintentional.

So imagine for a moment that you are the system administrator for a Linux box that has a large number of users and that one of those user accounts is running resource hogs – large jobs that suck up CPU time and memory, which slows the tasks being run by other users to a crawl. They all come complaining to you. What do you do?

These issues can be corrected immediately by killing all of the processes – or at least the offending ones – belonging to the user owning them.

It is even better to prevent these problems in the first place by setting limits on the amount of system resources that a user, users, or groups can consume. The /etc/security/limits.conf file can be used to set limits for system resources to levels that will affect other users not at all or at least only marginally. A related option is to add a local config file to the /etc/security/limits.d directory. This prevents making changes to the main configuration file that might be overwritten such as what might occur during updates or complete reinstallations.

There are soft and hard limits that can be set. A soft limit sends a message when it is met or exceeded, while a hard limit prevents completion of the command that triggered it. Both hard and soft limits can be set on a resource so that the user first receives a message and then is prevented from continuing. The limits set in this file are monitored and enforced by the pluggable authentication module (PAM) system, which we will encounter again later in this volume.

Limits can be applied to individual users, to groups such as dev or accounting, and to lists of users or groups, as well as to all users or groups.

EXPERIMENT 40-14: SETTING RESOURCE LIMITS ON USERS

This experiment is performed in part as the root user and in part as the student1 user.

First, as the root user, open /etc/security/limits.conf with less and just view its contents for now. Read the comment sections of this file to understand the system resources that can be restricted using this file and its overall structure as well as the syntax used in creating a limit specification. It is fine to leave this file open for reference.

Some of the configurable resources need a bit additional clarification. So Figure 40-4 lists all of the resources over which we can exert some control and the descriptions as found in the limits.conf file. In some cases I have added comments of my own.

Resource	Description	Comments
core	Limits the core file size (KB)	This refers to the core dump files in the event of a kernel or other system error.
data	max data size (KB)	The maximum amount of RAM that can be used for data.
fsize	maximum filesize (KB)	
memlock	max locked-in-memory address space (KB)	This type of memory is locked into RAM and cannot be swapped out. This limits the maximum amount of RAM that can be locked into RAM by a user's processes.
nofile	max number of open file descriptors	Each open file has a file descriptor. Effectively limits the total number of open files.
rss	max resident set size (KB)	The maximum virtual memory, RAM + swap, that can be allocated.
stack	max stack size (KB)	The stack is a temporary storage location for programs to store some types of data during operation. This limits the total stack space available to the user or group.

Figure 40-4. *The system resources that can be controlled with the limits.conf file*

Resource	Description	Comments
cpu	max CPU time (MIN)	The maximum amount of CPU time in minutes per day that can be allocated to a user or group. NO additional CPU time can be allotted to the user or group after a hard limit is reached so they would be done for the day.
nproc	max number of processes	
as	address space limit (KB)	The total amount of address space that can be allocated including, program, data, and stack.
maxlogins	max number of logins for this user	Limits the total number of concurrent logins by individual users.
maxsyslogins	max number of logins on the system	Limits the total number of concurrent logins on the system as a whole.
priority	the priority to run user process with	Allows setting low (or high) priorities on user processes. Usually used to lower priorities for users that do not run critical processes, thus allowing the more critical users to have more CPU time if it is required.
locks	max number of file locks the user can hold	File locks allow multiple users to access a single file while preventing all but one – the one with the lock – from altering the file. This limits the number of files a user can have open for modification.

Figure 40-4. *(continued)*

Resource	Description	Comments
sigpending	max number of pending signals	We looked at signals in Chapter 23. It is possible to use Ctrl-C to exit from a process (or other signals) multiple times but if the process is not responding, the signals are queued. This limits the size of that queue.
msgqueue	max memory used by POSIX message queues (bytes)	
nice	max nice priority allowed to raise to values: [-20, 19]	
rtprio	max realtime priority	

Figure 40-4. *(continued)*

Rather than change the default file, we will add a new file local.conf to the /etc/security/ limits.d/ directory. Create the local.conf file there and open it with Vim. Add the following line to set the number of logins for student1 to 3. The settings in this local file override the default settings:

```
student1          -          maxlogins          3
```

A reboot is not required. However, if a user already has the specified number or more of logins already open, the existing logins are not affected, but no additional logins will be allowed.

Use virtual consoles 2 through 5 to log in as the student1 user. If you have those consoles logged in as another user, log out and then log in as student1. When you try to log in on VC5, you will get the following error indicating that the number of logins has been exceeded:

```
student1@studentvm1's password:
There were too many logins for 'student1'.
Last login: Thu May 11 16:07:09 2023
Connection to studentvm1 closed.
```

Look at the number of logins:

```
[root@studentvm1 limits.d]# w -u student1
 16:09:24 up 3 days,  7:58,  7 users,  load average: 0.49, 0.53, 0.26
USER     TTY         LOGIN@   IDLE   JCPU    PCPU WHAT
student1 tty1        16:07    3days  1.39s   1.39s /usr/libexec/Xorg -core
-noreset :0 -seat seat0 -auth /run/lightdm/root/:0 -nolisten tcp vt1 -novt
student1 pts/5       16:06    3:07   0.02s   0.02s -bash
student1 pts/6       16:06    2:42   0.02s   0.02s -bash
```

This is the maximum number of logins allowed for this user.

Resource limitations must be considered with care, especially when applying them to groups and multiple users. This is an excellent way to ensure that the desires of the few do not outweigh the needs of the many.

Chapter Summary

This chapter has taken us through the processes of creation, modification, and deletion of user accounts. We have also explored the various configuration files that support user accounts and their creation. We have created user accounts using the command-line tools and have also used Vim to add a new user by direct editing of the passwd, group, and shadow files.

We have also looked at user account security in general and password security in particular. This included exploring configuration tools that can force users to change their passwords on a regular basis as well as to enforce some aspects of password security policy.

We have also explored multiple methods to deal with resource allocation problems and how to kick users off the system who are abusing resources.

Exercises

Perform these exercises to complete this chapter:

1. What are the file modes for /etc/passwd and /etc/shadow?

2. Why are the user passwords stored in /etc/shadow?

3. Why might a SysAdmin want to generate a password using the pwgen command and pipe it directly to the useradd command, thus creating an initial password that is not known to anyone?

4. The command `cp -r /etc/skel/.[a-z]* /home/tuser5 ; ll -a tuser5` was used to copy the files from /etc/skel to the home directory of tuser5 in Experiment 40-10. Why is the syntax /etc/skel/.[a-z]* used instead of just /etc/skel/.*?

5. Remove the tuser5 account by editing the user account files. Also remove the home directory for the account.

6. The tuser3 account was removed in Experiment 40-12 without also removing the account's home directory. Remove that home directory.

7. Set a hard limit of five minutes of CPU time on a user other than the student user. You could use the student1 user. Then start a cpuHog program and watch what happens.

8. Devise and run an experiment to verify that setting the number of allowed logins on a user to a number smaller than the current number that are open does not affect the open ones.

9. Set the shell on the student1 account as /sbin/nologin. What happens when you try to log in as that user?

CHAPTER 41

Managing the Firewall

Objectives

In this chapter you will learn to

- Describe the function of a firewall.

- Define and describe the term "port."

- Use firewalld zones for firewall management under different sets of circumstances.

- Set a default zone.

- Assign network interfaces to a zone.

- Modify existing zones.

- Create a new zone to meet a set of specifications.

- Integrate Fail2ban dynamic firewall software with firewalld to automate protection against specific Internet attacks.

Introducing Firewalls

Firewalls are a vital part of network security, so it's important for a SysAdmin to be familiar with how they work. If you understand firewalls, you can keep your network secure by making intelligent choices about the traffic you allow in and out.

© David Both 2023
D. Both, *Using and Administering Linux: Volume 2*, https://doi.org/10.1007/978-1-4842-9615-8_41

Because "firewall" is such an exciting name, people often imagine an intricate Tron-style[1] neon battle happening on the outskirts of a network, with packets of rogue data being set alight to protect your users' techno fortress. In reality, a firewall is just a piece of software controlling incoming and outgoing network traffic.

Ports

A firewall is able to manage this traffic by monitoring network ports. In the world of firewalls, the term *port* doesn't refer to a physical connection like a USB, VGA, or HDMI port. For the purpose of firewalls, a port is an artificial construct created by the operating system to represent a pathway for a specific type of data. This system could have been called anything, like "contacts," "connections," or even "penguins," but the creators used "ports," and that's the name that we still use today. The point is there's nothing special about any port; they are just a way to designate an address where data transference happens.

There are a number of ports that are well known, but even these are only conventions. For instance, you may know that HTTP traffic occurs on port 80, HTTPS traffic uses port 443, FTP uses port 21, and SSH uses port 22. When your computer transmits data to another computer, it adds a prefix to the data to indicate which port it wants to access. If the port on the receiving end is accepting data of the same protocol as the data you are sending, then the data is successfully exchanged as seen in Figure 41-1.

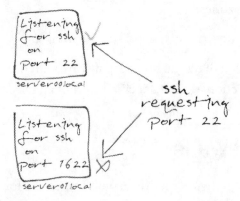

Figure 41-1. *An SSH – or any other – connection can only be made if the server is listening on the correct port*

---

[1] Wikipedia, Tron, https://en.wikipedia.org/wiki/Tron

You can see this process in action by going to any website. Open a web browser and navigate to example.com:80, which causes your computer to send an HTTP request to port 80 of the computer serving the example.com website. You receive a web page in return. Web browsers don't require you to enter the port you want to access every time you navigate to a URL, however, because it's assumed that HTTP traffic accesses port 80 or 443.

EXPERIMENT 41-1: TESTING PORTS

You can test this process using a terminal-based web browser. The curl command also returns some statistics that are displayed before the HTTP code that makes up the first four lines of the web server's response:

```
[root@studentvm1 ~]# curl --connect-timeout 3 "http://example.com:80" |
head -n4
  % Total    % Received % Xferd  Average Speed   Time    Time
Time  Current
                                 Dload  Upload   Total   Spent    Left  Speed
100  1256  100  1256    0     0  12337      0 --:--:-- --:--:-- --:--:-- 12435
<!doctype html>
<html>
<head>
    <title>Example Domain</title>
[root@studentvm1 ~]#
```

Tip The example.com website is a valid site that has been created for use by anyone who needs to test some basic network functions such as simple pings, traceroute, HTTP connections, and more. The sites example.org and example.net are also available for testing.

Using the same notation, you can force rejection by navigating to a website using a nonstandard port. Navigate to an arbitrary port, example.com:79, for instance. Your request for a web page is declined:

```
[root@studentvm1 ~]# curl --connect-timeout 3 "http://example.com:79"
curl: (28) Failed to connect to example.com port 79 after 1703 ms: Connection
timed out
[root@studentvm1 ~]#
```

The correlation between ports and protocols is merely a convention mutually agreed upon by a standards group and a user base. These settings can be changed on individual computers. In fact, back in the pioneer days of computing, many people felt that just changing the port number of popular services would prevent an attack. Attacks are a lot more sophisticated now, so there's little value in surprising an automated port scanner by changing which port a service listens on.

Instead, a firewall governs what activity is permitted in or out on any given port.

Firewall Rules

By default, most firewalls have rule sets that block all incoming packets unless explicitly allowed. Certainly this is true for Fedora and other Red Hat–based distributions that use firewalld or iptables. This, plus the fact that most server services are not needed so are not installed or not enabled, means that Linux is very secure right from the initial installation. Outbound packets are not blocked by the firewall so that we don't need to add rules for protocols like email, SSH, and web browsers just to access remote hosts using these services from our client hosts.

The flow of packets as they enter the Linux host is generally from start to finish through the rule set. If a packet matches one of the rules, the action defined in the rule is taken. Ultimately, each packet will be accepted, rejected, or dropped. When a packet matches a rule that has one of these three actions, that action is taken, and the packet travels no further through the rules. The three possible actions require just a bit of explanation:

- **Accept**: The packet is accepted and passed to the designated TCP port and a server such as a web server, Telnet, or SSH, to which it is addressed.

- **Reject**: The packet is rejected and sent back to the originator with a message. This message allows the host on the other end to know what happened and try again if need be or to terminate the connection.

- **Drop**: The packet is dropped and proceeds no further through the rules. No message is sent back to the originator. This action maintains the connection for the timeout period specified on the sender's end. This is useful when blocking IP addresses of known spammers so that when they attempt a connection, their sending host must wait through the timeout to try again, thus slowing down their attacks significantly.

All Linux firewalls are based on a kernel protocol called netfilter,[2] which interprets and enforces the rules. Netfilter.org[3] is the organization responsible for netfilter and its functions. The administrative tools we use simply allow us to add, modify, and remove netfilter rules that examine each data packet and determine how to handle it.

Firewall Tools

There are three primary tools that are commonly used to manage netfilter firewall rules, iptables, nftables, and firewalld. All are intended to make firewall management a bit easier for SysAdmins, but they differ in how they approach that task, and the use cases at hand can determine which tool is best. Fedora installs all three tools by default.

Red Hat's online documentation, "Configuring and managing networking,"[4] contains recommendations for using these tools:

When to use firewalld, nftables, or iptables

The following is a brief overview in which scenario you should use one of the following utilities:

- *firewalld: Use the firewalld utility for simple firewall use cases. The utility is easy to use and covers the typical use cases for these scenarios.*

- *nftables: Use the nftables utility to set up complex and performance-critical firewalls, such as for a whole network.*

---

[2] Wikipedia, netfilter, https://en.wikipedia.org/wiki/netfilter

[3] Netfilter.org, www.netfilter.org/index.html

[4] Red Hat, "Configuring and managing networking," https://access.redhat.com/documentation/en-us/red_hat_enterprise_linux/8/html/configuring_and_managing_networking/index

- ***iptables:*** *The iptables utility on Red Hat Enterprise Linux uses the nf_tables kernel API instead of the legacy back end. The nf_tables API provides backward compatibility so that scripts that use iptables commands still work on Red Hat Enterprise Linux. For new firewall scripts, Red Hat recommends to use nftables.*

These tools use different user interfaces and store their data in different formats. We will cover firewalld in some depth in this chapter.

My reading indicates that iptables is more or less obsolete and will probably be discontinued. I have already converted most of my hosts to firewalld and will be completing the rest soon. I like firewalld and it appears to meet my needs, including the ability to manage a true dmz. The use of nftables, because it is designed for very complex rule sets, is outside the scope of this course.

Block (Almost) Everything

Common advice when configuring a firewall is to first block everything and then open the ports you know you actually need. That means you have to know what you need, though, and sometimes figuring that out is an afternoon's job all its own.

If your organization runs its own DNS or DNS caching service, for instance, then you must remember to unblock the port (usually 53) handling DNS communication. If you rely on SSH to configure your servers remotely, then you must not block that port. You must account for every service running on your infrastructure, and you must understand whether that service is internal-only or whether it needs to interact with the outside world.

In the case of proprietary software, there may be calls made to the outside world that you're not even aware of. If some applications react poorly to a strict firewall recently put in place, you may have to reverse engineer (or talk to the application's support line) to discover what kind of traffic it's trying to create and why. In the open source world, this issue is less common, but it's not outside the realm of possibility, especially in the case of complex software stacks (e.g., today even media players make calls out to the Internet, if only to fetch album art or a track listing).

Crunchy on the Outside

I have encountered many networks in my career that SysAdmins say are "crunchy on the outside, soft and gooey on the inside."[5] This refers to some types of candy that have a hard shell but are quite soft in the middle. Networks can be like that. When the firewall on the edge of the network is cracked, no matter how hard that was, the rest of the network is laid open to plunder.

As a result, Linux distributions all ensure that they are installed with an active firewall that allows access only by a small number of necessary services.

As you will see in this chapter, I have experimented with reducing the number of open ports even smaller because I like to ensure the maximum level of security on all Linux hosts in my network. This includes an active firewall on every one.

firewalld

firewalld is the default firewall management daemon used by current releases of Fedora and many other distributions. It has superseded but not yet replaced iptables, which has been around for many years. firewalld provides some interesting features such as runtime rules vs. permanent rules. Runtime rules can be used to meet temporary conditions and can be left active until a reboot, or they can be manually removed, or they can be set to expire after a predefined period of time. Permanent rules – as their name suggests – are persistent through reboots.

firewall-cmd uses preconfigured zones as presets, giving you sane defaults to choose from. Doing this saves you from having to build a firewall from scratch. Zones apply to a network interface, so on a server with two Ethernet interfaces, you may have one zone governing one Ethernet interface and a different zone governing the other.

Standard `systemctl` commands are used to start, stop, enable, and disable firewalld. All other interactions with firewalld are through its own set of tools.

Changes made to firewalld are instant. The firewalld.service does not need to be restarted. There are a couple circumstances that require you to reload the firewalld configuration. I will point those out.

---

[5] Extreme Networks blog, `https://academy.extremenetworks.com/extreme-networks-blog/networks-hard-crunchy-on-the-outside-soft-gooey-on-the-inside/`, 2019

The firewalld.org website has excellent documentation you can use.[6]

firewalld Zones

The firewalld service can provide a complex and intricate set of rules for a firewall. It uses the concept of zones to collect related rules in such a way as to create levels of trust. Each zone represents a level of trust that can be independently modified without affecting other zones. firewalld has several predefined zones.

Each network interface is assigned a zone, and all network traffic to that interface is filtered by the rules in that zone. Network interfaces can be easily switched from one zone to another if necessary, thus making preconfigured changes easy. These zones are arbitrary constructs developed to meet a specific set of needs in a firewall. For example, a network interface that is connected to the internal network would be placed in the trusted zone, while an interface that connects to the Internet would be placed in the external or dmz zone, depending upon the logical and physical structure of the network.

firewalld has nine predefined zones that can be used as is or modified to meet local needs. Figure 41-2 lists the predefined firewalld zones and a short description of each.

[6] firewalld.org, Documentation, https://firewalld.org/documentation/concepts.html

Zone	Description
drop	Any incoming network packets are dropped, there is no reply. Only outgoing network connections are possible.
block	Any incoming network connections are rejected with an icmp-host-prohibited message for IPv4 and icmp6-adm-prohibited for IPv6. Only network connections initiated within this system are possible.
public	For use in public areas. You do not trust the other computers on networks to not harm your computer. Only selected incoming connections are accepted.
external	For use on external networks with IPv4 masquerading enabled especially for routers. You do not trust the other computers on networks to not harm your computer. Only selected incoming connections are accepted.
dmz	For computers in your demilitarized zone that are publicly-accessible with limited access to your internal network. Only selected incoming connections are accepted.
work	For computers in your demilitarized zone that are publicly-accessible with limited access to your internal network. Only selected incoming connections are accepted.
home	For use in home areas. You mostly trust the other computers on networks to not harm your computer. Only selected incoming connections are accepted.
internal	For use on internal networks. You mostly trust the other computers on the networks to not harm your computer. Only selected incoming connections are accepted.
trusted	All network connections are accepted.

Figure 41-2. The default firewalld zones

Exploring the Firewall

Your work infrastructure may have a server in a rack with the sole purpose of running a firewall, or you may have a firewall embedded in the router – or modem – acting as your primary gateway to the Internet. You probably also have a firewall running on your personal workstation or laptop. All of these firewalls have their own configuration interface.

firewall-cmd is a front-end tool for managing the firewalld daemon, which interfaces with the Linux kernel's netfilter framework. This stack probably isn't present on the embedded modems common in small- to medium-sized businesses, but it's on or available for any Linux distribution that uses systemd.

Let's do some initial exploration of firewalld. In Experiment 41-2 we'll poke around a bit and make a simple change.

EXPERIMENT 41-2: INITIAL EXPLORATION OF FIREWALLD

Without an active firewall, firewall-cmd has nothing to control, so the first step is to ensure that firewalld is running:

```
[root@studentvm1 ~]# systemctl enable --now firewalld
```

This command starts the firewall daemon and sets it to auto-load upon reboot.

Firewall Status

View the status of the firewalld.service. This does not show anything about the firewalld configuration such as which ports are open or which zones are in use:

```
[root@studentvm1 ~]# systemctl status firewalld.service
● firewalld.service - firewalld - dynamic firewall daemon
     Loaded: loaded (/usr/lib/systemd/system/firewalld.service; enabled;
     preset: enabled)
     Active: active (running) since Sun 2023-05-14 14:26:35 EDT; 15h ago
       Docs: man:firewalld(1)
   Main PID: 1109 (firewalld)
      Tasks: 2 (limit: 19130)
     Memory: 50.6M
        CPU: 807ms
     CGroup: /system.slice/firewalld.service
             └─1109 /usr/bin/python3 -sP /usr/sbin/firewalld --nofork --nopid
```

```
May 14 14:26:30 studentvm1 systemd[1]: Starting firewalld.service -
firewalld - dynamic firewall daemon...
May 14 14:26:35 studentvm1 systemd[1]: Started firewalld.service -
firewalld - dynamic firewall daemon.
```

The firewalld command-line tool can show whether it is running, but that is all so it is not especially helpful. This command is useful when used in a script used to automate firewall and network actions:

```
[root@studentvm1 ~]# firewall-cmd --state
running
```

This next command shows all of the supported zones in sorted order with uppercase first:

```
[root@studentvm1 ~]# firewall-cmd --get-zones
FedoraServer FedoraWorkstation block dmz drop external home internal nm-
shared public trusted work
```

One important bit of data to know is what the default zones are for the running systems:

```
[root@studentvm1 ~]# firewall-cmd --get-default-zone
public
```

This shows that the default setting is one of the most restricted zones. However, this command does not show the currently assigned zones for the installed network interfaces. For that we do the following, which lists each zone and displays the interfaces assigned to that zone:

```
[root@studentvm1 ~]# firewall-cmd --get-active-zones
public
  interfaces: enp0s3 enp0s9
```

We now know that both interfaces on my VM are in the public zone. Your VM will only have a single interface, enp0s3.

This leads us to determining the actual configuration for the public zone. This command displays the configuration for the active zones. Only the public zone is active. It also shows the interfaces assigned to this zone:

```
[root@studentvm1 ~]#   firewall-cmd --zone=public --list-all
public (active)
  target: default
```

```
icmp-block-inversion: no
interfaces: enp0s3 enp0s9
sources:
services: dhcpv6-client mdns ssh
protocols:
forward: yes
masquerade: no
forward-ports:
source-ports:
icmp-blocks:
rich rules:
```

You can see the services listed in the services field for the public zone. Now let's look at the permanent settings for the public zone:

```
[root@studentvm1 ~]# firewall-cmd --zone=public --list-all --permanent
public
  target: default
  icmp-block-inversion: no
  interfaces:
  sources:
  services: dhcpv6-client mdns ssh
  protocols:
  forward: yes
  masquerade: no
  forward-ports:
  source-ports:
  icmp-blocks:
  rich rules:
```

Do you see the difference? There are no interfaces assigned because this is a configuration and the actual assignments are performed when firewalld is activated at boot time or is restarted.

Adding a New Zone

Although the preexisting zones may meet our needs, sooner than later there will be a need that none of them can meet. We could simply modify one of these original zones, but I think it wise to create a new zone and leave the originals intact.

EXPERIMENT 41-3: ADDING A NEW ZONE

To create a new zone, use the --new-zone option. This creates a zone file that rejects everything because it contains no rules to open any specific ports such as SSH. All firewall-cmd actions persist only until the firewall or the computer running it restarts. Anything you want to be permanent must be accompanied by the --permanent flag.

First, make /etc/firewalld/zones the PWD. Then create a new permanent zone called corp, and then reload the firewall rules so that your new zone activates:

```
[root@studentvm1 zones]# firewall-cmd --new-zone corp --permanent
success
[root@studentvm1 zones]# ll
total 12
-rw-r--r--  1 root root  54 May 17 13:34 corp.xml
-rw-rw-r--. 1 root root 353 May 17 09:05 public.xml
-rw-rw-r--. 1 root root 388 May 12 11:03 public.xml.old
[root@studentvm1 zones]#
[root@studentvm1 zones]# firewall-cmd --reload
```

Before assigning any network interface to this new zone, add the ssh service so you can access it remotely. Use the --permanent option to make this addition persist across reboots:

```
[root@studentvm1 zones]# firewall-cmd --zone corp --add-service ssh
--permanent
[root@studentvm1 zones]# cat corp.xml
<?xml version="1.0" encoding="utf-8"?>
<zone>
  <service name="ssh"/>
</zone>
```

Your new zone, called corp, is now active, rejects all but SSH traffic, and is assigned to no specific network interface. We'll look at zone files in more detail in another experiment in this chapter.

To make corp the active and the default zone for the network interface you want to protect (enpOs3 in this example), use the --change-interface option:

```
[root@studentvm1 zones]# firewall-cmd --change-interface enpOs3 --zone corp
--permanent
The interface is under control of NetworkManager, setting zone to 'corp'.
success
```

By making corp the default zone, all future commands are applied to corp unless the --zone option specifies a different zone. Whether you want to set corp as the default depends on whether you plan for this zone as your new primary zone. If so, the following does the job:

```
[root@studentvm1 zones]# firewall-cmd --set-default corp
```

To view the zones currently assigned to each interface, use the --get-active-zones option:

```
[root@studentvm1 zones]# firewall-cmd --get-active-zones
corp
  interfaces: enpOs3
public
  interfaces: enpOs9
```

This finally shows that each of the two interfaces I have on my VM is assigned to a different zone.

Zones in a Complex Environment

Adding a new zone seems to be simple at first glance. In a host where there is only one NIC that has not been explicitly assigned a zone, it is quite simple. Just create your new zone and set that as the default zone. There is no need to assign the interface to a zone. Without any zone assignment, all interfaces are protected by the default zone, no matter which one that might be.

In a host where at least one NIC has been explicitly assigned to a zone, it becomes a bit more complicated. I have experimented with this extensively, and whenever you want to change the assignment of an interface to a different zone, it is actually quite simple. The real problem is that everything I have read seems to overcomplicate the process.

```
┌────────────────────────────────────────────────────────────────┐
│    EXPERIMENT 41-4: REASSIGN A NIC TO A DIFFERENT ZONE           │
└────────────────────────────────────────────────────────────────┘
```

Start with a reboot and then verify the current status of the network interfaces. It is always good to verify the beginning state of things – anything – before you change it:

```
[root@studentvm1 ~]# firewall-cmd --get-zone-of-interface=enp0s3
corp
[root@studentvm1 ~]# firewall-cmd --get-active-zones
corp
  interfaces: enp0s3
public
  interfaces: enp0s9
[root@studentvm1 ~]#
```

You can reassign the enp0s3 interface to the dmz zone by removing it from the current zone. This action reverts the interface to the default zone:

```
[root@studentvm1 ~]# firewall-cmd --remove-interface=enp0s3 --zone=corp
--permanent
The interface is under control of NetworkManager, setting zone to default.
success
[root@studentvm1 ~]# firewall-cmd --get-active-zones
public
  interfaces: enp0s9 enp0s3
[root@studentvm1 ~]#
```

This is part of what had me confused at first. Now assign the interface to the dmz zone and verify the change:

```
[root@studentvm1 ~]# firewall-cmd --change-interface=enp0s3 --zone=dmz
--permanent
The interface is under control of NetworkManager, setting zone to 'dmz'.
success
[root@studentvm1 ~]# firewall-cmd --get-active-zones
dmz
  interfaces: enp0s3
public
  interfaces: enp0s9
[root@studentvm1 ~]#
```

Reboot one more time and again verify that enp0s3 is assigned to the dmz zone. What services are allowed by the dmz zone?

```
[root@studentvm1 ~]# firewall-cmd --list-services --zone=dmz
ssh
[root@studentvm1 ~]# firewall-cmd --info-zone=dmz
dmz (active)
  target: default
  icmp-block-inversion: no
  interfaces: enp0s3
  sources:
  services: ssh
  ports:
  protocols:
  forward: yes
  masquerade: no
  forward-ports:
  source-ports:
  icmp-blocks:
  rich rules:
[root@studentvm1 ~]#
```

The dmz zone is the least trusted of any zone that actually allows any inbound connections. It allows only SSH as an inbound connection. The two zones that have no trust at all are drop and block. You can read the differences in Figure 41-2.

Note that changing the runtime zone is not necessary. Neither is reloading nor using the runtime-to-permanent sub-command. The reboots we did were not necessary to complete the task; they were only for us to verify that the changes were verifiable and persistent through a reboot.

We have seen in Experiment 41-4 that it is important to understand exactly how adding services – and ports – to a zone works. This set of guidelines is based on my experiments and describes how it can be expected to work:

1. **The public zone is the default by – ummm – default.** The default zone can be changed. A different zone can be designated as the default, or the configuration of the default zone can be altered to allow a different set of services and ports.

748

2. **All interfaces that are not specifically assigned to any zone use the designated default zone.** In this event all interfaces, whether there is only one as in our VMs or ten or fifty in a complex router environment, use the default zone whatever that may be. Typically in Fedora that is the public zone. If the default zone is changed, for example, from the public zone to the work zone, all of these interfaces immediately start using the work zone.

3. **All interfaces are explicitly assigned to a zone.** This use case is the least likely to cause unexpected problems and confusion. Changing the default zone does not affect any interface in any manner. Interfaces can be reassigned to different zones, and the zone configuration can be changed.

4. **Some interfaces are explicitly assigned to a zone, while other interfaces are not.** In this use case, changing the default zone affects only those interfaces that are not explicitly assigned to a zone. All of the unassigned zones begin using the new default zone.

5. **Deleting the zone assignment for an interface.** The interface is unassigned and reverts to using the default zone.

6. **Changing the configuration of the default zone.** All interfaces using the default zone, whether by explicit assignment to that zone or by having no assignment, immediately reflect the configuration change.

Adding and Deleting Services

As an old – um, mature – SysAdmin, I tend to think in terms of ports when working with firewalls and network services. Sometimes I need to look up a port number associated with a particular service, but that is no big deal because they are all defined in /etc/ services, although this listing has been around long before firewalld.

```
┌─────────────────────────────────────────────────────────────────┐
│              EXPERIMENT 41-5: LISTING SERVICES                    │
└─────────────────────────────────────────────────────────────────┘
```

Look at the list of services in the /etc/services file:

[root@studentvm1 ~]# **less /etc/services**
/etc/services:
$Id: services,v 1.49 2017/08/18 12:43:23 ovasik Exp $
#
Network services, Internet style
IANA services version: last updated 2021-01-19
#
Note that it is presently the policy of IANA to assign a single well-known
port number for both TCP and UDP; hence, most entries here have two entries
even if the protocol doesn't support UDP operations.
Updated from RFC 1700, ``Assigned Numbers'' (October 1994). Not all ports
are included, only the more common ones.
#
The latest IANA port assignments can be gotten from
http://www.iana.org/assignments/port-numbers
The Well Known Ports are those from 0 through 1023.
The Registered Ports are those from 1024 through 49151
The Dynamic and/or Private Ports are those from 49152 through 65535
#
Each line describes one service, and is of the form:
#
service-name port/protocol [aliases ...]   [# comment]

tcpmux   1/tcp   # TCP port service multiplexer
tcpmux   1/udp   # TCP port service multiplexer
rje   5/tcp   # Remote Job Entry
rje   5/udp   # Remote Job Entry
echo   7/tcp
echo   7/udp
discard   9/tcp   sink null
discard   9/udp   sink null
systat   11/tcp   users
systat   11/udp   users
daytime   13/tcp
```
```

```
daytime        13/udp
qotd           17/tcp        quote
qotd           17/udp        quote
chargen        19/tcp        ttytst source
chargen        19/udp        ttytst source
ftp-data       20/tcp
ftp-data       20/udp
# 21 is registered to ftp, but also used by fsp
ftp            21/tcp
ftp            21/udp        fsp fspd
ssh            22/tcp                        # The Secure Shell (SSH) Protocol
ssh            22/udp                        # The Secure Shell (SSH) Protocol
telnet         23/tcp
telnet         23/udp
<SNIP>
```

This command eliminates the comment lines and counts the remaining lines. Notice that Telnet is on port 23.

```
[root@studentvm1 ~]# grep -v ^# /etc/services | wc -l
11472
[root@studentvm1 ~]#
```

The services file contains 11,472 entries. Many ports are listed for both TCP and UDP.

We can also list the services explicitly understood by firewalld:

```
[root@studentvm1 ~]# firewall-cmd --get-services
```

The output of this command is a simple space-separated list of 209 services. These are the services that can be added to a zone by name. Any services not listed here must be added to a zone by port.

The firewalld firewall works perfectly well with services, but for those that are not defined, it also supports the use of port numbers. In Experiment 41-6 we first add a port to a zone and then remove it. Working with ports like this requires the use of both the port number and the protocol specification of either TCP or UDP.

EXPERIMENT 41-6: ADDING/REMOVING A PORT

I have arbitrarily selected the Telnet[7] service from this list so that we can use it to add to and delete from our dmz zone. First, install and enable the Telnet server and client so we can test our work:

```
[root@studentvm1 ~]# dnf -y install telnet telnet-server
```

Start Telnet. The command to do so does not start the server itself. It starts a socket that listens for connections on port 23 and only starts the server when a Telnet connection is initiated on port 23[8]:

```
[root@studentvm1 ~]# systemctl enable --now telnet.socket
Created symlink /etc/systemd/system/sockets.target.wants/telnet.socket → /
usr/lib/systemd/system/telnet.socket.
[root@studentvm1 ~]#
```

Now we add the service to the firewall:

```
[root@studentvm1 zones]# firewall-cmd --add-service=telnet --zone=dmz
success
[root@studentvm1 zones]# firewall-cmd --info-zone=dmz
dmz (active)
  target: default
  icmp-block-inversion: no
  interfaces: enp0s3
  sources:
  services: ssh telnet
  ports:
  protocols:
  forward: yes
  masquerade: no
```

---

[7] Telnet is a very old and vulnerable communications protocol. It provides no means for encrypting data transferred over the network so is completely insecure. SSH has replaced it as a secure choice. I use it here only for illustrative purposes.

[8] This process is very similar to the xinetd service used by the SystemV init system. xinetd listened for connections for Telnet and other services and only started them when a connection was made.

```
  forward-ports:
  source-ports:
  icmp-blocks:
  rich rules:
[root@studentvm1 zones]#
```

Let's test to ensure that the Telnet service works as expected:

```
[root@studentvm1 ~]# telnet studentvm1
Trying fe80::a00:27ff:fe01:7dad%enp0s3...
Connected to studentvm1.
Escape character is '^]'.

Kernel 6.1.18-200.fc37.x86_64 on an x86_64 (5)
studentvm1 login: student
Password: <Enter student password>
Last login: Sun May 21 15:41:47 on :0
```

Log out of the Telnet connection:

```
[student@studentvm1 ~]$ exit
logout
Connection closed by foreign host.
[root@studentvm1 ~]#
```

And now remove the Telnet service from the dmz zone:

```
[root@studentvm1 zones]# firewall-cmd --remove-service=telnet --zone=dmz
success
[root@studentvm1 zones]# firewall-cmd --info-zone=dmz
dmz (active)
  target: default
  icmp-block-inversion: no
  interfaces: enp0s3
  sources:
  services: ssh
  ports:
  protocols:
  forward: yes
  masquerade: no
  forward-ports:
```

```
  source-ports:
  icmp-blocks:
  rich rules:
[root@studentvm1 zones]#
```

Of course we would have used --permanent if we intended to make these changes persistent. We can also do this using the port number rather than the service name:

```
[root@studentvm1 zones]# firewall-cmd --add-port=23/tcp --zone=dmz
success
[root@studentvm1 zones]# firewall-cmd --info-zone=dmz
dmz (active)
  target: default
  icmp-block-inversion: no
  interfaces: enp0s3
  sources:
  services: ssh
  ports: 23/tcp
  protocols:
  forward: yes
  masquerade: no
  forward-ports:
  source-ports:
  icmp-blocks:
  rich rules:
[root@studentvm1 zones]#
```

Remove port 23:

```
[root@studentvm1 zones]# firewall-cmd --remove-port=23/tcp --zone=dmz
success
```

Verify that it has been removed.

When using firewalld for firewall services, it is always a good idea to be consistent and add new rules using the service name rather than the port number. It may be necessary to use the port number for a service that is not predefined although it is also possible to add a new service file to /etc/firewalld/services with a name of the form <servicename>.service. These files are all in XML and should be easily understandable.

Most of us will never need to modify or even look at these files, that is, unless you are running a Linux box as a router and play a lot of 1990s games with their own weird and wild takes on how networking should work.

Adding a Service for a Specific Period of Time

I have sometimes needed to open a port in my firewall for a limited period of time for one reason or another. This can be done easily using the --timeout option in the command to add the service.

EXPERIMENT 41-7: ADD A SERVICE FOR A LIMITED TIME

We will use Telnet again for this experiment. Add the service, this time using the timeout for ten minutes. Then verify that Telnet was added to the dmz zone:

```
[root@studentvm1 zones]# firewall-cmd --add-service=telnet –zone=dmz
--timeout=10m
success
[root@studentvm1 zones]# firewall-cmd --info-zone=dmz
dmz (active)
  target: default
  icmp-block-inversion: no
  interfaces: enp0s3
  sources:
  services: ssh telnet
  ports:
  protocols:
  forward: yes
  masquerade: no
  forward-ports:
  source-ports:
  icmp-blocks:
  rich rules:
[root@studentvm1 zones]#
```

Test as we did previously to verify that Telnet is listening. After ten minutes check the zone information again to verify that the Telnet service has been removed:

```
[root@studentvm1 ~]# firewall-cmd --info-zone=dmz
dmz (active)
  target: default
  icmp-block-inversion: no
  interfaces: enp0s3
  sources:
  services: ssh
  ports:
  protocols:
  forward: yes
  masquerade: no
  forward-ports:
  source-ports:
  icmp-blocks:
  rich rules:
[root@studentvm1 ~]#
```

The timeout= option takes it arguments as a plain number, which is interpreted as seconds. It also recognizes three trailing characters, where *s* is seconds, *m* is minutes, and *h* is hours.

So timeout=3m sets the timeout at three minutes and 4h sets it at four hours.

Timeout mode is incompatible with the --permanent option. It would be counterproductive to use a permanent timeout.

Wireless

Some quick experiments on my laptop systems show that, like wired connections, the default zone is applied to wireless connections unless they are assigned to a specific zone. Since many of the wireless connections we use out in public are completely unprotected, I strongly recommend assigning the drop zone, which just ignores all incoming connection attempts. This does not block your outbound connections such as web pages, email, VPN, or others.

Even those public networks that have some level of encryption are usually quite easy to crack into. Many crackers even use their own devices to spoof the public network so that users will log in to the cracker's network device instead. Once logged in, your computer is completely vulnerable unless you have a decent firewall applied to your wireless interface.

In Experiment 41-8 I cover the complete process of migrating one of my laptops from iptables to firewalld and assigning the wireless interface to the drop zone.

Tip   If you don't have a laptop that's running Linux, you still may be able to do this experiment. There are a number of USB wireless adapters available for under $20. To perform this experiment on your VM, you can insert the USB wireless adapter into the physical host and then connect the adapter to the VM. This will work exactly like it does on a physical laptop.

```
EXPERIMENT 41-8: ASSIGNING THE WIRELESS INTERFACE TO THE DROP ZONE
```

First, check the name of the wireless interface. On my laptop it is wlp113s0. All wireless interface names start with the letter "w":

```
[root@voyager zones]# nmcli
enp111s0: connected to Wired connection 1
        "Realtek RTL8111/8168/8411"
<SNIP>

wlp113s0: connected to LinuxBoy2
        "Intel 8265 / 8275"
        wifi (iwlwifi), 34:E1:2D:DD:BE:27, hw, mtu 1500
        inet4 192.168.25.199/24
        route4 192.168.25.0/24 metric 600
        route4 default via 192.168.25.1 metric 600
        inet6 fe80::44e5:e270:634d:eb20/64
        route6 fe80::/64 metric 1024
<SNIP>
```

View the configuration of the drop zone. All packets are sent directly to the DROP target. This means that they are ignored and no response of any kind is sent back to the originating host:

```
[root@voyager zones]# firewall-cmd --info-zone=drop
drop
  target: DROP
  icmp-block-inversion: no
  interfaces:
  sources:
  services:
  ports:
  protocols:
  forward: yes
  masquerade: no
  forward-ports:
  source-ports:
  icmp-blocks:
  rich rules:
[root@studentvm1 ~]#
```

The drop zone is safer than using the block zone, which blocks the packets but sends a rejection back to the source. That tells the cracker that there is a responsive computer on that IP address, so they may keep attacking, looking for an exploitable vulnerability.

Now we can disable iptables and enable firewalld. I needed to do this to make the conversion, but you won't need to if your host is already running firewalld:

```
[root@voyager ~]# systemctl disable --now iptables
Removed "/etc/systemd/system/multi-user.target.wants/iptables.service".
[root@voyager ~]# systemctl enable --now firewalld.service
Created symlink /etc/systemd/system/dbus-org.fedoraproject.FirewallD1.service
→ /usr/lib/systemd/system/firewalld.service.
Created symlink /etc/systemd/system/multi-user.target.wants/firewalld.service
→ /usr/lib/systemd/system/firewalld.service.
```

Now that firewalld is running, whether it was to begin with or you had to switch to it as I did, verify the default zone. It is public for both wired and wireless interfaces, which is what should be expected:

```
[root@voyager zones]# firewall-cmd --get-active-zones
public
   interfaces: enp111s0 wlp113s0
```

Now we change the wireless interface and add it to the drop zone:

```
[root@voyager zones]# firewall-cmd --change-interface=wlp113s0 --zone=drop
--permanent
The interface is under control of NetworkManager, setting zone to 'drop'.
success
[root@voyager zones]# firewall-cmd --get-zone-of-interface=wlp113s0
drop
[root@voyager zones]# firewall-cmd --get-active-zones
public
   interfaces: enp111s0
drop
   interfaces: wlp113s0
```

Setting the zone for the wireless interface works even if the interface is not currently connected to a wireless network.

Using --reload

The experiments I have performed on my VMs and my own physical systems in preparation for writing this chapter have taught me a couple things about managing with firewalld. I have seen a lot of misinformation about using the --reload command, most of which indicates that it should be performed more frequently than I have found to be truly necessary.

The times I have found it necessary to use firewall-cmd --reload are twofold. First, do it immediately after creating a new zone whether using the easy command-line technique you did in Experiment 41-3 or when creating a new zone file using an editor or copying a zone file from another host. The second instance is when first starting the firewalld.service after migrating from iptables or another firewall tool. Start firewalld. service and then run firewall-cmd -reload.

There may be other times when it is necessary, but I have not definitively identified them yet.

Zone Files

It's time to look at the zone configuration files in more detail. The default zone file is public.xml, and it is located in the /etc/firewalld/zones directory. Other zone files may be there also.

All of the predefined default zones are located in the /usr/lib/firewalld/zones directory. These files are never changed. If you were to reset firewalld to its defaults, the files in the /usr/lib/firewalld/zones directory would be used to restore the firewall to that condition. The /etc/firewalld/zones/ directory contains a file called public.xml.old, which is a backup created automatically when the zone configuration is changed.

These files are ASCII text files using the XML format for the data, but it is not necessary to be an XML expert to understand their content. XML stands for Extensible Markup Language. It is a markup language for documents using a format that is both human- and machine readable.

Let's look at a couple zone files and see how they are constructed.

EXPERIMENT 41-9: ZONE CONFIGURATION FILES

Because it is the most commonly used, we will start by examining the default public zone file. It contains enough information for us to understand.

Make /etc/firewalld/zones the PWD. Then examine the public.xml file:

```
[root@studentvm1 zones]# cat public.xml
<?xml version="1.0" encoding="utf-8"?>
<zone>
  <short>Public</short>
  <description>For use in public areas. You do not trust the other computers
  on networks to not harm your computer. Only selected incoming connections
  are accepted.</description>
  <service name="ssh"/>
  <service name="mdns"/>
  <service name="dhcpv6-client"/>
  <forward/>
</zone>
[root@studentvm1 zones]#
```

The first line specifies the version of XML used by the file and the language encoding. The second line, <zone>, identifies the beginning of a zone file. There is a closing line at the end of the file, </zone>. All other statements are enclosed by these two statements.

The short name is the one displayed when you use commands that show the zone names:

```
[root@studentvm1 zones]# firewall-cmd --get-zones
FedoraServer FedoraWorkstation block corp dmz drop external home internal nm-
shared public trusted work
```

The description field is a place to store a longer description of the zone. I have not found a command that displays the description. It appears to be only visible when you edit or cat the file.

The next three lines list the services that are allowed to connect to this host, in this case, ssh, mdns, and dhcpv6-client. This seems to be a common set of services in the home, internal, public, and work zone files. The home and internal zones have an additional service:

```
[root@studentvm1 zones]# cat internal.xml
<?xml version="1.0" encoding="utf-8"?>
<zone>
  <short>Internal</short>
  <description>For use on internal networks. You mostly trust the other
  computers on the networks to not harm your computer. Only selected incoming
  connections are accepted.</description>
  <service name="ssh"/>
  <service name="mdns"/>
  <service name="samba-client"/>
  <service name="dhcpv6-client"/>
  <forward/>
</zone>
```

The samba client is a Linux version of the Microsoft SMB (Server Message Block) protocol and allows Linux hosts to participate in Windows networks.

The forward statement in these zones allows TCP/IP packets entering the host on the interface assigned to this zone to be forwarded to other interfaces on the same host computer.

The external zone has an interesting statement:

```
[root@studentvm1 zones]# cat external.xml
<?xml version="1.0" encoding="utf-8"?>
```

```
<zone>
  <short>External</short>
  <description>For use on external networks. You do not trust the other
  computers on networks to not harm your computer. Only selected incoming
  connections are accepted.</description>
  <service name="ssh"/>
  <masquerade/>
  <forward/>
</zone>
```

The masquerade entry is typically used only on the firewall and is for packets that are outbound to the external network – usually the Internet. That entry causes the firewall to change the source IP address of the outbound packet from that of the originating computer in the internal network to that of the firewall computer. The firewall keeps track of the packets using connection IDs. Any inbound packets addressed to the firewall computer with that connection ID will be sent to the computer in your network that originated the request. Thus, a request from a computer inside your network to www.example.com on port 80 to retrieve a web page will contain a connection ID. When the packets returned from that website contain that ID, they are sent to the computer in your network that originated the request.

Masquerading is common, and it allows computers inside a network to communicate to the outside world through the firewall. The external computers cannot identify the specific computer inside your network because its IP address is not contained in the data packet – only the IP address of the firewall computer is.

Remember that the zone files provided with firewalld are intended as basic sets of rules that can be modified as required to meet your needs. As I have already mentioned, you should leave the existing zone files intact and create new ones based on the existing one that most closely meets your needs.

Minimum Usable Firewall Configuration

While writing this chapter, I have experimented with various aspects of firewalld in my own environment. One of the issues I was exploring was the question, "What is the minimum set of firewall rules needed on a workstation?" Put another way, "How secure can I make the computers in my network and yet keep them talking to each other?"

I have a fairly simple setup. All of my workstations use DHCP to obtain their network configuration from my one server. That server also provides name services, email, NTP, and multiple websites. I also have a host that serves only as a firewall and router. My primary workstation is also my Ansible hub. All of my administrative interactions with various hosts in my network are handled using SSH, and Ansible uses SSH and nothing else.

So all of my workstations and the server need only SSH for me to manage my network and its hosts.

The server needs incoming SMTP, IMAP, NTP, HTTP, and DNS from the internal network. It also needs SMTP, IMAP, and HTTP from the outside Internet. The firewall uses port forwarding to direct email and web requests from the Internet to the server.

It's not especially complex. Aside from email and the websites on the server and firewall, the only service that is needed on my network is SSH. I do however have one other inbound port open on all of the hosts in my internal network. I won't tell you what it is, but I use it on my primary workstation to remotely manage an application that runs on all of my hosts.

Panic Mode

We now have a well-protected host that is located inside a well-protected network. But vulnerabilities can still be exploited into a full-blown breach by the crackers.

What do you do then?

firewalld has a panic mode that you can set. It blocks all inbound and outbound packets, effectively creating a logical isolation of the host. The caveat is that you must have some level of physical or direct access to the host in order to turn panic mode off. Panic mode is not persistent so does not survive a reboot – so if all else fails …

EXPERIMENT 41-10: PANIC MODE

Panic mode is easy to activate. If you activate it remotely, you get no response and the terminal will freeze. You will need direct access to the host, physical or virtual, to deactivate panic mode.

Perform this experiment from the StudentVM1 command line in a terminal on the desktop. First, turn panic mode on:

```
[root@studentvm1 ~]# firewall-cmd --panic-on
success
```

Ping a remote host to verify that you cannot access the outside world. After a short wait, exit from the ping using Ctrl+C. Also try a ping to the virtual router:

```
[root@studentvm1 ~]# ping -c3 example.com
^C
PING 10.0.2.1 (10.0.2.1) 56(84) bytes of data.
^C
--- 10.0.2.1 ping statistics ---
3 packets transmitted, 0 received, 100% packet loss, time 2120ms
[root@studentvm1 ~]# firewall-cmd --panic-off
success
[root@studentvm1 ~]# ping -c3 example.com
PING example.com (93.184.216.34) 56(84) bytes of data.
64 bytes from 93.184.216.34 (93.184.216.34): icmp_seq=1 ttl=50 time=13.7 ms
64 bytes from 93.184.216.34 (93.184.216.34): icmp_seq=2 ttl=50 time=13.6 ms
64 bytes from 93.184.216.34 (93.184.216.34): icmp_seq=3 ttl=50 time=13.7 ms

--- example.com ping statistics ---
3 packets transmitted, 3 received, 0% packet loss, time 2012ms
rtt min/avg/max/mdev = 13.642/13.711/13.748/0.049 ms
[root@studentvm1 ~]#
```

When panic mode is on, no communication is allowed, either in or out.

Like other firewalld settings, panic mode can be turned on for a specified period of time. Normal access using your configured firewall zones will resume at the expiration of the timer. However, I recommend against doing so as it's not possible to predict how long it will take to correct the problem that caused us to set panic mode in the first place.

firewall-config GUI

In addition to the command-line tools, firewalld has a well-designed and useful GUI interface. Like many GUI tools, it may not be available on the hosts you will need to administer such as servers and hosts used as firewalls. When it is available, however, it can make firewalld management at least a little easier. We still need to understand what is really happening behind the scenes, and that's why we spend so much time on command-line tools – that and the fact that they will always be available even when the GUI ones are not.

nftables

The nftables rules and the nftables.service, along with the nft command-line tool, are a complete firewall solution. However, when using firewalld, the nftables service is disabled.

The zone files we use to define the firewall characteristics for network interfaces are used, along with the other configuration files in /etc/firewalld, to create rule sets using the nftables file formats. firewalld is used to create nftables rules that are used by the appropriate kernel modules to examine every network packet and determine its final disposition.

You can view all of the current nftables rules, but even though they are human readable, they are not very understandable.

EXPERIMENT 41-11: VIEWING THE NFTABLES RULES

This command displays all of the nftables rules for the currently active zones:

```
[root@studentvm1 ~]# nft list ruleset | less
table inet firewalld {
        chain mangle_PREROUTING {
                type filter hook prerouting priority mangle + 10;
                policy accept;
                jump mangle_PREROUTING_ZONES
        }

        chain mangle_PREROUTING_POLICIES_pre {
                jump mangle_PRE_policy_allow-host-ipv6
        }

        chain mangle_PREROUTING_ZONES {
                iifname "enp0s9" goto mangle_PRE_public
                iifname "enp0s3" goto mangle_PRE_dmz
                goto mangle_PRE_public
        }
<SNIP>
```

Search on the string "dmz" to locate the rules pertaining to that zone. You can also search on network interface names like enp0s3.

These rules cannot be accessed and changed directly. You must use one of the command-line tools, `firewall-cmd` for firewalld or `nft` for nftables, to manipulate the firewall as an entity. I find it easier to use `firewall-cmd`, and the strategies and logical structure of firewalls created by fircwalld are much easier to understand than nftables.

Outbound Blocking

I mentioned at the beginning of this chapter that outbound network traffic from a given host is not blocked so as to ensure that we as users can access external websites, send email, use SSH to communicate with remote hosts in our own network as well as those that are even more remote, and more. However, there is a use case in which outbound blocking can be appropriate.

In the event that a host becomes infected with certain types of malware, this may be an effective tool to prevent other hosts from being infected. Malware that sends spam email or that can propagate itself to other computers or that can participate in coordinated denial of service (DOS) attacks is a major problem – although primarily on Windows hosts. For example, a firewall can be configured such that the only email allowed to pass through to the Internet can only originate from a known and trusted internal email server. Thus, direct spamming is thwarted.

The most secure networks are also those that prevent internal problems from escaping to the outside world and the internal network as well.

Fail2ban

A great firewall is one that can adapt as the threats change. I needed something like this to stem the large number of attacks via SSH I had been experiencing a few years ago. After a good bit of exploring and research, I found Fail2ban, an open source software that automates what I was previously doing by hand and adds repeat offenders to a block list in firewalls. The best part is that it integrates nicely with firewalld.

Fail2ban has a complex series of configurable matching rules and separate actions that can be taken when attempts are made to crack into a system. It has rules for many types of attacks that include web, email, and many other services that might have vulnerabilities. Fail2ban works by detecting attacks and then adding a rule to the firewall that will block further attempts from that specific, single IP address for a specified and configurable amount of time. After the time has expired, it removes the blocking rule.

Let's install Fail2ban and see how it works.

EXPERIMENT 41-12: FAIL2BAN

Perform this experiment as the root user. First, install Fail2ban. This only takes a minute or so and does not require a reboot. The installation includes the firewalld interface to Fail2ban:

```
[root@studentvm1 ~]# dnf -y install fail2ban
```

Fail2ban is not started as part of the installation, so we will need to do so after we perform a bit of configuration. Make /etc/fail2ban the PWD and list the files there. The jail.conf file is the main configuration file, but it is not used for most configuration because it might get overwritten during an update. We will create a jail.local file in the same directory. Any settings defined in jail.local will override ones set in jail.conf.

Copy jail.conf to jail.local. Edit the jail.local file and ignore the comment near the beginning that tells you not to modify this file. It is, after all, the file we will be modifying.

Find the line **# ignoreself = true**, which should be line 87. Remove the comment hash, and change it to **ignoreself = false**. We do this so that Fail2ban will not ignore failed login attempts from the local host. It can and should be changed back to true after finishing this chapter.

Scroll down to the line **bantime = 10m** (line 101) and change that to one minute (1m). Since we have no other hosts to test from, we will test using the local host. We do not want the local host banned for long so that we can resume experiments quickly. In the real world, I would set this to several hours so that the crackers cannot get more attempts for a long time.

Change **maxretry = 5** to 2. This is the maximum number of retries allowed after any type of failed attempt. Two retries are a good number for experimental purposes. I normally set this to three because anyone failing three retries to get into my systems using SSH does not belong there.

We could also change both of these configuration options in the [sshd] filter section, which would limit them to sshd while the global settings we just changed apply to all filters.

Read the comments for the other miscellaneous options in this section of the file, and then scroll down to the [sshd] section in JAILS.

Add the highlighted line that enables the sshd jail. The documentation is not clear about needing to add this line. In previous versions the line was **enabled = false**, so it was clear that changing false to true would enable the sshd jail:

```
[sshd]

# To use more aggressive sshd modes set filter parameter "mode" in
jail.local:
# normal (default), ddos, extra or aggressive (combines all).
# See "tests/files/logs/sshd" or "filter.d/sshd.conf" for usage example and
details.
enabled = true
#mode    = normal
port     = ssh
logpath = %(sshd_log)s
backend = %(sshd_backend)s
```

Do not enable Fail2ban, but start it:

```
[root@studentvm1 ~]# systemctl start fail2ban.service
```

Now ssh to the local host and log in using a bad user account or password on a good user account. It takes three failed attempts to log in, not three failed password entries. After three failed login attempts, the following error message is displayed:

```
[student@studentvm1 ~]$ ssh localhost
<snip>
ssh: connect to host localhost port 22: Connection refused
```

This means that the sshd jail is working. Look at the iptables firewall rules. Remember that these Fail2ban rules are stored in memory and are not permanent. The iptables rejection lines are removed after one minute, so if you don't see that line, force the failed logins again:

```
[root@studentvm1 ~]# iptables-save
# Generated by iptables-save v1.8.8 (nf_tables) on Tue May 23 10:53:07 2023
*filter
:INPUT ACCEPT [0:0]
:FORWARD ACCEPT [0:0]
:OUTPUT ACCEPT [0:0]
:f2b-sshd - [0:0]
-A INPUT -p tcp -m multiport --dports 22 -j f2b-sshd
```

```
-A f2b-sshd -s 127.0.0.1/32 -j REJECT --reject-with icmp-port-unreachable
-A f2b-sshd -j RETURN
COMMIT
# Completed on Tue May 23 10:53:07 2023
[root@studentvm1 ~]#
```

Wait – what?! Why iptables??

Yes, `iptables-save` shows the firewall rules for fail2ban. However, the following output shows that the rules are actually interpreted by nftables. List the nftables rules and page to the bottom to find the following entries:

```
[root@studentvm1 ~]# nft list ruleset | less
table ip6 filter {
        chain INPUT {
                type filter hook input priority filter; policy accept;
                meta l4proto tcp tcp dport 22 counter packets 68 bytes 11059
                jump f2b-sshd
        }

        chain f2b-sshd {
                ip6 saddr ::1 counter packets 4 bytes 320 reject
                counter packets 54 bytes 9939 return
        }
}
table ip filter {
        chain INPUT {
                type filter hook input priority filter; policy accept;
                meta l4proto tcp tcp dport 22 counter packets 62 bytes 9339
                jump f2b-sshd
        }

        chain f2b-sshd {
                ip saddr 127.0.0.1 counter packets 2 bytes 120 reject
                counter packets 54 bytes 8859 return
        }
}
```

Now let's look at a couple log files. In /var/log, first look at /var/log/secure. You should see a number of entries indicating failed passwords. These are the log entries checked by Fail2ban for failures.

Look at the /var/log/fail2ban.log file. This log file shows the times that triggering entries were found in the secure log and the ban and unban actions taken to protect the system.

Be aware that the f2b-sshd chain entries do not appear in the iptables rule set until the first time a ban is triggered. Once there, the first and last lines of the chain are not deleted, but the lines rejecting specific IP addresses are removed as they time out. It took me a bit of work to figure out this bit.

The installation of Fail2ban installs the configuration files needed for logwatch to report on Fail2ban activity. It is possible to create your own filters and actions for Fail2ban, but that is beyond the scope of this course.

Be sure to look at the various jails in the fail2ban.local file. There are many different events that can trigger Fail2ban to ban source IP addresses from access to a particular port or service.

Chapter Summary

Security is a big part of our job as SysAdmins, and firewalls are a major tool in keeping our networks safe. While Linux is quite secure as initially installed, any device connected to a wired or wireless network is always a target for crackers. A good firewall on the edge of your network where it interfaces with the Internet is a good first step in ensuring that your network is hardened. However, without appropriately configured firewalls present on every host in the network, a cracker who breaches the firewall host also gains immediate access to every host in your network.

The best approach to setting up any firewall is to start by blocking everything. Only then should you start considering the specific services that should be allowed to access your network. firewalld does an excellent job as the default firewall using the public zone because it blocks almost everything. Like I did, you should experiment to see whether an even more restrictive zone configuration might provide all of the access needed into your hosts and network while making them even more secure.

I do recommend that you not change the preinstalled zone files. I suggest that you do what I do and copy the existing zone file that most closely meets your needs and modify it as necessary. firewalld provides some basic yet very secure zone files to start. You may find that one of those is perfect for your needs on some or all of your hosts.

We explored zones as a concept and the reality of how they work and how they can be adapted to better meet your needs. This was done in the context of a workstation rather than a server or designated firewall to protect your network.

We also looked at using Fail2ban with firewalld to automatically block persistent crackers who make multiple failed access attempts in a short period of time.

In Volume 3 we will explore ways to refine a firewall so that we can run email and web servers and accept inbound packets to those servers from both the Internet and our own internal network. We will also look at more active security measures, such as SELinux, root kit hunters, and intrusion detection in Volume 3.

Exercises

Perform the following exercise to complete this chapter.

This is a single exercise to add a new zone to your firewall. The following list describes the functions required of the zone and some specific instructions and requirements you need to follow to successfully complete this task:

1. You must copy an existing zone file to create a new one. *Don't* use the **firewall-cmd --new-zone** command. Name the new zone "telnet".

2. The zone must block all external access except for SSH and Telnet.

3. Forwarding and masquerading are not required.

4. Do not make this new zone the default. Your default zone should be the public zone. If not make it so.

5. Explicitly assign the enp0s3 interface to the new zone.

6. Test the new zone to ensure that both SSH and Telnet are listening and accepting connections in this zone.

7. For cleanup exit from all Telnet and SSH connections and disable telnet.

8. Remove the zone from the network interface and ensure that it has reverted to the public zone default.

Index

A

Address
  burned-in, 394
  hardware, 394, 459
  IP, 362–364, 394, 395, 397–402, 404–410,
      413–415, 418, 422–429, 431–434,
      439, 440, 447, 456, 459, 461, 466,
      468, 470, 737, 758, 762, 766, 770
  IPV4, 391, 398–400, 406, 408, 409, 419
  IPV6, 392, 399, 419, 440
  locally administered address
      (LAA), 395
  loopback, 400, 426
  MAC, 394–398, 402, 404, 405, 417
  network, 408–410, 440
  universally administered address
      (UAA), 394
anacron
  anacrontab, 365, 378
ASCII
  ASCII plain text, 23, 152, 187, 199, 208,
      446, 537
  ASCII text, 164, 176, 180, 193, 194, 197,
      199, 206, 208, 284, 421, 463, 511,
      567–569, 760
Authentication, 675
Automation
  automate everything, 245, 284, 511
  Bash scripts, 281–320, 357
  Chrony, 358–360, 365, 388
  scripts, 714
  shell scripts, 282–285, 288, 307, 319

B

Bash
  configuration files
    ~/.bashrc, 709
    ~/.bash_profile, 709
    /etc/bashrc, 188, 189, 195, 197, 198
  environment, 297
  global configuration directory
    /etc/profile.d, 709
  program, 156, 159, 161, 189, 234,
      236–237, 264, 278, 301, 316, 341,
      344–347, 365, 376, 581
  shell options, 258
  shell scripts, 170, 278, 282, 369, 685
  syntax, 79
  variables, 239
Bash commands
  compound, 245, 246, 252
Binary
  executable, 510, 517, 525
BIOS
  POST, 588
  SMBIOS, 212
Books
  "The Art of Unix Programming", 313, 567
Boot, 46, 47, 52, 54, 61, 108, 124, 146, 147,
    212, 230, 309, 310, 325, 360, 382,
    392, 425, 508–509, 511, 518–520,
    524–530, 532–535, 543, 545, 570,
    574, 575, 588–590, 593, 595,
    609–611, 620, 631, 632, 648,
    676, 744

© David Both 2023
D. Both, *Using and Administering Linux: Volume 2*, https://doi.org/10.1007/978-1-4842-9615-8

N

Command list
A, B

C

D

E

Printed in the United States
by Baker & Taylor Publisher Services